P9-BZS-518

CYNIC SAGE or SON OF GOD?

A BRIDGEPOINT BOOK

BridgePoint,
the academic
imprint of
Victor Books, is
your connection
for the best in
serious reading
that integrates
the passion of
the heart with
the scholarship
of the mind.

CYNIC SAGE 'OR' SON OF GOD?

GREGORY A. BOYD

A
BRIDGEPOINT
BOOK

DEDICATION

To my loving wife and
dearest friend, Shelley J. Boyd.

Unless otherwise noted, all Scripture quotations are from
the *Holy Bible, New International Version®*.
Copyright © 1973, 1978, 1984 by International Bible Society.
Used by permission of Zondervan Publishing House.
All rights reserved.
Other quotations are from the
New American Standard Bible (NASB), © the Lockman Foundation
1960, 1962, 1963, 1968, 1971, 1972, 1973, 1975, 1977.

Editor: Robert N. Hosack
Designer: Andrea Boven
Cover Art: Natasha Beshenkovsky, miniature icon,
1985, enamel and metallic paint on wood.
From the collection of the Billy Graham Center Museum, Wheaton, Illinois.

Library of Congress Cataloging-in-Publication Data

Boyd, Gregory A., 1955–
    Cynic, sage, or Son of God? / Gregory A. Boyd.
        p.   cm.
    Includes bibliographical references and index.
    ISBN: 1-56476-448-6
    1. Jesus Christ – Person and offices. 2. Jesus Christ – Historicity. 3. Cynics (Greek philosophy)
4. Crossan, John Dominic. Jesus. 5. Mack, Burton L. The lost gospel. 6. Q hypothesis (Synoptics
criticism) 7. Christianity – Origin. I. Title.
BT205.B648 1995
232 – dc20   95-8773
                                                                                                                        CIP

BridgePoint is the academic imprint of Victor Books.

© 1995 by Victor Books/SP Publications, Inc.
All rights reserved. Printed in the United States of America.

1   2   3   4   5   6   7   8   9   10   Printing/Year   99   98   97   96   95

No part of this book may be reproduced without written permission,
except for brief quotations in books and critical reviews.
For information write
Victor Books,
1825 College Avenue,
Wheaton, Illinois 60187.

CONTENTS

Part 2
Jesus the Son of God

Section 4: Paul and the Historical Jesus

Section 5: Mark and the Historical Jesus

Section 6: The Early Church and the Historical Jesus

PREFACE

B eing an interdisciplinary work, there are a number of individuals from various fields who have helped me in bringing this book about. A word of appreciation needs to first be expressed to the fifteen superb students who comprised my 1993 Senior Seminar class in theology at Bethel College entitled "Christian Faith and the Historical Jesus: An Examination of the Cynic Thesis." The idea for this book first arose out of the lively discussions of this seminar. I am also indebted to a number of New Testament specialists for their comments on various chapters. Here I am especially grateful to Michael Holmes of Bethel College and Robert Stein of Bethel Seminary for their helpful comments. In this regard, thanks also goes to Martin Albl, Steven Enderline, and Randy Nelson, who offered their New Testament specialist critiques on various sections of this work. Thanks also goes to my good colleague Roger Olson, whose mastery of the German language I leaned upon when necessary, as well as to Robert Hosack, BridgePoint editor, whose patience and meticulous work throughout this project impressed me to no end. Tyler DeArmond, my exceptional teaching assistant, deserves much credit for going far beyond the call of duty in organizing my endnotes and helping out with the bibliography. And finally, my deepest word of appreciation must be expressed to my good friend Paul Eddy. Beyond providing invaluable research assistance, the material that comprises chapters 3, 4, and 7 was originally produced by Paul in a more technical format, which I have simply edited for a wider audience.

While whatever shortcomings and errors this work contains are wholly my own responsibility, whatever value it has is shared with each of these individuals.

Gregory A. Boyd
Bethel College

INTRODUCTION
The Challenge of
the Cynic-Sage Thesis

Not since David Strauss' *Life of Jesus* shook European Christianity to its foundation in the nineteenth century has any scholarly discussion of the historical Jesus made the impact on a popular level that the Jesus Seminar is presently making in North America. First convened in 1985 under the leadership of Robert Funk, and funded by the Westar Institute, the work of the Jesus Seminar has, quite intentionally, received an unprecedented amount of media attention. Their controversial work has been thoroughly, and repeatedly, covered by major newspapers around the country. Popular magazines have provided a remarkable amount of space to their work, including *Time* and *Newsweek* which made their work cover stories. They have recently published their first major work, *The Five Gospels* (Macmillan) in which they, by a process of voting with colored beads, determine that less than one fifth of the sayings of Jesus are likely to be authentic.[1] All early indications are that the work is destined to be a big seller. And the research of this seminar is now even forming the basis for a major Hollywood film to be directed by Paul Verhoeven, director of such films as *Robocop, Total Recall,* and *Basic Instinct.*[2] This is not exactly what one might call "par for the course" as scholarly research goes!

This remarkable popular impact is hardly accidental. The charter of the Westar Institute explicitly states that it is seeking to promote "religious literacy" by popularizing scholarly research. This motif was emphasized in Robert Funk's 1985 opening address to the Jesus Seminar participants in which he enjoined them to "quit the academic closet" and to "begin earnestly to report on our work to a wider public and then to engage the public in conversation and conference."[3] And it has been repeatedly stressed by various members of the Jesus Seminar themselves. John Dominic Crossan, for example, one of the leading spokespersons for the group, admits that, because they were seeking to "close the knowledge gap between scholarly discussion and popular awareness," the Jesus Seminar participants deliberately sought to "catch media attention" as a way of bringing their "findings" not only into "pew and pulpit but into the popular press and onto the television screen as well."[4]

Indeed, it would not be much of an overstatement to say that, at least among some members of the Jesus Seminar, there exists an almost "evangelistic" zeal to present to the public a persuasive new vision of who the historical Jesus was. Burton Mack, for example, believes that the "mythological" apocalyptic portrait of Jesus in the Book of Mark lies behind much of the ills of Western society. It must be exposed as myth, and replaced by a new understanding of the historical Jesus, if these ills are to be overcome and especially if the church is going to have any positive role to play in contemporary Western culture.[5] Another seminar participant, Hal Taussig, believes a new view of Jesus, based on critical scholarly research, is needed if the church is going to remain relevant to thinking people and come to terms with modern pluralism. Moreover, its proclamation of a "male savior" needs to be rethought if Christianity is going to remain relevant to modern feminist sensibilities. This, according to him, mandates that the findings of scholarly research such as occurs in the Jesus Seminar be aggressively publicized.[6]

The Jesus Seminar, then, is aimed at influencing the North American populace. And all indications are that they are carrying out their agenda extremely well.

CROSSAN, MACK, AND THE CYNIC THESIS

If this much is true of the Jesus Seminar in general, it is even more so of two early participants of the Jesus Seminar in particular: John Dominic Crossan and Burton Mack. While both of these men are recognized as outstanding scholars in New Testament studies within academic circles, they have both been very active in promulgating their scholarly views to a popular audience. They have, arguably, been the two most public exponents of the Jesus Seminar. They are both among the most quoted, and certainly the most controversial, contemporary New Testament scholars today in the American popular media. And they have both published their scholarly research in books written for a lay audience, works that have, because of their popularistic thrust, received an enormous amount of attention. In particular, Crossan's *Jesus: A Revolutionary Biography,* and Mack's *The Lost Gospel: The Book of Q,* are both very readable, persuasively argued, highly controversial, and becoming extremely popular. Both titles are found in general bookstores across the country and have together sold close to 110,000 copies to date.[7]

What is of even greater interest, however, is the incredible growing popularity of the radical view of the historical Jesus both of these men espouse. Indeed, their vision of the historical Jesus has justifiably been called a "new paradigm" of historical Jesus research.[8] While there are significant differences between their views, as we shall see (chaps. 3–4), both men espouse the view that the historical Jesus is best characterized as a Cynic philosopher. Behind the layers of myth and legend that constitutes the majority of the Gospels lies a Cynic sage who was simply a traveling teacher of unconventional wisdom. And the original followers of Jesus, both Mack and Crossan hold, were simply people interested in living out the countercultural teachings of their Master. They never thought of him as being "divine" in any sense of the word. They did not see any special significance in his death. And they knew nothing of a supposed "resurrection." These were later myths that were gradually attached to this figure sometime prior to the writing of the Gospels. This "Jesus as Cynic sage" view is not original with Crossan and Mack, but its present growing popularity at both a scholarly and popular level is largely attributable to them.[9]

The growing popularity of this new paradigm should be of significant concern for all Christians and not just New Testament scholars. If it was ever excusable for evangelical laypeople to ignore the latest trends in New Testament scholarship, it is no longer. The popularistic thrust of the Jesus Seminar and of the work of Crossan and Mack in particular, along with the success with which they are presently propagating their views, requires evangelicals to pay attention and prepare themselves to intelligently respond to such views (1 Peter 3:15). The proclamation that the Jesus of the first century is the Son of God and Savior of all who believe requires that we take very seriously scholarly historical revisionist accounts such as Mack's and Crossan's that significantly undermine this Good News. If the evangelical proclamation that the historical Jesus is the Son of God is to continue to have persuasive power in our increasingly post-Christian culture, orthodox believers must be willing to defend this claim against alternative perspectives on a historical basis. And we must be willing to do so in the public arena.

To date, however, no thorough response to this new paradigm of the historical Jesus has been provided from an evangelical perspective. This book is written to fill this caveat. It is my hope that this work will provide a serious critique of the Cynic thesis, while at the same time providing arguments that support the historic Christian view that Jesus Christ was more than a mere Cynic, and in fact more than a mere mortal. As all the New Testament authors and historic Christian church have proclaimed, it is my conviction that Jesus was, and is, the Son of God. And it is my belief that, when all the evidence is in, this view stands above all alternative views in terms of its historical plausibility.

Hence, it is my hope that this work will prove accessible and beneficial to scholars and laity alike who hold to this precious faith as they wrestle with the arguments and implications of this and other critical revisionist views of Jesus.[10]

THE NATURE OF THIS BOOK

It will be helpful to the reader if at the start two things are made clear about what this book intends and does not intend to do.

First, this work seeks to be more critical than constructive. That is to say, my primary purpose is to critique one dominant paradigm for understanding the historical Jesus—the Cynic-sage thesis—but I do not intend to offer anything like a thorough alternative reconstruction of the historical Jesus. Given the brevity and obviously sermonic nature of the Gospels, such historical reconstructions are certainly necessary for evangelicals and non-evangelicals alike to embark upon. But it is not my intent in this work to embark upon one.

As mentioned above, my critique of Mack and Crossan *will* carry me so far as to make the counterclaim that the evidence for the historical Jesus cannot be exhaustively accounted for within any strictly naturalistic schema. And to this extent I provide evidence supporting the view that Jesus was, as New Testament authors interpret him, the Son of God. Thus, I am arguing in favor of the traditional Christian paradigm of understanding Jesus as the Son of God over and against the revisionist paradigm espoused by Mack and Crossan. As needed as this critique is, however, it certainly stops far short of providing anything like a thorough historical account of who the historical Jesus was.

In sections 4 through 6 of this work I shall be examining the general historical trustworthiness of Paul's and Mark's portrayal of Jesus and of the portrait of the early church in Acts, but no attempt is made to go beyond this general point and discuss the very complex historical issues surrounding, for example, the self-consciousness of Jesus, the titles he used or didn't use of himself, the particular cultural meaning of his teachings, or the particular way each Gospel author redacted his material. I believe that these are all very important discussions to enter into, but they simply lie outside the restricted scope of this work.

Such discussions, leading to a probable reconstruction of the historical Jesus, also lie outside of my area of expertise, and this brings me to the second point which needs to be made about this work. I am a systematic and philosophical theologian, not a New Testament specialist, and this certainly affects the way in which I approach my critique of the Cynic thesis. My concern in this work is decisively *not* to make any new contributions to New Testament scholarship. I have no new theory about the historical Jesus, "Q," the Cross Gospel, Mark's redactional tendencies, or the like, to offer.

Rather, as a theologian examining a historical thesis that significantly intersects with my own field of study and has crucial relevance to the central tenet of my own faith, my sole concern in this book is to evaluate the internal coherence and historical plausibility of the Cynic Jesus thesis. I shall thus be seeking to expose the arbitrary presuppositions, the faulty lines of reasoning, the circular methodologies, and the speculative assumptions that characterize the Cynic thesis as put forth by Crossan and Mack. Moreover, relying heavily on the work of such New Testament scholars as N.T. Wright, Colin Hemer, and Martin Hengel, I shall seek to show that these assumptions and methodological faults have caused Crossan and Mack to minimize, or completely neglect, significant contributions from more conservative New Testament scholarship that pose significant challenges to their reading of the evidence. And in doing this, I shall be offering counter arguments that favor the evangelical perspective that the New Testament portraits of Jesus as the Son of God and of the early church as professing this faith from the beginning are in fact rooted in reliable history. But in all of this I am functioning as a systematician, not a New Testament scholar.

This work, then, can be best characterized as *a systematic critique of a historical thesis with an apologetic objective*. While Crossan and Mack have stated in writing numerous times that they are highly suspicious of any historical work done from a theological or apologetic perspective—as though their own works were "purely objective"—I rather regard this systematic and apologetic perspective to be a strength of this present work.

It is, quite rightly, often pointed out that there is far too little critical dialogue between Christian philosophers, apologists, theologians, and New Testament scholars in our age of increasingly myopic specialization.[11] It should be obvious why Christian philosophers, theologians, and apologists need to pay attention to the work of historical and exegetical specialists: the historical claims concerning the Christ and the meaning of the New Testament witness concerning him are not self-evident. But it should be (but usually is not) equally obvious that New Testament scholars need to pay attention to the work of Christian philosophers, theologians, and apologists, for their interpretations of historical evidence and their use of ancient texts are also not self-evident.

As I shall show in section 3 of this work, New Testament scholars such as Crossan and Mack work with a myriad of worldview and methodological assumptions, and these greatly affect how they evaluate and interpret the data they work with. Moreover, such scholars often engage themselves in faulty lines of reasoning and unwarranted speculations. And they can, willingly or unwillingly, become myopic in their research and treatment of the evidence, neglecting lines of argumentation that might adversely affect their own theories. Crossan and Mack, I shall argue, are guilty of just such oversights. But it often takes the eye of someone outside of the field—the eye of a philosopher, theologian, and/or apologist who has some stake in the matter—to expose these blind spots. Hence, the line of dependency between those within and without the community of academic New Testament scholars is not, or at least should not, be unidirectional.

This, I believe, is the strength of this book. With "the eye of an outsider," a nonspecialist in New Testament studies but a specialist in examining systematic issues, I am endeavoring to critically analyze the theories of Crossan and Mack. If my perspective is tainted by a prior philosophical commitment—and it certainly is—it is no less so than the perspectives of Crossan and Mack. But in neither case does this mean that a rational discussion in the direction of objective truth about the historical Jesus is impossible. The fact that Crossan and Mack as well as I write books to persuade others of our points of view rather presupposes that we each believe such a discussion is possible. This book, in any case, aims at just such a discussion, with just such an objective.

THE OUTLINE OF THIS BOOK

This work is divided into two major parts, six major sections, and thirteen chapters. Part 1, *Jesus the Cynic Sage* (chaps. 1–7) concerns itself with the background, exposition, and critique of the foundational features of the Cynic-Jesus thesis. Part 2, *Jesus the Son of God* (chaps. 8–13) concerns itself with a critique of Crossan's and Mack's use of the biblical data. Insofar as I am here seeking to argue, against Crossan and Mack, that the biblical data is historically reliable, I shall in this second half of the book be seeking to argue that we have solid historical grounds for accepting the New Testament's portrait of Jesus as the Son of God.

To be more specific, Section 1 (chaps. 1–2) provides the broad historical background to the Cynic thesis. Chapter 1 examines, in broad terms, the quest for the historical Jesus that ran from the eighteenth century up to our present time. Chapter 2 then proceeds to examine the contours of the present (chaotic!) state of scholarship concerning this quest. Without an understanding of this intellectual background and contemporary context, it is impossible to adequately understand, appreciate, or critique the Cynic thesis (or any contemporary revisionist portrait of Jesus for that matter).[12]

This material then provides the background against which I examine in section 2 the particular views of Crossan (chap. 3) and Mack (chap. 4). With little critical comment, I here attempt to examine the various historical and philosophical influences that have shaped the perspectives of these authors; the various arguments they use and various conclusions they arrive at through these arguments; and perhaps most importantly, the various philosophical and methodological assumptions they bring to their work which help shape, if not determine, the course their research takes.

My critique of the Cynic sage thesis works from the general to the specific, and thus in section 3 I critically examine the most general foundational aspects of Crossan's and Mack's work. In chapters 5 and 6 I seek to demonstrate that the broad assumptions that drive the Cynic Jesus thesis are unwarranted, that its methodology is largely circular, and that its use of extra-canonical sources is very questionable. And I follow this in chapter 7 with a critique of the four major lines of argumentation that hold the Cynic thesis together.

In chapters 8 and 9 (section 4) I turn to an examination of Burton Mack's arguments that Paul's understanding of Christ is mythological and not representative of what early followers of Jesus generally believed. Substantiating such a view is crucial to the plausibility of the Cynic thesis since Paul's letters constitute our earliest extant evidence of early Christianity, on the one hand, while he does not see Jesus as being anything like a Cynic sage, on the other. Paul's historical testimony must, therefore, be discredited. I shall, however, attempt to demonstrate that we have very good historical grounds for regarding Paul's views as both rooted in the historical Jesus and as generally representative of early Christianity.

For similar reasons, the historical testimony of Mark must be discredited by Crossan and Mack, and thus I examine and critique their arguments against this Gospel in section 5 (chaps. 10–11).[13] Against their views that this Gospel was written by an unknown person and is mostly "theological fiction," I argue that we have very good grounds for accepting it as generally reliable and as coming from John Mark under the authority of Peter as church tradition attests.

I argue in similar fashion in the final section of this work with regard to the Book of Acts and the early Christian faith in the resurrection of Jesus. Since the revisioning of Jesus as a Cynic requires a complete revisioning of the history of the earliest Christian communities, as we shall see, this thesis can only be true if the Book of Acts is historically false. But this, I argue, is altogether untenable.[14] More precisely, the Cynic thesis can only be true if Luke's testimony in Acts that the church was founded on a faith in Jesus' resurrection is false. And hence, I conclude my work in chapter 13 by critiquing Mack's and Crossan's arguments against the historical resurrection, attempting to demonstrate in the process that we in fact have very good historical grounds for affirming the historicity of this event.

If my sustained polemic throughout this work is successful, this book will have shown that we have far better grounds for holding to the biblical and traditional understanding of Jesus as the divine Son of God than we do for rejecting it in favor of a new paradigm for understanding Jesus as a Cynic philosopher.

·PART 1·

JESUS THE CYNIC SAGE

·SECTION 1·

The Background to the Cynic Thesis

1

THE SEARCH FOR AN "ALTERNATIVE" JESUS:
An Overview of the Quest for the Historical Jesus

It is impossible to adequately understand or appreciate any modern revisionist portrait of the historical Jesus without first acquiring some understanding of the two-century long "quest for the histori-cal Jesus" that lies behind it. Many believing Christians too quickly dis-miss, or ignore altogether, contemporary critical accounts of the histori-cal Jesus for this reason. They don't understand the motivation behind such endeavors, for they don't appreciate the problems and issues raised over the last two centuries of New Testament scholarship that gives rise to these endeavors. Working from the assumption that the Gospels are divinely inspired, such believers simply assume that the historical Jesus and the Jesus of the Gospels are one and the same. And thus, any attempt to "get behind" the Gospel portraits through historical-critical means and "discover" a different Jesus than the one portrayed there is viewed as being an unnecessary and faithless exercise in futility.

While the belief that the Gospels are inspired and thus that their portraits of the historical Jesus are substantially accurate is certainly de-fensible, holding to this belief as an *uncritical assumption* is not—not in our present culture, precisely because it has been significantly impacted by two centuries of critical New Testament scholarship. If the evangelical proclamation that Jesus is the Son of God is going to continue to be intellectually viable in our age, neither this two-century tradition of scholarship, nor the contemporary revisionist portraits of Jesus that arise from it, can be ignored. If we conclude that this tradition of critical scholarship with its contemporary revisionist exponents is in fact largely misguided, this conclusion must follow our historical and theological arguments to this effect, not our conservative theological assumptions.

Thus, in this and the next chapter we shall briefly examine the two centuries of historical-critical research that serves as the background to the particular revisionist portrait of Jesus we wish to critique: the view that Jesus was a Cynic sage. This present chapter shall broadly outline the "quest for the historical Jesus" that lies behind all modern historical-critical approaches to Jesus, while the next one shall focus more particularly on the major developments and trends of the last several decades which form the specific background of the Cynic-sage thesis.[1]

HERMANN REIMARUS AND THE RISE OF BIBLICAL CRITICISM

It is understandable that most believing Christians today simply assume that the historical Jesus is identical with the Jesus of the Gospels, for this has been the working assumption of the church throughout most of its history. The Gospels, it has been traditionally assumed, are divinely inspired and are written by the authors to whom they are credited. And thus it has been assumed that their portraits of Jesus can in detail be trusted as being historically accurate. This is not to suggest that prior to the rise of the historical-critical method Christians did not notice problems within the Gospel accounts: they certainly did. But never did they take this to imply that the Gospels were not altogether trustworthy.[2]

With the rise of rationalism and the Enlightenment, however, things began to change. Seventeenth-century deism brought with it the first buds of modern biblical criticism. Attacks on the notions of miracle and revelation in general soon gave way to an explicit focus on the biblical texts themselves. Figures as diverse as Thomas Hobbes, Benedict Spinoza, Isaac La Peyrere, and Richard Simon laid the groundwork for what would eventually emerge as the mature historical-critical method in subsequent centuries.[3]

The Beginnings of the Quest

With the eighteenth century came the beginnings of the "quest for the historical Jesus." Following Albert Schweitzer, most target 1778 as the inaugural year.[4] Here, the story is as intriguing as the quest itself. From 1774 to 1778, Gotthold Lessing published a number of "fragments" of a text that was clearly written from a deist perspective. Lessing claimed to have found these anonymous fragments in the Wolfenbüttel Library in Hamburg, Germany. Although early suspicions existed, these fragments were eventually confirmed to have come from the pen of Hermann

Samuel Reimarus (1694–1768), a German professor of Semitic languages. Reimarus had written a controversial text from which the fragments were excerpted, but decided not to have it published for fear of the consequences it would bring. Instead, upon his death, his daughter gave it to Lessing to publish as he saw fit.[5]

In terms of the quest, it is the seventh and final fragment that is most important: *On the Intention of Jesus and His Disciples.*[6] In this work, Reimarus argues for a sharp dichotomy between the Jesus of history and the portrait of Christ found within the four Gospels. He begins by noting that Jesus himself wrote nothing; thus we are entirely dependent upon the writings of his disciples for knowledge of his teachings and deeds. This insight leads Reimarus to a critical conclusion.

> I find great cause to separate completely what the apostles say in their own writings from that which Jesus himself actually said and taught, for the apostles were themselves teachers and consequently present their own views.[7]

In essence, Reimarus argues that Jesus' own intentions were rooted in nothing more than a reaffirmation of the Jewish faith and a renewed call to its ethical imperatives. Jesus had no intention of inaugurating a new religious faith or doing away with the Levitical law. Rather, he envisioned himself as a political messiah, called by God to "build up a worldly kingdom, and to deliver the Israelites from bondage."[8] When Jesus was faced with crucifixion rather than coronation, however, his messianic hopes were dashed, and with them the hopes of his disciples.

At this point the story takes an unfortunate turn, according to Reimarus. Rather than simply accepting the death of their would-be messiah-king, the disciples concocted a scheme to keep their movement alive. Within twenty-four hours, they managed to steal the body of Jesus from the tomb and, after a strategic waiting period of several weeks, went on to proclaim him as the resurrected Lord.[9] And they didn't stop there. The ideas of Jesus as the Savior of the world and of his imminent return were quickly added to the growing conspiracy. Thus, by Reimarus' account, "the new system of a suffering spiritual savior, which no one had ever known or thought before, was invented only because the first hopes had failed."[10]

Finally, Reimarus traces out the motivation behind the disciples' "intentional, deliberate fabrication." According to Reimarus, the disciples were originally attracted to Jesus because of his aspirations to kingly power — not to mention his promises to them that they would share in his rule and reign. And so, just as it had motivated them before Jesus' death, so "the possession of worldly wealth and power was also the object of the apostles in the fabrication of their new doctrine."[11]

The Enduring Legacy of Reimarus

Although most of the specifics of Reimarus' reconstruction of the historical Jesus have long since been abandoned, important aspects of his general approach have remained central to the quest down through the years. First and foremost is the idea of a fundamental discontinuity between the "Jesus of history" and the "Christ of faith." While few contemporary scholars follow Reimarus in characterizing the disciples and Gospel writers with such harsh terms as blatant fraud and deception (though Mack and Crossan, we shall see, come close to saying this much about the author of the Gospel of Mark), many nonetheless assume that the early Christians were involved in a significant amount of mythmaking—or as it is sometimes more politely termed, "creative activity"—with regard to the Jesus record. Thus, it is a fundamental assumption of the quest that the actual Jesus of history is recoverable only to the degree that one can penetrate back through the embellished Gospel portraits to the historical kernels upon which they were originally based. Since the Jesus of the Gospels is assumed not to be historical, we must look for an "alternative" Jesus behind these accounts.

Second, an important aspect of Reimarus' thesis has proven to become a central issue of the ongoing quest: the question of Jesus' eschatology. For Reimarus, Jesus' eschatological convictions are fundamental to understanding his general religious intentions. His starting point is Jesus' proclamation: "Repent, for the kingdom of heaven is at hand" (Matt. 4:17). Jesus' eschatology is characterized by its rooting in the common Jewish conception of the day, which for Reimarus means not a spiritual or apocalyptic intervention, but a thoroughly temporal and political messianic hope. Nonetheless, Reimarus' thesis is based on the notion that the conviction of a *divine reversal in the form of an imminent event* lies at the heart of the message of the historical Jesus.[12] More than a century after Reimarus' death, Schweitzer would assess his contribution to the quest as

> perhaps the most splendid achievement in the whole course of the historical investigation of the life of Jesus, for he was the first to grasp the fact that the world of thought in which Jesus moved was essentially eschatological.[13]

In Schweitzer's view, Reimarus does end up with a flawed conception of first-century Jewish eschatology; in actuality it was apocalyptic rather than merely earthly and political. Nonetheless, he credits Reimarus with rediscovering the eschatological core of Jesus' message, an insight that had been buried under "eighteen centuries of misconception."[14] As we shall see, the question of the nature and significance of Jesus' eschatology was going to be a central factor in the course of the twentieth-century quest for the historical Jesus, and it continues to play a central role in contemporary quests.

Finally, Reimarus is critically important to any study of the question of presuppositions and motives operative in the quest. The twentieth century has provided the type of distance and discussion necessary for an accurate historical analysis of the beginnings of the quest itself. As noted above, Schweitzer saw virtually nothing in the way of precedent for Reimarus' "historical" investigation of Jesus.[15] Contemporary research, however, has revealed the deep intellectual debt that Reimarus owed to others. As Colin Brown has noted, Reimarus was a "synthesizer and translator of English Deism in a form which directly challenged German Protestant orthodoxy." He was equally "a child of the Enlightenment," as demonstrated by the desupernaturalizing, secularizing nature of his project.[16] Thus, the "father" of the quest, like the "fathers" of the general historical-critical method, were themselves children of a very definite, historically identifiable stream of philosophical and religious thought.

This stream of thought, we might further add, was self-consciously set against anything like the traditional orthodox Christian conceptions of the Bible and the Jesus it presents. It is this deistic Enlightenment mind-set that supplied both the historical-critical method and the quest for the historical Jesus with their original philosophical and religious presuppositions.

Chief among these presuppositions was the rejection of the ideas of the supernatural and divine revelation, presuppositions that were, *a priori*, at odds with the biblical worldview and its claims. As we shall subsequently see, the legacy of these original presuppositions was, in various ways, carried on throughout the quest for the historical Jesus and continue to lie at the heart of most contemporary revisionist portraits of Jesus. These presuppositions entail that the search for the "historical" Jesus is, almost by definition, a search for an alternative, "de-supernaturalized" Jesus. This presupposition, with its accompanying definition of the kind of Jesus scholars are questing after, is most decisively embraced by Crossan and Mack, as we shall see.

THE EARLY "LIVES" OF JESUS

The First "Semi-Rationalist" Lives of Jesus

When it comes to the first quest, Schweitzer remains to this day the uncontested master chronicler. The purpose of his *The Quest of the Historical Jesus,* published in 1906, is nothing less than the exposition and analysis of the first 125 years of the quest—the period now dubbed the "Old Quest." Following Reimarus, Schweitzer's account of the first quest moves next to a treatment of "the lives of Jesus of the earlier rationalism."[17] Here he investigates the work of J.J. Hess, F.V. Reinhard, E.A. Opitz, J.A. Jakobi, and J.G. Herder. A number of these men were associated with the Neology movement of the last half of the eighteenth century. This effort sought to move beyond orthodoxy and pietism in order to restate Christianity in a manner that was more compatible with the increasingly rationalistic thought of the day, yet without abandoning the essence of the historic faith.[18]

In fact, many of these early attempts to discover the historical Jesus behind the Gospels remained close to orthodox teaching. For example, against Reimarus, many held that an adequate rational account of Jesus' life was impossible unless one admitted the presence of the supernatural in his ministry.[19] For this reason, Schweitzer characterizes these "early rationalist" accounts of Jesus as being something less than truly rationalistic. On his account, they rather represented a sort of "half-and-half rationalism" that was "as yet not wholly dissociated from a simple-minded supernaturalism."[20] Their Jesus, in other words, was not yet thoroughly "de-supernaturalized," and hence their views were not yet thoroughly rationalistic.

Methodologically, these early "semi-rationalist" works tended to trade historical stringency in for contemporary relevance. Their portraits of Jesus were largely painted in the hues and textures of eighteenth- and nineteenth-century Europe. While the presence of some supernatural features of Jesus' ministry was generally admitted, the primary emphasis of these works was clearly upon Jesus' ethical teachings and their correlation with the rationalistic thought of the day. The Jesus they "discovered" was one who was, for the most part, not terribly offensive either to orthodox Christian or Enlightenment rationalistic sensibilities.

BAHRDT AND VENTURINI

Other "lives of Jesus," however, were more thoroughly rationalistic and consequently ventured farther away from orthodoxy. The two most comprehensive and influential works of this period that convey a thoroughly rationalistic orientation are K.F. Bahrdt's eleven-volume *An Explanation of the Plans and Aims of Jesus* (published 1784–1792) and K.H. Venturini's four-volume *A Non-supernatural History of the Great Prophet of Nazareth* (published 1800–1802).[21] These two works share a number of significant features in common. Both works, for example, make a valiant attempt to explain away all of the miraculous elements of the Gospel accounts in thoroughly naturalistic terms. For example, Venturini suggests that Jesus' healings were attributable to his pharmacological skills—he never went anywhere without his "portable medicine chest." The raisings from the dead were simple cases of coma. And the miracle of the wine at Cana was explained by Jesus bringing, as a wedding gift, several jars of good wine.[22] The only thing that could be said in favor of such speculations, of course, is that they allowed one to not admit a miracle. But given the rationalistic and naturalistic spirit of the time, this was just about sufficient. Hence such speculations became extremely popular, and even more spectacular, among liberal-minded thinkers throughout the nineteenth century.

Even more interesting, however, is the fact that both studies present Jesus as the prime player in a conspiracy orchestrated by an underground movement of Essenes. From the time of his childhood, Jesus was supposedly watched over by the Essene Order. In time, he and his cousin, John the Baptist, were groomed for a position of spiritual leadership. Ultimately, according to Barhdt and Venturini, Jesus was crucified and, with the help of the covert Essene operative Joseph of Arimathea, was later revived in the tomb. Again, there is, of course, no shred of evidence in support of such views. But they have the "advantage" of preserving a thoroughly naturalistic Jesus.

The precedent set by Barhdt and Venturini was soon to be followed by a number of subsequent questers. Indeed, Schweitzer ends his account of Venturini's work with the fairly accurate observation that it

> may almost be said to be reissued annually down to the present day, for all the fictitious "Lives" go back directly or indirectly to the type which he created. It is plagiarized [sic] more freely than any other Life of Jesus.[23]

Indeed, the precedent set by these two liberal scholars is yet followed by certain contemporary writers. While few scholars follow either Bahrdt's or Venturini's sometimes extravagant naturalistic accounts of miracles, a number of popular works make use of their conspiracy theory. Especially since the 1947 discovery of the Dead Sea Scrolls, a number of popular accounts of Jesus have been published which make the wild speculation that Jesus had an intimate connection with the Essenes and which postulate some sort of conspiracy theory to account for his life and ministry. While entertaining reading, they are, on a scholarly level, no more convincing today than they were 200 years ago.[24]

THE PINNACLE OF RATIONALISM: H.E.G. PAULUS

The rationalistic tendencies, and the propensity to explain the miracles of Jesus in naturalistic terms, becomes even more pronounced in the works of subsequent rationalistic questers such as K.A. Hase and especially H.E.G. Paulus.[25] Indeed, Paulus' two-volume work, *The Life of Jesus as the Basis of a Purely Historical Account of Early Christianity* (1828), has been justifiably characterized as the pinnacle of rationalistic accounts of the life of Jesus. Like Venturini before him, Paulus explains Jesus' miracles as embellished accounts of his unusual ability to utilize folk medicines. He also ventured what appeared to him as plausible naturalistic explanations for the nature miracles. Jesus' feat of walking on water, for example, is explained as a simple misconception of the disciples. In truth, Jesus was merely walking in the shallows near the shore. Similarly, the "miraculous" feeding of the 5,000 is explained in natural terms. Following Jesus' lead, the rich people in the crowd shared their food supply with the poor; thus, no one went hungry that day.[26]

In spite of his thoroughgoing rationalism in regard to the miraculous, however, Paulus did not remove God from the picture altogether. In fact, as Schweitzer explains, Paulus clearly viewed God as the ultimate cause of all events, including those described in miraculous terms in the Gospels. Thus, he saw himself as merely illuminating the rational, naturalistic secondary causes related to these events, over against the naive "miracle" explanations found in the text.[27] For Paulus, the wonder of Jesus was not to be located in his supposed miracles, but rather in his remarkable character – "the miraculous thing about Jesus is he himself."[28]

In this way Paulus could retain something of the significance of Jesus and even of the supposed "miracles" while not admitting that anything miraculous actually occurred. While the implausibility of Paulus' extravagant naturalistic explanations was to soon be conceded, his attempt to retain the significance of Jesus for faith while wholly denying any supernatural dimension to his ministry or character was to form a central component of most subsequent quests.

DAVID FRIEDRICH STRAUSS

The Gospels as Myth

In terms of importance to the first quest, between Reimarus and Schweitzer there stands one figure above the rest: David Friedrich Strauss (1808–1874). Strauss' main contribution to the quest is his *The Life of Jesus Critically Examined* (1835), a book that has been described as "the most revolutionary religious document written since Luther's Ninety-Five Theses."[29] Though its reception within scholarly circles was mixed, it certainly had more immediate impact at a popular level than any other critical work on the historical Jesus up to that time, or since, with the present work of certain participants of the Jesus Seminar (especially that of Crossan and Mack) being the only possible rival.

In this work, Strauss takes the critical approach to the Gospels to a radically new level. Previous rationalistic accounts of Jesus' life had assumed that the Gospel accounts were generally historically reliable, at least to the extent that they believed they had to explain away the various miraculous accounts about Jesus in naturalistic means. With Strauss, however, this reliability is dismissed. The Gospel accounts, he maintains, are so saturated with impossible-to-believe supernatural accounts and are so full of irresolvable contradictions that the only adequate explanation for them is that they are not historical accounts at all.[30] Rather, they are, almost in their entirety, "myth."[31] Previous critical scholars had hesitantly applied the category of "myth" to sections of the Gospels, but Strauss boldly applies it in almost a *carte blanche* fashion. As Schweitzer notes, the previously frightful possibility that there was next to nothing of genuine historical information in the Gospels held "no terrors" for Strauss.[32]

In relation to the Gospels, Strauss defines myth as a narrative relating directly or indirectly to Jesus, which may be considered not as the expression of a fact, but as the product of an idea of his earliest followers.[33] Thus, the Gospels do not so much record who the historical Jesus was as they do the mythological ideas his followers had about him. Hence, the ultimate aim of Strauss' *Life of Jesus* is not to provide a sketch of the historical Jesus, but rather to highlight the mythmaking process at work among his followers that comes to be recorded in the Gospels.

The methodology used throughout *The Life of Jesus* to accomplish this is accurately summarized by Baird when he writes:

> In discussing the material from each section, Strauss repeatedly presents his main line of interpretation: the accounts describe super-

natural events and thus are not historical; attempts to explain them by rationalistic methods are mistaken, even ridiculous; therefore, mythological interpretation is the only viable alternative.[34]

Like Paulus before him, but on totally different terms, Strauss concludes his *Life of Jesus* by attempting to show that his work is not ultimately disastrous for Christian thinking – though most of his immediate readers at a popular level drew just this conclusion. To put it in a word, Strauss attempts to locate the significance of the myths that surround Jesus within Hegel's dialectical understanding of world history. As in Hegel, for example, the myth of the incarnation for Strauss comes to mythologically represent the union of God with the human race being aimed at through world history.[35]

The Enduring Legacy of Strauss

It is remarkable to discover just how many subsequent trends in New Testament scholarship are foreshadowed in Strauss' work. His focus on the nature of the oral Gospel tradition – including his account of the mythmaking process at work within it – contained the seeds of what would eventually blossom into twentieth-century form-critical studies. Similarly, his interest in the history of religions foreshadowed the rise of the history-of-religions school at the turn of the century. And the parallels between his application of the category of religious myth to the Gospels – albeit in a less nuanced fashion – and Rudolf Bultmann's work can hardly be missed.[36] In all these areas Strauss was something of a pioneer.

But Strauss was also a forerunner in another important aspect of subsequent biblical studies: namely, in the manner in which he explicitly allowed philosophical and theological presuppositions to determine his historical research. But Strauss, unlike some modern critics, was very self-conscious and forthright about this fact. He frankly admitted that his historical work was guided by Hegelian presuppositions.[37] In one particular revealing article, for example, Strauss wrote about his work in the New Testament, "I am no historian; with me everything has proceeded from a dogmatic (or rather anti-dogmatic) concern."[38] And the clear target for Strauss' anti-dogmatic sentiments was, throughout his scholarly career, the foundational presupposition of the traditional Christian faith – the transcendent yet personal God. Hence he writes:

> For transcendence is indeed the one enemy – in its eschatological form, the final enemy – with which speculative criticism has to contend in all forms, and wherever possible to overcome.[39]

And again:

> [T]he one personal God . . . [has] resolved himself into the impersonal but person-shaping All. This same idea forms the ultimate point of departure . . . of our Cosmic conception.[40]

Hence, the traditional Christian notion that the one personal and transcendent God was decisively working through the life, death, and resurrection of Jesus Christ is, on philosophical grounds, rejected by Strauss. As with so many others within the quest, the Jesus Strauss was looking for—and thus found—was a de-supernaturalized Jesus. Given his philosophical presuppositions, it could have been no other way.

In the end, however, the Jesus discovered, or created, out of Strauss' philosophical presuppositions was one who held no significance to modern people. Even the later Strauss did not find his Hegelian attempt to salvage the Christian significance of Christ from his critique convincing. In his last work, *The Old Faith and the New,* published two years before his death, the significance of either the historical Jesus or the myths that arose from him is totally gone. Here Strauss describes Jesus as an "enthusiast" and infers from this that, "we shall not be desirous to choose him as the guide of our life. He will be sure to mislead us, if we do not subject his influence to the control of our reason."[41] With admirable forthrightness, Strauss concludes by admitting, "if we would speak as honest, upright men, we must acknowledge we are no longer Christians."[42]

Here too Strauss anticipates certain subsequent trends within the quest. Toward the turn of the century, as we shall shortly see, several other very influential thinkers would announce that the Jesus remaining after the historical-critical quest for him is complete is one who has nothing to say to contemporary people.

THE RISE OF SOURCE CRITICISM

Another extremely important aspect of the historical Jesus quest was coming into play around the time of Strauss in the form of source-critical studies. Prior to the mid-nineteenth century, most scholars—following Augustine—held that Matthew was the first Gospel to be written.[43] The increasingly critical orientation toward tradition that was taking place in the mid-nineteenth century, however, allowed the question of the sources and interrelationships of the Gospels to be reopened. One line of thought, which tended to downplay the literary interrelationships of the Gospels, emphasized the influence of an early, common oral tradition on each of the Gospel writers. This view was aided by the work of J.G. Herder and was vigorously supported by J.C.L. Gieseler and F.L. Godet.[44] Although it has suffered serious attrition over the last century, recent years have brought new reformulations, primarily from more conservative scholars.[45]

Another line of thought was pursued by J.J. Griesbach who attempted to preserve Matthean priority within the Synoptic relationships, but with a new twist. The "Griesbach hypothesis" – which postulates Matthean priority, Luke's use of Matthew and, finally, Mark's use of both the above – exerted a considerable force within Gospel studies in the first half of the nineteenth century. Adherents included F.C. Baur, the great Tübingen scholar, and Strauss. Ironically, many have attributed the demise of this theory to these two influential men as well. By the mid-nineteenth century, both Strauss' historical skepticism in regard to the Gospels and Baur's Hegelian-influenced "Tübingen hypothesis" had come under severe attack.[46] In what some consider a classic case of guilt by association, the Griesbach hypothesis was thus shunned by many as well. If, it was felt, this theory of Synoptic Gospel relations could support the type of historical skepticism propounded by Strauss, then another hypothesis must be found – one that could help to establish some type of historical base once again. This new theory would turn out to be the now-dominant "two-source" or "two-document" hypothesis.

The roots of the two-source theory can be traced back to the early nineteenth century. Critical to this enterprise, of course, was the establishment of both Markan priority and the "Q" hypothesis.[47] In regard to the former, an 1835 essay by Karl Lachmann argued that Mark represents the earliest Gospel tradition. In 1838, both C.G. Wilke and the philosopher C.H. Weisse contended that Mark was not only the earliest Gospel, but was also a common source for Matthew and Luke. Weisse, however, did not stop here. Like Schleiermacher before him, Weisse took Papius' famous Matthean "logia" statement at face value, and thus surmised that a pre-canonical Matthean sayings collection existed early on. Combining this with his view of Markan priority, he concluded that both Matthew and Luke were privy to Mark and this "sayings source"; thus, the two-source theory was born. It was left to H.J. Holtzmann, in 1863, to provide the first comprehensive presentation of the two-source theory. The common sayings source behind Matthew and Luke was given the title "Q" by Johannes Weiss in 1890, who derived it from the German word Quelle, meaning "source."[48]

With the assistance of the two-source hypothesis, scholars could hope once again—in the face of Strauss' historical critique of the Gospels—for a firm footing upon which to base the continuing quest for the Jesus of history. As Craig Evans notes:

> Mark was now understood as an early account (happily lacking the embarrassing infancy narrative) that provides the basic historical framework of Jesus' life. On the other hand, "Q" was understood as providing Jesus' basic teachings and, unlike Mark, did not contain any accounts of exorcism. From these two "documents" scholars would be able to reconstruct a life of Jesus.[49]

The Later "Lives" of Jesus

The quest continued along several different tracks throughout the nineteenth century. In Germany, a number of authors kept the basic framework of Venturini's Essene conspiracy theory alive.[50] Others, like Strauss, took the route of radical skepticism. Bruno Bauer, for example, adopted the theory of Markan priority as did most others. But instead of utilizing this theory to increase confidence in our ability to arrive at historically reliable information about Jesus, Bauer argued that this work was a literary creation pure and simple. And since the other Gospels depend on Mark, there is no reason to think that there is anything that is historical in any of the Gospels. Hence, he concluded that the historical Jesus most likely never even existed.[51]

While few followed Bauer in his wholesale denial of Jesus' existence, his attempt to thoroughly undermine the historicity of Mark was to be picked up by Wilhelm Wrede and others at the turn of the century and is recently experiencing something of a resurgence among New Testament scholars. The Cynic thesis, we shall later see, is significantly rooted in just this skeptical perspective on Mark. And hence, demonstrating Mark's historical reliability shall be an important aspect of our critique of this thesis (see chaps. 10 and 11).

Ernest Renan

While the most radical proponents of the quest for the historical Jesus tended to come from Germany, the quest certainly continued to be carried on in more moderate forms outside of Germany as well. One of the classic works from the latter half of the century—one that has been characterized as "[w]ithout question, the most popular life of Jesus ever written"—was published in France in 1863: Ernest Renan's *Life of Jesus*.[52]

More a popular than a scholarly work, Renan's book was infused with brilliantly descriptive narratives, fostered by his own experience of the Holy Land during archaeological excavations. Renan's Jesus is one who begins as a wise and gentle teacher of moral precepts and the loving Fatherhood of God, but who is gradually transformed into an apocalyptically motivated messianic aspirant. In the process, and largely against his own predilections, Jesus is drawn into the role of miracle-working "thaumaturgist and exorcist in spite of himself."[53]

Integral to Renan's thesis is the notion that, in tandem with this radicalizing process, Jesus also experiences a growing alienation and, finally, rejection. In the end, Jesus' apocalyptic orientation drives him toward martyrdom and thus the cross. The book ends with Renan's hesitant speculation about how the legend of Jesus' resurrection originated. With characteristic rhetorical flare, Renan writes:

> Let us say . . . that the strong imagination of Mary Magdalen played in this circumstance an important part. Divine power of love! Sacred moments in which the passion of one possessed gave to the world a resuscitated God![54]

Like the earlier lives of Jesus, we see, Renan yet considers the Gospel accounts reliable enough to warrant an explanation. But his explanations are, on the whole, much less extravagant, and hence more plausible, than were the rather crass explanations of Venturini and Paulus. What is more, the Jesus he portrays, and the manner in which he portrays him, was extremely attractive to both the rationalistic and romanticist sensibilities of his age. These factors in large measure account for why the popularity of this book dwarfed the popularity of all earlier lives of Jesus.[55]

Methodologically, Renan has a good deal in common with his more radical German contemporaries. Like them, he shares a sort of two-source hypothesis about the Synoptic relations and, increasingly throughout the thirteen editions of his book, a distrust in the historicity of the fourth Gospel.[56] But the most decisive aspect of Renan's methodology which he shared was his thoroughly rationalistic attitude toward the miraculous.

In the preface to the thirteenth edition, for example, Renan writes:

> If the miracle has any reality, this book is but a tissue of errors. If the Gospels are inspired books, and true, consequently to the letter, from beginning to end, I have been guilty of a great

wrong. . . . If, on the contrary, the miracle is an inadmissible thing, then I am right in regarding the books which contain miraculous recitals as histories mixed with fictions, as legends full of inaccuracies, errors, and of systematic expedients.[57]

Like Paulus before him, however, Renan asked that he be recognized not as a "skeptic" but merely as a "moderate critic"; he did, after all, "extract something historical" from the Gospels rather than reject them wholesale.[58] Next to Strauss and Bauer, after all, Renan does indeed look conservative. But his desire to not be considered radical did not lead him to equivocate in the least on the question of the admissibility of the supernatural. This was, he correctly noted, the question that is "[a]t the bottom of all discussion" concerning the historical Jesus. And for Renan, as with most nineteenth century questers, it had to be answered "anterior to exegesis." Hence he writes:

Miracles are things which never happen. . . . We reject the supernatural for the same reason that we reject the existence of centaurs and hippogriffes; and this reason is, that nobody has ever seen them. It is not because it has been previously demonstrated to me that the evangelists do not merit absolute credence that I reject the miracles which they recount. It is because they do recount miracles that I say, "The Gospels are legends; they may contain history, but, certainly, all that they set forth is not historical."[59]

For all of his attractive romanticist features, the Jesus of Renan's work is a thoroughly de-supernaturalized Jesus.

Conservative "Lives of Jesus"

While the majority of those who engaged in the quest for the historical Jesus operated with anti-supernaturalistic assumptions and thus "discovered" a Jesus who was significantly different from the one portrayed within the Gospels, there were those in the nineteenth century who resisted this philosophical bias. Most significant is the conservative tending work of several nineteenth-century British thinkers who brought a wealth of scholarship and insight to the quest for the historical Jesus. Because they did not share the scholarly consensus concerning the possibilities of miracles, their work was generally not taken as seriously as others by their contemporaries. And, in fact, modern reviews of the quest frequently minimize or, as with Schweitzer, ignore their contributions altogether. Nevertheless, their contributions to the quest, especially as providing a critique of the overly rationalistic and skeptical methods and findings of their contemporaries, are substantial and must be considered.[60]

The first substantial British life of Jesus, published in 1874, was F.W. Farrar's *Life of Christ*.[61] As his book indicates, Farrar was well-acquainted with the methods and results of critical German scholarship of the day. But, drawing upon the scholarly work of the Cambridge trio of J.B. Lightfoot, B.F. Westcott, and F.J.A. Hort, as well as upon more conservative German scholarship, he arrived at very different conclusions than they. In his view, the radical conclusions of the New Testament critics of his time were necessitated by the presuppositions they carried out their historical-critical method with: they were not necessitated by the historical-critical method itself. Farrar correctly saw that where one ends up in his or her research is significantly determined by where one starts. And for Farrar, the starting point was certainly not Enlightenment rationalism or Hegelian idealism, as it was for Strauss. Rather, for Farrar, the starting point of historical research was the Christian faith. Hence, at the beginning of his *Life of Christ* he writes:

> [T]his Life of Christ is avowedly and unconditionally the work of a believer. Those who expect to find in it new theories about the divine personality of Jesus, or brilliant combinations of mythic cloud tinged by the sunset imagination of some decadent belief will look in vain.[62]

Working with the presupposition that there is a personal and transcendent God, and thus that miracles are possible, Farrar contends that there is nothing in the historical evidence that leads to the naturalistic Jesus of so many other questers. Those who embrace this view do so for philosophical, not historical, reasons.

Perhaps even more significant in this vein is Alfred Edersheim's meticulous work, *The Life and Times of Jesus the Messiah*. In the words of Pals (intended as a compliment), "[This] book was . . . British scholarship on a German scale."[63] Edersheim's deep knowledge of the ancient Jewish world and its various writings was arguably unrivaled by any in the mid-nineteenth century. Though he is clearly at home within the historical-critical method, his work evinces a complete confidence in the historical trustworthiness of the Gospel accounts, including John. While holding to Markan priority, he nonetheless maintained (on solid grounds) the traditional apostolic authorship of – or influence on – the four Gospels. And he altogether rejected the anti-supernaturalistic bias of the age, as is clear from his comments on the account of Jesus' raising of the widow's son.

> [T]he only real ground for rejecting this narrative is disbelief in the Miraculous, including, of course, rejection of the Christ as the Miracle of Miracles. But is it not vicious reasoning in a circle, as well as begging the question, to reject the Miraculous because we discredit the Miraculous?

And in the light of what he believed was evidential historical support for a miracle-working Jesus along with the incredible stretches of imagination required to explain these miracles on naturalistic grounds (as exemplified by Venturini, Paulus, and others), Edersheim adds, "[D]oes not such rejection involve much more of the incredible than faith itself?"[64] The point is well taken.

As with Farrar, one finds in Edersheim the conviction that it is not historical evidence itself that leads one to reject the Gospels and their portraits of Christ. The evidence, they insist, leads to the opposite conclusion. Nor does a scholarly critical approach to history itself lead one to skeptical conclusions. What leads the radical critics to their radical conclusions, according to Farrar and Edersheim, is the worldview assumptions that saturate their methodology and distort their treatment of the evidence.

Colin Brown in essence agrees with their evaluations when he writes:

> From the Deists and Reimarus to Strauss and Renan, the world view that was brought to the study of the Gospels was decisive in the interpretation of Jesus. . . . The history of the study of Jesus in European thought in the eighteenth and nineteenth centuries is as much a history of changing philosophies, theologies, and world views, as it is of growing refinements in historical techniques.[65]

Farrar and Edersheim did not share the Enlightenment rationalistic assumptions of most of their scholarly contemporaries, and thus their research did not lead them to the same conclusions as most of their scholarly contemporaries. But it was, unfortunately, their contemporaries' assumptions that were to win the day within the academy. And hence their contributions and insights remain largely unappreciated by the scholarly world at large.[66]

THE END OF THE FIRST QUEST: ALBERT SCHWEITZER

The legacy of the nineteenth-century rationalistic quest continued on into the early twentieth century. Carrying on the tradition established with the earlier lives of Jesus, liberal scholars such as Albrecht Ritschl, Adolph Harnack, Ernst Troeltsch, and Walter Rauschenbusch conceptualized Jesus as being first and foremost a moral reformer and teacher of a universal spiritual religion.[67] As with their predecessors, these scholars accepted as historical basic features of Mark's Gospel but rejected, or at least radically reinterpreted, both the supernatural features of Jesus' ministry and the New Testament's portrayal of him as divine. The only Jesus that could be relevant for faith in the modern age, they believed, was one who was freed from the mythological trappings of his first-century world.

For a variety of reasons, however, other scholars at the turn of this century began to question the very possibility of finding a "relevant" historical Jesus behind the Gospel portraits. While such a move had already been carried out by the later Strauss, it did not significantly alter the course of the quest until the turn of this century when it was reformulated on different terms by Johannes Weiss and, most significantly, by Albert Schweitzer. In his 1892 study of Jesus' understanding of the kingdom of God, Weiss argued that the Jesus we find behind the traditions collected in the Gospels is not the ethical reformer of Ritschl and Harnack: he is, rather, a misguided eschatological prophet who lived in expectation of the imminent, apocalyptic end of the world.[68] As such, argued Weiss, he is simply not relevant to those who do not share his first-century apocalyptic worldview.

Weiss' view, however, made little impact upon the scholarly world until it was picked up and expanded upon in 1906 by Albert Schweitzer in a book that was to function as the symbolic terminus for the "Old Quest," his now famous *The Quest of the Historical Jesus.* In this brilliant work, as previously noted, Schweitzer chronicles the quest from Reimarus to himself. And the motif that runs throughout his chronicling is "the eschatological question." That is, throughout the book Schweitzer constantly forces the issue of the manner in which the eschatological worldview, so evident in the New Testament, had been systematically avoided by nearly all of the scholarly participants in the quest up to his time. Only on this basis, he argues, could they arrive at the view of Jesus as an ethical teacher or moral example who they believed was so relevant for their time. But the relevance, according to Schweitzer, was bought at the price of historical-critical integrity. In his view, Jesus the ethical reformer "never had any existence. He is a figure designed by rationalism, endowed with life by liberalism, and clothed by modern theology in an historical garb."[69]

On the score of Jesus' strange eschatology, only Weiss had dared to come clean with the evidence, according to Schweitzer. And the evidence is that, insofar as we can know anything at all about the historical Jesus, we know him to be an apocalyptic preacher whose entire worldview was radically alien to our own.[70] If Jesus "reigns" at all, as the church has always proclaimed, in Schweitzer's view he reigns as an enigma. Hence, in one now classic passage, Schweitzer summarizes the essence of his position as follows.

> There is silence all around. The Baptist appears, and cries: "Repent, for the Kingdom of Heaven is at hand." Soon after that comes Jesus, and in the knowledge that he is the coming Son of Man lays hold of the wheel of the world to set it moving on that last revolution which is to bring all ordinary history to a close. It refuses to turn, and He throws Himself upon it. Then it does turn; and crushes Him. Instead of bringing in the eschatological conditions, He has destroyed them. The wheel rolls onward, and the mangled body of the one immeasurably great Man, who was strong enough to think of Himself as the spiritual ruler of mankind and to bend history to His purpose, is hanging upon it still. That is His victory and His reign.[71]

As Strauss had earlier concluded, Schweitzer discovered that when one begins with naturalistic presuppositions and carries out the historical-critical method on this basis, the only historical Jesus one can honestly come up with is one who refuses to be understood within these presuppositions. He is "alien" to our modern world — unless we are willing to adjust our assumptions about the modern world.

THE PERIOD OF "NO QUEST": FROM SCHWEITZER TO KÄSEMANN (1906–1953)

One of the most significant repercussions of Schweitzer's work was that it significantly undermined the two-century-old liberal agenda of discovering a Jesus who was both de-supernaturalized and relevant to contemporary life. A wild-eyed apocalyptic failure was hardly the sort of person that twentieth-century humanity wanted or needed. Schweitzer was more than gentle in his statement of this problem when he wrote:

The study of the Life of Jesus has had a curious history. It set out in quest of the historical Jesus, believing that when it found Him it could bring Him straight into our time as a Teacher and Savior. . . . But He does not stay; He passes by our time and returns to His own.[72]

This disappointing conclusion, argued with force throughout Schweitzer's book, contributed to what has come to be called a period of "No Quest," one which extends from Schweitzer's time up to the early 1950s. It was a period where the general optimism of discovering a relevant historical Jesus behind the portraits of the Gospels, an optimism which fueled the "Old Quest," was lost. Many New Testament scholars simply abandoned the entire project of "finding" the historical Jesus as hopeless. And others, attempting to salvage something of significance from the Christian faith on the wreckage of the first quest, tried to argue that the historical Jesus was, after all, irrelevant to the Christian faith.

But it would be a gross oversimplification to attribute the demise of the "Old Quest" and the ensuing period of "No Quest" to Schweitzer alone. In truth, a number of factors contributed to bringing about this situation. Four stand out as warranting our attention.

Factors Contributing to the "No Quest"

First, Schweitzer's critique of the "Old Quest" not only produced a Jesus that was unappealing to modern minds: it also forced the question of whether one can, in fact, write anything like an objective account of the historical Jesus. Schweitzer aptly demonstrated that the tendency of the liberal scholars of the eighteenth and nineteenth centuries was to "find" a Jesus "after their own image." As George Tyrrell stated it in a now-classic analogy, in gazing into the deep well of the New Testament texts, scholars tend to find their own reflection gazing up. They discover, in other words, what they want to discover.[73] Schweitzer's stringent presentation of the decisive role the nonhistorical motivations of the researcher play in "discovering" the historical Jesus had the effect of producing widespread skepticism about any possibility of arriving at an "objective" account of the historical Jesus.

Secondly, much of the optimism of the "Old Quest" in recovering the "real" Jesus had come to be rooted in the reliability of Mark which was, on the generally accepted two-source hypothesis, seen as being the earliest Gospel and the foundation of Matthew and Luke (John had generally been long since dismissed). While the two-source hypothesis remained intact, the reliability of Mark did not. Toward the turn of the century several scholars began to follow in the footsteps of Bruno Bauer and assess this work as being more theological than historical.

By far the most influential voice in this new movement was William Wrede. In his highly influential book on Mark, *The Messianic Secret*, Wrede argued that the priority of Mark was no advantage for a recon-struction of who the historical Jesus was. For this work, he argued, is as thoroughly governed by nonhistorical theological concerns as are the other Gospels. "[A]s a whole," he writes, "the Gospel no longer offers a historical *view* of the real life of Jesus." While a "pale residue" of histori-cal reminiscences remains, the work as a whole "belongs to the history of dogma" rather than historical record.[74]

If Mark cannot be trusted, however, then we have virtually nothing to work with in our attempts to discover the historical Jesus. Hence many scholars closed the book on the "Old Quest" as a hopeless, mis-guided endeavor.

An extremely important third factor that contributed to the period of "No Quest" was the rise of form criticism. The foundations for this discipline had been anticipated in the work of Strauss and Wrede, and were picked up and expanded upon in the following decades by K.L. Schmidt, Martin Dibelius, and most importantly, Rudolf Bultmann.[75]

Form criticism attempts to investigate the oral tradition behind the Gospels. Ultimately, it seeks to identify the original setting (*Sitz im Leben*) of a particular piece of the tradition by tracing its formal development through oral and literary stages. The earliest practitioners of the method combined a number of philosophical presuppositions with the form-critical enterprise, and these have tended to govern its use up to the present. These presuppositions include: (1) particular conceptions of the process of oral transmission; (2) the conviction that the oral Jesus tradi-tion was a mixture of historical remembrances and early Christian fabri-cations — or, more politely, "creations" — both of which were "freely elab-orated, reinterpreted, and transformed" by the various Christian communities;[76] and, of course, (3) a naturalistic worldview that precludes the possibility of the miraculous in history. Thus, in effect, form criticism served to place an apparently immovable wall of early Christian distor-tion between the Gospel texts and the historical Jesus, which served to further undermine any confidence that we can ever accurately recover the original historical Jesus.[77]

A fourth and final factor that fed into the general abandonment of the quest project was a new theological perspective on the historical

Jesus. As early as 1892, Martin Kähler expressed the conviction that the quest for the historical Jesus was theologically unnecessary, even illegitimate. It was, in essence, an interesting trip down "a blind alley."[78] The heart of Kähler's critique of the quest is theological in nature: "*the historical Jesus of modern authors conceals from us the living Christ.*"[79] For Kähler, this fundamental issue involves a variation of the faith and reason problematic. He writes:

> [h]istorical facts which first have to be established by science cannot as *such* become experiences of faith. Therefore, Christian faith and a history of Jesus repel each other like oil and water as soon as the magic spell of an enthusiastic and enrapturing description loses its power.[80]

According to Kähler, the vicissitudes of historical research with their more or less probable results could never provide a foundation for faith. In fact, they hindered faith. Hence, for Kähler, the quest for the historical Jesus is at best irrelevant, and at worst a formidable obstacle, to genuine faith in Jesus as the Christ.

The post-World War I rise of neo-orthodoxy served to strengthen the type of sentiments found in Kähler. Virtually all of the major figures across the neo-orthodox spectrum held a negative view of the historical quest, primarily for theological reasons.[81] Hence, attention was shifted from the "Jesus of history" to the "Christ of faith." Both Barthian dialectical theology and Bultmannian existential theology agreed that contemporary Christian faith could not be rooted in anything as fluctuating and tenuous as historical Jesus reconstructions which were, in any case, now falling on hard times.

What is more, the attempt to rest one's faith upon an "objective" foundation—historical arguments and reconstructions, for example—was seen by neo-orthodoxy as a challenge to the central Protestant principle of "justification by faith alone."[82] A new (and highly questionable) epistemological twist was given to Luther's (and Paul's) foundational theological conviction which resulted in an intensely irrationalistic fideism. In any event, neo-orthodoxy followed Kähler in seeing faith and historical reason as relating like oil and water.

RUDOLF BULTMANN

In terms of New Testament scholarship, the most influential figure during the "No Quest" period was unquestionably Rudolf Bultmann. Indeed, his thought continues to exercise a strong influence in some scholarly circles, including the circle out of which the Cynic thesis has arisen. Hence we will do well to consider his thought in a more particular fashion.

Bultmann's general attitude toward the quest has already been sketched above: for all practical purposes the quest was seen by him as being both methodologically impossible and theologically illegitimate. These sentiments, however, did not stop Bultmann from authoring his own book on Jesus. The intensity of Bultmann's skepticism concerning the historical Jesus is expressed early on in his *Jesus and the Word* when he writes:

> I do indeed think that we can know almost nothing concerning
> the life and personality of Jesus, since the early Christian
> sources show no interest in either, are moreover fragmentary
> and often legendary; and other sources do not exist.[83]

Indeed, for Bultmann, the only certain knowledge we can have concerning the historical Jesus is the sheer "thatness" *(Dass)* of his historical existence and (perhaps inconsistently) that he died on the cross. But this bare minimum of historical information is, he believes, all that is required for Christian faith. It is sufficient to be used by God to call us to live an authentic existence, which is, according to Bultmann, what the Christian proclamation, the kerygma, is all about.

Following Strauss, however, Bultmann believed that the kerygma itself was hopelessly shrouded in first-century mythology. In his view, there was no possibility of penetrating behind this mythology to discover the real Jesus as a foundation for faith. That was the naive hope of the now abandoned "Old Quest." But, again like Strauss, he nevertheless believed that there was the possibility of reinterpreting the mythology of the New Testament in terms that would rescue its significance for modern people. This was the agenda of Bultmann's now famous "demythologizing" hermeneutic.[84]

The central key to this new hermeneutic is Heideggerian existentialist philosophy. From this perspective, the heart of the Gospel is understood to be the existential call to radical decision, and thus to authentic existence. Through its mythology, the New Testament directs "man to the fact that he is . . . brought before God, that God stands before him," and thus it directs him "into his Now as the hour of decision for God."[85] Hence, the eschatological emphasis of the kerygma which Weiss and Schweitzer pointed out is admitted, but demythologized, in Heideggerian terms.

As with most of his predecessors of the quest, it is very clear that Bultmann's New Testament work is driven by naturalistic presuppositions. Indeed, like Stauss and Renan, Bultmann was admirably forthright about this. In a revealing essay entitled "Is Exegesis without Presuppositions Possible?" Bultmann argues that while it is incumbent upon all biblical scholars to avoid "presupposing the results of their exegesis," there is, nonetheless, "one presupposition that cannot be dismissed": namely "the historical method of interrogating the texts."[86] And for Bultmann, this historical method was unequivocally committed to

> the presupposition that history is a unity in the sense of a closed continuum of effects. . . . This closedness means that the continuum of historical happenings cannot be rent by the interference of supernatural, transcendent powers and that therefore there is no "miracle" in this sense of the word.[87]

Armed with these presuppositions, Bultmann's reading of the New Testament as largely nonhistorical "mythology" was virtually guaranteed.

> The whole conception of the world which is presupposed in the preaching of Jesus as in the New Testament generally is mythological. . . . This conception of the world we call mythological because it is different from the conception of the world which has been formed and developed by science since its inception in ancient Greece and which has been accepted by all modern men. In this modern conception of the world the cause-and-effect nexus is fundamental. . . . In any case, modern science does not believe that the course of nature can be interrupted or, so to speak, perforated, by supernatural powers.[88]

While the radical skepticism of Bultmann was to soon disappear among his followers, as we shall see, the intensity of his conviction that miracles and modernity are mutually exclusive, a conviction he himself inherited from his predecessors, has not waned among most contemporary questers. Moreover, the meticulous manner in which he applied form criticism to the New Testament, and the stringency with which he argued his largely skeptical conclusions, presented a case that all subsequent scholars would have to wrestle with.

Parenthetically, it should perhaps be noted that, while Bultmann's radically skeptical views dominated the scene during the last three decades of the "No Quest" period, there were significant dissenters. And, as was the case in the nineteenth century, these dissenting voices were primarily British. Scholars such as T.W. Manson and C.H. Dodd refused to follow their German counterparts in embracing the skeptical mood of the time.[89] Their general perspective toward the "No Quest" proponents is captured by D.M. Baillie as he writes toward the end of the "No Quest" period:

> I cannot believe that there is any good reason for the defeatism of those who give up all hope of penetrating the tradition and reaching assured knowledge of the historical personality of Jesus. Surely such defeatism is a transient nightmare of Gospel criticism, from which we are now awakening to a more sober confidence in our quest of the Jesus of history.[90]

The "New Quest" (1953–1970s)

While the "transient nightmare" of radical skepticism Baillie spoke of has continued on in certain quarters up to our time, its dominance within the New Testament scholarly community began to wane shortly after he penned the above comment. In October 1953, Ernst Käsemann, a student of Bultmann, delivered a lecture to a group of Bultmann's former students that launched what has come to be known as the "New Quest for the historical Jesus."[91] Käsemann did not object to any significant feature of Bultmann's critical methodology or naturalistic worldview. But he wanted badly to avoid his devastating skeptical conclusions. As has been the case throughout this saga of the quest, this "New Quest" was birthed not primarily out of considerations for the historical evidence, nor because new methods of research were developed (for the "New Quest" scholars generally remained close to Bultmann's methodology). No, the "New Quest" was birthed primarily out of theological considerations.[92]

To put the matter succinctly, Käsemann realized that Bultmann's radical skepticism led necessarily to a type of docetic christology.[93] In other words, the "No Quest," with its emphasis on the Christ of faith and its practical disregard for the earthly Jesus, threatened to divest the church's Christ of his *humanity*. If the Christ of faith wasn't significantly related to the actual human Jesus of history, Käsemann saw, the Christian faith was in danger of being reduced to an existential dream. To salvage the relevance of the Christian faith, the historical-critical method had to salvage more of the historical Jesus than the previous generation of critical scholars had generally done.

Thus, one might say that the "New Quest" was essentially a quest for different conclusions by means of the same methodology that had conditioned the "No Quest" period. And, one can't help but further note the irony that, for this reason, the "New Quest" was carried out in an opposite direction from that of the "Old Quest." Whereas the "Old Quest" was launched in search of locating the *discontinuity* between the Christ of faith and the Jesus of history amidst the assumed continuity that existed between them, the "New Quest" was launched in an attempt to locate the *continuity* between the Christ of faith and the Jesus of history amidst an assumed discontinuity.

The first full-scale product of the "New Quest" appeared in 1956, Günther Bornkamm's *Jesus of Nazareth*.[94] The difference between the "Old Quest" and the "New" is clear from the very beginning of this work. "No one is any longer in the position to write a life of Jesus," Bornkamm admits.[95] Hence, little attention is paid in this work to such questions as the chronology of Jesus' life or his self-understanding, matters that the "New Quest" yet concedes to be irrecoverable from history. Nonetheless, Bornkamm displays a new post-Bultmannian confidence that certain strands of pre-Easter history within the Gospels' tradition can be recovered. And it is from these strands that he attempts to reconstruct the central teachings of Jesus. Other works, most notably those of Ernst Fuchs, Hans Conzelmann, and Gerhard Ebeling, were soon to follow and would attempt to carry out similar projects.[96]

Chronologically speaking, the new critical method of redaction criticism arose in tandem with the "New Quest."[97] Viewing the Gospels' writers as creative authors rather than merely as "scissor-and-paste men," redaction criticism focuses on the effects of the authors' own literary and theological tendencies upon the Gospel texts. Whereas form criticism sought to undercover the oral traditions preceding the Gospels, redaction criticism sought to discern how the individual authors themselves influenced how these traditions were worked into their works. Somewhat ironically, given the "New Quest's" aspiration to discover the continuity between the Christ of faith and the Jesus of history, redaction criticism has tended to raise a new barrier between the reader of the Gospels and the historical Jesus: namely, the "creativity" of the biblical authors themselves.[98] Redaction-critical studies have centered on the Gospel authors' use of earlier traditions, but have more recently also come to be applied to the hypothetical document Q as well.[99] As we shall see, such redactional speculations factor in strongly to Mack's project of establishing the historical Jesus as a Cynic sage.

While redactional criticism has remained quite strong up to the present, the fanfare that surrounded the "New Quest" was quite short-lived. There were a number of reasons for this. It produced little that was distinctly different from the "Old Quest," with some questioning whether it should be called "New" at all.[100] Others criticized some "New" questers for salvaging little more of the historical Jesus than what Bultmann had himself arrived at.[101] Still others, like Norman Perrin, began to challenge the basic assumption that initially drove the "New Quest" that Christian faith needs a significant continuity between the Christ of faith and the Jesus of history.[102]

A final factor that contributed to the general demise of the "New Quest" was that a number of scholars, both inside and outside of Germany, began turning out progressive works that were clearly independent of Bultmannian and post-Bultmannian assumptions.[103] Such works suggested (and continue to suggest) that the continuity between the Christ of faith and the Jesus of history can be established on terms not considered by the "New Quest," and that certain aspects of the Bultmannian form-critical enterprise which the "New" questers inherited were misguided. This school of thought, which has evolved over the last two decades into what some are calling the "Third Quest," will be important to us in our subsequent critique of the post-Bultmannian Cynic thesis.

Together, these factors served to put an end to the "New Quest" as originally conceived. As will become clear in the next chapter, however, this did not in the least mean that aspirations for the quest disappeared in post-Bultmannian circles. To the contrary, in a number of transformed ways, the post-Bultmannian school continues to engage in the quest for the historical Jesus and continues to exercise a dominating influence within contemporary New Testament scholarship. Indeed, most contemporary New Testament scholarship can be understood either as arising from this post-Bultmannian school of thought, or as arising from the "Third Quest" which is largely a reaction to it.

It is within these two distinctive trajectories of contemporary scholarship that the Cynic thesis must be understood. And thus, before we turn to explicating the Cynic thesis in section 2, we will do well to briefly survey the various methodologies and conclusions of these two movements. To this task we turn in the next chapter.

2

A SCHOLARLY HOUSE
DIVIDED AGAINST ITSELF:
An Overview of the Contemporary Quest

One might have thought that the demise of Käsemann's "New Quest" would have led many scholars back to something like Bultmann's "No Quest" position. For a variety of reasons, however, exactly the opposite has occurred. The last two decades have witnessed a veritable explosion of scholarly investigations of the historical Jesus.[1] Recent descriptions of the present state of the scholarly quest for Jesus struggle to capture the variety of phenomena in simple terms and categories.[2] Because of the current state of ferment, it is difficult to simply and neatly classify the amazing variety of conflicting theories and models being explored within Jesus research today. Nonetheless, with the assistance of various scholarly assessments of the field, it is possible to construct a framework that will provide the basis for a heuristic sketch of the contemporary quest.

Following the fresh insights of the British New Testament scholar N.T. Wright, it seems best to begin by viewing the new developments in the field in terms of two broad movements.[3] Though contemporary New Testament scholarship is very much a house divided against itself, there is a single discernible dividing line that can be located. On the one hand, as we mentioned in chapter 1, the legacy of the post-Bultmannian "New Quest" continues on in a transformed way with renewed vigor. As was the case in the "New Quest," most of these post-Bultmannians seek to avoid Bultmann's wholesale skepticism toward the quest. But, also as in the "New Quest," they tend to continue to operate within the methodological paradigm established by him. And it is primarily this methodological continuity with Bultmann and among themselves that justifies the classification of them as "post-Bultmannians."

On the other hand, numerous scholars have identified a burgeoning new phenomenon in Jesus research today. Its ultimate origins can perhaps be located in the counter-Bultmannian works of the fifties and sixties previously cited, though it did not blossom into anything like an identifiable distinct movement until the late seventies. Still, as early as 1973, the Swedish scholar Gustav Aulen brought attention to a "new phase" that he believed historical Jesus studies were entering into.[4] One of this movement's first major representatives, Ben Meyer, has referred to this new "phase" or "movement" as "the new questioning."[5] James Charlesworth heralds this new trend in a number of writings and has dubbed it "Jesus research" in order to distinguish it from the "Post-Bultmannian Quest."[6] And N.T. Wright has analyzed it as well, crowning it with a grand title—one that we will utilize as well—the "Third Quest."[7]

Thus, while keeping in mind the danger of simple classifications, we will throughout this chapter analyze the contemporary quest under the two broad categories of the "Third Quest" and the "Post-Bultmannian Quest."[8] This shall lay the foundation for our discussion of Crossan and Mack who come out of the post-Bultmannian camp (in section 2) as well as our critique of their approach which significantly borrows from the "Third Quest" (in section 3). We shall consider the "Third Quest" first.

CHARACTERISTICS OF THE "THIRD QUEST"

One of the distinguishing marks of this new movement is the variety of different scholars from a broad spectrum of religious backgrounds and methodological perspectives who have been classed within its ranks: liberals and conservatives, Jews, Christians, and agnostics—all are represented in the "Third Quest." To date, central figures in the movement include Geza Vermes,[9] Ben Meyer,[10] John Riches,[11] Anthony Harvey,[12] Marcus Borg,[13] E.P. Sanders,[14] and N.T. Wright.[15]

In spite of the variety of perspectives represented in the "Third Quest," however, several important distinctive characteristics are recognizable. While it is true that not all "third questers" can be identified by each of these, there is, nonetheless, enough continuity within the movement to constitute something of a "family resemblance" relationship.

Openness to the Supernatural

One of the most significant hallmarks of the "Third Quest" is that a number of those within its ranks self-consciously move beyond the methodological strictures of the Bultmannian paradigm. Ben Meyer, for example, identifies two of these: (1) the view that "the universe is a closed system," and (2) the view that "the only way to judge the past is by the present"—better known as Troeltsch's "principle of analogy."[16] As we have seen in our analysis of Bultmann and others, both of these presuppositions serve to rule out miracles and the supernatural in general. Meyer identifies these Bultmannian assumptions as rooted in particular "epistemological assessments," inherited from Enlightenment rationalism and the "Old Quest", that have, he believes, been shown to be "defective."[17] Many others within the "Third Quest" clearly resonate with such sentiments.[18] This new openness to the supernatural—or at least the extraordinary—in history sets the "Third Quest" apart from the dominant rationalistic strand of the quest for the historical Jesus up to this time.

Less Stringent Authenticity Criteria

There is also a general agreement within the "Third Quest" that the authenticity criteria that developed within the "New Quest" are far too stringent. Authenticity criteria are tests by which one determines whether a particular saying or action attributed to Jesus in the Gospels actually derives from the historical Jesus rather than from a later "creative" moment within the church. And, according to proponents of the "Third Quest," the tests employed by Bultmann and his followers were simply unrealistic.

For example, form critics who follow Bultmann often employ a "double dissimilarity criterion" to the sayings of Jesus. This criterion states that only those sayings of Jesus that are dissimilar to both first-century Jewish teaching and early church traditions can be safely attributed to Jesus. But this has been criticized by those within the "Third Quest" as being (among other things) quite arbitrary,[19] for there is no good reason to assume that Jesus never repeated teachings known in his culture and no good reason to assume that the traditions of the church couldn't have been influenced by Jesus' teaching.

New Approaches to Oral Tradition

Third, the stifling effects of other aspects of classical form-critical methods are often rejected—or at least drastically modified.[20] In this regard, it is interesting to note the influence of Birger Gerhardsson's work within the "Third Quest."[21] Since the early 1960s, Gerhardsson has honed a critique of the classic form-critical conception of the transmission process of the oral Gospel tradition.[22] In essence, he argues, on the basis of Rabbinic parallels to the Synoptic tradition, that there is much more continuity within the period of oral transmission than the Bultmannian model of form criticism allows for. Thus, within the "Third Quest" there is a general consensus that the Gospels offer a firm basis for genuine historical information about Jesus. Sanders expresses this sentiment well.

> The dominant view today seems to be that we can know pretty well what Jesus was out to accomplish, that we can know a lot about what he said, and that those two things make sense within the world of first-century Judaism.[23]

This point shall be explored more fully in chapter 5 when we critique the methodology of post-Bultmannians such as Crossan and Mack.

Emphasis on Jewishness of Jesus

This leads to a fourth general characteristic. There is, among most scholars within the "Third Quest," an emphasis on seeing *Jesus as a Jew*, and thus on understanding him within the context of first-century Judaism.[24] Such an emphasis has a decisive impact on how one understands Jesus and the early church. For example, it is because of this emphasis that "third questers" are frequently suspicious of the above mentioned double dissimilarity criterion. If we understand Jesus within the context of first-century Judaism, they reason, we have no reason whatsoever to reject as inauthentic those aspects of his teaching that reflect first-century Judaism. Similarly, it is because of this emphasis that many within the "Third Quest" are inclined to presuppose a great deal of continuity between early church traditions, found in the Gospels and the epistles, and the life and teachings of the historical Jesus. For within first-century Judaism, as Gerhardsson has argued, a strong emphasis was placed on accurately passing on the teachings of a master religious instructor.

No Controlling Presupposition

Finally, the wide diversity of backgrounds and perspectives within the "Third Quest" has led to the observation that, unlike earlier ones, this quest was not initiated by any one set of controlling *a priori* theological and/or philosophical presuppositions.[25] While its results will no doubt have theological implications, and while a variety of theological methodologies and convictions inform its various members, there is no one theological "school" directing the investigations of the "Third Quest." This fact allows for a greater possibility of self-correcting dialogue within the movement itself. Thus, in conclusion, it is safe to say that as a broad paradigm within contemporary Jesus research, the future of the "Third Quest" looks very promising.

EVANGELICALS AND THE THIRD QUEST

Generally speaking, it is clear that evangelicals would naturally be pre-disposed to the "Third Quest" paradigm. To begin with, because of the apparent attempt within the "Third Quest" to submit second-order philosophical and theological convictions to first-order historical endeavors, its methodologies are generally not controlled by presuppositions that *a priori* dismiss the idea of the supernatural or miraculous.[26] This is not to equate the "Third Quest" as a whole with a "new conservatism," but rather to simply observe that, for the most part, the type of blanket rationalism and skepticism concerning the possibility of miracles that was characteristic of the previous three defining moments of the quest (viz., the "Old," "No," and "New" quests) is not found within the ranks of the "Third Quest." In this sense, the "Third Quest" is clearly a part of what Craig Evans has referred to as the "post-mythological era" of Jesus research.[27]

It is also the case that the comparative confidence with which most "third questers" approach the Gospels in regard to historical material is much more in line with evangelical convictions than most of the work done during the prior quests. And the emphasis on Jesus' Jewishness is another point at which evangelical and "Third Quest" concerns intersect.

To date, a number of evangelical scholars have contributed to the endeavors of the "Third Quest," including N.T. Wright, Craig Evans,[28] and Ben Witherington III.[29] In fact, Wright is currently in the midst of producing a projected five-volume work—two volumes of which have been released—that promises to be one of the definitive statements from within the movement at the end of the twentieth-century.[30] As shall be clear in the subsequent critique of the Cynic thesis, this work is very much indebted to the work of these New Testament scholars.

While the "Third Quest" is flourishing in many quarters, however, it can hardly be said to be dominating the contemporary scene, for the renewed post-Bultmannian movement is yet very strong, especially in Germany and America, and it shows no signs of waning. It is out of this movement that the increasingly popular Cynic thesis has arisen, and thus it is to this movement that the rest of this chapter, and indeed the rest of this book, will be devoted.

THE ORIGINS OF THE POST-BULTMANNIAN QUEST

One of the more interesting aspects of the new "Post-Bultmannian Quest" is that its greatest impetus has come not from Germany, but rather from North America. To understand this phenomenon, one must trace that transplantation of Bultmannian seeds from German to North American fields of New Testament study. Two of Bultmann's former students figure prominently here: Helmut Koester and James Robinson.[31] Through their students, Koester and Robinson—New Testament instructors at Harvard and Claremont respectively—have spread their influence throughout North America, as witnessed by the dominating presence of both Harvard and Claremont graduates within many of its New Testament departments. The force of what William Farmer has called "the Harvard-Claremont connection" is also currently at work within the high-profile Jesus Seminar and within a variety of sectors of the prominent Society of Biblical Literature as well.[32]

One can trace the first buds of the North American post-Bultmannian renaissance to the early 1970s. In 1971, Koester and Robinson collected a number of earlier essays and, with additions, published them as a programmatic work entitled *Trajectories through Early Christianity*.[33] Since that time, their original program has been supplemented and developed through a wide variety of books and essays, often through the work of their students. Several aspects of their ongoing project are fundamental to the renewal of the "Post-Bultmannian Quest." In fact, each of them plays a significant role in the rise of the Cynic thesis.

CHARACTERISTICS OF THE POST-BULTMANNIAN QUEST

Beyond a shared continuity with Bultmann's presuppositions and form critical methodology, there are a number of specific features that proponents of the "Post-Bultmannian Quest" tend to share.

Radical Early Christian Diversity

First, Koester and Robinson have revitalized Walter Bauer's thesis on early Christian beginnings—a thesis that, in Koester's words, "destroyed the wholly legendary edifice of orthodox wishful thinking."[34] In a 1934 German work, Bauer argued that, rather than being marked by categories like "orthodoxy" and "heresy," early Christianity initially exhibited a remarkable diversity of interpretations of Jesus.[35] Thus, "heresy" only became such when one particular Jesus tradition among several—the one eventually known as "orthodoxy"—gained enough power and influence to pronounce it so. At the heart of this theory is the conviction that some of the developments within early Christianity that have been theologically and historically marginalized due to labels of "heresy" may actually represent traditions more primitive and initially widespread than so-called "orthodoxy."

Koester and Robinson's rejuvenation of Bauer's radical early Christian diversity thesis has created a context within which quite disparate renditions of "early Christianity" are recognized as simply one of any variety of equally valid expressions of primitive Christian "trajectories." Thus, the notion of radical early Christian diversity has become a central presupposition of the contemporary "Post-Bultmannian Quest," and certainly functions as a central presupposition of Crossan and Mack's Cynic thesis, as we shall see.

The Primacy of "Extra-Canonical Gospels"

A second factor which rides on the coattails of the first involves a shift in attention to apocryphal or extra-canonical "gospels." Koester and Robinson have called for the instatement of various noncanonical works into the data pool from which reconstructions of early Christianity — and thus the historical Jesus — are derived.[36] Chief among these documents is the group of largely gnostic writings found in Egypt during the 1940s known as the Nag Hammadi library.[37] Koester concludes an influential 1980 article that analyzes five apocryphal gospels with the claim that these works

> are perhaps at least as old and as valuable as the canonical gospels as sources for the earliest developments of the traditions about Jesus.[38]

The "Post-Bultmannian Quest" has tended to follow Koester in this type of assessment. In fact, Crossan himself has played a very prominent role in this regard.[39] By expanding the historical Jesus data pool to include a wide variety of noncanonical documents, particularly the Nag Hammadi library, the post-Bultmannians hope to escape the "tyranny of the synoptic Jesus."[40] As we shall see, the portraits of Jesus being spun out of this camp, including the portrait of Jesus as a Cynic sage, are on the whole more indebted to these extra-canonical sources than to the canonical ones.

It should also be said that it is largely this maneuver to expand the data pool of material relevant to the historical Jesus that has given the "Post-Bultmannian Quest" its renewed vigor. As we saw in the last chapter, Bultmann's skepticism concerning the historical Jesus was largely fueled by the fact that his form criticism had discredited the Gospels as reliable historical sources. But, in his case, there were no other sources from which to draw, hence his skepticism. While the discreditation of the Gospels remains among post-Bultmannians, however, the lack of extra-canonical sources does not. If certain works from the Nag Hammadi library and certain apocryphal gospels can be argued to be early, or at least to contain early traditions, then there is, after all, something to work with. Their use of these sources, we shall see, is very debatable. But, as we shall also see, without it the revisionist views of Jesus put forth by post-Bultmannians like Crossan and Mack could hardly get off the ground.

The Gospel of Thomas

One particular work from the Nag Hammadi library has come to play a very special role in the "Post-Bultmannian Quest": the Gospel of Thomas (GosThom). With the 1945 discovery of GosThom, scholars quickly recognized its general affinities with the hypothetical document Q, discussed in the previous chapter. Among other things, approximately 35 percent of GosThom's sayings have parallels in Q.[41] Thus, the discovery of GosThom ostensibly provides tangible evidence that something very much like Q did indeed exist in at least some Christian circles.

An important issue for GosThom research is the question of its relationship to the canonical Gospels. The standard assessment until recently has been that GosThom is essentially dependent upon the canonical Gospels and thus does not represent a significant independent source for new knowledge about Jesus.[42] Those contemporary scholars who stand within the North American post-Bultmannian tradition, however, are now almost unanimous in their agreement that GosThom represents a tradition that is independent from the canonical Gospels and that derives from an "early stage in the sayings traditions."[43] A number of studies — primarily by students of Koester and Robinson — have served to further develop these convictions. The work of John Sieber,[44] Stephen Davies,[45] Stephen Patterson,[46] and Ron Cameron[47] is particularly important here.

The Sayings Source "Q"

While the likely existence of a "sayings source" behind Matthew and Luke has been generally acknowledged by scholars for over a century (with significant exceptions noted in the previous chapter), it is only with the "Post-Bultmannian Quest" that it has come to play a decisive role in the quest. This too is a defining feature of this movement.

Since the work of H.E. Töedt in the 1950s, it has become a consensus position within the post-Bultmannian camp that Q functioned as a full-fledged "gospel" for its community, rather than merely as supplementary teaching material.[48] Based upon this conviction, the apparent lack of a passion and/or resurrection narrative in Q—as well as in GosThom—has served the post-Bultmannian thesis of radical early Christian diversity quite well. Coupled with Graydon Snyder's work on early Christian iconography (in which he concludes that the cross and other symbols of Christ's suffering and death did not become popular until the fourth century), this thesis serves to dethrone the historic orthodox conviction that Jesus' sacrificial death and resurrection lay at the center of the Christian faith from the start.[49] In Kloppenborg's words:

> What Paul held to be the heart of his theology, and what in the canonical gospels achieves prominence through the sheer bulk of the passion narratives, seems not to have been widely celebrated outside of the literary elites responsible for the production and transmission of these documents.[50]

This also leads to a particular view of Q's understanding of salvation.

> "Easter," if one can still use that term in respect to Q, is not a narratible [sic], temporal event, but a hermeneutical one. In this sense we may say, paraphrasing Bultmann, that for the Sayings Gospel "Jesus arose in his words."[51]

With this understanding of Q as a presupposition, the "Post-Bultmannian Quest" has devoted an incredible amount of time to the study of this hypothetical document.[52] In a foundational essay, originally presented in 1964, Robinson proposed a *Gattung*—or genre—trajectory, which he termed "sayings of the sages," that extends from Jewish wisdom collections (e.g., the Book of Proverbs) to gnostic collections.[53] He argues that both Q and GosThom can be easily accommodated within this genre trajectory. Koester eventually went on to argue that such a collection of Jesus' sayings—a long-lost "gnosticizing wisdom book"—was vital to the early Christian movement, actually functioned as "scripture," and was a primary source of both GosThom and Q.[54] Based on this hypothesis, he further conjectured that the other non-wisdom elements in Q—particularly the "apocalyptic orientation" and its "christology of the coming Son of man"—must be seen as "due to a secondary redaction" of the "older wisdom book."[55]

It was left to John S. Kloppenborg to finally tackle the problem of Q "stratification" postulated by the Robinson-Koester thesis. Kloppenborg's investigation is two-pronged: he examines Q in regard to both composition/redaction and genre.[56] The results of Kloppenborg's study have led to the well-known thesis of a triple-layered Q. The earliest "strata" of Q ("Q-1") was essentially discernible as "sapiential instruction." A second redactional layer ("Q-2") is characterized by the addition of chreiai (wisdom sayings added to short narratives), polemical words of prophetic judgment, and "apocalyptic."[57] And the final recession ("Q-3") further developed the already prevalent tendency toward narrative-biographical material by adding the temptation story.

Kloppenborg's understanding of Q has become the predominant model within the "Post-Bultmannian Quest"; both Koester and Robinson, among many others, have adopted it.[58] And from this speculative redaction of this hypothetical document, they are now in a position to drastically rewrite the earliest history of the church. The development of the earliest Jesus communities, it could now be argued, mirrored the development of the various strata of Q.[59] As we will see in the next two chapters, Crossan, and especially Mack, rely heavily on Kloppenborg's thesis of a triple-layered Q to construct their revisionist portraits of Jesus and the early church.

The Non-Apocalyptic Jesus

Yet another central aspect of the "Post-Bultmannian Quest," one that flows naturally out of the previously discussed aspects, is the fairly recent trend toward viewing Jesus in decidedly non-apocalyptic terms. From Schweitzer to Bultmann, there had been an almost unanimous consensus that Jesus' worldview was fundamentally apocalyptic in nature. Post-Bultmannians began to move toward a non-apocalyptic Jesus, however, as a number of Bultmann's former students began to reject the authenticity of the "future Son of Man" sayings in the Gospels on the basis of certain form-critical considerations.[60]

Koester made new strides in the de-apocalypticizing of Jesus when he introduced his thesis, discussed above, of an early "wisdom book" composed of sayings of Jesus that served as the primary source for both Q and GosThom. According to Koester, this early sayings collection, "must have been a version of Q in which the apocalyptic expectation of the Son of man was missing."[61] Kloppenborg's work on Q has served to confirm this reading of Q within post-Bultmannian circles. His triple-layer Q thesis recognizes the "apocalyptic" sayings as secondary (Q-2) additions to Q-1.[62]

More recently, Kloppenborg has further distanced Q from any real apocalyptic influence by arguing that even Q-2's apparent apocalyptic eschatology is best understood in terms of an essentially non-apocalyptic, "symbolic" eschatology.[63] And so, armed with GosThom and Kloppenborg's triple-layered Q—two supposedly early, non-apocalyptic documents—the post-Bultmannian questers "discover" an original non-apocalyptic Jesus.[64] And just as the new de-apocalypticizing of Q leaves a "wisdom" book in its wake, so the de-apocalypticized Jesus leaves a "wisdom" savior in its wake. For when the (supposedly) later apocalyptic features of Jesus' teachings are stripped away, it is argued, the only Jesus that remains is *"a teacher of subversive wisdom."*[65] As we shall see below, this trajectory of Jesus as sapiential sage finds its culmination in the Cynic-Jesus thesis.

History-of-Religions Approach

The "Post-Bultmannian Quest" has also come under the influence of a renewed history-of-religions approach to early Christianity. The history-of-religions school was a small but significant movement that developed at the turn of the century.[66] Members included Wilhelm Bousett, Hermann Gunkel, Ernst Troeltsch, Johannes Weiss, and William Wrede. Methodologically, they applied the conclusions of various historical studies, Oriental studies, ethnology, and the history of religions to the biblical texts. As a result, a picture of early Christianity emerged that suggested syncretistic phenomenon with a deep indebtedness to first-century Greco-Roman religion. In the words of advocate Kurt Rudolph:

> For the history of religions, there has never been a "pure religion"; this would be an ahistorical construct. Indeed, every religion is a syncretistic phenomenon.... [I]t is an axiom arising from scientific insight and integrity that this knowledge should be employed in future work.[67]

The classic work to appear from this school, Bousett's *Kyrios Christos*, assumed a sharp distinction between the primitive Palestinian community and the later Hellenistic Christianity.[68] He argued that the latter was heavily influenced by both pagan mystery religions and the *"Kyrios* cult." Bultmann himself was strongly influenced by the history-of-religions approach. He too posited a radical dichotomy between Palestinian and Hellenistic Christianity, emphasizing the influence of gnosticism on the latter.[69]

However, with the turn to neo-orthodoxy in Europe, the history-of-religions school along with the sociological analysis it had spawned was soon eclipsed.[70] Since Koester and Robinson's "trajectories" thesis, however, the history-of-religions approach has been given new life, if in a distinctly transformed state. While many of the particular conclusions of the old history-of-religions school are rejected, and while there is a new emphasis on sociological and political factors in early Christianity that was absent in the old school, the basic methodology of assuming that early Christianity can be almost exhaustively accounted for as a synthesis of previous first-century religious ideas and practices is very much in place among many post-Bultmannians.[71]

One can see the effects of the renewed history-of-religions perspective within the contemporary "Post-Bultmannian Quest" in several regards. First, there is the strong emphasis among some (e.g., Mack) that Jesus and the origins of Christianity are far from unique in the history of religions. In fact, like Bousett and others before him, Mack begins with the *a priori* assumption that *no* religion can be "unique" in any fundamental sense. The comparative religions scholar Jonathan Z. Smith — to whom Mack is self-consciously indebted — puts the matter bluntly.

> The "unique" is an attribute that must be disposed of, especially
> when linked to some notion of incomparable value, if progress
> in thinking through the enterprise of comparison is to be made.[72]

Such a presupposition, of course, forces one to dismiss out of hand the idea that the historical Jesus was exceptional among religious founders, let alone the possibility that he was God incarnate.

Second, in contrast to the emphasis of those within the "Third Quest," the history-of-religions approach fosters an inclination toward painting Jesus and early Christianity primarily against a Hellenistic rather than Jewish backdrop. The Cynic-Jesus thesis itself is a striking example of this tendency.

The Sociological Turn

As Marcus Borg has noted, one of the universal characteristics of the contemporary quest — third and post-Bultmannian questers alike — is the increased attention given to the social world of first-century Palestine.[73] This tendency parallels a fairly recent development that has taken place within biblical studies in general. Since the 1970s, two closely related trends have emerged in the field. First, there has been an increased focus on *social history and description*, which makes use of archaeological, historical, and literary sources contemporaneous with the biblical texts. This

trend has produced a wide variety of works that can assist one in reconstructing a general sketch of first-century Palestine within which to understand Jesus.[74]

Second, there has been a growing use of *sociological methods and
models* which involve the application of the theories of various social-
scientific disciplines (e.g., sociology, cultural anthropology) to the biblical
texts.[75] Dominic Crossan has been one of the pioneers of this trend and,
together with Mack, continues to be one of its most influential exponents. The relationship between these two trends and the appropriateness of the second constitute one of the most debated topics in the field
of New Testament studies today. Many scholars, especially those within
the "Third Quest," argue that the attempt to understand all early Christian beliefs and practices on the basis of supposed "universal laws" of
social behavior is illegitimate.[76] We shall in subsequent chapters have
occasion to employ this criticism.

Nevertheless, this social-scientific approach has come to characterize
the "Post-Bultmannian Quest," especially in North America.[77] Indeed,
some have argued that this new interdisciplinary approach to the quest
among post-Bultmannians is now replacing the older, strictly historical
approach to the quest.[78] The old approach of trying to explain early
Christian mythology by reference to a unique historical Jesus is being
replaced with a new approach that tries to understand it by reference to
universal laws of social group formation. The quest for the historical
Jesus is thus being replaced with a quest for the sociological factors at
play in the early church. And the assumption is that when these factors
have been understood, the early church's mythological views of Jesus
will have been explained and one will see that the very idea that Christianity had one unique point of origin in a unique historical person is
simply a "myth of Christian beginnings" that can itself be explained
sociologically.[79] Jesus did not so much create social groups with social
issues as the social issues of certain groups created Jesus.

This perspective has contributed to the rise of a new and strikingly
innovative authenticity criterion within some post-Bultmannian circles:
the "social formation" criterion. This criterion states that

> no material can be attributed to the historical Jesus if that mate-
> rial contains evidence of dealing with some situation or issue for
> which considerations of community formation are dominant.[80]

As we shall subsequently see, this criterion, when combined with
the post-Bultmannian assumption that what early Christian faith and

practice is "really" about is social group formation, has the result of rendering inauthentic the vast majority of everything Jesus was supposed to have taught according to the Gospels.

THE JESUS SEMINAR: THE "POST-BULTMANNIAN QUEST" IN ACTION

The "Mission" of the Jesus Seminar

Since 1985, the revived "Post-Bultmannian Quest" has been provided with a new and high-profile focal point. In that year, Robert Funk inaugurated the Jesus Seminar. Interestingly, both Crossan and Mack were on the original five-person organizing committee, and Crossan continues as a co-chairman of the seminar.[81] The heart of the seminar is a sizable group of "fellows," biblical scholars from various North American learning institutions.[82] It should be clarified here that the seminar is not exclusively a "post-Bultmannian" organization. In fact, it has even included several evangelicals over the years, though most have eventually disassociated. To this day, several of its members would be classified within the "Third Quest." For the most part, however, the group is governed by post-Bultmannian convictions.[83] Thus, the Jesus Seminar offers the best general portrait of the contemporary "Post-Bultmannian Quest."

The seminar was organized in order to "renew the quest of the historical Jesus."[84] In his inaugural address to the Jesus Seminar, Funk set the grand mood that has come to characterize its ventures.

> We are about to embark on a momentous enterprise. We are going to inquire simply, rigorously after the *voice* of Jesus, after what he really said.[85]

The seminar's distinctive method of ascertaining just what Jesus said has become renowned—a sort of Jesus-by-ballot box. The seminar meets twice yearly. After presentations and group discussion, the fellows vote on the authenticity of the individual Jesus sayings under consideration. Each participant casts one vote by placing a colored bead in a voting box. Four voting options are possible: a red bead signifies a vote of confidence in the saying's authenticity; pink signifies a positive but qualified vote; gray a qualified skepticism; and a black vote signifies certain inauthenticity.[86] The Jesus Seminar has finally published its conclusions on the sayings of Jesus in the 1993 *The Five Gospels*.[87] Currently, the seminar continues to meet, with their attention now focused on the deeds of Jesus.[88]

As mentioned in the introduction, one very important facet of the Jesus Seminar is its commitment to the dissemination of its ideas and conclusions to the wider public.[89] In his inaugural address, Funk makes this commitment abundantly clear:

> We are going to carry out our work in full public view; we will not only honor the freedom of information, we will insist on the public disclosure of our work and, insofar as it lies within our power, we shall see to it that the public is informed of our judgments.[90]

The success of the seminar in this regard is evident from the amount of attention that it and its members have garnered in the general media.[91]

Explicit within this commitment to public proclamation is the seminar's conviction that it has something worth saying that the masses need to hear. Here one finds an interesting tension with regard to the Jesus Seminar. On the one hand, the seminar has made much of the fact that its members

> are critical scholars. To be a *critical* scholar means to make empirical, factual evidence — evidence open to confirmation by independent, neutral observers — the controlling factor in historical judgments. Non-critical scholars are those who put dogmatic considerations first and insist that the factual evidence confirm theological premises.[92]

On the other hand, however, the seminar — or at least significant persons within its leadership — appears to be committed to a particular theological agenda. Funk, for example, has expressed his own theological agenda very clearly when he writes:

> What we need is a new fiction that takes as its starting point the central event in the Judeo-Christian drama and reconciles that middle with a new story that reaches beyond old beginnings and endings. In sum, we need a new narrative of Jesus, a new gospel, if you will, that places Jesus differently in the grand scheme, the epic story. Not any fiction will do. . . . We require a new, liberating fiction, one that squares with the best knowledge we can accumulate and one that transcends all self-serving ideologies. And we need a fiction that we recognize to be fictive.[93]

Another high-profile member of the group, Hal Taussig, has added his own clarifications in an article entitled "The Jesus Seminar and Its Public." Here, with Tina Turner, Taussig declares that "we don't need another hero."

> Jesus, updated or not, is not what American society needs. The Jesus Tradition, on the other hand, may be a bit more helpful, because it chronicles a dramatic (one of the most dramatic) accomplishment of social formation within cultural chaos. . . . [Thus] the needs of the American public to understand how groups cooperate and cohere appear much greater than their need for an update of the Great Man from another age.[94]

Thus, there are clearly some very definite theological presuppositions at work within the Jesus Seminar. Such explicit assumptions about the public's religious needs, mixed with the generally evangelistic tone of its stated mission, as well as the presence of a distinct persecution complex, serve to seriously question the supposed purely "neutral" and "objective" nature of its endeavors.[95] As has been the case with much of the quest from its inception as we saw in chapter 1, this quest seems to be largely driven by theological, philosophical, and sociological presuppositions.

The strict scholarly neutrality of the Jesus Seminar is further called into question by Robert Funk's recent call for a "canon council" to be convened in conjunction with the group. The purpose of this council, he says, is

> to reconsider the configuration of the biblical canon . . . to consider whether to add any of the newly discovered documents to the Bible, and whether to include as separate documents any of the hypothetical sources, such as J, E, D, and P of the Pentateuch and the Sayings Gospel Q. The Council will also want to consider whether any of the traditional books of the canon, or parts of those books, either Roman Catholic or Protestant, should be dropped.[96]

It is, to say the least, not clear what qualifies certain critical New Testament scholars to make theological judgments about what should and should not be included in the church's canon. But, in any case, the fact that such a proposal has been taken seriously, and indeed appears likely, is enough to reveal a strong theological mission behind the supposed neutrality of the Westar Institute and the Jesus Seminar it is funding.

The "Jesus" of the Jesus Seminar

In concluding this discussion of the Jesus Seminar, and in preparation for what is to follow, it will be helpful to provide a succinct general consensus outline of the Jesus that has emerged from the seminar's endeavors. Generally speaking, the most influential participants of the Jesus Seminar hold that the historical Jesus was (1) a *non-apocalyptic,*[97] possibly quite Hellenized, Galilean who (2) both taught and lived "*subversive forms of social behavior.*"[98] (3) He was quick with the *aphoristic wit.*[99] (4) Not only did he have *no consciousness of being in any way, shape, or form God incarnate,* but he would have blanched at the idea. Indeed, he most probably did not even think of himself as the coming messiah or Christ.[100] (5) His *concept of salvation* was framed in terms of sharing *the wisdom and knowledge that could immediately usher one into the kingdom of God, a present reality in the here-and-now.*[101] Thus, in his own mind, he was at most a proclaimer—never the one to be proclaimed. (6) Although he spoke to many, it is "crystal clear" that *he never intended to found an organized following.*[102] (7) His *death* was certainly unfortunate, but neither he nor his initial followers read any theological significance into it. It was simply "an accident of history."[103] Hence, the belief in the resurrection is understood to be a later Christian myth.

Such appears to be the general consensus emerging out of the various projects within the "Post-Bultmannian Quest." As we shall see, both Mack and Crossan have played very influential roles in these developments. It is easy to see how this conception of Jesus both follows from, and fulfills, the theological mission of discovering, and disseminating, a view of Jesus who is not only palatable, but attractive, to contemporary people.

JESUS AS CYNIC SAGE: A NEW MODEL FOR THE HISTORICAL JESUS

There are a number of post-Bultmannian works on the historical Jesus that fill in the details of this general outline. But the view that is presently enjoying the most influence at both a scholarly *and* popular level and which this book shall henceforth be concerned with is the portrait of Jesus as a Cynic sage. This view is most fully developed, and most persuasively argued, by John Dominic Crossan and Burton Mack. The following chapters shall provide a full explication and critique of the views of these two scholars. But before engaging in this, it will be helpful to set the stage for this critique by providing the specific background to Crossan's and Mack's versions of the Cynic thesis.

The Ancient Cynics

It is traditionally held that ancient Cynicism arose with Socrates' student Antisthenes in the fourth century B.C.[104] One of Antisthenes' students, Diogenes of Sinope (404–323 B.C.), has come to represent the epitome of the Cynic philosopher. The name "Cynic" most likely derives from the Greek term for "dog" (kyōn). Thus from the time of Diogenes, the Cynics were popularly known as the "dog" philosophers, a name not unbefitting some of their public actions. The principal source of knowledge regarding these early Cynics is the sixth book of Diogenes Laertius' *Lives of Eminent Philosophers*, written in the third century A.D.[105]

We hear virtually nothing of Cynicism during the second and first centuries B.C. in which time it apparently waned. But with the first century A.D., something of a renewal occurs with the rise of Imperial Cynicism.[106] During this period, Cynics such as Demetrius, Dio Chrysostom, Demonax, and Oenomaus of Gadara attained a certain degree of notoriety.[107] One Cynic from this period, Peregrinus Proteus of Parium (110–165), is of particular interest for our purposes in that he was originally a prominent Christian who later adopted the Cynic way of life after being excommunicated from the church. In the following centuries the influence of Cynicism waned until it all but disappeared in the fifth and sixth centuries.

Cynicism was quite distinct among the Greco-Roman philosophies in that the Cynics generally shunned speculative philosophy. Thus Cynics were identified primarily by their behavior and appearance — both of which exemplified their basic life-principles — rather than by a particular philosophical system. The Cynics were committed to the concepts of *radical personal freedom and independence*, with the bounds of *nature* as their only convention. Ethically, whatever violated nature was wrong; whatever did not was permissible. Thus, the ideal Cynic was one who reveled in the freedom that only a life of contented asceticism brings, rejected the shackles of social custom, and did what could be done to open the eyes of the surrounding society to its plight. Often the latter was accomplished by loud harangues in the marketplace accompanied by socially unacceptable behavior, which included "using violent and abusive language, wearing filthy garments, performing acts of nature (defecation, sex) in public, feigning madness."[108]

The appearance of the Cynic was quite distinctive as well. They generally went barefoot, kept their hair and beard long, wore a rough and ragged cloak, and carried a walking staff and a carrying pouch. This, combined with the fact that they generally rejected conventional ways of supporting oneself, meant that they were usually identified as beggars by their contemporaries.[109]

The Rise of the Cynic-Jesus Thesis

The recognition that certain aspects of ancient Cynicism parallel certain aspects of early Christianity is not new. Throughout this century various scholars have noted certain mostly incidental similarities.[110] But it has only been in the last few decades that these similarities have been explored in a comprehensive way, and only during this time that the thesis that much of early Christianity, including the life of Jesus, can be understood along Cynic lines was developed.[111]

The stage for viewing Jesus as a wandering Cynic was set in 1972 by Gerd Theissen who argued that "Jesus did not primarily found local communities, but called into being a movement of wandering charismatics."[112] In this respect, Theissen maintained, Jesus' ministry was similar to that of " many itinerant cynic philosophers and preachers of the first two centuries."[113]

Other scholars soon expanded upon Theissen's thesis and argued for more particular commonalties between Jesus and his earliest disciples and ancient Cynics. According to Stambaugh and Balch, for example, both groups were examples of "wandering moralists" that are known to have traveled throughout the Roman Empire.[114] Moreover, both groups supposedly taught and lived a generally ascetic life. Such parallels are especially evident, it is claimed, in Jesus' mission charge to his disciples in Luke 10:1-16 and parallels, a passage that has received a good deal of attention in this regard.[115] The style of ministry Jesus dictates to his disciples in this passage, it was argued, sounds remarkably similar to the style of living and teaching exemplified by itinerant Cynic philosophers as they wandered about the Roman Empire.[116]

In recent years, some have taken this line of thought yet a step further and have argued for the *direct influence* of Cynicism upon early Christianity. Indeed, a small but significant group of scholars have taken the final step and have argued not only for a direct influence on Jesus and his followers from Cynicism, but for an *essential identification* of Jesus and his followers as itinerant Cynics. One of the first and most prolific advocates of this view is the British theologian Gerald Downing. Since 1982, Downing has developed and defended the Cynic-Jesus thesis in a variety of essays and books.[117] He argues that Jesus must be understood as a Jewish Cynic and that "a Christian Cynicism" must be seen as one of the early strands of thought influencing the early Christian movement.[118]

The parallels, he maintains, are simply too close, and too frequent, to stop short of any other conclusion.[119]

Several factors serve to distinguish Downing's approach from that of the North American Cynic theorists associated with the "Post-Bultmannian Quest" such as Crossan and Mack. First, Downing tends to allow for a more *Jewish* Cynic than do the post-Bultmannians who rather tend to emphasize Hellenistic influences on Jesus. Second, Downing doesn't base his arguments on the sort of complex redactional programs that characterize the North American post-Bultmannians, such as Kloppenborg's stratification of Q.[120] And finally, and perhaps most significantly, Downing goes out of his way to show that his suggestion of a Cynic Jesus does not necessarily rule out the doctrine of the incarnation. Indeed, Downing himself affirms this doctrine.

> I trust that God made his own the life of this Cynic Jesus. God accepted his experience of trying to share this Jewish-Cynic vision, and his dying. The measure but also the actuality of God's self-involving and vulnerable love is his identification of himself with this Jesus. . . . The Jewish-Cynic Jesus I have been sketching did not think he was God incarnate; it cannot be imagined that such a thought ever crossed his mind. But when God accepted the conditions of a human life, these Jewish-Cynic ideals were the ones he lived and tried to share.[121]

Affirming significant "Cynic" aspects of Jesus' life, we see, no more necessitates a denial of his divinity than does affirming (say) many Jewish aspects of Jesus' life. If God is to become incarnate in a particular human life, that life is, quite obviously, going to necessarily reflect aspects of the particular culture(s) it is apart of. What threatens the doctrine of the incarnation is not so much locating Cynic aspects of Jesus' life and teaching, but the direction one pushes these conclusions. And as we shall see, North American post-Bultmannians, and Crossan and Mack in particular, have pushed these conclusions in rather unfortunate directions.

The Cynic Thesis — Post-Bultmannian Style

For a relatively small but highly influential group of scholars within the "Post-Bultmannian Quest," the Cynic model has become the operative paradigm by which to understand Jesus and earliest Christianity. Here, Kloppenborg's claim of an early, sapiential, non-apocalyptic layer of Q (Q-1), combined with the renewed interest in a Greco-Roman history of religions approach – particularly Cynic-Christian parallels – have become grist for this radical new proposal regarding Christian origins.

Crossan and Mack are currently the two most high-profile advocates of the Cynic thesis within the North American post-Bultmannian camp, but they are hardly alone in their Cynic interpretation. Another emerging voice for the Cynic thesis is Leif Vaage, a professor at Emmanuel College, Toronto, and Fellow of the Jesus Seminar. Vaage's 1987 dissertation focuses on the question of the social identity of the earliest Q community.[122] He works from the basis of a reconstructed formative layer of Q quite similar to Kloppenborg's Q-1.[123] Central to his thesis is Jesus' mission charge in Q (Luke 10:3-16), mentioned above, in which he argues that Jesus' instructions "compare quite thoroughly and closely to traditions of Greco-Roman Cynicism."[124] And from his source and redactional criticism of this and other passages in Q, Vaage concludes that

> [t]he persons whom Q represents were like Cynics, Greco-Roman Cynics. They were more like them than any other comparable persons or group. If it is clear that they were not identical with them . . . it is unclear that the differences are more notable than the similarities. In search of an identity for the persons whom Q represents . . . no better appellation presently exists than Cynic.[125]

More recently, Vaage has gone on to investigate the implications of his reconstructed Q-1 layer for the historical Jesus, and, not surprisingly, a Cynic-like Jesus again materializes.

> The man emerges here as neither apocalyptical seer nor sapiential sage. He was rather a bit of an imp, in Socrates' terms a social gad-fly, an irritant on the skin of conventional mores and values, a marginal figure in the provincial context of Galilee and Judea whose style of life and appeal to others was to go a different way than the "normal" one. The "religious" character of this posture is neither primary nor secondary. It is simply part of the cultural setting in which Jesus will have lived and moved.[126]

Ron Cameron, professor at Wesleyan University and Jesus Seminar fellow, has taken the Cynic thesis one step further yet. In what Mack has referred to as a "watershed study," Cameron cuts the Gordian knot that had plagued the non-eschatological Cynic Jesus thesis: namely, the problem of accounting for Jesus' (supposed) decisive break with John the

Baptist's eschatological vision.[127] How was one to account for Jesus' Cynic-like non-eschatological orientation when his predecessor was so thoroughly eschatological? The solution, according to Cameron, is found in a critical analysis of Q/Luke 7:18-35 which shows that John the Baptist was also a non-eschatological Cynic-like figure! Like Jesus, he argues, the original Q envisioned John in non-eschatological terms. It was only with later redactions of Q (viz. Q-2) that John, like Jesus, received an apocalyptic orientation. His solution has received quick support.[128]

The force of the Cynic thesis is beginning to show within post-Bultmannian circles, including the Jesus Seminar.[129] Both Crossan and Mack have played a central role in this regard. With the remarkable rising popularity of their work outside of the academic world, they will no doubt play just as crucial a role in the wider expansion of this new paradigm's sphere of influence. If the evangelical conviction that Jesus was and is the Son of God is going to continue to be expressed with intellectual viability within our culture, we shall need to take very seriously views such as this. With this in mind, we turn to an examination of the work of Crossan and Mack in the next two chapters of this work.

›SECTION 2›

The Case for the Cynic Thesis

3

JESUS, THE REVOLUTIONARY JEWISH CYNIC:
The Work of John Dominic Crossan

T he historical Jesus was, then, a *peasant Jewish Cynic*."[1] Thus concludes Crossan's well-crafted and extremely popular work, *The Historical Jesus: The Life of a Mediterranean Jewish Peasant*. This magisterial study represents the fruit of over two decades of research for Crossan. One commentator has suggested that it "could be the most important book on the historical Jesus since Albert Schweitzer's *Quest of the Historical Jesus*."[2] The purpose of this chapter is to provide an exposition of his study. We will begin with a brief overview of Crossan's scholarly development in order to set the context for his later Cynic thesis and then conclude with a discussion of his thesis itself.[3]

SETTING THE STAGE: EARLIER WORK AND INFLUENCES[4]

The New Hermeneutic and Structuralism

John Dominic Crossan, an Irish Roman Catholic and former priest, commenced serious work on the historical Jesus in the early 1970s.[5] Throughout that decade, his time was largely spent focusing on the parables of Jesus.[6] A penchant for literary-poetic analysis, carried out along post-Bultmannian lines, has characterized his work from the start. Crossan's work during this period shows a marked dependency on three major movements that significantly affect his understanding of parables. First, Crossan's work is clearly influenced by "the new hermeneutic," a school of thought that arose concurrent with the "Post-Bultmannian New Quest" and which was heavily influenced by Bultmann's brand of existentialism. The hallmark of this movement, if we can put it in a word, is that it stresses language as "event" over language as "information."

Communication occurs not so much as information is conveyed, but as language creates an "event" in which the personal world of one intersects and impacts the personal world of another. Applied theologically, the "word of God" is here no longer seen as propositional communication by God but, in the words of Gerhard Ebeling, as "an event in which God himself is communicated . . . word and deed are one: his speaking is the way of his acting."[7] For Professor Crossan, as we shall see, the parables of Jesus function as just such an event, but with a radically unexpected twist.

Crossan's work during this time also shows a clear dependency on the sociolinguistic theories of Peter L. Berger and Thomas Luckmann. In their acclaimed work, *The Social Construction of Reality*, Berger and Luckmann argue that a society's views of reality are largely shaped and sustained through language.[8] Language does not simply convey information about reality; it also creates it. The application of this perspective to literary-critical approaches to the New Testament opened up new methods of interpretation in the 1960s and 1970s, and they continue to be employed today, especially in the area of parable studies.[9] The early Crossan was very much a part of this new enterprise.[10]

But Crossan was to soon move beyond the views of Berger and Luckmann in subsequent works, owing largely to a third influential movement in his scholarly work: namely, structuralism.[11] To grossly oversimplify this school of thought, language is here seen not only as shaping and reinforcing a view of reality: according to structuralism, *language is reality*. The only world we know, or ever can know, is the world of our linguistic conventions. In Crossan's words, "reality is language," and (echoing Acts 17:28!) it is in "the story" (worldview) our language embodies that we "live, move, and have our being."[12] Outside of our linguistic conventions, there is nothing — at least nothing we can ever know or speak. As we shall see, this perspective has monumental implications for Crossan's understanding of what Jesus was about with his use of parables.

The Priority and Nature of Jesus' Parables

According to the Crossan of the early 1970s, the search for "the historical Jesus" was, in essence, a hunt for the "language of Jesus." And this language, he believed, was centered on the parables. Indeed, "The term 'historical Jesus,' " he writes, "really means the language of Jesus and most especially the parables themselves."[13] What was most distinctive about this parabolic language, according to the early Crossan, was its irreducibly *metaphorical* nature. One misses the point of a parable, he argues, if one sees it as secretly conveying a literal truth, or even if one interprets it in a symbolic or allegorical fashion. The meaning of a parable, Crossan rather maintains, is found in the way in which it uses language in an unconventional (metaphorical) way in order to disclose an unconventional way of seeing reality. Hence, the meaning of Jesus' parables, according to Crossan's perspective, is found in the way they metaphorically realize a new vision of reality which he calls "the Kingdom of God."[14]

Crossan expanded upon this view in a radical fashion in his subsequent work on parables, owing largely to the influence of structuralism on his thought. In his *The Dark Interval* (1975) and *Raid on the Articulate* (1976), as well as in a number of other writings during the 1970s, Crossan argues that the metaphorical quality of parables is centered on their *paradoxical* and *subversive* quality.[15] Functioning something like a Zen koan, parables intend to subvert a hearer's conventional understanding of reality by jarring their worldview with its paradoxical quality. Hence, parables are

> *paradoxes formed into story by effecting single or double reversals of the audience's most profound expectations.* The structure of parable is a deliberate but comic reversal of the expected story.[16]

As such, parables seek to subvert the "very foundation of opinion, logic, thought, communication, and therefore of itself."[17] And, according to Crossan, herein lies the heart of a parable's paradoxicality: its success is measured by the extent to which it subverts even itself.[18]

Parables, Comic Eschatology, and the Kingdom of God

During this same period, Crossan developed a distinctive reading of Jesus' eschatology that was rooted in his structuralist linguistic theory and analysis of the parables as subversive paradoxes. From the start, Crossan rejected the traditional apocalyptic understanding of Jesus' proclamation of the kingdom of God. Jesus, he maintained, was "not proclaiming that God was about to end this world." Rather, seeing the prevalent Jewish eschatology of his day "as one view of the world, he was announcing God as the One who shatters world, this one and any other before or after it."[19] In other words, the "end" that Jesus was proclaiming was the end of all worldviews — including the Jewish eschatological one. Indeed, Crossan maintains that Jesus, through his parables, was jarring the very idea — the Jewish monotheistic idea — that God was moving history toward any definitive end, or even moving history at all!

Hence he calls Jesus' eschatology a "comic eschatology." Its "comic" quality is due to the fact that it is

> the ending of endgame, the silent laughter at our invention of a divinity whose coherent plan is moving, imminently or distantly, towards some final consummation. Comic eschatology laughs at the idea of a final ending which, by teleological retrojection, might clarify and justify all preceding events.[20]

In Crossan's view, then, the paradoxical and subversive quality of Jesus' parables are to have the effect of creating in his audience the awareness that they are "making it all up within the supreme game of language."[21] In keeping with his structuralist convictions, *every* worldview is seen by Crossan as a linguistic invention, and the thrust of Jesus' parables, he holds, is to laugh at it.[22]

From this perspective, Jesus' references to "the kingdom of God" are interpreted as references to the radical vision of a reality that has woken up to its comic linguistic nature. And Jesus' radical call to discipleship is interpreted as the call to abandon all in following the paradoxical force of the parable to its world subverting conclusion, a conclusion that in the end—paradoxically—subverts even the paradox and the call itself, as we saw above. Hence Crossan again writes:

> The Kingdom demands our "all," demands the abandonment not only of our *goods* and of our *morals* but, finally, of our *parables* as well. The ultimate, most difficult and most paradoxical demand of the Kingdom is for the abandonment of abandonment itself.[23]

If the world is seen in structuralist terms as a linguistic convention, then Jesus is portrayed here as the master deconstructionist. And it is not surprising to find that, as Crossan moves into the 1980s, there is a distinct tendency in his thought to cross over from structuralist to post-structuralist thinking.[24]

The Wider Backdrop: Crossan's Religious Worldview

If the only reality we can know is the reality of our invention, and if the thrust of Jesus' parables is to expose the arbitrary nature of our "supreme language game" conventions, then one must wonder what place, if any, a belief in God has for Crossan (and his Jesus). For, quite clearly, any view of God we might have is, by definition, understood as *our* creation. Crossan himself poses the problem well when he writes:

If there is only story, then God, or the referent of transcendental experience, is either *inside* my story and, in that case, at least in the Judeo-Christian tradition I know best, God is merely an idol I have created; or, God is *outside* my story, and I have just argued that what is "out there" is completely unknowable. So it would seem that any transcendental experience has been ruled out, if we can only live in story. In all of this I admit most openly a rooted prejudice against worshipping my own imagination and genuflecting before my own mind.[25]

Still, Crossan is unwilling to draw from this line of structuralist thinking the atheistic, or at least the radically agnostic, conclusion that it seems to entail. Rather, Crossan attempts to find some place for an experience of transcendence in the very awareness of our inability to know transcendence. In other words, he attempts to arrive at a sort of "theology of negation," and he uses Derrida's deconstructionism to do it.[26] The experience of God — the transcendent — begins precisely where the deconstruction of all worldviews as linguistic convention ends. It is found "only at the edge of language and the limit of story." And, given what we have seen about the subversive (deconstructionist) nature of parables above, all of this is to say that transcendence is experienced through parable.[27]

This deconstructionism-in-service-to-transcendence was, according to Crossan, what Jesus was all about. Jesus took the "mosaic iconoclasm" inherent in the Jewish monotheist tradition — the rejection of all "graven images" of God — and turned it upon language itself. Not only can the transcendent not be expressed in matter: God cannot be expressed in words.[28] Hence, the only knowledge one can have of the transcendent is that It is *not* this, and *not* that. Yet, in the very act of attaining this negative knowledge, one opens oneself up to experiencing, in some form, the transcendent, the "kingdom of God."

This understanding of Jesus' teaching, of course, bears little resemblance to the Jesus of Christian tradition. But he bears a remarkable resemblance to, and has much relevance for, contemporary structuralist thinkers who have abandoned any hope of knowing a personal, transcendent God. The remarkability of this contemporary relevance and significance, however, is itself grounds for suspicion toward Crossan's perspective. George Tyrrell's observation, noted earlier, that we tend to see our own reflection in the "deep well" of the historical data comes to mind.[29]

THE 1980S: THE QUEST FOR THE APOCRYPHAL JESUS

While never abandoning his radical views on the parables, Crossan's attention shifts to Jesus' "aphorisms" (his non-narrative sayings) in the early 1980s.[30] His primary objective in his work *In Fragments* (1983) was to conduct a "transmissional analysis" of these sayings whereby he would trace the pre-canonical history of the various traditions of the Jesus-sayings of the Gospels.[31] While many of Crossan's particular conclusions are intriguing and warrant attention, the most important effect of this study for our present purposes is that it led him to an investigation of the noncanonical Jesus traditions, a move that was to permanently condition his perspective on the historical Jesus, as we shall see.

In his next major work, *Four Other Gospels* (1985), Crossan investigates four important noncanonical texts: GosThom, the "Unknown Gospel" of Egerton Papyrus 2 (EgerP 2), the Secret Gospel of Mark (Secret Mark), and the Gospel of Peter (GosPet). Following the precedent set by Koester, Crossan concluded that each of these works, or at least crucial sections of them, derive from traditions that are early and independent of the canonical Gospels. Indeed, Crossan here goes so far as to argue, against the general consensus of previous New Testament scholarship, that it is the canonical Gospels that are significantly dependent on these noncanonical sources! The "core challenge" of this book, Crossan maintains, is that anyone who follows his meticulous comparison of the canonical Gospels with these four "other Gospels" — these "pale ghosts that haunt the corridors of canon" — will "never see the former the same way again."[32] If his arguments are accepted, he is surely right.

The most significant of these "other Gospels" in terms of their impact on the canonical Gospels was, according to Crossan, the GosPet. Hence his next work developed his views of this gospel. In his 1988 *The Cross that Spoke*, Crossan conducts a meticulous source-critical analysis of GosPet in order to isolate a "Passion-Resurrection Source" (now dubbed the "Cross Gospel") as the earliest of three strata in GosPet. This "Cross Gospel," he argues, was originally independent of the rest of GosPet. Indeed, in its original version, it predates all the canonical Gospels and was, in fact, used by Mark as the primary source of his passion narrative. And, given his view of Markan priority, this further entails that this "gospel" served as the indirect source for the passion narratives of the other canonical Gospels as well.[33]

As we shall see, this perspective on GosPet, combined with his earlier views on the parabolic-paradox Jesus, lays the groundwork upon which Crossan's magnum opus, *The Historical Jesus*, is built.

Crossan's Historical Jesus: The Methodology

Crossan's New Methodological Synthesis

Crossan begins his own reconstruction of the historical Jesus by observing, quite correctly, that *"Historical Jesus research* is becoming something of a scholarly bad joke."[34] As we saw in the previous chapter, contemporary New Testament scholarship is witnessing an explosion of works on the historical Jesus. And while this explosion can roughly be broken down into two camps—the "Third Quest" and the "Post-Bultmannian Quest"—it nevertheless remains true that the diversity of conclusions these works are arriving at is something of an embarrassment. The house of the academy is, within New Testament circles, badly divided against itself.

The problem, judges Crossan, is due mainly to the fact that there is no accepted methodology that governs these diverse works. And thus Crossan begins his work by attempting to cut through this "academic embarrassment" by establishing a solid methodology. The methodology he arrives at is one he has been refining for years, and insofar as it determines all the particular conclusions of his work, it can justifiably be said to constitute "the most important element in *The Historical Jesus*."[35]

Interestingly, however, in many respects Crossan's methodology appears quite different from what one might expect, given his prior work. There is, for example, little explicit mention of contemporary literary-critical theory and its jargon. Instead, social-scientific and cross-cultural anthropological methods and models largely steer the course. Things have also changed for Crossan in terms of authenticity criteria. Whereas he had previously praised the new quest's foundational "criterion of dissimilarity" (discussed in the previous chapter) as "a necessary and negative discipline," one finds it seemingly upstaged in his recent work.[36] Instead, criteria involving the *earliest chronological strata and multiple independent attestations* take pride of place. On the whole, the synchronic, postmodern, literary-critical ethos of Crossan's prior work, while not altogether absent, has at least been reined back into ostensive harmony with—even submission to—a more traditional diachronic, historical method.[37]

The Triple-Triadic Methodology

Crossan describes this method in terms of "a triple triadic process: the campaign, the strategy, and the tactics."[38] First, the broad "campaign" is conducted on three symbiotic fronts:

a macrocosmic level using cross-cultural and cross-temporal social *anthropology*, a mesocosmic level using Hellenistic or Greco-
Roman *history*, and a microcosmic level using the *literature* of
specific sayings and doings, stories and anecdotes, confessions
and interpretations concerning Jesus.[39]

In terms of the first component, Crossan is indebted to the anthropological models of social status and conflict produced by such theorists
as Gerhard Lenski, Ted Gurr, Brian Wilson, and James Scott.[40] As his
eventual portrait of Jesus will reveal, he also borrows quite heavily from
both anthropological and historical studies of illness and sickness, healing and magic, eating and meals.

Crossan's second methodological triad moves to the heart of the
matter—his handling of the *literary* material involving Jesus. He prefaces
this discussion with some comments on the "literary problem" of the
Jesus tradition. In brief, Crossan recognizes three layers in the Jesus
tradition: (1) the *retention* of at least the essential core of the historical
words and deeds of Jesus; (2) the *development* of this material as the early
Christians applied it to new problems and situations; and (3) the wholesale *creation* of new material, both in terms of creating sayings and stories
about Jesus, and, "above all, composing larger complexes that changed
their contents by that very process."[41] While the last category would no
doubt prove troublesome to those of us concerned with the historical
reliability of the Gospel record, it holds no pejorative connotations for
Crossan: "Jesus left behind him thinkers not memorizers, disciples not
reciters, people not parrots."[42]

The second methodological triad serves to cut through the "literary
problem" by analyzing the various textual data. The first step is that of
collating a comprehensive *inventory*, consisting of "all the major sources
and texts, both intracanonical and extracanonical, to be used."[43] The second step is *stratification* of the various texts in a chronological sequence.
Finally, the third step is *attestation*, which "presents that now stratified
data base in terms of multiplicity of independent attestation" for each
saying of the Jesus tradition. In other words, one must determine the
number of occurrences of each particular saying of Jesus in independent,
that is *unrelated*, texts.[44]

Crossan's final methodological triad involves the interpretation of
the results derived from the process of triad two. First, one must give
attention to the *sequence of strata:* the earlier the chronological strata, the
greater the chance that one is dealing with original material. The second

principle involves the *hierarchy of attestation*. The greater number of independent attestations for a given saying, the greater likelihood that it stems from Jesus himself. Finally, Crossan *brackets all singularities*: any saying that has only one attested occurrence is methodologically bracketed from the data pool — even if it occurs in the first stratum. It cannot be significantly factored into a reconstruction of the historical Jesus.

In applying his methodology to the New Testament texts, Crossan arrives at a data pool of 131 sayings, those that pass the two tests of first stratum location and plural attestation. From these he reconstructs his historical Jesus.

PRELIMINARY REFLECTIONS ON CROSSAN'S METHOD

A number of scholars have commented on the rigor and appropriateness of Crossan's tripartite methodology. Clearly, in his attempt to rectify the present academic embarrassment, he has taken great pains to develop a methodology that fosters control over idiosyncratic assumptions and conclusions. However, Crossan's practical employment of his method reveals that even apparent rigor cannot always filter out fundamental presuppositions. Specifically, one can detect a variety of post-Bultmannian assumptions at work within Crossan's development of this ostensibly neutral methodological framework.

A Preference for Extra-Canonical Sources

First, one notes in Crossan's inventory a clear presence of the previously mentioned post-Bultmannian tendency to take very seriously a wide variety of extra-canonical sources, even preferring these over canonical sources. Many of these extra-canonical sources, however, are quite problematic for one reason or another. For instance, within his inventory one finds: (1) the *"Cross Gospel,"* which even among his own post-Bultmannian colleagues finds very little support;[45] (2) the highly controversial *Secret Gospel of Mark;* and (3) a number of *hypothetical textual reconstructions,* typically based upon highly speculative stratigraphies that, in turn, derive from various, often idiocyncratic, redactional theories. For instance, Crossan puts substantial weight on the ideas of a two-layered GosThom and a triple-layered Q (following Kloppenborg), the two documents that have revitalized the post-Bultmannian quest as we have seen. This allows him to place significant portions of both of these documents in his first stratum, a stratum where, not surprisingly, *none* of the canonical Gospels finds room to reside.[46]

Questionable Dating Procedures

The manner in which Crossan chronologically stratifies his inventoried sources is also problematic. Here again he betrays a distinctly post-Bultmannian preference for extra-canonical sources. Hence, the GosThom is assigned a very early date. So too, the Cross Gospel and Secret Mark are dated before the canonical Gospels. Conversely, the canonical Gospels are assigned the latest imaginable (many would say *unimaginable*) date.[47]

The questionableness of Crossan's radical redating of the available documents, combined with the speculative nature of his application of source criticism to these documents, renders Crossan's portrait of the historical Jesus somewhat tenuous, especially when one considers that for Crossan, *everything* is based on these initial methodological moves. A brief look at Crossan's earliest stratum illustrates this and shows once again the influence of post-Bultmannian assumptions on his project.

There are, for Crossan, a total of thirteen sources that qualify for his earliest strata. Of these, five are hypothetical reconstructions: an "early" layer of GosThom,[48] a triple-layered Q, a Miracles Collection, an Apocalyptic Scenario, and the "Cross Gospel." Three are obscure fragments of papyrus texts: EgerP 2, P. Vienna G. 2325, and P. Oxy. 1224. And one is known only from several patristic citations: the Gospel of the Hebrews. Only the remaining four are fully extant documents – and these all happen to be canonical: 1 Thessalonians, Galatians, 1 Corinthians, and Romans.

This already may seem like a meager data pool from which to reconstruct a historical Jesus, but in practice the situation is worse. For the papyri fragments are of such little value, and the secondary references to the Gospel of Hebrews so few, that little use is made of either by Crossan. Moreover, and most significantly, because of Crossan's understanding of Paul, virtually no use is made of his epistles (the only four extant documents he has!). Hence, functionally speaking, Crossan's historical Jesus is completely reconstructed from a data pool that has been largely reduced to a hypothetical "early" layer of GosThom, a hypothetical "Cross Gospel," and a hypothetical triple-layered "Q Gospel."

Drawing Arbitrary Parameters

Even apart from such dubious dating and speculative source critical procedures, however, the manner in which Crossan chronologically defines his various strata in which he places his sources is questionable and contributes further to the tenativeness of his whole project. Most significantly, Crossan, without explanation, draws the parameters of his "first" and primary strata—the contents of which alone are allowed as material for his reconstruction—as being A.D. 30 to 60. What is strange about this is that we have no extant literary input from A.D. 30 to 50 by anyone's count. Hence, the decade of the fifties is made by Crossan to function as a sort of magical ten-year period which alone speaks for the historical Jesus. But even here, the four epistles of Paul that Crossan accepts and which comprise the bulk of what was written during this decade—and the only documents in his first strata we can date with certainty—are dismissed as irrelevant to a reconstruction of the historical Jesus![49]

But, beyond this point, it is not clear why one should grant this period such a privileged status. It seems quite arbitrary. If one were to shift these parameters (say) ten years later one might immediately allow for other voices, perhaps even synoptic voices, to join the early Jesus choir.[50] But the manner in which Crossan arbitrarily defines his foundational parameters rules out all voices except those he (with a questionable dating and source critical procedure) is willing to allow to speak for the historical Jesus.

Problematic Attestation Criterion

Finally, Crossan's criterion of multiple attestation is problematic, if only because it is so thoroughly enmeshed in his first two methodological processes. Put simply, Crossan's consistently overoptimistic judgments regarding the "independence" of the extra-canonical sources actually serve to determine the presumably prior questions of what sources make it into the inventory pool and their dating.[51] The whole enterprise smacks of circularity and contributes further to the tenuousness of Crossan's project.

In the end, 131 sayings complexes make it through Crossan's methodological net (first stratum, plural attestation) and of these only 75 are finally judged by Crossan as deriving from historically specific incidents in the life of Jesus. These sayings are reproduced at the beginning of the book as "The Gospel of Jesus," and it is from this list that Crossan embarks on his reconstruction of the historical Jesus.

CROSSAN'S HISTORICAL JESUS: THE RESULTS

Crossan's application of his methodology delivers a Jesus quite different from the portrait of the canonical Gospels. The heart and soul of this Jesus, his central programmatic concern, is summarized by Crossan as follows.

[T]he historical Jesus proclaimed and performed the Kingdom of God, and empowered others to do likewise, as a community of radical egalitarianism negating not only the ancient Mediterranean's pivotal values of honor and shame, patronage and clientage, but culture and civilization's eternal round of hierarchies, discriminations, and exclusions. That vision and program was focused, as it had to be for a peasant talking primarily even if not exclusively to other peasants, on the body. It emphasized free healing, or egalitarian sharing of spiritual and religious resources, and open commensality, or the egalitarian sharing of material and economic resources.[52]

In short, Jesus was a *peasant Jewish Cynic* who proclaimed a new kingdom wherein a *radical social egalitarianism*—in the midst of oppressive hierarchies at every turn—reigned, and which he demonstrated by the sharing of *free healings* and *open commensality* or, more simply, "magic" and "meal."[53] We will now discuss each of these aspects of Crossan's portrait.

Jesus as a "Peasant Jewish Cynic"

Each of the terms, "peasant," "Jewish," and "Cynic" is critical to Crossan's reconstruction of Jesus. The first two parts of Crossan's three-part work are taken up with various socio-historical background studies that eventually come together to provide the interpretive framework for these three terms and thus for his historical Jesus.

The most important element of Crossan's designation of Jesus as a "peasant" concerns the *social and economic oppression* that characterized first-century peasantry. In the first part of *Historical Jesus*—entitled "Brokered Empire"—Crossan develops a model of peasantry, drawn primarily from G.E. Lenski's work on agrarian societies, that "is characterized by the iron plow and abysmal social inequality separating the upper classes from the lower classes."[54] Crossan focuses intently both on the social stratification of the Greco-Roman world and the conventions that secured such a state of affairs. More particularly, he details the social realities of the ancient Mediterranean systems of patronage and clientage, honor and shame, aristocracy and peasantry. In all of this, according to Crossan, "brokerage" was the name of the game. Power, prestige, and resources were all brokered through the various layers of the complex hierarchical social strata. And in such a system, for anyone to inch their way up the social ladder meant stepping on a lower person's neck in one way or another.[55]

Such was the world of Jesus the peasant. While Crossan believes that it is more likely that Jesus was a peasant farmer rather than a carpenter, as the Gospels portray him, either way he envisions Jesus as possessing an acute awareness of suffocating social and economic oppression. This awareness is central to Crossan's reconstruction project.

Secondly, Jesus was a peasant *Jew*. The second part of *Historical Jesus*, entitled "Embattled Brokerage," is devoted to exploring the social turmoil that characterized first-century Palestine. Using Josephus extensively, Crossan masterfully brings the reader into the sociopolitical tensions of Jewish peasants living under Roman rule in the first century. This section is arguably Crossan's finest, and the wealth of scholarship he brings to his task greatly illumines our understanding of first-century Palestine, even if one cannot accept some of the conclusions he draws from his argumentation.

One significant aspect of Crossan's portrayal of first-century Jewish life that should be critically noted, however, is Crossan's preference for ethnic over religious categories. Indeed, Crossan's interest in first-century Jewish socioeconomics nearly eclipses any interest in first-century Jewish religion. This preference is demonstrated in his self-conscious reading of Josephus in "socioeconomic" terms.[56] Hence, for Crossan, the phrase "Jewish peasant" functions far more as an ethnic tag than it does a religious tag.

This orientation has significant repercussions for Crossan's reconstruction. Instead of seeing Jesus as being dominated by the basic religious worldview of first-century Judaism — with its foundational pillars of covenantal monotheism, election, and eschatology — Crossan's Jesus thrives on a largely secular vision, motivated most decisively by socioeconomic factors.[57] This emphasis sets Crossan decisively against the emphasis on Jesus' Jewishness found in many "Third Quest" scholars, noted in the previous chapters.

Finally, according to Crossan, Jesus was a peasant Jewish *Cynic*. Although Crossan calls for an equal emphasis on "Jewish" and "Cynic" when it comes to Jesus, it becomes clear that *in terms of worldview and programmatic vision,* "Cynic" takes the upper hand. The model of Jesus as Cynic supplies Crossan with a countercultural radical in the face of a radically oppressive culture. As we saw in the last chapter, Cynicism's moral vision was this-worldly, and its attendant lifestyle challenged the values and conventions of the brokered Roman Empire.

Making use of the work of Downing and Vaage, Crossan bases his historical ties between Jesus and Cynicism on Jesus' aphoristic, socially subversive wit and the parallels between the Q Mission Charge and typical Cynic itinerancy and dress.[58] This is not to suggest that Crossan sees no distinction between the two, however. Jesus operated in a rural setting, while Cynics typically preferred an urban environment. Cynics usually carried a knapsack, while Jesus forbade his followers to carry one (showing the importance of sharing and dependence for his followers). And Jesus, Crossan further admits, performed healings and exorcisms (of a sort, as we shall see) while the Cynics did not. Still, on the basis of the commonalities of the teachings of the Cynics and the teachings of Jesus (as contained in Crossan's "first strata"), Crossan believes that Jesus can be justifiably categorized as a Cynic.

SAPIENTIAL WISDOM AND MAGIC

Crossan locates two further distinctive features of the historical Jesus that fill out his portrait of this first-century peasant Jewish Cynic. The first is Jesus' "sapiential" (wisdom-oriented) understanding of the kingdom of God as opposed to the apocalyptic conception that was prevalent in his day. As we have seen, Crossan, along with many other post-Bultmannians, interprets Jesus' references to "kingdom of God" in non-eschatological terms and sees this as constituting his break with his early mentor, John the Baptist.[59] In contrast to John the Baptist (at least as he is portrayed in the canonical Gospels), Jesus arrived at a sapiential interpretation of the kingdom which viewed it not in terms of a future event but rather as "a mode of life in the immediate present."[60] As we have seen, Crossan interprets Jesus' parables as the means by which he sought to create this "mode of life" in his followers.

Secondly, Crossan understands Jesus in the context of "the *thaumaturgists*, the miracle workers, [and] the magicians," of his culture.[61] Unlike some of his post-Bultmannian counterparts, Crossan maintains that certain aspects of the Gospel miracle accounts are rooted in history. This does not, however, signify anything "supernatural" according to Crossan. He rather understands Jesus' "miracles" along anthropological lines, seeing Jesus as similar to the medicine men and shamans of "primitive" cultures today. Put in a word, Jesus was able to produce extraordinary *psychosocial effects* in his ministry.[62] On this basis Crossan can now revise the traditional picture of Jesus as a passionate religious Jew in terms of Jesus as "a popular first-century Jewish magician."[63]

This "magic" dimension of Jesus' ministry is actually fundamental to Crossan's historical Jesus portrait. "His vision of the Kingdom," he writes, "was but an ecstatic dream without immediate social repercussions were it not for those exorcisms and healings."[64] Jesus, in Crossan's view, *demonstrated* the truth of his egalitarian vision, the "kingdom of God," through the magic he performed, and this is what gave his ministry such force. Curiously, however, Crossan does not take this quite *un-*Cynic-like activity as evidence that Jesus was operating with a first-century Jewish worldview. One might have thought that admitting that Jesus performed exorcisms — which seems to presuppose a strongly dualistic and eschatological view of reality — would have led him to just this conclusion, a point we shall explore more fully in chapter 7. To the contrary, however, Crossan reinterprets the "magical feats" of Jesus' ministry as symbols of Jesus' Cynic-like countercultural vision for society.[65]

This reinterpretation of the Gospel miracle accounts in psychosocial terms relies heavily on the distinction made by some medical anthropologists between "disease" (i.e., "organic pathologies and abnormalities") and "illness" (i.e., "the secondary psychosocial and cultural responses to disease").[66] Jesus' healings and exorcisms, according to Crossan, took place in the realm of the latter, not the former.[67] Jesus did not actually heal people's diseases, but he did symbolize his egalitarian vision for society by overcoming the conventional negative social implications of that person's disease — their "illness." Crossan summarizes his views here in a discussion of Jesus' healing of a leper.

> I presume that Jesus, who did not and could not heal that disease or any other one, healed the man's illness by refusing to accept the disease's ritual uncleanness and social ostracization. . . . By healing the illness without curing the disease, Jesus acted as an alternative boundary keeper in a way subversive to the established procedures of his society. Such a position may seem to destroy the miracle. But miracles are not changes in the physical world so much as changes in the social world.[68]

Such an interpretation of Jesus' "miracles," of course, is not without problems. Beyond the obvious criticism that Crossan has brought to the Gospel texts a thoroughly naturalistic presupposition — something Crossan himself admits — there is the historical question of whether such a "symbolic" action would have impressed anyone in first-century peasant society. Marcus Borg makes the point succinctly when he writes:

> [C]an "healing illness" without "curing disease" make much sense in a peasant society? Are peasants (or anybody else, for

that matter) likely to be impressed with the statement "your illness is healed" while the physical condition of disease remains?[69]

In any event, the miracle and exorcism accounts in the Gospels certainly do not easily lend themselves to Crossan's naturalistic reinterpretation. In these accounts, it was the actual change in "the physical world," not simply the change in the "social world," that impressed the multitudes.

CROSSAN'S JESUS AND THE EARLY CHURCH

When Crossan draws all these strands of thought together, the resulting portrait is of a peasant Jewish Cynic magician whose central mission was to proclaim and demonstrate radical egalitarianism in the midst of a Greco-Roman culture dominated by brokered hierarchies. Jesus' vision for society was taught in witty Cynic-like aphorisms, realized in his parables, symbolized in his "magic," and lived out by his open meals in which he sat at table with all segments of the down-and-out of his society.[70]

According to Crossan, the earliest followers of Jesus understood him in these terms. He was a revolutionary teacher and the charismatic founder of their new egalitarian community, no more. These earliest followers, according to Crossan, never dreamed of attributing to Jesus any supernatural, let alone divine, qualities. They did not believe he made any divine claims for himself (for in Crossan's view, he made none). And they did not find any special significance in their Master's untimely death. Indeed, according to Crossan, the earliest followers knew next to nothing about their Master's death, and they most certainly entertained no concept of his resurrection.[71] If this group believed in any sort of "salvation" at all, it was simply connected with living in accordance with the countercultural wisdom of their founder: it had nothing to do with the "later" Christian notion of redemption through Jesus' death and (supposed) resurrection.[72]

Hence, Jesus' earliest followers were simply about living out the radical egalitarian vision of their founder, nothing more. They continued to center themselves around open meals (which eventually became "communion") and continued Jesus' practice of healing and exorcism as a means of demonstrating their egalitarianism. And they recalled, discussed, developed, and occasionally wrote out the teachings of their master. Q and GosThom represent the earliest such records of these communities, according to Crossan, as do (at a slightly later date) the other documents that compose the first strata of Crossan's chronological scheme. And it is these documents, according to Crossan, that ground the view that Jesus was a Cynic sage who founded a new community with his egalitarian vision.

Obviously, however, this is not the view represented by the extant New Testament documents. In Paul's epistles, in the Gospels, and in the Book of Acts, we find a very different understanding of Jesus and the early church. For in each of these sources, Jesus is generally understood in divine terms (viz., as the Son of God), and salvation is intrinsically connected with his death and resurrection. Moreover, the earliest communities are portrayed in these documents (especially Acts) as being founded upon and centered on Jesus' resurrection. For Crossan (as for Mack as we shall see), this simply means that all of these documents are mistaken. For both Crossan and Mack, these documents represent later Christian "mythmaking" about Jesus. They do not represent either the historical Jesus or his earliest communities.

Crossan's case for the historical Jesus as a Cynic sage thus hangs upon his case for preferring certain noncanonical documents such as "Q" and GosThom over the extant New Testament documents. For his view to be embraced, one must accept both his arguments for the existence and/or priority of these noncanonical works as well as his view that Paul, Mark (as the earliest canonical Gospel), and Acts are fundamentally unreliable. In section 3 of this work (chaps. 5–7), I shall argue on methodological and historical grounds that his views of the documents that compose the first strata of his chronological scheme are untenable. And in sections 4, 5, and 6 (chaps. 8–13), I shall challenge his skeptical views of the New Testament documents. In all of this I shall attempt to make the case that we have every reason to accept these documents as providing for us a generally reliable portrait of the historical Jesus, and very little reason for accepting Crossan's use of his first strata non-canonical documents.

But first we must investigate the arguments of the second major defender of the Cynic thesis, Burton Mack. It is, therefore, to this task that we turn in the following chapter.

4

JESUS,
THE JEWISH SOCRATES:
The Work of Burton L. Mack

There is a rather interesting irony in Burton Mack coming to hold a central place within the recent North American resurgence of interest in the historical Jesus. For, as one makes his or her way through Mack's corpus, it soon becomes clear that his own personal interest in the historical Jesus is quite secondary. What most interests Mack, rather, is what happened *after* Jesus: namely the rise and development of the various groups that traced their socioreligious heritage back to Jesus. Thus, "Christian origins," rather than the historical Jesus, is Mack's subject of choice.

Nonetheless, in the course of spelling out his new and radical hypothesis on the Christian origins question, Mack has settled upon an interesting conclusion regarding Jesus of Nazareth: as far as we can tell, the life lived by the historical Jesus would have been most easily construed by his contemporaries as that of a "Cynic sage."[1] With this insight in the mid-1980s, Mack was propelled into the Cynic-Jesus debate, like it or not.[2] More recently, in light of his own further study as well as rapid developments within the Cynic thesis itself, Mack has stated that the thesis "has grown on me."[3]

This chapter focuses on Mack's characterization of Jesus as Cynic sage. We will begin with a look at Mack's earlier work and the important influences that have come to guide his project. Next, we will offer a summary of his thesis on Christian origins, since it is largely out of this context that his views on Jesus have arisen. And third, we will examine the central planks of Mack's Cynic-Jesus thesis. We shall in particular examine the heavy use Mack makes of (supposed) pre-Markan pronouncement stories and of (supposed) early Q material.

SETTING THE STAGE: EARLIER WORK AND INFLUENCES

Burton Mack's 1967 Göttingen dissertation, directed by Hans Conzelmann, seems to have set his scholarly course in life in a number of ways. His research focused on the relationships between *Logos* and *Sophia* in Hellenistic Judaism.[4] Here Mack argues that Hellenistic-Jewish Wisdom theology developed from a synthesis of appropriated categories from Egyptian Isis mythology and subsequent Jewish mythological constructions. Several interrelated themes involved in this project have become lifelong research interests of Mack: namely, Hellenism, the "wisdom" motif and literature, and mythology. We will take a brief look at where Mack has gone with each of these, since they all inform his revisioning of Christian origins in a significant way.

The Hellenistic Turn

Mack's interest in Hellenism extends back at least to the early 1960s and his predoctoral days at San Francisco Theological Seminary where he focused his studies on Hellenistic religions. His doctoral work in Germany furthered this interest, particularly in the form of Hellenistic Judaism and its wisdom texts.

In conjunction with his New Testament work, Mack has maintained strong interests in Hellenistic Judaism. For example, he has played a significant role in Philo studies over the years, having served as one of the original editors of the *Studia Philonica* series and more recently has written on the Book of Sirach.[5] It will subsequently become clear that this interest in Hellenism—especially as it relates to Second Temple (i.e., intertestamental) Judaism—fosters a bias toward reading Palestine (specifically Lower Galilee) in exaggerated Hellenistic terms (a point to be critiqued in chap. 7). It is only on this basis that he can construe this locale as a perfect incubator for his thoroughly Hellenized Cynic view of Jesus.

Mack's early interest in Hellenistic religions has also remained with him. It was no doubt reinforced during his time under Conzelmann in Germany. A line of influence can be surmised that extends from the early history-of-religions school, through Bultmann and Conzelmann, on up to Mack. As noted above, the Egyptian Isis myth proved to be decisive for Mack's early work on Jewish wisdom literature. In the same way, we shall see that the first-century Hellenistic religious milieu of Northern Syria, Asia Minor, and Greece provides the crucial context for Mack's theory about the development of the "Christ myth." For, on Mack's account, this "myth" is a synthesis of mythological elements found in each of these quarters. One can readily detect here the pattern of the old history-of-religions school (discussed in chap. 2).

Another facet of Mack's interest in Hellenistic thought has been his work on *Greco-Roman rhetoric* and its application to New Testament texts.[6] With other practitioners of rhetorical criticism, Mack utilizes ancient rhetorical techniques to investigate various aspects of a text, including the method and form of argumentation, the author's intention, and the basic issues and problems that lie behind a particular discourse. In the process, one can hope to reconstruct at least a partial picture of the sociological positioning of the author and audience.

Mack goes significantly beyond standard rhetorical criticism, however, in that he views the New Testament texts *primarily* – if not entirely – in terms of rhetoric, and this entails that he views these texts primarily – if not entirely – in *sociological* terms. The meaning and function of a text, in other words, can and should be exhaustively discovered in understanding its social situation. In Mack's words:

> Rhetoric cautions against taking the literature of the New Testament either at face value or as coded language for hidden theological truths whether timeless or recently revealed. Instead, rhetorical criticism explores the human issues at stake in early Christian social formation and its discourse.[7]

Mack suggests that the sociological moves and motives that rhetorical criticism can uncover in the New Testament will inevitably prove disturbing to those who look to these books for their religious grounding – namely, the Christian community. For such study highlights the fact that "the rhetorics were harsh, divisive, and based upon non-negotiable claims to authority."[8] Much of the New Testament, in other words, arises out of, and must therefore be understood in terms of, a fight for power among early Christians. For Mack, this implies that there is little that is relevant in any positive sense to modern people in the New Testament. Indeed, Mack suggests that its real relevance to modern people may be in teaching us how *not* to treat and speak to one another. And thus,

> the hermeneutical value of a rhetorical criticism of the New Testament may therefore lie ... in its challenge to the very notion of biblical hermeneutics as an essential grounding and guide for Christian faith and practice.[9]

Finally, Mack's research on ancient rhetoric has involved a significant focus on the chreiai, largely in conjunction with the Claremont

Chreia Project through the 1980s. A chreia is "a saying or action that is expressed concisely, attributed to a character, and regarded as useful for living."[10] The fact that ancient chreiai were predominantly connected to the anecdotes of Cynic philosophers, and that apparently strong similarities exist between chreiai and the "pronouncement stories" (that is, sayings of Jesus attached to brief narratives) in the Gospels, have proven to be a strong impetus in the development of Mack's Cynic-Jesus thesis.[11]

Wisdom

Second, the motif of *wisdom* has remained a central focus of Mack's over the years. The important intersection between these first two themes — Hellenism (particularly Hellenistic Judaism) and wisdom — is the wisdom literature of Second Temple Judaism, an intersection around which Mack's work has largely centered.[12] From his dissertation on, Mack has consistently sought to understand this important literature along syncretistic lines. While he has modified the old history-of-religions approach in significant ways, the program he inherited from Conzelman and Bultmann of attempting to trace the influence of Hellenistic religions on Jewish thought has remained a constant.[13]

In recent years, Mack's ongoing interest and approach to the concept of "wisdom," understood along Hellenistic lines, has led to readings of Second Temple Judaism and early Christianity that radically undermine more conventional views. For instance, Mack has consistently argued against the conventional view that the concept of "messiah" in Second Temple Judaism was a fundamental, content-specific, religious concept. Rather, argues Mack, it was simply one among a class of concepts that expressed "ideal figures" during this period. All of these figures, he argues, were intrinsically linked to the concept of "wisdom," and all had a sociological foundation. The mythological views of "ideal figures," like the mythological views of wisdom herself, arose in answer to "the problems of societal experimentation and change in an era of uncertainty."[14]

His syncretistic and sociologically rooted understanding of "wisdom" has become foundational for Mack's understanding of early Christianity as well. According to Mack, not only Q and GosThom, but the pre-Pauline material in Paul's epistles and even the earliest material of the passion narrative, reveal "assumptions" and "modes of reasoning" that are characteristic of "wisdom imagery and thought."[15] Indeed, the early Christians, in Mack's view, were doing little different than what other Jews in the intertestamental period were doing: namely, attempting to answer "problems in societal experimentation" through wisdom inspired mythological concepts of "ideal figures." The only significant difference was that the early Christians located their idealization in a historical person.[16]

FROM RELIGIOUS MYTHOLOGY TO RELIGION AS MYTHOLOGY

In conjunction with his historical studies in Hellenism, Second Temple Judaism, and early Christianity, Mack has developed a full-blown theory of religion in general that both expresses, and reinforces, his particular views on these topics. His theory centers around the concepts of "myth" and "mythology" and the sociological roles they play in various communities.[17] If we are to adequately understand Mack's views on early Christianity, it is crucial that we understand his theory of religion in general.[18] In this section, therefore, we shall briefly discuss two primary influences on Mack's theory of religion and then provide an overview of the theory itself.

Two Important Influences on Mack's Theory of Religion

Mack's theory of religion can be largely understood as deriving from two influential contemporary schools of thought. The first is a recent version of the cultural-anthropological approach to religion, represented most forcefully by René Girard and Jonathan Z. Smith.[19] The aspect of this school of thought that has most impacted Mack is the understanding of religious myth and ritual as "mythic rationalizations" of social group formation. Myths and ritual are, in essence, always about conflict resolution and the establishing of group identification within a community. They establish what the group is about, what behavior is and is not appropriate, who's in charge and who's not, what values are and are not endorsed, and so on.

It is crucial to note that Mack's *Myth of Innocence* is worked out entirely from this perspective. In his introduction to this work he writes:

Jonathan Z. Smith's constructive theory of religion, more than any other, informs the position taken in this book. According to Smith, myths, rituals, and symbols are ways of thinking about, or making sense of, social practices and orientations to the world. . . . For Smith, what has come to be called religion is actually a social mode of thinking about social identity and activity.[20]

Mack expands upon this theory further in a different context when he writes:

Religion is the way in which a people make their world work, position themselves in their world, acknowledge their agreements, reflect upon their relationships, inculcate their manners and codes, rectify displacements, and meditate upon their social system in light of accident and the impingements of history. The theory is based in a thoroughly social, rational, and constructive anthropology.[21]

Hence, religious beliefs, stories, and rituals are never *really* about what they on the surface seem to be about. While they may *look* like they are about supernatural beings performing supernatural deeds, what they are really about, says Mack, is establishing social identity. Such a presupposition, obviously, has radical implications for how one reads the Gospels. Clearly, with such a stance, one could only conclude the "gospels are not history. . . . They are myths claiming to be history."[22] And behind these myths, it is assumed, lurks issues of social identity. The only historical root the Gospel myths have, therefore, is the history of community creation and conflict that gives rise to them.

A second significant influence on Mack's theory of religion has already been touched on in our discussion of Crossan: namely, post-structuralism, especially in its deconstructionist application as espoused by Derrida and Foucault.[23] Mack's indebtedness to deconstructionist literary theory is most evident in *Myth of Innocence,* although as Vernon Robbins has noted, Mack's actual application of it is " 'subtle' because it relies on understatement, implication, and occasional innuendo to make its points."[24] Such post-structuralist commitments — especially in the Foucaultian vein — include the ideas that "reality" is fully a matter of social construction, that claims to "truth" are always fundamentally bound up with power plays, and that the critic's job is first and foremost to "read a text against itself" in order to expose its originatory social location, its fundamental ideological commitments, and its rhetoric by which the author is attempting to impose his/her (typically *his*) authority over the "other" (the reader).

With such a perspective, one necessarily reads texts "suspiciously." Behind and within the "apparent" meaning of any "truth claim," one always suspects an ulterior motive. And so it is with Mack's approach to the Gospels. As the very title of Mack's work on Mark (*The Myth of Innocence*) indicates, Mack is highly suspicious of Mark's motives in writing ("fabricating") his Gospel. Indeed, disclosing his (supposed) hidden agenda is what Mack's book is all about.

It is, at least in part, also this post-structuralist line of influence that leads Mack well beyond his ostensively "disinterested" religious studies approach to engage in a radically scathing attack on traditional Christianity. Mack is not simply concerned with "objective" scholarship, but with ridding the Western world of the "dangerous" ideology that it inherited from Christianity—mostly owning, he believes, to the canonization of Mark's Gospel. Hence, Mack not only "discovers" Mark's hidden agenda: he also traces the damaging effects of his "myth of innocence" into the twentieth century. He finds it lurking in the collective American conscious at large, as is demonstrated by such epitomizing hero figures as the Lone Ranger, Superman, and—from the realm of real-life—Ronald Reagan.[25] Because of Mark's "myth," he believes, Westerners tend to possess a mythic mentality that concentrates "innocence and power in a single figure." And this, Mack believes, is dangerous in our present world.[26]

What we need, Mack believes, is a new view of Jesus to inspire our imaginations: a Jesus who is not contaminated by (viz., "is prior to") Mark's "myth of innocence," a Jesus who does not monopolize power over others (viz., as "Lord"), but rather empowers others and affirms them all on equal footing. What we need is a Jesus who critiques the world's (and Mark's!) system of hierarchical authority. Fortunately, a historical critical quest for Jesus reveals just such a person, according to Mack. This, we shall later argue, is hardly coincidental.

Owing to these influences, the most fundamental critique one could make of Mack's theory of religion is that it is thoroughly reductionistic.[27] Social formation and identity are here not simply a *part* of religion: they *are* religion. Everything about religious faith and life is reduced to sociological categories. All beliefs ("myths") about a personal transcendent God, a savior, or salvation are, we are told, "really" about social group formation.

All of the particulars of Mack's theory on Christian origins, to be discussed below, follow from this basic assumption. And it is just that: an *assumption*. Never once does Mack actually *argue* for his theory of religion. He merely adopts and henceforth *assumes* it, while likewise assuming the incorrectness and general irrelevance of any other. It is the spectacles through which he chooses to see the world and assess historical evidence. And no sustained argument is given as to why one should adopt this "way of seeing" over any other way.

MACK'S THEORY OF CHRISTIAN ORIGINS: A SUMMARY

Mack's theory of religion, when applied to his New Testament studies, has resulted in a distinct theory of Christian origins and consequently of the historical Jesus. His theory is best documented in his *Myth of Innocence*, from which the following summary is largely drawn. The reductionistic and anti-supernaturalistic bias that characterizes his whole project is laid out early in this work as Mack states emphatically what is *not* needed to explain Christian origins.

> [T]he emergence of early Christianity and its literatures can be understood without recourse to assumptions or caveats with regard to miracles, resurrections, presences, or unusual charismatic phenomena.[28]

Such a declaration, of course, is an inherent assumption of both the historical-critical program as originally conceived, as well as Mack's broad theory of religion. With this theory as his starting point, and through textual analyses that depend upon a variety of critical methods — most importantly redactional, rhetorical, and sociological — Mack weaves a radical and intriguing theory of early Christianity. Not that the work is convincing to one not already disposed to accept its basic premises and subsidiary theories. To the contrary, by Mack's own admission, this work is more of an "essay" than it is a "monograph."[29] Much of his theorizing therefore comes by way of assertion rather than argumentation.

Frequently Mack simply states, and henceforth assumes, a number of debatable conclusions regarding a variety of different issues.[30] What *is* compelling about Mack's overall theory — if it is compelling at all — is its overall plausibility as a way of accounting for the whole of early Christianity on a strictly naturalistic basis — "without recourse . . . to miracles, resurrections, presences, or unusual charismatic phenomena." If one begins where he begins, his arguments to take one where he ends might have some force.[31]

Since a number of the more specific aspects of his theory shall be dealt with in subsequent chapters as we critically interact with this theory, here I shall simply provide a general overview of the most significant major points of his theory.

A Cynic Jesus, Some Table-Talk, and Radical Diversity

Mack argues that Jesus, a Cynic sage with no real intentions of launching a program of any kind, became a founder figure for a number of diverse groups involved in innovative "social experiments." Mack divides these groups into two categories: the *"Jesus movements"* of Palestine and southern Syria, and the *"Christ cults"* of northern Syria, Asia Minor, and Greece.[32] Mack emphasizes time and again the *radical diversity* that characterized the beliefs and practices of these various groups in relation to one another, particularly with regard to their understandings of Jesus himself. In this he represents the epitome of the previously discussed post-Bultmannian early Christian radical diversity thesis.

> It is very important to see that everyone did not think the same about Jesus. Even among those who thought him very important and especially among those who knew him well there was no agreement.[33]

In fact, Mack highlights only one real continuity between these various groups, a phenomenon that he traces within the various groups and thus back to the historical Jesus: namely, the practice of meeting together for meals enveloped by unconventional table-talk. Mack writes:

> Jesus at social occasions would not be difficult to imagine at all, for there would be no need to ask about any grand design or formal recognition of the practice. . . . Meals together would be the perfect occasion for aphoristic discourse, parables, reports, poking fun, and serious discussions about staying alert and living sanely in the midst of cultures in transition. A sense of the unconventional may very well have prevailed, supposing the company was mixed and the conversation somewhat self-reflective. . . . Supposing the Jesus movements continued such a social practice, the history of group formation known to have occurred is quite understandable. Without a clear charter and agenda, groups meeting regularly would have to work out the times, purposes, and practices as best they could under the leadership of those willing and eager to assume leadership.[34]

With some form of table fellowship and a nod to Jesus as the only ties that bind, Mack offers the following characterization of Christian origins.

The "Jesus Movements"

Mack proposes that there were five different types of "Jesus movements." What justifies seeing each of these types as belonging to the same group is that they all "kept the memory of Jesus alive and thought of themselves in terms of Jewish reform."[35] What is more, in sharp contrast to the "Christ-cults" (e.g., Paul and the Hellenistic congregations), none of the Jesus movements saw any significance in Jesus' death. Nor did they hold any beliefs concerning Jesus' resurrection, his posthumous appearances, or his continuing spiritual presence in the communities. Nor did they recognize Jesus as being, in any sense, the "Lord" of a new religious society. And neither did they believe in any sort of "conversion" process that separated a person's present participation in their group from his or her past.[36]

These Jesus movements, Mack contends, represent a closer tie to the actual teachings of the historical Jesus than do the Christ-cults. Since it is clear, however, that the New Testament documents themselves do not reflect this perspective — their perspective, as we shall see, is much closer to the "Christ cults" — one might wonder how Mack infers the existence of these Jesus movements. The answer is that two of the groups are inferred by references in Paul's epistles and the Gospels, while three of the groups are inferred on the basis of hypothetical documents that Mack believes can be "uncovered" in the four Gospels through various critical methods. These documents are (of course) "Q," a collection of miracle stories, and a collection of pronouncement stories.

A word about each of these five groups is in order, since they factor in significantly to Mack's theory on Christian origins.

Galilean Itinerants: The Q People

The first, and in some respects the most important, of the five Jesus movement groups were the "itinerants in Galilee" as represented by the "Q" document (which, Mack contends, functioned as their handbook). According to Mack, this group was composed of "Cynic-like preachers" and as such probably represents the group that maintained the most continuity with the historical Jesus. They were devoted to preaching the message of the "kingdom of God" which, Mack (along with Crossan) would emphasize, must not be confused with the apocalyptic rendition of that theme developed in the Gospel of Mark. Instead, this group's conception of the kingdom — like that of the Cynic Jesus — was rooted in Hellenistic-Jewish wisdom and even in Cynic thought.[37] Hence, in Burton Mack's view:

> A broadside critique in the Cynic mode, and a dare to be different on the basis of a wisdom view of the world, may have been about as far as it went with Jesus and those who came to share his views and ways.[38]

Mack develops his views on this hypothetical community more fully in his recent book *The Lost Gospel*. Mack here offers his full-scaled reconstruction of the social history of the "Q people." He takes as his starting point the earlier mentioned conclusions of Kloppenborg regarding a triple-layered Q.[39] From this starting point, Mack claims to uncover five distinct stages of Q's social history.

First, there is a "pre-Q-1" stage, recognizable only from the reconstruction of a set of aphorisms and aphoristic imperatives selected for reworking by a (supposed) Q-1 redactor. It is in this stage of social formation that Mack locates a "fascination with what might be called an egalitarian view of social roles and ranking."[40] Also, and most importantly for our purposes, it is at this stage that Mack sees clear remnants of Cynic elements — namely, the aphoristic saying-cores within the blocks of Q-1 material. Accordingly, these "crisp sayings of Jesus in Q-1 show that his followers thought of him as a Cynic-like sage."[41]

Second, Mack finds a Q-1 stage in which he detects a "heightened awareness of belonging to a movement . . . and a social vision." Earlier "injunctions" (from the pre-Q-1 stage) have now evolved into "rules for the group," complete with supporting argumentation.[42]

Mack then posits a post-Q-1/pre-Q-2 interim stage in order to account for the peculiar phenomena eventually found in Q-2. Here, one must surmise the rise of "social conflict within close circles of acquaintance," brought on by the Q community's novel social experiment.[43] The language of judgment that comes to characterize Q-2 must have had its beginnings during this stage, Mack believes, no doubt in response to severe criticism Q people were receiving from outsiders.

Next Mack discovers a Q-2 stage which is supposedly characterized by a recognition of the deep investment that the movement had come to hold for its members. This intensification of group identity set the stage for the "mythmaking" that one finds in Q-2 which involves "creative borrowing and the clever rearrangement of fascinating figures from several other vibrant mythologies of the time."[44] An important element of the emerging "myth of origins" includes the expanding vision of Jesus. In contrast to the radical egalitarianism of the earliest stages of this community, Jesus is now beginning to be revisioned as an authority figure. Indeed, the people of Q are, at this stage, beginning to tap into the wisdom mythology of their culture and to invest Jesus with superhuman knowledge and wisdom.

Finally, Mack postulates a Q-3 stage, occurring sometime after the Roman-Jewish war, in which a wisdom mythology of the previous stage is expanded further to arrive at a view of Jesus as a semi-divine son of God. Here too, he argues, one finds an increasingly Jewish focus as the Q people begin to make use of temple imagery and Jewish Scripture.[45]

Shortly after this final stage, Mack holds, the handbook of this community, Q, was incorporated into, and transformed by, Mark. Unfortunately, Q disappeared as an independent document after its incorporation, and can now only be "discovered" by the source-critical analysis of scholars as they work on Mark, Matthew, and Luke. Mack supplies the text of this document, complete with his Kloppenborgian stratification, in *The Lost Gospel*.[46]

The Remaining Four Jesus Movements

None of the other five groups play as central a role in Mack's thesis and thus can be reviewed more briefly. The second group within the "Jesus movements" Mack postulates are called "the Pillars in Jerusalem." Their distinct existence as a group is inferred by Mack largely on the basis of references in Paul's epistles, especially in Galatians 1 and 2. According to Mack, this group "laid the foundations for a Jewish sect of hasidism who interpreted the law by appeal to Jesus' authority."[47] It is also responsible for the "myth" of the Jerusalem origin of Christianity.

Mack identifies a third distinct group of Jesus people on the basis of several references to Jesus' family in the Gospels, and hence calls them "the Family of Jesus." According to Mack, from Jesus' own family a group of Jesus people formed in Transjordan and eventually became the Jewish-Christian sect of the Nazareans. Judging from Q, which downplays the importance of Jesus' actual family, Mack supposes that this group had conflicts with the Q community on the issue of authority.[48]

Mack dubs a fourth Jesus group "the Congregation of Israel," which he postulates upon the basis of hypothetical "miracle stories" collections purportedly discovered within the Gospels of Mark and John. Here, Mack notes both the group's existence and its odd choice of miracle collections as a literary basis upon which to mythologize.

> Because they are collections, and because they betray a certain kind of meditation on Jesus' activity, they are evidence for yet another early Jesus movement. Miracle stories do seem an unlikely vehicle for a group's mythmaking. It would be more natural to think that miracle stories simply traveled from group to group as entertainment.[49]

Nevertheless, developing a mythology on the basis of a collection of miracle stories is precisely what the "Congregation of Israel" did, according to Mack.

Finally, Mack postulates a fifth Jesus group called "the Synagogue Reform" movement, which he infers on the basis of the (again, hypothetical) "pronouncement stories document" that has been "interwoven into Mark's narrative designs."[50] According to Mack, this group became involved in a heated conflict with the Pharisees as both attempted synagogue reform within various locales. The Pharisees, of course, "had to win" at this game. They had "arguments, institutional precedents, and practical considerations" on their side. The "Jesus people," however,

> had only their unconventional table fellowship to share, plus the liberal kingdom talk that went with it, and appeals to a recent sage who had excited the imagination. What sounded good around the table of the Jesus people may not have been convincing in the service at the synagogue.[51]

Thus, this group's reform movement failed, as the high polemic attached to the pronouncement stories incorporated into the Gospels suggests. The lasting legacy of this group is not limited to the polemical stories they passed on to the Gospel traditions, however, for it was supposedly out of this group that the greatest Christian myth weaver of all time, the author of Mark, arose.[52]

In all of this, Mack's post-Bultmannian proclivity toward positing radical diversity within early Christianity should be noted. For every distinct aspect of the early Christian tradition—references to "pillars," Jesus' family, miracle stories, pronouncement stories, chreiai, Q, the differing emphases of Q—Mack posits a distinct document and a distinct group behind the document (and/or a distinct phase of a social history of the group behind the document). The diversity of Jesus groups Mack "discovers" is breathtaking, as is the hypothetical nature of the entire enterprise. And we have not yet even discussed the second major hypothetical group that the historical Jesus inspired. To this group we now turn.

The "Christ-Cults"

The second major group that would identify themselves as associated with Jesus are the "Christ-cults," whose existence is, for the most part, inferred from Paul's epistles. In Mack's estimation, the Christ-cult must have arisen out of a Syrian Jesus movement. Antioch, that "great sea of Hellenistic culture," is a probable location, where the mix of Jews and

Gentiles is just as the reconstruction calls for.[53] In any case, this group quickly distinguished itself in several ways. First, the table gatherings of this movement began to take on ritualized tones "on the model of the [Hellenistic] mystery religions."[54] Second, and most significantly, in contrast to all the Jesus movements, from this group "a mythology sprang up about Jesus as a divine being," which "focused on Jesus' resurrection."[55] Thus, it is only within the Christ-cults that the title "Christ" is used, where it signifies the dying and rising One.

Accounting for how this group arose, and how they developed such an exalted mythology around a recently departed Jewish Cynic sage, is one of the central burdens of Mack's theory, as he himself acknowledges.[56] Mack must, in a word, attempt to "reconstruct the logic by which Jesus came to be thought of as a god."[57] This is no small task, but Mack attempts to carry it out by identifying an all-important clue to this "logic" in the Christ-cult's (that is, Paul's) notion that Christ died "for us" — that is, for the congregations of the Christ. In keeping with both his history-of-religions approach and his orientation toward Hellenism, Mack postulates the origin of Paul's concept of vicarious suffering in non-Jewish sources.

> Such a notion cannot be traced to old Jewish and/or Israelite traditions, for the very notion of a vicarious human sacrifice was anathema in these cultures. But it can easily be traced to a strong Greek tradition of extolling a noble death.[58]

The majority of New Testament scholarship (and, we might add, the mass of evidence) does not support Mack's position, but his particular version of Christian origins requires it. While perhaps acknowledging the influence of a Hellenistic martyrological motif, the majority of scholars locate the primary background to Paul's concept as the Old Testament.[59] For Mack, however, the Christ-cults are seen as being indebted to Hellenistic conceptions at every term, just as the "true" origins of the Jesus movements are conceived of as Hellenistic in that they derived from a Hellenistic Cynic sage (Jesus). The fundamental Jewish worldview of Jesus and his earliest followers is first watered down and thus marginalized by Mack through the claim of a radically diverse first-century Judaism.[60] And in the midst of this (Mack created) ideological chaos, "Hellenism" becomes the primary cohesive factor that solidifies all the different "Judaisms" and then all the diverse "Jesus movements." Hellenism thus becomes, for Mack, the conceptual matrix that alone holds the generative key to virtually every question. In this sense, one could argue that Mack weaves his own "Hellenistic myth of Christian origins." The question of Paul and the "Christ-cult" thesis will be taken up again in chapters 8 and 9.

THE GOSPEL OF MARK: THE CREATION OF THE GRAND CHRISTIAN "MYTH"

According to Mack, the creation of the Gospel of Mark constitutes the most critical turning point in the evolution of early Christianity. Mack suggests that the Markan author, a member of one of the "Synagogue Reform" Jesus movements, began by collecting the very diverse traditions associated with the various Jesus movements on the one hand (including Q),[61] and the entirely different traditions of the Hellenized Christ cults on the other. These in hand, the Markan author then literally interwove them together – creating the chronological narrative framework along the way – into a single, grand myth of Christian origins. What were formerly disparate, even conflictive, movements whose similarities included nothing more than dining clubs and a generally obscure founder figure (whose true Cynic-like character had, oddly enough, been "erased" by virtually every one of the groups he had spawned!), were now joined together in Mark to create the illusion of a single, unified front. For Mack, then, Mark becomes a classic example in the study of high-level mythmaking as self-justifying rationalization for the purpose of social formation. Mack's (and Crossan's) reading of the Gospel of Mark will be critiqued in detail in chapters 10 and 11.

According to Mack, the authors of Matthew and Luke-Acts, taking their clue from Mark, carried on his grand tradition with their own "myths of origin," even if toning down some of his apocalyptic eccentricities along the way. This means, of course, that the church's own history book of its earliest days – the Acts of the Apostles – is patently "unreliable," a claim that will be contested in chapter 12.[62] John, who was even more imaginative, nonetheless remained indebted to the original Markan plot. Thus, in summary, "Mark's Gospel must be seen as the origin of the Christian view of Christian origins."[63]

MACK'S HISTORICAL CYNIC-LIKE JESUS

We have already seen the outline sketch of Mack's historical Jesus. Again, since his greatest concern is in tracing out a theory of Christian origins that is commensurate with his general theory of religion, he spends far less time on the specifics of Jesus than most contemporary questers. In fact, given his basic thesis concerning the mind-boggling extent to which rampant mythmaking was going on in each and every diverse sector of early Christianity, the basic question arises as to how he avoids the implications of an even more formidable wall of "myth" between the historical Jesus and the early church than that set up by either Strauss or Bultmann. It is clear that he does have sentiments in this radically skeptical direction—hence his conscious focus on the early church rather than Jesus.[64] Nonetheless, Mack somehow penetrates the mythological veil, only to discover a historical Cynic sage. We must now take a brief look at just how—and equally importantly *why*—this curious feat is pulled off.

Mack's Cynic-Jesus Thesis: The Foundations

Mack has noted at least four areas of current research that serve to strengthen the wider foundations of the Cynic-Jesus thesis.[65] First, there are the recent studies by classicists that provide a greater measure of understanding in regard to ancient Cynicism.[66] Presumably Mack's point is that such studies provide surer ground for accurate comparisons.

Second, Mack points to a "shift" in scholarly perspective with regard to the Hellenistic influence of Galilee in Jesus' day. In his words, "Galilee was in fact an epitome of Hellenistic culture on the eve of the Roman era."[67]

Third, Mack suggests that recent readings of a variety of early Christian sources—he lists GosThom, Mark, Matthew, Didache, and Luke—"no longer stand in the way of a Cynic hypothesis for the historical Jesus."[68] Mack is here referring to the emerging, largely post-Bultmannian, view that the early Jesus traditions and the "kerygmatic" (that is "Pauline") interpretation of Christ's death and resurrection are simply not compatible with one another. Thus, according to Mack, "The gap between a Cynic Jesus and the Jesus traditions is not as great as that between Jesus and the Pauline Christ."[69] Finally, Mack appeals to recent explorations into the rhetorics of both Jesus and Paul as suggesting important Cynic connections for both.[70]

Mack's Cynic-Jesus Thesis: The Textual Evidence

Mack's central arguments for the Cynic thesis are, of course, *text*-based. Recently, he has put forth three lines of evidence, derived from textual studies of the Synoptics, that must "bear the weight" of the Cynic hypothesis.[71] Each will now be briefly summarized in turn.

First, there is the Cynic-like nature of *the rhetoric of the chreiai* found at the core of the Gospels' pronouncement stories. In Mack's words, in these stories, "Jesus is depicted in a certain situation; someone questions what he is saying or doing; and Jesus gives a sharp response."[72] Mack argues that when one cuts through the later elaborations of the pronouncement stories to the core chreiai, one finds that oftentimes they compare remarkably well with ancient chreiai associated with the Cynics.[73]

More specifically, Mack suggests that many of Jesus' responses in the Gospels' chreiai do not reflect the "ethical maxims and truisms" one finds in the conventional wisdom sayings of stable, traditional settings. This more conventional wisdom, however, affected the later elaborations on the chreiai into the present form of the pronouncement stories, and hence in-depth critical analysis is needed to recover the original chreiai. When this is done, however, Mack contends that the recovered chreiai betray a "logic and cleverness" that characterized the way in which ancient Cynics would respond to their critics who were trying to catch them in inconsistencies with regard to their unconventional lifestyles.[74] Thus, Mack concludes that the Gospels' pronouncement stories reveal that, just like the Cynics, "at some early stage in the Jesus movement playful rejoinder may have been enough to justify an unconventional practice in the face of askance convention."[75]

The validity of Mack's comparison here, of course, depends on accepting his view that the pronouncement stories in the Gospels are in fact literary elaborations upon an original chreia. One could, however, as easily argue in an opposite direction: the Gospel pronouncement stories are in fact in their original form, but Mack chooses to see them as elaborations so that he can strip away the supposed "elaborations" to "discover" a (not surprisingly) Cynic-like "original" chreia.

The second piece of Mack's textual evidence for the Cynic thesis involves the *aphorisms* found in Q. Again, he assumes Kloppenborg's layering of Q, and goes on to argue that at the heart of many of the Q-1 sayings-clusters one can isolate the "aphoristic maxims" that represent the original community rules of the Jesus movement.[76] According to Mack, these sayings "illustrate the aphoristic nature of the wisdom attributed to Jesus and bristle with the pointed style of Cynic maxims."[77] The "Cynic flavor" increases when Mack adds to such maxims a number of behavioral injunctions that suggest that the "Jesus people were apparently taking up what we would call an alternative lifestyle."[78]

Just what this alternative lifestyle looked like is all-important to

Mack's Cynic thesis. After listing no less than sixteen tenets of the Q-1 lifestyle—including such Cynic hallmarks as "criticism of the rich and their wealth," "fearlessness in the presence of those in power and authority," "a call to voluntary poverty," "disentanglement from family ties," "a challenge to fearless and carefree attitudes," "a strong sense of independent vocation," and "etiquette for unashamed begging"—Mack concludes:

> This list of themes makes a set. The set spells out a program. And the program fits the popular profile of the Cynic in antiquity. The conclusion must be that, were this program the only feature distinguishing the Jesus people, their first century acquaintances would have thought they were Cynics.[79]

Mack goes on to summarize the general code that would have guided both the Cynics and the Q-1 people.

> "Live naturally," both said, "Do not be guided by the rules that now govern the social situation. And don't worry. Protecting your own personal sense of integrity is worth it."[80]

The validity of Mack's comparison here, of course, depends on one's acceptance of his convictions that (a) Q exists; (b) that it served the "handbook" purpose he believes it served; and (c) that his Kloppenborgian stratification of Q is accurate. One could, however, easily argue in an opposite direction: what counts as belonging to Q-1 is *defined ahead of time* as what will look Cynic-like (hence all authoritative statements of Jesus and apocalyptic elements are ruled to be later), and thus it is hardly surprising that Mack "discovers" a Cynic-like Jesus in this supposed earliest strata of Q.

Third, and finally, Mack takes what at first glance appears to be a strike against the Cynic thesis and parlays it into his third line of textual evidence in its favor. As we have already seen, on Mack's account both the chreiae and the aphorisms have been "elaborated" into pronouncement stories and sayings clusters that are clearly *not* in line with a Cynic ethos. They have, rather, been transformed in a more "conventional" manner, being supported with illustrations and argumentation from "conventional logic."

This may initially seem like an unexpected history for sayings that were, per hypothesis, originally characterized by their unconventional, if not outright subversive, character. But Mack attempts to argue that this is exactly what one would expect, and in fact sees this history as further conformation of his original Cynic Jesus. For, as we have seen, social groups are always struggling for a solid self-definition. And in an unstable internal environment such as the early Jesus movements had, and an unstable external environment such as the Greco-Roman world they lived in, people are inclined to turn to more stable conventional wisdom for their self-definition. Hence we find, Mack argues, the "people of Q" and the "synagogue reform movement" attempting to work out their internal and external struggles by increasingly moving away from their radically egalitarian beginnings toward a "safer" authoritarian Jesus who is invested with divine significance.

According to Mack, then, we find these early Jesus people increasingly abandoning their originally carefree, lighthearted, countercultural movement in favor of a more conventional, but self-absorbed, somewhat defensive, and all-too-serious "social experiment." And with each step, the original sayings of Jesus are revisioned away from their original radical character.

> By the very simple means of manipulating the sayings of Jesus rhetorically, the synagogue reform movement turned a Cynic sage into an imperious judge and sovereign.[81]

Thus, through his social history scheme, Mack not only derails a potential threat to his Cynic thesis, but argues that just such a phenomenon is what one could expect given the community's pattern of development. The validity of this analysis, of course, depends on one accepting (a) Mack's theory of social group formation, (b) his postulation of the Jesus movements as distinct from the Christ cults, and (c) his reconstructed social histories for these groups. Again, however, one could easily argue in the opposite direction: it is only the assumption that the original Jesus was Cynic-like that leads one to look for and find an original Cynic-like chreia behind the pronouncement stories and thus to reconstruct a hypothetical history of a hypothetical group to account for how these sayings became "unCynic" like!

MACK'S JESUS: THE SHADOWY CYNIC SAGE

The Secular Jesus

In concluding his argument for the Cynic thesis, Mack states that he "sees no way around it. . . . The Cynic-like data from Q and Mark are as close as we shall ever get to the real Jesus of history. Punkt."[82] For Mack, then, Jesus is, almost without qualification, a Hellenistic Cynic. Indeed, in several important respects, Mack takes the Cynic parallels even further than Crossan.

For example, Mack is much less hesitant than Crossan in making the sweeping claim of a thoroughly non-eschatological Jesus.[83] He also goes further than Crossan in denying *any* fundamental historical linkage between the historical Jesus and the miracle-worker and exorcist traditions about him. In fact, one strains to catch a real hint that Mack's Jesus is about "religion"—in anything like the traditional sense of the term—at all. Even when it comes to judging just what *type* of Cynic Jesus was remembered as, Mack concludes not for the rigorous ascetic model, but rather for the "hedonistic variety."[84] He has to admit that Jesus must have endorsed "a religious piety of some kind," for even on Mack's account Jesus' view of the kingdom involves a belief in God, and his followers eventually came to understand themselves in terms of the Jewish traditions. But if it were not for these two points, virtually nothing would separate the essentially a-religious Hellenistic Cynics from the Jewish Cynic Jesus. And thus his piety can be largely attributed to the accidental fact of his Jewish ethnic identity.[85]

The Importance of the Cynic Jesus for Mack's Theory of Religion

Mack does not shy away from flushing out the full ramifications of his portrait of Jesus and his earliest followers. In essence, his portrait tells us

> that the Jesus of history was not nearly as important for the emergence of Christianity as the intellectual energies generated by his followers while experimenting with a novel social vision. Mythmaking is hard work. It is not the clever insight or the dramatic moment of vision that counts. It is the elaboration.[86]

It is important to note that this understanding of the historical Jesus and the creative mythmaking histories of his followers is exactly what Mack's theory of religion requires. It constitutes, in fact, simply one dramatic application of this theory to New Testament studies. Everything about early Christianity is naturalistically explained in sociological terms, and *nothing is unique.* Every piece of the early Christian portrait of Jesus is accounted for by reference to other religious and social phenomenon. Both Mack's sociological reductionism and history of religions approach to religion are clearly evidenced in this account. Indeed, everything in his account is clearly *determined* by his approach.

It is the non-uniqueness of Jesus and Christianity that Mack's religious theory produces that provides us with an answer to our earlier question about why Mack has entered into the historical Jesus quest when his own proclivities would suggest a generally "No-Quest" attitude. According to Mack, the search for the historical Jesus has been largely carried out on the assumption that there existed one unique and extraordinary person behind the extraordinary "mythologies" of the New Testament.[87] Just this notion, however, is altogether ruled out by the sociologically reductionistic and comparative religions approach that Mack operates with.

By entering into the quest himself and recovering a Cynic Jesus that is fundamentally discontinuous with, and largely irrelevant to, later Christian ideas, Mack can "contribute" to New Testament scholarship the conclusion that any and all claims of a singularly unique Jesus as the actual historical impetus for the Christian tradition are unnecessary. The search for "the unique" is itself a misguided search, so no wonder the results of the quest have been so conflicting. To the contrary, Mack wants to demonstrate that

> the notion of a single, miraculous point of origin [is] . . . not a category of critical scholarship at all, but an article of faith derived from Christian mythology.[88]

Hence, the *real* material in need of explaining on the question of Christian origins is not related to the historical Jesus at all. It is the creative mythmaking of the earliest Christians – ironically, the very material upon which his theory of religion feeds and depends.[89]

CONCLUSION

Though they employ quite different methodologies, and hence come at it from very different directions, both Crossan and Mack conclude that the historical Jesus was, more than anything else, a Cynic sage. While Crossan is willing to grant that Jesus healed "illnesses," both agree that he never cured diseases. Both agree that he made no divine claims. Both agree that his earliest followers saw him as a teacher and leader, no more. Both agree that his earliest followers saw no special significance in his death. And both agree that they held no concept of a resurrection. Hence, both agree that the central thrust of the New Testament portrait of Jesus is largely mythological and hence fundamentally unreliable.

This last point, while it is simply a consequence of Crossan's and Mack's methodological starting point, constitutes the fundamental arena in which their theories must be tested. For if one can successfully argue against their fundamentally skeptical attitude toward the New Testament documents, their entire program with its revisionist view of Jesus falls to the ground. That is, if one can demonstrate that Paul's view of Jesus is rooted in early Christian tradition (viz., it is not a mythological creation of a "Christ-cult"), that the Gospel of Mark is solidly rooted in history (it is not a fabrication), and that Luke recorded reliable church history (against Crossan's and Mack's reconstructed histories), then one will have thereby demonstrated the fallaciousness of Crossan's and Mack's conclusions.

How one evaluates the evidence for and/or against the reliability of these documents, however, is largely determined by the presuppositions one brings to the table of their evaluation, as we have already seen. Hence, before we take issue with Crossan's and Mack's attitude toward the New Testament, it will be beneficial to first critically examine the general presuppositions, methodological assumptions, and general perspectives they work out of. Our argument shall be that, even apart from their particular views of the New Testament documents, their projects are seriously flawed at a foundational level on a number of points. To this issue we now turn.

·SECTION 3·

A Critique of the Foundations of the Cynic Thesis

5

BEGINNING AT THE CONCLUSION:
A Critique of Post-Bultmannian Assumptions

Having laid out the central features of the "Post-Bultmannian Quest" and the specific theories of Crossan and Mack in the previous three chapters, we are now in a position to begin a critical analysis of the Cynic thesis. We shall work from the general to the particular in this critique. Hence, this segment of the work shall thoughtfully analyze foundational aspects of the Cynic thesis. More specifically, in this chapter I shall critically examine the most general control beliefs that characterize the "Post-Bultmannian Quest" and attempt to demonstrate that these control beliefs lead them to neglect important aspects of scholarship that argues, against their views, that the canonical Gospels are in fact generally reliable. The next chapter shall concentrate on a critical analysis of the post-Bultmannian use of extra-canonical sources, while chapter 7 shall concern itself with a critical analysis of the main arguments specifically employed by defenders of the Cynic thesis. This shall then pave the way for a critical examination of the Cynic thesis' case against Paul, Mark, and Luke in sections 4, 5, and 6 of this work.

THE ASSUMPTION OF NATURALISM

The Influence of the Anti-Supernaturalistic Presupposition
In recounting the quest from Reimarus up to Crossan and Mack (chaps. 1–2), I argued that religious and philosophical presuppositions have dramatically influenced the manner in which questers interpreted the available evidence regarding the historical Jesus. These foundational control-beliefs have played a major role not only in the quest, but in the larger historical-critical enterprise of which it is a part. Over the years,

there has been intense debate on the question of whether one can in principle separate these religious and philosophical assumptions from a strictly historical methodology or not.¹ But, however one resolves this philosophical debate, several observations concerning the past and present quest for the historical Jesus regarding the influence of religio-philosophical presuppositions are undeniable.

First, as our earlier review of the quest demonstrated, most practitioners of the historical-critical method, and thus most of the key players in the quest, have adopted blatantly anti-supernatural, anti-dogmatic, and generally reductionistic *a priori* religio-philosophical control-beliefs. The post-Bultmannian quest, as both Crossan's and Mack's work has shown, very much continues this trend. While there have always been some who have withstood this tide, and while there are an increasing number of those within the "Third-Quest" camp who are now rejecting these presuppositions (see chap. 2), they are generally marginalized and written off as less than serious historical scholars by those within the post-Bultmannian camp.²

Second, these naturalistic presuppositions have decisively influenced the general attitude and approach of modern critical scholarship to the biblical texts by dictating what these texts are and are not allowed to witness to.³ To be specific, if the possibility of the intervention of a personal God into history is ruled out on an *a priori* basis, then clearly the New Testament worldview and many of its historical claims must be viewed as nonhistorical "myth" at best, and outright nonsense – possibly orchestrated deception – at worst. The *a priori* rejection of the New Testament worldview necessarily leads to a skeptical assessment of all of its historical and theological claims.⁴ If it is decided ahead of time that the texts *cannot* be accurately speaking about what it *seems* they are speaking about – for example, a miracle-working, resurrected Jesus – then the only alternative is to view them as mythological and/or fraudulent. The most fundamental difference between this skeptical approach to the biblical texts and a more conservative approach that concludes that these texts are generally historically reliable is just this presupposition.⁵

Third, it must be noted that critical scholars within this liberal tradition have usually *not* been self-critical of the presuppositions they work with, and not self-critical of the very clear "non-scholarly" motives that influence their work (such as the need for acceptance within the scholarly community). As Elisabeth Schüssler Fiorenza has argued, critical biblical scholars have tended to operate from within a "positivistic paradigm" that naively assumed that the historical-critical enterprise was value free, a-political, and entirely objective.[6] But such has certainly not been the case. The historical-critical enterprise has been as driven by value-laden presuppositions and ulterior motives as any intellectual enterprise could be. And it is perhaps time for this enterprise to own up to this fact and subject their control-beliefs and motivations to the same critical assessment to which they've previously subjected the biblical texts. Thomas Oden speaks to this point when he writes:

> The hermeneutic of suspicion has been safely applied to the history of Jesus but not to the history of the historians. It is now time for the tables to turn. The hermeneutic of suspicion must be fairly and prudently applied to the critical movement itself. This is the most certain next phase of biblical scholarship – criticism of criticism. Why has it taken so long?[7]

The Demise of Naturalism

This naïveté concerning their own control-beliefs and motivations is all the more surprising given the recent postmodern critique of the rationalistic, positivistic modern worldview out of which the post-Bultmannians operate. To be sure, postmodernism has penetrated this camp in its "deconstructive" literary form (as with Derrida's and Foucault's influence on Crossan and Mack), but not as a foundational critique of the rationalistic worldview itself.[8] Were this wider postmodern perspective appropriated, the arbitrary nature of the rationalistic assumptions that drive the post-Bultmannian school would become more evident and their dogmatic skepticism regarding Scripture perhaps more qualified.[9] Instead, however, the spirit of Bultmann's dogmatic anti-supernaturalism yet looms large.

The irony in this is that, while Bultmann originally adopted this stance to accommodate Christianity to the modern "secular" mind-set (through his hermeneutic of "demythologization"), Bultmann's attitude itself is now becoming profoundly out of sync with contemporary Western culture. The secular, mechanistic, and hence anti-supernaturalistic attitude that has largely dominated Western intellectual culture for the last two centuries is, by most accounts, in the process of surrendering its reign. Quite a number from within the scientific community, for instance, are presently rethinking the adequacy of the old mechanistic worldview, with important implications for our understanding of the relationship between science and theology.[10] More broadly, vast segments of "(post)modern" Western culture at large – Christian and not – are having no trouble at all integrating the supernatural into their worldviews and everyday life experience.[11]

In short, the advance of technology and knowledge has not, as the earlier modernists predicted, brought an end to religious experiences or worldviews. In fact, since the 1960s, an entirely new spiritual quest has arisen in the Western world that flies in the face of the secularistic predictions of Marx, Nietzsche, and Freud. Contrary to the working presuppositions of the post-Bultmannian quest, reports of religious experiences with a transcendent personal God (or of other supernatural beings) are anything but in short supply today.[12] It seems, then, that if a portrait of the historical Jesus is going to be relevant to contemporary postmodern Western culture—a predominant concern for many post-Bultmannians—it will not look anything like Bultmann's demythologized portrait.

PRESUPPOSITIONS AND METHODOLOGY

All can agree that rigorous methodology is important in any scholarly discipline. What is important to see from our earlier discussions, however, is that rigorous methodology does not necessarily insure that one's control-beliefs will be critiqued, or even identified, as part of the scholarly discipline. Mack's theory of religion and the impact it has on his methodology is a very good example of this. His (fully) sociological theory of Christian origins can only be true if, in fact, there is no personal transcendent God behind the events and movements that gave birth to Christianity. But this perspective is not something Mack argues for: he simply *assumes* it. In almost every one of his more recent publications, his assumed theory of religion determines the course of his investigation.[13] Yet his theory itself always lies in the background.

This is certainly true of his *Myth of Innocence.* One need only read his introduction with its sustained *a priori* rejection of the idea of religious uniqueness to surmise the sort of Jesus he is going to end up within this work. Any view that would suggest that Jesus could have been radically unique and the originator of a radically unique movement is ruled out at the start—not on the basis of the evidence, but on the basis of Mack's *starting assumptions.*

Crossan's work is, in a different way, another example of this. While Crossan *intends* to weave a tight methodological net that filters out idiosyncratic presuppositions, his own post-Bultmannian assumptions, nevertheless, determine *how* this net is woven, and thus determine what this net does and does not catch, as we have seen. And what it does *not* catch is Crossan's own idiosyncratic assumptions. The "formal procedures" of his methodology (e.g., his concern to create a data base, organize it chronologically) are sound enough. But the *way* these procedures are followed through are heavily indebted to *a priori* assumptions. Hence, his preference for Q, the Gospel of Thomas, and the Cross Gospel over Mark and Paul do not strictly follow from the formal aspects of his methodology, but from the assumptions that give his methodology material content.[14]

CONTROL-BELIEFS AND THE HISTORICAL JESUS

Because foundational control-beliefs strongly influence a scholar's methodology and assessment of the historical evidence, they very much influence their reconstructions of the historical Jesus. This is true in both a negative and positive way. Negatively, the control-beliefs of a scholar determine what *kind* of Jesus he or she is looking for by defining what kind of Jesus *is and is not possible.* One can, obviously, only reconstruct a historical Jesus that one can conceive of as *possible.* For Crossan and Mack, this entails that the notion that Jesus was the Son of God—that the personal transcendent God was present in, and revealed through, Jesus in a decisive way—is ruled out *a priori.* The religiophilosophical presuppositions of both Crossan and Mack rule out such a concept as a possibility. Hence, no amount of historical evidence could ever be interpreted as counting for such a view. Both Crossan's negative theology and Mack's sociological reductionism render, *on a metaphysical basis,* anything like the traditional conception of Jesus unintelligible.

The control-beliefs of a scholar also function positively, however, for they predispose a scholar to "discover" a certain kind of Jesus. We should not, for example, be surprised to find Crossan "discovering" a Jesus who is a parabolic-paradoxical egalitarian, for this Jesus happens to perfectly reflect Crossan's own post-structuralist understanding of the "divine" and how we go about experiencing it (see chap. 3). He thus describes Jesus' (reconstructed) vision of the kingdom as "necessarily, gloriously, and explosively paradoxical from the very first moment of its conception."[15] Such a characterization, however, sounds more like the enthusiasm of a true believer than the cautious description of a "disinterested" scholar.[16]

Mack's understanding of Jesus as Cynic, on the other hand, differs from Crossan's at just the points one would expect, given his reductionistic sociological theory of religion. Jesus is *not* a miracle worker, an exorcist, or anything else that would cause him to stand out as "unique." In fact, Jesus is hardly even religious! His concerns are almost exclusively sociological. All this is just what one guided by Mack's sociological theory of religion would expect to find.

For both scholars, then, the Jesus that is "discovered" is in perfect sync with the Jesus their religiophilosophical presuppositions incline them to discover. Their understandings of Jesus' life and message reflect the type of theme that is conducive to what their worldviews can most easily imagine. For Mack, with his sociological reductionism, the essence of Jesus' message was, "See how it's done? You can do it also."[17] For Crossan, with his parabolic-paradoxical negative theology, the essence of the message was, "The Kingdom is here, you don't need even me."[18] In both cases, the centrality of Jesus as a person is marginalized while his (reconstructed) teachings are given central place. And in both cases, there is, by methodological necessity, nothing that approximates the traditional Christian notion of Jesus as God incarnate.

THE HEART OF THE DIFFERENCES AMONG THE VARYING PORTRAITS OF JESUS

Mack and Crossan's portraits of the historical Jesus differ remarkably from those offered by scholars within the "Third Quest" and certainly differ from the portraits offered by scholars who operate with a traditional Christian faith, primarily because of the different worldview assumptions each holds. This is not to suggest, however, that there is no point in these scholars from various traditions discussing the concrete historical evidence among themselves, for the scholarly ideal of objectivity – discovering "what is actually the case" – is held by all within that community. The foundational assumption of this community is that the evidence should be allowed to speak for itself as much as possible and thus that not all ways of assessing the historical evidence are equally valid. The line of influence between presuppositions and evidence can, and should, flow in both directions. Were this assumption not present, no one would bother to write books arguing *on the basis of the evidence* for their particular portraits of the historical Jesus.

Still, the truth of the matter is that the widely divergent ways in which the evidence is assessed, and the widely divergent portraits of Jesus this creates, is due primarily to the widely different control-beliefs scholars bring to their projects. And precisely because such control-beliefs function so decisively in the scholarly enterprise, and precisely because scholars strive for objectivity in their endeavors, these various control-beliefs need to be acknowledged, rendered explicit, and, in the interests of the theoretical objectivity all scholars strive for, subjected to criticism. There thus needs to be critical dialogue within and between these differing schools of thought concerning the influence, and legitimacy, of the presuppositions that significantly steer the course of their various historical projects.

Just this is largely lacking within the New Testament scholarly community, however, particularly within the post-Bultmannian camp. It must frankly be said that there is, within this camp, a distinct tendency to write and speak as if they were the sole scholarly voice for the contemporary quest. One observes in this camp a distinct uncritical posture toward their own presuppositions, as well as a predilection to downplay or simply ignore scholarship that calls foundational aspects of their project into question.[19] While this posture was perhaps somewhat understandable in Bultmann who, in his day, was indeed widely regarded as *the* voice of critical New Testament scholarship, it is altogether unwarranted among his contemporary followers who operate in a scholarly world that offers a host of plausible alternative approaches that must, in the interest of objectivity, be taken seriously.[20]

AN ALTERNATIVE APPROACH TO THE GOSPELS

Perhaps the most important, yet most neglected, area of "alternative" scholarship that the post-Bultmannian camp needs to take seriously at a methodological level surrounds the issue of the reliability of the canonical Gospel traditions. Here one discovers most clearly the profound role presuppositions play in a scholar's work, and one discovers it at precisely that point that is most crucial for any quest for the historical Jesus. For, quite obviously, how one evaluates the traditions contained within the Gospel narratives largely determines what kind of Jesus one is going to eventually end up with in their scholarly research.

As noted above, if one begins with a control-belief that dictates that everything *must* be understood in terms of a natural law of cause and effect, then one *has* to adopt a radically skeptical stance concerning the trustworthiness of the Gospels such as characterizes the post-Bultmannian camp.[21] Since the Gospels *cannot* be accurately speaking about what they seem to be speaking about—God working in history in unique and unrepeatable ways—they *must* be speaking about something different—about myths, social agendas, and the like. Scholars who do not operate with these control-beliefs, however, often come up with a very different estimation of the reliability of the Gospels. Having no *a priori* grounds for dismissing as a-historical what the Gospels speak of, these scholars rather argue that we actually have *very solid historical grounds* for believing that they speak of historical matters quite accurately.

In the remainder of this chapter, therefore, we shall review what a number of scholars who do not share Crossan and Mack's post-Bultmannian assumptions are saying about the reliability of these foundational Christian sources. Whereas we shall examine in detail Mack's and Crossan's radical reassessment of Mark in section 5 of this work, our focus here shall be on what certain scholars are saying about the *most general features* of the traditions behind all of the Gospels. And the argument shall be that the approach of these scholars who do not *a priori* reject the supernatural makes much better sense of the available evidence concerning the traditions behind the Gospels than do the conclusions guided by post-Bultmannian control-beliefs. As such, this scholarship serves as a critique and corrective of the post-Bultmannian enterprise. And as such, it should be (but usually is not) taken seriously by post-Bultmannians.

THE EARLY JESUS TRADITION

The Gospels and Historical Interest

To begin, a number of scholars have pointed out that, given the strong Jewish constitution of the early church (and thus the distinct conviction of a personal God at work in history) as well as the clear evidence from the texts themselves, the Gospel writers (and the early Christians in general) were very concerned with *history*.[22] The manner in which they wrote, the types of things that interested and concerned them, all point toward the fact that *what had actually happened in the past, including Jesus' earthly past,* was both critically important and was meant to be remembered and passed down in a faithful manner.[23]

There is, in this regard, much to be learned from the careful attitude expressed in the prologue to Luke's Gospel (Luke 1:1-4; also Acts 1:1). It evidences a serious concern within early Christianity for "reliable tradition and faithful traditionists."[24] It informs us that when the Gospel writers *look* like they were intending to write history, we have reason to assume that they indeed *were* intending to write history.[25] Relatedly, many scholars have argued that the notion that ancient writers were largely gullible and uninterested in historical accuracy – being unable to adequately distinguish fact from fiction, reality from myth — is simply not tenable in the face of the evidence.[26] Such an observation makes the post-Bultmannian view of the Gospels as largely a-historical in interest and content, and thus as largely comprised of myth, very difficult to accept.

Jewish Oral Traditions and the Gospels

The historical interest, and historical reliability, of the Gospel authors has received strong support from the pioneering work of Birger Ger-hardsson.[27] Gerhardsson's original work argues that, based on clear par-allels of oral transmission processes between early Christianity and Rab-binic Judaism, one could conclude that the oral Jesus tradition was passed along with a high degree of care and continuity. This thesis emphasizes Jesus' role as a Rabbinic-like teacher and the common Rab-binic practice of word-for-word memorization.

Gerhardsson's thesis immediately came under attack on several fronts. Some argued that using the Rabbinic model is anachronistic, giv-en Jesus' A.D. pre-70s situation.[28] This thesis also suggests that Jesus be understood as a Jewish "rabbi," something that he technically was not. The anachronism charge is less than devastating once one considers that the later careful Rabbinic practices most likely did not spontaneously arise *ex nihilo;* they no doubt were tapping into an earlier pervasive Jewish attitude of reverence for religious traditions. And while Jesus was technically not a rabbi, he was clearly a teacher, and thus he quite likely made use of similar *teaching methods.* Here, it is important to recognize the place that ancient Jewish educational practice gave to the memoriza-tion of both oral and written tradition. In regard to first-century educa-tion of children, Safrai writes:

> The teacher explained the halakic item or the Midrash and en-couraged the student to participate actively in asking questions and explaining them, but he also demanded memory-work and a constant effort to remember the actual text. . . . Individual and group study of the Bible, repetition of passages, etc., were often done by chanting them aloud. . . . This was the only way to overcome the danger of forgetting.[29]

Over the last thirty years, Gerhardsson and others have refined his original thesis, often in the light of critical responses.[30] The work of Rainer Riesner is particularly important in this regard. Riesner has done a thorough study both of educational practices within first-century Juda-ism, as well as the evidence within the Gospels' tradition related to Jesus and his teaching methods. He has concluded—quite apart from a dependency upon Rabbinic parallels—that *memory* of sacred teachings and traditions was a vital part of both Jewish life in general and Jesus' teaching program in particular.[31]

Another important related area of study is that of oral folklore tradition. Studies by anthropologists such as Albert B. Lord and Jan Vansina have demonstrated that the transmission of traditions in oral societies follow a generally fixed, if flexible, pattern—similar to the type of pattern witnessed to in the Gospels themselves.[32] Related to this, contemporary psycholinguistic studies have served to confirm that the techniques that characterized Jesus' oral teaching methods would have made for "very accurate communication between Jesus and his followers" and would have "ensured excellent semantic recall."[33] Thus, it is safe to say that, even if some of the particular points of Gerhardsson's thesis remain debatable, its overall thrust is sound. Indeed, outside of post-Bultmannian circles (and even, to some extent, within this camp), there is a growing acknowledgment of the general reliability of the Gospel traditions as a result of this scholarship. For example, W.D. Davies, one of Gerhardsson's more vocal critics in terms of specifics, has nonetheless conceded that the thesis has

> made it far more historically probable and reasonably credible, over against the skepticism of much Form-Criticism, that in the Gospels we are within hearing of the authentic voice and within sight of the authentic activity of Jesus of Nazareth.[34]

This perspective on the Gospel tradition flies squarely in the face of the post-Bultmannian foundational assumption that much, if not most, of the material within the Gospels is not historically reliable. Given the original Jewish context out of which the earliest oral traditions about Jesus sprang, we have every reason to suppose the opposite.

The Gospels and the *Sitz em Leben* of the Early Church

Gerhardsson's perspective on the traditions behind the Gospels also flies in the face of another fundamental tenet of the post-Bultmannian camp, one that plays a crucial role in Crossan's and Mack's work: namely, the assumption that the Jesus traditions within the Gospels were created by the early church to meet various needs and address the assorted issues it confronted. It is not just that the Gospel authors had a view toward the needs and issues of the communities they were a part of when they composed their works—something everyone admits. Rather, in the

Bultmannian and post-Bultmannian view, these needs and issues *created* the material utilized by these Gospel authors.

Such a view, of course, runs directly counter to Gerhardsson's arguments concerning the accurate transmission of oral tradition within first-century Jewish culture. But this prevalent form-critical assumption has been challenged on several other grounds as well. First, a number of scholars, such as Heinz Shürmann, have persuasively argued that a good amount of the Jesus tradition can be demonstrated to have had its rooting within *a pre-Easter situation* in the life of the historical Jesus.[35] In more specific terms,

> within the context of the disciple-teacher setting of Jesus' minis-
> try, and above all in his sending out of the disciples to preach
> and heal, we have a natural context for the passing on of the
> Jesus traditions to the disciples.[36]

This insight adds further weight to Gerhardsson's contention that Jesus' disciples—and especially the Twelve—played an important role in the transmission and preservation of the Jesus tradition, an idea that the radical form-critics have had trouble with since the time of Bultmann.[37]

Secondly, the frequently held position that it was "prophets" in the early church, speaking in the name of the resurrected Lord, who created much of Gospel material to address issues in the early church has been questioned on a number of accounts.[38] Chief among these is the fact that this view is almost totally devoid of historical evidence. We simply do not have any clear examples of prophets in the early church functioning in this way and certainly no examples of prophetic material taking on a narrative historical form, as this theory requires. Hence, as David Aune concludes, "[T]he historical evidence in support of the theory lies largely in the creative imagination of scholars."[39]

Yet a third criticism of the form-critical assumption that the Gospel material was created to suit the needs of the church is this: if the early Christians created sayings (whether under "prophetic" inspiration or not) to meet the needs of the church and then retroactively placed them in the mouth of Jesus, why do we find so little of what we know were issues in the early church addressed in the Gospels? If this thesis were correct, one would expect to find ostensive "Jesus sayings" directed toward a wide variety of early Christian issues and problems such as circumcision, dietary issues, church polity, and glossolalia. The fact that this is simply not the case counts strongly against this form-critical assumption and counts strongly in favor of the view that the Gospels are expressing traditions that pass on material that likely derives from the historical Jesus himself.[40]

A fourth and final criticism that can be raised against this form-critical assumption is that it simply lacks inherent plausibility. It is difficult to imagine relatively unknown early church "Christian prophets" creating sayings that were creatively woven into a narrative form and received as authoritative by this same early church. This difficulty is intensified when we consider the above mentioned Jewish context in which this is occurring: there were cultural restraints on this sort of creativity. This difficulty is intensified further when we consider the temporal proximity in which this creativity was supposed to have taken place to the historical Jesus: there were contemporaries of Jesus still around—many of them hostile—who presumably would have called such a practice into question. And this difficulty is intensified still further when we consider that the Apostle Paul—himself a prophet—felt it necessary to clearly differentiate between his own words and those of the historical Jesus (see 1 Cor. 7:10, 12).[41]

All of this suggests that we have no good reason to follow the post-Bultmannian hypothesis that the Gospels are largely early church creations and are, as such, fundamentally unreliable on historical matters. This is not to say that the way they present their material is not affected by concerns their authors have for their audience. But it is to say that we have every reason to suppose that the basic content of what they present as historical is, in fact, rooted in history.

This historical content, however, is not one that can be accepted if one assumes that the miraculous is impossible or that nothing radically unique can occur in the history of religions. And this, to a large extent, perhaps explains why this more conservative scholarship is frequently not given due consideration by post-Bultmannians. One looks in vain, for example, to see either Mack or Crossan wrestle with, or even acknowledge, the work of Gerhardsson in their respective recent works on the historical Jesus and the early church.

The Gospels Tradition in Literary Form

The skepticism with regard to the Gospels tradition has been bolstered by the long-standing Bultmannian conviction that the tradition experienced a long period of purely *oral* transmission before anything substantial was put into writing. Given our above discussion on the reliability of oral traditions in a Jewish context, the skepticism of the post-Bultmannian enterprise would not be warranted even if this assumption were granted. But it is not obvious that even this much should be conceded. Indeed, a number of scholars have recently argued that we actually have good reason to think that "some written formulations of Jesus' teachings were being transmitted among his followers already during his earthly ministry."[42]

Among other considerations, the manuscript finds at Qumran have rendered this Bultmannian and post-Bultmannian assumption unnecessary. It was (and yet is) often assumed in post-Bultmannian circles that an apocalyptic movement, such as early Christianity, would not have been interested in writing down and codifying their ideas and their histories. Hence, it was held, we must assume little if anything in writing behind the Gospel traditions, and we must assume that these Gospel traditions are written late (viz., toward the end of the first century or early second century) when the apocalypticism of early Christianity was (it is speculated) waning.

But here in Qumran we find a thoroughly apocalyptic group doing just this! Though they expected an imminent end of the world, they nevertheless took great care in composing volumes. Hence, however we construe the apocalypticism of Jesus' early movement, we have no reason to think they would not have been, from the start, involved in writing. There is, therefore, no reason to suppose a purely oral period of tradition behind the canonical Gospels, and this further increases the likelihood that they contain reliable historical information.[43]

The Burden of Proof

It is evident that the case for the general reliability of the canonical Gospels is quite strong. At the very least, it implies that we should approach the Gospels with no more of a skeptical orientation than we do other ancient works that are ostensively concerned with historical matters. And this entails that the "burden of proof" should *not* lie on the Gospels to prove in every instance that they *are* historically trustworthy: it should rather lie on the historian who in any particular instance wants to argue that they are *not* trustworthy. Such is the standard historiographical procedure adopted by historians in treating other texts, and there is no cogent reason to prohibit its application to the Gospels as well.[44]

For those in the post-Bultmannian camp, however, the burden has always been on the side of the Gospels. Indeed, the Jesus Seminar has declared that one of the "seven pillars of scholarly wisdom" is that the Gospel traditions are unreliable unless proven otherwise.[45] Working from this assumption—beginning at the conclusion—it is hardly surprising that they have determined that less than a fourth of the sayings attributed to Jesus in the Gospels are authentic.

But, we must ask, what warrants this overly skeptical posture? It flies in the face of standard historiographical procedure. It neglects and negates the above mentioned general considerations of the Gospels and their first-century Jewish environment. And, as we shall see (sec. 5), it denies many other facets of the Gospels that testify to their historical reliability. Its only consistent feature is that it squares with the naturalistic mind-set that dictates that any accounts that contain reports of supernatural activities must be generally unreliable. But this, as we have seen, is a philosophical prejudice that should not be allowed to override all other considerations.

The Nature and Problems of the Gospels

There are two important qualifications that need to be made in the light of the preceding discussion, one concerning the nature of the Gospels, the other concerning historical problems in them. First, to say that the Gospels are reliable enough to place the burden of proof on any who would argue against their historical veracity is not to suggest that they are simply "objective," issue-free chronicles of the life of Jesus on par with the attempts of modern "disinterested" historiography. Such is demonstrably not the case. As Robert Guelich has pointed out, the Gospels do not simply provide verbal "snapshots" of Jesus. Yet neither do they merely comprise "abstract paintings" of him, as the more skeptical scholarship would suggest. Rather, he contends, they give us living "portraits."[46] Each of the Gospel writers has specific audiences to address, definite emphases regarding the earthly Jesus that he needs to communicate, and particular circumstances within which these things are to be accomplished. And their handling of their preexisting oral and written material, as well as the expression of their own material, certainly reflects this fact. They are, again, "portraits," not "snapshots."

Still, contrary to post-Bultmannian assumptions, we have every reason to suppose that the portraits these evangelists created are *reliable reflections* of the earthly Jesus. Though the reflection comes through the colored lens of their own perspectives, interests, and creativity, it is, nevertheless, the reflection of the historical Jesus that comes through. There are simply no good historical grounds for denying the general reliability of the traditions behind the Gospels or for assuming that the Gospel authors' "lens" (e.g., their redactional tendencies) seriously distorted these sources.[47]

Second, to argue that we have good grounds for having confidence in the general reliability of the Gospels is not to suggest that these documents are devoid of discrepancies between them or of historical problems. The crucial issue is what one makes of these apparent problems. A methodology that works from the premise that the Gospels are generally reliable will be inclined to seek for an explanation of the discrepancies and/or ostensive historical inaccuracies—as historians customarily do regarding other texts—while an approach that works from the premise that they are generally unreliable will be inclined to see in these discrepancies or historical inaccuracies further justification of their skeptical stance.[48] It is the latter stance that has largely characterized the historical quest for Jesus and clearly characterizes the present post-Bultmannian endeavor.[49] It is the former stance, however, that seems most consistent with general considerations of the Gospel traditions and with standard historical protocol.

CONCLUSION

This chapter has attempted to flesh out and critique the foundational religiophilosophical assumptions that are operative in Crossan and Mack's Cynic thesis and demonstrate how these lead them to revision a certain kind of Jesus while minimizing or ignoring a significant portion of scholarship on the reliability of the Gospel traditions that could, and should, call their project into question. In contrast to their post-Bultmannian agenda, we have seen that we have good grounds for placing confidence in the general reliability of the Gospel traditions. It seems that it is primarily an anti-supernaturalistic prejudice that leads certain scholars to a different assessment.

This confidence, we shall later argue, is significantly increased when we examine in detail Mark (as the canonical counter-Cynic portrait of Jesus) and Acts (as the canonical counter-Cynic portrait of the early church) in sections 5 and 6.[50] But enough has already been said to establish the basic illegitimacy of Crossan and Mack's project on a methodological level as it concerns their approach to the biblical texts.

While their Cynic thesis requires one to accept the fundamental unreliability of the portrait of Christ and the early church found in Paul, Mark, and Acts, and thus while a demonstration of the reliability o[f] sources shall serve as a decisive refutation of their views, thei[r] thesis is *not* built on these sources. To the contrary, the canonical s[o] are, for the most part, what they need to *explain away* to rende[r] view plausible. Their actual theories, flowing from their post-Bult-mannian assumptions and worked out in accordance with their distinct methodologies, are built upon other sources, and employ other arguments. In a word, they are carved out of various understandings of Cynics, of Galilee, and of certain noncanonical sources such as Q, GosThom, and the Cross Gospel. Hence, before we turn to investigate their treatments of the canonical material, we need to critically examine the arguments and materials they use to positively construct their theses. We now turn to this task in the next two chapters.

6

ARGUING IN CIRCLES AND GRASPING AT STRAWS:
A Critique of the Post-Bultmannian Use of Extra-Canonical Sources

Having discussed in general terms the nature and roles of various control-beliefs within the post-Bultmannian camp and the effect this has on their assumptions regarding the canonical Gospels, we are now in a position to address the material content of this school of thought, out of which Crossan's and Mack's Cynic theses are constructed. I shall first critique the post-Bultmannian view of the early church as radically diverse, a view which functions as a critical presupposition for everything that follows. This shall be followed by an examination of the extra-canonical documents the North American post-Bultmannians tend to draw upon in their constructions of various "alternative" (noncanonical) views of Jesus. Finally, this chapter will conclude with a critique of one crucial aspect of the alternative Jesus many post-Bultmannians, including Crossan and Mack, arrive at from their use of extra-canonical sources: their understanding of Jesus as non-eschatological.

EARLY CHRISTIANITY:
RADICAL DIVERSITY OR NORMATIVE TRADITION?

The post-Bultmannian conviction of radical early Christian diversity, discussed in chapter 2, is fundamentally important to the Cynic-Jesus thesis. Only on the supposition that the earliest Christian communities held to a variety of differing and contradictory interpretations of Jesus, none of which were "normative," can Crossan and Mack plausibly replace the (mythologized) Gospel portraits with their (historical) Cynic-sage portrait. For, on this account, the Gospel portraits of Jesus were just several of a multitude of very conflicting views circulating in the decades following his death. Conversely, if it can be shown that the portrait of the historical Jesus found in the Gospels was in fact *normative* among early Christians, then it would be exceedingly difficult to argue that the "true" picture of Jesus is very much *unlike* this one (viz., that Jesus was a Cynic sage). Among other things, one would have a difficult time explaining how the normative picture became normative if it was, in fact, fundamentally historically inaccurate.

Hence, the post-Bultmannian assumption of a radically pluralistic early Christian movement is vital to the Cynic thesis. Cynic theorists fundamentally rely on a sort of "divide and conquer" approach to the New Testament. The view of Christ in the New Testament must be rendered as a multiplicity of contradictory views among a multitude of other noncanonical contradictory views if their own view of Jesus as a Cynic sage is to gain in plausibility as *the correct* view. Unfortunately for their view, however, there is little to support the assumption of radical plurality and much to support the view that Christianity was founded upon normative beliefs and practices from the start. We shall discuss this issue in detail when we consider Mack's treatment of Paul (chap. 8), but a general critical overview of the issue is in order here.

First, Walter Bauer's thesis regarding the anachronism of applying notions of "orthodoxy" and "heresy" to the earliest church – a thesis that has functioned as the principle foundation upon which Koester and Robinson have based their own radical diversity thesis – has been subjected to some very cogent criticism since its original appearance in the 1930s. Both in terms of its general thesis (that what came to be called "heresy" was both earlier and more widespread than so-called "orthodoxy") as well as on some of its more specific arguments, it has been found wanting by recent scholarship.[1]

This is not to say that a romantic, idealized view of the early church's unity is called for.[2] The epistles of Paul, and even the Gospel portrayals of the ministry of Jesus, clearly reveal that the early Christian movement from its inception was engaged in countering, and assimilating, diverse understandings of what Jesus was all about. The correct point in Bauer's thesis, as I. Howard Marshall has noted, is that ". . . *there was variety of belief in the first century*."[3] But, by the same token, this diversity does *not* entail that there was *nothing normative* within earliest Christianity. Rather, the conflicts within the early church *presuppose* some foundational normative elements.

These normative elements, according to many scholars, are readily discernible within the New Testament if it is allowed to speak for itself and not read with the *presupposition* that a normative strand is lacking within it.[4] For example, in his recent book, *The Rise of Normative Christianity*, Arlund Hultgren demonstrates that

> a *normative* type of Christianity arose that is exemplified in the twenty-seven books of the New Testament and in other early Christian literature. This type of Christianity was the precursor of, and then the dominant voice at, the ecumenical councils, beginning with the Council of Nicaea in A.D. 325.[5]

This normative Christianity, a legacy that stems from both the earthly Jesus and his first interpreters, is characterized by belief in

> the God of Israel as Creator, the Father of Jesus, and the Father of all humanity . . . the essential humanity of Jesus, on the one hand, and his role in redemption made possible by his crucifixion and exaltation/resurrection by God . . . [the understanding] that a new era has been inaugurated in consequence of the cross and resurrection, attested to by the presence and power of the Holy Spirit in the lives of believers . . . [and the conviction that] believers constitute communities of faith that are marked by an ethos in which the individual gives himself or herself over to others in love and service, which is inspired by and modeled on Jesus' own giving himself over.[6]

Whether we consider the Apostle Paul, the Gospel authors, or other canonized epistles, argues Hultgren, we find this normative substratum of teaching more or less reflected. The diversity found amidst this unity is either a diversity *within* these broad normative parameters (e.g., the difference between Gentile and Jewish Christianity) or a polemic against those who are *outside* those parameters (e.g., Paul's polemic against opponents). But there is simply no evidence within the New Testament that there were no parameters![7] Indeed, it is the unity of the New Testament that this theory has to *explain away* (as retroactive idealization) in order to make room for its speculation that "in reality" there was a radical diversity.

But the New Testament evidence is stubborn, and hence the "reality" of an original radical pluralism is hard to locate. For example, despite the post-Bultmannian insistence that Paul represents a fundamentally different kind of Christianity from that of the Gospels, it is very difficult to get around the fact that Paul's kerygmatic formulations look very much like "mini-versions" of the basic story line about Jesus found in narrative form in each of the Gospels.[8] Relatedly, it is very difficult to explain away Paul's explicit references to his essential agreement with all the other leaders in early Christianity (e.g., Gal. 2:9; 1 Thes. 2:14). And, as such scholars as Hultgren and Wright have so effectively argued, it is extremely difficult to dismiss the foundational story line – the new story of Israel's covenantal relationship with the one true God, now centered on Jesus – which weaves itself throughout each of the New Testament documents.[9]

This case for the essential normativity of the New Testament's portrait of Christ already puts the Cynic thesis in jeopardy. For it means that the New Testament documents resist the "divide and conquer" approach necessary to get such a thesis off the ground.

THE EXTRA-CANONICAL JESUS VS. THE CANONICAL JESUS

It is, however, only by ruling out the normative element in early Christian teaching that the post-Bultmannians can escape what they consider to be the stifling "tyranny" of the canonical Jesus.[10] Having freed themselves from this "tyranny," they are now able to create a revisionist Jesus along other lines. But it should not be thought that this entails that post-Bultmannians in general envisage no "normative" Christianity. In practice, their notion of "radical diversity" is emphasized just long enough to dethrone the traditional New Testament portrait of Jesus. Once this takes place, the post-Bultmannian tendency is to reinvest *another* stream of the tradition with priority in their search for the "historical Jesus." It is just this type of process that has produced the structure of the Cynic-Jesus thesis.

The stream of tradition that the post-Bultmannians have crowned with "most favored status," as we have seen, is that represented by the apocryphal gospels in general and the Gospel of Thomas and the hypothetical Q Gospel in particular.[11] Scholars within the post-Bultmannian camp tend to view the apocryphal gospels as *independent* of the canonical Gospels' tradition and as containing very *early* tradition. Beyond the Gospel of Thomas, the "Gospel of Peter" (out of which Crossan extracts the hypothetical "Cross Gospel") and "The Secret Gospel of Mark" (a work supposedly cited by Clement of Alexandria in the late second century) are vital to their project.[12] Many post-Bultmannians see this latter work as reflecting an earlier book by the author of Mark and one that served as a source for canonical Mark.[13]

THE GOSPEL OF PETER AND SECRET MARK

Numerous scholars, however, have taken serious issue with this preferential treatment of these documents. Concerning the Gospel of Peter, many have cogently argued that there is clear literary evidence that it is dependent upon the canonical Gospels and is, as a whole, to be dated in the late second or early third century.[14] And, as mentioned in chapter 3, few scholars, even within the post-Bultmannian camp, find Crossan's argument for a pre-canonical "Cross Gospel" within this document to be compelling.

Regarding the Secret Gospel of Mark, there are strong suspicions on the part of many scholars regarding the authenticity of Clement's letter which purportedly quotes this work. The fact that no one except Smith has actually seen the Mar Saba copy of Clement's letter (beyond photographs taken by Smith in 1958), despite visits to this monastery for this very purpose, strikes some scholars as suspicious.[15] But even if the document is accepted as an authentic letter of Clement, there is no compelling reason to grant the work it cites (in the late second or early third century!) privileged status over canonical Mark or any of the canonical Gospels. Indeed, what little we can surmise about the contents and composition of this questionable document suggests that it is, if anything, also dependent upon the canonical Gospels.[16] Nor is it surprising that Clement would mistakenly endorse this esoteric work as authoritative. As is well-known, Clement had a strong proclivity toward "ideas of secrecy, esoteric teaching, mystical experiences and the like," and thus was in general "far more open than most patristic writers to accept the authenticity of purportedly apostolic writings. . . ."[17] At the very least, neither this hypothetical document, nor the Gospel of Peter, constitute very solid grounds upon which to reconstruct a portrait of the historical Jesus.

As important as the Gospel of Peter and Secret Mark are to many within the post-Bultmannian quest their significance is dwarfed in comparison to the Gospel of Thomas and especially the "Q Gospel." Hence, most of the scholarly discussion has centered around the use made of these two pillars of the post-Bultmannian enterprise. And thus we shall need to take a more in-depth critical look at how these two documents are employed by post-Bultmannians like Crossan and Mack.

THE GOSPEL OF THOMAS

Several points can be raised with regard to the post-Bultmannian use of the Gospel of Thomas. First, as with the other apocryphal sources discussed above, the post-Bultmannians characteristically take as optimistic a view as possible with regard to Thomas' *independence* from the canonical Gospels. Numerous scholars, however, have argued that such a position is untenable. For example, ever since the 1964 landmark study of Wolfgang Schrage, much of German scholarship has been convinced that Thomas is largely dependent upon the canonical Gospels, or at least upon traditions that stem from the canonical Gospels.[18] Indeed, many international scholars, representing a wide variety of methodological persuasions and theological interests, have come to similar conclusions: Thomas does not represent much in the way of reliable independent early church traditions.[19] The summary statement of Klyne Snodgrass helps to nuance this general opinion.

> The dependence of *Thomas* on the canonical Gospels is not . . . a direct literary dependence. Rather, it is an indirect dependence, probably at some distance and apparently mediated through oral tradition that had shaped and harmonized the Gospels. The author of *Thomas* has also continued the redaction of the sayings. No doubt there is independent tradition in *Thomas* as well, but the bulk of the material seems to have its origin in the canonical Gospels.[20]

Such conclusions, of course, have a direct bearing on the *date* of Thomas and the traditions it contains. Once it is recognized that Thomas is significantly dependent upon the canonical Gospels, the recent post-Bultmannian push for an early date (A.D. 50–70) for its content is no longer feasible. In fact, most of the scholars who did the pioneering work on GosThom date it around A.D. 140.[21] Among other considerations, we have no independent attestation of the existence of this work until the early third century when it is cited by Hippolytus and Origen – an unexpected silence if this is, in fact, a first-century work. What is more, GosThom reflects a distinct gnosticizing tendency which renders a second-century dating most feasible.

Some within the post-Bultmannian camp, recognizing this fact, have attempted to minimize, or deny altogether, Thomas' gnostic elements.[22] But their case is extremely vulnerable. It is, for example, hard to get around the gnostic-tending ascetic dimension of the following dialogue of GosThom.

> Simon Peter said to them, "Let Mary leave us, for women are not worthy of Life." Jesus said, "I myself shall lead her in order

to make her male, so that she too may become a living spirit resembling you males. For every woman who will make herself male will enter the Kingdom of Heaven (GosThom, 114).

Such an understanding of spirituality and of sexuality is hard to attribute to any first-century Christian movement, even after due consideration is given to Hellenizing influences. But it is quite intelligible (though hardly more palatable) in a second-century gnostic-tending milieu.

Similarly, it is difficult to escape the conclusion that the talk about "the kingdom of God" or "the kingdom of the Father" in GosThom is often attributable to a gnostic-tending reworking of the canonical material.[23] In GosThom, this phrase is taken to indicate "the present secret religious knowledge of a heavenly world."[24] Hence, for example, the Jesus of GosThom says,

[T]he Kingdom is inside of you, and it is outside of you. When you come to know yourselves, then you will become known, and you will realize that it is you who are the sons of the living Father. But if you will not know yourselves, you dwell in poverty and it is you who are that poverty (GosThom, 3).

The concept of "the kingdom of God," of course, is a thoroughly Jewish, and thoroughly biblical, concept. And, indeed, one can detect a canonical teaching of Jesus (Luke 17:20-21) behind this passage (again, a possible example of Thomas' dependency).[25] But the concept has here been given a distinctly gnostic twist. And it is, as Wright has argued, extremely difficult to see this gnostic-like view of the kingdom as preceding the traditional Jewish view.

It is unthinkable that this motif should be introduced into a community from scratch with the meaning that it comes to have in *Thomas*. . . . If there has been a shift in the usage one way or the other, it is far more likely to have been *from* this Jewish home base into a quasi-Gnostic sense, rather than from a Gnostic sense, for which there is no known, or imaginable, precedent, to a re-Judaized one—a shift which, on the hypothesis, must have taken place somewhere between an early *Thomas* and a later Mark.[26]

The same might be argued for a significant portion of GosThom. Indeed, many scholars have argued that whenever "details not found in the Synoptics . . . appear [in GosThom], they can almost always be explained as conscious, Gnostic redactions."[27] In this light, the conclusion reached by Boudewijn Dehandschutter seems reasonable.

> To put it in categories of the Robinson-Koester approach of "trajectories": the [Gospel of Thomas] should be situated more at the end of the trajectory than at the beginning.[28]

Despite these formidable objections to the early dating of GosThom, the post-Bultmannian enterprise in general, and Crossan and Mack (especially the former) in particular, continue to use this work as a foundational pillar to their revisionistic portraits of Christ. And this, at the very least, must render their portraits extremely tentative.

THE "Q GOSPEL"

Even more important than GosThom to the post-Bultmannian quest, however, is the "Q Gospel." Indeed, it is hardly an overstatement to say that the whole of the present post-Bultmannian quest stands or falls with their particular theories regarding this hypothetical document. There are, however, three lines of argumentation that are devastating to their general theory of Q. The first concerns the speculativeness of their theories; the second addresses problems in Kloppenborg's stratification of Q; and the third concerns issues surrounding the nature of Q. We shall consider each of these three lines of argumentation in order.

The Speculativeness of Post-Bultmannian Views of Q

First, the post-Bultmannian views of Q are, at best, highly speculative and extremely tentative. And hence, any portrait of Jesus and the early church that is significantly based on such views must, *a priori*, be considered highly speculative and extremely tentative. As M. Eugene Boring and others have demonstrated, the various layered Q theories of the current post-Bultmannian enterprise (of which Kloppenborg's triple-layered Q is but the most recognized) are predicated upon no less than *six levels* of hypothetical speculation.[29]

The first two of these speculative assumptions are that (a) Q existed; and (b) that it was a written document. While a majority of contemporary New Testament scholars hold to the two-source theory regarding the Synoptic problem (and thus the Q hypothesis), this theory (and thus Q) is coming under attack in a number of quarters today. For example, the Ropes-Farrer-Goulder hypothesis holds to Markan priority, but finds that it can quite easily dispense with Q by positing a direct use of Matthew by Luke.[30] Similarly, the Neo-Griesbach hypothesis challenges the need for the Q postulation by arguing for Matthean priority, Luke's use of Matthew and, subsequently, Mark's use of both Matthew and Luke.[31] Other scholars question the need for the Q hypothesis on other grounds, for example, on the basis that the phenomenon of Synoptic parallels can be adequately accounted for by reference to the pre-canonical oral tradition.[32]

While one may or may not regard such arguments as being decisive against the Q hypothesis, they serve to at least highlight the reality that the existence of Q, and the nature of Q as a written document, is only a *hypothesis—a debatable* hypothesis. This seems to be frequently forgotten. Hence these "alternative" views serve to demonstrate that any revisioning of the historical Jesus and of the earliest Jesus communities which relies heavily on Q's hypothetical existence must, for this reason, be regarded as speculative. The elaborate edifices built upon this hypothetical foundation by the post-Bultmannians, however, suggest that they are not as aware of this fact as the situation calls for.[33]

The third level of post-Bultmannian speculative assumption is that the *general contents* of this hypothetical written document can be inferred from the common tradition in Matthew and Luke. But this too is highly questionable. Even if Matthew and Luke (and according to Mack, Mark as well) possessed such a document, on what basis can we infer what its general contents were? We, at most, could only know how these authors *used* this document. What it did and did not have in its supposedly "original form" is simply unavailable to us. Yet Mack claims to provide his readers with "the text of the lost gospel." Indeed, he presents his readers with two versions of the lost gospel: the original book of Q and the complete book of Q.[34] Not only this, but, as we shall see in section 4 of this work, both Crossan and Mack go further and draw incredible conclusions about what the earliest communities of Jesus did *not* believe on the basis of what this hypothetical text does *not* say!

The last three layers of speculative assumptions which constitute the post-Bultmannian use of Q and which Boring speaks of are the assumptions (a) that the *original wording* of Q can be accurately reproduced, (b) that the *original order* of Q's contents can be accurately determined, and (c) that the literary *pre-history of Q* can be accurately uncovered through redactional and genre analysis. Clearly, however, if the postulation of the very existence, nature, and general contents of Q are themselves speculative leaps, these last three assumptions must be viewed as taking us out of the realm of speculative plausibility. Given that *everything* we actually know about this document (if it exists) is dependent on what Matthew and Luke have in common, and given that their phrasing and placing of the hypothetical contents of this supposed document varies significantly, the attempt to arrive at its original wording and order must be regarded as extremely tentative. And the attempt to apply redaction criticism to this document on the basis of this guesswork must be regarded as even more speculative.

But the guesswork, unfortunately, does not stop here. Remarkably enough, Mack and others have gone yet a step further and are now assuming that there was a discernible "community" behind this document. They are further assuming that we can know a good deal about this hypothetical "community" from a "critical analysis" of Q – including, as was said, what this community did *not* believe. And they are, most remarkably, attempting to reconstruct the *socio-historical stages of the supposed "Q community"* on the basis of the supposed literary stages Q went through! Hence, for example, the wisdom motif in Q supposedly represents an early stage in the "social experiment" of this community, while the apocalyptic motifs supposedly represent a later stage when the community came under attack.

But, it must be asked, what warrants any of these various assumptions? If Q existed, why not suppose that there was an individual, and not a community, behind its creation? And, if some supposed final community which possessed the "complete book of Q" saw no problem in holding together the various motifs in Q all at once, why suppose that *any* community would have had problems doing so? Even if, for the sake of argument, one grants that there was a written document whose general contents, exact wording, and original order we can discern, why create unnecessary and baseless hypotheses about the social history of a supposed community behind it on the basis of what we think are discrepant motifs – when the only Q we know about obviously *doesn't* find these motifs discrepant?

In any event, the entire project is extremely speculative. One might have suspected that the intensely hypothetical nature of this approach would lead post-Bultmannians to express their reconstructions of the historical Jesus in very cautious and hypothetical terms. But, unfortunately, this is generally not the case. One usually finds in the writings of the chief proponents of this view a surpassing air of confidence which at times borders on naïveté. Mack's opening lines to his popular work, *The Lost Gospel*, are not wholly untypical of this attitude.

> Once upon a time, before there were gospels of the kind familiar to readers of the New Testament, the first followers of Jesus wrote another kind of book. Instead of telling a dramatic story about Jesus' life, their book contained only his teachings. They lived with these teachings ringing in their ears and thought of Jesus as the founder of their movement. But their focus was not on the person of Jesus or his life and destiny. They were engrossed with the social program that was called for by his teachings. Thus their book was not a gospel of the Christian kind. . . . Rather, it was a gospel of Jesus' sayings, a "sayings gospel." His first followers arranged these sayings in a way that offered instruction for living creatively in the midst of a most confused time, and their book served them well as a handbook and guide for most of the first Christian century. . . . Then the book was lost.[35]

The statement reads like straightforward factual history, when, in truth, it is simply a piece of creative guesswork.

The Dubiousness of Kloppenborg's Stratification of Q

The second line of argumentation against the post-Bultmannian use of Q involves the standard redactional theory that has come to dominate the camp — namely Kloppenborg's triple-layered Q. Even if we grant, for the sake of argument, that Q existed as a written document, that we can know its general contents, precise wording, the order of these words, and that a community was behind this document, the *particular way* in which Kloppenborg redacts this document has to be regarded as questionable.

To put the matter succinctly, Kloppenborg's redaction seems at times inconsistent, arbitrary, and circular. As to its consistency, several scholars have called into question the cogency of Kloppenborg's all-important divide between Q-1 and Q-2 layers. In particular, the contention that Q-1 is characterized by wisdom motifs while Q-2 is characterized by a (later) apocalyptic/prophetic theme has received serious criticism. It has been pointed out that Kloppenborg's Q-1 stratum contains *prophetic* material and that its content is not all that "sapiential" in character.[36] Conversely, it has been pointed out that it is within Q-2 — not the supposedly wisdom-oriented Q-1 — that the *figure of Wisdom* arises.[37] Others have gone further and argued that Kloppenborg's Q-3 (the Temptation narrative) should be located in the *earliest* portion of Q.[38] Hence, his clearly defined layers of Q do not appear to be all that clearly defined.

Some projects that make use of Kloppenborg's conclusions can also be criticized on the grounds that they are arbitrary and circular. For example, why think that the sapiential Q material comes *before* the prophetic and apocalyptic material? Why could it not as easily be the other way around? Why, indeed, could they not coexist together? It might be responded that it is easier to explain how a sapiential community became prophetic and apocalyptic than it is to explain how an apocalyptic community became sapiential. The point is certainly debatable, but more fundamentally, it wholly begs the question. Why create the problem of "which came first" in the first place? Why not suppose that the "Q community" had sapiential, prophetic, and apocalyptic elements from the start? As Wright argues:

> [B]y what stretch of the imagination can we insist, in relation to a hypothetical document whose origin is supposedly found in otherwise unknown Jewish-Christian groups in first-century Palestine, that a firm distinction could be made between "sapiential" and "prophetic" traditions? . . . There is every reason, within the actual known history of first-century Palestinian religions, as opposed to the mythical model constructed by some scholars, why such a combination should be perfectly natural.[39]

As stated earlier, the very fact that the only Q we have (if we have even this) has no difficulty combining these different motifs should call into question the legitimacy of our insisting that they must have been separated at a hypothetical earlier stage. And it certainly must call into question the legitimacy of our then constructing (against the Book of Acts!) a whole social history in order to account for how these "originally distinct" motifs eventually became combined. The point becomes all the more forceful when we recognize that other literature of the period (e.g., Qumran) holds these types of motifs together very well.

Another response to the question of why sapiential material in Q should be dated earlier than the prophetic and apocalyptic material, however, could be, and indeed often is, that the sapiential material closely parallels the Gospel of Thomas which reflects the earliest Christian tradition and is devoid of apocalyptic elements.[40] The circularity of this response, however, is evident on several scores. First, the parallels between Q and GosThom are impressive only if one *first* extracts the prophetic and apocalyptic elements out from Q and isolates the wisdom material of Q.[41] But this practice of tearing apart Q is the very thing that is now under question. Second, there is, we have seen, no good reason to date Thomas early—other than the post-Bultmannian contention that it parallels an early, non-apocalyptic Q. But again, this begs the question of why we should think there is such a strata of Q. It also leaves totally unanswered the question of why one couldn't as easily suppose that a late Thomas borrowed from certain traditions stemming from the Q material in the Gospels.

The arbitrariness and circularity of the post-Bultmannian use of Q comes out in a remarkable way in Mack's work, especially in his book on Q, *The Lost Gospel*. Several examples will serve to illustrate this. Mack, for instance, observes in Q that, "[f]requently the way sayings are grouped or ordered makes a point. Sometimes a saying offers a specific interpretation of a preceding unit of material."[42] This is hardly surprising, however, since it is Mack (following Kloppenborg and others) who has ordered the sayings—on the basis of the points *they* think "the original Q" is making. Similarly, Mack notes that "the order and organization of material are . . . clear signs of the coherence of a particular layer of tradition" in Q.[43] But, of course, it is *Mack* (or his supporting Q theorists) who imposed on the Matthean and Lukan sayings a particular "order and organization," so arguing for a particular "layer of tradition" on this basis is less than compelling.

In similar fashion, Mack notes how in Q-1, as opposed to Q-2, "[t]here is no sign of hostility" toward those outside the community;[44] hardly surprising since Mack (again, following Kloppenborg) has decided ahead of time that any saying that exhibits "hostility" is to be placed in Q-2 (or Q-3) instead of Q-1. He notes with interest the "shift in tone that awaits the reader of Q-2," and notes how, "[i]n contrast to Q-1 the reader now encounters narratives, dialogue, controversy stories . . . warnings, and apocalyptic pronouncements."[45] But one wonders how it could have been otherwise, since all such material is methodologically ruled out of Q-1 early on!

The long and short of the matter is that, for Mack, and for the post-Bultmannian school in general, this use of Q can be shown to be quite inconsistent, arbitrary, and circular.[46] What further calls into question their perspective is that a large number of scholars outside of their camp, using different starting points and different criteria for redactional analysis, have come to very different understandings of Q.[47] And all of this, at the very least, has to cast a dark shadow of tentativeness over every reconstruction of the historical Jesus that makes use of such a questionable foundation.

The Nature of Q

A final line of argumentation against the post-Bultmannian use of Q concerns the foundational question of the *nature* and *purpose* of the original Q document (again, assuming that it really did exist). As noted in chapter 2, ever since the work of H.E. Töedt in the 1950s, post-Bultmannian scholarship has tended to assume that Q represents the defining Gospel of a particular community of early Christians. The problem this poses for the traditional Christian view of the early church lies in the observation that the passion and resurrection apparently play no real role in Q's understanding of salvation: it is not Jesus' *death* that saves, but rather his life-giving *words and teachings*.[48] And so, it is claimed, we are faced with an early Christian community whose soteriology was apparently nearer to that of the later gnostics than what came to be called "orthodox" Christianity. In this way, as William Farmer has correctly observed, the post-Bultmannian questers appropriate the Q hypothesis as another tool – probably their most important one – in their ongoing enterprise of "dismantling the church's canon."[49] Mack drives home this argument forcefully when he says:

> The remarkable thing about the people of Q is that they were not Christians. They did not think of Jesus as a messiah or the Christ. They did not regard his death as a divine, tragic, or saving event. And they did not imagine that he had been raised from the dead to rule over a transformed world.

Hence he adds:

> Q's challenge to the popular conception of Christian origins is therefore clear. If the conventional view of Christian beginnings is right, how are we to account for these first followers of Jesus?[50]

The Invalidity of Arguing from the Silence of Q

There are a number of responses that can be made to this position. First, and perhaps most fundamentally, this argument about the nature of Q assumes the validity of the earlier discussed post-Bultmannian view that early Christianity was characterized by radical pluralism. If one starts instead with the general conviction (demonstrated above) of a broadly defined normative unity among the early church, this entire argument from silence (arguing from what Q does *not* say) loses all of its force. If, as Hultgren has convincingly argued, the idea of Jesus' "role in redemption made possible by his crucifixion and exaltation/resurrection by God" was an integral presupposition of the broad stream of early normative Christianity, then *however* we understand Q, we should not be inclined to draw too quickly from it implications that would run counter to such a view.[51] We possess and understand a great deal about the New Testament documents, but we do not have Q and can only guess at its constitution. So, at the very least, it seems poor historical method to overturn what is known on the basis of what is not.

But, in fact, a number of plausible reasons can be given that render the ostensive silence in Q concerning Jesus' passion understandable, while not requiring us to overturn the clear normativity of central New Testament motifs. First, there is no basis for inferring from Q's silence that its author(s) had no knowledge of, or interest in, Jesus' death and resurrection. To cite an analogy, on the post-Bultmannian approach, one might be inclined to conclude from the Book of Acts that Luke was uninterested in the historical Jesus, or from the epistles of John that John was uninterested in the earthly Jesus. But we know from their *other* writings that they were very interested in the earthly Jesus (see the Gospels of Luke and John). This should already caution us toward making general assumptions about what an author, or community, does not believe, or is *not* interested in, on the basis of what one (hypothetical) document does *not* say.[52]

A second and closely related point is simply that it is altogether unwarranted to expect any single document (including Q) to relate all of the theological concerns and beliefs of a given community. This is especially true if Q is, as most scholars have believed, primarily intended to be a "sayings gospel." While theological and teaching interests are clearly present, there is simply no justification for requiring of this "sayings gospel" that it provide us with anything like an exhaustive compendium of the earliest community (if they existed) that birthed this document.

This point stands all the more firm when we consider the likelihood that there already existed other documents within the Christian communities that performed some of these other functions (see chap. 5). Hence, the argument from silence used by Mack, Crossan, and other post-Bultmannians must not only assume more than we know about Q, but more than we know about the state of literature contemporary with Q.

Graham Stanton summarizes the situation well when he argues:

> There is no reason to assume that Q contains all the theological convictions of the Q community. . . . [I]n view of the fact that both Matthew and Luke (and presumably their communities)

had access to two very different and originally separate kinds of material about Jesus (Q and Mark), is it not at least possible that the Q community also had two different kinds of material? If so, we might envisage traditions which set out the teachings of Jesus, but underlined the grounds of his authoritative words and actions, being used in instruction of those within the community and also in an evangelistic context. And, alongside Q, traditions which told the story of the ultimate rejection of Jesus by men, but proclaimed his vindication by God — such traditions being used primarily in the worship of the community.[53]

The pre-Pauline hymns about Christ (to be discussed in chap. 8) are perhaps echoes of the kinds of sources Stanton is speaking of. This postulation of other contemporary sources is speculative, to be sure. But it is no more so than the post-Bultmannian assumption of Q as a theological compendium with its requisite denial of such contemporary sources. And, in contrast to this latter position, Stanton's speculation does have *some* precedent in the available evidence. In any case, it demonstrates how tentatively all arguments from silence based on Q must be taken. Unfortunately for Crossan and Mack, however, just such arguments function foundationally for their revisionist reconstructions of Jesus and the early church.

Finally, the assumption that Q is altogether silent about Jesus' death and resurrection is itself dubious. A number of noteworthy scholars deny this. Hultgren, for example, has identified no less than seven passages that reveal Q's acquaintance with "traditions about Jesus' death and resurrection."[54] Similarly, Edward Meadors has documented a variety of telling allusions, several of which refer to "passages in Isaiah which complement rather than contradict Mark's portrait of Jesus as the suffering Son of Man."[55] So too, Malcolm Peel argues that a belief in the resurrection is presupposed in Q in its portrayal of Christ as an endtime messenger who will return and vindicate his word (e.g., Luke 11:30; 12:8-10, 40; 17:24-30).[56] Hence, the claim that Q is devoid of all knowledge of and/or concern for the passion tradition is very debatable.

There is, then, nothing to compel one to follow the post-Bultmannian tendency to invest a good deal of historical and theological significance in what Q does *not* say. This ground is simply not solid enough to bear much (if any) theoretical weight. And the whole procedure of arguing from silence is itself questionable. Historical theories should be built upon the foundation of what is *present* in *concrete* evidence that is *available*; not in what is *absent* in *hypothetical* evidence that is altogether *unavailable*.

JESUS AND THE QUESTION OF ESCHATOLOGY

When, however, one approaches the question of the historical Jesus with this skewed methodology, the picture of Jesus discovered will significantly differ from the one found by those who begin with another methodology. It will certainly differ remarkably from the portrait discovered by those who place more confidence in the Gospel's ability to transmit historical reminiscences than in any contemporary scholar's ability to accurately infer what a hypothetical community did not believe on the basis of what a hypothetical document does not say after it has been broken down into hypothetical layers.

One of the most fundamental differences in perspectives is that the Jesus portrayed in the Gospels (and, indirectly, in most of the canonical literature) is eschatological in outlook; the Jesus discovered from the post-Bultmannian use of Q often is not. This, in any case, is the view of North American Cynic theorists such as Crossan and Mack. Unlike the Judaism of that day, unlike John the Baptist, and unlike the early church—but very much like the Cynics—this position contends that the historical Jesus held no distinct belief about God acting decisively in the future to bring history as we know it to a close.[57] Indeed, such a position constitutes the "fifth pillar" of "scholarly wisdom" of the Jesus Seminar![58] It now needs to be critically examined.

The Motivation behind the De-Eschatologized Jesus

The first thing that should perhaps be said in response to this view is that it is difficult to justify calling this position a "pillar of scholarly wisdom" when so many scholars disagree with it. Indeed, outside of the post-Bultmannian camp, one finds scholars claiming that, "one of the strongest consensuses in New Testament research" involves the conviction that Jesus' message of the kingdom of God was fundamentally apocalyptic.[59] At the very least, whatever else may be reflected in this "fifth pillar of scholarly wisdom," it does not reflect scholarly consensus—at least not outside the Jesus Seminar![60]

A good many scholars, for example, completely reject the position of the Jesus Seminar that the so-called "future Son of Man" sayings that predict a coming eschatological event are inauthentic. Many rather argue that the historical-critical grounds for affirming the authenticity of these sayings are as good as many other sayings of Jesus that are generally affirmed as authentic by the scholarly community (including scholars within the Jesus Seminar!).[61] Indeed, many further argue that what actually fuels the post-Bultmannian de-eschatologization of Jesus is not the textual evidence itself so much as it is a desire on the part of some scholars to find a Jesus whose worldview does not clash with their own thoroughly naturalistic one.

The view that there is a personal God who will, through Jesus (or any other means), someday bring an end to history as we know it, is simply inconsonant with the modernist worldview that structures the post-Bultmannian paradigm. And hence, this argument goes, in the interest of having a "relevant" Jesus, his eschatological sayings are judged to be inauthentic. The assumption on the part of some post-Bultmannians that futurist eschatologies lead to religious exclusivism and even militant madness further fuel the drive to portray Jesus as a non-eschatological teacher.[62]

Three things can briefly be said in response to this. First, concerning this last point, it can be argued that, far from leading to "militant madness," the biblical eschatological worldview actually functions as the foundation for a vibrant "theology of hope."[63] There is, in any case, certainly no *necessary* connection between eschatological thinking as such and the destructive mind-sets and behaviors some may adopt for eschatological reasons. Second, the *a priori* dismissal of an eschatological worldview reflects an arbitrary metaphysical prejudice against the supernatural in general that is itself based on an increasingly outdated modernist worldview, as we have seen. And third, and most foundationally, it is simply illegitimate to allow one's own metaphysical assumptions to significantly influence one's historical exegesis. This is the perennial danger of trying to "discover" a relevant Jesus.[64]

The Meaning of Jesus' Eschatological Vision

A second important point to be addressed in regards to the post-Bultmannian rejection of an apocalyptic Jesus concerns the meaning of the terms "eschatology" and "apocalyptic" as they are applied to Jesus' teaching. No small part of the present controversy over the question of Jesus and eschatology has arisen from the fact that a variety of meanings can be attached to the various terms involved.[65] What is entailed by affirming, or denying, that Jesus was "eschatological" and/or "apocalyptic" depends on what meaning one gives these words.

For example, many post-Bultmannians who reject the notion that

Jesus was eschatological mean that he held *no* belief in *any* future divine intervention which would bring history as we know it to a close. Other scholars who reject the notion that Jesus was eschatological, however, mean only that Jesus did not expect history as we know it to come to a close "in his generation" — though he *did* hold a view that God would *eventually* bring the present order to some type of culmination.[66] Conversely, many scholars who affirm that Jesus was eschatological in his outlook mean that he expected the imminent end of the world, and thus, following Schweitzer, hold that Jesus was simply mistaken and that he is, in this respect, irrelevant to modern people.[67] Others who affirm this, however, mean that Jesus was "future oriented" — believing that the kingdom of God would *someday* be fulfilled in history by a divine intervention — but not that he held any particular belief that this would happen *in the immediate future.* Jesus, in this view, did announce the imminence of *the kingdom of God,* but *not* the imminence of *the end of the world.*

This latter position represents an "already-but-not-yet" understanding of the eschatological reign of God. It affirms Jesus' understanding of an imminent kingdom, but not of an imminent end of history. And, over and against the post-Bultmannian understanding of eschatology Crossan and Mack work with, there are at least six arguments that can be made in its favor.[68]

First, as we have already indicated, the post-Bultmannian claim that Q betrays an early, non-eschatological layer followed by a later eschatological one is, in fact, very difficult to substantiate.[69] As we have said, it seems to be driven more by a desire to discover a certain kind of historical Jesus (a non-apocalyptic Jesus) than by hard evidence.[70] But even if this stratification of Q were granted, there is no justification for equating "earlier" with "authentic" and "later" with "inauthentic."[71] One could, as Koester himself has noted, easily argue that the authentic eschatological sayings of Jesus circulated early but were not incorporated into Q until later.[72]

Indeed, Kloppenborg himself argued in just this direction. Hence, for example, in relationship to the sapiential and apocalyptic elements of Q, he writes:

> To say that the wisdom components were formative for Q and the prophetic judgment oracles and apothegms describing Jesus' conflict with "this generation" are secondary is *not* to imply anything about the ultimate tradition-historical provenance of any of the sayings.[73]

While we may regard Kloppenborg's stratification of Q as being itself overly speculative, the point he is here making is a sound one, and it is crucial. One cannot legitimately equate the history of a document's composition with the actual chronology of the various materials within a document's layers. And thus, one cannot infer stages in the life of the (hypothetical) community on the basis of the layers one finds in the document they produce. Yet it seems Kloppenborg's cautious position is rarely followed by those post-Bultmannians (such as Mack) who consistently employ his stratification in service to a non-eschatological Jesus thesis. If Kloppenborg's cautious position *were* adopted, *no* solid inference about how Christianity historically developed could be made from the stratification of Q.[74] One could not, for example, use Q to argue that a sapiential understanding of Christ preceded an apocalyptic understanding, for either view, according to Kloppenborg (and Koester) might have *in actual history* preceded the other. Hence, even if the priority of sapiential over apocalyptic literary elements is granted in Q, this does not imply that the historical Jesus was more likely to have been a sage rather than an apocalyptic prophet.

Secondly, the post-Bultmannian tendency to locate the traditions in GosThom early seems to stand in tension with their tendency to locate apocalyptic traditions late, for there is, as many have noted, a distinct *anti-apocalyptic* polemic which runs throughout this work. Most notably, the Jesus of GosThom is portrayed as correcting his disciples' apocalyptic conceptions of the kingdom.[75] This polemic presupposes, of course, that the apocalyptic understanding was *already in place.* However early one dates GosThom, then, the apocalyptic understanding of the kingdom must be dated earlier.

Third, it is difficult to maintain that Jesus' worldview was fundamentally discontinuous with that of John the Baptist, on the one hand, and the early church, on the other. But just this is required in order to maintain a non-eschatological Jesus.[76] Among other considerations, one wonders how it was that the (supposedly) later traditions came to (mistakenly) see Jesus as embodying the same outlook as John, if "in reality" Jesus' views were radically different from his.[77]

Fourth, outside of post-Bultmannian circles, a good many scholars argue that the eschatological aspects of Jesus' teaching must, on historical-critical grounds, be regarded as generally authentic. For example, as we mentioned earlier, many argue that the "future Son of Man" sayings of Jesus must be understood as deriving from Jesus himself. Among many other considerations, the uniqueness of Jesus' concept of "the Son of Man" is more easily understood as deriving from a unique historical figure than from a latter community of faith, especially in light of the fact that the phrase "Son of Man" quickly fell into disuse as a christological title in the early church.[78]

Fifth, as we have already indicated, the post-Bultmannian tendency to treat "apocalyptic" and "wisdom" mind-sets as fundamentally opposed represents a false dichotomy.[79] The supposed incompatibility is based on an overly literalistic imminentist understanding of Jesus' (and the New Testament's) eschatology, for one thing. And, for another, the textual evidence of the period clearly demonstrates that the two motifs were in fact frequently combined (as in the "final" version of Q).[80] Indeed, according to some, the two themes are frequently combined in prophetic writings, which is perhaps one of the best indications that understanding Jesus along the lines of a Jewish prophet (as many third questers are now doing) squares with the available evidence more easily than understanding him as a Hellenistically oriented Cynic sage.[81]

A final argument in favor of an eschatological understanding of Jesus' thought world squares with the nature of Jesus' ministry as an exorcist. Very few players in the contemporary quest deny that the historical Jesus engaged in something like "deliverance" activity (Mack is among the few). What is frequently unnoticed, however, is that this activity, as it is portrayed in the Gospels, is fundamentally bound up with a *thoroughly eschatological worldview.*[82] In a word, Jesus' exorcisms are, quite remarkably, portrayed as anticipations of the final struggle between the kingdom of God and the kingdom of Satan. As Graham Twelfree carefully argues in his insightful and comprehensive study of this topic:

> *Jesus was the first to make the connection between exorcism and eschatology. For him, his exorcisms were the first or preliminary binding of Satan who would finally be destroyed in the eschaton.*[83]

Jesus' exorcisms, in other words, manifested the "already-but-not-yet" quality of the kingdom he was preaching and embodying. The kingdom of God was already present — over and against that of Satan — though its full realization would only be accomplished in the future.

All of these arguments, we may contend, count decisively against the post-Bultmannian portrait of Jesus as a non-eschatological teacher in general and Crossan and Mack's portrayal of Jesus as a Cynic sage in particular. They argue in favor of understanding Jesus as one who expected God to intervene decisively in human history at some point in the future and who saw his own ministry as the definitive precursor to this eschatological event.

CONCLUSION

The post-Bultmannian enterprise, we have seen, begins with the assumptions that the Gospels are not reliable and that the early church was not significantly unified in its view of Christ. Working from these assumptions, they then elevate extra-canonical sources such as GosThom and the hypothetical Q document over the canonical material as the primary "data pool" out of which their portrait of the historical Jesus is to be derived. And, not surprisingly, the portrait of Jesus that is then painted by these scholars has little in common with the view of the New Testament itself. Instead of being the Son of God, the one through whom God decisively worked and in whom God decisively dwelt, Jesus is here generally viewed as a non-eschatological sage who simply went about espousing a form of countercultural wisdom.

But, we have further seen, there is little to commend this approach to the historical Jesus. Not only do we have no compelling reason to approach the Gospels more skeptically than we would other ancient documents (cf. chap. 5), but the arguments employed to elevate certain extra-canonical documents above the Gospels must be viewed as highly tenuous, overly speculative, and often circular. Therefore, the whole approach can be said to be "arguing in circles and grasping at straws."

We are on much firmer ground, historically speaking, if we use the canonical material as our primary data pool to arrive at an understanding of who the historical Jesus was. And, as sections 4 through 6 will demonstrate, the closer we look at this material, the firmer our ground becomes—if we do not look through the metaphysically prejudiced eyes of naturalism. However, there is one further dimension of Crossan's and Mack's arguments for Jesus as a Cynic sage that needs to be investigated.

Working from the general to the particular in this critique, we have thus far been arguing against the general methodology, assumptions, and use of historical material of the post-Bultmannian enterprise out of which the exponents of the Cynic thesis come. We have, however, not yet analyzed those arguments that are employed by Cynic theorists in *particular* to establish their view that Jesus was a Cynic. It is to this task that we turn in chapter 7. The argument here shall be that if the post-Bultmannian enterprise is already stretching a plausible thread of speculation thin, Cynic theorists stretch it even thinner.

7

STRETCHING A
THIN THREAD THINNER:
A Critique of the Central Arguments
for the Cynic Thesis

There are three central lines of argumentation that are generally employed by Cynic theorists such as Crossan and Mack. The first concerns a particular reading of Q and GosThom, the second a particular understanding of the Hellenistic nature of Galilean culture, and the third a particular interpretation of Cynicism's influence on Jesus and the early church. Each of these lines of argumentation are problematic. If the post-Bultmannian enterprise itself hangs on a thin thread of tentative speculation, the Cynic thesis, I shall now argue, stretches this thread even thinner.

THE CYNIC-JESUS READING OF Q AND GOSTHOM

The Cynic-Jesus thesis is wholly dependent upon the post-Bultmannian preference for extra-canonical traditions over canonical ones. This is hardly surprising, since the portrait of Christ in the canonical Gospels is hardly that of a Cynic sage. Their case is rather argued on the basis of a particular reading of the hypothetical "Q Gospel" and GosThom. It is, in a word, argued that the model of a Hellenistic Cynic philosopher offers the best way of explaining the historical person who lies behind the earliest traditions found in these two documents.

Three critical observations can be made which call this argument into question. First, we have already seen that the practice of establishing layers in Q is highly speculative, largely arbitrary, and quite circular. What is more, the practice of locating decisive chronological stages in the development of early Christianity from the (supposed) literary stages of this hypothetical document is unwarranted, as Kloppenborg himself states.[1] Hence, the practice of using Q – and more particularly, the "earliest" strata of Q – as the central means of defining the historical Jesus must be rejected. In the light of the discussion in the previous chapter, Harold Attridge's assessment must be deemed quite accurate when he writes

> a focus on Q, and particularly Q-1, as the surest path to the origins of Christianity is methodologically flawed . . . the originating figure was a much more complex individual than Q-1 gives him credit for being.[2]

The identification of Q-1 is simply too tentative to bear the foundational weight this thesis places on it. Among other considerations, the objectivity of the criteria used to establish Q-1 is questionable, as we have seen. A Cynic Jesus is inferred from Q-1 because it is primarily Cynic-like material that is (quite artificially) extracted out of Q and defined as what constitutes Q-1. But even if the establishment of Q-1 were to be granted, this would hardly warrant limiting our perspective on the historical Jesus – at the expense, say, of the later canonical material – to this strata of Q. The Cynic-Jesus approach, then, is myopic in its focus on the very data it speculatively, and circularly, creates for itself.

Secondly, the use made of GosThom to establish a Cynic Jesus is questionable on several accounts. The more reasonable dating of GosThom within the second century, combined with the fact that it betrays dependence upon the canonical Gospels at a number of junctures and contains an anti-apocalyptic polemic, is enough to call into question the use of this document as a pillar for any reconstruction of the historical Jesus and of earliest Christianity. But what is more, it is not altogether clear the GosThom, whenever it is dated, supports a Cynic understanding of the historical Jesus. Most scholars, after all, do not readily identify the Jesus of GosThom as a Cynic sage.

The Cynic reading of GosThom is arrived at only through (a) a debatable interpretation of key passages, and (b) the employment of the same sort of questionable source criticism that was embarked on to arrive at a Cynic Jesus behind Q. This last point is particularly crucial. For Crossan, for example, GosThom is composed of at least two fundamental strata, and only that material that is paralleled in early Q material (or other "early" fragments) is identified as belonging to the earliest strata.[3] Beyond its conjectural nature, however, this strategy once again invites the charge of circularity.

Wright argues this point when he suggests that the post-Bultmannian practice of discovering the earliest tradition in what the "early" Q material and GosThom have in common is, in all likelihood, not due to post-Bultmannians having "made a brilliant guess at how to strip off redactional layers." Rather, it is due to

(a) a desire on the part of some modern readers to imagine early Christianity as very similar to the religion of Thomas and (b) the consequent critical activity of pulling apart what is already a purely hypothetical document, Q, in order to reveal an "early version" which just happens to fit the history-of-religions theory.

And thus he concludes, quite appropriately:

Frankly, some of the arguments advanced along the way within the suggested model look suspiciously naive; others, manifestly and damaging circular.[4]

Finally, as previously argued (chap. 5), the intensely skeptical view toward the canonical Gospels that lies behind their preference of Q and GosThom is unwarranted. We shall expand upon this line of argumentation, in a more specific fashion, concerning the Gospel of Mark in part 5. But enough has already been said to establish the point that these works should be treated with the same degree of confidence and/or skepticism we generally approach other ostensively historical works with: no more and no less. Hence, if they are to be considered untrustworthy at points, the burden of proof ought to be placed on the one who would seek to prove this. The Cynic thesis, however, completely relies on the shoe being on the other foot. Its entire methodology, and the whole of its portrait of the historical Jesus it arrives at from this method-ology, *requires* that the Gospels be considered *fundamentally unreliable.* And in the light of the evidence, this is one further weakness of this theory.

First-Century Lower Galilee: A Hellenized Cynic Haven?

A second foundational line of argumentation that is employed by expo-nents of the Cynic-Jesus theory concerns the nature of the social land-scape first-century Galilee. To make their portrait of Jesus as a Jewish Cynic plausible, Cynic theorists must create a general portrait of the cultural milieu in which Jesus operated as being a *thoroughly* Hellenized environment. Their theory is plausible only to the extent that the region of Galilee can be construed as a likely place for a Jewish Cynic to arise. Although the evidence certainly indicates that Galilee was Hellenized in important ways, the exponents of the Cynic thesis must seriously exaggerate the significance of this evidence to render their thesis plausible.

A Survey of Recent Scholarship

Over the last several decades there has been a veritable explosion of scholarship addressing the social, intellectual, and cultural milieu of first-century Galilee. A number of historical and archaeological discoveries have suggested that Galilee, especially lower Galilee, was influenced by Hellenistic culture to a greater degree than was previously supposed.[5] Of particular importance for our purposes has been research related to the ancient city of Sepphoris, the urban center closest to Nazareth. Studies suggest that this city in most respects resembled other Greco-Roman cities in terms of its general Hellenistic influence.[6] Among the various claims that have been made on the basis of such studies, one of the most controversial has come to play a central role among Cynic theorists: namely, the claim that Nazareth's proximity to Sepphoris most likely had a significant Hellenizing effect upon Jesus and other Nazarenes.[7]

Utilizing this recent research, Cynic theorists have attempted to construct a picture of a thoroughly Hellenized milieu for Jesus and his followers, one in which the influence of Cynic philosophers is almost to be expected. There are, however, several observations that should caution our acceptance of their conclusions.

Going Beyond the Data

First, it is instructive to note the difference in tone between the historians and archaeologists on the one hand, and the Cynic theorists on the other. While the former are generally careful and hesitant with regard to drawing definitive conclusions from their data, the latter tend to argue as though the case was closed. The historians and archaeologists seem to be more aware of how easy it is to run ahead of the data with one's interpretation of it. The data, many of these scholars suggest, is at the present time simply inconclusive. At this stage, we simply cannot say, with any degree of confidence, just what ramifications follow for our perception of Jesus and the early Christians from the apparent Hellenization of first-century Galilee.[8]

Nazareth and Sepphoris

A second observation concerns the significance Cynic theorists invest in the proximity of Nazareth to Sepphoris. It is, more than anything else, this proximity which allows them to portray Jesus as being significantly influenced by Hellenistic culture. The assumption at work here is that geographical proximity implies cultural influence.

This assumption is questionable on any account, but it is most certainly erroneous as applied to Nazareth and Sepphoris. A number of historians and archaeologists have aptly argued that the evidence suggests that there frequently existed cultural rifts between Hellenistic urban centers (like Sepphoris) and the smaller villages that surrounded them (like Nazareth).[9] This rift seems to have been particularly intense between Sepphoris and its surrounding Jewish villages, owing in part to the pacifistic, pro-Roman position Sepphoris adopted during the First Jewish Revolt against Rome—a position that infuriated the surrounding Galileans.[10]

This observation renders the supposition that Sepphoris exercised a significant *positive* cultural influence upon a first-century Nazarene unlikely. When we consider further that there is nothing but a deafening silence with regard to Sepphoris and other such cities in the early Jesus tradition, the supposition of a positive cultural influence becomes more unlikely still. If there was any influence at all, it most probably would have been negative.

Were There Cynics in Galilee?

A third observation is this: even if we were to accept the notion that the cultural world of Sepphoris exercised a positive influence on its neighboring villages, the evidence does not justify our concluding that this would render it more likely than not that Jesus would have adopted a specifically Cynic outlook. For there simply is no solid evidence that Cynics inhabited Sepphoris, or Jewish urban centers in general.

Against this, Downing has suggested that Dio Chrysostom's comment concerning the presence of Cynic preachers on the street corners and in the temple gates of Alexandria can serve as a basis for extrapolating to a Cynic presence in Palestinian cities. But his case is weak. For one thing, Dio's statement is somewhat hyperbolic, and thus should not be taken too literally. For another thing, Dio does not claim that Cynics are found on *every* street corner, as Downing implies. And, in any event, his reference is specifically to Alexandria, not to "a city like" Alexandria.[11] Hence there is simply no good reason to take Dio's statement as inferring anything about the presence of Cynics in Jewish centers like Sepphoris.

A more convincing argument in this direction, however, has been offered by Theissen. Since we know that Menippus, Meleager, and Oenomaeus (each of whom was a Cynic) came from Gadara, in Southern Syria, we may, he contends, conclude that Cynicism was prevalent over a significant period of time in this area.[12] And from this, one could argue, it is not much of a stretch to assume that Cynics were present in Galilee as well.

Several considerations count against this argument, however. First, although these Cynics originally hailed from this region, there is no evidence to suggest that they lived and taught there.[13] Secondly, none of them can be dated to the early first century.[14] Indeed, it is significant to note that, while Cynicism was very popular in ancient Greece, it seems to have significantly waned in the second and first centuries B.C. until it experienced a revival (generally called "Imperial Cynicism") in the mid-first century with Demetrius in Rome, and hence *after* the life of Jesus.[15] This doesn't itself rule out the theoretical possibility of Cynics being present in many cities, including Galilee, before this time. But it does reveal that there is no evidence of such a presence. Hence, if we stick to the evidence, we must agree with Harvey that "there is no evidence whatever for [a Cynic presence] in Palestine in the first century A.D.," and with Hans Dieter Betz that to presume otherwise is "mostly fanciful conjecture."[16]

Galilean Judaism and Hellenistic Culture

One final and very significant observation concerns first-century Galilean religious life. In spite of the degree to which some factors of the empire-wide Hellenistic ethos such as language, architecture and, to a lesser extent, the arts had permeated Galilean life, it is nonetheless the case that Galilee, along with Judaism in general, maintained a close vigil over their inherited *religious life*. The scholars who have made the study of first-century Galilee their central concern are virtually unanimous in concluding that, at least since the time of the Hasmoneans prior to the turn of the millennium, the Jews of Galilee deeply identified with the traditional Jewish religious worldview. The Jewish covenant with their one God, along with its concomitant notions of sacred land, sacred Torah, and sacred temple, was deeply embedded in the minds of Galilean Jewish people.[17] Indeed, far from compromising the Judaism of these people, the influence of Hellenism in their culture seems to have actually *intensified* it. As Meyers argues:

Despite five centuries in which Greeks, Greek language and culture, artifacts and numerous architectural structures and decorative arts were adopted in the land of Israel, Semitic modes of intellectual reasoning were still dominant. The land of Israel had not lost its distinctive character in the first century; its peoples had not compromised its values and traditions. Rather, the inroads of Hellenism spawned a sterner and stricter sort of attitude among segments of the Jewish population.[18]

Thus, just as many of the Diaspora Jews tended to bond even more closely with their Jewish religious traditions *because* of the close proximity of pagan and/or Hellenistic influence, so the Hellenization of Galilee on various cultural levels actually served to buttress the religious worldview of the Galilean Jews.[19] With specific regard to Sepphoris, Meyers has noted that, despite its clear Hellenistic features, its first-century population was deeply *Jewish* both ethnically and religiously, and that archaeological remains reveal "a Torah-true population."[20]

In this light, Louis Feldman has called for a refocusing of the question of how Hellenized the Jews were.

The question is not so much how greatly Jews and Judaism in the Land of Israel were Hellenized, as how strongly they resisted Hellenization. In other words, what was the power of Judaism to remain strong despite the challenge of Hellenism and later of Christianity?[21]

Thus, to suggest, as the Cynic theorists must, that Galilee (and in particular Sepphoris) would have provided the type of context within which a Nazarene Jew could likely be converted to Cynicism seems, in the light of the evidence, quite implausible. Cynicism, we must remember, was a decidedly anti-religious Hellenistic philosophy that centered on the notions of complete self-sufficiency, freedom from law, and the practice of any and all sorts of "shameless" behavior in the attempt to transgress community mores. Such notions violated the most fundamental tenets of the religious worldview that the Jews of first-century Galilee embraced.[22] And as such, the suggestion that a first-century Jew could have, or would have, converted to this philosophy is almost unthinkable.

In sum, while the largely nonreligious, non-Jewish Jesus revisioned by Cynic theorists in many (but not all) ways squares with what we know about ancient Cynics, it simply stands in diametric opposition to

everything we know about Palestinian Jews. And Jesus was most decisively a Palestinian Jew.[23]

CYNICISM, PAUL, AND JESUS

The third foundational line of argumentation employed by exponents
of the Cynic thesis is that, all other considerations aside, there exists
significant parallels between the earliest traditions of Jesus' teaching and
that of early Christianity in general, on the one hand, and the teachings
of ancient Cynics, on the other. These parallels must be taken seriously
and accounted for. And, it is argued, the easiest way to do this is by
positing a line of influence from one to the other. We shall first address
the Cynic theorists' case for a Cynic influence on Paul and then turn to
the more significant issue of their case for a discernible Cynic influence
on Jesus.

Parallels between Paul and Ancient Cynicism

To buttress their general portrayal of Cynicism as an influential force on
Jesus, certain defenders of the Cynic-Jesus theory have made much of
the parallels between Paul and Cynics in terms of literary styles and
practical activities.[24] Attention has been given to Paul's use of the Cynic
"diatribe" style, as well as to a variety of Hellenistic moral *topoi* (com-
monplace themes), some of which are shared by Cynics.[25] Ronald Hock
has even correlated Paul's tent-making trade with certain Cynic attitudes
regarding work and self-sufficiency.[26] While recognition of these similarities is helpful for a full-orbed understanding of Paul's rhetorical style
and even content, several observations will serve to reveal that the attempt by Cynic-Jesus theorists to read a strong Cynic influence upon
Paul it unjustifiable.

First, even in those places within the Pauline corpus that one discovers ostensive Cynic parallels, there are always significant features that
serve to strongly *distinguish* Paul's thought from Cynicism. For example,
although Paul uses the term *parresia* ("boldness of speech"; 1 Thes. 2:2) –
a term that expressed a fundamental aspect of the Cynic ideal – he does
so "in a way different from the Cynics."[27] Malherbe notes that while the
Cynic philosopher was

> impelled by an awareness of his own moral freedom, acquired
> by reason and the application of his own will, to speak boldly to
> the human condition and demand its reformation, Paul regards

his ministry, as to its origin, motivation, content and method, as being directed by God.[28]

Similarly, Paul's use of moral *topoi* and other stylistic features common to Cynic material is very selective. While Paul no doubt made use of a wide variety of Hellenistic rhetorical and stylistic devices that were a part of the cultural air of the day, it is clear that he would consistently shape and transform them at will to fit his particular Christian needs.[29] Again, while Paul practiced an asceticism that has been compared to Cynicism's voluntary poverty, the similarities are skin-deep at best. The all-important question is *why* each party took an ascetic route. For the Cynics, it is an end in itself; for Paul, it is merely a practical means to very specific ends: namely, the furthering of his ministry to the budding church.[30]

Finally, one can point to the places in Pauline literature where he takes an explicitly critical view of Cynic-like qualities. The first letter to the Thessalonians has in particular received much attention in regard to the question of Cynic parallels in Paul. In 1 Thessalonians 4:9-12, for example, Paul makes use of a number of Hellenistic moral *topoi*. However, as Paul Eddy has noted,

> for all of its similarities with Hellenistic literary conventions and moral *topoi* . . . this section functions as a blunt Pauline warning against adopting an attitude and life-style characteristic of either the Epicureans or the Cynics. . . . By calling these common Hellenistic moral *topoi* into service in a uniquely Christian manner, Paul both distinguishes Christians from, and warns them against, the philosophical attitudes and life-styles of the surrounding culture.[31]

Thus, while the style and even some of the content of Paul's moral exhortation exhibits numerous similarities with other types of Greco-Roman (including Cynic) paraenesis, there are equally striking differences, the most prominent of which are

> the Christian motivation (regard for God and his call to holiness) and means (the transformative power of the Holy Spirit) for living the ethical life. Finally, the eschatological hope serves as the distinctive Christian foundation for present consolation and future glory.[32]

In short, all "Cynic" parallels in the Pauline corpus can be explained in terms of rhetorical, stylistic, and thematic commonalties that were available within the empire-wide Hellenistic culture of that day. To suggest anything more in the way of a Pauline-Cynic connection is to fly in the face of the clear differences noted above.[33]

Parallels between Jesus and Ancient Cynicism

The Cynic-Jesus thesis places much of its weight upon the claim that the teaching style of Jesus shares significant similarities with Cynic rhetoric. As noted earlier, Mack suggests that both the core chreiai in the supposed pre-Markan pronouncement stories as well as the aphorisms of Q-1 display a Cynic-like wittiness in the service of a countercultural subversive wisdom. This Cynic Jesus is not concerned with renewing Judaism and its covenant relationship with God. In fact, such a Jesus is hardly religious at all. Rather, in Cynic fashion, he partakes in social critique for its own sake, committed to a "wisdom" view of the world that offers a largely secular ethic.[34] He is, therefore, more of a Hellenistic sage than he is "Jewish."

Beyond what has already been said against the (circular) methodology used by Cynic theorists to determine which aspects of which pronouncement stories are "core" and which aspects of Q are "earliest," several things may be said that minimize the significance of these supposed parallels.

First, it must be noted that the ancient Cynics hardly cornered the market on chreiai and aphoristic forms of speech. However such patterns of speech evolved (a debatable issue), by the first century such styles of speech were available for use throughout the Mediterranean world. What is more, Henry Fischel has documented the adaptation of chreiai within Hebrew culture. They are, he argues, especially prevalent in certain Rabbinic literature. Hence the use of this style by Jesus was hardly unique, even within Jewish culture. And, as such, the attribution of a specifically Cynic influence on him to account for it is unnecessary.[35]

Secondly, while the Cynic theorists have aptly highlighted the wisdom aspects of Jesus' teaching—Jesus was certainly a sage—they have erred, it seems, in thinking that this implies that Jesus could not have also been thoroughly Jewish in his worldview.[36] To the contrary, the evidence suggests he was, in fact, *a Jewish sage.*

In terms of his sapiential teaching, this model fits Jesus far better than that of a Cynic sage. An objective look at the content and style of Jesus' teaching bears this out. When Jesus utters characteristic wisdom sayings, he consistently reflects Jewish rather than Cynic values, if these sayings are understood in their proper Jewish context. It is only by extrapolating these sayings out of their Jewish context and reading them in an artificial non-Jewish light that their Jewishness can be missed. One good example of this is found in the way certain Cynic-Jesus theorists' read Q/Luke 14:26. Here Jesus proclaims:

> If anyone comes to me and does not hate his father and mother, his wife and children, his brothers and sisters—yes, even his own life—he cannot be my disciple.

According to Vaage, this authentic saying of Jesus' suggests, in good Cynic fashion, that "the first requirement for going with Jesus [is] the breaking of familial bonds."[37] According to Crossan, Jesus is here confronting the abuse of power in families again in good Cynic (and egalitarian) fashion.[38] But both views miss the point of the passage if it is allowed to speak out of its original Jewish context. In truth, the passage represents a classic example of Jewish hyperbole.[39] Jesus is not instructing anyone to *literally* hate any other family member. He is, rather, saying (in good *Jewish* fashion) that following him must take priority over all familial relationships.

Even if the Cynic theorists' non-Jewish and overly literalistic reading were granted, however, the passage would *still* not be a good candidate for a genuine Cynic parallel. For one must note the *reason* why the social norm of loving family members was (supposedly) here violated. It is, in this passage, not on the basis of a countercultural self-reliant freedom, as it would have been for a Cynic. Rather, quite remarkably, it is on the basis of *Jesus' authority* over the disciple. This is hardly what one would expect from a Cynic![40]

The Jewishness of Jesus' sapiential teachings becomes even clearer as our purview of his teachings broadens. In the light of the above passage, one might, for example, emphasize Jesus' strong admonitions concerning the honoring of one's parents, against divorce, and so on (Mark 7:9-12; 10:2-10). This is not characteristically Cynic, but it *is* characteristically Jewish. What is more, it is highly significant that Jesus' most characteristic form of teaching—the parable—has no real Cynic parallels. It is, rather, a distinctly *Jewish* pedagogical device.

Hence, the model of Jesus as a Jewish sage is much more feasible than the model of Jesus as a Cynic sage. Whatever parallels one might be able to find between the teachings and styles of the Cynics and of Jesus, they are "at best only secondary, general and indirect."[41] In essence, he is Jewish through and through. Bernard Scott nicely summarizes the situation.

Beside the obvious problems with wonder-working and eschatology, there are even more substantial grounds against a Cynic
interpretation of Jesus. The primary *forms* of the synoptic and
Thomas traditions are forms closely identified with the Jewish
wisdom tradition. . . . Second, the *content* of these forms is Jewish. The debate issues are Jewish in their interest and background. . . . [T]he problems with identifying the root of the wisdom tradition with Cynic wisdom remains irresolvable: the
forms as well as the content are Jewish.[42]

Finally, the claim that the Q Mission Discourse reflects strong Cynic
connections must be challenged. As noted earlier, this Discourse is typically cited as decisive evidence of an original Cynic ethos for Jesus' early
followers. But a closer analysis reveals that almost the opposite is the
case. For example, on the surface Q/Luke 10:4 seems to call for a meager
way of life that compares favorably to the Cynic lifestyle: "Do not take a
purse or bag [*pera*] or sandals; and do not greet anyone on the road."
However, the explicit charge in the mission discourse against carrying a
pera – that is, a begging bag – suggests otherwise. The *pera* was one of the
defining elements of Cynic dress. Not only did it serve the practical
purpose of functioning as a begging bowl, it came to symbolize the
Cynic's *self-sufficiency*. This Jesus *forbids*!

Relatedly, in a parallel charge (Luke 9:3), Jesus' missionaries are
instructed to go *without* a staff as well – another common feature of
Cynic apparel. Given that a critical component of Cynic self-understanding was its particular *dress* – including the *pera* and the walking staff –
the mission instruction against these things is very significant.[43] And
lastly, the charge to refrain from *greeting* anyone along the way would
seem to fly in the face of the Cynic virtue of "boldness of speech." In this
light, far from constituting a decisive parallel with Cynicism, the Q mission charge can justifiably be understood "almost as anti-Cynic."[44]

CONCLUSION

The central lines of argumentation used to establish the Cynic thesis, we
see, are all seriously flawed. Its arguments from Q and GosThom are
tentative at best, viciously circular at worst. Its portrayal of a hyper-
Hellenized Galilee, so foundational to the plausibility of its revisionist
portrait of Jesus, is not supported by the available data. And the supposed parallels it locates between Paul, Jesus, and Cynicism, do not

generally stand up under scrutiny, and certainly do not warrant identifying this philosophy as a significant (let alone primary) influence on these two figures. When we add to this the previously discussed problems with the whole post-Bultmannian enterprise, upon which the entire Cynic-Jesus theory is built, the case for seeing Jesus as a Cynic sage looks quite poor. The thin thread of tentative speculation that was already stretched too far in the general post-Bultmannian enterprise has here been stretched even further.

The most decisive refutation of this view, however, has not yet even been addressed: namely, *the New Testament itself.* The most compelling argument against any revisionist account of the historical Jesus is not the exposition of its internal weaknesses, as crucial as that is. It is, rather, the *positive* evidence for the reliability of the New Testament's portrait of Christ. For all of its rich variety, Jesus Christ is, according to the canonical collection, portrayed as being the Son of God. All "alternative" views of Jesus are weak if for no other reason than because the evidence for the foundation of *this* view is so strong.

It is to this evidence that we now turn in part 2 of this book. The primary focus shall continue to be on a critical analysis of the Cynic thesis. Because the Cynic thesis completely relies on a particular assessment of Paul, Mark, and Luke (in Acts) as fundamentally mistaken (or intentionally deceptive) in their portrayals of Christ, our attention will be directed toward refuting Crossan's and Mack's views on these three figures. But, in the process of this refutation, the counter evidence supporting these New Testament authors shall necessarily be presented. And to this extent, their understanding of Jesus as the Son of God, in contrast to Crossan and Mack's understanding of him as a Cynic sage, shall be historically established.

8

CHRIST-CULT LEADER OR REPRESENTATIVE SPOKESMAN?

A Critique of Mack's Portrayal of Paul

With few exceptions, all scholars agree that the earliest extant documents we have of the early Christian movement are the letters of the Apostle Paul.[1] From the early 50s to the early 60s Paul wrote a number of epistles addressing issues that concerned various new Christian congregations throughout the Roman Empire.[2] As such, one might be inclined to assume that these letters would be of inestimable value to the historian of early Christianity, providing him or her with our earliest direct evidence of what the early church believed and what it was like.

Working from this assumption, one would quickly conclude that the earliest Christian communities viewed Jesus as the Messiah, the Christ, and that this title had strong overtones of divinity (Rom. 1:4; 5:8; 7:25; 8:9-11, etc.).[3] One would further conclude that these believing Jews and Gentiles worshiped Jesus in song and prayer, calling him "Lord" and "Son of God" while ascribing the activities and attributes of Yahweh himself to him (Phil. 2:6-11; 1 Cor. 1:2-3; 8:6; Rom. 1:3-4; 10:9-13; Gal.2:20, etc.).[4] One would also quickly conclude that this surprising activity of these early communities surrounding this historical person in the recent past was centrally connected to their belief that Jesus had died for their sins, had risen from the dead, had been exalted by God, and was soon going to return (Rom. 4:24-25; 1 Cor. 15:3, 9, 17, 51-54; 1 Thes. 4:13-18). And, given the occasional and incidental nature of such references as well as the discernible presence of creedal material in Paul's epistles, one would likely conclude that these early Christians had been engaging in this surprising activity *for some time,* certainly before Paul wrote to them. Such, in fact, has been the customary reading of Paul's letters.

How does this early testimony square with the view that the "real" historical Jesus was simply a wandering Cynic and that the earliest "Jesus people" communities held no particular beliefs about him, but were merely engaged in a radical social experiment? How does Paul's portrayal of the earliest believing communities being centered on Jesus as the crucified and risen Lord fit with Mack and Crossan's view that the earliest Jesus people never saw him in divine terms, saw no particular significance in his death, and never entertained the thought that he rose from the dead?

The answer, in a word, is that the two views of earliest Christianity do *not* at all square with one another. Indeed, they are, as Mack and Crossan both acknowledge, worlds apart from one another. Following in the footsteps of Bauer, Bousett, and Bultmann, Mack and Crossan generally see the Christianity of Paul as constituting a completely different religion from the "Christianity" of the Jesus people that Q represents.[5] One became detached from the historic Jesus and centered on the myth of a dying and rising savior – the "Christ-cult" – while the other (the "people of Q") was more rooted in the Jesus of history and was originally concerned only with his teachings on a radically egalitarian way of life. And, since the sapiential and egalitarian views of "the people of Q" are seen as being earliest, the congregations Paul represents are viewed as being "a peculiar aberration."[6]

Paul's letters, then, while being the earliest extant documents we have, are not after all the best reliable guides to what the early church was like, according to Mack and Crossan. They only provide evidence for what a marginal cult fringe of the early church believed in Northern Syria, Asia Minor, and Greece.[7]

It should be clear that this position concerning Paul's letters and "Hellenistic Christianity" is no incidental addendum to the Cynic thesis.[8] Seeing Jesus as a Cynic sage largely depends on whatever case can be made for viewing the earliest extant evidence for Christianity as *non-representative* of earliest Christianity, for this initial evidence for Christianity certainly does *not* present Jesus as a Cynic sage.

The Cynic thesis, in other words, largely hangs upon Mack's and Crossan's ability to prove that Paul is *not representative* of what early followers of Jesus generally believed. And their ability to defend this thesis hangs entirely on their ability to provide a coherent and compelling account for how this supposedly "aberrant" Hellenistic movement departed so quickly, and so radically, from the original Jesus movement.

The argument of this chapter is that Mack and Crossan have not succeeded on either of these scores. Since Crossan has to date provided remarkably little in the way of detail about his views on how the Christ-cult developed (remarkable given how much of his thesis hangs on this point), our discussion in this chapter shall necessarily center around the arguments of Mack who has had a great deal to say about this matter. Our contention shall be that Mack's account is burdened with insurmountable problems and that the simplest reading of the available evidence suggests that Paul is in fact representative of early Christian faith. And this, we shall further argue, spells disaster for the Cynic-Jesus thesis.

THE HELLENISTIC CHRIST-CULT ABERRATION

The Beginnings of the Christ-Cult

According to Mack, the Christ-cult aberration resulted from Jesus people moving their "social experiment" out from Galilee and Judea into the more cosmopolitan and pagan environment of Antioch and Northern Syria. The radically multicultural and egalitarian emphasis of the group, centered around its open table fellowship, was attractive to diaspora Jews as well as to Gentiles. And the mixed fellowship that resulted from this provided a stimulating context in which Greek thought and mythology could be taken up and creatively fused with the ideals of the Jesus people.[9] The freedom of the Jesus people to engage in novel Hellenized mythmaking was also reenforced by their geographical separation from Judea, for this meant that their ties to Judaism were weakened.

The myth of Jesus that ultimately resulted from this mingling of ideas was that Jesus was a heavenly being, the "Son of God" and "Lord," who had "died for" the cause of the group and was vindicated by God raising him from the dead.[10] The central intent of the myth was not to explain the historical Jesus: the historical Jesus all but drops out of the picture in this mythmaking process, according to Mack.[11] Rather, in keeping with his general theory of religion (see chap. 4), Mack understands the central function of this myth as being the justification of the group's ethnically diverse composition. Like all myths, the Jesus myth is created in order to "rationalize a social formation already under way."[12]

Such a myth, argues Mack, was needed by the Hellenistic Jesus people. In their new social environment, the simple aphoristic teachings of Jesus could not carry the day. A myth of origins was needed to justify the open inclusion of Gentiles within a group that claimed to be the representation of Israel.[13] The social experiment thus needed a mythically imagined event to ground it. As Mack states it:

Separated from the synagogue, constituted by a [cultural] mix in
need of justification, Christians decided upon an event instead
of a teaching to say how things got started. The event was,
mythically imagined, the crucifixion and resurrection of Jesus
Christ . . . the Christ myth was born in the desire to justify a
novel experiment in social inclusiveness."[14]

The Literary Roots of the Christ Myth

This perhaps explains the motive for the myth making, but how are we
to account for the actual content of this surprising myth? According to
Mack, the origins of the myth are to be found in Greek myths of martyrdom and Hellenistic Jewish stories of God vindicating his righteous people.[15] From Greek stories of heroes dying a noble death "for the cause" of
their city, Hellenistic Jesus people derived the concept of Jesus "dying
for" the cause of their movement. Such a notion, according to Mack,
could have only arisen in a predominently Gentile environment since
"the idea of vicarious human sacrifice was anathema" within Jewish
culture.[16] And from Hellenistic Jewish stories of God reversing the fate of
righteous people who were threatened by death, or who had already
died, the Jesus people of Northern Syria and beyond created the story of
Jesus being vindicated by God by being raised from the dead. The two
motifs of martyrdom and vindication were already somewhat combined
in a Hellenistic Jewish environment in 4 Maccabees and the Wisdom of
Solomon, and thus "it would not be surprising to learn that the crucifixion of Jesus also could be understood by his followers in a similar way."[17]

This is not to undermine the unique way in which the Hellenistic
congregations applied these mythical motifs to their founder. The application had to be unique, for the questions the myth was designed to
answer were. Hence, whereas other martyrs died for existing social institutions, Jesus had to be imagined as dying for a new institution, and
doing so in such a way that its composite cultural nature was justified.
Hence, according to Mack, Jesus was imagined as having "died for sinners"—meaning, he died not only for Jews ("the righteous") but "for
Gentiles."[18] His death, according to this scheme, demonstrated his faith
(*pistis*)—his resolve to die for the cause of the new inclusive social experiment he began. And God honored this faith by vindicating his death
by raising him up from the dead and exalting him.[19]

This divine vindication, according to Mack, was further understood
as God's endorsement of the inclusive social program Jesus died for.
Jesus' death was understood to be a supreme manifestation of God's

righteousness, now redefined in terms of the new society's inclusive ethnic makeup.[20] And his resurrection demonstrated that this new society layed claim to being the true representation of Israel.[21] Hence, all those who shared Jesus' faith in the new inclusive society could lay claim to being made righteous, "justified."[22] For the Hellenistic Christians, then, "What made the Gentile (and the Jewish members) righteous was simply belonging to the society 'for' which Jesus had died."[23] All of Paul's language about "the righteousness of God apart from the law" and about "justification by faith" is to be understood along these lines. It taps into the myth of the vindicated martyr in order to rationalize the radical mix of the Hellenistic Jesus people.[24]

Such a development already set the Hellenistic Jesus people apart from their Jerusalem brothers and sisters. The people represented by the Q and GosThom, we have seen, had little knowledge of, and no special interest in, the death of their founder, according to Mack and Crossan. And they certainly entertained no concept of a resurrection. But the differences between the two groups was to intensify much further as the myth of the vindicated martyr played itself out in the largely pagan locale of Northern Syria, Asia Minor, and Greece.

A New Mystery Religion

Following quickly the myth of Jesus' vindication and exaltation was the further idea of Jesus as the rightful heir of God's kingdom for which he died.[25] The new society could thus now be imagined as "a realm over which Jesus as the Christ presently ruled."[26] The term "Christ," according to Mack, had been introduced by Jewish members "in the course of trying out ideas about Jesus as the sovereign ('king') of the 'kingdom' he had founded." And while the term originally simply meant "annointed," before long "the term became simply the name of the god of the cult," making Christ "the patron deity of a religious association."[27]

With this move, the movement that had originally begun as a movement *by* Jesus became a movement *about* Jesus. The Jesus movement, in a word, became a Christ-cult. It "turned a prophet-teacher into a divine soveriegn."[28] In this wild mixture of Jewish and Gentile mythologies, these congregations could then move on in the development of their mythology by reimagining Christ as the heavenly "Son of God" who had descended to earth and ascended back to heaven, and as the "Lord" not only of the cult congregations, but of the entire universe.[29] The end result was a "spirited cult formed on the model of the mystery religions" whose mythology was actually closer to Greek thought than Jewish thought.[30] Like the mystery cults, this one had its cultic god, its apotheosis of a hero, its entrance baptism, its rites of recognition (the holy kiss), and its ritualized meals (the Lord's Supper).[31]

And with each further step in its developing mythology, the Christ-cult moved further away from the Judean Jesus people and thus further away from the historical Jesus. "With such a dramatic mythology focused on the death and resurrection of Jesus as the Christ, the congregations of the Christ no longer needed to cultivate the memories of Jesus as a teacher."[32] Nor did they care to keep alive any memory of Jesus' historical activity.[33] Hence, in time, the view of Christ as the heavenly savior erased all historical recollection of Jesus the teacher.[34] Its mythology, though conceptualized as taking place within history, actually had nothing to do with history.[35] The " 'event' of the cross and resurrection was . . . placed in a thoroughly mythological once upon a time."[36] And it is for this reason, according to Mack, that we find no information about, or interest in, the historical Jesus in Paul.

What Has Athens to Do with Jerusalem?

The end result of the development of this mythological process is that the Jesus people in Northern Syria, Asia Minor, and Greece evolved into a wholly different religion from the movement that gave rise to them. Mack expresses this radical difference when he admits:

> With such a difference in social sensibilities and mythologies, one would hardly imagine that Jesus people and Christ people would ever be able to recognize one another, much less find a way to accomodate both types of social experimentation and mythology in a single configuration.[37]

Such is a brief overview of the case Mack presents of the development of Hellenistic Christianity. If it is judged persuasive, then we may have grounds for accepting his hypothetical reconstructed Q-community as providing us with a more trustworthy perspective on the faith and practice of the earliest Jesus people than we have with the letters of Paul. A number of considerations, however, lead us to judge his account to be altogether implausible. We will now explore these.

THE MYTH OF RADICAL DIVERSITY

Perhaps the first issue that needs to be addressed, since it is foundational to all the others, concerns the supposition that the early Jesus people of the diaspora developed a form of Christianity that was significantly different from—indeed, *unrecognizable* to—the Jesus people of Palestine. While the radical juxtapositioning of "Gentile" and "Jewish" Christian expressions had (for good reason) largely fallen into disfavor among scholars after the second world war, it is now regaining momentum in post-Bultmannian circles.[38] And the distinct form it takes in Mack's account is central to the overall plausibility of his thesis. Hence a brief critical word is in order.

Paul and the Jerusalem Community

The most telling and oft repeated criticism against this view is that it simply lacks any support in the available evidence.[39] Proponents of this view have always made much of the fact that Paul reflects some tension with the Jerusalem party in Galatians 2. With this tension in mind, other polemical references in Paul's letters can be interpreted as perhaps referring to associates of this group (e.g., 1 Cor. 1:12; 2 Cor. 5:16; 11:4; Gal. 6:3). But it is certainly going beyond, if not against, the known evidence to follow Baur's old Hegelian approach (see chaps. 1 and 6) and read into such references a polemic against a Jerusalem-based "Petrine" wing of Christianity.[40]

Mack (and Crossan) do not seem to give sufficient weight to Paul's own testimony about his essential theological agreement with the "pillars" of the Jerusalem community (Gal. 2:9). Indeed, Paul encourages the Thessalonians to follow the example of "God's churches in Judea" (1 Thes. 2:14)—hardly what one would expect if they were his opponents. And in Galatians 2:4 he speaks of these Judaizing "false brothers" in *distinction* from the Jerusalem apostles with whom he is in agreement in terms of "the truth of the gospel" (2:5, 7-9). First Corinthians 15:1-11, moreover, presupposes his essential agreement with the "pillars" of Jerusalem (concerning Jesus' resurrection). Nor does Mack give sufficient consideration to Paul's own stress on the unity of Christ's church, a unity that, as Stephen Neill has argued, Paul himself demonstrated by his concern for the *Jerusalem* churches![41] All of this is very difficult to square with any view that would posit a radical distinction between Paul's supposed "Hellenistic" Christianity and the Christianity of the Jerusalem-centered communities.

Where there were differences between Paul and certain "pillars," Paul makes no attempt to conceal them (Gal. 2:11-21). But these differences, as Hengel has noted, actually presuppose their essential agreement on foundational matters.[42] For example, for Paul to confront Peter on his inconsistency in living out the Gospel presupposes that they shared a common conviction about what the Gospel was and what it entailed. There is, one must note, virtually no indication that any points of doctrine were at stake in the discussion.[43]

Nor does Mack take seriously enough the possibility that the portrayal of Paul's close alignment with the Jerusalem church in Acts may not be a complete idealization.[44] It is not Antioch, but Jerusalem that centrally stands behind Paul's missionary activity in Acts – a view that is, interestingly enough, somewhat substantiated by Paul's own letters which betray an affiliation to Jerusalem but make little mention of Antioch, even (as in Rom. 15:19) where we might expect him to.[45] Moreover, as we shall argue subsequently (chap. 12), there are very good historical grounds for having some confidence in Luke's ability to relate generally reliable history.

Paul, Q, and GosThom

The only other evidence that can be appealed to in support of this view of a radical dichotomy between Paul and Jerusalem – and this has been what has fueled the modern revival of this old thesis – is the evidence of a "radically different" kind of Christianity from that of Paul in Q and GosThom. But as we have already argued (section 3), this line of reasoning is tenuous on a number of accounts. Among other things, the reconstruction, and certainly the stratification, of Q is highly speculative, and inferring the history of a religion from this stratification is more so. Further, basing these inferences largely on the *silence* of a hypothetical document is still more tenuous.[46] And, finally, there is no plausible way of dating the traditions in Thomas contemporary with, let alone prior to, Paul. The very best that can be said about this whole approach, then, is that it has not yet provided sufficient grounds for overturning all the evidence from Paul and Acts that, despite their diversity, the early Christians were relatively unified in their views of Jesus.

INHERENT PLAUSIBILITY

Do People "Decide Upon" Foundational Myths?

A second criticism which needs to be raised against Mack's account is that it simply seems inherently implausible. In a word, it is difficult to picture the earliest Jewish and Gentile Christians of the Hellenistic world engaging in the kind of self-conscious mythmaking behavior Mack's theory requires. It is hard to imagine them, or really any group of people, simply constructing stories from preexisting mythological material, without any concern for historical truth, in order to justify their new social program. It is even harder to imagine them accomplishing all of this in the incredibly short span of time they are said to have performed it in. Still harder is it to picture this when these people originated in a Jewish context where strong cultural tendencies existed *against* this sort of activity (recall chap. 5). And, most decisively, it is virtually impossible to imagine them doing this in relation to a Jewish man who had lived no more than two decades earlier — about whom many living eyewitnesses would presumably have something to say!

N.T. Wright speaks to this problem in relation to Bultmann's views of the Gospels as myth when he writes:

> Myths of the basic kind Bultmann envisaged (quasi-folk tales, articulating the worldview of a people) characteristically take a long time to develop. . . . But the first generation of Christianity is simply too short to allow for such a process. . . . The hypothesis about the early church necessary to support the idea that the first Christians told "foundational myths" to legitimate their faith and life is far too complex to be credible.[47]

People do not simply "decide upon" foundational myths. They do not generally embark, in any kind of self-conscious way, on "constructing a symbolic world in which to live."[48] And they certainly do not succeed in doing this, at the level of a foundational worldview, in ten to twenty years — especially when this supposed foundational myth is centered on a person who lived ten to twenty years before![49] This is simply not how foundational myths are generally formed within religious communities. They evolve naturally, and mostly unconsciously, over decades and centuries. They are not intentionally composed about a figure in the recent past to self-consciously justify a particular way of life. The history of religion is replete with foundational myths constructed by religious communities, but there is no genuine parallel to what Mack is proposing here with regard to how Hellenistic Christianity's view of Christ, and of themselves, came into being.[50]

When we add to this the fact that these congregations were headed up by, and largely composed of, first-century Jews who possessed a strong monotheistic-covenantal worldview that was not amenable to a-historical mythological thought (chap. 5), the credibility of the Cynic-thesis account of Hellenistic Christianity is weakened still further. First-century Jews, as well as first-century Gentiles, knew very well the difference between fact and fable.[51] And in the case of the early Christians, we have every reason to suspect that they would be intensely interested in distinguishing between the two as it pertained to the person on whom they were now basing their life, Jesus Christ.[52]

A Presumptuous Assumption

Relatedly, it must be observed that there is virtually no independent evidence that the "Christ-myth" of the Hellenistic Christians functioned in the rationalizing way Mack portrays it as functioning. While their belief in Christ as the Lord and Savior of both Jews and Gentiles certainly had far-reaching implications for their mixed fellowship, and while an interest in Jewish-Gentile relationships was certainly central to Paul's thinking, only a naturalistic assumption and reductionistic methodology could lead us, as it led Mack, to the conclusion that this mixed fellowship *created* their belief in Christ as Lord and Savior as a way of justifying itself.

To significantly understate the case, this is putting the cart before the horse. Mack *starts* with the assumption that all early Christian literature is to be "viewed as evidence for the investments early Christians made in their new social formations and their rationalizations." He *starts* with the presupposition that the whole of the New Testament, including Paul's letters, form a "literary residue of extremely thoughtful and calculated reflection upon the grounds and purposes of new social formations," and that the differing views of Jesus arrived at are "the result of various attempts to give an account of new social identities."[53] With such starting points, of course, the whole of Paul's thought can *only* be read as one major rationalization.[54] But what, one must ask, justifies such a starting point?

Clearly neither Paul nor the Hellenistic Christians understood themselves to be doing what Mack assumes they were doing. If anything is clear from Paul's writings, it is that he and his audience held deep convictions about the story of Christ they were basing their lives on. *They believed it was true.* Now, one can certainly argue that they were wrong and that their story was in fact made up. But we need to seriously question whether anyone 2,000 years removed from the situation is in a position to assume that their fundamental motivation for believing their story in the first place was not what *they* thought it was. Such an approach does not constitute a reasonable historical treatment of the textual evidence. It rather constitutes a presumptuous, speculative, psychologizing of the evidence. The evidence is not here *explained* so much as it is *explained away.*

If we had independent compelling evidence that these early Christian communities were creating myths to justify their social program, that would, of course, be another matter. For in this event we would be *arriving at* a conclusion, not *working from* an assumption. But no such evidence is available. And the fact that what Paul and his audience believe may not fit into the naturalistic worldview of the historian examining Paul's letters cannot itself justify the presumption of telling the apostle and his audience what they were "really" doing.

Hence, Mack's account must be judged as being circular as well as inherently implausible. Its conclusions are thoroughly rooted in an unwarranted assumption and misguided methodology.

THE JERUSALEM CENTER

Closely related to this last point is a third problem with Mack's depiction of Hellenistic Christianity. The supposition that the Jewish missionaries who first carried the Gospel to Northern Syria would have, or could have, severed their ties to the Jerusalem community as thoroughly, and as quickly, as Mack's view requires is highly questionable. *Prima facie*, one would expect close ties between the Jerusalem church and this new missionary endeavor, especially in light of the fact that the original apostolic witnesses were located in Jerusalem. And, in fact, all the evidence we have suggests that this is precisely what took place.[55]

From Paul's letters, Acts, and the other New Testament epistles as well, we get the picture of an early movement composed of multitudes of congregations that were very much in communication with each other. There was a good deal of traveling around and networking.[56] Hence, for example, 1 Corinthians 9:5 assumes that the leaders in Jerusalem traveled around, a view confirmed in an incidental way by Galatians 2:9-11 which speaks of Peter's visit to Antioch. Relatedly, 1 Corinthians 1:12 implies familiarity with Peter on the part of the Corinthian communities. And Acts depicts Peter as traveling far and wide in Christian circles. He and John travel to Samaria to confirm Philip's evangelism there (8:14-25). He later visits Christian groups in Lydda and Joppa (9:32-43), and preaches the Gospel in Caesarea to Cornelius (10:24-48).[57]

The great New Testament historian Stephen Neill sums up the matter well when he writes:

If we take the picture given us by every single source on which we depend for our knowledge of early Christianity, even allowing fully for every variety of detail in the presentation, it is as different as possible from the imaginary picture given us by Bultmann and his disciples. Here are no isolated groups, forging their own theology in independence of what other Christians elsewhere might be thinking or doing. The picture is one of constant coming and going.

And, quite significantly, he adds, "But always in the background is the mother church at Jerusalem."[58]

The postulation of a radical break between the two forms of Christianity is thus difficult to accept. But even more difficult is the supposed extent and speed with which these missionary congregations of the Diaspora are supposed to have been transformed by Greek mythology. It, of course, cannot be denied that some significant transformation took place as the original Gospel was contextualized in these new missionary environments. Their language, thought forms, and worship clearly set them apart from their Jerusalem counterparts, as most scholars recognize.[59]

But it must again be remembered, as even Mack admits, that the leaders of these new congregations were *Jewish* believers who had recently come up from Palestine. This has to put a *significant* check on how much alteration of content we suppose to have taken place in these congregations. Paul himself was an orthodox Jew, a Pharisee of Pharisees (Phil. 3:5; 2 Cor. 11:22), a fact that has to be given due consideration. He certainly would not have been eager to assimilate pagan ideas.[60] Nor do we have any reason to suppose that the paganism of his missionary field would have softened him on this point. Indeed, judging from the way Hellenism often intensified (rather than compromised) the convictions of many of his fellow Jews (recall chap. 6), we should be more readily inclined to suppose that the heathen environment of Paul's missionary activity would have had the *opposite* effect on him.

Hence, the suggestion that these congregations, under this sort of Jewish leadership, broke their ties with Jerusalem, evolved into an unrecognizably new and largely pagan religion, developed a radically new, a-historical, "divinized" view of Jesus as well as a whole new societal self-understanding largely modeled after mystery religions, seems most unlikely. Indeed, the suggestion stretches historical credibility to the breaking point.

When it is, again, further suggested that this all took place within twenty years after Jesus' death – at the outside! – we have moved beyond what historical credibility allows.[61] Mack himself calls it "astounding,"[62] but he nevertheless postulates it in order to preserve his normative view of Q. A more reasonable approach, however, would rather consider the presence of a Jewish leadership, the shortage of time, combined with the complete lack of supporting evidence, to be fatal to the theory, and would thus suggest rethinking what the hypothetical Q implies in the light of Paul instead of the other way around.

THE PROBLEM OF CHRISTOLOGICAL DEVELOPMENT

Twenty years is not enough time to account for the development of a "Christ-myth" among the Hellenistic Christians. But, as it turns out, we do not even have anything close to twenty years with which to work. For it is beyond dispute that a good bit of material contained in Paul's letters can be identified as pre-Pauline, and much of this material constitutes precisely what is supposed to have resulted at the *end* of the mythological development within the Hellenistic congregations, according to Mack. This brings us to our fourth criticism of Mack's thesis: namely, the problem of rendering Paul's christology coherent within his history-of-religions framework when much of Paul's christology is pre-Pauline.

Pre-Pauline Christological Material

The confession of Jesus Christ as Lord (1 Cor. 12:3; Rom. 10:9; Phil. 2:11) certainly predates Paul and in all probability goes back to the Jerusalem community, as the Aramaic prayer of 1 Corinthians 16:22 certainly suggests.[63] The hymn of Philippians 2 which constitutes one of Paul's strongest statements of Christ's divinity is undoubtedly mostly pre-Pauline, as are such creedal statements of Romans 1:3-4 and 1 Corinthians 8:6.[64] And, of course, we have the traditional statements about the Lord's Supper and his resurrection in which Paul is self-consciously passing on material he had received (1 Cor. 11:23-26; 15:3-8), the first involving information about Christ's vicarious death, the second his resurrection. The traditional liturgical nature of this material pushes back the time allowed for mythological development, and thus further damages the theory that significant mythological development took place at all.[65]

Related to this is the observation that Paul everywhere assumes in place many of those features of the society Mack must say evolved over time. So, for example, Paul simply mentions in passing that the Corinthians, like all believers, call upon the name of the Lord Jesus Christ (1 Cor. 1:2). Worshiping Christ and praying to him is obviously a firmly established practice in these congregations. Paul himself – a former Pharisee! – invokes Christ in the same breath as he prays to God the Father (1 Thes. 3:12-13; 2 Thes. 2:16-17; cf. 2 Cor. 12:7-10). Whenever this surprising practice began, it obviously didn't begin with Paul, or any time shortly before Paul. So too, there is not a hint of novelty in the way Paul refers to Jesus as preexisting, as the "Son of God," the "Savior," and, in all probability, even as "God" (Titus 2:13; Rom. 9:5).[66] Whatever else we say about Paul on these matters, it is clear that he was not espousing new ideas.[67] "[H]e treats his doctrine of Christ as though it were firmly established and required no defense."[68]

The Impossible "Jump" from Sage to "Lord"

Mack tries to construct a plausible scheme in which these Hellenistic communities, under the influence of pagan ideas, evolved from talking about Jesus as "the Christ" (the anointed one) to talking about him as "Son of God" and "Lord" because "[t]he jump from Jesus the sage to Jesus the Lord is simply too great to have been taken all at once."[69] And he admits that accounting for how this "surprising phenomenon" happened is "one of the most difficult challenges confronting the historian."[70]

I certainly agree that, on naturalistic presuppositions, the jump from Cynic sage to Son of God is too great to have taken place all at once. But the evidence, I would add, also rules out the possibility that the "jump" from one to the other occurred over *any* significant period of time. The task is not just "difficult": it is impossible.[71]

The only reliable information we have about the Hellenistic communities before Paul is found in the pre-Pauline material of his epistles (and Acts, if we allow it), and we find here that "the jump" had already been taken![72] This is indeed "surprising," and "astounding," but the evidence requires us to admit that it was substantially *there all along*. The evidence suggests that it is not a supposed "jump" from sage to Son of God that is astounding and difficult to explain: it is, rather, the historical Jesus who is from the start the catalyst behind the whole movement! In truth, the question is not, "What must the Hellenistic communities have been like to evolve this view of Jesus?" but "What must the historical Jesus have been like to have created these sorts of communities?"

How Pagan Was "Gentile" Christianity?

We have thus far argued that it is difficult to suppose the Hellenistic Christianity would have, or could have, significantly evolved in a pagan direction away from the views of the original Jerusalem community. However, we might be moved to overturn all of this and accept this difficulty if persuasive evidence existed that the Hellenistic congregations did in fact assimilate significant doses of Hellenistic mythology. If, for example, significant parallels existed between the Hellenistic communities as known from the letters of Paul and ancient Greco-Roman mystery religions, we might be more inclined to follow Mack, in spite of the above mentioned difficulties, and hold that the Hellenistic communities were significantly modeled after these mystery cults.

Our fifth criticism of Mack's portrayal of Hellenistic Christianity, however, is that no such evidence exists. We shall first consider Mack's argument that the significance which the Hellenistic congregations found in Christ's death and resurrection was created out of preexistent Hellenistic sources and then examine his attempt to draw historical links between these congregations and ancient mystery religions.

Jesus' Death and Hellenistic Martyr Stories

It can hardly be denied that there are certain linguistic parallels between Paul's talk about Jesus' sacrificial death and the martyr motif found in certain Greek stories, as well as between his talk of Christ's resurrection as divine vindication and the motif of "righteousness vindicated" found in Hellenistic Jewish literature. This much has been established.[73] But it is not clear how much is to be made of this. At the very least, it would seem that we are wringing too much out of these parallels if we draw the conclusion that the *origin* of Hellenistic Christian communities' view of Jesus' death and resurrection is to be found here. Showing parallels and proving origin are simply two very different matters. We have evidence of the former, but none for the latter.[74]

It is not even clear whether or not these parallels demonstrate that Paul's talk about Jesus "dying for sinners" is directly dependent on any prior sources. His language parallels these sources to be sure, but the issue is whether it does so to any extent greater than would be expected given the fact that he is expressing *a similar concept*. In other words, if Paul wants to express his belief that Jesus "died for" people, he is naturally going to express it in contemporary relevant terms that are similar to any talk of someone "dying for" a cause. So too with his talk of Jesus being divinely vindicated. It should not be surprising if it parallels other contemporary religious talk about righteous people being vindicated, especially by God after death.

Finally, it is uncertain whether Mack is correct even in locating the thought world of Greco-Roman mythology as the primary background for understanding Paul's concept of Jesus' sacrificial death. Paul was, after all, an orthodox Jew, as were the leaders of the Hellenistic congregations. Hence, the influence of the Old Testament on their thinking and language must not be minimized. Both of the themes of sacrificial death and divine vindication can be found – with strongly Messianic overtones – in Isaiah and throughout the Psalms (and perhaps other passages of Scripture as well).[75]

Isaiah 53, for example, speaks of the righteous servant of Yahweh being "pierced for our transgressions" and "crushed for our iniquities" (v. 5). He bears the punishment of Israel to bring them peace and bears wounds to bring them healing (v. 6). Yahweh lays on him the iniquity of Israel and he is stricken for the transgressions of God's people (v. 8). He thus bears the sin of many and makes intercession for the transgressors (v. 12). Hence his death becomes "a guilt offering" (v. 10). Nevertheless, Yahweh vindicates him. Yahweh will "see his offspring and prolong his days" and "the will of the Lord will prosper in his hand" (v. 10). The righteous servant will see the effect of his suffering and be satisfied as many will be justified because of him (v. 11). And the Lord will "give him a portion among the great, and he will divide the spoils with the strong, because he poured out his life unto death, and was numbered with the transgressors" (v. 12).

In the light of passages such as these, Mack's attempt to explain the origin of Paul's notion of Jesus' sacrificial death by appealing to Greco-Roman martyr myths seems to be both unnecessary and implausible. While the way Paul expresses himself is undoubtedly and understandably influenced by the missionary context he is speaking in, the *substance* of his concept of Jesus' vicarious death certainly need not be read as evidence for his indebtedness to Hellenistic mythology.

Hellenistic Christianity and Mystery Religions

Even more tenuous, however, is Mack's conjecture that the Hellenistic congregations were modeled after Greco-Roman mystery religions. As we saw in chapters 1 and 3, the practice of explaining the origins of certain beliefs and practices in Hellenistic Christianity by showing (or creating) parallels between it and the mystery religions had its heyday early in this century in the history of religions school. The general consensus of New Testament scholarship for the last fifty years, however, has been that the whole endeavor was pretty much misguided. It is only within certain segments of the post-Bultmannian camp that it is now enjoying a (hopefully brief) new lease on life. Beyond the general comments offered earlier, two more specific critical words are in order here, given the central place Mack gives to this post-Bultmannian perspective.[76]

First, all of the material on which we base our knowledge of the mystery religions comes after the first century, most of it coming in the third and fourth centuries. This does not, of course, mean that there were no mystery cults in the first century (there undoubtedly were), but it does render any attempt to draw a historical line of influence from the mystery religions to early Christianity extremely tenuous. Given the eclectic nature of the mystery religions and the relatively non-eclectic nature of Jewish thought, any supposed lines of influence should probably be seen as running in the opposite direction. The observation that in many instances there had been a Christian presence for some time in the locales where we find evidence for the mystery religions reinforces this probability.[77]

Secondly, the supposed "parallels" this comparative religion approach bases itself on are simply not impressive. Indeed, even in its heyday many scholars argued that such parallels were largely contrived.[78] It is true, for example, that many mystery religions seemed to center on the myth of a dying and rising god-figure. But, as has been generally recognized, this bears little if any resemblance to the early Christian view of Jesus' resurrection. Jesus' death is located in (very recent) history: the mystery religions speak of a "once upon a time." Jesus' death and resurrection occurred once, and was "for sin": the resuscitated figures in the mystery religions die annually and are usually connected with vegetation and fertility concerns. And Jesus is viewed as dying voluntarily, and his death is triumphant: the resuscitated gods of the mystery cults die involuntarily as a temporary defeat and rise only to a temporary resuscitation. The parallels are simply weak, if they can legitimately be called "parallels" at all.[79]

Similar things could and have been said about the parallels posited between the mystery religions and the early Christian views of salvation, communion, and baptism. Almost all religions have some sort of concept of salvation, but one need only appeal to the almost universal human sense of being dissatisfied with physical life alone to explain this. Moreover, the mystery religions tended to locate salvation in an ecstatic experience, a notion quite foreign to the New Testament. And, finally, the evidence for mystery religions speaking about "rebirth" in a way that is arguably close to the New Testament is meager (three instances in all) and very late (fourth century).

The supposed parallels between the "ritual meals" and "ceremonial washings" of the mystery religions and communion and baptism within Hellenistic Christianity—something Mack alludes to[80]—are hardly more persuasive.[81] It is simply asking too much to see any significant commonality or posit any historical causal link between the Dionysian cult's practice of eating the raw flesh and drinking the blood of a dismembered animal in the context of a drunken orgy and the early Christian practice of communion. It is no less of a stretch to posit any commonality or historical line of influence between the Mithraic practice of "baptizing" an advanced cult initiate in the blood of a bull and the early Christian practice of baptizing new converts in water as an expression of their identity in Christ (Rom. 6:1-4). Since Paul was Jewish, and writing in the first century, a far more plausible supposition is that Paul's practice of baptism had Jewish proselyte baptism as its historical antecedent.

For good reason, then, New Testament scholarship in the latter part of this century closed the door on this line of research. Unless Mack has some new evidence or new line of argumentation to offer, we see no need to reopen it.

How Jewish Was Gentile Christianity?

We have thus far seen that the concrete evidence for a substantial pagan influence on so-called "Gentile Christianity" is minimal at best. Conversely, there are a number of indications from Paul's epistles that these Hellenistic congregations retained much of the Jewish heritage of the original Jesus movement in Jerusalem. Whereas Mack overemphasizes what he sees as evidence of a Greco-Roman influence on these congregations, he seems to minimize these strongly Jewish aspects of Paul's letters. And this is our sixth criticism against his portrayal of "the Christ-cult" as a Hellenistic aberration of the early Jesus movement. His thesis is weakened to the extent that it can be shown that the Christian congregations receiving Paul's letters remained within the Jewish thought world of the original Jesus movement.

The Jewishness of Paul

We have already demonstrated (chap. 7) that the Jewish *religious worldview* was largely resistant to any external influences that could serve to undermine its central conceptual pillars. This is particularly clear in the case of Paul.[82]

The most noteworthy feature of Paul's letters that indicates the retention of a thoroughly Jewish worldview amidst the "Gentile" congregations he is writing to is the manner in which he everywhere *presupposes* the story of Israel as the backdrop against which the story of Jesus and the church are to be understood.[83] His working assumption is that "the God and Father of our Lord Jesus Christ" is one and the same as "the God of Israel." He thus understands his own calling along the lines of the Israelite prophetic tradition (Gal. 1:15; cf. Jer. 1:5; Isa. 49:1) and views the calling of the church as a continuation of Israel's call (e.g., Rom. 4:13-16; Gal. 3:16-19, 29), even to the point of calling the church "the Israel of God" (Gal. 6:16).

Moreover, Paul's way of understanding the significance of Jesus and the Spirit is within the distinctly Jewish categories of how the one true God acts within history. All of Paul's talk about Jesus as the Christ and the Holy Spirit only makes sense in the context of Israel's distinctive language about the Creator being active within his creation (paralleling, for example, Jewish talk about the Torah, God's Wisdom, Israel, and the Shekinah).[84] Seen in this context, his concept of Jesus' messiahship (the Christ) is world's removed from any concept of "a patron deity of a religious association," as Mack contends.[85]

Similarly, Paul's understanding of the nature and organization of the church is very much in keeping with Jewish reflection on the synagogue. With few exceptions, the issues he wrestles with, the questions he asks, and the solutions he proposes throughout his corpus only make sense in the context of Israel's story. And, quite remarkably, given the Gentile milieu he is writing in, throughout his letters Paul assumes the divine authority of the Old Testament and presupposes a good deal of familiarity on the part of his readers with this authority!

It may thus be concluded, as N.T. Wright has argued, that the entirety of Paul's thought "only makes sense if it is still seen . . . as Jewish theology. It is emphatically not a variant on paganism."[86]

On Romans 9–11

All of this is clearly seen, to cite one noteworthy example, in Paul's discussion of Israel's relationship to God and to the church in Romans 9–11. The congregation(s) of Rome appears to have been composed mostly of Gentiles, perhaps more so than any other congregation Paul addresses, as signified (among other things) by his reference to "you Gentiles" (Rom. 11:13). Yet his discussion here is as thoroughly Jewish as any writing in the first century could be. The entire treatise is carried out in conversation with the Old Testament, and the familiarity he presupposes with this Scripture on the part of his readers is hardly less than what one might expect were he writing to a synagogue.

Paul presupposes, as already in place, a familiarity with, and acceptance of, the Jewish view of God's singularity, sovereignty, character, election, covenant, and salvation plan, as well as a thorough acquaintance with significant portions of the Old Testament narrative. The new pieces Paul adds to the Jewish story (e.g., about the Gentiles being "grafted in" to move the Jews to jealousy; Rom. 11:11-24) only make sense in the overall context of these already established pieces. This is hardly what one would expect if Paul's readers were defining themselves as participants in a new religious association along the lines of a mystery religion with Christ as their new cult god.

Now it is, of course, possible, and probably even likely, that Paul was "shooting over the heads" of some of his readers throughout much of his argument (cf. 2 Peter 3:15-16). But this in no way weakens the point that the overall context of Paul's thought, in Romans 9–11 and elsewhere, is thoroughly Jewish, and that he presupposes a thoroughly Jewish belief system on the part of his "Gentile" readers. He is, for all intents and purposes, treating them the way a rabbi might be expected to treat Gentile proselytes to the synagogue. And this observation has monumental repercussions for our understanding of "Gentile" Christianity.

It means, at the very least, that any view that characterizes early Christianity as being radically split between Jewish and Gentile cultural factions has to be ruled out. Indeed, it means, as Hengel argues, that the very notion of a "Gentile Christian" community, distinct from "Jewish Christianity," must be judged as being a "fabrication" and "incredible fiction."[87] There was no "Gentile Christianity" that was not in its outlook more Jewish than "Gentile." While we should not minimize the cultural differences between the Jesus movement in Jerusalem and Judea and those in Northern Syria, Asia Minor, and Greece, it must also be insisted that the church, in *all* its cultural manifestations, appeared "under the shade of the Synagogue."[88] This is as true of Paul's Hellenistic communities as it is of Matthew's – or James' – communities. And it was this shared worldview – the story of Israel reaching its climax in the story of Jesus – that constituted the unity of the church amidst all of its diversity. As Wright says concerning the diverse expression of the Christian faith in the first century:

> Their diversities were diverse ways of construing that basic point: their disputes were carried on not so much by appeal to

fixed principles . . . but precisely by fresh retellings of the story which highlighted the points at issue. . . . Right across the spectrum of fixed points within the first Christian century, the early church lived and breathed within a symbolic universe which was . . . emphatically Jewish rather than pagan. . . . The lens through which the Christians viewed the whole of reality was a recognizable variation on the Jewish worldview.[89]

The recognition of the shared christocentric Jewish vision between Paul's Hellenistic congregations and the original Jesus movement of Jerusalem accounts for how it is that the church could enter the second century, having grown and spread with breathtaking speed across the Roman world, without having dissipated into a myriad of differing sects with little family resemblance between them. This is something of a mystery on Mack's and Crossan's accounts, as it is on all accounts that postulate an original radical diversity.[90]

It should also be said that this shared vision is what we should expect given the short span of time separating the Hellenistic congregations from the Jerusalem congregations. It is what we should expect given the authoritative presence of Jewish missionaries among these congregations. It is what we should expect given the busy missionary networking that occurred between these two culturally distinct congregations. And it is what we should expect given the relative absence of pagan elements within these communities and the dominant presence of foundational Jewish dimensions. But it most certainly is *not* what we should expect if Paul's congregations were patterned after the pagan mystery religions!

In short, the supposition of a shared christocentric variation on Israel's monotheistic-covenantal story has everything going for it as a historical explanation and nothing against it, whereas we must conclude pretty much the opposite for Mack's account.

9

IMAGINED IN THE MIND OR ROOTED IN HISTORY?
An Investigation Concerning Paul and the Historical Jesus

Thus far I have argued that we have no good grounds for following Mack and Crossan in regarding Paul as being nonrepresentative of what early Christians in general believed. Relatedly, we have also argued that we have no good grounds for regarding his view of Christ as being the result of a syncretistic mythmaking process carried out under the influence of pagan notions circulating in the environment in which he operated. One final important aspect of Mack and Crossan's treatment of Paul, however, has not yet been directly addressed, and this concerns their view that Paul and the Hellenistic Christians were solely concerned with "Christ as savior" at the expense of the "Jesus of history."[1]

To state the matter succinctly, according to Mack and Crossan, there is in the Pauline corpus next to nothing that could possibly contribute to our understanding of the historical Jesus. Even in 1 Corinthians 11 in which, they agree, it *looks* like Paul is passing on historical information, Mack and Crossan nevertheless conclude that "cult legend," not "historical reminiscence," is what is taking place.[2] Neither Paul nor the Hellenistic congregations he founded have any significant interest in, and thus any significant information about, the actual Jesus of history.

It should at the outset be noted that this view of Paul is by no means incidental to the Cynic thesis. To the contrary, the Cynic thesis absolutely requires it. Indeed, such a view is really required by *any* strictly naturalistic revisionist account of the historical Jesus. For it is exceedingly difficult to suppose that Paul and others in the Hellenistic communities had significant knowledge of the recently deceased Jesus (who was, per hypothesis, simply a man [e.g., a Cynic sage]) while also supposing that they nevertheless went on to depict him in such heavily "mythological" terms as Lord of all creation and Son of God.

Conversely, if it can be demonstrated that Paul (and perhaps others in the Hellenistic communities) did in fact possess a signficant body of knowledge concerning the historical Jesus, this would presumably count against the notion that this Jesus was, after all, merely a Cynic sage (or merely a Jewish rabbi, or whatever view the naturalistic account postulates). The historical cause (the naturalistic Jesus) would not be adequate for explaining the historical effect (the exalted views of Jesus among the Hellenistic communities).

In short, if the Hellenistic communities with their exalted views of Jesus were in any significant sense connected with the Jesus of history, then Mack and Crossan's reconstructed view of Jesus, carried out largely on the basis of what the hypothetical "community of Q" supposedly believed, must be judged as having a very low probability of being correct. It is the contention of this chapter that this connection can be demonstrated. We shall argue that we have good grounds for believing that the Hellenistic communities Paul wrote to, and Paul himself, possessed significant information about the historical Jesus. And thus, we have further grounds for supposing that the Cynic-Jesus thesis is incorrect.

Two Preliminary Observations

The Historical Kerygma

Before examining the evidence itself, however, two preliminary observations should first be made. First, given the chronological proximity of the Hellenistic congregations to the events surrounding the Jesus they are believing in, it seems counter-intuitive to assume that these believers would *not* have at least *some* interest in the historical Jesus. As Hengel has argued:

> Those to whom the earliest Christian missionaries preached were no less curious than we are today. Certainly, they too will have wanted more information about the man Jesus. In other words, it was only possible to describe the exalted Jesus by telling of the earthly Jesus, his work and his death.[3]

Indeed, it is difficult to understand how these early Hellenistic faithful could have become believers in the first place without a certain amount of historical information about Jesus. Unlike the mystery religions, the person these new converts were placing ultimate trust in was not some mysterious figure who appeared "somewhere, once upon a time." The concrete historical nature of the kerygma was arguably one of the appealing aspects of this new religion over and against the nebulous "gospel" of the mystery cults. The Savior of the early Christian kerygma was a person who lived in the recent past and in a very specific and not too remote region of the earth.[4] How these people could have embraced this faith without any information about (or interest in!) the historical Jesus is simply inexplicable — as is the question of how the earliest Hellenistic missionaries, such as Paul, could have themselves based their lives on this faith without such information. While these first-century people may not have had an Enlightenment critical approach to historical reports, they certainly were not altogether credulous, as I have previously argued. Nor were they like twentieth-century existentialist theologians who seem to have no problem separating their faith from history, as R.T. France has argued.[5] Hence, we have every reason to assume that the first converts to Christianity who put their ultimate trust in this Savior did so *because* they trusted some historical reports about him (not despite the fact that they had no historical reports about him).

When we add to this consideration the fact that Paul was a Jew whose whole Jewish belief system was centered on God's acts *in history* and that he was well-acquainted with the region Jesus ministered in (whether or not he actually knew Jesus during his lifetime), the notion that the Jesus Paul preached was divorced from actual history becomes even more improbable. This improbability is increased still further when we add to this the fact that the original leaders of the Hellenistic congregations were themselves mostly Jews who originated from the Jerusalem movement. And when we finally consider, once again, that the transformation from historical Cynic sage to mythological Son of God was supposed to have happened — among these Jewish leaders — within fifteen to twenty years at the outside, the improbability of these perspective becomes simply impossible.

The Purpose of an Epistle

A second preliminary observation is this: whatever case can be made for the presence of historical reminiscences in Paul's letter, it must be conceded at the outset that they are not at all dominant in Paul's expressed writings, and there is virtually nothing by way of any detailed references to the narrative history of Jesus. The question then is, what conclusions can be safely drawn from this? Does this entail, as Mack and many others have suggested, that Paul was unfamiliar with the stories about Jesus that were going to eventually make their way into the Gospels (or that such stories didn't yet exist)? Does it entail that historical references to Jesus were not part of the kerygma in "Gentile" missions?

Such a conclusion would certainly be supportive of the "aberrant" portrayal of Hellenistic Christianity, but a number of scholars, for a number of reasons, have argued that such a conclusion is quite unwarranted.[6] The most fundamental objection against this conclusion, and the only one we presently need to concern ourselves with, is the argument that an epistle, serving the purpose Paul had for it, is not the kind of document one should *expect* to find much historical narrative in. Since Paul's letters were not evangelistic—they are written to people already converted and already under the instruction of "elders"—we can't infer much about what historical content his missionary preaching did or did not include. Relatedly, since the purpose of Paul's epistles was to answer questions, correct problems, and to further doctrinal instruction, it seems unreasonable to expect that Paul would repeat at any length matters he (or some other evangelist) had already given them.[7]

We cannot, then, jump from an observed relative silence concerning the historical Jesus in Paul to the conclusion that he was largely ignorant and unconcerned about the historical Jesus. As we saw when discussing Q (chap. 5), one is methodologically on much safer ground when using positive evidence to discern what a person or community *did* believe than when using the absence of evidence to speculate about what a person or community *did not* believe.

Paul's Incidental Biographical Information on Jesus

So, adhering to this methodological principle, what can we say about what Paul and the Hellenistic congregations believed about the historical Jesus on the basis of his (not surprisingly) few references scattered throughout his epistles? For starters, Paul clearly knew that Jesus was born and raised as a Jew (Gal. 4:4) and that he was a descendant not only of Abraham but of David (Gal. 3:16; Rom. 1:3). Jesus' historical life, for Paul, modeled the kind of acceptance of other people his followers should aspire toward (Rom. 15:5, 7).

Paul was further informed that Jesus' life was characterized by service and humility (Phil. 2:5, 7-8) as well as meekness, gentleness, and self-sacrificial love (2 Cor. 10:1; Gal. 2:2). Paul himself sought to imitate Christ on these (and other?) matters and thus provide an example for others to follow (1 Cor. 11:1). Paul also knew that Jesus had a brother named James, who was still alive at the time of Paul's early writings, as well as other unnamed brothers (Gal. 1:19; 1 Cor. 9:5). And he was further aware that his disciple Peter was married (1 Cor. 9:5).

What is most significant about these scattered disclosures of Paul's knowledge of Jesus' life is that they are all completely incidental. Paul only states them in the interest of making a theological point, and "[i]t seems that, if another theological point were to be made, the author was capable of introducing further historical facts."[8] What is more, none of these allusions are given as new instruction. They are not given as instruction on historical matters at all! And, as such, they "presuppose that the readers know more."[9] The very fact that Paul appeals to Jesus' life as a model of Christian behavior requires such a supposition. These various references thus serve as pointers to a body of historical knowledge held by both Paul and his readers. We can confidently say no more about the actual content of this knowledge than what Paul alludes to. But given the incidental nature of his allusions, we *can* confidently say that his allusions do not exhaust its content.

The same inference can be drawn from the several references Paul makes to certain events in Jesus' life. Paul certainly knows and makes much of the fact that Jesus was executed by crucifixion (1 Cor. 1:17-18; Gal. 5:11; 6:12; Phil. 2:8; 3:18). He further knows of Jesus' historical betrayal (1 Cor. 11:23), that certain Jews in Judea were instrumental in getting him crucified (1 Thes. 2:14-15), and that he instituted a memorial meal on the night in which he was betrayed (1 Cor. 11:23-25). He is, finally, informed that Jesus was buried, that he rose again "on the third day," and that he was seen after his resurrection on a number of occasions by a number of witnesses whom Paul and his readers know by name (Rom. 4:24-25; 1 Cor. 15:4-8; cf. 1 Cor. 6:14; 2 Cor. 4:14; 6:4-9; 8:11, 34; Gal. 1:1; 1 Thes. 4:14).

What is again more impressive than the actual content of such passages (though the content is itself impressive, given its incidental nature) is the manner in which Paul assumed that his Hellenistic readers *already possessed* such information. This alone is enough to show that the view that Paul and the Hellenistic congregations "neither knew nor cared about Jesus as a figure in history" is mistaken.[10] One may perhaps wish to argue that the information they possessed was not accurate (but then must explain how it so quickly got distorted). But one cannot dispute the fact that they had some concern about the Jesus of history and at least *thought* they had some accurate knowledge about him.

The Shared Kerygma of Jewish and Gentile Christianity

One final dimension of Paul's awareness of the events of Jesus' life must be mentioned, and this concerns the way Paul's material correlates with other material we have on the historical Jesus, especially as related in the Gospels. Virtually everything Paul says about the historical Jesus confirms what we find about him in the Gospels. This must enhance our estimation of the reliability of both Paul and the Gospels, and it certainly is not what one would expect if Paul and the Hellenistic communities had for two decades been in the process of breaking away from the original Jesus people movement and forming their own aberrant Christ-cult. The historical core of what these Hellenistic Christians believed is, so far as we can know it, identical with the historical core of what other Christians, including the Christians in Judea, believed.

Even more significant, however, is the commonality which exists between the kerygmatic interpretation Paul gives to this historical core and the interpretation it receives in other Christian quarters. In a word, the kerygmatic formulations of Paul, based upon the historical core of information discernible in his letters, is almost identical to the central kerygma of the Gospels. As Richard Hays has demonstrated, there is a narrative substratum that is discernible within Paul's small kerygmatic formulations which looks remarkably like a mini-version of the narrative proclamation of the Gospels.[11] Passages such as Galatians 3:13-14, 4:3-6, Romans 3:24-26, 4:24-25, 5:6-10, 6:9-10, 8:3-4, and 10:3-4 and many others scattered throughout Paul's letters, provide an outline for the story of Jesus that is, in essence, the story told in the Gospels. As Wright argues:

> [A]t one fixed point in the early years of Christianity, the story which was being told has substantially the same shape as the story which we observed in Luke, Matthew and Mark. It is the Israel-story, fulfilled, subverted and transformed by the Jesus-story, and now subverting the world's stories. In its new form, it generates and sustains a symbolic universe, in which the writers of epistles and gospels alike understand themselves and their readers as living: the world in which this fulfilled Israel-drama is now moving towards its closure, its still unreached ending.[12]

It is, then, not just a discernible historical core of information that Paul has in common with other Christians of the time. He shares with them the radical kerygmatic interpretation of this information as well. He shares with them a thoroughly Jewish worldview that has been transformed by virtue of its christocentric center.

Such a commonality is virtually unthinkable if, in fact, Paul and the Hellenistic communities were anything like how Mack and Crossan portray them. As such, the presence of these common foundational elements must count against their thesis that the Hellenistic communities significantly strayed either from the original Jesus people or from the historical Jesus these people were formed around.

PAUL AND THE TEACHINGS OF JESUS

More problematic, however, is the relative absence of the tradition of Jesus as a teacher in Paul's epistles, for here we might at points reasonably expect Paul to reproduce Jesus' teaching. For example, one might have expected Paul to appeal to Jesus' teaching on what does and does not defile a person (Mark 7:14-23; cf. Matt. 15:10-20) when he addresses a similar issue in Romans 14. And one is puzzled as to why Jesus' teaching on such things as not repaying evil with evil, blessing those who persecute you, not judging others, and paying taxes, is not explicitly appealed to when Paul is seeking to make these same points (Rom. 12:14, 17; 14:13; 13:6; 1 Thes. 5:15). Does this entail that Paul and the Hellenistic congregations had no knowledge of the teachings of Jesus? And if this is so, how are we to square this with the fact, repeatedly emphasized by Mack and Crossan, that the teaching ministry of Jesus was centrally important to the Jesus people in Judea?[13]

Three things can be said about this. First, it should not surprise us if, in fact, Paul and the Hellenistic churches were unfamiliar with much of the teaching tradition of Jesus that became well-known *after* the publication of the Gospels. We are, after all, dealing with the very earliest stage of the Christian tradition, a stage in which the teachings of Jesus are in various forms yet being informally passed on in an oral or (perhaps) written form. And we have nothing more than guesses as to who knew what at any given time during this period. If we, in fact, conclude that Paul and the Hellenistic congregations knew little of the Jesus teaching tradition, this only need imply that the original missionary kerygma outside of Jerusalem centered more on the theological interpretation of Jesus' life, death, and resurrection than it did on the teachings of Jesus.

But, secondly, it may be that even this conclusion should not be arrived at too hastily. It may be that we are simply asking too much in expecting Paul to tell his readers he is citing a teaching of Jesus if the teaching is already well-known in the community, or if he is simply interested in conveying the content of the teaching and feels no need to buttress it with an appeal to Jesus' authority. The distinctive content of what Paul says may be enough to make it plausible (though never certain) that he is echoing a teaching of Jesus. To draw an analogy, James never explicitly cites Jesus as the originator of the tradition he is drawing on. Yet it is almost universally acknowledged that his epistle draws heavily on the tradition of Jesus' teaching, particularly on the material that comes to constitute Matthew's Sermon on the Mount.[14]

Hence it may be that we can after all discern a Jesus tradition behind a number of Paul's own teachings. When Paul tells the Romans to "bless those who persecute you" (Rom. 12:14), the cultural uniqueness of the teaching and its linguistic closeness to the Q saying of Matthew 5:44 and Luke 6:28 make it quite reasonable to suppose that we are dealing with a piece of the Jesus teaching tradition here. Similarly, it is nearly impossible to deny that Jesus' very distinctive use of "Abba" in prayer lies behind Paul's use of this Aramaic term in Galatians 4:6 and Romans 8:15.[15]

A similar case could be argued for Paul's teaching on not repaying evil for evil (Rom. 12:17), on giving tribute to whom it is due (13:6-7), on love fulfilling the law (13:8-10; Luke 10:25-28), on the Lord's returning "as a thief in the night" (1 Thes. 5:2-5; Luke 12:39-40), on not judging others (Rom. 14:4, 10; Matt. 7:1), and on eating what is set before you (1 Cor. 10:27; Luke 10:7). Such allusions certainly don't *prove* that Paul is tapping into a Jesus teaching tradition, but they do render such a supposition quite plausible, especially if (a) we have no other more convincing way of explaining the parallels, and (b) we have other grounds for supposing that Paul in fact knew and cared about a Jesus teaching tradition.[16]

EXPLICIT CITATIONS OF JESUS' TEACHING IN PAUL

We have thus far attempted to argue that there are good grounds for affirming that Paul was aware of, and made some use of, Jesus' teaching tradition. The fact that Paul and the other leaders of the Hellenistic communities were Jewish and hailed from Jerusalem suggests as much. The conservative nature of the Jewish milieu as it concerns the transmission of authoritative oral material, combined with the rather technical rabbinic language of *paradosis* (1 Cor. 11:2, 23; 15:1, 3; 1 Thes. 2:13; 4:1; 2 Thes. 2:15; 3:6), further suggests this.[17] And the commonalities shared by Paul and the Gospel authors as it concerns the framework for the kerygma suggests this as well.

But, we must now add, we also have several direct allusions to this tradition which, while they are not plentiful by any means, further suggest that Paul was in touch with some form of the Jesus teaching tradition. Thus, Paul makes explicit that he is passing on a received tradition when he quotes Jesus' words at the Last Supper (1 Cor. 11:23-26), words that ultimately find their way into all four Gospels in a form that is remarkably close to the way Paul gives them here.[18] He also makes a direct reference to Jesus' teaching on divorce and remarriage and distinguishes it from his own teaching in 1 Corinthians 7:10-11. He cites, as a command of the Lord, Jesus' teaching on the laborer deserving his wages (1 Cor. 9:14; Matt. 10:10; Luke 10:7; cf. 1 Tim. 5:18). And he is emphatic that it is "according to the Lord's own word" that the Lord shall return and receive believers, whether they are alive at the time or have already died (1 Thes. 4:15-17). Each of these passages warrants a brief comment.

The Lord's Supper

First Corinthians 11:23-26 is significant not only because of its self-consciously traditional structure, but because Paul incidentally lets us in on the fact that he is reminding the Corinthians of something they *already* knew (v. 23). Had the Corinthians not been misbehaving so badly at communion (1 Cor. 11:20-22) we never would have known this. This is yet another caution for all who would want to draw unwarranted conclusions from silence. The impression we get is that, did other circumstances require it, Paul could have given other instruction from the Lord as well.

Also significant in this passage is the way in which it informs us that, at the earliest stage in Christian development, the meal around which Christians gathered was not, as Crossan and Mack so strongly insist, simply a meal celebrating "open commensality."[19] From the very start, even *before* the time of Paul's writing (as Crossan acknowledges), the "ritual meal" of the Christian community was centered on the death of Jesus Christ.[20] Crossan and Mack attempt to make much of the fact that the Didache does not mention the bread and wine as the body and blood of Christ or connect it with a supposed "last supper" (which they take to be a later legendary development).[21] But aside from the fact that they are making far too much of what the Didache does *not* say (the argument from silence again), the traditional nature of 1 Corinthians 11 simply pulls the rug out from any scheme that would try to postulate any "line of development" from an informal meal of open commensality to a legendary meal celebrating Jesus' sacrifice. The fact that the Didache is to be dated at the end of the first century at the earliest simply makes such a conjecture all the more untenable.[22]

Support for Missionaries

First Corinthians 9:14 is noteworthy not only for its incidental nature, but because Paul's "quote" from the Lord is so loose that, had he not told us he is citing the Lord's teaching, it is unlikely we would ever have guessed it.[23] First Corinthians 9:14 certainly bears far *less* resemblance to any teaching of Jesus we know on the subject than do most of the earlier cited parallels where Paul *doesn't* tell us he is drawing from a teaching tradition. This opens up the possibility that there may be a number of passages in Paul that draw on some version of the Jesus teaching tradition, but their source is not acknowledged or the reference is too loose (or the tradition he is in touch with is too different from the Gospel traditions) for us to discern them. The point, again, is that we must be extremely cautious about drawing conclusions about what Paul did *not* know from what we *think* is Paul's silence. We may even be wrong about his being silent![24]

The Return of the Lord

Finally, 1 Thessalonians 4:15-17 is noteworthy chiefly because it doesn't seem to reflect any teaching of Jesus we know of through the Gospels. This may mean, as Jeremias has quite persuasively argued, that Paul is tapping into an independent and authentic piece of the Jesus teaching tradition that didn't make its way into the Gospel.[25] Or, it may mean that Paul is referring to a prophetic word from the Lord, not to the teaching of the historical Jesus. Or, finally, this may be another instance of Paul loosely citing a teaching of the Lord which became part of the Gospel tradition. It might be significant that Paul here says, "According to the Lord's own word, *we* tell you . . ." implying, perhaps, that Paul is here giving more of an interpretation and application of something Jesus taught than he is a direct quotation.[26]

Hence, it may be possible that behind this passage lies some form of Jesus' eschatological teaching from which Paul is deriving his relatively new teaching.

In any event, the important point to note is that, though Paul was primarily concerned with the soteriological significance of Jesus' death and resurrection and the implications this had for the believer's life, he does reflect significant biographical information about the historical

Jesus and some awareness of his teachings. Even more importantly, the incidental way he reflects this material makes it difficult to resist the conclusion that both he and the Hellenistic communities possessed more information on these matters then he disclosed in his occasional epistles. And this, finally, is just what we would expect since Paul and the other leaders of these congregations were people who possessed a first-century Jewish belief system centered around the conviction that God acts *in history*.

This, again, renders the view that the Hellenistic communities veered off in an a-historical mythological direction and became an aberrant Christ-cult unrecognizable to the original Jerusalem Jesus people a most unlikely occurrence.

CONCLUSION:
PAUL AND THE QUESTION OF THE CHRISTIAN FAITH

In the light of the considerations of this and the previous chapter, we conclude that Mack and Crossan's portrayal of "Gentile Christianity" as an aberration of the earliest Jesus movement is quite unfounded. While earliest Christianity was obviously divaricated, there is no evidence that this plurality concerned the foundational picture of Jesus as the one through whom God completes the story of Israel. The retention of a Jerusalem center as well as the presence of Jewish leadership and missionaries in the Hellenistic congregations insured this much continuity.

Nor is there any compelling reason to accept Mack's inherently implausible notion that the Hellenistic communities created myths to justify their social program and modeled themselves after the mystery religions. The evidence of a high christology within the pre-Pauline material, the absence of any significant demonstrable parallels with the contemporary pagan culture, and the strong pervasive presence of a presupposed Jewish belief system renders such a contention all the more implausible.

And finally, as we have just seen, the evidence of a substratum of historical information about Jesus and his teachings in Paul and the Hellenistic communities is further evidence that these congregations were no cultic aberration of the original Jesus movement. Their faith was not divorced from history. They were causally connected to the same historical Jesus that the original Jerusalem Jesus people were.

Hence, we have every reason to believe that the faith in Christ reflected in these earliest extant documents of the Christian faith is more or less representative of what the earliest Christians believed. And, to say the least, what we find here is that they certainly did *not* believe that Jesus was a Cynic sage. They rather believed that he was the divine Son of God, the Lord of all creation, the Savior of all who believe, and one who is deserving of prayer and worship.

And this leaves us with some rather awkward historical questions: How are we to account for such an extravagant mythology (if we regard it as such) in light of the fact that these believers were yet closely connected to the historical Jesus in their very recent past? And what must the historical Jesus have been like to almost immediately evoke this sort of radical and unexpected response from orthodox Jews and Gentiles alike? If this incredible faith is seen as the historical *effect*, what must the *cause* have been like? Or perhaps we should ask, *Who* must the cause have been like?[27]

The Gospels provide us with a ready answer, but it is not an answer most naturalistically inclined Westerners, and certainly most Western trained academic historians, want to accept. Here we find several pictures painted of a person whose life, teachings, claims, authority, deeds, death, and most decisively, resurrection and transformation from the dead, give a sufficient historical explanation to the unprecedented response we find to him presupposed throughout Paul's letters. If Jesus was like *that*, then we can perhaps understand why the earliest Christians were like *this* (viz., as we find them through Paul's letters). Indeed, one is almost tempted to argue in the other direction: unless Jesus was something like *that*, we can't possibly understand why the earliest Christians were like *this*.

In any event, the Gospels present us with several remarkable portraits of a historical person who, if these reports are understood to be more or less rooted in history, sufficiently accounts for the faith we find throughout Paul's letters. So the crucial question now becomes, are these portraits rooted in history? Or are Mack and Crossan correct in seeing them as mostly nonhistorical fabrications of creative, mythologically inclined, second and third generation Jesus people? It is with this all-important question that we shall concern ourselves in the next section of this work.

Mark and
the Historical Jesus

10

CREATIVE FABRICATION OR RELIABLE REPORT?
A Critique of Crossan and Mack's View of Mark

A s we have seen, the epistles of Paul can justifiably be read as representations of what Christians generally believed at the earliest stage at which we can know anything certain about the church. Within twenty years of his earthly ministry, Jesus' followers were ascribing to him titles and activities appropriate to God and were worshiping him as such. Moreover, the occasional nature of these documents, the way in which they assume an established understanding of Jesus, and the clearly discernible presence of pre-Pauline christological material in these letters has compelled us to further maintain that this exalted view of Jesus significantly predates Paul's letters. To be sure, we have every reason to follow Hengel, Dahl, and many other scholars in maintaining that the essence of this christology goes back to the very beginnings of the post-Easter Jerusalem Christian communities.

To say, with Mack, that the development of this incredible faith in a historical figure of the recent past is "astounding" is to understate the case significantly. The immediate creation of such a "foundational myth" would be astounding (if not unprecedented) in *any* historical context, however pagan. But the presence of such a phenomenon among communities significantly influenced by a *Jewish* worldview, even after due consideration is given to the Hellenistic influences, goes well beyond "astounding."

Indeed, it likely goes beyond anything that can be cogently accounted for on any strictly naturalistic basis. It forces us to entertain the possibility that the historical Jesus who was the ultimate catalyst for this faith among both his Jewish and Gentile followers cannot be exhaustively explained within the naturalistic categories of the historical-critical

203

method. It forces us to reckon with the likelihood that Mack's goal of reconstructing early church history without reference to "miracles, resurrections, divine appearances . . . or unusual charismatic phenomena" is a futile endeavor.[1]

Still, while there is certainly an interest in the historical Jesus discernible in Paul's letters, there is so little information given that the identity of Jesus would probably have to largely remain an unsolvable historical puzzle did we not have other sources of information about him. It is the claim of the Gospels that they provide just such information. If taken as generally reliable, they can be seen as filling out the skeletal outline of Jesus' life provided in Paul's letters and as doing so in such a way that they sufficiently explain why Jesus' followers so quickly developed such an exalted view of him. If their portraits of him accurately convey his essential teachings, deeds, and personal characteristics, then the faith-filled, worshiping response on the part of his earliest followers, as represented in Paul, makes sense. But embracing such an explanation, of course, requires abandoning the sovereignty of the constraints of the naturalistic critical approach to history to be accepted.[2] For the Jesus these documents portray certainly goes beyond naturalistic explanations.

Many historical-critical scholars, including Mack and Crossan, are simply unwilling to qualify the sovereignty of these historical-critical constraints in this fashion. They must, therefore, attempt to account for both the phenomenon of Paul's letters and of the Gospels by strictly naturalistic means, however difficult this is to do.[3] We have thus far reviewed Mack's attempt to explain the former and have judged it unsuccessful. We must now examine Mack's and Crossan's attempts to explain the latter. We shall argue that they are unsuccessful on this score as well.

The issue largely boils down to the historical reliability of Mark. On the assumption that Matthew and Luke (and John?) borrowed heavily from Mark, if Mark can be proven to be generally untrustworthy, then the reliability of the other Gospels is brought into question. Thus, at the very center of Mack's and Crossan's revisionist views of Jesus is a theory about Mark. Indeed, Mack's *Myth of Innocence* is about nothing else. Everything hangs upon this.

Thus the next two chapters will be devoted to this issue. In this chapter I shall consider Crossan and Mack's understanding of Mark as being largely a fabrication, while the next chapter shall concern itself with the authorship and dating of this Gospel. Through all of this, I shall be arguing that we have far better grounds for accepting Mark's narrative as reliable history than we do for accepting Crossan and Mack's view that it is largely creative fabrication.

A REVIEW OF MACK AND CROSSAN'S VIEW OF MARK

The Nature of Mark's Gospel

As we have seen in chapters 3 and 4, Mack and Crossan see little of historical value in the Gospel of Mark, and thus in any of the other Gospels as well. The Gospels are "neither histories nor biographies, even within the ancient tolerances of those genres."[4] While there are occasional echoes of the teaching and deeds of Jesus in Mark's Gospel, the work as a whole is judged by both to be largely a "fantastic fabrication."[5] It is, quite simply, a piece of historical and theological fiction[6] created by Mark's "stupendous manipulation of imagery."[7]

While many historical-critical scholars have imagined Mark's Gospel to contain significant elements of pious legend, Mack and Crossan align themselves with that small minority of scholars who, following the hypercritical tradition of Bauer and Strauss (see chap. 1), hold that even the basic narrative structure of this Gospel is nonhistorical.[8] And while it is a rather common view within historical-critical circles to view Mark as naively recording legendary stories passed down to him, Mack and Crossan stand largely alone in maintaining that the author of this Gospel was emphatically *intentional* in much of his mythmaking. To be sure, they are not above imputing "dishonest" and even "vicious" motives to him in his supposed re-creation of history.[9]

Hence, concerning Mark's passion narrative, that aspect of his Gospel which most scholars believe served as the structuring framework for his entire narrative, Mack writes:

> The intention of the rewriting [of the kerygma] was not innocent. It was not merely a matter of giving narrative form to the kerygmatic report. It cannot be explained as the natural desire to flesh out the historical point of contact for the cosmic event, as if the kerygma implicitly invited such explication. . . . Time, place, agents, and consequences are all spelled out in the predictions and identifiable in the passion account. They purport to be the ingredients of a historical event, but this story does not derive from history. History was written according to the script of the persecution story.[10]

And again:

> The schema is mythic. There is no "earlier" report extractable from the story, no reminiscence. This is the earliest narrative there is about the crucifixion of Jesus. It is a Markan fabrication.[11]

Crossan largely agrees. Hence, of the trials of Jesus in Mark's passion narrative he writes:

> It is impossible, in my mind, to overestimate the creativity of Mark, but those twin trials must be emphasized for what they are, namely, consummate theological fictions. . . . It is magnificent theological fiction, to be sure, but entailing a dreadful price for Judaism.[12]

At its core—the passion narrative—Mark's Gospel is seen as being an intentional and very damaging fabrication.[13]

The Motive of Mark

The motive of this unknown author in producing this theological fiction in the early A.D. 70s was to create a new "myth of origins" to rationalize the social history of the Jesus people in the light of recent historical developments. The original Jesus movement had been a dismal failure. Instead of gaining widespread acceptance, it had met with resistance and persecution. Instead of transforming the synagogue, it had been totally rejected by the synagogue. This failure had, according to Mack, produced an increasingly hostile view toward the "outside world" among the Jesus people and hence had given them an increasingly apocalyptic orientation in general. Such a development, it is argued, can already be discerned in the second strata of Q. It also produced an increasing need on the part of the Jesus people to justify their unique social existence. Hence, a new "social self-definition" was called for, and Mark provides it.

What is more, the external struggles of the Jesus people had, according to both Mack and Crossan, produced many internal struggles as well. The once egalitarian movement became especially divided over issues of who had what authority, as well as over how the authority of their founder was to be conceived. The rift that had already erupted between the Jesus people and the Christ-cult was now, in different forms, working its way into the Judean movement itself. In a word, the movement was disintegrating due to a "loss of loyalties, diversity of leadership, and competitive christologies and ideologies."[14] If the movement was to be salvaged, something radical had to be done. To this end Mark created his new Gospel.

Finally, in Mack and Crossan's view, the already tottering Jesus movement had just gone through the trauma of the Jewish-Roman war. They had just experienced the cataclysm of the fall of Jerusalem and the destruction of the temple. The Jewish-based Jesus people movement was ·thus left to wonder, along with all Jews, what theological significance this cataclysm had. Such an event had to be made to fit into the self-understanding of this already weakened movement. Again, Mark rose up to the occasion.

The Achievement of Mark

According to Mack, these internal and external conflicts, combined with the general disarray of the society they were part of, produced an environment in which "the past was ripe for reconstruction" and in which new "fantasies and mythic imageries" could be envisioned.[15] Into such a situation stepped the creative mind of the author of Mark. With a single bold and daring stroke, Mark fused together material from the Christ-cult and Jesus people traditions and created a narrative in which all these issues were addressed and resolved.[16] By structuring his myth not as new revelation, but as history, he was able to reconceptualize the identity of his movement in such a way that it appeared that all that their society had been through had been part of a divine plan, centered on their movement from the beginning. His revisionist historical approach allowed him to create a supernatural Jesus who had anticipated the entire struggle and insured the ultimate victory of his followers. And in doing this, Mark gave his founder a superhuman authority under which the beleaguered community could now unite.

Mack sums up the perspective he is arguing for well when he writes:

> Mark's apocalyptic imagination was generated in the seventies as a reaction and response to contemporary social history. There were certain advantages, however, in presenting his views, not as a new revelation in the traditional genre of apocalyptic, but as the teaching of Jesus. Not only could the authority of Jesus be called upon to give the instruction legitimacy, the import of Jesus' appearance could be aligned with the apocalyptic scheme. All of the events at the beginning could be cast as powerful, mysterious, and absolutely determinative for the subsequent

course of history in spite of the fact that the intervening history was not all that glorious. Reasons could be given for the rejection from the synagogue and for the confusions within the community by linking them, not to the failure of the movement, but to the nature of the kingdom and the enigmatic manner and authority of Jesus himself. . . . Mark made the connection at the level of social history and its rationalizations. He projected them back upon the time of Jesus by creating a narrative setting of conflict and rejection for the teachings and activities of Jesus. . . . To imagine Jesus' teachings as predictive apocalyptic instruction solved social historical issues nicely.[17]

The narrative structure of Mark's "fantastic reconstruction"[18] thus united the Jesus people against the hostile world that rejected them by investing their founder with absolute divine authority and apocalyptic wisdom, and by reimagining his history as being, like their own, a history of conflict with the Jews. This new view of Jesus, of course, had "little to do with the historical Jesus, much, however, with the recent history of the Jesus movement to which Mark belonged."[19] To achieve the needed social justification, the original egalitarian Cynic-sage was traded in for an "imperious judge and sovereign" who "rules by fiat."[20] And, of course, this changing image of the founder had radical implications for (and was itself in part the result of) the community's own changing self-understanding.

The desire originally underlying the whole program was for social reform, open borders, the presence of the new social spirit, the affirmation of plural pasts, and invitational discourse. The apocalyptic solution to the failure of the program meant that all of the original desires were abrogated, sacrificed to the new desire for self-justification. In the place of a social experimentation and its constructive visions, sectarian existence was now governed by absolute loyalty to a power effective only in events of vindictive transformation.[21]

It was, according to Mack, this novel and bold literary experiment on his part that has given "to the Christian imagination its sense of a radical and dramatic origin in time,"[22] a myth that Mack feels rises up again every time a scholar feels the need to posit some sort of stupendous (if not supernatural) event to explain the rise and growth of early Christian faith.[23] It was this apocalyptic narrative that ultimately buried the soul of the original Jesus movement (now only vaguely discernible in Q and GosThom). And, as we saw in chapter 4, it was this daring story of Mark's that is, according to Mack, largely responsible for most of the ills that plague Western, and especially American culture.[24] Most importantly, the "us-them" mentality – where "we" are conceived to be "innocent" and God is on "our side" – which Mack believes pervades our culture, is largely the legacy of Mark's original "myth of innocence."

ONCE AGAIN, WHERE IS THE EVIDENCE?

What are we to make of this understanding of Mark? As with any historical hypothesis, the first question always to be asked is, how does it square with the data? Does Mack and Crossan's reconstruction account for all the data in a manner that is superior to (e.g., simpler, more plausible) alternative views? And does their hypothesis explain otherwise hard to explain data? It is difficult to see how it does.

First, it must emphatically be pointed out, once again, that there is no independent evidence for the supposed embattled history and development of the Jesus people Mack and Crossan are imagining, and this must from the start be considered quite damaging to their theory. Of course, if one grants that there was a Q community that believed only what the Q material in the Synoptic Gospels explicitly contains; and if one grants that this document can be accurately reconstructed and accurately stratified; and if one grants that GosThom is to be dated earlier than the Synoptics; and if one grants that Mark knew and used Q; and if one further grants that Paul and the Hellenistic communities radically departed from the historical Jesus and the original Jesus communities; and if one is willing to grant that Mark knew and used material from this Christ-cult; and, finally, if one grants that Mark's narrative should be read as theological fiction for the purpose of social self-definition so that the narrative conflicts of Jesus can be assumed to be "really" about the conflicts of the Jesus people community; then it can perhaps be agreed that there is some evidence for Mack and Crossan's reconstruction. Certainly the postulation of some such history of the Jesus people makes sense as a way of explaining this "evidence."

But, as I have previously shown (sec. 3), there is little reason to grant each of these, let alone all of these, assumptions. Each assumption is highly questionable, so the tenuous portrait that results from stringing them all together, and the reconstructed history offered to explain this portrait, can't be considered all that compelling.

Relatedly, we must seriously question the value of material that only looks like "evidence" in light of the assumed truth of the positions it is supposed to be justifying. For example, Mack and Crossan's view that the original Jesus people invested no special significance into the life and death of Jesus and held no belief in the resurrection hangs completely on Mack and Crossan's view of Q and GosThom. But Q and GosThom can only be read as evidence for such an original community if we are willing to grant not only Crossan's and Mack's controversial views of Q and GosThom, but a significant portion of the other assumptions mentioned above as well. We must, for example, also be willing to grant their radically marginalized understanding of the "Christ-cult," as well as their radically skeptical reading of Mark. But if we ask why we should regard Paul and Mark in this fashion, the evidence that is pointed to is – Q and GosThom!

Each of their assumptions, in other words, hangs on the others, but it is not clear what the whole web of assumptions itself hangs on. One assumption is taken as evidence for the other, but the collection *as a whole* lacks evidence. In short, nothing exists that counts as evidence *outside of the assumptions themselves.* And this must certainly lower our estimation of the whole program as a plausible historical hypothesis.

SUSPICIOUS COMPLEXITY AND "DEALING WITH THE DATA"

A second observation that needs to be made concerns the complexity of Mack's and Crossan's theses. If simplicity is a central ingredient in any plausible historical (or generally scientific) hypothesis, as is generally assumed, then the very complexity of the above mentioned web of assumptions needed to be made by Crossan and Mack to sustain their Cynic thesis must be considered suspect.[25]

Crossan and Mack's approach certainly doesn't constitute the simplest and most straightforward way of understanding the data. The multitude of assumptions that must be made to carry the weight of the theory itself testifies to this. Perhaps their strongest "selling point" is that their reconstruction of early Christian history allows them to explain on a strictly natural basis how a Cynic sage ended up being seen as the Son of God. However, the tenuousness and convoluted nature of the reconstruction they offer and the assumptions they must make to arrive at this point should lead us to suspect that perhaps something is amiss with the point they are attempting to arrive at.

N.T. Wright speaks to this point when he writes concerning the revisionist scheme typified by Bultmann and Mack.

Such a scheme is incredibly complex, and looks very much like a reconstruction designed to save the phenomena of the gospels without damaging a hypothesis (that Jesus was a certain type of person and that the early church was uninterested in him) which is threatened by the actual evidence.

And he adds:

When it is suggested that these developments took place within forty years at the outside, it becomes not just incredibly complex but simply incredible.[26]

We may, in fact, go further and argue that, far from *utilizing* the extant data available on the historical Jesus in support of their views, the Cynic-sage thesis actually requires that the vast majority of the evidence at hand be *explained away* as not presenting to us the "real" historical Jesus. The apparent historical value of the primary data (from Mark, Paul, Luke/Acts, and the other Gospels) must be exchanged for a hypothetical social history of a community, the unprovable fabricating motive of an author, the tenuous use of other literary fragments, and a sometimes overly symbolic reading of the Markan text (see below). The program must, in a nutshell, assume that our ability to reconstruct what "actually" happened is more reliable than the available primary reports about what happened — which have to themselves be explained away on the basis of the reconstruction!

But we need to question whether or not such a program can be said to have genuinely "dealt with the data."[27] As Wright has argued, it certainly rather looks like the program is "threatened" by the data. And we have to begin to suspect that in their attempt to explain away the "myth of Christian origins" perhaps Mack and Crossan have simply created a new "myth of origins" of their own.[28]

An observation of Hengel's may here apply when he points out that

those authors who apply radical criticism to early Christian narrators like Mark or Luke ... often invent facts of their own which have no basis in the sources and indeed go directly against them.[29]

It seems that the need to explain away the data to preserve their Cynic thesis forces Mack and Crossan's reconstruction to be so complex and speculative. To explain why the biblical data is misleading about who Jesus "really" was, a very complex and speculative picture of social developments has to be imagined.[30] Unprecedented mythological imaginings and unprovable trajectories of historical influences have to be posited. Marginal documents must be made central and redated, and the basic integrity of key figures (e.g., Mark) have to be undermined. And there is hardly a shred of evidence for any of this outside of the sheer explanatory power the overall picture has in accounting for why the data does not give us the "real" Jesus![31]

The complexity, speculativeness, and circularity of this enterprise must certainly be considered damaging to the thesis it services. What counts above all else in arriving at a good historical hypothesis is "getting in the data, and simplicity."[32] On both accounts, however, Crossan's and Mack's thesis must be judged to have faired quite poorly.

INHERENT IMPLAUSIBILITY

A third criticism that must be raised against Crossan's and Mack's account concerns its inherent plausibility as a historical hypothesis, even if we were willing for the moment to grant the numerous assumptions that hold their accounts together. In a word, we must wonder how likely it is that someone, working from within a Jewish environment, would have thought of fabricating a mythological narrative account about a person in recent history in the way that Crossan and Mack imagine Mark doing.

In their view, after all, Mark is not just sincerely passing on stories that have acquired some legendary elements. Nor is he sincerely expressing a worldview through a nice edifying story. Nor is he simply redacting prior material and organizing it in a creative fashion – something everyone acknowledges. For Crossan, and even more so for Mack, Mark is doing nothing less than creating a radically new self-understanding for his community by producing a new "foundational myth." And he is achieving this by *intentionally fabricating history.*

To state the matter most bluntly, Mark is, for self-serving reasons, intentionally deceiving people about who Jesus was, what he did, who persecuted him, and what happened to him. He is pretending to record history, and he is, both Crossan and Mack admit, very "clever" at doing it. But it is, as Mack and Crossan both acknowledge, a fundamentally deceptive endeavor.

So the question that must be addressed is, how inherently plausible is this supposition? Does this "explanation" ring true? Is this how people ordinarily operate? If not (as assuredly is the case), are there good grounds for supposing that Mark did not share the sort of honesty we normally assume on the part of other people?

Moreover, we must wonder whether or not a first-century Jew (or Gentile) could have pulled off this entirely new genre of historical fiction as successfully as he did.[33] And does the motivation required for such a view of Mark fit in easily with the hostile context in which he is writing, a context in which being a Christian could cost one a good deal (recall that Nero's slaughter of the Christians was not yet ten years old—even on Crossan and Mack's late dating of Mark)?

And finally, does this "explanation" help provide a coherent understanding of the available data that is otherwise difficult to account for? Does it accord easily with the actual text of Mark's Gospel? Does it have explanatory advantages over the view that, for all his theological interests, Mark was nevertheless sincere and honest in what he wrote (however good or bad he was at recording history)?

A review of the evidence shows nothing that would compel one to answer any of the above questions in the affirmative. The assumption that Mark was an intentional fabricator of theological fiction in a narrative mode simply does not "ring true." Like all of the other varieties of "conspiracy" theories proposed throughout the history of the quest for the historical Jesus (see chap. 1), this one lacks inherent plausibility. Indeed, given the ostensively historical nature of this Gospel and the nature of the first-century context in which he wrote, we must agree with Thomas Oden in regarding this supposition as "patently absurd."[34] *Whatever* explanation is posited to explain the portrait of Jesus in Mark, no explanation seems less likely than that he simply made it up.[35]

Indeed, the supposition really "explains" nothing—except for how we can suppose that a Jewish peasant Cynic sage could be transformed into the Son of God in a mere forty years within a Jewish milieu. But that, of course, is the very hypothesis which needs to be substantiated by *the historical data!* And, unless we have solid independent grounds for thinking otherwise, writing off the primary data as deceptive can hardly be said to count as an "explanation."

THE AUTHORITY OF MARK'S GOSPEL

Thus, it is difficult to understand how and why Mark would or could have created the fantasy that Crossan and Mack imply. What is even more difficult to understand, however, is how this fabrication could have been *believed* by the Jesus people in Mark's own generation, and this constitutes my fourth criticism of their theory. Even if this unknown author had concocted such an account, how could his contemporaries have failed to recognize this Gospel for being what it was? How could this Gospel have possessed any credibility to Mark's community which, per hypothesis, had up to this point held a very different view of Jesus than the one Mark gives? Indeed, how are we to understand the astounding authority this work quickly attained—to the point that it (on the two-source hypothesis) formed the foundation for at least two subsequent canonical Gospels shortly after its composition?

The problem is a difficult one for Crossan and Mack, and neither one has provided us with a plausible answer. On Mack's own admission, Mark's (supposed) incorporation of significant elements of previously alien Pauline elements into his narrative would have struck some of his own community as "strange if not obnoxious."[36] These "people of Q," after all, had up to this point never conceptualized Jesus as a suffering savior, a divine being, or a risen god (all pagan concepts on Mack's account). But, in this case, how are we to account for these very same people accepting this fused together story and basing their lives on it?

Perhaps the problem can be solved by appealing to the authoritative stature of the author of this Gospel. The sheer weight of his authority made this new Gospel credible. Unfortunately, Crossan and Mack deny this as well. The author of this Gospel was not John Mark, or anyone connected to the original inner circle of Jesus. And this denial intensifies their problem.

How are we to conceive of this "Mr. Nobody" (to use Hengel's phrase) undertaking the "revolutionary innovation of writing a gospel,"[37] doing so within a nonhistorical apocalyptic framework, fusing together traditions that were previously unrecognizable to each other, and having the whole thing accepted and given authoritative status on a widespread scale within the span of a decade or so?[38] Frankly, the picture is not an easy one to accept.

Indeed, if accepting Mack's view that the Hellenistic congregations produced an exalted mythology of the Christ figure within the space of ten to twenty years is difficult, then believing that the Jesus people accepted a similar view (now embedded in narrative form) almost overnight with little historical precedent is even more so. Even if we for the moment grant that steps had already been taken in this direction within the community as "evidenced" by the (supposedly) increasingly apocalyptic second and third strata of Q and by the Cross Gospel, it nevertheless requires us to suppose an incredible disinterest in historical truth and an astounding gullibility on the part of the Jesus people to suppose that they would readily accept the fantastic revisionist story this un-known author was now telling. Did *no one* think of asking where all of this (fabricated) information that comprised Mark's Gospel had been hiding for forty years? Why did no one object to the fact that Mark was giving them a radically different religion than the one they had been previously adhering to?

When we consider that this is all taking place within a largely Jewish framework where what God does *in history* — not imagination — is what is of supreme importance, Mack and Crossan's case becomes yet more strained. The supposition that Mark (or any of the Gospel authors) was writing intentional fiction is not only counter-intuitive: it stands in direct antithesis to the basic creational monotheistic worldview they all shared. Wright's argument is to the point when he states:

> If someone, say, in 75 A.D. were to tell a Jew a fiction . . . and to claim that in this very story the long hope of Israel had finally been fulfilled, the response would have been not just that he was a liar, but that he had not understood what the Jewish world view was all about.[39]

Hence, the supposition that Mark intentionally fabricated the bulk of his story renders him not only dishonest: it also renders him thoroughly non-Jewish. And this, in turn, renders the supposition itself inherently implausible and makes it very difficult to understand why his work was so widely and so quickly regarded as historically true and authoritative.

Mack and Crossan's case is weakened still further when we consider that oral traditions and historical memory were highly esteemed and transmitted with a remarkable degree of reliability within this culture (as discussed in chap. 5). It is not, after all, as though the Jesus people would have had no historical recollection of who Jesus actually had been and what he actually had said until Mark fictionalized his own view. Further, little time had elapsed for these people to forget all of this. Within the first century Jewish milieu, even after due consideration has been given to Hellenistic influences, it is simply implausible to posit "a lack of con-cern for history . . . a freely creative oral tradition . . . [and a] rapid loss of historical perspective" concerning Jesus on the part of the Jesus people.[40]

Thus, I reiterate that it seems quite unlikely that a member of the Jesus people community would have attempted to pull off what Mack and Crossan attribute to Mark. But even if he had, we have every reason to suppose that his fabricated narrative would have significantly collided with the traditions about Jesus that were already in place. So we again are left wondering how and why these Jesus people moved past what must have at points seemed a "strange if not obnoxious" story to a whole new kind of faith in the one Mark was now portraying in apocalyptic terms.

One especially wonders how the surviving *eyewitnesses* to Jesus who were undoubtedly still around, eyewitnesses who must have exercised some influence within these communities, responded to Mark's supposed rewriting of history.[41] One must ask how Mark could have thought that he could get his piece of historical fiction past these eyewitnesses. And, finally, how could this fabrication not only be accepted, but serve to motivate the followers of Jesus to the point where they quickly took this "new" Gospel and risked their lives evangelizing the entire Mediterranean world? As Thomas Oden writes, on the supposition that Mark (and all the Gospels) are creative fiction:

> One wonders how these deluded believers of early centuries gained the courage to risk passage into an unknown world to proclaim this message that came from an imagined revolution of a fantasized Mediator. The "critical" premise itself requires a high threshold of gullibility.[42]

In short, unless something more than Mark's shrewd creativity stands behind his basic narrative, the passion with which the early church so quickly believed and preached his message is utterly inexplicable. Crossan and Mack's account of Mark thus suffers from the same inherent implausibility that conspiratorial theories on the origins of Christianity have suffered since the time of Reimarus. This inherent implausibility could perhaps be overcome if there was a wealth of convincing evidence supporting the theory. But as we have seen, this too is lacking. In the words of Hengel, the supposition that Mark created his work as a theological fiction, along with the earlier mentioned web of corollary assumptions posited to support it, looks like one more example of, "[w]hat is supposed to be 'critical' scholarship . . . positing things . . . which cannot be proved."[43]

BEGINNING WITH AN ASSUMED MOTIVE

A fifth and closely related criticism of Mack and Crossan's treatment of Mark concerns the manner in which they assume, in an *a priori* manner, that Mark does not intend to write historically. A fabricating motive –

despite appearances in the text to the contrary – is assumed at the start and conditions the entire treatment of the text of Mark. Hence Mack states:

> If one wants to understand the origins of the Christian gospel of origins, one must study the way in which Mark fabricated his story, and determine why he wrote it the way he did.[44]

There is no question here of *whether* Mark fabricated his account or not: the only open issue, therefore, is understanding "the *way* . . . Mark fabricated" (emphasis mine). So too, according to Mack, Mark's text must be studied "in relation to [the] social setting [of the early church] in order to determine why it was that Jesus was reimagined in just the way he was."[45] That Jesus was "reimagined," we see, is settled: the only question is, why was he "reimagined" that way. And to answer this question, the text of Mark's Gospel "must be construed as imaginative constructions functional within a much larger set of factors at work in the social formation of early Christian groups."[46] Again, that Mark's portrait of Jesus' life and ministry is composed of "imaginative constructs" is a settled issue at the start: the only remaining task is for Mack to now dissect them according to his theory of group formation and mythmaking.

But if one asks why we should assume this motive on the part of Mark in the first place, there is no clear answer. And, given the ostensively historical nature of his narrative, this absence of an answer must be considered a weakness of Mack's approach.

Working from the Unknown to the Known

All of this, of course, *assumes* that such "reimagining" occurred and that we know something about "the social formation of early Christian" groups *before* we come to the texts. It also assumes from the start that Mark's concern *isn't* historical: it is purely sociological. Indeed, it assumes that we know in general *why* Mark wrote even before we know in particular *what* he wrote and we arrive at an understanding of the latter only through the assumption of the former. It begins with what is most tenuous, for nothing is more difficult than prying into the ultimate motives of an author, and ends with a total reconstruction of what seems most apparent – the author's desire to proclaim Christ by telling history.[47] In essence, this approach allows a preconceived hypothesis (viz., Mark's motive of fabrication) to control the evidence (Mark's texts).

Conveniently enough, this methodology makes it difficult for any evidence *within* Mark's Gospel to count against the hypothesis. The motive has (per hypothesis) already been established: we need now only reinterpret all the evidence. Indeed, on the assumption that Mark is fabricating his story, one can in principle reconstruct "the truth"—what is "really" going on—behind any particular passage of this Gospel in any way one pleases. For the hypothesis is no longer constrained by the evidence: rather, the evidence is controlled by the hypothesis. If it is assumed that all the available data is misleading, then we can speculate without much concern for data.[48]

So it is posited by Mack and Crossan that Mark is largely creating his account, and behind it all lies a Cynic-sage Jesus and an original Jesus people movement who saw him as such. As we have seen, the independent evidence for such a view is quite meager. But once the theory is in place, whatever in Mark's Gospel does *not* square with this Cynic portrait can be, and must be, explained away by his (supposed) motives to fabricate his account. The end result is that Mark is not allowed to do what it *looks* like he is trying to do: namely, relate history. When it appears that this was his intention, the radical critics, here functioning as "masters of suspicion" (to use Ricoeur's phrase), are in place to better inform us as to what is "really" going on.

Exegesis Versus Eisegesis

This approach puts the proverbial cart before the horse. Instead of allowing the text to inform us concerning Mark's meaning and motive, it postulates a motive which then dictates the meaning of the text. Instead of reading out of the text (exegesis), it reads meaning into the text (eisegesis). Instead of letting the text tell us what it really means, this approach decides ahead of time what the text cannot mean (viz., historical narrative) and then seeks to construe what the text must "really" be saying.

Several examples from Mack and Crossan's work will help illustrate the misguidedness of this approach. According to Mack, all of Mark's stories of the conflict of Jesus and his disciples with Jewish authorities (e.g., Mark 2:15-28; 3:1-6), are to be read as really being about the recent conflicts the Jesus people had with the synagogue, and materially constitute "the way Jesus people wanted to imagine the conflict and its resolution in retrospect."[49] Mark's records of Jesus being charged with blasphemy (3:28-30; 14:57-65) are really a "crafty" way of getting at "the old distinction between the Jesus people who admitted 'sinners' into the group and the synagogue people who held to the code of purity. Social contamination is the charge against Jesus."[50] And the story of the woman anointing Jesus with expensive oil, an act which in Mark's narrative provoked objections about wasting money, is actually a "dishonest" but "clever" reworking of an originally Cynic-like saying which simply had a woman of ill repute anointing Jesus, and Jesus saying, "that was good."[51] Again, the redefining of social boundaries is the real issue being addressed. One would never surmise any of this, of course, unless he or she approached the text with the strong suspicion that what it appears to be saying is not at all what it is really saying.

So too, Mark's miracle stories, according to Mack, "are not historical reports." They are, rather, really about the social boundaries the new Jesus movement have crossed, picturing Jesus after the model of Elijah or Moses.[52] Mark's portrayal of Jesus referring to himself as "the Son of Man" is really "a stupendous manipulation of imagery," and his use of exalted christological titles throughout his narrative simply "reveals the pressures upon Mark for another rationalization of a new set of social circumstances."[53] And, finally, while Mark portrays Jesus as instituting the communion meal at the Last Supper, Mack insists that, "[a] more reasonable account would be to recognize the common meal [of the Jesus people movement] as the important thing . . . and the ritual meal as evidence for the way in which early Christians noticed its importance."[54] In other words, what is really going on in the Last Supper story is the Jesus people telling a story to justify the importance it already had within the community.[55]

But again, one could only agree with Mack's account of what is "really" going on in these texts if he or she first accepted his premise that the surface meaning of the text is fundamentally deceptive. Working from such a premise, a "social setting" is imagined (about which we know nothing on the basis of independent evidence) which provides the "true" meaning of the text and helps explain why the apparent meaning of the text is misleading.

Mark receives similar treatment from Crossan. To again cite but a few examples: When Mark tells us of the execution of John the Baptist (Mark 6:17-29), according to Crossan he is really telling us "marvelous fiction" in order to draw parallels between John and Jesus after the model of Livy's story of a morbid woman at Placentia who asked Flaminius to execute a criminal before her.[56] When Mark reports the incident of Jesus exorcising the Gerasene demoniac and sending the demons into swine (Mark 5:1-17), Roman imperialism is being symbolically exorcised out of Judea, according to Crossan.[57]

Similarly, when Mark tells us of Barabbas being chosen over Jesus on his day of execution (Mark 15:6-15), Mark is excusing Pilate and blaming the Jews while symbolically dramatizing Jerusalem's fate because of their choice of an armed rebellion over an unarmed savior.[58] And the Marcan story of Joseph of Arimathea offering his tomb to Jesus (Mark 15:42-46) is a rather desperately created fiction enabling Mark to hold that Jesus didn't die a "cursed" death by not being buried. By fabricating a member of the council who was also a believer, Mark creates a person who would have both the motive to bury Jesus and the authority to do so.[59]

Such understandings of what Mark is "really" about are not obvious. They certainly presuppose a good deal more about (1) the history of the Jesus people community and (2) what was going on in Mark's mind, than we in fact know.[60] But given the assumption that Mark is pretending to do history with primarily sociological motives, such readings are to be expected. If the appearance of historical narrative is (it is assumed) only an appearance, then the *real* meaning of the narrative *must* lie somewhere behind the narrative in the hidden histories of Mark's community.[61]

Now there can be no question that Mack and Crossan bring an incredible wealth of scholarship to bear on their revisionist readings of Mark. Nor is there any question that their revisionist readings are at times remarkably clever and at times plausible—once one accepts the premise that Mark's motivation is not at all historical. But again, the all-important question is, why should one accept this premise? Is it fair to approach Mark, or any ancient document that looks like it is attempting to relate history, with this assumption? Is it ever justifiable to begin with an assumption about what is in principle unknowable and to then reconstruct what one knows on this basis?

The "Common Courtesy" of Historical Methodology

It goes without saying, of course, that we must always allow for biases, "redactional tendencies," exaggerations, legendary accretions, mistaken information, and the like in the study of ancient (and modern) documents. But, as I argued in chapter 5, what is also crucial to note is that it is customary to always assume that an author is "innocent until proven guilty."[62] Historians generally assume that an author's intent is to write history if it *appears* he or she is trying to write history. And while we may judge the history reliable or unreliable, depending on what the evidence dictates, we in general trust the account unless we have reasons *not* to do so.[63]

The burden of proof, in short, is always assumed to rest on historians to demonstrate that a work is untrustworthy; it does not rest on documents to in every instance prove the opposite. And it certainly does not rest on ancient authors to prove that they are not intentionally making stories up! Unless such a commonsensical assumption were made, it is difficult to see how the discipline of writing ancient history could ever get far off the ground.

Thus, no historian doubts the essential integrity of Herodotus, Dio Cassius, Josephus, Suetonius, Tacitus, or even any of the many ancient Greco-Roman biographers, however extravagant or mistaken particular accounts of theirs may be judged. We routinely judge their accounts *at points* to be prejudiced, mistaken, or legendary, of course. But the exceptions prove the rule. We do not impugn their motives without good reason.

Hence, it seems quite unwarranted by standard historiographical procedure to assume that Mark is not doing what it clearly appears he is. We would be refusing him the "common courtesy" customarily extended to all other ancient (and modern) authors.[64] And thus, however ingenious a reconstruction of what he is supposedly "really" about may be, it lacks plausibility to the extent that it is not first demonstrated that such a reconstruction is necessary.

MARK AND HISTORICAL INTEREST

Mark and Ancient Histories

I have thus far been assuming that Mark is interested in relaying reliable history, even if this is not his primary interest. And I have argued that assuming the opposite, as Mack and Crossan do, is unwarranted by common historical procedure. We need to now examine more closely the case for maintaining that Mark's interest does include transmitting historical material.

I have already conceded (chap. 5) that neither Mark nor any other of the Gospel authors were attempting to write anything like a modern biography of Jesus. The fact that they all include very little by way of biographical information on Jesus and focus almost exclusively on the last few years of his life itself evidences this. The freedom with which they modify the words of Jesus, relate the deeds of Jesus, and freely play with the chronology of his ministry is further evidence of this.[65] So too, the manner in which they combine historical reports with kerygmatic proclamation puts them well outside the domain of what we would in contemporary terms call "historical writing."

But does this imply that the Gospel authors are not interested in history or that their history is unreliable? Certainly the sheer fact that Mark's standards do not conform to modern standards of historiography can't be held against him. Such a move would undermine not only the historical reliability of Mark, but also that of virtually *all* ancient authors. No ancient historian or biographer wrote with the sort of care and precision expected of historians today. From our perspective, all of them played "fast and loose" with their sources. They all possessed a freedom to modify and rearrange their materials according to their own purposes that is very much out of step with the way the discipline of history is conducted today.[66] Still, it is very clear that ancient writers generally knew good history from bad history, exercised some critical judgment in adjudicating between their reliable and unreliable sources, and in general produced some generally trustworthy histories.[67]

Hence, the fact that Mark and the other Gospels do not share our modern assumptions about doing history should not have excessively negative implications for our understanding of their historical interests. As Hengel notes, "Though they are set in the context of antiquity and do not come up to modern standards in this respect, they claim to be accounts of what really happened, and not literary fictions."[68] It is also worth noting in this regard that the most common way of referring to the Gospels in the early church was by calling them "reminiscences."[69] If Mark and the other Gospels were not intending to write history, it is difficult to see how their earliest readers assumed that they wrote just that.[70]

Proclamation and History

Nor can the fact that Mark's narrative is clearly composed to express and inspire faith be used against him, for this too would undermine the historical reliability of all ancient authors. They certainly did not share with us moderns the (unattainable) ideal of arriving at pure objective historical reporting. They were never concerned with "history for the sake of history," but were rather always interested in making a moral, political, or religious point with their history. In other words, they all wrote (as all modern historians also write!) from some committed perspective.[71] This stance must, of course, always be taken into consideration in the critical evaluations of their histories. But it certainly does not itself preclude our concluding that they nevertheless wrote good histories.

So too, it is not clear why Mark's faith perspective should itself be taken to undermine the historical reliability of what he is reporting. The odd notion that faith and historical interest are somehow incompatible with each other is a modern prejudice that cannot be read back onto the authors of the Gospels without inviting the charge of anachronism.[72] This is an assumption that has led contemporary critical scholarship down many wrong paths, as we saw in chapter 1.[73] From their own perspective—their Jewish creationist monotheistic perspective—the two were rather intertwined with one another. Hence, "The engagement of faith and the pathos of the [Gospel] accounts," writes Dahl, "do not exclude a historical interest on the part of the evangelists, but rather include it."[74] Though they are "theological through and through," says Wright, "they are not for that reason any less historical. The fact of their being interpretations does not mean that they are not interpretations *of events*."[75] Their passion to proclaim who Jesus is rivals their passion to say who Jesus *was*. If anything, one could argue that their reliability is enhanced, not weakened, precisely by the passion of their faith.[76]

Apocalyptic, Ancient Biographies, and History

The fact that Mark's basic narrative has, as Crossan and Mack point out, a thoroughly apocalyptic framework doesn't change this.[77] For it is, as Wright has thoroughly argued, simply a modern misconception to think that apocalyptic and history are mutually exclusive. The intent of apocalyptic, he argues, was not to negate the world, but rather to affirm it by investing it with a new divine significance. Apocalyptic does not spell the literal *end* of history and the space-time world, but the *interpretation* of history and the space-time world.[78] Hence, to agree that Mark is heavily apocalyptic (as Wright does) in no way entails that he is disinterested in "this world" history. Quite the opposite. It *presupposes* that he is talking about real events in real history.

A literary analysis of Mark bears this out. While his work differs markedly from Hellenistic biographies, it does so by being more, not less, concerned with historical matters.[79] A host of recent studies have shown—against the classical Bultmannian form-critical dogma—that the Gospels reflect similar themes, interests, subject matters, and even styles as do the Hellenistic biographies.[80] But, as Wright has again emphasized, Mark and the other Gospel authors each do so in *a distinct Jewish way*. They tell the biographical story of Jesus, but in such a way that they also tell the story of Israel coming to its climactic destiny within God's providence.[81] In the life, death, and resurrection of Jesus, and in the destiny of his people, the calling of Israel finds its fulfillment.

What is for our purposes important to note here is that this unique fusion of Hellenistic and Jewish genres only served to enhance the historical interest of the Gospel authors, not detract from it. Mark intended to write history, *precisely because* he was writing about "theology." As Hengel has argued, neither Mark nor any of the canonical Gospels bare any resemblances to the pieces of religious fiction that were generally looked down upon even in their own day. "People did not look to them for edifying entertainment which bore no relation to the truth." Rather, Hengel argues, "they claim to be accounts of what really happened."[82]

Hence, when Mark tells us that Jesus cast a legion of demons out of a possessed man and sent them into a herd of swine, for example, we may question his theological interpretation of what happened, and we may legitimately wonder what redactional purpose he might have had in placing the event where he did in his narrative, and we may (if we have historical grounds for doing so — recall "the burden of proof") even question whether any such event actually happened. But we have no reason to doubt that, at the very least, Mark *believed* that some such event as this really happened! Reading into this account a symbolic rejection of Roman imperialism at the expense of the historical interest of the passage simply doesn't do justice to the kind of book the Gospel of Mark is.

MIRACLES AND HISTORY

Finally, it must once again be argued that this historical interest of Mark's is not compromised by the fact that his record includes miracles. It is arguably this aspect of his record that, more than anything else, causes modern historians to treat him (and the other Gospel authors) with a more intense skepticism than they treat other ancient works. Mack captures the general secular sentiment succinctly when he remarks that "Scholars and miracles don't mix well."[83] The assumption that all reports of miracles are legendary has certainly been one of the main driving forces behind the various quests for the historical Jesus, as we have already seen (chaps. 1, 5).

Several things need to be said about this. First, even if one insists on considering all of the miraculous aspects of the Gospel narratives as legendary, this in no way justifies rejecting outright the historical integrity of the work that includes them. Nor does it relieve the historian of the responsibility of trying to find "the historical nucleus" within the account, or of asking "why it was produced in the first place."[84] It does not, in other words, justify simply dismissing the account as a wholesale fabrication. This is not how historians treat other ancient historical accounts, even when they do contain what might be regarded as legendary material.

Secondly, as was argued in chapter 5, the legitimacy of dismissing everything that does not easily fit our twentieth-century "closed universe" worldview needs to be seriously questioned. In truth, it seems quite presumptuous to self-consciously enshrine one's own worldview as the final arbiter of what could and could not have happened in history.[85] By what metaphysical authority can we confidently claim that we secular twentieth-century people have "arrived" at the definitively accurate worldview?[86] And, as Wright has argued, with what justification can we call our enterprise "scientific" if we do not even allow for the possibility that our own worldview might be incorrect?[87]

What history should concern itself with is historical data, not metaphysics. If a report of an event cannot be explained within the ordinary system of historical cause and effect relations, and if we have other grounds for considering the report reliable, perhaps the issue of what exactly lies behind the report should simply be left open. But the integrity of the data should not be compromised simply because it suggests that our present worldview might be limited.[88]

This does not just apply to the Gospel accounts. History is full of reported events that stretch our ordinary sensibilities (not surprisingly, for the mundane is rarely worth recording). And, as historians, we should allow them to do so if the evidence warrants it. For example, it certainly goes against our ordinary view of things to read Arrian's unbelievable account of Alexander the Great redesigning an entire landscape and erecting a massive causeway of tree trunks to cross the ravine to the Rock of Chorienes. But both Arrian's general reliability and now recent archaeology suggest that the event actually took place.[89] Relatedly, when we read Tacitus' report that numerous eyewitnesses attest to the fact that Emperor Vespasian healed a blind man and a cripple, we may not be able to explain what happened, but we must not for that reason discredit Tacitus' report which in all other respects smacks of reliable history.[90]

Hence, if the Gospels contain surprising feats on the part of Jesus, we should not, as historians, be too quick to dismiss them out of a preconceived metaphysical prejudice.[91] Indeed, given the kind of unprecedented response he elicited from his followers, we should perhaps anticipate discovering some pretty amazing things about Jesus. If Jesus had never performed any such feats, it would be hard to understand how he inspired such a robust faith in his followers. The difficulty Mack has in accounting for this faith without any appeal to the miraculous is itself evidence of just how hard such a naturalistic understanding is to maintain.

And thirdly, it must be noted by way of reminder that the old form-critical dogma that the stories of Jesus' supernatural feats were late Hellenistic developments of the Gospel traditions has by and large been rejected by contemporary scholarship (though Mack, owing to his view of miracles stories as justifying social agendas, still seems to be influenced by it).[92] As an increasing number of scholars are conceding, there is strong evidence which suggests that many of the miracle stories go back to the earliest stages of the Gospel traditions and cannot plausibly be extracted out of the overall portrait of Jesus they provide.[93] Indeed, it is difficult to even prove a redactional tendency on the part of Mark or the other evangelists to exaggerate the miracle stories already present in their sources.[94]

What is more, it is increasingly recognized that the Gospel portraits of Jesus as a miracle worker have very little in common either with the pagan stories of magicians and wonder workers or with the pagan or later Christian legendary romances of mythic heroes (including later accounts of Jesus). The Gospel accounts are remarkably restrained, sober, and detailed and altogether lack the mythic and superstitious quality found in these other accounts.[95] Indeed, one could perhaps argue that this very distinctness of Jesus' miracles is, on the basis of the criteria of dissimilarity, itself evidence of their historicity.[96]

In any case, we have no reason for supposing that the presence of supernatural reports in Mark's Gospel implies that he is not interested in real history – even if some might be inclined to doubt (on whatever historical grounds they find) the historical accuracy of the supernatural reports themselves.

CONCLUSION: MARK AND HISTORY

We find, then, no compelling reason to follow Mack and Crossan in their assumption that Mark is largely an intentional fabrication. The view lacks independent evidence, is inherently implausible, runs counter to ordinary historical protocol which generally gives historical texts the benefit of the doubt, and collides with what is a clearly discernible historical interest in Mark's actual narrative.

This implies that the reports in Mark's narrative should be taken seriously and that any attempt to undermine them must carry the burden of proof in demonstrating its case. And it certainly implies that views that write major portions of Mark off as fabrication should be treated with a great deal of suspicion—unless there is compelling external evidence to substantiate their claim. But, in the case of Crossan and Mack, we have found that this is lacking.

But showing the historical interest of Mark does not yet say anything about his actual historical reliability. To begin to establish this— beyond the "general courtesy" extended to all historical texts—we shall need to investigate the authorship, sources, and perhaps date of this document. Of course, even if Mack and Crossan are correct in maintaining that Mark was written in the 70s or 80s by an unknown author who enjoyed no direct connection to the original witnesses of Jesus, writing off this work as being largely imaginative would still be unwarranted. But if we have grounds for accepting the church tradition concerning this work—that it was composed by John Mark under the influence of Peter—then our estimation of its reliability, and our argument against Crossan and Mack, cannot help but be enhanced. And if there are internal grounds for regarding the work as being early and relaying reliable eyewitness testimony, our case is made all the stronger. It is to this task that we now turn.

11

OBSCURE NOBODY OR APOSTOLIC AUTHORITY?
An Investigation Concerning the Authorship and Date of Mark

Mack and Crossan, in keeping with the general trend of contemporary New Testament scholarship, take for granted that the author of the Gospel of Mark is not John Mark, that the received tradition that Peter significantly influenced this Gospel is fictitious, and that this Gospel is to probably be dated *after* A.D. 70. These points, in their view, hardly need to be argued. In this view Mark was an obscure "Mr. Nobody" (to use Hengel's phrase again), not an apostolic authority. It was only after his Gospel became accepted and influential within the Jesus communities that the title of this work, "The Gospel According to Mark," was attached to this document.

Such a position is really required of the Cynic thesis and any thesis that must presuppose the untrustworthiness of Mark. It would obviously be difficult for Crossan or Mack to maintain their low estimation of this Gospel's historicity if they did not hold to this position. Whoever composed this (supposed) theological fabrication, it is difficult to suppose that he was closely related to the original inner circle of Jesus' ministry (such as John Mark was). And he must have written and published this work far enough removed from the original events that his fabrication could have some degree of credibility among the Jesus people.

If, however, we can with some probability show that John Mark did author this Gospel (he was *not* a "nobody"), that he did so under the influence of Peter (he had apostolic authority), and perhaps that he did so prior to A.D. 70 (he was *not* far removed from the events he records), this will provide further evidence that Mack and Crossan's view of Mark, and by implication, their Cynic thesis, is misguided. It would also greatly increase the likelihood that we are here dealing with some substantially accurate information in this Gospel and thereby increase the likelihood that Mark's Jesus and the historical Jesus are not as far apart as Mack and Crossan supposed.

To this end we shall in this chapter consider arguments favoring the Markan authorship of, and Petrine authority behind, the Gospel of Mark. Furthermore, we shall argue that the evidence suggests that it relates very early material and was probably composed sometime before A.D. 70.

THE TITLES OF THE GOSPELS

The case for Markan authorship must begin with the fact that this work, as it has come down to us, bears the title "The Gospel According to Mark." Whereas this was assumed to represent reliable tradition throughout church history, the last seventy years of liberal scholarship has by and large dismissed it without serious discussion.[1] Martin Hengel, however, has called for a reopening of the issue, and has in fact argued that the title of Mark's Gospel (and indeed of the other Gospels as well) is probably accurate, stemming from traditions that go back to the initial publication of the Gospel. While a full exposition of his (typically) meticulous and thorough case cannot be presented here, the seven main arguments that form his case can be summarized as follows.[2]

1. The original readings of the Gospels for liturgical purposes in the early Christian communities would have probably required titles to establish their authority and avoid confusion. It is, Hengel argues, difficult to envisage the earliest communities using these works in this fashion had these works remained anonymous for long.

2. The unanimity of the second-century testimony regarding the titles of each of the four Gospels further suggests that these documents received their titles very early (more on this below). This, for Hengel, is a crucial point. If the titles of the Gospels were added in the mid to late second century, we should expect a diversity of suggestions as to who authored them (as we find, for example, with a number of apocryphal Gospels). Instead, and quite remarkably, we find absolutely no variants from the received tradition.

3. Many incidental statements made by authorities early in the second century serve to further substantiate this unanimous testimony regarding the authorship of the canonical Gospels. Tertullian, for example, critiques Marcion's edited version of Luke for not having a name attached to it. This demonstrates the general relationship between the

perceived authority of a work and the (already) traditional title it bore.[3] The former depended on the latter.

4. The Gospels took on their titles prior to their canonization: they did not receive them as a means of justifying their canonization. The titles are present before the issue of canonization is present. And the fact that the sequence of the Gospels varies in second- and third-century citations while the titles never do also suggests that the titles were not ascribed to promote canonization.

5. In the case of Mark and Luke, it is difficult to see why they would have acquired the titles they did (and not, say, the authorship of more prestigious persons) had their titles been made up.

6. The unique manner in which the four canonical Gospels are titled ("The Gospel According to . . .") also argues against the common belief among contemporary scholars that they received their titles in the second century, according to Hengel. All fabricated titles follow their example, for which there is no clear precedent.

7. Finally, concerning Mark in particular, Hengel argues that the internal evidence suggests that the traditional title of this Gospel, and the tradition that Peter lies behind it, is correct (more on this below).

Hengel's argument, of course, falls short of *proving* that the four titles of the Gospels are historically correct. But it does suggest that they most likely go back to the earliest stages of each Gospel's circulation, which increases the probability that the titles are accurate. At the very least, his argument must be considered strong enough to invalidate the prevalent assumption that the early church is simply wrong in regarding the titles as accurate.

Our estimation of Hengel's argument for the traditional authorship of the Gospels in general, and of Mark in particular, increases when we consider several other lines of argumentation that support this position, to which we now turn. Given our focus on Mark as the foundational Gospel, our concern shall be specifically with this Gospel.

SECONDARY ATTESTATION

Papias and His Detractors

We have already noted that the secondary attestation to the authorship of Mark is unanimous in the second and third centuries. We need now to take a closer look at these witnesses.

The most important piece of secondary attestation to Mark's Gospel comes from Papias, as recorded in Eusebius. Between A.D. 120 and 130,

Papias relates information he says comes from the presbyter John whom he was a disciple under.

> Mark indeed, since he was the interpreter of Peter, wrote accurately, but not in order, the things either said or done by the Lord as much as he remembered. For he neither heard the Lord nor followed Him, but afterwards, as I have said, [heard and followed] Peter, who fitted his discourses to the needs [of his hearers] but not as if making a narrative of the Lord's sayings; consequently, Mark, writing some things just as he remembered, erred in nothing; for he was careful of one thing—not to omit anything of the things he had heard or to falsify anything in them.[4]

This is an extremely valuable piece of information. As Hengel says, "Here Papias is not advancing something that he has made up himself, but an old tradition guaranteed by the presbyter, which goes back to a time towards the end of the first century."[5] There is as yet no convincing reason to doubt the historical accuracy of this statement. It certainly predates any concern to artificially give Mark's Gospel apostolic clout in order to get it canonized, as has been sometimes argued.[6] Moreover, the incidental and unpretentious nature of the statement itself testifies against such a supposition. Indeed, far from serving an apologetic purpose, Papias' statement can be read as being somewhat disparaging of Mark's Gospel, emphasizing that it is largely secondhand and inferior to oral tradition, though nevertheless accurate.[7]

Nor is the frequently mentioned objection that form criticism has discredited Papias' statement by showing Mark to be a collection of originally individual stories conclusive. As I. Howard Marshall notes:

> [W]hile it may be granted that the Gospel contains come community tradition, this does not rule out the presence of some Petrine material also, and the latter could well have attained some of the forms characteristic of oral material simply as a result of Peter's having often recounted his memories when he was preaching and teaching in the church.[8]

It would, in fact, be quite remarkable if Peter's preaching did *not* in many respects parallel community tradition. He was, after all, a foundational spokesperson for just this tradition!

Nor are there any grounds for dismissing Papias' statement on the basis that it contradicts anything else we know about Peter or John

Mark. To the contrary, the tradition he is passing on squares perfectly with what we elsewhere find. Luke informs us that John Mark's house was a meeting place of believers in Jerusalem who seemed to have special ties with Peter (as opposed to James? Acts 12:12-17; cf. Gal. 1:18-19). While he was initially considered a burden to Paul, a fact that separated Paul from John Mark's cousin Barnabas (Acts 15:37-39), he later became his companion (Phile. 24; cf. 2 Tim. 4:11). But his closest ties seem to have remained with Peter, who later affectionately refers to him as "my son" (1 Peter 5:13), a reference that probably implies something of a "surrogate father relationship going back to Jerusalem in the thirties and forties."[9] Also noteworthy, as F.F. Bruce argues, is that Peter is "the chief preacher of the Gospel in the early chapters of Acts."[10] Unless we have grounds for supposing this canonical information to be altogether untrustworthy (see the next chapter) or that the tradition Papias is quoting was artificially contrived on the basis of this biblical information, we must simply be impressed with how well it squares with it all.[11]

Hence, we again find no basis for the customary dismissal of Papias' remark as having no significant bearing on the question of who authored the Gospel of Mark. And we are puzzled as to why Mack and Crossan don't so much as mention it in their most recent major works. Given the centrality their revisionist treatment of Mark has in their Cynic thesis, one might expect at least a refutation.

Arguments Supporting Papias' Statement

But we may go yet further and say that, not only are there no good reasons for dismissing this statement, there are actually a number of considerations that support it. First and foremost among these is the observation that Papias' statement is subsequently confirmed by virtually everyone who mentions the subject. Both the authorship of Mark and his connection with Peter are attested to by Justin, Irenaeus, Origen, Clement of Alexandria, as well as the so-called "anti-Marcionite" prologue. And while one can perhaps argue that Irenaeus, Origen, and Clement are simply repeating received tradition from Papias, the attestation of Justin and the anti-Marcionite prologue seem quite independent.[12]

What further confirms the independence and credibility of the anti-Marcionite prologue's reference in particular is that it incidentally mentions that the Mark who authored this Gospel was called "stubby-finger" because of his noticeably short fingers.[13] Such a personal derogatory aside suggests that the author(s) of this prologue was in touch with a reliable tradition that went back to Mark himself. There is clearly no discernible *apologetic motive* for making up such a comment!

In any case, it is difficult to overturn such a strong, early, unanimous tradition. Certainly the modern tendency among more radical critics to prefer their own speculations over such ancient testimonies is unwarranted.[14] The early tradition has to be seriously wrestled with, and any attempt to replace it is going to have to include a plausible alternative to their testimony as to how this Markan-Petrine tradition got started, and why it was so quickly, and universally, accepted. But this has not yet been done.

Secondly, as we have already mentioned, the widespread acceptance of Mark, and (if we accept Markan priority) his almost wholesale inclusion in Luke and Matthew, is difficult to account for if Mark was simply an unknown author with no apostolic authority behind him. Indeed, the very fact that this Gospel continued to live on in the church, despite the fact that after Matthew and Luke he had little distinctive to say, is most easily explained on the supposition that Papias' statement is accurate: the work is authored by John Mark under the guidance of the Apostle Peter.[15]

INTERNAL CONSIDERATIONS OF PETRINE AUTHORITY

A number of internal considerations of Mark's Gospel also support Papias' received view that Peter stands behind this Gospel. Mark's Gospel is certainly constructed around Peter more than any other Gospel, mentioning him twenty-five times in all. He is the first disciple mentioned (1:16) and he stands at the head of all the lists of the disciples and of the Twelve (3:16-18; 5:37; 9:2; 13:3). This "cannot be explained as mere convention; there must be profound historical reasons behind it."[16] Moreover, Peter is consistently portrayed as standing within Jesus' most intimate circle (5:37; 9:2; 13:3; 14:33), and with two exceptions (9:38-41; 10:35-40) Peter is the only individual to stand over and against Jesus throughout Mark's narrative (8:29, 32-33; 9:5; 10:28; 11:21; 14:29-31).[17]

But the distinct focus on Peter is not all praiseworthy; this also is very significant. While Peter is the first to acknowledge Jesus' messiahship, he is rebuked by him in the harshest possible terms (8:29-30, 32-33). His exemplary willingness to follow Jesus at all costs is matched, if not surpassed, by his abysmal failure to actually do so (14:29-31, 37, 66-72). And his spiritual insight is often portrayed as being quite dull (9:5-6; 10:28). To a number of scholars, the "true-to-life" quality of this account testifies to its authenticity and perhaps indicates that Peter's own reflections lay behind it.[18] Indeed, given Peter's later status in the church, it is difficult to conceive of such disparaging insights coming from anyone other than Peter himself.

At the very least, were Mark's narrative composed with a post-Easter motive either to buttress or to undermine Peter's position within the church—both views have their defendants—one would think the portrayal would be more unambiguous one way or the other. Instead, what we find in Mark is stark realism.

The distinctly Petrine perspective of this Gospel is also signified in a number of other incidental ways. Several examples must suffice. The personal nature of the report of Jesus' healing of Peter's mother-in-law and the way the episode awkwardly fits into the overall framework of Mark's narrative perhaps suggests Peter's own reminiscences behind it (1:29-31). Indeed, the incidental way Peter's house is repeatedly mentioned throughout this Gospel is itself significant (1:35-36; 2:1; 3:20; 7:17; 9:33). It makes perfect sense if the story is ultimately being told from Peter's perspective.

Relatedly, instead of simply referring to "the people" seeking after Jesus while he was praying (as in Luke 4:42), Mark mentions "Simon and his companions" (1:36). Similarly, what is pointed out as being significant about Andrew is that he is Simon's brother (1:16). Also noteworthy is that the failure of the disciples to stay awake with Jesus in Gethsemane is driven home in a personal and poignant way in relation to Peter when Jesus singles him out and asks, "Simon, are you asleep? Could you not keep watch for one hour?" (14:37) Indeed, the personal address of "Simon" here, after he has already received his honorific surname "Peter" (3:16), is arguably another indication of Petrine reminiscence standing behind the narrative.[19]

Moreover, psychological comments are made about Peter throughout Mark's narrative that are not made of the other disciples and are most unlikely to have been contrived (11:21; 14:72). And, finally, when the women receive their angelic instructions upon discovering the empty tomb, they are, most significantly, told to tell the news to Jesus' disciples "and Peter" (16:7).

EYEWITNESS FEATURES OF MARK'S NARRATIVE

Several other general features of Mark's narrative perhaps suggest that Papias' statement about Peter standing behind it is accurate.

The "They" Passages of Mark

First, while too much should not be made of this, it has with some plausibility been argued that behind many of Mark's uses of the third person plural is an original first person plural that reflects Peter's perspective (e.g., 1:29-31; 8:22; 9:30; 11:12; etc.). The group activity mentioned in such passages fits well with the view that Peter originally told the story to Mark in the first person plural. A comparison with Matthew's and Luke's use of Mark (if we follow Markan priority) reveals that this perspective has largely been dropped out of the picture. This suggestion, first made by C.H. Turner in 1928, is, of course, highly speculative, but it gains in plausibility to the extent that we have *other* reasons for already suspecting that Peter stands behind Mark's Gospel.[20]

Incidental Names and Graphic Description in Mark's Narrative

If we read Mark in a straightforward manner and do not at the outset presuppose that he is an artistic genius in fabricating historical realism, the remarkable vividness and detail that characterizes much of his narrative is most easily explained as deriving from the recollections of an eyewitness.[21] One cannot, for example, help but be somewhat impressed by the specificity with which Mark identifies people, especially those that don't factor into his overall narrative framework. In this fashion we learn of such people as Barabbas (15:6-15), Simon of Cyrene, the father of Alexander and Rufus (15:21, see below), Mary the mother of James the younger and of Joses, as well as Salome and Joseph of Arimathea (15:40, 43; 16:1). To suggest that figures such as these were simply created out of thin air by Mark to serve some hypothetical problem he was facing is to betray the incidental nature of these references and to thereby create more problems in interpreting this Gospel than one is supposedly solving.

Similarly, the wealth of incidental detail found throughout Mark's Gospel is impressive. If read at face value, passages such as 4:35-38, 6:39-40, and 9:14-29 betray an almost "photographic image" of the episode Mark is narrating.[22] He is equally as graphic at picking up, in a most incidental fashion, the emotions of people throughout his narrative. Thus, for example, the anticipation of a crowd at sunset, facing the door of the house Jesus was staying in, doesn't go unnoticed by Mark (1:32-33). Nor does the realistic combination of sorrow and scorn of the friends and relatives of a deceased child (5:38-41).[23] The somber fear and amazement of the disciples as they follow behind Jesus (another interesting incidental detail) as he heads into Jerusalem for the last time also reflects Mark's realism and attention to detail (10:32).[24] And no attempt is made by this author to soften either the angry and biting question of the disciples toward Jesus, nor his harsh reply, when they were together caught in a storm at sea (4:38-40; cf. Matthew's possible softening—assuming Markan priority—in Matt. 8:24-25). It is hard to escape the conclusion that such incidental detail and realism, even when it is damaging to the "heroes" of the story, betrays the influence of an honest eyewitness.

Relatedly, the deep, and surprisingly realistic, emotions of Jesus as he responds to different situations with pity (1:40-44), love (10:17, 21), anger (10:13-16), anxiety (14:33-34), and alienation (15:34) are also captured by Mark, some of which one would think would be left out of a fabricated account.[25] So too other incidental and unexpected features about Jesus' behavior are noted by Mark, such as his expressions and gestures (7:33; 9:36; 10:16) as well as the interesting (if not cryptic) fact that on a number of occasions Jesus paused to purview those around him (3:5, 34; 5:32; 10:23; 11:11). His surprising and scandalous association with women in Mark's Gospel must also be noted, for this would hardly be a selling point for a fictitious account in the first century.[26] It is, however, what one might expect from an eyewitness influenced account that is interested in saying "what actually happened."

Detail of Time and Place in Mark

Combined with all of this is Mark's remarkable descriptive detail about the time and place of events. While Papias himself has told us that one cannot derive a detailed chronology of Jesus' activity and teaching from Mark (something form criticism later "discovered"), we must nevertheless note that his narrative is interlaced with historical allusions to particular times and places.[27] This further serves to root his Gospel in history and to suggest the influence of an eyewitness such as Peter behind it.

So, for example, Mark notes not only that Jesus "approached Jerusalem," but also that he "came to Bethphage and Bethany at the Mount of Olives" (11:1). He then entered Jerusalem and went to the temple. He looked around and was apparently disturbed, but "since it was already late he went out to Bethany with the Twelve" (11:11). This sort of vivid geographical and temporal reference one finds throughout Mark. Indeed, his entire narrative is strung together by such vivid references. And while it is not impossible that such allusions are literary devices, one would only come to this conclusion if they already assumed that

Mark was not relaying historical reminiscences. If, however, Mark is taken at face value, such allusions readily suggest that the recollection of an eyewitness lies behind this work.[28]

The renowned philologist and Homeric scholar Wolfgang Schadewaldt speaks to this point when he says:

> [W]e cannot be other than captivated by the experiential vividness with which we are confronted. The conditions of their time stand before us: nature, the landscape of Palestine, the Sea of Galilee, places from the coast to the far side of the Jordan, and Nazareth with its sheer cliff. If only we read the text simply enough, we can imagine Jesus traveling here and there — a situation which we misunderstand if we see the repeated "on the way" . . . as no more than literary decoration. . . . I know of no other area of history-writing, biography or poetry where I encounter so great a wealth of material in such a small space.[29]

Such a wealth of detail, argues Schadewaldt, betrays as much an eyewitness influence when found in the Gospels as it does when found in Homer, Plato, or Shakespeare. And, he concludes, only a hypercritical approach to these documents — an approach long abandoned in literary studies! — could deny this.[30]

To insist, as both Mack and Crossan do, that such detailed references as these are the result of Mark's creative imagination is, at best, to treat Mark unfairly. If Mark's narrative *lacked* this wealth of detail, one suspects they would draw the exact same conclusion. One has to ask, if this sort of incidental detail doesn't at least *count toward* the historicity of a document (whether or not it does so decisively is another matter), what would? Certainly not its absence! As we seek to ascertain the historical value of this document, what more can be asked of any ancient biography beyond what Mark has given us?

When these considerations are combined with the above mentioned supporting secondary evidence, it seems that the simplest and best historical explanation for this detailed historical flavor of Mark is not that it is the result of the "clever" imagination of an otherwise unknown person, but that it is due to its being significantly influenced by Peter.

THE "LITTLE APOCALYPSE" AND THE DATING OF MARK

If the Markan authorship and Petrine authority of the Gospel of Mark is regarded as established, very little hangs upon the actual dating of this work. And that is fortunate, for very little can be said with any degree of certainty about this matter. Insofar as we are generally inclined to reckon accounts more reliable the closer they are to the events they record, however, a brief word on the subject is in order.

The primary reason why Mack and Crossan – and a majority of historical-critical scholars – date Mark after A.D. 70 is that Mark has Jesus prophesy the destruction of the temple in Mark 13, what is known as the "little apocalypse" of Mark.[31] Since it is assumed that neither Jesus nor Mark could have had knowledge of this event ahead of time, a post-70 date is required. The "prophecy," in other words, is a *vaticinium ex eventu* (prophecy after the event). Three general considerations, however, lead us to judge this argument inconclusive.

First, while we can empathize with that line of historical reasoning that would be *inclined* to read prophecy as "retroactive history" and thus would be *inclined* to date Mark after the "fulfillment" of this prophecy, we cannot agree that this consideration alone should settle the issue. For, as I have already argued, there is no good reason to rule out the possibility that our post-Enlightenment "closed continuum" worldview might be limited. Thus, if we have other reasons for dating Mark early, and other reasons for regarding him as relaying generally reliable history, then we must weigh these considerations against the view that Mark 13 is a *vaticinium ex eventu* and thus against an A.D. post-70 dating. We may, in fact, perhaps have to entertain the possibility that the historical Jesus could, at times, predict the future.

Secondly, certain features of Mark 13 seem incompatible with the view that this passage is a *vaticinium ex eventu*. For one thing, 13:1 implies that the temple was still standing at the time the narrative was written.[32] Even more importantly, however, on the traditional understanding of apocalyptic imagery, Jesus seems to connect the destruction of the temple with the end of the world. When pressed on the question of when this terrible event will happen (vv. 3-4), Jesus says that there first will be worldwide wars and numerous earthquakes and famines (v. 9). Followers of Jesus will be severely persecuted and made to stand before "governors and kings as witnesses to them" (v. 9). In the course of preaching the Gospel "to all nations," believers will be turned over by their own families and will be hated "by all men" because of Christ (vv. 12-13). The sun and moon will be darkened, and stars will fall from the sky (vv. 24-25). And then the Son of Man will appear (vv. 26-27).

The passage raises certain exegetical difficulties for those of us who want to affirm both the historicity of this passage and that Jesus was accurate in making these predictions. But my present point is that the passage raises far more serious difficulties for any view that would want to read this as Mark retroactively putting words into Jesus' mouth. For surely Mark would know that not all of this took place when, or before, the temple was destroyed![33] The widespread wars, earthquakes, famines, and worldwide evangelism had not occurred. So, one naturally wonders ·why Mark would have had Jesus associate his prophecy with such phenomenon. We should, in other words, expect a retroactive prophecy to be much more tidy in squaring with recent history than what we actually find in Mark 13.

A third point, however, is this: it is not perfectly clear that one need even appeal to any supernatural ability on Jesus' part to see him predicting the destruction of the temple. The theme of the destruction of the temple, resulting from God's judgment on Israel's infidelity to him, was a widespread prophetic theme dating back hundreds of years before Jesus.[34] In this light, it is not too difficult to see the prophet Jesus, sensing the increasing tension between Jews and Romans, and distressed by the state of Israel's faith, predicting in customary apocalyptic language the temple's destruction. Nor is it difficult to accept that Mark could have recorded such a prediction years before the event actually happened. Indeed, we know of several contemporaries of Jesus who were saying the exact same thing.[35] So far as we can discern, this consideration alone pulls the rug out from under the argument that uses this passage to argue for an A.D. post-70 dating of this Gospel.

INTERNAL EVIDENCE OF EARLY MATERIAL IN MARK

As to exactly when this Gospel was written, little more than a guess can be made, though internal considerations point in the direction that it was early.[36] In 15:21 Mark refers, without explanation, to "A certain man from Cyrene, Simon, the father of Alexander and Rufus" who was forced to help Jesus carry his cross. The statement is utterly inexplicable except on the assumption that Mark's audience was well-acquainted with Alexander and Rufus.[37] Matthew and Luke, interestingly enough, make no reference to them.[38] This not only further entrenches this work in actual history away from any view of it as theological fiction; it also most probably locates it within the first generation of Christian believers.[39]

Similarly, Mark mentions Pilate without feeling the need to tell his readers who he was (Matthew and Luke note that he was "governor"), and, conversely, Mark refers to "the high priest" without feeling the need to name him (whereas Matthew and Luke correctly name him as Caiaphas) (Mark 15:1; 14:53-54). The most natural explanation of this is that Mark's audience did not need to be told what position Pilate held or who held the distinctive position of "high priest" when Jesus was crucified. Since Pilate ceased to be governor in A.D. 36, and Caiaphus ceased to be high priest in A.D. 37, the farther away from these dates we move in dating Mark's Gospel, the less intelligible these Markan assumptions become.[40] We are again led to the conclusion that, whenever Mark's Gospel was written, it couldn't have been all that late.

A third consideration that possibly suggests an early dating of Mark concerns the fact that Mark accurately reflects, in quite a detailed manner, the contours of Palestinian Judaism before the time of the fall of Jerusalem. "His work is still wholly oriented on this period."[41] Thus, in Mark's Gospel, the "scribes," who (accurately) form a distinct class from the Pharisees and Sadducees, come to Galilee from Jerusalem which, prior to A.D. 70, was the center of Torah study (e.g., 3:22; 7:1). The "scribes of the Pharisees" (2:16, NASB) are portrayed (accurately) as the intellectual leaders of the Pharisaic party and are mentioned more frequently in Jerusalem than they are in Galilee (in contrast to the Pharisees themselves), while the Sadducees are completely absent from Galilee.[42] And, perhaps most remarkably, Mark's delineation of the members of the Sanhedrin, the "elders," "chief priests," and "teachers of the law" (8:31; 10:33; 11:18, 27; 14:1, 10, 43, 55; 15:1, 3, 10-11, 31), groups that ceased to exist with the destruction of the temple, is on all accounts accurate.

What makes this impressive, as Hengel notes, is that "After 70 this whole pluralistic political and religious landscape, which Mark depicts quite accurately in broad outline, was destroyed."[43] The fact that he gets it right, and does so in detail, seems to suggest that an A.D. pre-70 dating is more reasonable than an A.D. post-70 dating.

One final consideration of the "primitiveness" of Mark's Gospel concerns his view of who is important and who is not in earliest Christianity. To be specific, Mark always places James immediately after Peter and before John in his lists of disciples (9:2; 14:33; 5:37; 9:2; cf. 1:29; 3:17; etc.), though James died early and was quickly surpassed in significance by his brother John, something perhaps reflected in Luke's tendency to reverse their order (Luke 8:51; 9:28).[44] Mark's repeated reference to "the Twelve" is also indicative of a very early Christian tradition (cf. 1 Cor. 15:5), as is his rare and informal use of "apostle" (6:30).

All in all, such incidental features of Mark's Gospel lend further credibility to the view that we are here dealing with a fairly early and reliable document. While attempting to fix a more exact date for the composition of this Gospel would lead us too far astray from the restricted scope of this work, we may with some confidence conclude that the perspective we find in Mark is not at all the perspective one might reasonably expect were he simply creating a story to meet the needs of a disintegrating community sometime after A.D. 70.

CONCLUSION: MARK AND THE HISTORICAL JESUS

One simply has to undermine the historical credibility of Mark to maintain that the real historical Jesus was a Cynic sage, for Mark's portrait of Jesus is anything but that. Like all the other attempts of the various "quests" to find a natural Jesus behind the supernatural portrait of the Gospels (see chap. 1), Mack and Crossan must get over this hurdle if their portraits are to be judged credible.

We have in the last two chapters examined Mack's and Crossan's attempts to do this and have concluded that, on a number of scores, they are unsuccessful. Their views of Mark are unsupported by any evidence outside of other assumptions made within their overall schema. Their accounts do not constitute the easiest way of reading the evidence, but rather seem unnecessarily complex in attempting to explain away the evidence. Nor do their accounts have the kind of inherent plausibility that would render them easy to believe. Among other things, they leave insufficiently answered the question of how and why an unknown author would or could contrive such an account, within a Jewish worldview, and be so readily accepted as a definitive authority within the early Christian movement.

We have also seen that Mack and Crossan's treatment of Mark appears unwarranted in the light of customary historiographical protocol in which the burden of proof is always on the historian to demonstrate error, not vice versa. Relatedly, I have attempted to demonstrate that, for all his kerygmatic interest, Mark does nonetheless intend to record history, and that he should therefore be judged by the same standards as other ancient historians. And finally, I have argued that Mack's and Crossan's views do not square with the very solid external and internal evidence that this Gospel was composed by John Mark, under the guidance of Peter, and at a relatively early date.

While all of this, of course, falls short of proving that Mark is to be considered reliable in all respects, the evidence in favor of accepting the church tradition on his authorship and authority certainly goes a long way in establishing his general reliability. It is, in fact, about as solid as historical evidence ever gets. And it certainly is enough to render most improbable Mack and Crossan's view that Mark is largely the result of intentional mythmaking.

In concluding section 4, I posed the awkward historical question Paul's epistles force upon us: Namely, what must the historical Jesus have been like to have created a movement that so quickly (if not immediately) came to see him in the incredibly exalted fashion it did? How do we explain first-century Jews coming to the point of worshiping a contemporary human being and speaking of him as the Creator of the world?

I shall conclude this chapter by noting that Mark's Gospel, if it is judged reliable, provides us with a ready answer. It involves no speculations about unknown social histories and unprovable motives; it isn't dependent upon tenuous conclusions drawn from hypothetical documents; it doesn't require of us that we read Mark more cynically than we'd read any other ancient book that purports to tell history; and in terms of simplicity as a hypothesis, it stands alone. It is, quite simply, that Jesus was, in fact, the kind of person Mark said he was. If his portrait is at all accurate, then all the evidence from Paul and Mark becomes intelligible (including Q!), just as it stands. If it is not, however, then the sort of highly complex speculations and tenuous conclusions of Mack and Crossan are the best we can hope for.

What I have attempted to demonstrate in the last two chapters is that we have no compelling reason to opt for Mack's and Crossan's speculations over the portrait given in Mark. We have very good grounds for regarding Mark's portrait as basically historically reliable. This portrait is no "myth of origins": it is, in all probability, written by an early follower of Jesus and governed by an apostolic eyewitness of Jesus. Moreover, on its own internal merits it gives us every reason to regard it as generally trustworthy.

And all of this entails that, for all intents and purposes, this document brings us face to face with the person the Pauline communities were worshiping and ascribing divine titles and activities to. And in doing this, it answers the question of how a historical figure could have inspired such an astounding phenomenon. If Jesus was like *this*, it is not altogether surprising that the earliest Christian communities were like *that*. A Jesus who was as Mark portrays him could conceivably have inspired a movement that exhibits the features displayed in Paul's letters. A lesser Jesus obviously could not.

The supernatural Jesus of Mark's Gospel, of course, is difficult for many twentieth-century people to accept. It is not the kind of portrait a modern could be expected to accept *were there not good evidence in its favor*. But the evidence is there. And, rather than adjusting the evidence to make this Jesus more palatable to twentieth-century sensibilities, it seems more reasonable to leave it intact and to simply allow the enigma of this first-century Jew to confront our twentieth-century sensibilities. It just may be that history is, after all, *not* a closed continuum!

The evidence which forces this conclusion upon us, however, is by no means restricted to the evidence from Paul and Mark alone. Further evidence that the historical Jesus was as Mark portrays him, and that the earliest Christian communities were as Paul reflects them, is found in Luke's earliest record of the history of the early church, *The Acts of the Apostles*. This record too must be thoroughly overturned by all who would insist on a "closed continuum" view of history and who would therefore seek to construct a revisionist portrait of Jesus compatible with this view of history. For Luke's portrait of the early church as being birthed soon after Jesus' death, as being centered on the person of Jesus Christ as the Son of God, and as being founded on a faith in his bodily resurrection, is completely incompatible with any view that supposes that Jesus was a mere man and that his earliest followers understood him as such.

Unfortunately for such revisionist accounts, however, the evidence that Luke records accurate history is very strong, as I shall now show in the next chapter. And the evidence that the resurrection of Jesus was a historical event is inescapable, as I shall show in our final chapter.

·SECTION 6·

The Early Church
and the Historical Jesus

12

ACTS OF LUKE'S MIND
OR ACTS OF THE APOSTLES?
An Examination of the
Trustworthiness of Acts

T he understanding of the historical Jesus as a Cynic sage, we have seen, requires a very definite understanding of how the early church developed. The church began as a small, loosely defined, Galilean social experiment in radical egalitarianism. Struggling against social pressures and in search of a social self-identity, it gradually broke into several disparate branches, each developing its own distinct mythologies about Jesus to justify their own evolving self-understanding.

As we have seen, for both Crossan and Mack, Q-1 and early GosThom represent communities that remained closest to the teachings of the historical Jesus. They based their distinct identity on a body of Cynic-like sayings. They did not conceive of Jesus as the Son of God, as a miracle worker, or as having been raised from the dead. In time, however, the original Q community evolved a more exalted, and more apocalyptic, mythology about their founder, while the community behind GosThom veered off in a more gnostic direction.

Such mythological developments were mild, however, compared to the extravagant understandings that evolved in the Christ-cult congregations of Paul, the apocalyptic narratives of Mark, and the congregations behind the fully developed mythologies of John. The mythological tendencies of these congregations, hammered out under internal and external pressures put upon them, moved well beyond anything that the people of Q or Thomas ever envisioned, as we have seen. For here Jesus was envisioned as the divine Son of God, coming down to earth to save believers through his death, and as being enthroned as the apocalyptic judge of the world through his resurrection.

In each case, the mythological view of Jesus arrived at was the direct result of the group's need to work out internal conflicts (especially of authority) and to justify its floundering social experiment to a world that was not inclined to accept it. And, as we have seen, the ultimate result of the whole process was that the heart of what the original Jesus people were originally fighting for—radical egalitarianism—was largely sacrificed for the myth used to defend it (which is why it now takes such careful critical scholarship to "rediscover" this "original" movement).

It is again crucial to note that this conception of the multifarious and haphazard development of the Jesus-people congregations is no mere addendum to the Cynic thesis. Without it, the Cynic thesis could not for a moment stand. It is this revisionist understanding of early church history alone that provides Mack and Crossan with a framework within which they can attempt to provide a coherent account of how a Cynic sage naturally evolved into a divine Son of God. Take away this revisionist account of the floundering social experiment of the Jesus people and you've taken away the only means the Cynic thesis has for rendering itself at all plausible.

This understanding, however, obviously flies directly in the face of the earliest account we possess of the history of the early church, Luke's Acts of the Apostles. Far from being a multitude of differing groups evolving quite contradictory mythical portraits of Christ, Acts depicts the history of the early church as being from the start a largely unified and dynamic force, centered on an exalted view of Christ. Indeed, the differences between the portrait of the early church provided in the Book of Acts and the revisionist understanding of Mack and Crossan could hardly be greater. Hence, if Mack and Crossan are close to being correct, Luke's narrative history must be judged as being almost totally devoid of historical value.[1] It must be, as they in fact contend, a very late piece composed largely of Christian lore by someone who was not close to the original Jesus movement.[2] Conversely, if Luke's narrative can in fact be shown to be rooted in reliable history, then there is no possible way that Mack and Crossan can be close to the truth in their own reconstructions.

So the all-important question is who is to be trusted. And this question largely reduces down to the issue of the historical reliability of Acts.[3] It is a question that can only be settled by an examination of the concrete evidence, something that is frequently lacking in many contemporary literary-critical approaches to Acts.[4] Are there historical grounds for supposing that this work provides for us a more trustworthy account than that of Crossan and Mack's reconstruction?

In this chapter I shall argue for an affirmative answer to this question. We have remarkably good grounds for accepting the portrait of the early church in Acts as being quite reliable. And these same grounds constitute further proof that Mack and Crossan's view of the historical Jesus as a Cynic sage is fundamentally flawed.

THE AUTHOR OF ACTS

As with all the Gospels, the traditional authorship of Acts is unanimously attested to in the early church. Luke, the "beloved physician" and companion of Paul (Col. 4:14; cf. Phile. 24; 2 Tim. 4:11), composed Acts as the second part of his two-volume work. The first surviving explicit references to Luke as the author of Acts come from the second century. Irenaeus, Clement of Alexandria, Tertullian, and Origen all attest to his authorship, and they do so in incidental ways showing that in their day the point needed no argumentation. His authorship is also attested to in the Muratorian fragment and the Anti-Marcionite prologue of Luke.[5] The antiquity and unanimity of this witness must impress us. So must the fact that there is no discernable ulterior motive on the part of the tradition for naming Luke as the author: he certainly plays no prominent authoritative role in the early church.

Internal considerations of the work give us no reason to doubt the trustworthiness of this tradition. It is almost beyond doubt that the author of Acts is the same as the author of the third Gospel.[6] His opening reference to his "former book" and his renaming his primary reader as "Theophilus" is itself almost enough to establish as much (1:2; cf. Luke 1:1-4). The close similarity and style of both works also points to the same conclusion.[7] And the overall distinctive outlook of the two works are essentially the same. Both works, for example, share a distinctive universal scope, a sympathetic treatment of women, a concern for Gentiles, a similar apologetic tendency, and an identical christology. A host of other more incidental considerations also indicate that one author wrote the two works as a two-volume set.[8]

It is also clear from a straightforward reading of the text that the author of Acts was at times a companion of the Apostle Paul. This further attests to Lucan authorship as well as for the general reliability of his narrative. His detailed knowledge of Paul's life, confirmed by Paul's own letters but evidencing no dependence on them (see below), already points in this direction. But the most impressive indication of his companionship with Paul is the incidental way the author switches from the usual first person singular to the first person plural at certain junctures in his narrative (16:10-17; 20:5–21:18; 27:1–28:16).[9] Such switches are too subtle and infrequent to constitute a fictitious apologetic ploy or be seen as mere literary convention.[10] And attempts to postulate an earlier written source to explain them are speculative and create unnecessary theoretical sources: a move, as we have seen, that always weakens any hypothesis.[11] Nor is there a shred of literary evidence to support such a view.[12]

The frequent attempts to override this evidence by appealing to supposed discrepancies between Paul's and Luke's theology are not convincing, for several reasons.[13] First, even if certain differences in theological perspective are granted, it is not clear why this would in and of itself preclude seeing Luke as a disciple and companion of Paul. Companions frequently share different perspectives on matters, and disciples frequently do not fully capture the depth of their mentors.[14] But secondly, the supposed differences are all minor when the different purposes of Acts and Paul's epistles are taken into consideration. While Luke certainly has a driving theological interest, he is writing as a historian. One should not, therefore, expect of him the sort of theological insight and precision one finds in Paul.

Hence, for example, when Luke paraphrases Paul as saying, "Through him [Christ] everyone who believes is justified from everything you could not be justified from by the law of Moses" (13:39), one should not press him too far and suppose that he is saying, in contradiction to Paul, that people could nevertheless be justified from *some* things by the Law of Moses. This is, as Robinson notes, a "typical 'lay' summary of a theologian's position: inadequate in precision of statement . . . but sufficient in general intention."[15] As such, it constitutes no basis for overriding the literary evidence from Acts that Luke was indeed an occasional companion of Paul.

Nor is the fact that the Paul of Acts was willing to have Timothy circumcised (16:3) and to participate in a temple ceremony involving four men taking a Nazirite vow (21:23-24) evidence that Luke's portrait essentially contradicts the "real" Paul who clearly broke from Judaism, and especially from the practice of circumcision (Gal. 5:6; 6:15). For while the Paul we find in the Pauline epistles was certainly opposed to finding any salvific significance in Jewish rites, he nevertheless was extremely flexible on matters of social propriety (Rom. 14:5-23; 1 Cor. 9:19-23).

We find, therefore, no convincing arguments against, and a number of convincing arguments for, the traditional view that Luke, a companion of Paul, authored this work. And this is very significant for our estimation of the reliability of the work. It means, in a nutshell, that the author of Acts was a close follower of Paul, and thus was clearly in a good position to "carefully investigate everything from the beginning" (Luke 1:3).[16] And this already entails that any revisionist account of the early church that must suppose that this work is fundamentally unreliable in its portrayal of the early church is going to have to go to great lengths to prove it.

THE DATE OF ACTS

The date we assign to Acts is of some consequence to our assessment of its historical value. While one can theoretically hold to a later date for this work and yet regard it as quite reliable, it is nevertheless true that one's estimation of the historical value of this work (and usually of any work) tends to diminish the later it is dated from the events it records. Establishing an early date is important, as Hemer has argued, because one's dating of this work "influences the formulation of questions, and excludes inapplicable lines of argumentation." More specifically, "[t]heories of tradition-historical reinterpretation by the early church tend to require time, and to become more difficult with early datings."[17] Hence, the earlier this work is understood to have been written, the more difficult it is to assume that the traditions it embodies have undergone significant transformation. And hence, the more likely it is that it conveys reliable history.

Response to Second-Century Datings

Crossan and Mack are in line with the most radical strand of contemporary scholarship in dating Acts in the early to mid-second century.[18] This radical tradition goes back to F.C. Baur who postulated such a late date for Acts primarily because it fit his dialectical understanding of the early church. In his view, "Luke" was the major synthesizer of the previously antagonistic Petrine and Pauline branches of Christianity, and such a synthesis could not be understood to have occurred until the mid-second century.[19]

More recent scholarship within this tradition has not altogether abandoned Baur's view — Acts is frequently seen as an example of the kind of "early catholicism" found in Ephesians (also dated very late) and among the second-century Apologists[20] — but the emphasis now tends to be on the political climate presupposed in Acts. In a word, Luke is thoughout his narrative clearly concerned to present the Roman government in a positive light and to show that Christians, unlike the Jews, present no threat to them (e.g., Acts 5:33-39; 13:7, 12; 16:35-39; 18:12-17; 24:1-26; 26:32; 27:3, 43; 28:30-31). The same may be said of his first volume in which Jesus is portrayed as encouraging the paying of taxes (Luke 20:20-25) while in his trial Pilate is exonerated and the Jews blamed (23:1-25). This apologetic agenda, it is argued, makes more sense in the mid-second century than it does in the first.

However, there are a host of considerations which, if taken together, count decisively against this view. First, the view does not square easily with the above mentioned literary evidence that we are in Acts hearing from a companion of Paul. Nor does it easily account for the remarkably detailed accuracy exemplified in this document concerning matters in the mid-first century, a point to be discussed below. Nor does it readily explain other internal factors (e.g., Luke's abrupt ending in A.D. 62) — again, to be discussed below — that also point to an early dating. Nor does it explain why no use is made of the writings of its central figure, Paul, for on the supposition that we are dealing with a late apologetic for Paul one might have expected his (now circulated) writings to be at least referred to.[21]

Neither is it necessary to postulate a late date to explain Luke's "catholicism." For, as we have seen in previous chapters, the postulation of a radical break between Pauline and Petrine communities that Luke is supposed to have mended is itself an unwarranted postulation.[22] And, finally, the supposition of a mid-second century date for this work cannot readily explain the likelihood that this work is quoted by various authors as authoritative prior to 120. It is, for example, arguable that 1 Clement 2:1 (A.D. 96) refers to Acts 20:35; that the Epistle of Barnabas 19:8 (A.D. 100?) cites Acts 4:32; that Ignatius (A.D. 110) cites Acts 1:25; and that Polycarp (A.D. 120) refers to Acts 2:24 and 10:42 in 1:2 and 2:1 respectively of his epistle.[23] Unless the proximity with the Acts passages can be accounted for another way, a first-century date for this work seems to be required.

Even more fundamentally, however, there is no reason to accept the supposition that Luke's apologetic purpose only makes sense in the mid-second century. As Bruce points out, "Any period of tension between church and Roman state might serve" to explain Luke's apologetic purpose. And the mid-first century is just as good a candidate for such a period as is the mid-second century.[24] The supposed parallels between the second-century Apologists and Acts do not tip the scales decisively in favor of the latter. For it is, first of all, not clear how much should be made of such supposed parallels: some scholars have argued that the enormous differences in motive, style, and content between Acts and the Apologists render all commonalities largely coincidental.[25] But, secondly, even if the parallels are granted, there is no reason to rule out the possibility of understanding Acts to be a precursor to the (later) works of the second-century Apologists.[26]

Finally, placing Acts in the second century must be seen as being more speculative than placing it in the first, if only because we know much less about the general relationship of the church with the state in the second century than we do in the first. While we certainly know of local persecutions against the church and of local governors trying to arrive at a policy about them (e.g., Pliny), we cannot confidently assert what the situation was like in the locale of the author of Acts, assuming a second-century date. The evidence is in fact ambiguous enough so that Koester can actually argue for a second-century dating of Acts on the basis of how *peaceful* the church-state relations were at the time![27]

The Ending of Acts and the Fall of Jerusalem

By contrast, the evidence for a mid-first century dating is quite strong. One fact that strongly impressed Adolf von Harnack, and a number of scholars after him, is that the narrative of Acts breaks off abruptly with the trial of Paul at Rome. Given the centrality of Paul to this work, this is difficult to explain except on the supposition that Paul had not yet been martyred when Luke wrote his narrative.[28]

It is sometimes responded that such a "happy ending" fits Luke's apologetic purposes. But it is certainly difficult to suppose that Theophilus, or any later reader, would have been very impressed with Luke's intentional glossing over the obvious truth that Paul, along with "a vast multitude" of believers (Tacitus), were mercilessly martyred under Nero.

Another response has been to argue that, while Luke doesn't end his work with Paul's martyrdom, the prediction of Acts 20:25 shows that he is nevertheless aware of it. But it is not at all clear that 20:25 is a prediction of Paul's death or just an indication of Paul's missionary resolution. And even if it were the former, this does nothing to explain why Luke would omit the fulfillment of this prophecy in his own work.[29] The less frequent responses that the original ending of Luke has been lost, or that Luke had intended a third volume, are even weaker.[30] In reality, they only serve to demonstrate how desperately *some* explanation for Acts' abrupt ending is called for.[31]

Related to this, not only is Paul's martyrdom not mentioned, but the deaths of Peter and James are omitted as well. This is surprising in light of the fact that Luke is quick to note the earlier martyrdom of lesser figures such as Stephen (7:57-59) and James the brother of John (12:2) while Paul, Peter, and James are obviously key figures throughout Luke's narrative.[32] The omission of James' death is particularly significant, for according to Josephus, it took place at the hands of the Sanhedrin *against* the Roman authorities. If part of Luke's apologetic scheme is to say that it is unbelieving Jews, not the Roman government, that constitute the real enemies of the Gospels, then "[n]o incident could have served Luke's apologetic purpose better"—had he known about it.[33]

We may, in fact, go further and say that the total absence of any allusion to Nero's persecution or the Jewish Roman war—though Luke is elsewhere interested in church/state and Jewish/Roman relations—is likewise difficult to explain except on the supposition that Luke was writing *before* these events took place. One particular facet of this omission stands out as most remarkable: namely, Luke's omission of any reference to the fall of Jerusalem and the destruction of the temple.

For an author whose narrative is centrally structured around Jerusalem (Luke 24:13; Acts 1:8) and who makes frequent mention of the temple (Acts 2:46; 3:1-2, 8, 10; 5:20-25; 21:28-30, etc.), this omission is most surprising. For an author who took the time to mention the much less significant expulsion of the Jews from Rome under Claudius (18:2), this omission is indeed astounding. And for an author who is interested in how persecutions of the church helped spread the Gospel around the world (e.g., 8:1-4), this omission comes close to being inexplicable—except on the supposition that he had no knowledge of these events!

But what presses this point even further is the recognition that the Jesus of Luke's first volume prophesies the destruction of this temple (21:6).[34] Since one of the driving motifs of Acts is to show how the ministry of Jesus was continued and fulfilled in the life of the church (Luke 1:1-4; Acts 1:1-2), Luke's failure to record how this central prophecy of Jesus' was fulfilled is difficult to explain unless we suppose that he was writing *before* its fulfillment. These considerations, taken together, strongly suggest a date of composition sometime before the fall of Jerusalem, the start of the Jewish-Roman war, and even before Nero's persecution in A.D. 62.[35]

Incidental Considerations

Several other pieces of internal evidence from the Book of Acts point in the same direction. First, a significant portion of Luke's theological vocabulary appears very primitive. His reference to the Jews as "the people," to the eucharist as "breaking of bread," and to Sunday as "the first day of the week" (instead of "the Lord's day"; Rev. 1:10; Didache 14:1) is arguably evidence for the primitiveness of his sources.[36] And while a great deal of caution must be exercised in talking about a "developing christology" — full-blown "high" christologies exploded onto the scene immediately after the resurrection event, as we have seen (chap. 8) — one should still point out that at least the Evangelist Luke's way of expressing his christology appears very Semitic and very archaic. His use of "son of man," "servant of God," and "Christ" as christological titles are particularly noteworthy, for such terms quickly dropped out of common usage (and "Christ" functioned as a proper name) and would, therefore, be much more out of place in the second century than they would be in the middle of the first.[37]

Secondly, the issues that Luke addresses in Acts, and the way he addresses them, suggests a pre-70 time of composition. His portrayal of the Holy Spirit falling on different groups of people (Jewish, chap. 2, Samaritan, chap. 8, and Gentile, chap. 10) and his clear division between Palestinian and Hellenistic Jews (chap. 6) fits in better with the situation before the fall of Jerusalem than afterward. So too, his positive portrayal of the temple and of the Pharisees squares best with an A.D. pre-70 dating, as does his portrayal of the terms of Gentile admission into church fellowship. Moreover, his concern for Jewish-Gentile coexistence, mediated by the food requirements of the apostolic decrees, makes much less sense after A.D. 70 than before.

On top of this, Hemer notes a number of other incidental considerations of Luke-Acts which generally strengthen a pre-70 dating.[38] These include: (1) "the prominence of the popular assemblies rather than administrative councils in city life"; (2) "the importance of Roman citizenship and the status of dual citizenship"; (3) "an early phase in the history of Roman provincial administration, exemplified in Paul's trial experiences"; (3) "a tone and feel of civic life which finds its nearest parallels in the first century writers Strabo, Josephus and Dio Chrysostom"; (4) "provinicial terminology appropriate to the period preceding Vespassian's reorganization in A.D. 72"; and (5) "reference to the *sicarii* (21:38), as suiting the period between Felix and the fall of Jerusalem."

When all of this is combined with the general accuracy of his account, to be discussed shortly, the case for dating Acts in the 60s and for seeing it as written by a close follower of Paul appears very solid. Such a supposition, of course, wreaks havoc with the customary critical datings of all the New Testament documents, as J.A.T. Robinson realized.[39] For if Acts is to be dated in the 60s, the Gospel of Luke must also be (shortly before) this time. And if Luke used Mark, this work must be earlier still. And this simply does not allow enough time for many of the operative assumptions in much New Testament critical scholarship to work. But this clearly constitutes no grounds for dismissing the arguments for the early date of Acts – unless one has no concern for avoiding vicious circularity.[40]

At the very least, all of this evidence is enough to judge the position of Mack and Crossan that Acts is largely a second-century collection of Christian lore as being quite implausible. And this, we maintain, already implies that the perspective of the Book of Acts on the early history of the church is more likely to be accurate than is their speculative reconstructions.

LUKE AND OTHER ANCIENT HISTORIANS

Luke's Historical Interest

No one disputes that Luke's two-volume work is driven by strong theological concerns. Like the Gospels (including his own), Luke is, in Acts, telling the creationist-monotheistic story of how the story of Israel has climaxed in the story of Jesus and is being carried out in the story of the church.[41] But, as we have seen in considering Mark's historical interest (chap. 10), we must resist the modern ill-conceived assumption that this theological interest in any way precludes a healthy historical interest. Rather, as Wright insists, Luke's theological story "only means anything if it takes place within public, world history."[42] As I.H. Marshall has argued, Luke is both a theologian *and* a historian; indeed, "Luke can be properly appreciated as a theologian only when it is recognized that he is also an historian."[43]

His prefatory remarks to his two volumes (Luke 1:1-4) tell us this much, for they place him squarely within the ranks of other ancient historians.[44] Following ancient historiographical literary convention, Luke tells Theophilus that he is seeking to write reliable history ("an orderly account," 1:3) by "carefully investigating" reliable sources ("handed down to us by those who from the first were eyewitnesses," 1:2). Neither Josephus, Thucydides, Lucian, Tacitus, or Suetonius ever expressed a historical interest more clearly.[45]

And the evidence indicates that Luke carried out his historical intention very well.[46]

CORROBORATIONS WITH OTHER SOURCES

The first piece of evidence that bolsters one's confidence in the historical accuracy of Luke's record is that it is, at a number of significant points, corroborated by other ancient sources, especially Josephus. Thus, Luke's unusual account of the sudden death of Agrippa I (ca. A.D. 44) is confirmed in detail (and even in theological interpretation!) by Josephus (12:20-23; cf. *Jewish Antiquities* [henceforth *Anti.*] 19:344-49). His report of a major famine "in the days of Claudius" is also confirmed by Josephus (11:28; cf. *Anti.* 220:101), as is his naming of Ananias as high priest (ca. A.D. 47) (23:2; 24:1; cf. *Anti.* 20:103) along with his record of an unknown Egyptian prophetic revolutionary who led thousands to their death (21:38; cf. *Jewish War,* 2:261).[47]

Similarly, Luke's identifying Gallio as proconsul of Achaia in A.D. 51 has been confirmed by a discovered inscription at Delphi (18:12). His report of Claudius' expulsion of the Jews from Rome around A.D. 49 is referred to by Suetonius (*Life of Claudius;* 25:4). His incidental reference to Felix as Roman procurator along with his Jewish wife Drusilla is corroborated by both Josephus and Tacitus (24:24; cf. *Anti.* 20:131-43; *Jewish History* 5:9; *Annals* 12:54). His identification of Festus as Felix's successor is likewise confirmed by Josephus and Suetonius (*Anti.* 20:182; *Claudius* 28). And his mentioning of Agrippa II and Bernice, elder sister of Drusilla and widow of Herod, is again corroborated by Josephus (25:13; cf. *Anti.* 20:145).

This degree of confirmation concerning public figures and events is impressive. This is not, of course, to suggest that there are no points of tension between Luke and these other ancient sources.[48] So much is to be expected in analyzing parallel accounts of any two ancient (or modern) historical sources. But the number of apparent contradictions are relatively few and can be readily explained without impugning the basic veracity of any of the ancient authors.

Two Historical Problems

The two most difficult discrepancies warrant our brief attention, if only because they are regularly appealed to as evidence of Luke's untrustworthiness. First, Luke's reference (in the mouth of Gamaliel) to an uprising led by Theudas before an uprising led by Judas apparently stands in tension with Josephus who locates Theudas' uprising a good forty years *after* Judas' revolt (5:36; cf. *Anti.* 20:97-98). Does this mean that Luke is mistaken?[49] One could, of course, just as easily apply this argument in the other direction – it is Josephus who is in error – but, in fact, neither recourse is necessary. When we consider how common a name Theudas was at the time, and how frequent uprisings were during this tumultuous period (as both Luke and Josephus attest, 21:38, cf. *Anti.* 17:269), the likelihood that we are dealing with two different revolutionaries with the same name is apparent.[50] Indeed, Josephus himself mentions four men named Simon in a space covering forty years and three named Judas within ten years who were all instigators of rebellion.[51] And, of course, we know of two different persons within the space of forty years who were named Jesus and who were both branded as revolutionaries!

Given this situation, and given that "Luke's background information can so often be corroborated," Hemer's conclusion seems reasonable: "it is wiser to leave this particular matter open rather than to condemn Luke of a blunder."[52]

A second, and even more noteworthy, problem concerns Luke's naming Quirinius as governor of Syria at the time of Jesus' birth (Luke 2:2). Crossan in particular cites this as evidence of Luke's untrustworthiness,[53] though, unfortunately, he never discusses the other evidence in Luke's two volumes which might argue in an opposite direction. In any case, Quirinius is only known to have held this office from A.D. 6–9, hence about ten years after the time of Christ's birth. Does this imply that Luke was mistaken?[54]

First, even if this (and the previously mentioned) "mistake" were granted, this wouldn't warrant any negative conclusion about Luke's general reliability. If he were *generally* unreliable, it is difficult to explain how he got so many other details in his narrative right. But secondly, given Luke's otherwise demonstrable reliability, it seems appropriate to exercise some caution before concluding that Luke was here mistaken. This is not special pleading. It is the sort of courtesy extended to all historical documents that give us other reasons for placing any degree of trust in them.

There are two possible ways of accounting for this apparent error of Luke. First, we learn from Tacitus (Annals 3:48) and Florus (*Roman History* 2:31) that Quirinius led large military expeditions in the Eastern provinces of the Roman Empire a decade before his holding the governor's office in A.D. 6. He thus obviously held some significant leadership position at this time. It is not unlikely, therefore, that Luke, in using the general participle *hegemoneuo*, is referring to this "governing" position, or possibly even to an official joint rule, at this time prior to his becoming formal governor in A.D. 6. Ramsey, in particular, was convinced that this was the case.[55] Moreover, two Latin inscriptions, discovered by Ramsey, seem to suggest that Quirinius held some sort of joint office in Northern Syria while heading up his military expeditions.[56]

A second possibility is to translate Luke 2:2 as: "This census was *before* that which Quirinius, governor of Syria, held."[57] There is no doubt that Luke's construction, *prota geneto hagemoneuontos*, can bear this meaning, though it is admittedly more awkward than the standard translation. Still, in light of Luke's otherwise accurate record of official titles and reigns, it is not unreasonable to accept it, alongside the first explanation, as a possible way of reconciling Luke's account with known history.

In any event, the degree to which Luke's narrative about first-century events is corroborated by other sources must evoke a good bit of confidence in his record. It is the kind of accuracy one might expect by a careful researcher, close to the events, writing in the mid-first century, but not at all what one might expect from a collector of Christian lore in the second century.

LUKE'S KNOWLEDGE OF TITLES, GEOGRAPHY, AND CUSTOMS

More impressive than his grasp of major figures and events, however, is Luke's accuracy in recording the various titles of various officials in the mid-first century. "Experience shows," writes Stephen Neill, "that nothing is more difficult than to get titles exactly right."[58] If this much is true generally, it is all the more true in the very complex, ever changing, political-religious Greco-Roman world of the first century. The status of provinces along with the titles of their officiaries changed with some regularity.[59] We cannot, therefore, help but be impressed when Luke drops a host of names and titles within his record and, almost without exception, indisputably gets them right. A quick survey of the confirmed evidence must presently suffice.

In Acts, the governors of senatorial provinces in Cyprus (13:7), Achaia (18:12), and Asia (19:38) are accurately termed "proconsuls" *(anthupatoi)*, whereas those over imperial provinces such as Syria and Judea are correctly termed *hagemon* (Luke 2:2; 3:1; Acts 23:24; 26:30).[60] Relatedly, Herod is not called "king" of Galilee, but "tetrarch" (Luke 3:1; Acts 13:1), while other members of the Herod family, Agrippa I and II, are properly titled "king" *(basileus*, Acts 12:1; 25:13).

Similarly, Luke notes, quite incidentally, that Phillipi is a Roman colony (16:12) whose magistrates are therefore called "praetors" (*stratagoi*) and whose officers are called "lictors" or "sergeants" (*rabdouxoi*) (16:35). In Thessalonica (17:6), however, the chief authorities are called "politarchs" (*politarxai*), a term not found elsewhere in extant literature but six times confirmed by archaeological findings in Thessalonica. "Exactly the right title is used at exactly the right time and place," concludes Neill.[61]

With a similar unpretentious display of accuracy, Luke portrays the "town clerk" (*grammateus*) of Ephesus (19:35) as functioning as the liaison officer between civic administration and the Roman goverment in the province of Asia as well as taking part in the town assemblies (19:39). His portrayal of the Ephesian Artemision is likewise accurate in detail (19:35), and his specific naming of the head of the artisans of the temple (*texnitai*) as "Demetrius" can only bolster our confidence in his account. So too, Luke's naming of "Publius" as the "chief official" of the island of Malta (*to proto tas nasou*) can hardly be thought to be fabricated, especially in light of the fact that he demonstrably got his title right (28:7).

Sir William Ramsey, who himself was won over from an earlier low estimation of Acts by evidence such as this, sums up the matter well:

> The officials with whom Paul and his companions brought in contact are those who would be there. Every person is found just where he ought to be: proconsuls in senatorial provinces, asiarchs in Ephesus, strategoi in Philippi, politarchs in Thessalonica, magicians and soothsayers everywhere.[62]

We would hardly hold it against a writer if he occasionally got such matters confused, even if he was writing relatively close to the events and was in other regards quite reliable. That Luke consistently gets them right, therefore, cannot help but bolster our confidence in his overall historical ability.

What has also impressed a good number of scholars is the manner in which Luke accurately portrays the political regions, geography, roadways, and various means of travel of the mid-first century.[63] The frequent, and very understandable, errors on such matters found in other contemporary historians such as Tacitus, Pliny the Elder, Strabo, and even Josephus are almost wholly absent from Luke.[64] For example, Luke correctly identifies Lystra and Derbe as "Lycaonian cities" (Acts 14:6), though they were actually located within Phrygia and labeled as such by later writers (e.g., Hierax, ca. A.D. 50).[65] And he correctly does not locate Caesarea within Judea (12:19), owing, presumably, to its unique status as a "city state" over and against other local regions.[66]

One other example on this matter is especially noteworthy. Many scholars have long been impressed with the wealth of knowledge about localities and about ship travel in the mid-first century evidenced in Luke's account of Paul's shipwreck in chapter 27.[67] This chapter constitutes the most detailed passage in the entire work and has been called "one of the most instructive documents for the knowledge of ancient seamanship."[68] While the literary form of this passage has been convincingly argued (by Dibelius and others) to be influenced by similar famous "lost at sea" accounts (e.g., Jonah, the Odyssey), the accuracy of its many incidental, meticulous, nautical details suggests not only its historicity, but its having been composed by an eyewitness (it is the third "we" passage in the work).[69] Luke's thorough description of the three ships involved, of precise references to geography, and of life at sea are all as accurate as they are vivid.[70] And with Hemer, we conclude that "these inconsequential details are hard to explain except as vivid experiences recalled at no great distance in time."[71]

Luke's ability to correctly capture the various cultural textures of various regions has also been noted. His above mentioned depiction of Ephesus as steeped in magic and centered on the temple of Diana (19:18-19) is an example of this. His portrayal of the Athenians with their insatiable intellectual curiosity and love of open debate (17:21) in contrast to the highly pagan and superstitious crowds of Lystra (14:8-18) also squares with everything we know about these locales in the first century. So too his general portrayal of the easily excited and quite intolerant crowds of Jerusalem — in marked contrast to the more eclectic melting pot atmosphere of Antioch (11:19-30) — is remarkably "true to life."[72] And he consistently evidences a knowledge of Jewish customs and beliefs within Jerusalem (e.g., 3:1; 8:27; 21:27-40; 24:6, 13). "He gets the atmosphere right every time."[73]

Finally, a number of scholars have made a solid case for Luke's accuracy in describing the diverse and highly complex legal matters of the various regions he was concerned with. Luke's various references to the nature of Roman citizenship; to Roman, Greek, and Jewish judicial procedures; to the right to appeal to Caesar; and to the various relationships that pertained between magistrates of various states and between cities of various sizes all square with what we know about Roman law in the first century.[74] It was on the basis of evidence such as this that Sherwin-White, who is widely considered to be the ablest historian of ancient Roman law in our time, concluded:

> [T]he confirmation of historicity [in Acts] is overwhelming . . .
> any attempt to reject its historicity even in matters of detail must
> now appear absurd. Roman historians have long taken it for
> granted.[75]

Among a plethora of examples that could be given, one might in
particular note Luke's account of Paul's trials in Jerusalem and Caesarea
(21:27–26:32). Here, Luke accurately depicts the precise legal arrange-
ments between Jews and Romans and the somewhat tenuous internal
legal system of the Roman government itself in the region of Judea
during this tumultuous time. Indeed, he even correctly captures the
particular situations of the main players of his narrative. As Hengel
argues, the entire passage

> fits admirably into the strange—one might almost say maca-
> bre—milieu in Judea in the time of the last procurators: Felix,
> under whose long administration the political situation wors-
> ened to an acute degree, Festus, Albinus and after them Gessius
> Florus.[76]

And thus he concludes:

> [I]n my view the account must ultimately derive from an eye-
> witness. It demonstrates the political uncertainty in Judea to-
> ward the end of Felix's period of office. . . . His knowledge of
> conditions in Judea during roughly the last fifteen years before
> the outbreak of the Judean war and his special concern [in
> Luke] with the destruction of Jeruslem [sic] show how he was
> affected by these events and stood relatively close to them; this
> makes it impossible to date his work in the second century.[77]

In the light of all of this evidence, it is difficult to see how any
contemporary account of the development of the early church—*especially*
one such as Mack and Crossan's that seeks to lay out a theory that is
radically at odds with this work—could fail to seriously wrestle with
Acts. However one dates Acts, and however one estimates his theological agenda, the work clearly deserves to be taken seriously.

ACTS AND THE PAULINE EPISTLES

One final dimension of Luke's narrative warrants our brief attention,
and this concerns the way in which his material intersects with material

from Paul's epistles. While there are, predictably, points of tension between these two sources, a judicious comparison still leads to the conclusion that Luke had a substantial knowledge of Paul's life and activity. The complete lack of any reference to Paul's epistles—a fact, we might note, that is more surprising on a late dating of Acts than it is on an early dating—suggests that this information is independent of these writings.[78] The incidental way in which such material filters into Acts also makes points of corroboration between these two sources all the more impressive. Again, a brief summary of the matter must presently suffice.[79]

To begin with, Luke's record that Paul's original name was Saul (7:58) squares well with Paul's own testimony that he belonged to the tribe of Benjamin (Rom. 11:1; Phil. 3:5), since Saul was the most famous name associated with that tribe.[80] His portrait of Paul as a Pharisee (23:6; 26:5) who persecuted the earliest Christian communities (8:3; 9:1-2; etc.) is explicitly confirmed by Paul's own testimony to this effect (Phil. 3:5-6; Gal. 1:13; 1 Cor. 15:9). Moreover, his conversion near, and later escape from, Damascus (9:1-2, 24-25) is corroborated by Paul's own record— though there are enough differences here to demonstrate the independence of Luke's account.[81]

Similarly, Paul's association with, and later break from, Barnabas is recorded in both sources (11:25-26, cf. Gal. 2:1-2; 15:36-40, cf. Gal. 2:13)— though the reasons given for the breakup differ.[82] Both sources also mention Paul's later association with Silas and Timothy (Acts 16:11-12; 2 Cor. 1:19; 1 Thes. 1:1-2). And Luke's above mentioned detailed account of Paul's shipwreck (chap. 27) finds confirmation in Paul's own account (2 Cor. 11:25).

In the same fashion, while there are significant gaps in Luke's highly abbreviated narrative, and while there are several aspects of Paul's own account of his earliest travels that are difficult to square with the portrait in Acts, it is nevertheless true that the general chronology of Paul's missionary activity in Acts is confirmed by Paul's own accounts in his epistles.[83] Hence, for example, the general sequence of visits to Philippi, Thessalonica, Athens, Corinth, Ephesus, Macedonia, and Achaia in Acts 16:12–20:2 is completely substantiated by Paul's own record (Rom. 15:26; 1 Cor. 16:8; 2 Cor. 1:16; 9:2; 12:14; 1 Thes. 2:2; 3:1). So too, Paul's intent to go to Rome after his visit to Jerusalem in Acts (19:21) squares with Paul's own statement to this effect (Rom. 15:22), though Luke apparently did not know of Paul's private aspirations to go from there into Spain (Rom. 15:24). He perhaps was aware, however, that the visit to Jerusalem involved a relief fund (Acts 24:17).

We might finally note the manner in which incidental details of Paul's life and activity in Acts are at times confirmed by his own letters. For example, Luke's portrayal of Paul preaching to Jews in the synagogue first and then to Gentiles may be echoed in Paul's own statement that the Gospel is "first for the Jew, then for the Gentile" (Rom. 1:16; cf. 2:9). So also, Paul's own expressed concern over "the unbelievers in Judea" to the Romans (Rom. 15:31) is filled out by Luke's account in Acts 21:27-36. And Luke's depiction of Paul as earning his own living while preaching (18:3; 20:34) finds confirmation in Paul's own repeated statements to this effect (e.g., 1 Thes. 2:9; 2 Thes. 3:7-10; 1 Cor. 9:15-18).

Even if disputable points of tension remain, the extent of corroboration Paul's letters provide for the material we find in Acts is impressive. We again find that insofar as we are able to cross-check Acts against other sources of information in the mid-first century – this time, with Paul's letters – it comes out looking remarkably good. And this cannot help but to reinforce our overall positive estimation of Luke's ability to relate generally accurate history.

This does not, of course, in any way minimize the importance of understanding the theology of Luke, his use of sources (insofar as this is knowable), and his literary conventions which recent works on Acts have emphasized. Nor does it establish the reliability of Luke on every matter on which he speaks.[84] But it does imply that one should exercise some caution in drawing from these studies any conclusion that suggests that Luke is not *also* interested in history and that he reports it very well. And this further implies that, if and when errors on Luke's part are to be posited, the burden of proof is on the critic to demonstrate such.[85]

CONCLUSION

We have good grounds for regarding the early church history provided for us in Acts as being basically trustworthy. If Luke is so accurate in matters of Roman imperial and senatorial provinces, we cannot easily dismiss his narrative about the Day of Pentecost as a piece of Christian lore. If he was astute enough to catch the right titles of various officials, we cannot readily write off his narratives of Peter and Paul as being of little historical value. And if he is demonstrably accurate in his recording of the legal proceedings of various locales, we cannot quickly dismiss his record that the early church was, from the start, united in its proclamation that Jesus was the Son of God who was crucified and rose again from the dead.

What also counts decisively in Luke's favor, however, is that his portrait of the early church squares well with the evidence of early Christian belief in Paul and Mark which we have examined earlier. Luke's understanding that the early church from the start proclaimed a crucified and risen Savior is precisely what the evidence from Paul's epistles implies. His portrait of the early church as being essentially unified and as networking together also squares perfectly with the evidence we've previously discovered in Paul. And the understanding of Jesus Christ in both Acts and Paul's epistles lines up well with the portrait of Jesus Christ provided for us in Mark (and, of course, from Luke's own Gospel), a portrait, we have seen, that we have every reason to believe derives from an authoritative eyewitness.

The available data, in a word, allows us to conclude from these three witnesses that the earliest followers of Jesus understood him as being anything but a Cynic sage. On the basis of his teachings, deeds, life, death, and especially on the basis of his resurrection, they from the start believed that he was the Son of God. And, as Luke and Paul testify (and other sources attest), this conviction led to a zealous missionary explosion that covered the entire Mediterranian world within a century, a fact that is itself difficult to account for on any scheme that fundamentally discredits their testimony.

For Crossan and Mack's view of the historical Jesus to be accepted, *all* of this evidence must be overturned. Paul, Mark, and Luke must be judged — against the evidence here given — as being unreliable guides to who the historical Jesus was and what the earliest Christians believed about him. To arrive at the "true" picture of Jesus and the early church, in other words, these earliest records of Jesus and the early church must all be rejected. This is, to say the least, unusual historical procedure.

And what is the evidence available that justifies this radical move? We have Q, a hypothetical document; the Gospel of Thomas, a second-century gnostic-tending work; Secret Mark, an obscure secondhand, second-century fragment; and the Cross Gospel, an extracted narrative from a second- or third-century apocryphal Gospel. And even these, we have seen, are only of use when accompanied by circular methodological procedures, highly questionable dating techniques, disputable assumptions about the Hellenistic climate of Galilee, and very speculative conclusions drawn from a questionable redaction of the hypothetical document, Q. Paul, Mark, and Luke are to be traded in *for this*.

This trade, in our modern parlance, "is not a good deal." Its only "advantage" is that it allows for a naturalistic historical Jesus, whereas taking the New Testament documents seriously brings us face to face with an unavoidably supernatural Jesus. But, while we may concede that coming to grips with a Jesus who refuses to fit into our twentieth-century naturalistic categories can be difficult—in this sense the natural Jesus is perhaps an "advantage"—fidelty to the facts simply shuts down this option. The price tag attached to the natural Jesus is simply too high!

Hence, the only Jesus of history we can know, if we restrict ourselves to the evidence, is the disturbing Jesus reflected in Paul's epistles and Mark's Gospel and who gave rise to that disturbing Christian community reflected in Luke-Acts. The earliest followers of Jesus proclaimed him to be the Son of God, and basic historiographical reasoning suggests that they were right!

But we have not yet considered the most foundational reason these believers give us as to *why* they believed Jesus was the Son of God. We have not yet considered the New Testament's claim that Jesus was proclaimed to be the Son of God *because he rose from the dead*. The historical evidence for this event constitutes both the strongest evidence that the early believers' perception of Jesus was correct, and the most formidable obstacle any naturalistic account of Jesus and the early church must overcome, if it is to be regarded as a plausible account. It is, then, to this topic that I now turn in the final chapter.

13

DEVOURED BY BEASTS OR RAISED FROM THE DEAD?

A Critique of Crossan's and Mack's Explanations for the Resurrection Faith of the Early Church

For all their diversity, the various New Testament portraits of Jesus are remarkably unified in their understanding that he was more than an ordinary man. Whether he is viewed as being the embodiment of God's personified wisdom, of God's Word, of God's kingdom, and/or as the prophet of God par excellence, he is on all accounts viewed as being divine.

I have been making the case that we have no good grounds for supposing that the "real" historical Jesus "behind" this uniform witness was radically different from the corporate portraits. More specifically, I have argued that Crossan and Mack fail to make a convincing case for supposing that the "real" Jesus was, in contrast to this testimony, a mere Cynic sage.

This work would be incomplete, however, did we not take at least a cursory look at the most fundamental reason the New Testament authors give concerning why they hold this most peculiar view of Jesus. And this brings us directly to the question of Christ's resurrection. The testimonies of Paul, the Gospels, Acts, and most of the other New Testament epistles are in agreement in proclaiming the resurrection of Christ as being the central event of Jesus' ministry, and the foundational reason for their faith.[1] "God has raised . . . Jesus to life, and we are all witnesses of this fact," proclaims Peter in Acts (Acts 2:32). And without this event, as Paul puts it, the Christian faith would be utterly meaningless (1 Cor. 15:14-15). From a New Testament perspective, everything hangs upon the resurrection.

I have attempted to demonstrate that we have good grounds for seriously doubting Crossan's and Mack's revisionist accounts of Jesus and early Christianity and good grounds for trusting the accounts of Paul, Mark, and Acts as being generally reliable. But because of its centrality to the Christian faith, the issue of Christ's resurrection warrants more particular attention. We thus need to conclude this work by examining in a more specific way Crossan and Mack's explanation of the resurrection. Here too, I shall argue, we have very good grounds for regarding Crossan and Mack as being misguided, and very good grounds for regarding the New Testament witness as being substantially reliable.

My goal in this chapter, therefore, shall be to raise up a number of objections (or better, sets of objections) which, I believe, demonstrate the inadequacy of Crossan's and Mack's accounts. And in doing this, I shall by contrast provide a number of reasons for regarding the New Testament faith in Jesus' resurrection as being rooted solidly in historicity.

CROSSAN ON THE RESURRECTION

Crossan speculates that the body of Jesus became "a corpse for the wild beasts."[2] If his body was buried at all, it would have been in a common shallow grave where wild dogs and preying birds would have quickly devoured it. Being part of a mass crucifixion, the only ones who would have known where his body had been buried would have been the Roman soldiers. Hence, argues Crossan, "those who cared [about the body of Jesus] did not know where it was, and those who knew did not care."[3] The earliest followers of Jesus, then, "knew almost nothing whatsoever about the details of his crucifixion, death, or burial."[4]

According to Crossan, the brutality of Jesus' unexpected execution and the ignominy of how his body was disposed of forced his followers to wrestle with the question of how this could have happened if, in fact, Jesus was God's chosen one. And to answer this they turned to the Scriptures. They searched them to find "texts that show death not as end but as beginning, not as divine judgment but as divine plan, not as ultimate defeat but as postponed victory for Jesus."[5]

Hence, over the next five to ten years, Crossan speculates the earliest followers of Jesus found and pieced together texts that, they thought, addressed this matter. They collected them, reinterpreted them, and eventually began to splice them together into a narrative form. The disappointment of the end of Jesus' ministry thus fueled the rewriting of history. According to Crossan, the "Cross Gospel" constitutes the earliest written narrative of this reworking of history. This narrative was then taken up and reworked by each of the four canonical Gospels. The passion narratives of these latter works, he holds, can "all be adequately and plausibly explained as layers of redactional expansion on that single primary source."[6]

There is, then, almost nothing of historical value in the Gospel passion narratives. They are highly creative fictions even down to their smallest details. The story of Joseph of Arimathea, for example, is viewed by Crossan as being completely Mark's creation, as we have seen (chap. 10). Mark invented this person as a way of resolving a problem in the growing legend about Jesus (Mark 15:42-46).[7] According to Crossan, Mark (following the Cross Gospel) was unwilling to accept that the body of Jesus was left above ground for the dogs. Indeed, he wanted to say not only that Jesus was buried in a dignified manner, and in a legitimate tomb, but that he rose out of this tomb on the third day. Yet, how could such a view be sustained if in fact Jesus was buried in a shallow grave by Roman soldiers (or not buried at all)? Mark must, then, contrive a way to have Jesus being buried by his followers.

But how could his followers conceivably have had an opportunity to bury him, since they had no social or political authority? The problem is resolved, argues Crossan, by Mark creating a person who is at once a follower of Jesus *and* a person in political authority. Hence we find in his narrative a certain Joseph of Arimathea who is a follower of Jesus, while also being a respected member of the council. Following Mark, the Evangelists Matthew, Luke, and John all "try to improve on that creation."[8] Matthew adds that he is "rich" to explain "why he has access to Pilate." And the dignity of Jesus' burial is enhanced by being buried in "a new tomb" (Matt. 27:57-60). Luke follows Mark more closely but clarifies that, though Joseph was part of the council, he had not agreed to their plan of action to crucify Jesus (Luke 23:50-54). And John climaxes this movement toward dignifying Jesus' death by explaining that Joseph was a "secret disciple" and then, supposedly, by greatly refining and expanding the burial procedure Jesus underwent (John 19:38-42). All such creations are "deliberate" and "almost desperate" attempts to get around the horror of picturing the body of Jesus as being left to wild animals.[9] There is, again, nothing of historical value in them.

The same holds true for Crossan's understanding of the resurrection accounts. As we have already seen (chap. 8), both Mack and Crossan hold that the concept of Jesus' resurrection originates from the Christ-cult. It played no role in the earliest thinking of the Jesus people, as "evidenced" by its omission in Q and GosThom. Crossan holds that

Paul's use of this concept must be rooted in some sort of trance experience he had[10] and that it eventually worked its way into the Cross Gospel, Mark, and then the other Gospels in a narrative form. Each of these accounts, however, are devoid of genuinely historical information. Paul's own account in 1 Corinthians 15 is governed by a concern to establish his own apostolic authority,[11] while the accounts in the Gospels are governed by a need to establish ecclesial authority within the earliest communities.

This last point is especially noteworthy, for it colors Crossan's exegesis of all the Gospel material he associates with the resurrection motif. To give just a few examples of this, Crossan argues that the point of Luke 24:33-35 is to emphasize the authority of a specific leader (Peter) over the general community (represented by the two unnamed disciples on the way to Emmaus). He deduces this from the fact that the eleven *first* tell the two disciples about Jesus' appearance to Simon Peter *before* they are allowed to tell them about Jesus' appearance to them.[12] A similar political theme is found in John 20 which recounts Peter and John's discovery of the empty tomb. From Luke 24:12 Crossan argues that an earlier tradition emphasized Peter's authority by having him alone run to the tomb and looking inside of it. The Johannine community, however, wanted to exalt John over Peter, and so they have John and Peter both race to the tomb, but here "Peter loses badly."[13] In "deference to the tradition," however, "Peter is allowed . . . to enter the tomb first." But "only the beloved Disciple is said to *believe*. That takes care of Peter."[14] In both passages (and numerous other examples could be given), historical narrative is simply created to justify a particular view of ecclesiastical hierarchy, according to Crossan.

The same sort of political exegesis is applied not only to the other units in the resurrection narrative, but also to the pre-resurrection "nature miracles" of Jesus in the Gospels as well, for Crossan maintains that these are all derived from the post-resurrection apparition motif.[15] Hence, for example, the "symbolic message" of Luke 5:2-9 which tells of the disciples' miraculous catch of fish is that "Jesus chooses Peter's boat above the other one, and it is from there that he teaches and catches fish."[16] He finds a political tension, however, in a similar story (Crossan maintains it is in essence the *same* story) told in John 21:2-8. For here John is given some authority alongside of Peter as signified by the fact that he first recognizes Jesus along the shore and tells Peter this.[17] Peter yet has preeminence here, however (unlike John 20), for it is he who jumps overboard to swim to Jesus. In each case, we see, the stories are read "not . . . as historical but as fiction units, as competing visualizations about priority and primacy."[18]

MACK ON THE RESURRECTION

Mack doesn't supply detailed exegesis of how the resurrection narratives function, as Crossan does. Nor does he speculate about what actually happened to the body of Jesus. But he is no less convinced than Crossan that both the resurrection account of Paul and those of the Gospels are devoid of historical reminiscence.

According to Mack, as we have seen, the concept of Jesus' resurrection was hit upon within the Christ-cult communities primarily by their reflection on the significance of Jesus in the light of Hellenistic stories about vindicated martyrs.[19] Like Crossan, Mack holds that Paul's own particular account in 1 Corinthians 15 is driven not by a desire to recount history, but by a desire to justify his own apostolic authority.[20] Mark takes up Paul's notion of Christ's resurrection as vindication, but he does it in such a way that it is clear that "his sympathies were still with the Jesus people, not with the Christ cult."[21] His sparing resurrection narrative, according to Mack, was not constructed to convey the message that "Jesus was alive and available as a spiritual presence, but that Jesus was absent until the eschaton and that one should not go looking for him."[22] Later Gospels, however, would build upon this resurrection narrative until we reach the Gospel of John where the crucifixion and resurrection are seen as the central events of "history."[23] All of these accounts, in Mack's view, are simply "imaginative accounts" and examples of extravagant mythmaking. As such, they "have no claim as historical accounts."[24] Whatever actually happened to this Cynic sage after he was crucified, one thing for Mack is clear: he did not rise from the dead.

The question that must be asked, of course, is how plausible these accounts are as explanations for the unanimous New Testament proclamation that Jesus rose from the dead. Are their arguments cogent, and do they adequately account for the available data? We will argue that neither account fairs well on this score.

In what follows I shall briefly outline seven sets of objections against Crossan's and Mack's treatments of the Gospel accounts and six objections against their treatment of 1 Corinthians 15. This is by no means meant to provide anything like a thorough defense of the historicity of the resurrection, nor even an exhaustive critique of Crossan's and Mack's views on this matter.[25] As I said at the outset, my goal in this chapter is simply to say enough to demonstrate the general implausibility of Crossan's and Mack's particular denials of the historicity of the resurrection by arguing against the most fundamental features of their revisionist accounts of the New Testament resurrection accounts. And to this extent, I shall be arguing in defense of the historical resurrection.

1. CROSSAN AND THE CROSS GOSPEL

Crossan's explanation for how the Gospels' passion and resurrection narratives came about is wholly dependent upon his early dating of the (hypothetical) "Cross Gospel" and his claim that Mark reworked this narrative in the composition of his own narrative. In chapter 6, however, I argued that both of these positions are highly problematic. With few exceptions, scholars have not followed Crossan on this score. Crossan's hypotheses that this narrative had an earlier circulation prior to its incorporation in the Gospel of Peter, that it is to be dated before Mark, and that Mark used it are all very speculative and tenuous, and this must significantly weaken his theory as an alternative to the New Testament's own account that Jesus in fact rose from the dead.

Relatedly, Gerald O'Collins contends that Crossan's theory about the Cross Gospel and its relationship to Mark suffers from another problem: namely, it does not seem altogether internally coherent. That is, his hypothesis about Mark's use of this narrative seems to stand in tension with his hypothesis about Mark's narrative creativity. If Crossan wants to hold that "it is impossible to overestimate the creativity of Mark,"[26] we must then wonder how he can confidently set about reconstructing how Mark supposedly used this proposed earlier narrative. For if Mark was in fact as creative in making up "historical narratives" as Crossan contends, one would think that it would be very difficult, if not altogether impossible, to trace his creative use of a previous source. Hence, O'Collins argues, "[T]he more Crossan emphasizes Mark's creativity, the more precarious become any hypotheses about the genesis and composition of the second gospel."[27] Indeed, if Mark was as creative as Crossan contends, it becomes difficult to see why he would even bother to rework a previously existing source in the first place.

2. "HISTORICIZED PROPHECY" IN THE FIRST CENTURY

Crossan's and Mack's accounts of the origins of the resurrection narratives assume that the (supposed) early Christian practice of creatively rewriting recent history in the light of their own experience and their own reading of Scripture was not unique. Crossan is in particular very explicit on this, holding that the creative historicizing of Old Testament prophecies was a "pervasive process."[28] Only by such an assumption can Crossan and Mack's view of the genesis of the Gospel resurrection narratives be rendered plausible in light of their claim that these accounts are ·almost devoid of genuine historical information.

This assumption, however, has been seriously called into question by a number of recent scholars. Joel Green, for example, argues that Crossan has "failed to consider substantial works of the last decade on the hermeneutics of late Judaism" which argue that the line of influence in popular Judaistic hermeneutics was not from text to event, but "from event to biblical text."[29] In keeping with this research, Green maintains that neither in the Qumran community, nor in post-biblical historiography, nor even in contemporary apocalyptic literature do we find "historical events" being retroactively *created* on the basis of Old Testament prophecy. Historical events determine what counts as prophecy in these communities, and they obviously heavily influence how Old Testament texts are interpreted. But the "given," around which everything else is worked, is the historical event itself. As O'Collins puts it, "The O.T. references and resonances help to tell the story, not to create it."[30]

If this line of argumentation is accepted, it significantly affects the plausibility of Crossan and Mack's thesis. For it means that there is no clear cultural precedent for Jews in the first century doing what Crossan and Mack maintain the early Christians did. If in fact Mark (and following him, the other Gospels) simply created the story of the passion and the resurrection on the basis of Old Testament texts, we must regard them as doing something quite novel. But this renders that thesis inherently improbable.

3. THE UNWARRANTED SKEPTICISM OF THE FABRICATION HYPOTHESIS

What also weakens the hypothesis that the Gospel authors simply created the passion and resurrection narratives is that it cannot be proven without presupposing its own truth. That is, one can only read the Gospels' passion and resurrection narratives as creative fiction if one first *assumes* that they are writing creative fiction. There is nothing in the texts themselves which requires this view. Indeed, the texts themselves suggest the opposite. As we have previously argued (chap. 10), these narratives *look* very much like the sort of literature we find in both Greek and Jewish antiquity that intends to record history (though, as we've pointed out, this was never the sole purpose behind these writings).

So we need to ask, what justifies treating the Gospels' passion and resurrection narratives more skeptically than one would treat the narratives of Lucian or Thucydides? Or, to pose the question in a different way, if (for the sake of argument) the Gospel authors *had* wanted to write the kind of historical narratives we find elsewhere in antiquity, how might their accounts have differed from what we in fact find?

To the response that they would have lacked such supernatural elements as angels, darkened skies, and, of course, a resurrected body had they been writing history, four replies can be made. First, this objection rests on a naturalistic assumption that we have elsewhere (chaps. 5 and 10) exposed as being arbitrary. It certainly was not an assumption most first-century authors would have shared, and it seems not only arbitrary, but presumptuous, to impose our "superior" worldview onto them—lest we fall prey to committing what C.S. Lewis called "chronological snobbery."

Second, even if some or even all of the supernatural features of these narratives are dismissed as legendary, this does not excuse the historian from seeking to find the historical core of the story, as Hengel has argued.[31] It does not, in other words, justify dismissing wholesale the narratives as complete fabrications, any more than finding some supernatural or legendary elements in Livy or Tacitus leads anyone to dismissing wholesale their accounts.[32]

Third, the facts that Paul provides for us a report of Jesus' resurrection without these "legendary" features and that this report is remarkably early should arguably incline us to regard the resurrection as part of the historical core of these narratives, even if other elements are (rightly or wrongly) regarded as legendary. Quite obviously, the resurrection of Jesus, which all the narratives have in common, plays a far more crucial role to these narratives than does the occasional presence of angels, concerning which there is little agreement. The point is that it is one thing to write off an incidental detail of a narrative as being legendary (if one has grounds for doing so), and quite another to dismiss the whole account as being an intentional legendary creation.

Fourthly, the Gospel accounts, for all their supernatural features, are nevertheless remarkably restrained and sober. They are, in all other respects, devoid of the kind of things one is accustomed to finding in standard mythological stories.[33] Not only are the accounts remarkably subdued, but they altogether lack the sort of obvious theologizing that characterizes the later apocryphal Gospels. Their willingness to leave unexpected features of the story unexplained, such as Jesus' odd prohibition of Mary touching him (John 20:17), stands in stark contrast to the later apocryphal tales (such as the Gospel of Peter!) where sensationalism abounds and very little is left unexplained.[34]

It should also be pointed out that these accounts contain very little that can be explained away by reference to an apologetic motive. If, as many scholars hold, these narratives of the empty tomb were created as an apologetic for the Christian proclamation of the resurrection, they carried out their task very poorly. As Stephen Davis argues:

> If the story [of the empty tomb] is an apologetic legend invented by later Christians, why does it (in Mark's original version) lead only to fear, flight, and silence on the part of the women? If the story is an apologetic legend . . . why is it so openly admitted that some of Jesus' followers were suspiciously in the vicinity of the tomb early on the morning of the discovery of the empty tomb? And why is there no mention made of any thorough investigation of the tomb or its environs, or of some verifying word from Joseph of Arimathea? As an apologetic argument, this one seems weak.[35]

And finally, a good case can be made that certain linguistic and cultural features of the Gospel narratives argue against viewing them as creative fictions.[36] To be specific, the accounts are filled with Semitic expressions and customs that suggest that they derive from early sources in a Palestinian environment. Hence, for example, such phrases as "on the first day of the week" (Mark 16:2), "angel of the Lord" (Matt. 28:2), "bowed down with their faces to the ground" (Luke 24:5), "answering said" (Matt. 28:5, author's trans.), and "Miriam" (Matt. 28:1, author's trans.) are easily accounted for on the supposition that the material for the Gospel narratives relies on early traditions. They are, however, difficult to account for on the assumption that each account was a late legendary creation.

These considerations, we may argue, count further against Crossan's and Mack's dismissal of these accounts as instances of creative myth-making.

4. The Resurrection and Q

We have seen that one of the foundational reasons Crossan and Mack deny that the resurrection was part of the earliest Christians' belief system is that it is not found in Q. This, however, is very dubious reasoning on a number of accounts. First, as we have earlier argued, we only know Q to the extent that Matthew and Luke incorporated it into their narratives. With Q we possess a hypothesis, not a document. Hence, even if we accept the independent existence of such a source, we certainly can have no confidence concerning the contents of Q as it was (per hypothesis) before it was incorporated into these Gospels. And we can have even less confidence in any argument from silence about what the earliest believers did *not* believe based on what is not included in the (unknown) contents of Q prior to its (hypothetical) use by Matthew and Luke!

Secondly, the Q that we infer from Matthew and Luke seems to constitute more of a "sayings source" than it does a manual of doctrines. Hence, even if we did possess the whole of Q in Matthew and Luke, we yet could not confidently infer anything about what the earliest Christians did not believe on the basis of what it does not contain. Such an inference would only be justified if we had reason for thinking that Q intended to exhaustively reflect early Christian belief. But there is virtually nothing to support this, as was argued in chapter 6.

And thirdly, the very notion that the resurrection motif is wholly absent in Q is debatable. Some scholars, such as Malcolm Peel (who certainly has no conservative ax to grind), argue that Q evidences some awareness of Christ's resurrection, at least as much as could be expected of a document that is primarily a sayings source. Among other things, the resurrection of Jesus seems to be presupposed in Q's portrayal of Christ as an end-time messenger who will return and vindicate his word (Luke 11:30; 12:8-10, 40; 17:24-30 and parallels).[37] At the very least, some sort of postmortem vindication is here assumed. And this is enough to further weaken the already flimsy assumption that the earliest believers held no belief in Jesus' resurrection.

When we couple this consideration with our certain knowledge from Paul's epistles that there were many believers contemporary with the hypothetical Q community for whom a belief in the resurrection was normative and central to their faith, Peel's argument takes on even more plausibility, and Crossan's and Mack's arguments appear even more implausible. If the only *certain* evidence we have of the earliest Christians is that they believed in the resurrection, finding this belief reflected in Q's sayings about Jesus' vindication cannot be too quickly dismissed. And, at the very least, the attempt to overturn this certain knowledge from Paul by making him nonrepresentative of early Christian faith (recall chap. 8), and doing this largely on the basis of an uncertain inference from an uncertain document, has to be judged as being misguided — especially now that it is probable this document in fact reflects the very belief Crossan and Mack are seeking to overturn!

5. THE DISTINCTNESS OF THE FOUR RESURRECTION TRADITIONS

We have seen that Mack and Crossan attempt to dismiss the Gospels' portrayal of Jesus as the Son of God in favor of their view of him as a Cynic sage by arguing that Mark is generally unreliable in depicting history. Since, it is assumed, the other Gospels used Mark as a foundational source for their own distinctive stories, showing Mark to be unreliable has the effect of undermining the historical reliability of the other Gospels as well. We thus do not have four independent witnesses to historical events: we have one creative author of fiction followed by three others who borrow from him and who further embellish and/or correct his story.

We have earlier attempted to counter this critique by arguing for the general reliability of Mark (chaps. 10–11). What must now be said, however, is that even if Crossan and Mack's skeptical approach were to be accepted in general, it does not work in the particular case of the Gospels' resurrection narratives. For if there is anything that is clear about these four accounts, it is that they do not all derive from the same single source. "Our gospels represent distinctly different traditions."[38] While the central facts of certain women finding an empty tomb and of Jesus appearing to various disciples are shared by each account, almost all of the details surrounding these core facts are different, so different that it is impossible to explain them as mere editorial alterations of a single source.[39]

These differences, of course, have often been used in attempts to discredit these sources as reliable witnesses. But, in fact, a good case can be made for thinking that these differences actually serve to *enhance* the basic reliability of the testimony of each author by demonstrating the relative independence of the tradition each author draws on.[40] While it may well be that Matthew and Luke (and John?) utilized Mark to a large extent in their narratives of Jesus' ministry, it is very clear that they do *not* do so in their resurrection narratives. And while the differences between these accounts (and Paul) should not be minimized and certainly need to be explained, the core facts shared by each of these independent traditions cries out even louder for explanation.[41] Differences among four largely independent historical accounts is what one would expect: fundamental similarities among four independent legendary accounts is not. Hence, however difficult explaining the differences among the four accounts might be, it is nothing next to the difficulty of explaining how it is that these four different narratives came to share the same core of their stories if, in fact, none of the stories is rooted in history![42]

Hence, Crossan and Mack's all-too-easy approach of explaining away Mark's narrative as fabrication doesn't accomplish much here. One has yet to account for Luke, and then Matthew, and then John, and finally Paul. And if, as Wright argues, it is questionable historical procedure to dismiss historical data by chalking it up to a person's or community's "creativity," how much plausibility are we to attribute to a theory that would require this of us five times in regard to five relatively independent accounts?[43] And it *still* would not have accounted for why these divergent "fabrications" have the core of their stories in common!

6. THE DETAILS OF THE RESURRECTION NARRATIVES

On top of the questionability of dismissing these five divergent accounts as creative fiction, there are a number of features of the Gospel accounts that many scholars argue are not compatible with seeing them as fictional accounts. Only a cursory sampling of these can presently be given.

The Central Role of Women

Most impressive, perhaps, is the central role that women play in each of the resurrection accounts. Though the particular women named in each account differs depending on the interests of the author, the fact that it is women in each account who first visit the tomb, first receive word about the resurrection, and first proclaim this to the other (male) disciples is surprising. For the inclusion of women in any story in first-century Jewish culture could only serve to undermine the credibility of the story. In this heavily patriarchal culture, the testimony of women generally counted for nothing. Indeed, in most circumstances they were not even allowed to testify in court. Thus, there is no reason why each of the Gospel authors would have (independently?) included them in their accounts were they simply creating narratives for an apologetic purpose.[44] The only discernible motive they could have had for including them is that they were interested in saying what happened, and it happened that these women were in fact the first ones to discover the tomb empty.

Incidental Details

The wealth of other incidental details included in these accounts is also arguably evidence of their historical reliability. John, for example, notes how John outran Peter to the tomb (20:4) and how he "bent over and looked at the strips of linen lying there but did not go in" (v. 5). Peter then arrives and goes into the tomb, wherein he sees what John had ·seen but also notices "the burial cloth that had been around Jesus' head" (v. 7). John then notes how the burial cloth was folded, and where it was placed in relation to the strips of linen (v. 7). What is important to note here is that none of this incidental information contributes anything to the main story line. It is just reported. And such incidental details, when found elsewhere in documents that look like historical narratives, are generally taken to strengthen confidence in the historicity of the report.[45]

Crossan, we have seen, attempts to locate a hidden political motive for why this narrative incorporates the detail about John outrunning Peter: the author wanted to exalt John as a spiritual authority over Peter (see above). Such a motive, however, is not apparent from a straightforward reading of the text. It is, in fact, pure speculation. And, in any case, it doesn't yet explain the details about Jesus' discarded clothes; why the account mentions that *neither* John nor Peter yet understood that Jesus had risen from the dead (v. 10), a point that doesn't enhance *either* Peter's or John's spiritual authority; or why either the author of the narrative or his intended audience would have assumed that running faster symbolized greater spiritual authority in the first place!

Joseph of Arimathea

A number of such details could be cited, but one more must suffice. While Crossan, as we have seen, dismisses Joseph of Arimathea in each of the passion and resurrection accounts as being a fictitious character, the mention of such a person can easily be argued in the other direction as adding credibility to the accounts. Unless there exists reasons for thinking otherwise, the citing of particular people, places, and times in a document's recording of an event is usually taken as evidence for its trustworthiness.

In any case, it is, for most scholars, difficult to imagine Mark simply making such a person as Joseph of Arimathea up. Why this particular name? And why this particular obscure village? And if Mark were going to make such a person up, would he have had him be such an overtly public figure as one of the seventy-one leaders who served on the Sanhedrin? Knowledge about who served on the Sanhedrin was common in

Jewish circles, and fabricating such a person would make exposing his narrative as a lie very easy.[46]

Jesus' Cursed Death

Not only this, but Mark's motives for making such a person up in the first place are not perfectly clear. According to Crossan, as we have seen, it was ultimately to have Jesus buried in a dignified way and not in a way that would suggest, following Deuteronomy 21:22-23, that he was "cursed." But such a suggestion leaves several questions unanswered. If Mark (and the others following him) were concerned enough about ensuring that Jesus did not die a "cursed" death that they would go to the extent of rewriting actual history to get around this, why did they even leave in his death on the cross? If getting around Deuteronomy 21:22-23 was a paramount concern, and if "what actually happened" exercised no constraint on them, why leave even this much of Jesus' actual death in?

Similarly, if their concern was to soften the debacle of Jesus' death, why leave in (or worse, create) in their accounts the "cursed" cry of Jesus on the cross, "My God, my God, why have you forsaken me?" (Mark 15:34; Matt. 27:46) If they were as free to rewrite history as Mack and Crossan envisage, and if they were driven by a need to minimize the scandal of Jesus' death and burial, one would suppose that at least this much of their account would have been left out.

Conversely, if out of a modicum of genuine historical interest the Gospel authors had to admit that Jesus died on the cross, and if they had no problem with admitting (or contriving) that their Chosen One cried out to God in horror while dying on a cross, what did they find so repulsive about his being thrown into a common shallow grave? And why didn't their modicum of historical interest carry over to admitting that this was how he was in fact disposed of? It seems that their fictitious resurrection stories, if entirely concocted, could have easily incorporated this fact without having lost anything.

Taking these narratives at face value, it doesn't appear that any of the Gospel authors had a vested interest in "tidying up" the horror of what actually happened to Jesus. From Paul's letters we can discern that the notion that Jesus died a cursed death actually played a positive soteriological role in the theology of the early church. Indeed, far from trying to avoid the implication that Jesus died a cursed death on the basis of Deuteronomy 21:22-23, as Crossan contends, we find Paul quoting this passage to prove that Jesus *did* die a cursed death (Gal. 3:13).

The Gospel authors arguably share something of this conviction, which explains, among other things, their inclusion of Jesus' cry on the cross. So if, as Crossan contends, the body of Jesus had been disposed of in a "cursed" manner, we have no reason to think that the Gospel authors would have been unduly embarrassed by this fact.

There is, then, no clear motive for why Mark would have invented Joseph of Arimathea. And as such, the inclusion of this detail is arguably another piece of evidence in favor of the reliability of his account. It is on a par with Mark's incidental mentioning of Simon from Cyrene, "the father of Alexander and Rufus" (Mark 15:21), a remark that presupposes that the audience knows Alexander and Rufus and that is, on this account, impossible to treat as contrived.[47] What is more, there is no doubt that everything the Gospels say about the tomb of Joseph of Arimathea is historically accurate, a point that further substantiates the historicity of the entire account. The kind of tomb described in these accounts—hewed in rock, located by a garden, low entrance (Peter has to stoop to go into it, John 20:5)—is consistent with what we have learned from archaeology about wealthy tombs of this time.[48] Hence, the external as well as the internal evidence argues against Crossan's view that this Joseph is a Markan creation and in favor of viewing this reference as one more indication of the Gospels' substantial reliability.

7. THE ROLE OF EYEWITNESSES

There is one final important criticism that can be raised against Crossan and Mack's dismissal of the Gospel resurrection accounts, and this concerns the role of eyewitnesses in the early church. In a word, even if the Gospels are dated fifty or sixty years after the death of Christ, it is difficult to explain how the four different resurrection narratives came into being and how they were so readily accepted, if these narratives are not rooted in history. For one has yet to account for the presence of eyewitnesses of Jesus' ministry within the Christian communities and hostile eyewitnesses outside of the Christian communities. Crossan and Mack's supposition that the resurrection narratives were simply created by certain mythmakers in the early church requires us to believe that neither the sympathetic nor hostile eyewitnesses of the historical Jesus, nor those who closely associated with them, exercised any significant constraints on what the early church said about Jesus. But this, we must contend, is a most unlikely thesis.

Simply put, is it plausible to suppose that stories about Jesus' empty tomb and resurrection appearances were created, circulated, and widely (if not universally) accepted while there were people within and without the early Christian communities who had known the historical Jesus, as well as others who were close associates of those who had known the historical Jesus, and could have confirmed that these new stories about Jesus simply were not true? And is it plausible to suppose that names like Peter, John, Mary Magdalene, Mary the mother of Jesus, and James the brother of Jesus, could have been attached to these creations and accepted as historical by communities that had known these people in the very recent past? If the resurrection narratives are anything, they are not stories about something that occurred in some distant nebulous past. They are concrete stories, told in a stunningly realistic fashion, about a very recent past event. And they name names that everybody would know. Such a phenomenon is unintelligible on the supposition that these narratives are sheer literary creations.

This point is strengthened when we further consider that Paul had already associated the resurrection kerygma with the founding "pillars" of the church *while these people were still alive* (more on this below). Indeed, as presented by Paul in the early A.D. 50s, the resurrection of Jesus as attested by all the founding figures of the church is assumed to be an already established teaching of the church. The point is strengthened further still when we consider the internal evidence within these Gospel narratives that they derive from eyewitnesses and contain early material. And it is verified even further when we consider that there are good arguments against the late dating of the Synoptic Gospels in the first place (see chap. 11).

In sum, therefore, the supposition that the four resurrection narratives of the Gospels are literary creations goes against not only the internal evidence these narratives provide for us in their historicity, but given the presence of an eyewitness influence in the early church, it lacks inherent plausibility as well.

1 CORINTHIANS 15 AND THE RESURRECTION

We have, however, not yet addressed the Achilles' heel of Crossan and Mack's revisionist understanding of the resurrection. As damaging as the above considerations are to Crossan's and Mack's hypotheses, the weakest component of their hypotheses is found precisely where they need to be strongest. First Corinthians 15 constitutes our earliest written report of Jesus' resurrection. Indeed, as we shall see, it gives us compelling evidence for thinking that the central material used here significantly predates Paul's own writing. Its very antiquity entails that this material constitutes the most important data to be accounted for in any historical hypothesis about the early Christian faith in the resurrection. Hence, the ability, or inability, of any hypothesis to adequately and easily explain what is going on in this passage must significantly determine our estimation of the plausibility or implausibility of this hypothesis.[49]

In my estimation, at no point do Crossan's and Mack's hypotheses fair worse than they do when they attempt to account for this all-important material. Even if their accounts of the Gospel narratives were to be accepted, their weakness in adequately explaining 1 Corinthians 15 would be enough to cast serious doubts on their explanations of the early Christian faith in the resurrection. We shall first briefly outline this passage, then give Crossan and Mack's explanation of it, and conclude with a refutation of their explanation.

AN OUTLINE OF 1 CORINTHIANS 15

Paul begins by telling his readers that he is reminding them of something that he has already preached to them (vv. 1-2). He then tells them that the Gospel he "passed on" (*paradidomi*) to them "as of first importance" is the same one he had "received" (*paralambano*). As most scholars recognize, the language used here denotes the passing on of authoritative traditional material, a point confirmed by the creedal structure of the kerygma contained in verses 3-8. This pushes the antiquity of this material back considerably, some noteworthy scholars arguing that it likely goes back to the beginning of the Christian movement itself.[50] Verse 3 also informs us that this kerygma was regarded as being the center of the Christian faith Paul inherited and passed on.

The contents of the traditional kerygma that Paul "received" and "passed on" was that "Christ died," "was buried," and "was raised on the third day according to the Scriptures" (vv. 3-4). He then appeared to "Peter," the "Twelve," and then to "more than five hundred of the brothers at the same time" (vv. 5-6). Most of these brothers, Paul adds, are still alive: the implication being that they were available to be cross-checked if any of his readers wished to do so. Christ then appeared to "James, then to all the apostles" (v. 7), and last of all to Paul "as to one abnormally born" (v. 8).

Paul then attaches to this Gospel a word about his own calling. He is, he admits, "the least of the apostles" and does not "even deserve to be called an apostle" (v. 9). Yet he has, by God's grace, been called to preach the same message as the other apostles (vv. 10-11). This is then followed by his lengthy discourse on the nature of the resurrection of believers in relation to the resurrection of Christ (vv. 12-58).

This passage obviously raises a serious historical question. What sufficiently explains the message that Jesus was buried and raised being circulated and believed well before A.D. 55 (which is by all accounts the latest possible date that can be assigned for this letter)? Within twenty-five years of his death, the proclamation that Jesus rose from the dead is being passed on as *already established creedal material!* And what adequately explains the many references to particular noteworthy people, and to the more than 500 brothers, who had seen the resurrected Lord? As was said, most of these named and unnamed persons would still have been alive at the time of this writing and could have readily been sought out.

The simplest explanation is to admit that the church from its beginning believed and preached that Christ rose from the dead and that the people Paul cites as seeing the risen Lord in fact believed they had seen him. Beyond its simplicity, this explanation also has the advantage of squaring with the central material of the Gospel accounts (though matters such as the order of appearances are yet different and need further explanation). This explanation, of course, doesn't itself prove that Jesus actually rose from the dead. But given the strong improbability of mass hallucinations, combined with the fact that neither Paul's account nor the Gospel stories suggest that the appearances were of this nature, it is difficult to admit the genuineness of Paul's record here without coming to this conclusion.[51]

CROSSAN'S AND MACK'S EXPLANATIONS OF 1 CORINTHIANS 15

Crossan and Mack, however, reject this explanation and hence must try to explain this passage in other ways. According to Crossan, Paul in 1 Corinthians 15:1-11 is "not primarily interested in trance, ecstasy, apparition, or revelation, but in authority, power, leadership, and priority."[52] Paul is, in other words, not so much interested in proving the resurrection as he is in insisting that he is himself an apostle, on an equal par with the other apostles.[53] This is, Crossan argues, why he distinguishes between "the Twelve" and "the apostles," for while these two groups were sometimes regarded as being synonymous in the early church, Paul knew he could never be one of "the Twelve." He could, however, claim to be an "apostle," one sent by God.

It is, Crossan holds, in order to establish his own authority that Paul attempts to equate "his own experience of the risen Jesus with that of all others before him."[54] On the basis of the three accounts of his conversion provided in Acts, Crossan is certain that this experience was of a "trance" nature. But Crossan does not believe that this experience can be taken as "the model for all the others."[55] In different ways these other authorities all believed in Jesus' continued influence or "presence" within their communities. But, according to Crossan, only Paul expresses this in terms of "resurrection" and "appearance." For political reasons, however, he sought to put his experience on a par with the other Christian authorities.

Crossan also believes that it is extremely significant that there are three types of recipients mentioned in Paul's account: specific leaders, such as Peter, James, and Paul himself; two leadership groups, the Twelve and the apostles; and one general community, the 500 brethren.[56] The significance of this is that it shows that this account, like all the Gospel accounts, is primarily concerned with "the origins of Christian leadership, not the origins of Christian faith."[57] All these accounts aim at expressing "who is in charge."[58] In the case of 1 Corinthians 15, Paul's aim is to put himself in charge, alongside of the other "apostles." As such, neither Paul's account, nor the Gospel accounts, are to be understood as containing any historically reliable information.

Mack's explanation of 1 Corinthians 15 is slightly different, but it arrives at the same conclusion. Mack argues that verses 3-5 originally circulated as an independent creedal formulation and that it was Paul who tacked on the other appearances to various persons in verses 5-7. Moreover, he maintains that a critical analysis of verses 3-5 reveals that statements about Christ's death were originally circulated apart from (and before) those about his resurrection, and that the references to the significance of the event (viz., dying "for our sins") originally "attached only to statements about the death."[59] It was only when Jesus' death became associated with the "martyr myth" in which a martyred hero is vindicated that a belief in Jesus' resurrection arose.[60] All of this was accomplished, argues Mack, in order to rationalize the unique egalitarian social structure of the Hellenistic Jesus people. And even he is impressed with the speed with which this mythological rationalization was accomplished.[61]

But what is to be made of Paul's report that Christ appeared to a significant number of individuals, most of whom were still alive at the time of his writing? Mack acknowledges that this is problematic, if only because Paul here inverts the normal pattern, found throughout religious history, of myths giving rise to visions. For Paul, the "vision" of Christ precedes the faith in Christ—the "mythmaking."[62] Despite this problem, however, Mack is yet convinced that the report is devoid of historical information. With Crossan, Mack believes that Paul's report is "quite self-serving" and is contrived for the purpose of enhancing his own spiritual authority. He writes:

> By attributing appearances to the Jerusalem leaders, Paul achieved two important objectives . . . objectives that countered what he considered to be serious challenges to his authority. One objective was to argue that he also should be regarded as a founder figure among the founder figures. . . . The other objective was to claim that his version of the gospel was the standard from the beginning.[63]

By making the Jesus that he preached and presumed be the same as the Jesus preached and seen by the other authorities, Paul successfully validated his message as well as his apostolic authority. But the whole thing, according to Mack, is as contrived as are the Gospel resurrection accounts. At the time of Paul's writing, according to Mack, neither Peter, James, nor any of the other apostles, were preaching a kerygmatic form of Christianity, certainly not one that included a resurrection of Jesus at its core. As such, both Paul's account and the later Gospel versions "are of no value to the historian who wishes to reconstruct and understand the early history itself."[64]

Six Objections to Crossan's and Mack's Explanations of 1 Corinthians 15

Such is the account Crossan and Mack give of 1 Corinthians 15. If successful, they have offered readers a plausible way of coming to grips with this crucial passage without having to admit the puzzling presence of an empty tomb and hard-to-explain post-resurrection appearances of Jesus to large groups of people. On a number of scores, however, we may judge their accounts as unsuccessful. This chapter will conclude by briefly elucidating six objections that can be made against their use of 1 Corinthians 15.

1. The Failure to "Deal with" the Data

First, as we did with their treatment of Mark (chap. 10), we must wonder whether any historical hypothesis can legitimately be said to have genuinely "dealt with" the historical data when it simply dismisses as a fabrication the data in need of explanation. On one level, this strategy can be read as amounting to nothing more than an open admonition that this data does not square with the hypothesis being argued for. In other words, since Paul's testimony in 1 Corinthians 15 (the "data") doesn't square with the hypothesis of Crossan and Mack, Paul must be twisting the truth in 1 Corinthians 15. But surely this is not sound historical methodology.

Similarly, one wonders what could ever conceivably count against such a hypothesis since all the historical data that could count *against* it is dismissed as deceptive. At the very least, the employment of this strategy to save a hypothesis can hardly strengthen our confidence in the hypothesis. And when we further recall that this strategy must be used five times against all five of the distinct testimonies of Christ's resurrection, we must begin to wonder whether the self-serving purpose of recreating history is on the part of the ancient authors or on the part of the authors of the hypothesis who need to use this strategy so often to save their ideas.

2. Starting with the Unknown

Secondly, the *manner* in which Paul's account is dismissed is suspicious. As they did in interpreting Mark's Gospel, Crossan and Mack seize upon what is most difficult to discern — Paul's motives — to reinterpret what is most apparent — Paul's references to certain people seeing the risen Lord. Rather than taking Paul at face value and wrestling with his testimony, Crossan and Mack impugn his motives so as to excuse themselves from taking seriously his testimony. Such a strategy is as inappropriate here as it was in their treatment of Mark.

However one explains either Paul's or the Gospels' resurrection accounts, the attempt to write them off on the basis of a projected deceptive motivation must be judged as illegitimate. The liberal historical Jesus scholar E.P. Sanders speaks to this point and offers a more reasonable stance toward the biblical data when he writes:

> I do not regard deliberate fraud as a worthwhile explanation. . . . That Jesus' followers (and later Paul) had resurrection experiences is, in my judgment, a fact. What the reality was that gave rise to the experiences I do not know.[65]

While we must be open to the possibility that an actual resurrection lies behind the resurrection experiences — if the data is inexplicable on any naturalistic scheme – Sanders preference for agnosticism over dismissing the data outright as deceptive, as Crossan and Mack do, is admirable. If Paul tells us that he saw the resurrected Lord, and if he tells us that the other leaders in the early church as well as over 500 brethren had a similar experience, we must at least assume that he believes he is telling us the truth. If we have no way of naturalistically explaining how he arrived at this belief, so be it.

3. The Integrity of Paul

If it is always illegitimate to explain away evidence by impugning the motives of an ancient author, doing so when we have good evidence that the writer was a man of high integrity must be considered especially unwarranted. And this is our third criticism. Crossan and Mack's supposition that Paul fabricated information for self-serving purposes in 1 Corinthians 15 flies in the face of everything else we know about the apostle.

It is, for starters, difficult to see how a man who says he received his revelation of Christ as "one abnormally born" (v. 8) can be accused of fabricating history for the sake of bolstering his own authority. It is difficult to see how such a motive can be ascribed to a man who further adds that he is "the least of the apostles" and admits that he does not "even deserve to be called an apostle" (v. 9), especially when he inserts this in the middle of the account he is supposed to have fabricated *as a way of bolstering his own authority!* If Paul is in fact seeking to establish his own authority, he certainly gives away a good deal of ground in the process.

Now verses 7 through 9 could, of course, be read as a display of "false humility." Paul could be seen as trying to sneak his authority in the back door, as it were, by coming across as being humble. Such a conclusion can be reached, however, only by first assuming the disingenuousness of Paul. It certainly doesn't itself constitute evidence of Paul's insincerity. If one at the outset *assumes* that Paul is disingenuous, then of course he *must* here be read as exhibiting "false humility." But the issue is, what evidence is there that Paul is disingenuous in the first place? And the answer, we submit, is none.

Paul's letters clearly reveal a man who had a deep sense of divine vocation and who at times had to fight to establish his authority against opponents. But they do not reveal a man obsessed with his own authority.[66] His letters consistently reveal a man who possessed a high degree of ethical consciousness, humility, love, and integrity, and who encouraged other people to follow his example, as he followed Christ's (1 Cor. 4:6; 11:1).[67] He was, moreover, a man who was willing to be persecuted, and if need be, martyred for his beliefs (Rom. 8:35-37; 1 Cor. 4:9-13; 2 Cor. 1:8-12; 4:8-12; 6:4-10, etc.).[68] In short, he does not come across as the kind of person who would intentionally distort the truth for self-serving purposes.

This is not to say that there was absolutely no issue of authority behind *how* Paul spoke in 1 Corinthians 15. But it is to say that we have no good reason to suppose that this motivation led Paul to contrive *what* he said in this passage. If taken at face value, it certainly *looks* like Paul is doing in this passage exactly what he himself says he's doing: namely, reminding the Corinthians of a central feature of the Gospel he passed on to them, the belief in the resurrection of Jesus Christ (1 Cor. 15:1-2). And it therefore seems quite illegitimate to overturn the genuineness of this expressed motivation and sincerity of this expressed content on the basis of whatever agenda Paul may also have had to establish his own apostolicity.

4. The Distinctness of Motivation and Material Content

Closely related to this is a fourth objection. Even if one accepts that a strong political motivation is discernible in this passage, this does not itself justify the conclusion that Paul is making up the resurrection appearances to Peter, James, the Twelve, the apostles, and the 500 brethren. It is a long way from establishing a *redactional motive* to explaining *material content*. At most, conceding that Paul was here motivated by issues of authority would only mean that Paul was *using* his information on the resurrection for this purpose. It would not rule out the possibility that he was *also* using this material for his own stated purpose of instructing the Corinthians. And it certainly wouldn't rule out the possibility, or even impugn the likelihood, that Paul is here telling us the truth when he says that he is passing on received tradition, not *creating* it, and that he shares this tradition with all the other apostles.

Hence, the view that Paul is here artificially putting his own "vision" of Jesus on a par with the other disciples who never actually had such "visions" is really a separate hypothesis from the one that Paul is being influenced or even controlled by political motives. As such, even if the political motivation in this passage is granted, a different line of argumentation and evidential support is needed to substantiate it. But Crossan and Mack do not provide this.

Appeal could, of course, be made at this point to Q and Thomas which, it is argued, lack a concept of Jesus' resurrection. This, one could argue, proves that the earliest Jerusalem Christian communities, and hence the earliest leaders of these groups, did not believe in a resurrection. Thus, it proves that Paul is in 1 Corinthians 15 creating history, not simply passing it on. But the fallacy of arguing along these lines has already been exposed at a number of points in our study. Among other things, the case for an early dating and normative reading of GosThom is very tenuous, as is the case for arguing from silence on the basis of Q. At the very least, it seems quite misguided to dismiss the testimony (and integrity) of Paul (and the authors of the Gospels) on such a flimsy basis. If the case against the historicity of Paul's account hangs on the early dating and normative reading of GosThom as well as on an argument from silence from Q, we can assuredly have a good deal of confidence in the historicity of Paul's report.

5. The Improbability of Paul's Fabrication

A fifth objection concerns the inherent improbability of Paul naming specific noteworthy church leaders and referring to an extraordinarily large group of people who purportedly "saw" what he "saw" if in fact these leaders and this group never had such an experience. If Paul is stretching the truth here, would not such a procedure invite disaster? Given that Paul was dealing with a number of people at Corinth who were doubting his message of the resurrection, and given that there were influential spokespersons who opposed him and who had influence in Corinth, could Paul have dreamed that he would get away with such a maneuver if in fact he was fabricating the parallels between himself and the other apostles? Would this not be very easy to expose? Would Paul have wagered everything on the hope that no one would think of inquiring of these other leaders and supposed witnesses to the resurrection about whether what Paul was saying of them was true? And would Paul have invited such an invitation by reminding the Corinthians that most of the eyewitnesses were still alive? (15:6) The supposition seems most unlikely.

As we have seen, of course, Crossan and Mack portray the Hellenistic Christian communities of Paul as being worlds removed from the Jerusalem Jesus people and thus they could perhaps hold that the Corinthians would have had no knowledge about, or concern with, the Jerusalem "pillars." Hence Paul could safely get away with his artificial strategy of citing these people as a means of establishing his own apostolic authority.

There are at least two problems with this response, however. First, as we have already argued, all the evidence indicates that these different clusters of believers were, for all their differences, networked together (chaps. 5 and 10). Indeed, 1 Corinthians 1:12 suggests that the Corinthians had some familiarity with Peter, a point confirmed by 9:5 which presupposes not only that Peter traveled around to different communities but that the Corinthians were well-acquainted with this fact. Paul's incidental reference to the way early churches networked (Gal. 1:18-24), his own report about his and Peter's travels (Gal. 2:1-11), and the picture painted in Acts all serve to confirm the view that the earliest communities were anything but independent and isolated congregations. Hence, in citing Peter, James, the Twelve, and the apostles as witnesses to the resurrection, we cannot understand Paul to be referring to people who would be unknown to the Corinthians.

Secondly, the response actually seems to argue against itself. For if the Corinthians were so unfamiliar with the Jerusalem leaders, why would Paul feel such a great need to put his own experience of the risen Lord on a par with them before his Corinthian audience? Or, to ask this question another way, if the Corinthians were acquainted enough with these leaders that Paul had to bolster his own authority by artificially appealing to them, why would they not be acquainted enough with them to verify whether or not what Paul was saying was true — especially if what he was saying was relatively new? The point is that one can't plausibly explain Paul's motivation for artificially putting himself on a par with the other apostles without at the same time making the suggestion that he actually did so most implausible.

6. Paul and the Other Apostles

A final and closely related objection to Crossan and Mack's treatment of 1 Corinthians 15 is that it seems to stand in tension with what Paul tells us elsewhere about his communication with the other apostles. Are we really to believe that Paul, Peter, James, and the apostles didn't discuss the resurrection when they met together for extended periods of time (Gal. 1:18), twice after Paul's conversion? (Gal. 1:18-24; 2:1-11) Given the centrality of the resurrection in Paul's theology and the fact that he tells the Galatians that he went down to Jerusalem for his second visit to "set before them the gospel that I preach among the Gentiles" (Gal. 2:2), is it really conceivable that their differences on this matter (if they had any) would not have surfaced? If Paul's teaching on the resurrection wasn't talked about, what was? And if a disagreement about living out the

Gospel surfaced (2:11), how could a disagreement about its essence not have surfaced? The idea seems ludicrous. If the other apostles had not held to a belief in Christ's resurrection, there is no conceivable way that Paul could have left these meetings feeling like he and the other disciples were preaching the same Gospel (Gal. 2:6-10).

What is more, if the other apostles didn't believe in the resurrection, we must wonder who Paul was referring to when he says he "received" what he also "passed on": Jesus died and was raised again from the dead. From whom did Paul "receive" this tradition if not from these authorities? If he didn't get the content of 1 Corinthians 15:2-8 during the fifteen days he visited with Peter and James (Gal. 1:18), who did he "receive it" from and when? And again, we must in this case wonder what Paul, Peter, and James talked about during their fifteen-day visit.

All such difficulties are immediately resolved the moment one simply admits that Paul wasn't fabricating his material in 1 Corinthians 15. Deny this, however, and a deluge of insurmountable difficulties beset you. And it is these difficulties that require one to engage in the many tenuous speculations which characterize the hypotheses of Crossan and Mack.

CONCLUSION:
THE RESURRECTION OF THE HISTORICAL JESUS

The Cynic thesis, we have earlier seen, is quite unsuccessful in attempting to explain away the view of Christ and the early church given to us in the New Testament documents. The evidence from Paul, Mark, and Acts is too compelling to be overturned by the questionable speculations about Q, GosThom, Secret Mark, and the like offered us by Cynic theorists. What we have seen in this chapter is that this view is equally unsuccessful in its attempts to explain away the foundational *reason* given us in the New Testament documents for why the early church held the view of Christ it did: namely, his resurrection from the dead.

This issue boils down to this: How are we to account for the widespread belief that Jesus rose from the dead – held as an already established piece of the church tradition a mere twenty to twenty-five years after the historical Jesus lived? And how are we to account for the fact that those who were closest to Jesus during his lifetime (e.g., James, Peter, John) shared this belief? Moreover, how are we to counter the fundamental commonalities shared among the four post-Pauline resurrection accounts, accounts which on other matters clearly exhibit independence from one another? And how are we to counter the internal evidence in these accounts, and in Paul, that suggests that we are here dealing with reliable historical reminiscence, and not fabricated mythology?

The simplest explanation, and the only one that accounts for all the data, is to admit that Jesus' tomb was empty and that a number of his disciples believed that they saw him in a postmortem state shortly after his death. If this much is not conceded, observers have to necessarily get very speculative and complex in their explanations. For they can no longer build their theory *upon* the available data: they must rather build their theory *around* the available data. And that, we have seen, is illegitimate as a historical methodology and is, in any case, exceedingly difficult to do.

Of course, admitting that the tomb was empty and that many early disciples believed they witnessed the resurrected Lord doesn't itself prove that Jesus actually rose from the dead. Historical reasoning necessarily stops short of this. Affirming the historical resurrection, therefore, is fundamentally an act of faith. But admitting this much *does* render this act of faith very reasonable. Indeed, if a "leap" is required to affirm Jesus' resurrection, it is far less than the "leap" required to deny it. To insist that Paul and Mark were fundamentally deceptive; to affirm that Q and GosThom give us a more solid foundation for understanding the early church than Paul or Acts; to insist that the Jerusalem pillars had little or no contact with the Hellenistic churches—*that* requires faith!

Thus, whether one holds that Jesus was the Son of God and was raised from the dead, or whether one believes that Jesus was a Cynic sage whose body was eventually devoured by wild beasts, faith is necessarily involved. The point of this whole book, however, has been to establish this: the first act of faith is firmly rooted in all the available evidence: the second is rooted only in human speculation. A concern for rational integrity, to say nothing about a concern for salvation, should therefore compel the reader to "leap" in the direction of the former.

NOTES

Introduction: The Challenge of the Cynic Thesis

1. For a trenchant review of this work by an esteemed New Testament scholar (Richard Hays), see *First Things* 43 (May 1994): 43–48.

2. See Paul Verhoeven, "Update: Christ the Man," *Fourth R* 4/1 (January 1991): 5–8.

3. R. Funk, "The Issue of Jesus," *Foundations and Facets Forum* 1/1 (1985): 10.

4. J.D. Crossan, "Why We Must Seek the Historical Jesus: His Message Goes Beyond the Gospels," *The Boston Sunday Globe*, 26 July 1992, 59. The seminar's decision to vote on sayings with colored beads, e.g., was calculated to get media attention. Says Crossan, "We thought the colors would be more photogenic." Quoted in R. Watson, "A Lesser Child of God," *Newsweek*, 4 April 1994, 54.

5. Burton L. Mack, *A Myth of Innocence: Mark and Christian Origins* (hereinafter referred to as *MI*) (Minneapolis: Fortress, 1988), 378–86. Mack's understanding of "the cost of the Markan legacy" shall be discussed more fully in chap. 10.

6. H. Taussig, "The Jesus Seminar and Its Public," *Foundations and Facets Forum* 2 (1986): 71–72.6.

7. This figure is based sales information given by HarperSanFrancisco during a phone interview, 28 March 1995.

8. J.H. Charlesworth, "Jesus Research Expands with Chaotic Creativity," in *Images of Jesus Today*, ed. J.H. Charlesworth and W. Weaver (Valley Forge, Pa.: Trinity, 1994), 16–19.

9. The background to the Cynic-sage thesis shall be given in chap. 2.

10. Since I am seeking to make my critique accessible to lay readers, I have kept technical discussions on various scholarly issues to a minimum within the text. When such discussions are called for, I have generally placed them in the notes. Consequently, some of my notes are content oriented and will be of limited interest to the nonspecialist.

11. See, for example, Colin Hemer's comments in *The Book of Acts in the Setting of Hellenistic History*, ed. C.H. Gempf (Tübingen: Mohr, 1989), 3.

12. Readers already well-acquainted with "the quest for the historical Jesus" may consider chap. 1 optional, however, and those well-acquainted with the post-Bultmannian and "Third Quest" trajectories of contemporary scholarship may want to bypass chap. 2 as well.

13. My concentration is on Mark, instead of Matthew, Luke, and/or John, because Crossan and Mack, along with the majority of New Testament scholars, assume that Mark lies behind Matthew and Luke (and perhaps John

as well). Hence the issue of the reliability of the Gospels largely boils down to an issue over the reliability of Mark.

14. It should be said, for the sake of lay readers, that I shall content myself with providing evidence for "the general reliability" of Paul, Mark, and Acts. I have no interest here in further attempting to argue for their divine "inspiration" or their "infallibility." The case against revisionist historical portraits of Jesus must be made on historical, not doctrinal, grounds. The methodological significance of this for my work is that "general reliability" is a much looser category than is "infallibility," and hence the admission of occasional contradictions and inaccuracies that might bother the latter do not affect the former at all. While I believe that a strong case for biblical inspiration can be defended on historical grounds, such a defense lies outside the scope of this work; and thus, I shall be concerned with matters of contradictions and inaccuracies only to the extent that they impact our estimation of the historical reliability of the canonical documents.

Chapter 1: The Search for an "Alternative Jesus"

1. For more detailed discussions of the history and nature of the quest from various perspectives, see C.C. Anderson, *Critical Quests of Jesus* (Grand Rapids: Eerdmans, 1969); E. Hurth, *In His Name: Comparative Studies in the Quest for the Historical Jesus,* EUS (Frankfurt/New York: Lang, 1989); W.S. Kissinger, *The Lives of Jesus: A History and Bibliography* (New York/London: Garland, 1985); I.H. Marshall, *I Believe in the Historical Jesus* (Grand Rapids: Eerdmans, 1977); A. McGrath, *The Making of Modern German Christology, 1750–1990,* 2nd ed. (Grand Rapids: Zondervan, 1994); W.B. Tatum, *In Quest of Jesus: A Guidebook* (Atlanta: Knox, 1982); H. Zahrnt, *The Historical Jesus,* trans. J. Bowden (London: Collins, 1963). For extensive bibliographies related to the quest, see C.A. Evans, *Life of Jesus Research: An Annotated Bibliography,* NTTS 13 (Leiden: Brill, 1989); and the student edition, idem, *Jesus,* IBRB 5 (Grand Rapids: Baker, 1992).

2. For discussions of precritical attitudes toward biblical complexities and difficulties, see W. Kümmel, *The New Testament: The History of the Investigation of Its Problems,* trans. S. Gilmour and H.C. Kee (Nashville: Abingdon, 1972), 13–39; C. Blomberg, *The Historical Reliability of the Gospels* (Downers Grove, Ill.: InterVarsity, 1987), 1–5.

3. On various aspects of the rise of the historical-critical method, see W. Baird, *History of New Testament Research, Volume 1: From Deism to Tübingen* (Minneapolis: Fortress, 1992); C. Brown, *Jesus in European Protestant Thought, 1778–1860* (Durham, N.C.: Labyrinth, 1985), 29–55; Kümmel, *The New Testament,* 51–61; G. Reedy, *The Bible and Reason: Anglicans and Scripture in Late Seventeenth-Century England* (Philadelphia: Univ. of Pennsylvania Press, 1985); H.G. Reventlow, *The Authority of the Bible and the Rise of the Modern World,* trans. J. Bowden (Philadelphia: Fortress, 1985).

4. While Schweitzer's date functions as a helpful heuristic, to suggest—as he seems to—that the quest began virtually *ex nihilo* at this point is simply inaccurate. See Brown, *Jesus,* 29–55.

5. For a detailed discussion of the "fragments" of Reimarus, see Brown's, "The Fragments Controversy: A Chapter in the Theology of the Enlightenment," in his *Jesus,* 1–55.

6. See *Reimarus: Fragments,* ed. C.H. Talbert, trans. R.S. Frazer (Philadelphia: Fortress, 1970).

7. Ibid., 64.

8. Ibid., 150.

9. Ibid., 249–50.

10. Ibid., 151.

11. Ibid., 243.

12. Ibid., 123–29.

13. A. Schweitzer, *The Quest of the Historical Jesus: A Critical Study of Its Progress from Reimarus to Wrede*, trans. W. Montgomery (New York: Collier/Macmillan, 1968), 23.

14. Ibid.

15. Ibid., 13, 26.

16. Brown, *Jesus*, 52.

17. Schweitzer, *Quest*, 27–37.

18. See Brown, *Jesus*, 8–16.

19. Ibid., 161.

20. Schweitzer, *Quest*, 27–28.

21. Ibid., 38–47.

22. Ibid., 44.

23. Ibid., 47.

24. E.g., see J. Allegro, *The Dead Sea Scrolls and the Christian Myth* (Buffalo: Prometheus, 1984); M. Baigent and R. Leigh, *The Dead Sea Scrolls Deception* (New York/London: Summit, 1991); and most recently, B. Thiering's fantastically speculative work, *Jesus and the Riddle of the Dead Sea Scrolls: Unlocking the Secrets of His Life Story* (San Francisco: HarperSanFrancisco, 1992). For a concise critique of Thiering, see N.T. Wright, *Who Was Jesus?* (London: SPCK, 1992), 19–36. On the perennial reappearance of such conspiracy theories see G. O'Collins and D. Kendall, "On Reissuing Venturini," *Gregorianum* 75/2 (1994): 241–65.

25. See Schweitzer, *Quest*, 48–67.

26. Ironically, all the attention that has been given to Paulus' reworking of the miracle accounts runs counter to the author's intentions. In the preface of his book, he wrote: "My greatest wish is that my views on the miraculous narratives should by no means be taken for the chief matter. O, how empty would be devotion or religion, if the truth depended on whether one believed in miracles or not." Cited in Brown, *Jesus*, 165.

27. Schweitzer, *Quest*, 51.

28. Cited in Baird, *History of New Testament*, 202.

29. Baird, *History of New Testament*, 246. The most recent edition of this work is, *The Life of Jesus Critically Examined*, ed. P.C. Hodgson, trans. G. Eliot (Philadelphia: Fortress, 1972). In 1864, Strauss wrote a second account of Jesus, ostensibly designed for a wider, non-scholarly audience, entitled *A New Life of Jesus*, 2 vols. (London: Williams and Norgate, 1865). And the following year, he came out with *The Christ of Faith and the Jesus of History*, a critical reply to Schleiermacher's posthumously published lectures on the life of Jesus. See *The Christ of Faith and the Jesus of History: A Critique of Schleiermacher's The Life of Jesus*, ed. and trans. L.E. Keck (Philadelphia: Fortress, 1977). For a helpful survey of Strauss' life and thought, see H. Harris, *David Friedrich Strauss and His Theology* (Cambridge: Cambridge Univ. Press, 1973).

30. Strauss gives "the most convincing argument" for his view of the Gospels when he writes: "If the mythical view be once admitted, the innumerable, and never otherwise to be harmonized, discrepancies and chronological contradictions in the gospel histories disappear, as it were, at one stroke" (*Life of Jesus*, 56–57). This is not to suggest that Strauss held that there was nothing of historical value within the Gospel, only that the *genre* of the Gospels was mythological, not historical.

31. On sources of Strauss' concept of myth, see E.G. Lawler, *David Friedrich Strauss and His Critics: The Life of Jesus Debate in Early Nineteenth-Century German Journals*, TR 16 (New York/Berne: Lang, 1986), 21–45.

32. Schweitzer, *Quest*, 79.

33. Strauss makes a distinction between "pure" and "historical" myth. "Pure myth" has two sources: (1) the messianic ideas and expectations, rooted in the Old Testament; and (2) the "impression" of Jesus' life, character, and fate that was left on his early followers (*Life of Jesus*, 86). "Historical myth," on the other hand, ultimately derives from "a definite individual fact" that has been embellished with mythic ideas drawn from "the idea of the Christ" (p. 87).

34. Baird, *History of New Testament*, 251–52.

35. Strauss, *Life of Jesus*, 777–81.

36. See the brief comparison of Strauss and Bultmann in Harris, *Strauss*, 272–73.

37. Shortly after the publication of his *Life of Jesus*, for example, Strauss noted: "My criticism of the life of Jesus was from its origin intimately related to Hegelian philosophy." Cited in Brown, *Jesus*, 203.

38. Ibid., 204.

39. From his 1840 *Glaubenslehre*; cited in P.C. Hodgson, "Strauss's Theological Development," in *Life of Jesus*, xlvi. On the anti-orthodox polemical sentiment of the early biblical-critical movement in general, see W. Wink, *The Bible in Human Transformation: Toward a New Paradigm for Biblical Study* (Philadelphia: Fortress, 1973), chap. 1. For a general critique of anti-Christian presuppositions of "historical-critical theology" as a whole, see E. Linnemann, *Historical Criticism and the Bible: Methodology or Ideology?* trans. R. Yarbrough (Grand Rapids: Baker, 1990). The genuine insights of this latter work are largely lost, however, in the author's tendency to overstate her case in often vitriolic and extremely generalized terms. See my review of this work in *Christian Scholars Review* 22:1 (Sept. 1992): 106–9.

40. Strauss, cited in Hodgson, "Strauss's Theological Development," xlvi.

41. D.F. Strauss, *The Old Faith and the New: A Confession*, 2 vols., trans. M. Blind (New York: Holt, 1874), 1:92.

42. Ibid., 107, cf. 169. It's not insignificant to note that, toward the end of his life, Strauss embraced a form of cosmic evolutionary pantheism in which the figure of Christ played no role. See the discussions of Harris, *Strauss*, 238–49; Hodgson, "Strauss's Theological Development," xlv-vi.

43. See R. Stein, *The Synoptic Problem: An Introduction* (Grand Rapids: Baker, 1987), 129–30; W.R. Farmer, *The Gospel of Jesus: The Pastoral Relevance of the Synoptic Problem* (Louisville: Westminster/Knox, 1994), 15–18.

44. See Baird, *History of New Testament*, 296–98, 372–74.

45. See B. Reicke, *The Roots of the Synoptic Gospels* (Philadelphia: Fortress, 1986); J. Wenham, *Redating Matthew, Mark and Luke: A Fresh Assault on the Synoptic Problem* (London: Hodder & Stoughton, 1991); and, from a former Bultmannian scholar, E. Linnemann, *Is There a Synoptic Problem? Rethinking the Literary Dependence of the First Three Gospels* (Grand Rapids: Baker, 1992).

46. On Baur and the Tübingen school, see Brown, *Jesus*, 204–19; Baird, *History of New Testament*, 258–94. More extensively, see P.C. Hodgson, *The Formation of Historical Theology: A Study of Ferdinand Christian Baur* (New York: Harper & Row, 1966), and H. Harris, *The Tübingen School* (Oxford: Clarendon, 1975).

47. For extended discussions of the rise of the two-source theory, see W.R. Farmer, *The Synoptic Problem: A Critical Analysis* (New York: Macmillan, 1964), 1–47; Baird, *History of New Testament*, 295–311.

48. Much debate has surrounded the origins of the sygla "Q." For a discussion, see J.Y. Yieh, "The Study of Q: A Survey of Its History and the Current State," *Taiwan Journal of Theology* 8 (1986): 105–39. It should also be noted that there is a long-standing debate as to why the two-source theory "won" over the Griesbach theory, with the defenders of Matthean priority

arguing that Griesbach's theory was rejected primarily for religious, social, and political reasons, while the defenders of the two-source theory argue that the issue was fought, and won, primarily on the basis of demonstrable evidence. On the side of Griesbach, see H.U. Meijboom, *A History and Critique of the Origin of the Marcan Hypothesis, 1835-1866: A Contemporary Report Redis-covered,* ed. and trans. J.J. Kiwiet (Macon, Ga.: Mercer Univ. Press, 1993); H. Stoldt, *History and Criticism of the Markan Hypothesis,* ed. and trans. D.L. Niewyk (Edinburgh: T & T Clark; Macon, Ga.: Mercer Univ. Press, 1980); B. Reicke, "From Strauss to Holtzmann and Meijboom," *Novum Testamentum* ·29/1 (1987): 1–21; and Farmer, *Gospel of Jesus,* 125–60. On the side of the two-source theory, see Schweitzer, *Quest,* 121–36; C. Tuckett, "The Griesbach Hypothesis in the Nineteenth Century," *Journal for the Study of the New Testament* 3 (1979): 29–60; idem, *The Revival of the Griesbach Hypothesis: An Analysis and Appraisal* (Cambridge: Cambridge Univ. Press, 1983), 3–7; Stein, *Synoptic Problem,* 131–32; B. Henaut, "Is Q But the Invention of Luke and Mark?: Method and Argument in the Griesbach Hypothesis," *Religious Studies and Theology* 8 (1988): 15–32.

49. C. Evans, "The Historical Jesus and the Christ of Faith: A Critical Assessment of a Scholarly Problem," *Christian Scholar's Review* 18/1 (1988): 51.

50. See Schweitzer, *Quest,* 161–72.

51. Ibid., 137–60; Brown, *Jesus,* 227–31. For one of the few contemporary arguments for the non-historicity of Jesus, see G.A. Wells, *The Historical Evidence for Jesus* (Buffalo: Prometheus, 1982). Though no reputable New Testament scholar follows him, the philosopher M. Martin defends him in his *The Case Against Christianity* (Philadelphia: Temple Univ. Press, 1991), chap. 2. For a recent critique of this thesis, see G. Habermas, *The Verdict of History* (Nashville: Nelson, 1988).

52. Baird, *History of New Testament,* 375. On Renan, see Schweitzer, *Quest,* 180–92; Baird, *History of New Testament,* 375–84; and Brown, *Jesus,* 233–88.

53. E. Renan, *The History of the Origins of Christianity, Volume 1: Life of Jesus* (London: Mathieson, n.d.), 155.

54. Ibid., 249.

55. The book was so popular that, only four years after its release, Renan found himself making significant alterations in a *thirteenth* edition!

56. See Renan, *Life of Jesus,* 267–316 for a lengthy appendix on this topic, which he attached to the thirteenth edition. Here Renan reflects the increasingly skeptical attitude toward John that characterizes the mid-nineteenth century. On this growing skepticism, see Baird, *History of New Testament,* 249–50, 267–68, 311–19.

57. Renan, *Life of Jesus,* xi.

58. Ibid.

59. Ibid., xi-ii.

60. This is not to suggest that Britain did not have its radical critics who shared the anti-supernaturalistic bias of their German and French counterparts. As early as 1724, Anthony Collins prefigured Strauss and many contemporary scholars (including Mack and Crossan) when he argued that early Christians re-created history out of what they thought were Old Testament prophecies. See J. Drury, *Critics of the Bible, 1724–1873* (Cambridge: Cambridge Univ. Press, 1989), chap. 1., C.C. Hennell's *Inquiry Concerning the Origin of Christianity* (1838), and J.R. Seeley's *Ecce Homo: A Survey of the Life and Work of Christ* (1865) also constitute works that embody the naturalistic, rationalistic, and skeptic spirit of the times on British soil. For a discussion of these and other British ventures, see D.L. Pals, *The Victorian "Lives" of Jesus, TUMSR 7* (San Antonio: Trinity Univ. Press, 1982).

61. For an extended discussion of Farrar, see Pals, *Victorian "Lives,"* 78–85.

62. F.W. Farrar, *The Life of Christ* (Portland, Ore.: Fountain, 1972), 3.

63. Pals, *Victorian "Lives,"* 104. On Edersheim, see 104–8.

64. A. Edersheim, *The Life and Times of Jesus the Messiah,* 2 vols., 8th ed. (New York/London: Longmans, Greenman, 1896), 1:559.

65. Brown, *Jesus,* 275. On late nineteenth-century American conservative-evangelical responses to biblical criticism, see M. Noll, *Between Faith and Criticism: Evangelicals, Scholarship, and the Bible in America,* 2nd ed. (Grand Rapids: Baker, 1991), 11–31.

66. Another reason why the contributions of conservatives in the first quest is often overlooked is that, by the very nature of the case, their contributions were typically framed as *responses* to their more radical colleagues. For detailed discussions on conservative contributions during this time, see the several relevant sections in Baird, *History of New Testament;* and Brown, "Orthodoxy Modified," in his *Jesus,* 239–76. For discussions on conservative reactions to Strauss, see Lawler, *Strauss and His Critics,* 47–65; Brown, *Jesus,* 196–200. More broadly in this regard, see H.W. Frei, *The Eclipse of Biblical Narrative: A Study in Eighteenth and Nineteenth Century Hermeneutics* (New Haven: Yale Univ. Press, 1974).

67. On the work of these four, see C. Welch, *Protestant Thought in the Nineteenth Century,* 2 vols. (New Haven: Yale Univ. Press, 1985), vol. 2.

68. See J. Weiss, *Jesus' Proclamation of the Kingdom of God,* ed. and trans. R.H. Hiers and D.L. Holland (Philadelphia: Fortress, 1971).

69. Schweitzer, *Quest,* 398.

70. This is not to suggest that Schweitzer finds nothing of value in questers other than Weiss. To the contrary, Schweitzer argues that there are in fact three major contributors to the "Old Quest" who force a fundamental choice between two mutually exclusive alternatives. According to Schweitzer, Strauss forces us to choose between the "purely historical or purely supernatural" Jesus. Holtzmann forces us to choose between either a "Synoptic or Johannine" Jesus. And Weiss, of course, forces us to choose between either an "eschatological *or* non-eschatological" Jesus (see *Quest,* 238). For Schweitzer, an honest evaluation of the evidence makes a choice of the former over the latter in each case necessary.

71. Schweitzer, *Quest,* 370–71.

72. Ibid., 399.

73. For Tyrrell's original use of this analogy in regard to Harnack's Christ, see his *Christianity at the Cross-Roads* (London: Longmans, Green, 1913), 44. This criticism, I shall argue, can be justifiably raised against both Mack and Crossan. See chap. 6.

74. W. Wrede, *The Messianic Secret,* trans. J.C.G. Greig (Greenwood, S.C.: Attic, 1971), 131. For more recent discussion on the "messianic secret," see C. Tuckett, ed., *The Messianic Secret,* IRT 1 (Philadelphia/London: Fortress/SPCK, 1983).

75. Bultmann's work, *The History of the Synoptic Tradition,* has come to function as the classic touchstone for all subsequent ventures in the field. See R. Bultmann, *The History of the Synoptic Tradition,* rev. ed. (Oxford: Blackwell, 1963). On the rise and nature of form criticism, see E.V. McKnight, *What Is Form Criticism?* (Philadelphia: Fortress, 1969); Neill and Wright, "The Gospel Behind the Gospels," in their *Interpretation of the New Testament,* 252–312; Stein, "The Preliterary History of the Gospel Tradition" in his *Synoptic Problem,* 161–228.

76. E.E. Ellis, "Gospels Criticism: A Perspective on the State of the Art." In *The Gospel and the Gospels,* ed. P. Stuhlmacher, trans. J. Vriend (Grand Rapids: Eerdmans, 1991), 38.

77. One need not adopt these skeptical presuppositions in the use of form criticism. See, e.g., the classic work by Vincent Taylor, *The Formation of the Gospel Tradition* (London: Macmillan, 1953) and, for an evangelical employ-

ment of form criticism, Stein, *Synoptic Problem*, 217–28.

78. M. Kähler, *The So-called Historical Jesus and the Historic, Biblical Christ*, ed. and trans. C.E. Braaten (Philadelphia: Fortress, 1988), 46.

79. Ibid., 43 (emphasis in text).

80. Ibid., 74 (emphasis in text). For more detailed discussions of Kähler, see C.E. Braaten "Revelation, History, and Faith in Martin Kähler," in *The So-called Historical Jesus*, 1–38; Anderson, *Critical Quests*, 75–86. This perspective was anticipated by Søren Kierkegaard, who himself derived much from Gotthold Lessing. See S. Kierkegaard, *Concluding Unscientific Postscript*, trans. ·D. Swanson (Princeton: Princeton Univ. Press, 1941).

81. For representative citations and sources, see Braaten, "Revelation, History, and Faith," 33.

82. For further discussion, see W. Baird, *The Quest of the Christ of Faith: Reflections on the Bultmannian Era* (Waco, Texas: Word, 1977); J.M. Robinson, *A New Quest for the Historical Jesus* (London: SCM, 1959), 9–47.

83. R. Bultmann, *Jesus and the Word*, trans. L.P. Smith and E.H. Lantero (New York: Scribner's, 1958), 8.

84. On Bultmann's understanding of mythology and his demythologizing hermeneutic, see both his *Kerygma and Myth*, ed. H.W. Bartsch, trans. R.H. Fuller (London: SPCK, 1953), and *Jesus Christ and Mythology* (New York: Scribner's, 1958). See also Baird, *Quest of the Christ of Faith*, 95–118.

85. R. Bultmann, *Theology of the New Testament*, 2 vols., trans. K. Grobel (New York: Scribner's, 1951), 1:21.

86. R. Bultmann, "Is Exegesis without Presuppositions Possible?" in *Existence and Faith: Shorter Writings of Rudolf Bultmann*, ed. and trans. S.M. Ogden (Cleveland: Meridian; New York: World, 1966), 289, 291.

87. Ibid., 291–92. One of course wonders how Bultmann could continue to speak of God's call to radical decision if he applied this conviction consistently. What does speaking about "God's call" mean if it doesn't in some sense entail a divine interruption of the "closed continuum of effects"?

88. R. Bultmann, *Jesus Christ and Mythology* (New York: Scribner's, 1958), 15. In a similar discussion one finds Bultmann's famous statement: "It is impossible to use electric light and the wireless and to avail ourselves of modern medical and surgical discoveries, and at the same time to believe in the New Testament world of spirits and miracles." See "New Testament and Mythology," in *Kerygma and Myth*, vol. 1, ed. H.W. Bartsch, trans. R.H. Fuller (London: SPCK, 1964), 5.

89. See T.W. Manson, *The Servant-Messiah* (Cambridge: Cambridge Univ. Press, 1966); C.H. Dodd, *Historical Tradition in the Fourth Gospel* (Cambridge: Cambridge Univ. Press, 1963); idem, *The Founder of Christianity* (London: Macmillan, 1970). See also the longer list in J.M. Robinson, *A New Quest of the Historical Jesus*, SBT 25 (London: SCM, 1959), 9–10.

90. D.M. Baillie, *God Was in Christ: An Essay on Incarnation and Atonement* (New York: Scribner's, 1948), 58. See pp. 20–58 for his discussion of the implications of form criticism for historical Jesus study and Christology.

91. The term "New Quest" was coined by James Robinson in his book, *A New Quest of the Historical Jesus*. Käsemann's lecture is entitled, "The Problem of the Historical Jesus" and is found in his *Essays on New Testament Themes*, SBT 41, trans. W.J. Montague (London: SCM, 1964), 15–47. For various perspectives on the "New Quest," see C.E. Braaten and R.A. Harrisville, eds., *The Historical Jesus and the Kerygmatic Christ: Essays on the New Quest of the Historical Jesus* (Nashville: Abingdon, 1964); R.P. Martin, "The New Quest of the Historical Jesus," in *Jesus of Nazareth: Savior and Lord*, ed. C.F.H. Henry (Grand Rapids: Eerdmans, 1966), 23–45; B.L. Ramm, "The New Quest for the Historical Jesus," in his *An Evangelical Christology: Ecumenical and Historic* (Nashville: Nelson, 1985), 149–66; J. Reumann, "Jesus and Christology," in

The New Testament and Its Modern Interpreters, ed. E.J. Epp and G.W. MacRae (Philadelphia/Atlanta: Fortress/Scholars, 1989), 501–64; and Robinson, *New Quest.*

92. See Robinson, *New Quest,* 65–66.

93. Käsemann, "Problem of the Historical Jesus," 46. See also p. 34.

94. G. Bornkamm, *Jesus of Nazareth,* trans. I. and F. McLuskey and J. Robinson (New York: Harper & Row, 1960).

95. Ibid., 13.

96. E. Fuchs, *Studies of the Historical Jesus,* SBT 42, trans. A. Scobie (London: SCM, 1964); H. Conzelmann, *Jesus,* ed. J. Reumann, trans. J.R. Lord (Philadelphia: Fortress, 1973); G. Ebeling, "Jesus and Faith" and "The Question of the Historical Jesus and the Problem of Christology," in his *Word and Faith,* trans. J.W. Leitch (Philadelphia/London: Fortress/SCM, 1963), 201–46, 288–304. For statements and assessments of the "New Quest"–including a response by Bultmann–see Braaten and Harrisville, *Historical Jesus and the Kerygmatic Christ.*

97. On the rise and nature of redaction criticism, see N. Perrin, *What Is Redaction Criticism?* (Philadelphia: Fortress, 1969); R.H. Stein, *Gospels and Tradition: Studies on Redaction Criticism of the Synoptic Gospels* (Grand Rapids: Baker, 1992); idem, "The Inscripturation of the Gospel Traditions," in his *Synoptic Problem,* 231–72.

98. See S.S. Smalley, "Redaction Criticism," in *New Testament Interpretation: Essays on Principles and Methods,* ed. I.H. Marshall (Grand Rapids: Eerdmans, 1977), 181–95.

99. See J.S. Kloppenborg, "Tradition and Redaction in the Synoptic Sayings Source," *Catholic Biblical Quarterly* 46/1 (1984): 34–62.

100. E.g., see V.A. Harvey and S.M. Ogden, "How New Is the 'New Quest of the Historical Jesus,' " in *Historical Jesus and the Kerygmatic Christ,* 197–242.

101. See R.E. Brown, "After Bultmann, What?–An Introduction to the Post-Bultmannians," *Catholic Biblical Quarterly* 26 (1964): 24; J.I.H. MacDonald, "New Quest–Dead End? So What about the Historical Jesus," in *Studia Biblica 1978,* vol. 2: *Papers on the Gospels,* ed. E.A. Livingstone, *JSNTSS* 2 (Sheffield: JSOT, 1980), 151–70.

102. See N. Perrin, *Rediscovering the Teaching of Jesus* (New York: Harper & Row, 1967). See also the valuable review article by W.G. Kümmel, "Norman Perrin's 'Rediscovering the Teaching of Jesus,' " *The Journal of Religion* 49 (1969): 59–66.

103. E.g., see J. Jeremias, *New Testament Theology: The Proclamation of Jesus,* trans. J.S. Bowden (New York: Scribner, 1971); M. Hengel, *The Charismatic Leader and His Followers,* trans. J. Greig (New York: Crossroad, 1981); B. Gerhardsson, *Memory and Manuscript: Oral Tradition and Written Tradition in Rabbinic Judaism and Early Christianity,* 2nd ed. (Lund: Gleerup, 1964).

Chapter Two: A Scholarly House Divided against Itself

1. More than one commentator has likened it to a "renaissance" of the quest. M. Borg, "A Renaissance in Jesus Studies," *Theology Today* 45 (1988): 280–92; J.P. Meier, "The Historical Jesus: Rethinking Some Concepts," *Theological Studies* 51 (1990): 3.

2. E.g., see M. Borg, *Jesus in Contemporary Scholarship* (Valley Forge, Pa.: Trinity, 1994); C. Brown, "Historical Jesus, Quest of," in *Dictionary of Jesus and the Gospels,* ed. J. Green, S. McKnight, and I.H. Marshall (Downers Grove, Ill.: InterVarsity, 1992), 326–41; W.R. Telford, "Major Trends and Interpretive Issues in the Study of Jesus," in *Studying the Historical Jesus: Evaluations of the State of Current Research,* NTTS 19, ed. B. Chilton and C.A. Evans, (Leiden/

New York: Brill, 1994), 33–74; N.T. Wright, "Jesus, Quest for the Historical," in *The Anchor Bible Dictionary*, 6 vols., ed. D.N. Freedman, et al. (New York: Doubleday, 1992), 3:796–802. For an invaluable resource for understanding the contemporary quest, see Chilton and Evans, *Studying the Historical Jesus.*

3. See Wright, *Jesus and the Victory of God* (Minneapolis: Fortress, 1995), chap. 1; idem, "Jesus, Quest for the Historical," 796–802; idem, *Who Was Jesus?* (London: SPCK, 1992), chap. 1.

4. See G. Aulen, *Jesus in Contemporary Historical Research,* trans. I.H. Hjelm (Philadelphia: Fortress, 1976), 12–15.

5. B.F. Meyer, *The Aims of Jesus* (London: SCM, 1979), 20. Meyer notes that the phrase came from Heinz Schürmann.

6. See J.H. Charlesworth, "From Barren Mazes to Gentle Rappings: The Emergence of Jesus Research," *Princeton Seminary Bulletin* 7 (1986): 221–30; idem, "Research on the Historical Jesus in the Eighties" and Appendix 5: "A New Trend: Jesus Research," in his *Jesus within Judaism: New Light from Exciting Archaeological Discoveries, ABRL* (New York/London: Doubleday, 1988), 9–29, 187–207; idem, "Jesus Research: A Paradigm for New Testament Scholars," *Australian Biblical Review* 38 (1990): 18–32.

7. For Wright's original use of this term, see S.C. Neill and N.T. Wright, *The Interpretation of the New Testament: 1861–1986,* 2nd ed. (Oxford: Oxford Univ. Press, 1988 [1964]), 379–403; see also Wright's *Jesus and the Victory of God,* chap. 1.

8. Naturally, there are perspectives today that fall outside of these two major thrusts. E.g., the skepticism of the "No Quest" period continues on in a number of contemporary works. See, e.g., S. Ogden, *The Point of Christology* (San Francisco: Harper & Row, 1982); and W. Hamilton, *A Quest for the Post-Historical Jesus* (London: SCM, 1993).

9. G. Vermes, *Jesus the Jew: A Historian's Reading of the Gospels,* 2nd ed. (New York/London: Macmillan, 1983 [1973]); idem, *Jesus and the World of Judaism* (Philadelphia: Fortress, 1984); idem, *The Religion of Jesus the Jew* (Minneapolis: Fortress, 1993).

10. Meyer, *Aims of Jesus;* idem, *Christus Faber: The Master Builder and the House of God* (Allison Park, Pa.: Pickwick, 1992).

11. J. Riches, *Jesus and the Transformation of Judaism* (London: Darton, Longman, & Todd, 1980).

12. A.E. Harvey, *Jesus and the Constraints of History* (Philadelphia: Westminster, 1982).

13. M.J. Borg, *Conflict, Holiness and Politics in the Teachings of Jesus, SBEC* 5 (New York/Toronto: Mellen, 1984); idem, *Jesus: A New Vision* (San Francisco: Harper & Row, 1987); idem, *Meeting Jesus Again for the First Time* (San Francisco: HarperSanFrancisco, 1993); idem, *Jesus in Contemporary Scholarship.*

14. E.P. Sanders, *Jesus and Judaism* (Philadelphia: Fortress, 1985); idem, *The Historical Figure of Jesus* (London/New York: Penguin, 1993).

15. Neill and Wright, *Interpretation of the New Testament,* 379–403; Wright, *The New Testament and the People of God* (Minneapolis: Fortress, 1992); idem, *Jesus and the Victory of God.*

16. Meyer, *Aims of Jesus,* 16–17.

17. Here, Meyer argues from the epistemological perspective established by Bernard Lonergan. See Lonergan's *Insight: A Study of Human Understanding* (London/New York: Longmans, 1958); idem, *Method in Theology* (New York: Herder and Herder, 1972).

18. E.g., see Charlesworth, "From Barren Mazes to Gentle Rappings," 221–24; Wright, *New Testament and People of God.* For a related discussion, see C.A. Evans, "Life-of-Jesus Research and the Eclipse of Mythology," *Theological Studies* 54 (1993): 3–36.

19. E.g., see Sanders, *Jesus and Judaism,* 16–17; Charlesworth, *Jesus within*

Judaism, 4–5; W.P. Weaver, "Reflections on the Continuing Quest for Jesus," in *Images of Jesus Today*, ed. J. Charlesworth and W. Weaver (Valley Forge, Pa.: Trinity, 1994), xv-i. On authenticity criteria, see R. Stein, "The 'Criteria' of Authenticity," in *Studies of History and Tradition in the Four Gospels*, GP 2, ed. R.T. France and D. Wenham (Sheffield: JSOT, 1980), 225–63.

20. E.g., Wright, *New Testament and People of God*, 418–35; Sanders, *Jesus and Judaism*, 14–16; B. Witherington III, *The Christology of Jesus* (Minneapolis: Fortress, 1990), 3–22.

21. E.g., see Charlesworth, *Jesus within Judaism*, 204; B.F. Meyer, "Some Consequences of Birger Gerhardsson's Account of the Origins of the Gospel Tradition," in *Jesus and the Oral Gospel Tradition*, JSNTSS 64, ed. H. Wansbrough (Sheffield: JSOT, 1991), 424–40; Sanders, *Jesus and Judaism*, 14–16; Wright, *New Testament and People of God*, 422.

22. See Gerhardsson, *Memory and Manuscript: Oral Tradition and Written Tradition in Rabbinic Judaism and Early Christianity*, 2nd ed. (Lund: Gleerup, 1964 [1961]); idem, *Tradition and Transmission in Early Christianity* (Lund: Gleerup, 1964); idem, *The Origins of the Gospel Traditions* (Philadelphia: Fortress, 1979); idem, *The Gospel Tradition*, CBNTS 15 (Lund: Gleerup, 1986).

23. Sanders, *Jesus and Judaism*, 2. See also Borg, *Jesus: A New Vision*, 15; Evans, "Life-of-Jesus Research and the Eclipse of Mythology," 14–15, 34–36; Charlesworth, "Jesus Research Expands with Chaotic Creativity," in *Images of Jesus Today*, 5–7.

24. The very titles of many "Third Quest" works highlight this emphasis. E.g., Vermes, *Jesus the Jew*; Riches, *Jesus and the Transformation of Judaism*; Sanders, *Jesus and Judaism*; Charlesworth, *Jesus within Judaism*; J.H. Charlesworth, ed., *Jesus' Jewishness: Exploring the Place of Jesus within Early Judaism* (New York: Crossroad, 1991). This research into the relationship between Jesus and his Jewish context has been fostered in recent decades by new discoveries of ancient documents—the Dead Sea Scrolls, for instance, new archaeological finds, and a renewed appreciation for other ancient Jewish writings. See J.H. Charlesworth, "Research on the Historical Jesus Today: Jesus and the Pseudepigrapha, the Dead Sea Scrolls, the Nag Hammadi Codices, Josephus, and Archaeology," *Princeton Seminary Bulletin* 6/2 (1985): 98–115.

25. E.g., see Neill and Wright, *Interpretation of the New Testament*, 398; Charlesworth, *Jesus within Judaism*, 26–27.

26. E.g., see Meyer, *Aims of Jesus*, pt. 1; Wright, *New Testament and People of God*, 92–96; Witherington, *Christology of Jesus*, 156–58.

27. Evans, "Life-of-Jesus Research and Mythology," 35–36.

28. Evans, "Jesus of Nazareth: Who Do Scholars Say That He Is?" *Crux* 23/4 (1987): 15–19; idem, "The Historical Jesus and Christian Faith," *Christian Scholars Review* 18 (1988): 48–63; idem, "Jesus' Action in the Temple: Cleansing or Portent of Destruction?" *Catholic Biblical Quarterly* 51 (1989): 237–70; idem, *Life of Jesus Research: An Annotated Bibliography*; Evans and Chilton, *Studying the Historical Jesus*.

29. See Witherington, *Christology of Jesus*; idem, *Jesus, Paul and the End of the World: A Comparative Study in New Testament Eschatology* (Downers Grove, Ill.: InterVarsity, 1992); idem, *Jesus the Sage: The Pilgrimage of Wisdom* (Minneapolis: Fortress, 1994).

30. Wright's *The New Testament and the People of God* and *Jesus and the Victory of God* comprise volumes 1 and 2 of the larger project, which is entitled *Christian Origins and the Question of God*.

31. It is interesting to note that, while several aspects of Koester's work have fueled the post-Bultmannian quest, he himself has remained somewhat hesitant about the entire enterprise. See H. Koester, "The Historical Jesus and the Historical Situation of the Quest: An Epilogue," in *Studying the Historical Jesus*, 535–45.

32. Farmer, *Gospel of Jesus,* 163. See J. Robinson, "The Q Trajectory: Between John and Matthew via Jesus," in *The Future of Early Christianity: Essays in Honor of Helmut Koester,* ed. B.A. Pearson (Minneapolis: Fortress, 1991), 173.

33 Robinson and Koester, *Trajectories through Early Christianity* (Philadelphia: Fortress, 1971).

34. Koester, "GNOMAI DIAPHOROI: The Origin and Nature of Diversification in the History of Early Christianity," *Trajectories,* 126. See also, idem, "Epilogue: Current Issues in New Testament Scholarship," in *The Future of Early Christianity,* 470–71; idem, *Ancient Christian Gospels: Their History and ·Development* (Philadelphia: Trinity, 1990), xxix-xxxi.

35. See W. Bauer, *Orthodoxy and Heresy in Earliest Christianity,* 2nd ed., ed. R.A. Kraft and G. Krodel, trans. Philadelphia Seminar on Christian Origins (Philadelphia: Fortress, 1971).

36. Important statements include Koester's 1957 essay, recently translated as "The Extracanonical Sayings of the Lord as Products of the Christian Community," *Semeia* 44 (1988), 57–77; idem, "GNOMAI DIAPHOROI," *Trajectories,* 114–57; idem, "Gnostic Writings as Witnesses for the Development of the Sayings Tradition," in *The Rediscovery of Gnosticism,* vol. 1, *The School of Valentinus,* ed. B. Layton (Leiden: Brill, 1980), 238–61; and especially idem, "Apocryphal and Canonical Gospels," *Harvard Theological Review* 73 (1980): 105–30. See also Robinson, "Jesus from Easter to Valentinus (or to the Apostles' Creed)," *Journal of Biblical Literature* 101/1 (1982): 5–37.

37. See J. Robinson, ed., *The Nag Hammadi Library in English,* 3d rev. ed., trans. Coptic Gnostic Library Project (San Francisco: HarperSanFrancisco, 1990).

38. Koester, "Apocryphal and Canonical Gospels," 130.

39. See Crossan, *Four Other Gospels: Shadows on the Contours of Canon* (Minneapolis: Winston, 1985); idem, *The Cross That Spoke: The Origins of the Passion Narratives* (San Francisco: Harper & Row, 1988); idem, "Lists in Early Christianity: A Response to Early Christianity, Q and Jesus," *Semeia* 55 (1992), 235–43.

40. C.W. Hedrick, "Introduction: The Tyranny of the Synoptic Jesus," *Semeia* 44 (1988), 1–8. See the two special issues of *Semeia* devoted to this issue, C.W. Hedrick, ed., *The Historical Jesus and the Rejected Gospels, Semeia* 44 (Atlanta: Scholars, 1988) and R. Cameron, ed., *The Apocryphal Jesus and Christian Origins, Semeia* 49 (Atlanta: Scholars, 1990).

41. B. Mack, *The Lost Gospel* (San Francisco: HarperSanFrancisco, 1993), 34.

42. Since the landmark study of Wolfgang Schrage [*Das Verhältnis Des Thomas-Evangeliums Zur Synoptischen Tradition Und Zu Den Koptischen Evangelienubersetzungen*] (Berlin: Topelmann, 1964), the majority of German scholarship has held to the dependency thesis. See, e.g., M. Fieger, *Das Thomasevangelium: Einleitung Kommentar und Systematik* (Münster: Aschendorf, 1991). See also C. Blomberg, "Tradition and Redaction in the Parables of the Gospel of Thomas," in *The Jesus Tradition Outside the Gospels,* GP 5, ed. D. Wenham (Sheffield: JSOT, 1985), 177–205; B. Dehandshutter, "Recent Research on the Gospel of Thomas," in *The Four Gospels 1992: Festschrift Frans Neirynck,* 3 vols., ed. F. Van Segbroeck, et al. (Leuven: Leuven Univ. Press, 1992), 3:2257-62; K. Snodgrass, "The Gospel of Thomas: A Secondary Gospel," *The Second Century* 7/1 (1989–1990): 19–38; C.M. Tuckett, "Q and Thomas: Evidence of a Primitive 'Wisdom Gospel'?" *Ephemerides Theologicae Lovanienses* 67 (1991): 346–60.

43. "Koester, GNOMAI DIAPHOROI," *Trajectories,* 132 (emphasis added). See also idem, "One Jesus and Four Primitive Gospels," in *Trajectories,* 158–204.

44. Sieber, "A Redactional Analysis of the Synoptic Gospels with Regard to the Question of the Sources of the Gospel According to Thomas" (Ph.D. diss.,

Claremont Graduate School, 1964); idem, "Gospel of Thomas and the New Testament," in *Gospel Origins and Christian Beginnings: In Honor of James M. Robinson*, ed. J. Goehring, et al. (Sonoma, Calif.: Polebridge, 1990), 64–73.

45. Davies, *The Gospel of Thomas and Christian Wisdom*, (New York: Seabury, 1983). For an overview of his positions, see idem, "Thomas – The Fourth Synoptic Gospel," *Biblical Archaeology* 46/1 (1983): 6–17. Davies offers his analysis of GosThom's Christology in "The Christology and Protology of the *Gospel of Thomas*," *Journal of Biblical Literature* 111/4 (1992): 663–82.

46. Patterson, *The Gospel of Thomas and Jesus* (Sonoma, Calif.: Polebridge, 1993). See also his "Introduction" to Thomas in John Kloppenborg, et al., *Q-Thomas Reader* (Sonoma, Calif.: Polebridge, 1990), 77–127; S. Patterson and H. Koester, "The Gospel of Thomas: Authentic Sayings?" *Bible Review* 6/2 (1990), 28–39; idem, "The Gospel of Thomas and the Historical Jesus: Retrospectus and Prospectus," *SBLSP* 1990, ed. D.J. Lull (Atlanta: Scholars, 1990), 614-36; idem, "The Gospel of Thomas and Jesus," *The Fourth R* (May/June 1993): 8-13; idem, "The Gospel of Thomas and the Synoptic Tradition: A *Forschungsbericht* and Critique," *Foundations and Facets Forum* 8/1-2 (1992): 45–97.

47. Cameron, *The Other Gospels: Non-Canonical Gospel Texts* (Philadelphia: Westminster, 1982); idem, "Parable and Interpretation in the Gospel of Thomas," *Foundations and Facets Forum* 2/2 (1986): 3–39; idem, "The Gospel of Thomas and Christian Origins," in *The Future of Early Christianity*, 381–92; F.T. Fallon and R. Cameron, "The Gospel of Thomas: A *Forschungsbericht* and Analysis," in *ANRW* II. 25. 6, 4196–251.

48. H.E. Tödt, *The Son of Man in the Synoptic Tradition*, trans. D.M. Barton (Philadelphia: Westminster, 1965).

49. See Snyder, *Ante Pacem: Archaeological Evidence of Church Life before Constantine* (Macon, Ga.: Mercer Univ. Press, 1985).

50. Kloppenborg, "The Theological Stakes in the Synoptic Problem," in *The Four Gospels 1992*, 119. See also idem, " 'Easter Faith' and the Sayings Gospel Q," *Semeia* 49 (1990), 71–99.

51. Kloppenborg, " 'Easter Faith' and Q," 92.

52. Important works that have arisen from this endeavor include Kloppenborg, *The Formation of Q: Trajectories in Ancient Wisdom Collections* (Philadelphia: Fortress, 1987); idem, *Q Parallels: Synopsis, Critical Notes and Concordance* (Sonoma, Calif.: Polebridge, 1988?); idem, ed. and trans., *The Shape of Q: Signal Essays on the Sayings Source* (Minneapolis: Fortress, 1994); A. Jacobson, *The First Gospel: An Introduction to Q* (Sonoma, Calif.: Polebridge, 1992); Mack, *Lost Gospel*.

53. Robinson, "Logoi Sophon: On the Gattung of Q," *Trajectories*, 71–113.

54. Koester, "Gnostic Writings as Witnesses," 249–50.

55. Koester, "Apocryphal and Canonical Gospels," 113.

56. See Kloppenborg, *The Formation of Q*, based on his 1984 dissertation.

57. Ibid., 322.

58. See Koester, *Ancient Christian Gospels*, 149–62; Robinson, "Preface" to Kloppenborg's *Formation of Q*, xiii-iv. See also the various reactions to Kloppenborg's thesis in the special issue of *Semeia*: Kloppenborg and Vaage, eds., *Early Christianity, Q and Jesus, Semeia* 55 (Atlanta: Scholars, 1992). For a rival conception of Q within the post-Bultmannian school see Jacobson, *The First Gospel*.

59. Kloppenborg himself cautions against drawing conclusions about the historical development of the views of Jesus in the developing early church from the development of strata in Q, but few post-Bultmannians seem to heed his advice. See *The Formation of Q*, 244ff.

60. See Robinson's account of this move in "The Q Trajectory."

61. "One Jesus," *Trajectories*, 186. See also idem, "Q and Its Relatives," in *Gospel Origins and Christian Beginnings*, 49–63.

62. Kloppenborg, *Formation of Q,* 322.

63. J. Kloppenborg, "Symbolic Eschatology and the Apocalypticism of Q," *Harvard Theological Review* 80 (1987): 287–306.

64. See H. Koester, "Jesus the Victim," *Journal of Biblical Literature* 111/1 (1992): 3–15; A.D. Jacobson, "Apocalyptic and the Synoptic Sayings Source Q," *The Four Gospels 1992,* 1:403–19; M. Borg, "Portraits of Jesus in Contemporary North American Scholarship," *Harvard Theological Review* 84/1 (1991): 1–22. Interestingly, Borg—a scholar generally associated with the "Third Quest"—has emerged as one of the leading spokespersons for the non-·apocalyptic Jesus. He arrived at this conviction, however, not via post-Bultmannianism, but by way of the Oxford scholar George Caird. See Borg, "A Temperate Case for a Non-Eschatological Jesus," *Foundations and Facets Forum* 2/3 (1986): 81–102; idem, "An Orthodoxy Reconsidered: The 'End-of-the-World Jesus,' " in *The Glory of Christ in the New Testament: Studies in Christology in Memory of George Bradford Caird,* ed. L.D. Hurst and N.T. Wright (Oxford: Clarendon, 1987), 207–17.

65. Borg, "Renaissance in Jesus Studies," 287 (emphasis in text). Borg claims that such a view of Jesus has become a "consensus." Interestingly, however, each of his citations at this point are from those within the post-Bultmannian camp. Here, in placing *primary* emphasis on Jesus as subversive sage, Borg is once again something of an anomaly among most third questers. This is not to deny, of course, that the role of wisdom teacher was *one* important aspect of the historical Jesus. See Witherington, *Jesus the Sage.*

66. On the history-of-religions school see Kümmel, *New Testament,* 206–324. For introductions see K. Rudolph, *"Religionsgeschichtliche Schule,"* in *The Encyclopedia of Religion,* 16 vols., ed. M. Eliade (New York: Macmillan, 1987), 12:293–96; A.J. Malherbe, "Greco-Roman Religion and Philosophy and the New Testament," in *New Testament and Its Modern Interpreters,* ed. E.J. Epp and G.W. MacRae (Atlanta: Scholars, 1989), 3–26.

67. K. Rudolph, "Early Christianity as a Religious-Historical Phenomenon," in *The Future of Early Christianity,* 17–18.

68. See W. Bousset, *Kyrios Christos,* trans. J.E. Seely (Nashville: Abingdon, 1970).

69. See Bultmann, *Primitive Christianity in Its Contemporary Setting,* trans. R.H. Fuller (New York: Meridian, 1956); idem, *Theology of the New Testament.*

70. There were, in any case, a number of decisive criticisms that were raised against this movement which contributed to its speedy demise. We shall examine some of these in our critique of Mack's view of Paul (chap. 8), for he makes significant use of the history-of-religions school.

71. In a recent analysis of contemporary New Testament studies, Koester concludes that, "[T]he current issues of New Testament scholarship are the renewal of the agenda of the history-of-religions school in a more comprehensive political perspective." See Koester, "Epilogue: Current Issues in New Testament Scholarship," 476, as well as Rudolph's similar proposal, "Early Christianity as a Religious-Historical Phenomenon," 9–19.

72. J.Z. Smith, *Drudgery Divine: On the Comparison of Early Christianities and the Religions of Late Antiquity* (Chicago: Univ. of Chicago Press, 1990), 36. On Mack's indebtedness to Smith and the renewed history-of-religions approach, see *Myth of Innocence,* 20; idem, "Q and the Gospel of Mark: Revising Christian Origins," *Semeia* 55 (1992), 34–38.

73. M. Borg, "Jesus in Contemporary North American Scholarship," 2.

74. E.g., see S. Freyne, *Galilee, from Alexander the Great to Hadrian 323 B.C.E. to 135 C.E.: A Study of Second Temple Judaism* (Wilmington, Del.: Glazier/Notre Dame, Ind.: Univ. of Notre Dame Press, 1980); idem, *Galilee, Jesus and the Gospels: Literary Approaches and Historical Investigations* (Philadelphia: Fortress, 1988); A.J. Malherbe, *Social Aspects of Early Christianity,* 2nd ed. (Philadelphia:

Fortress, 1983); J.E. Stambaugh and D.L. Balch, *The New Testament and Its Social Environment* (Philadelphia: Westminster, 1986).

75. E.g., see J.H. Elliott, *What Is Social-Scientific Criticism?* (Minneapolis: Fortress, 1993); R.A. Horsley, *Sociology and the Jesus Movement* (New York: Crossroad, 1989); H.C. Kee, *Christian Origins in Sociological Perspective: Methods and Resources* (Philadelphia: Westminster, 1980); G. Theissen, *The Sociology of Early Palestinian Christianity*, trans. J. Bowden (Philadelphia: Fortress, 1978 [1977]); idem, *Social Reality and the Early Christians: Theology, Ethics, and the World of the New Testament*, trans. M. Kohl (Minneapolis: Fortress, 1992 [1979]).

76. For further discussion see S.R. Garrett, "Sociology of Early Christianity," *ABD* VI. 89–99; W.R. Herzog II, "Sociological Approaches to the Gospels," *DJG*, 760–66; B. Holmberg, *Sociology and the New Testament: An Appraisal* (Minneapolis: Fortress, 1990); C. Osiek, *What Are They Saying about the Social Setting of the New Testament* (New York: Paulist, 1992); D. Tidball, *The Social Context of the New Testament: A Sociological Analysis* (Grand Rapids: Zondervan, 1984). For a history of the sociological analysis of the New Testament, see G. Theissen, "Introduction: Sociological Research into the New Testament," in his *Social Reality and the Early Christians*, 1–29.

77. Post-Bultmannians are sometimes critical of "third questers" for not sufficiently employing the methods and findings of the social sciences. See, e.g., P.W. Hollenbach, "Recent Historical Jesus Studies and the Social Sciences," *SBLSP* 1983 (Chicago: Scholars, 1983), 61–78, who suggests that Meyer, Harvey, and Sanders—three prominent "third questers"—show insufficient interest in the social sciences.

78. Bernard Scott, e.g., has argued that "the historical quest for the historical Jesus has ended; the interdisciplinary quest for the historical Jesus has just begun." Cited in Borg, "Renaissance in Jesus Studies," 284.

79. Mack, *MI*, 8.

80. J.R. Butts, "Probing the Polling: Jesus Seminar Results on the Kingdom Sayings," *Foundations and Facets Forum* 3/1 (1987): 111. For an example of this criterion at work, see K. King, "Kingdom in the Gospel of Thomas," *Foundations and Facets Forum* 3/1 (1987): 48–97.

81. See R.W. Funk, "Form and Function [of the Jesus Seminar]," *Foundations & Facets Forum* 1/1 (1985): 51. For discussions on the Jesus Seminar, see Funk's "The Story of the Jesus Seminar" in *The Parables of Jesus: Red Letter Edition*, ed. R.W. Funk, B.B. Scott, and J.R. Butts (Sonoma, Calif.: Polebridge, 1988), ix-xv; M. Borg, "The Jesus Seminar and the Church," in his *Jesus in Contemporary Scholarship*, 160–81; J. Dart, "The Jesus Seminar," in his *The Jesus of History and Heresy: The Discovery and Meaning of the Nag Hammadi Library* (San Francisco: Harper & Row, 1988), 153–61. M. Wilkins and J.P. Moreland have recently completed editing a work that critically evaluates the Jesus Seminar from an evangelical perspective entitled *Jesus Under Fire: Modern Scholarship Reinvents the Historical Jesus* (Grand Rapids: Zondervan, 1995). And Randy Nelson of Rice University (Houston) is currently working on what will probably prove to be the first doctoral dissertation devoted to a critical analysis of the Jesus Seminar.

82. The actual membership in this group fluctuates. Compare, for instance, the membership lists found in Funk, et al., eds., *The Parables of Jesus* (1988), 93–97; Funk and M.H. Smith, eds., *The Gospel of Mark: Red Letter Edition* (Sonoma, Calif.: Polebridge, 1991), 240–43; Funk, R.W. Hoover, and the Jesus Seminar, *The Five Gospels: The Search for the Authentic Words of Jesus* (New York: Macmillan, 1993), 533–37.

83. Compare the obvious similarities between the characteristic elements of the "Post-Bultmannian Quest" discussed above with the basic assumptions of the Jesus Seminar as published in the Introduction to *Five Gospels*, 1–38.

84. Funk, et al., *Five Gospels*, 34.

85. Funk, "The Issue of Jesus," *Foundations & Facets Forum* 1/1 (1985): 7. Funk's Westar Institute in Sonoma, California continues to sponsor the seminar. Westar also operates its own publishing house (Polebridge Press) and sponsors two journals: *Foundations & Facets Forum* provides an outlet for scholarly articles, while *The Fourth R* focuses on a more popular audience.

86. For a description of voting and tabulation methods, see Funk, et al., *Five Gospels*, 36–37.

87. For description and critique of this work see D.A. Carson, "Five Gospels, No Christ," *Christianity Today*, 25 April 1994, 30–33; F. Neirynck, review of *The Five Gospels*, *Ephemerides Theologicae Lovanienses* 70/1 (1994): 160–62.

88. For a preliminary report concerning their findings on some of Jesus' miracles, see R. Funk, "Report on the Jesus Seminar," *The Fourth R* (March/April 1993): 12–16.

89. Its journal, *The Fourth R*, certainly has this audience in mind. Recently, several of its high-profile members—including both Mack and Crossan—participated in a panel discussion, "The Jesus Summit: The Historical Jesus and Contemporary Faith," held at San Francisco's Grace Cathedral, which was broadcast via satellite to over 70 down-links throughout North America.

90. Funk, "Issue of Jesus," 7.

91. E.g., see R.N. Ostling, "Who Was Jesus?" *Time*, 15 August 1988, 37–42; "Father, Son, and Holy Ghost Writer," *National Review*, 1 April 1991, 16, 18; J.L. Sheler, "What Did Jesus Really Say?" *U.S. News & World Report*, 1 July 1991, 57–58; R.N. Ostling, "Jesus Christ, Plain and Simple," *Time*, 10 January 1994, 38–39; K.L. Woodward, "A Lesser Child of God: The Radical Jesus Seminar Sees a Different Christ," *Newsweek*, 4 April 1994, 53–54; J. Simon, "Who Was Jesus?" *Life*, December 1994, 66–82.

92. Funk, et al., *Five Gospels*, 34.

93. Funk, "The Issue of Jesus," 12.

94. H. Taussig, "The Jesus Seminar and Its Public," *Foundations and Facets Forum* 2/2 (1986): 75–76.

95. Concerning the seminar's persecution complex, Funk's opening address ("Issue of Jesus," 7) makes much of the idea that the Jesus Seminar's chosen path "may prove hazardous. We may well provoke hostility." Subsequent publications have clearly identified the perceived enemy as "fundamentalists" and "conservative Christian groups." Those Christian denominations who hold seminar members within their ranks to a particular standard of Christian orthodoxy are branded as "latter-day inquisitors" who "have gone on a witch-hunt." See Funk, et al., *Five Gospels*, 35.

96. Funk, "Call for a Canon Council," *The Fourth R* (May/June 1993): 7. Funk suggests that the first three items up for discussion and "preliminary vote" should be (1) the Gospel of Thomas, (2) the order of the Gospels, and (3) the Book of Revelation. In regard to the last item, Funk states that a vote is "pertinent in view of the recent events that took place in Waco, Texas" (p. 13). See also J.L. Sheler, "Cutting Loose the Holy Canon," *U.S. News & World Report*, 8 November 1993, 75.

97. See Borg, "Temperate Case for a Non-Eschatological Jesus"; Butts, "Probing the Polling," 98–113; Funk, "The Jesus That Was," *The Fourth R* (November 1992): 2.

98. Funk, "The Jesus That Was," 6. See also Borg, "Renaissance in Jesus Studies," 287–88.

99. See Crossan, *In Fragments: The Aphorisms of Jesus* (San Francisco: Harper & Row, 1983).

100. Funk, "The Jesus That Was," 3.

101. See Funk, "The Jesus That Was," 4–5; M. Meyer, ed. and trans., *The Gospel of Thomas: The Hidden Sayings of Jesus* (San Francisco: Harper, 1992), 16.

102. Funk, "The Jesus That Was," 6.

103. R. Cameron, quoted at a Jesus Seminar meeting in Dart, *Jesus of Heresy and History*, 160.

104. There is an ongoing debate as to whether Antisthenes or Diogenes should be credited as the first Cynic (e.g., see respectively Höistad vs. Dudley and Sayre below). For introductory discussions on the ancient Cynics, see R.F. Hock, "Cynics," *ABD* I, 1221–226; E. Ferguson, *Backgrounds of Early Christianity* (Grand Rapids: Eerdmans, 1987), 275–81. For more extensive studies, see the three classics: D.B. Dudley, *A History of Cynicism from Diogenes to the 6th Century A.D.* (London: Methuen, 1937); R. Höistad, *Cynic Hero and Cynic King: Studies in the Cynic Conception of Man* (Uppsala: Bloms, 1948); F. Sayre, *The Greek Cynics* (Baltimore: Furst, 1948). For two excellent collections of recent studies, see M. Goulet-Cazé and R. Goulet, eds., *Le Cynisme Ancien et Ses Prolongements* (Paris: Presses Universitaires De France, 1993); B. Branham, ed., *The Cynics: The Cynic Movement in Antiquity and Its Legacy for Europe* (forthcoming).

105. Diogenes Laertius, *Lives of Eminent Philosophers*, 2 vols., LCL, trans. R.D. Hicks, (London:Heinemann/New York: Putnam's, 1925), 2:3–109.

106. On Imperial Cynicism see M. Billerbeck, "Greek Cynicism in Imperial Rome," in *Die Kyniker in der modernen Forschung*, ed. M. Billerbeck, BSZP 15 (Amsterdam: Grüner, 1991), 147–66; and especially M. Goulet-Cazé, "Le cynisme l' poque imperiale," *ANRW* II. 36. 4 (1990), 2720–833.

107. An important source of Cynic literature from this era is the collection of pseudonymous Cynic epistles. See A.J. Malherbe, *The Cynic Epistles: A Study Edition, SBLSBS* 12 (Missoula, Mont.: Scholars, 1977).

108. Ferguson, *Backgrounds of Early Christianity*, 276.

109. Abraham Malherbe accurately sums up the Cynic philosophy and lifestyle when he writes: "What made a Cynic was his dress and conduct, self-sufficiency, harsh behavior towards what appeared as excess, and a practical ethical idealism" (A. Malherbe, "Self-Definition Among Epicureans and Cynics," in *Jewish and Christian Self-Definition*, vol. 3: *Self-Definition in the Greco-Roman World*, ed. B.F. Meyer and E.P. Sanders [Philadelphia: Fortress, 1982], 49).

110. Some of the earlier sources include S. Dill, *Roman Society from Nero to Marcus Aurelius* (London: Macmillan, 1911), 361; Dudley, *History of Cynicism*, 173–75, 204–7; W.R. Halliday, *The Pagan Background of Early Christianity* (New York: Cooper Square, 1970 [1925]), 126, 169–71, 201–2; E. Hatch, "Greek and Christian Ethics," in his *The Influence of Greek Ideas on Christianity* (New York: Harper & Row, 1957 [1889]), 138–70; Höistad, *Cynic Hero and Cynic King*, 199, 221; G. Boas, "Christianity and Cynicism," in his *Essays on Primitivism and Related Ideas in the Middle Ages* (Baltimore: Johns Hopkins Press, 1948), 87–128.

111. The work of scholars such as Abraham Malherbe and Ronald Hock has served to highlight the Cynic background to various aspects of the New Testament. See Malherbe, *The Cynic Epistles*; idem, *Moral Exhortation, a Greco-Roman Sourcebook* (Philadelphia: Westminster, 1986); idem, *Paul and the Thessalonians: The Philosophic Tradition of Pastoral Care* (Philadelphia: Fortress, 1987); idem, *Paul and the Popular Philosophers* (Minneapolis: Fortress, 1989); R.F. Hock, "Simon the Shoemaker as an Ideal Cynic," in *Greek, Roman, and Byzantine Studies* 17/1 (1976): 41–53; idem, "Lazarus and Micyllus: Greco-Roman Backgrounds to Luke 16:19-31," *Journal of Biblical Literature* 106/3 (1987): 447–63; idem, "A Dog in the Manger: The Cynic Cynulcus among Athenaeus's Deipnosophists," in *Greeks, Romans, and Christians: Essays in Honor of Abraham J. Malherbe*, ed. D.L. Balch, E. Ferguson, and W.A. Meeks (Minneapolis: Fortress, 1990), 20–37; idem, "Cynics," *ABD*, I:1221–26; idem and E.N. O'Neil, *The Chreia in Ancient Rhetoric*, vol. 1, *The Progymnasmata TT 27/GRRS* 9 (Atlanta: Scholars, 1986).

112. G. Theissen, *Sociology of Early Palestinian Christianity*, trans. J. Bowden (Philadelphia: Fortress, 1978 [1977]), 8.

113. G. Theissen, "Itinerant Radicalism: The Tradition of Jesus Sayings from the Perspective of the Sociology of Literature," *Radical Religion* 2 (1975): 87. See also idem, *Sociology of Early Palestinian Christianity*, 14–15.

114. Stambaugh and Balch, *New Testament in Its Social Environment*, 143–45. See also M. Hengel, *The Charismatic Leader and His Followers*, trans. J. Greig (New York: Crossroad, 1981 [1968]), 27–34.

115. E.g., see L. Schottroff and W. Stegemann, *Jesus and the Hope of the Poor*, ·trans. M.J. O'Connell (Maryknoll, N.Y.: Orbis, 1986 [1978]), 38–66; J.S. Tashjian, "The Social Setting of the Q Mission: Three Dissertations," in *SBLSP 1988*, ed. D. Lull (Atlanta: Scholars, 1988), 636–44. We shall examine in detail the use made of this passage by Cynic theorists in chap. 7.

116. In the face of the similarities between the Cynics and Christians, however, most scholars are equally quick to highlight the obvious *differences*. See, e.g., Boas, "Christianity and Cynicism," 108; Hengel, *Charismatic Leader*, 30; Kee, *Christian Origins*, 68; Malherbe, *Paul and Popular Philosophers*, 8; M.L. Soards, "Reframing and Reevaluating the Argument of the Pastoral Epistles toward a Contemporary New Testament Theology," *Perspectives in Religious Studies* 19 (1992): 389–98; Stambaugh and Balch, *New Testament in Its Social Environment*, 144–45; Theissen, "Itinerant Radicalism," 88.

117. E.g., see F. Gerald Downing, "The Politics of Jesus," *The Modern Churchman* 25/1 (1982): 19–27; idem, *Jesus and the Threat of Freedom* (London: SCM, 1987); idem, *Christ and the Cynics: Jesus and Other Radical Preachers in First-Century Tradition*, JSOTM 4 (Sheffield: JSOT, 1988); idem, "Cynics and Early Christianity," in *Le Cynisme Ancien*, 281–304. Downing's *Cynics and Christian Origins* (Edinburgh: T & T Clark, 1992) represents his most complete argument to date and contains versions of several important previously published articles.

118. On Jesus the Jewish Cynic, see *Jesus and the Threat of Freedom*, 132f. On early Christian Cynicism, see his *Cynics and Christian Origins*, 5.

119. Here, see especially his book of parallels, *Christ and the Cynics*.

120. Downing argues that Q, in its present hypothesized form, is "quite like" the 'Lives' of Cynic philosophers, and thus proposes that the Cynic *Lives* offer the most fitting genre for understanding Q. See his, "Quite Like Q: A Genre for Q: The 'Lives' of Cynic Philosophers," *Biblica* 69 (1988): 196–225.

121. Downing, *Jesus and the Threat of Freedom*, 159.

122. L. Vaage, "Q: The Ethos and Ethics of an Itinerant Intelligence" (Ph.D. diss., Claremont Graduate School, 1987). Vaage's recent book, *Galilean Upstarts: Jesus' First Followers According to Q* (Valley Forge, Pa.: Trinity, 1994), is largely based upon his dissertation.

123. Vaage does take issue with some of Kloppenborg's judgments regarding the layering of Q. For the most part, however, they hold quite similar views. See Vaage, "The Formative Stratum of Q: Agreements and Disagreements with John S. Kloppenborg, *The Formation of Q*," Appendix 1 in his *Galilean Upstarts*, 107–20.

124. Vaage, "Q: Ethos and Ethics," 349. Here, and throughout, I will follow scholarly convention and refer to particular Q passages in terms of the Lukan text.

125. Ibid., 495.

126. "Q1 and the Historical Jesus: Some Peculiar Sayings (7:33-34; 9:57-58, 59-60; 14:26-27)," *Foundations and Facets Forum* 5/2 (1989), 175. See also idem, "The Son of Man Sayings in Q: Stratigraphical Location and Significance," *Semeia* 55 (1992), 125.

127. B. Mack, "Q and the Gospel of Mark: Revising Christian Origins,"

Semeia 55 (1992), 18.

128. R. Cameron, " 'What Have You Come Out to See?': Characterizations of John and Jesus in the Gospels," *Semeia* 49 (1990), 62. Vaage now also sees a Cynic-like Baptist. *Galilean Upstarts,* 87–106.

129. E.g., see J.S. Kloppenborg, "The Sayings Gospel Q: Recent Opinion on the People Behind the Document," *Currents in Research: Biblical Studies* 1 (1993): 26–28; S.J. Patterson, "Q: The Lost Gospel," *Bible Review* 9/5 (October 1993), 62; D. Seeley, "Was Jesus Like a Philosopher? The Evidence of Martyrological and Wisdom Motifs in Q, Pre-Pauline Traditions, and Mark," in *SBLSP·1989,* ed. D.J. Lull (Atlanta: Scholars, 1989), 540–49; idem, "Blessings and Boundaries: Interpretations of Jesus' Death in Q," *Semeia* 55 (1992), 131–46; idem, "Jesus' Death in Q," *New Testament Studies* 38 (1992): 222–34; M.G. Steinhauser, "The Violence of Occupation: Matthew 5:40-41 and Q," *Toronto Journal of Theology* 8/1 (1992): 28–37; W. Braun, "Symposium or Anti-Symposium? Reflections on Luke 14: 1-24," *Toronto Journal of Theology* 8/1 (1992): 70–84.

Chapter 3: Jesus, the Revolutionary Jewish Cynic

1. J.D. Crossan, *The Historical Jesus: The Life of a Mediterranean Jewish Peasant* (hereinafter referred to as *HJ*) (San Francisco: HarperSanFrancisco, 1992), 421.

2. M. Borg, "Portraits of Contemporary North American Scholarship," in *Jesus in Contemporary Scholarship* (Valley Forge, Pa.: Trinity, 1994), 33.

3. Although primarily engaging *HJ,* relevant aspects of his more recent and popular *Jesus: A Revolutionary Biography* (hereinafter referred to as *JRB*) and several essays will be noted as well. Crossan has recently added a third popular-level book to create something of a Jesus trilogy: *The Essential Jesus: Original Sayings and Earliest Images* (HarperSanFrancisco, 1994). This latter work was published too late to be used in this study.

4. For helpful discussions of this segment of Crossan's project, see F.B. Brown and E.S. Malbon, "Parabling as a Via Negativa: A Critical Review of the Work of John Dominic Crossan," *Journal of Religion* 64 (1984): 530–38; B.B. Scott, "to impose is not/To Discover: Methodology in John Dominic Crossan's *The Historical Jesus,*" in *Jesus and Faith: A Conversation on the Work of John Dominic Crossan,* ed. J. Carlson and R.A. Ludwig (Maryknoll, N.Y.: Orbis, 1994), 22–30; and Crossan, "Responses and Reflections," *Jesus and Faith,* 146–49. I am also indebted in this section to an unpublished paper by M.C. Albl, "J.D. Crossan's *The Historical Jesus:* A Critique" (Marquette University, 1993).

5. For an autobiographical reflection, see J.D. Crossan, "Almost the Whole Truth," *The Fourth R* (September/October 1993): 3–8.

6. An important impetus to Crossan's parable research was the formation of the SBL Parable Seminar, which he chaired.

7. G. Ebeling, *The Nature of Faith,* trans. R.G. Smith (Philadelphia: Fortress, 1968), 87, 90. On the New Hermeneutic, see J.M. Robinson and J.B. Cobb, Jr., eds., *The New Hermeneutic,* NFT 2 (New York: Harper & Row, 1964); A.C. Thiselton, "The New Hermeneutic," in *New Testament Interpretation: Essays on Principles and Methods,* ed. I.H. Marshall (Grand Rapids: Eerdmans), 308–33.

8. P.L. Berger and T. Luckmann, *The Social Construction of Reality: A Treatise in the Sociology of Knowledge* (Garden City, N.Y.: Doubleday, 1966).

9. E.g., see A.N. Wilder, *The Language of the Gospel: Early Christian Rhetoric* (New York: Harper & Row, 1964); N. Perrin, *Jesus and the Language of the Kingdom* (Philadelphia: Fortress, 1976). For discussion, see Crossan's study of Wilder's work, *A Fragile Craft: The Work of Amos Niven Wilder,* BSNA 3 (Chico,

Calif.: Scholars, 1981); W.E. Elmore, "Linguistic Approaches to the Kingdom: Amos Wilder and Norman Perrin," in *The Kingdom of God in 20th-Century Interpretation,* ed. W. Willis (Peabody, Mass.: Hendrickson, 1987), 53–65. On literary criticism and the New Testament, see W.A. Beardslee, *Literary Criticism of the New Testament* (Philadelphia: Fortress, 1970); E.V. McKnight, "Literary Criticism," *Dictionary of Jesus and the Gospels,* ed. J.B. Green, S. McKnight, and I.H. Marshall (Downers Grove, Ill.: InterVarsity, 1992), 473–81. On the application of this perspective to parables, see R.W. Funk, *Language, Hermeneutic, and Word of God: The Problem of Language in the New Testament and Contemporary Theology* (New York: Harper & Row, 1966), 123–222; D.O. Via, *The Parables: Their Literary and Existential Dimension* (Philadelphia: Fortress, 1967). For a more recent example within this trajectory, see B.B. Scott, *Hear Then the Parable: A Commentary on the Parables of Jesus* (Minneapolis: Fortress, 1989). This trend quickly moved beyond parables research; e.g., see R.C. Tannehill, *The Sword of His Mouth, SBLSS* 1 (Philadelphia: Fortress; Missoula, Mont.: Scholars, 1975). On the roots of this new turn in parables study, see A.C. Thiselton, *The Two Horizons: New Testament Hermeneutics and Philosophical Description with Special Reference to Heidegger, Bultmann, Gadamer, and Wittgenstein* (Grand Rapids: Eerdmans, 1980), 347–52. For evaluation from an evangelical perspective, see C.L. Blomberg, *Interpreting the Parables* (Downers Grove, Ill.: InterVarsity, 1990), 133–63; idem, "The Parables of Jesus: Current Trends and Needs in Research," in *Studying the Historical Jesus: Evaluations of the State of Current Research, NTTS* 19, ed. B. Chilton and C.A. Evans (Leiden/New York: Brill, 1994), 231–54. For a helpful recounting of the rise of modern parables research and a criticism of some of its general conclusions see Mack, *MI,* 135–71.

10. J.D. Crossan, *In Parables: The Challenge of the Historical Jesus* (New York: Harper & Row, 1973). This work is a collection of separately published essays from 1971 to 1973.

11. See J.D. Crossan, *The Dark Interval: Towards a Theology of Story* (Niles, Ill.: Argus, 1975). See also idem, "Perspectives and Methods in Contemporary Biblical Criticism," *Biblical Research* 22 (1977): 39–49. On structural analysis, see D. Patte, *What Is Structural Analysis?* (Philadelphia: Fortress, 1976); C. Armerding, "Structural Analysis," *Themelios* 4 (1979): 96–104. See also, Brown and Malbon, "Parabling as a *Via Negativa,*" 532, and A.C. Thiselton, "Structuralism and Biblical Studies: Method or Ideology?" *The Expository Times* 89 (1978): 329–35.

12. J.D. Crossan, *Raid on the Articulate: Comic Eschatology in Jesus and Borges* (New York: Harper & Row, 1976), 137; and idem, *Dark Interval,* 37, 47.

13. Crossan, *In Parables,* xiii.

14. Hence Crossan states, "Parable is the house of God." Ibid., 32–33.

15. This theme is pronounced not only in his *The Dark Interval* and *Raid on the Articulate,* but also in his *Finding Is the First Act: Trove Folktales and Jesus' Treasure Parable* (Philadelphia: Fortress; Missoula, Mont.: Scholars, 1979) and *Cliffs of Fall: Paradox and Polyvalence in the Parables of Jesus* (New York: Crossroad/Seabury, 1980).

16. Crossan, *Raid on the Articulate,* 98 (emphasis original). In this sense, a parable is the opposite of a "myth." Myths, in Crossan's view, work to reinforce a world viewwhile parables seek to subvert it. See Crossan, *Dark Interval,* 59; and *Raid on the Articulate,* 99.

17. J.D. Crossan, "Stages in Imagination," in *The Archaeology of the Imagination,* ed. C.E. Winquist, *JAARTS* 48/2 (Ann Arbor: Edwards, 1981): 56.

18. See Crossan, *Finding Is the First Act,* 120.

19. Crossan, *In Parables,* 27.

20. Crossan, *Raid on the Articulate,* 45. See also pp. 149–51. So too, concerning the end of history, Crossan states that, "[T]he Holy has no such plan at

all and that is what is absolutely incomprehensible to our structuring, planning, ordering human minds" (p. 44).

21. Ibid., 93.

22. Crossan says, "Paradox is language laughing at itself," in *Raid on the Articulate*, 93.

23. Crossan, *Finding Is the First Act*, 93 (emphasis original).

24. The thought of French deconstructionist Jacques Derrida becomes important in Crossan's *Cliffs of Fall* and "Difference and Divinity," *Semeia* 23 (1982), 29–40. On post-structuralism and deconstructionism, see P. Kamuf, ed., *A Derrida Reader: Between the Blinds* (New York: Columbia Univ. Press, 1991); C. Norris, *Deconstruction: Theory and Practice* (London/New York: Methuen, 1982); idem, *Derrida* (Cambridge: Harvard Univ. Press, 1987); M. Sarup, *An Introductory Guide to Post-structuralism and Postmodernism* (Athens: Univ. of Georgia Press, 1989); A. Jacobs, "Deconstruction," in *Contemporary Literary Theory: A Christian Appraisal*, ed. C. Walhout and L. Ryken (Grand Rapids: Eerdmans, 1991), 172–98. It should be noted, however, that although Crossan has made increasing and abundant use of various literary-critical methods, including deconstructionism, he has never dispatched with the more traditional historical-critical approach. Instead, he has viewed it as adding one perspective to the others. See his *Finding Is the First Act*, 1–2.

25. Crossan, *Dark Interval*, 40–41 (emphasis original).

26. See Crossan, "Difference and Divinity," 38. For P. Ricouer's skeptical response to Crossan's attempted appropriation of Derrida for a negative theology, see "A Response" (to Crossan's "Paradox Gives Rise to Metaphor: Paul Ricouer's Hermeneutics and the Parables of Jesus," 20–37), *Biblical Research* 24–25 (1979–1980): 71–76. For a counterresponse from Crossan—still maintaining assistance from Derrida for his negative theology—see Crossan, "Stages in Imagination," 49–62.

27. Crossan, *Dark Interval*, 45–46. Brown and Malbon have noted that Crossan's attempt to affirm transcendence—or anything else for that matter—in the face of his radical negative theology thoroughly conforms to his idea of incomprehensible paradox. On the other hand, "this may simply mean that Crossan needs to reexamine his theology or his theory of language, or both." See "Parabling as a *Via Negativa*," 538.

28. Crossan, *Raid on the Articulate*, 178. See also idem, *Cliffs of Fall*, 20.

29. Interestingly, Mack has criticized this now common understanding of the parables within contemporary scholarship—mentioning Crossan by name—as constituting another ploy to find a new hermeneutic by which to render the increasingly problematic Jesus tradition relevant for twentieth-century humanity. See Mack, *MI*, 4–7, 17, 138–47; idem, *Rhetoric and the New Testament*, (Minneapolis: Fortress, 1989), 100–101.

30. For a helpful summary of this shift, see J.D. Crossan, "Jesus and Gospel," in *The Biblical Heritage in Modern Catholic Scholarship*, ed. J.J. Collins and J.D. Crossan (Wilmington, Del.: Glazier, 1986), 106–30.

31. J.D. Crossan, *In Fragments: The Aphorisms of Jesus* (San Francisco: Harper & Row, 1983).

32. J.D. Crossan, *Four Other Gospels: Shadows on the Contour of the Canon* (Minneapolis: Winston/Seabury, 1985), 10–11.

33. See J.D. Crossan, *The Cross That Spoke: The Origins of the Passion Narrative* (San Francisco: Harper & Row, 1988). For a summary statement, see idem, "The Cross That Spoke: The Earliest Narrative of the Passion and Resurrection," *Foundations and Facets Forum* 3/2 (1987): 3–22. For the text and Crossan's stratification, see idem, Appendix 7: "Strata in the Gospel of Peter," in *HJ*, 462–66. Koester offers a critique of Crossan's thesis, but nonetheless concludes that the Gospel of Peter has preserved the most original passion narrative. See H. Koester, *Ancient Christian Gospels: Their History and Develop-*

ment (Philadelphia: Trinity, 1990), 216–30. Thus, with Crossan, he holds to its independence from the canonical Gospels.

34. Crossan, *HJ*, xxvii.

35. J.D. Crossan, "Why We Must Seek the Historical Jesus," *Boston Sunday Globe*, 26 July 1992, 59.

36. Crossan, *Raid on the Articulate*, 177. See also *In Parables*, 4–5. As recently as 1988, Crossan had formulated a "new first principle" for Jesus research in the form of a new authenticity criterion: "the criterion of adequacy." This criterion states that "*that is original which best explains the multiplicity engendered in the tradition.*" J.D. Crossan, "Divine Immediacy and Human Immediacy: Towards a New First Principle in Historical Jesus Research," *Semeia* 44 (1988), 125 (emphasis original). In *HJ*, however, he chose to forego its use as primary arbiter since it was "too subjective." See Crossan, "Responses and Reflections," 147–48.

37. No doubt his renewed turn to the historical has been largely influenced by his involvement in the Jesus Seminar and its methods. Reviewers have tended to read this mix of methods either in terms of ground-breaking brilliance or self-contradictory confusion. See, e.g., Scott, "to impose is not/To Discover"; N.T. Wright, "Taking the Text with Her Pleasure: A Post-Post-Modern Response to J. Dominic Crossan's *The Historical Jesus* (With Apologies to A.A. Milne, St. Paul and James Joyce)," *Theology* 96 (1993): 303–10; and Brown and Malbon, "Parabling as a *Via Negativa*," 535–36.

38. Crossan, *HJ*, xxviii.

39. Ibid.

40. See G. Lenski, *Power and Privilege: A Theory of Social Stratification* (New York: McGraw-Hill, 1966); T.R. Gurr, *Why Men Rebel* (Princeton: Princeton Univ. Press, 1970); B.R. Wilson, *Magic and the Millennium: A Sociological Study of Religious Movements of Protest Among Tribal and Third-World Peoples* (New York: Harper & Row, 1973; J.C. Scott, *Domination and the Arts of Resistance: Hidden Transcripts* (New Haven, Conn.: Yale Univ. Press, 1990). Unlike the first three theorists, Crossan does not mention Scott by name in *HJ*. However, in a subsequent article he states that his concept of "radicalism" is the "most important" model in regard to his project. See "Jesus the Peasant," *Dialogue* 26 (1993): 160.

41. Crossan, *HJ*, xxxi.

42. Ibid.

43. Ibid.

44. The results of Crossan's own inventory, stratigraphy, and attestation count are listed in appendix 1 of *HJ*, 427–50.

45. E.g., see J. White, "Jesus as Actant," *Biblical Research* 36 (1991): 22; Koester, *Ancient Christian Gospels*, 218–20.

46. Crossan's use of Q, GosThom, and Secret Mark will be critiqued in chap. 6.

47. We will discuss the dating of Mark in chap. 10 and the dating of Crossan's noncanonical works in chap. 6.

48. GosThom is fully extant only in the Coptic script (with some fragments in the Greek), but Crossan divides it into two hypothetically reconstructed layers and dates only the earliest in his first stratum.

49. Aside from some two dozen references to 1 Corinthians and four references to Galatians in his 505 page magnum opus (*HJ*), Crossan ignores Paul. And even these references contribute nothing to his reconstruction. Section 4 (Chaps. 8–9) shall argue that Paul has a great deal to contribute to our understanding of the historical Jesus.

50. It is interesting to note that between his 1988 "Materials and Methods in Historical Jesus Research," *Foundations and Facets Forum* 4/4 (December 1988): 9–10 and *HJ*, Crossan has adjusted the chronological parameters of his

own stratigraphy framework—i.e., compare stratum three in each case.

51. Crossan judges GosThom, the "Egerton Gospel" (EgerP 2), P. Vienna G. 2325, P. Oxy 1224, the Gospel of Hebrews, and the Gospel of the Egyptians to be independent of the canonical Gospels. The Cross Gospel and Secret Mark are judged to be not only independent of the canonical Gospels, but to actually serve as sources for them. For an insightful analysis of Crossan's inventory and the methodology by which it is gathered, see F. Neirynck, "The Historical Jesus: Reflections on an Inventory," *Ephemerides Theologicae Lovanienses* 70/1 (1994): 221–34. It is interesting to note in "Materials and Methods in Historical Jesus Research" that Crossan is aware of the potential problems of circularity associated with presumed genetic relations between texts (pp. 7–8). One wonders if this awareness arose during the construction of the stratification and data pool for *HJ*.

52. Crossan, "The Historical Jesus in Earliest Christianity," in *Jesus and Faith*, 1.

53. Crossan, *HJ*, 304.

54. Crossan, "Jesus the Peasant," 159. See also *HJ*, chap. 3: "Slave and Patron."

55. See Crossan, *HJ*, 59–68.

56. Ibid., 99. In all of this Crossan is self-consciously indebted to Richard Horsley's work on first-century Jewish life (see *HJ*, 100). For Horsley's views, see R.A. Horsley and J.S. Hanson's popular work, *Bandits, Prophets, and Messiahs: Popular Movements in the Time of Jesus*, NVBS (Minneapolis: Winston/Seabury, 1985); and R.A. Horsley, *Jesus and the Spiral of Violence: Popular Jewish Resistance in Roman Palestine* (San Francisco: Harper & Row, 1987).

57. On the religious worldview of Second Temple Judaism. see the excellent study by Wright, *New Testament and People of God*, pt. 3: "First-Century Judaism within the Greco-Roman World," esp. 215–79.

58. See e.g., *HJ*, 304; *JRB*, 102–22. See also Crossan's summary article, "Open Healing and Open Eating: Jesus as a Jewish Cynic?" *Biblical Research* 36 (1991): 6–18.

59. Crossan, *HJ*, 259.

60. Ibid., 304.

61. Ibid., 303.

62. See also *JRB*, 75–93, where Crossan further suggests that Jesus may have operated as an "*entranced healer*" who effected his healings through the use of "contagious trance as a therapeutic technique" (p. 93). For his discussion of the nature of trance as "*ecstasy, dissociation, or altered states of consciousness,*" see pp. 87–88.

63. Crossan, *HJ*, 310. For Crossan there is no clear-cut distinction between "religion" and "magic." Although he acknowledges the distinction made by some between religion as "humble submission to the deity" and magic as "attempting to force the supernatural powers to accomplish what he desires and avert what he fears" (see, e.g., A.A. Barb, "The Survival of the Magic Arts," in *The Conflict between Paganism and Christianity in the Fourth Century*, ed. A. Momigliano [Oxford: Clarendon, 1963], 100–125), he dismisses it in the end—in good postmodern fashion—by still chalking any such distinction up to nothing more than a political ploy. "We" practice religion, "they" practice magic (see *HJ*, 305).

64. Ibid., 332.

65. In doing so, he consistently misses the point of the exorcisms. This critique will be fleshed out below (chap. 6) in the context of a critique of the particular features of the post-Bultmannian non-apocalyptic Jesus.

66. E.g., see A. Kleinman, *Patients and Healers in the Context of Culture: An Exploration on the Borderland Between Anthropology, Medicine, and Psychiatry*

(Berkeley: Univ. of California Press, 1980), 72.
  67. Crossan, *HJ*, 336–37.
  68. Crossan, *JRB*, 82.
  69. Borg, *Jesus in Contemporary Scholarship*, 43, n. 88. For helpful discussions on Jesus' miracles—including healings and exorcisms—that either challenge such naturalistic assumptions and/or provide a more plausible historical account, see D. Wenham and C. Blomberg, eds., *The Miracles of Jesus, GP* 6 (Sheffield: JSOT, 1986); G.H. Twelftree, *Jesus the Exorcist: A Contribution to the Study of the Historical Jesus, WUNT* 2:54 (Tübingen: Mohr, 1993); and L. Sabourin, "The Miracles of Jesus (II): Jesus and the Evil Powers," *Biblical Theology Bulletin* 4/2 (1974): 115–75. On the wider, and more basic, question of miracles in the "modern" world, see C. Brown, *Miracles and the Critical Mind* (Grand Rapids: Eerdmans, 1984); J. Houston, *Reported Miracles: A Critique of Hume* (Cambridge: Cambridge Univ. Press, 1994); T.C. Williams, *The Idea of the Miraculous: The Challenge to Science and Religion* (London/New York: Macmillan, 1990).
  70. Crossan, *HJ*, 341–44.
  71. Crossan, *JRB*, 145. Crossan accounts for Jesus' missing body by suggesting that, whether left on the cross or buried in a shallow mass grave, it was eventually devoured by scavenging birds and dogs (see *JRB*, 154). Interestingly, this response hearkens back to that offered by Strauss in his *Life of Jesus for the German People*. I shall discuss and critique Crossan's and Mack's view of the resurrection fully in chap. 13.
  72. See Crossan, "Historical Jesus in Earliest Christianity"; idem, "Lists in Early Christianity," 241–43.

Chapter 4: Jesus, the Jewish Socrates

  1. Mack, *MI*, 77.
  2. Mack raised the possibility of a "Cynic characterization of Jesus" in a 1985 reflection, addressed to the members of the Jesus Seminar, regarding their first official meeting. See B.L. Mack, "Gilgamesh and the Wizard of Oz: The Scholar as Hero," *Foundations and Facets Forum* 1/2 (June 1985): 25. The initial seeds for this characterization apparently derive from Mack's study of the chreia in Greco-Roman rhetoric in conjunction with the Claremont Chreia Project in the early 1980s. We shall discuss his views on the chreia below.
  3. B. Mack, "Q and A Cynic-Like Jesus" (unpublished paper delivered at a conference on recent approaches to the historical Jesus, Ottawa, Ontario, 8–9 June 1993, 2, emphasis in text). Thanks goes to Professor Mack for permission to cite this paper.
  4. For the published results of his dissertation, see B.L. Mack, *Logos und Sophia: Untersuchungen zur Weisheitstheologie im hellenistischen Judentum, SUNT* 10 (Göttingen: Vandenhoeck & Ruprecht, 1973). For helpful reviews, see H.D. Betz, *Journal of Biblical Literature* 93 (1974): 606–8; R.E. Murphy, *Catholic Biblical Quarterly* 36 (1974): 130.
  5. Although the original *Studia Philonica* series ended in 1980, a new series, *The Studia Philonica Annual* was launched in 1989, with Mack as a consulting editor. For his recent work on Sirach, see B.L. Mack, *Wisdom and the Hebrew Epic: Ben Sirach's Hymn in Praise of the Fathers* (Chicago: Univ. of Chicago Press, 1985). Here he argues (against e.g., M. Hengel) that Sirach, far from representing a generally conservative Jewish reaction against Hellenism, is essentially a Hellenized "Man of Letters" himself. Other ventures into Hellenistic Judaism include his, "Under the Shadow of Moses: Authorship and Authority in Hellenistic Judaism," *SBLSP* 1982, ed. K.H. Richards

(Chico, Calif.: Scholars, 1982), 299–318; idem, "Decoding the Scripture: Philo and the Rules of Rhetoric," in *Nourished with Peace: Studies in Hellenistic Judaism in Memory of Samuel Sandmel*, ed. F.E. Greenspahn, E. Hilgert, and B. Mack, *SPHS* 9 (Chico, Calif.: Scholars, 1984), 81–115.

6. See B.L. Mack, *Rhetoric and the New Testament* (Minneapolis: Fortress, 1990).

7. Ibid., 94.

8. Ibid., 102.

9. Ibid. See also Mack, "Gilgamesh and the Wizard of Oz," 11–13.

10. R.F. Hock and E.N. O'Neil, *The Chreia in Ancient Rhetoric*, vol. 1, *The Progymnasmata, TT 27/GRRS* 9 (Atlanta: Scholars, 1986), 26. On chreia see also D.F. Watson, "Chreia/Aphorism," in *Dictionary of Jesus and the Gospels*, ed. J.B. Green, S. McKnight, and I.H. Marshall (Downers Grove, Ill.: InterVarsity, 1992), 104–6.

11. Mack did his chreia-pronouncement story work largely in conversation with V. Robbins, who was involved with the SBL Seminar on pronouncement stories. See B.L. Mack and V.K. Robbins, *Patterns of Persuasion in the Gospels* (Sonoma, Calif.: Polebridge, 1989); Mack, "Anecdotes and Arguments: The Chreia in Antiquity and Early Christianity," *Occasional Papers 10* (Claremont: Institute for Antiquity and Christianity, 1987), 1–48; idem, "Persuasive Pronouncements: An Evaluation of Recent Studies on the Chreia," *Semeia* 64 (1993): 283–87 (this issue of *Semeia* is devoted to the topic).

12. In addition to the works noted above, see B.L. Mack and R.E. Murphy, "Wisdom Literature," in *Early Judaism and Its Modern Interpreters*, ed. R.A. Kraft and G.W.E. Nickelsburg (Philadelphia: Fortress; Atlanta: Scholars, 1986), 371–410. An early impetus for Mack's interest in this concept, and thus for his dissertation, came in the form of an essay by Conzelmann, entitled "The Mother of Wisdom," in *The Future of Our Religious Past: Essays in Honour of Rudolf Bultmann*, ed. J.M. Robinson, trans. C.E. Carlston and R.P. Scharlemann (New York/London: Harper & Row, 1971 [1964]), 230–43.

13. For a discussion of the differences between the history-of-religions school and Bultmann on this matter, followed by Mack's own modified hypothesis, see B.L. Mack, "Wisdom Myth and Myth-ology: An Essay in Understanding a Theological Tradition," *Interpretation* 24 (1970): 46–60.

14. B.L. Mack, "Wisdom Makes a Difference: Alternatives to 'Messianic' Configurations," in *Judaisms and Their Messiahs at the Turn of the Christian Era*, ed. J. Neusner, W.S. Green, and E.S. Frerichs (Cambridge: Cambridge Univ. Press, 1987), 47. Here, Mack's starting point is the fairly recent contention that the Second Temple notion of "Messiah" was not as monolithic as once thought. For various perspectives on this controversial observation, see the above volume and J.H. Charlesworth, ed., *The Messiah: Developments in Earliest Judaism and Christianity* (Minneapolis: Fortress, 1992).

15. Mack, "The Christ and Jewish Wisdom," in Charlesworth, *Messiah*, 194.

16. E.g., see B.L. Mack, "Lord of the Logia: Savior or Sage?" in *Gospel Origins and Christian Beginnings, in Honor of James M. Robinson*, ed. J.E. Goehring, C.W. Hedrick, J.T. Sanders, with H.D. Betz (Sonoma, Calif.: Polebridge, 1990), 3–18.

17. From Conzelmann, Mack early on adopted a methodological distinction between "myth" and "myth-ology," where the latter refers to "the employment of myth for theological reflection." See Mack, "Wisdom Myth and Mythology," 48; idem, *Logos und Sophia,* 20, and Conzelmann, "Mother of Wisdom," 243. In his dissertation, this is worked out in relation to personified wisdom: this personification is not to be understood as myth, but as the result of reworking mythic materials in the process of theologizing (mythology).

18. It is important to note that Mack has always viewed himself *both* as a

New Testament scholar *and* a historian of religions. He has held (and yet holds) joint posts in both fields, and in a recent article describes himself under both titles. See his review essay of G. Habermas and A. Flew, *Did Jesus Rise from the Dead?* in *History and Theory* 28/2 (1989): 219, 223, n. 2.

19. Girard is best known in relation to biblical studies for his "scapegoat" theory of social violence, and the question of its application to the biblical notion of atonement. See R. Girard, *Violence and the Sacred*, trans. P. Gregory (Baltimore: Johns Hopkins Univ., 1977 [1972]); idem, *The Scapegoat*, trans. Y. Freccero (Baltimore: Johns Hopkins Univ., 1986 [1985]). On Smith, see J.Z. Smith, *Map Is Not Territory: Studies in the History of Religions, SJLA* 23 (Leiden: Brill, 1978); idem, *Imagining Religion: From Babylon to Jonestown* (Chicago: Univ. of Chicago Press, 1982); idem, *To Take Place: Toward Theory in Ritual* (Chicago: Univ. of Chicago Press, 1987); idem, *Drudgery Divine: On the Comparison of Early Christianity and the Religions of Late Antiquity, CSHJ* (Chicago: Univ. of Chicago Press, 1990).

20. Mack, *MI*, 20, n. 9. See also Mack, "Q and the Gospel of Mark: Revising Christian Origins," *Semeia* 55 (1992): 36–38.

21. B.L. Mack, "After Drudgery Divine," *Numen* 39/2 (1992):227.

22. Mack, "Innocent Transgressor: Jesus in Early Christian Myth and History," *Semeia*, 33 (1985), 155. For other sentiments along these lines, see the essays collected in J. Neusner, ed., *The Christian and Judaic Invention of History, AARSR* 55 (Atlanta: Scholars, 1990), where the opening pages of Mack's *Myth of Innocence* comprises a chapter.

23. For Mack's acknowledged indebtedness to these two men, especially their notion of "intertextuality," see *MI*, xi, 23 n. 10. For important texts, see J. Derrida, *Of Grammatology*, trans. G.C. Spivak (Baltimore: Johns Hopkins Univ. Press, 1976); M. Foucault, *The Order of Things: An Archaeology of the Human Sciences* (New York: Pantheon, 1971); idem, *The Archaeology of Knowledge*, trans. A.M. Sheridan Smith (New York: Pantheon, 1972). For discussions on his understanding of knowledge and power, see M. Foucault, *Power/Knowledge: Selected Interviews and Other Writings, 1972–1977*, ed. and trans. C. Gordon et al. (New York: Pantheon, 1980). On the Nietzschean underpinnings of Foucault's thought at this point, see M. Mahon, *Foucault's Nietzschean Genealogy: Truth, Power, and the Subject* (Albany: State Univ. of New York, 1992). For a helpful introduction to post-structuralist criticism of the New Testament, see S.D. Moore, *Poststructuralism and the New Testament: Derrida and Foucault at the Foot of the Cross* (Minneapolis: Fortress, 1994).

24. V.K. Robbins, "Text and Context in Recent Studies of the Gospel of Mark," *Religious Studies Review* 17/1 (1991): 20.

25. See *MI*, 368–76, and esp. B.L. Mack, "Innocence and Power in the Christian Imagination," *Occasional Paper* 17 (Institute for Antiquity and Christianity), 1989.

26. Mack, "Innocence and Power," 12.

27. Here, "reductionism" refers not simply to the employment of a single method (a charge that Mack wants to defend Smith from, see "After Drudgery Divine," 228), but rather to the *a priori* reduction of all religious phenomena to a purely naturalistic and thus anthropological and/or sociological level of reality. More will be said about this approach and the fundamental worldview to which it is committed in chap. 5.

28. Mack, *MI*, 23–24.

29. Ibid., 23.

30. The most important of these scholarly assumptions, which, again, are largely coterminous with those that characterize the "Post-Bultmannian Quest," will be analyzed in chaps. 5 and 6.

31. While generally regarded as highly controversial, Mack's theory of Christian origins has found a number of largely sympathetic ears. See, e.g.,

D.C. Duling, "Leaving One's Mark" (review of *A Myth of Innocence*), *Commonweal* 116 (11 August 1989): 445–46; M.P. Miller, "How Jesus Became Christ: Probing a Thesis," *Continuum* 2/2–3 (1993): 243–70; J. White, "Jesus as Actant," *Biblical Research* 36 (1991): 19–29. On the remarkable influence that Mack's thesis had on the Jesus Seminar's voting with regard to the kingdom sayings in Mark, see J.R. Butts, "Probing the Polling: Jesus Seminar Results on the Kingdom Sayings," *Foundations and Facets Forum* 3/1 (1987): 108–11.

32. While there are differences, Mack's two categories are analogous to the older Bousett/Bultmann notions of Jewish and Hellenistic Christianity, discussed in chapter 1.

33. Mack, *MI*, 91.

34. Ibid., 82–83.

35. Ibid., 96.

36. Ibid., 96–97.

37. Mack, "The Kingdom Sayings in Mark," *Foundations and Facets Forum* 3/1 (1987): 3–47; idem, *LG*, 123–30. More recently, however, Mack has revised his understanding of the Q people as "itinerants" and "prophets." See B.L. Mack, "A Myth of Innocence at Sea," *Continuum* 1/2 (1991): 143, n.1.

38. Mack, "Kingdom Sayings in Mark," 17. Mack's attack on the authenticity of the Markan notion of the kingdom of God was the primary factor that moved the Jesus Seminar to vote against the Markan kingdom sayings (which was helped along, of course, by the seminar's generally anti-apocalyptic mood). See Butts, "Probing the Polling," 108–11. Against Mack's locating of the concept of the kingdom of God away from Old Testament and apocalyptic and toward a primarily Hellenistic-wisdom orientation, see G.R. Beasley-Murray, *Jesus and the Kingdom of God* (Grand Rapids: Eerdmans, 1986), esp. chaps. 1–8; M. Lattke, "On the Jewish Background of the Synoptic Concept 'Kingdom of God,' " in *The Kingdom of God in the Teaching of Jesus, IRT 5*, ed. B. Chilton (Philadelphia: Fortress; London: SPCK, 1984), 72–91; D. Patrick, "The Kingdom of God in the Old Testament," in Willis, *Kingdom of God in 20th-Century Interpretation*, 67–79; M.J. Selman, "The Kingdom of God in the Old Testament," *Tyndale Bulletin* 40/2 (1989): 161–83; B. Witherington III, *Jesus, Paul and the End of the World: A Comparative Study in New Testament Eschatology* (Downers Grove, Ill.: InterVarsity, 1992), 59–74.

39. See *MI*, 59 n.4; *LG*, 35–38; "Q and the Gospel of Mark," 16.

40. Mack, *LG*, 121.

41. Ibid., 115.

42. Ibid., 121.

43. Ibid., 204.

44. Ibid., 149.

45. Ibid., 171–79. Mack had already developed this basic social history of Q by 1988. See Mack, "The Kingdom That Didn't Come: A Social History of the Q Tradents," *SBLSP 1988*, ed. D. Lull (Atlanta: Scholars, 1988), 608–35, which offers a good summary of his thesis.

46. Mack, *LG*, 71–102.

47. Mack, *MI*, 90.

48. Ibid., 90–91.

49. Ibid., 91.

50. Ibid., 94.

51. Ibid., 95.

52. In *LG*, 214, Mack has added a sixth Jesus group—the community "within which Luke was at home"—whose history is "sketchy" (in contrast to the others?) and whose distinguishing mark is "a distinctively human view of Jesus."

53. Mack, *MI*, 101.

54. Mack, *LG*, 220.

55. Mack, *MI*, 100.

56. Ibid., 101.

57. Mack, *LG*, 216.

58. Ibid., 216–17. See also *MI*, 102–13 for Mack's argument at this point. He is heavily dependent upon the work of D. Seeley—one of the Cynic Jesus exponents mentioned in chap. 2. Seeley argues that Paul's understanding of Christ's death owes virtually nothing to any Jewish background (neither to ideas of the Temple cultus, nor to Old Testament ideas such as the Suffering Servant, etc.), but rather to the pervasive Hellenistic notion of the "philosopher-martyr" and his "Noble Death." See D. Seeley, *The Noble Death: Graeco-Roman Martyrology and Paul's Concept of Salvation, JSNTSS* 28 (Sheffield: JSOT, 1990). In two subsequent articles, Seeley has located this same understanding of Jesus' death in the earliest stratum of Kloppenborg's triple-layered Q: namely at Q/Luke 14:27. He concludes that such an understanding is "familiar from Cynic and Stoic schools." See his, "Blessings and Boundaries: Interpretations of Jesus' Death in Q," *Semeia* 55 (1992): 132, as well as "Jesus' Death in Q," *New Testament Studies* 38 (1992): 222–34. Interestingly, in a recent review of Seeley's book, F.G. Downing—who finds Cynic parallels to the Jesus tradition everywhere—admits that Seeley's Greco-Roman thesis cannot account for the full evidence. See *Journal of Theological Studies* 42 (1991): 242–44.

59. E.g., see C.D.F. Moule, *The Origin of Christology* (Cambridge: Cambridge Univ. Press, 1977), esp. 107–26; B. Witherington III, *Paul's Narrative Thought World: The Tapestry of Tragedy and Triumph* (Louisville: Westminster/John Knox, 1994); N.T. Wright, *The Climax of the Covenant: Christ and the Law in Pauline Theology* (Edinburgh: T & T Clark, 1991), esp. 137–56. I shall critique Mack on this point more fully in part 4.

60. See Mack, *MI*, 27–52.

61. Although Mack does not press this thesis in *Myth of Innocence*, in a recent article he has argued for Mark's use of Q ("Q and the Gospel of Mark," 21–30). This, of course, works well with his larger theory of just what it was that Mark accomplished. While it is true that Mack is not alone in postulating such a textual relationship, it is at best a minority position. Beyond this, the questions it raises in regards to the basic Two-source hypothesis upon which contemporary New Testament studies rests are problematic to say the least, given that Q has customarily been *defined* as that material which Matthew and Luke have in common that is *not* found in—and therefore not accounted for by—Mark.

62. Mack, *MI*, 128.

63. Ibid., 357.

64. His feelings on this are made abundantly clear in his unpublished paper "Q and a Cynic-Like Jesus." Here, he describes his investigation of early Christian mythmaking, which is "the real attraction of the early Christian enterprise," in terms of traveling along the "high ridge" and "peaks." His forray into the Cynic-Jesus thesis, while somewhat interesting to him, is nonetheless described in terms of an inadvertent and largely unfortunate "slide" into the valley below (pp. 1, 20). In contrast to the generally optimistic tone of the third quest, Mack writes (in the course of a discussion on the passion narratives): "For now, only the fact of Jesus' crucifixion in Jerusalem can be entered as a datum in the quest of the historical Jesus. . . . There is at the moment no firm consensus about Jesus, the nature of his activity, or the reasons for the groups that formed in his name" (*MI*, 55–56).

65. In the currently unpublished "Q and a Cynic-Like Jesus." Again, thanks goes to Mack for permission to quote.

66. Here Mack notes the forthcoming volume, *The Cynics*, edited by B. Branham.

67. Mack, *MI*, 66.

68. Mack, "Q and a Cynic-Like Jesus," 3.

69. Ibid., 22 n.11. This statement, of course, begs the question of just *who* the historical "Jesus" is in the second comparison.

70. With regard to Jesus, Mack notes his own *Patterns of Persuasion in the Gospels*. Regarding Paul, appeal is made to R.F. Hock, *The Social Context of Paul's Ministry* (Philadelphia: Fortress, 1980), A.J. Malherbe, *Paul and the Popular Philosophers* (Minneapolis: Fortress, 1989); and S. Stowers, "Paul on the Use and Abuse of Reason," in *Greeks, Romans, and Christians: Essays in Honor of Abraham J. Malherbe*, ed. D.L. Balch, E. Ferguson, and W.A. Meeks (Minneapolis: Fortress, 1990), 253–86.

71. Mack, "Q and a Cynic-Like Jesus," 3.

72. Ibid., 4.

73. Mack lists sayings in the following verses: Mark 2:17, 19, 27; 7:15; 9:35; 10:18, 25; 11:27-28; 12:13-14, 17.

74. Mack, "Q and a Cynic-Like Jesus," 6–7.

75. Ibid., 10. For further elaboration of Mack's argument here, see *MI*, 179–200; *Patterns of Persuasion*, esp. 45–51, 65–67; "Anecdotes and Arguments," 39–42.

76. Mack, "Q and a Cynic-Like Jesus," 11. He points to sayings in the following verses: Luke 6:20, 38-39, 43; 9:58; 11:10; 12:2, 23-24, 34; 14:11, 34; 16:33.

77. Ibid., 12.

78. Ibid., 12–13. Here he lists sayings from: Luke 6:20, 28-30, 37, 42; 9:60; 10:2, 4, 7; 11:9; 12:7, 22, 33, 57; 14:26.

79. Ibid., 14. The other tenets of Q-1 lifestyle that Mack lists include: "A critique of hypocracy and pretention," "a challenge to renounce the supports usually considered necessary for human life," "etiquette for responding to public reproach," "nonretaliation," "concern for personal integrity and authenticity," "a challenge to live naturally at all cost," "a reliance on the natural order," "singlemindedness in the pursuit of God's kingdom," and "confidence in God's care" (pp. 13–14). The last two points are hardly "Cynic" commonplaces, and thus Mack is forced to try to give them the sort of radical Hellenistic spin necessary for that kind of linkage. We will take this up in more detail in chap. 7.

80. Ibid.

81. Mack, *MI*, 199.

82. Mack, "Q and a Cynic-Like Jesus," 19–20.

83. See Mack, *MI*, 53–77; "Lord of the Logia"; "Kingdom Sayings in Mark."

84. Mack, *MI*, 188.

85. E.g., see *MI*, 6–7, 75–77, 208–45.

86. Mack, "Q and a Cynic-Like Jesus," 20–21.

87. Mack, *MI*, 3–4.

88. Ibid., 8.

89. Despite Mack's claim that contemporary scholarship needs his work to dispell the remnants of its mythological faith in a unique origin to Christianity, a review of chap. 1 will quickly reveal that the central features of Mack's program are not all that new. While the specifics have changed, to be sure, the essence of this "mythological" trajectory can be traced from Reimarus' initial skepticism through Strauss' explicit myth theory and on through the early history-of-religions school to Bultmann. The logical, most radical, end point to this trajectory comes when one simply denies any historical existence to Jesus and attributes *everything* to myth. As we have seen, Bruno Bauer blazed this trail in the nineteenth century. There is in Mack's theory of religion, with its strong faith in people's incredible mythmaking power, nothing that *requires* a historical Jesus at all. Hence, it seems that there is little outside of Mack's confidence in isolating an earliest Q strata, and a shadowy Cynic-like figure behind it, that keeps him from completely following Bauer.

Chapter 5: Beginning at the Conclusion

1. Some assume (positively) or argue (negatively) that naturalistic presuppositions are fundamentally entwined with the historical-critical method. For the first position, see C. Hartlich, "Is Historical Criticism Out of Date?" in *Conflicting Ways of Interpreting the Bible, Concilium* 138, ed. H. Küng and J. Moltmann (Edinburgh: T & T Clark; New York: Seabury, 1980), 3–8. For the second, see G. Maier, *The End of the Historical-Critical Method*, trans. E.W. Leverenz and R.F. Norden (St. Louis: Concordia, 1977 [1974]); and G. Soares-Prabhu, "The Historical Critical Method: Reflections on Its Relevance for the Study of the Gospels in India Today," in *Theologizing in India*, ed. M. Amaladoss, et al. (Bangalore, India: Theological Publications in India, 1981), 314–67. Others, however, argue that they can be separated. See J.A. Fitzmyer, "Historical Criticism: Its Role in Biblical Interpretation and Church Life," *Theological Studies* 50 (1989): 244–59; and J.D. Kingsbury, "The Historical-Critical Method in Perspective," *Currents in Theology and Mission* 2/3 (July 1975): 132–41.

2. Mack is representative of this school when he argues that the notion that Christianity had a unique and miraculous origin is "not a category of critical scholarship at all" (*MI*, 8).

3. See M.L. Brice, "Reflections on Historical Criticism and Self-Understanding," in *Self-Definition and Self-Discovery in Early Christianity: A Study in Changing Horizons, Essays in Appreciation of Ben F. Meyer from Former Students, SBEC* 26, ed. D.J. Hawkins and T. Robinson (Lewiston, N.Y.: Mellen, 1990), 55–77; B.F. Meyer, "The Relevance of 'Horizon,' " *The Downside Review* 112 (January 1994): 1–14; M. Silva, "The Place of Historical Reconstruction in New Testament Criticism," in *Hermeneutics, Authority, and Canon*, ed. D.A. Carson and J.D. Woodbridge (Grand Rapids: Zondervan, 1986), 105–33.

4. Note, e.g., Koester's argument in his, "The Divine Human Being," *Harvard Theological Review* 78/3–4 (1985): 243–52. His negative attitudes toward just what the Christian idea of Jesus' divinity involves, where it derives from, and how us moderns should reject the notion of a uniquely "divine man," are all intimately bound up with his own, largely unstated, worldview assumptions about divinity (e.g., the recognition of "the presence of divinity in all human beings," p. 251), metaphysics, and so on.

5. For various insights on the presuppositional differences behind varying assessments of the biblical texts, see W.J. Abraham, *Divine Revelation and the Limits of Historical Criticism* (Oxford/New York: Oxford Univ. Press, 1982); M. de Jonge, "The Loss of Faith in the Historicity of the Gospels: H.S. Reimarus (ca. 1750) on John and the Synoptics," in A. Denaux, ed., *John and the Synoptics, BETL* 51 (Leuven, Belgium: Leuven Univ. Press, 1992), 409–21; E.E. Ellis, "Gospels Criticism: A Perspective on the State of the Art," in *The Gospel and the Gospels*, ed. P. Stuhlmacher, trans. J. Bowden (Grand Rapids: Eerdmans, 1991 [1983]), 26–33; C.A. Evans, "The Historical Jesus and Christian Faith: A Critical Assessment of a Scholarly Problem," *Christian Scholars Review* 18/1 (September 1988): 60–62; N.L. Geisler, ed. *Biblical Errancy: An Analysis of Its Philosophical Roots* (Grand Rapids: Zondervan, 1981); F. Hahn, "Problems of Historical Criticism," in his *Historical Investigation and the New Testament: Two Essays*, ed. E. Krentz, trans. R. Maddox (Philadelphia: Fortress, 1983 [1972]), 13–33; P. Helm, "Understanding Scholarly Presuppositions: A Crucial Tool for Research?" *Tyndale Bulletin* 44/1 (1993): 143–54; I.H. Marshall, "Historical Criticism," in *New Testament Interpretation: Essays on Principles and Methods*, ed. I.H. Marshall (Grand Rapids: Eerdmans, 1977), 126–38; J. Ratzinger, "Foundations and Approaches of Biblical Exegesis," *Origins* 17/35 (11 February 1988): 593–602; G.N. Stanton, "Presuppositions in New Testament Criticism," in *New Testament Interpretation*, 60–71; P. Stuhlmacher, *His-*

torical Criticism and Theological Interpretation of Scripture: Towards a Hermeneutics of Consent, trans. R.A. Harrisville (Philadelphia: Fortress, 1977 [1975]); T.F. Torrance, " 'The Historical Jesus': From the Perspective of a Theologian," in *The New Testament Age: Essays in Honor of Bo Reicke,* 2 vols., ed. W.C. Weinrich (Macon, Ga.: Mercer Univ. Press, 1984), 2:511–26; N.T. Wright, *The New Testament and People of God* (Minneapolis: Fortress, 1992), pt. 2. Also, a helpful book in this regard is awaiting publication: C.S. Evans, *Suffered Under Pontius Pilate: The Historicity of the Incarnational Narrative* (Oxford/New York: Oxford Univ. Press, forthcoming).

6. E. Schüssler Fiorenza, "The Ethics of Biblical Interpretation: Decentering Biblical Scholarship," *Journal of Biblical Literature* 107/1 (1988): 11. See D.A. deSilva, "The Meaning of the New Testament and the *Skandalon* of World Constructions," *Evangelical Quarterly* 64/1 (1992): 3–21; G. Soares-Prabhu, "Historical Critical Method," 319; W. Wink, *The Bible in Human Transformation: Toward a New Paradigm for Biblical Study* (Philadelphia: Fortress, 1973), esp. chap. 1.

7. T.C. Oden, *The Word of Life: Systematic Theology: Volume 2* (San Francisco: Harper & Row, 1989), 226. See Oden's perceptive discussion on pp. 217–28; and esp. idem, "The Critique of Criticism," in his *After Modernity . . . What? Agenda for Theology* (Grand Rapids: Zondervan, 1990), 103–47. In this regard, see also the insightful comments on Koester's project (comments that can be redirected at any number of post-Bultmannian projects) in F.W. Burnett and G.A. Phillips, "Palm Re(a)ding and the Big Bang: Origins and Development of Jesus Traditions," *Religious Studies Review* 18/4 (1992): 298–99. See also, J.D. Levenson, *The Hebrew Bible, the Old Testament, and Historical Criticism: Jews and Christians in Biblical Studies* (Louisville: Westminster/John Knox, 1993), 116, in which he raises the question of "suspecting the hermeneuts of suspicion" within modern historical-critical scholarship.

8. See D.R. Griffin, W.A. Beardslee, and J. Holland, *Varieties of Postmodernism* (Albany: State Univ. of New York Press, 1989), 3–4. In critical New Testament scholarship, as several have noted, one finds less a true "postmodernism" than an "arch-modernism." See N. Murphy and J.W. McClendon, Jr., "Distinguishing Modern and Postmodern Theologies," *Modern Theology* 5/3 (1989): 211–12. See also L. Dupre, "Postmodernity or Late Modernity?: Ambiguities in Richard Rorty's Thought," *Review of Metaphysics* 47/2 (1993): 277–95.

9. For the enlightening thoughts of one who has moved from Bultmannianism to a postmodern "paleo-orthodoxy," see Oden, *After Modernity . . . What? Agenda for Theology,* again esp. "The Critique of Criticism," 103–47. See also A. Dulles, "Theology for a Post-Critical Age," in *Theology Toward the Third Millennium: Theological Issues for the Twenty-First Century,* TST 56, ed. D.G. Schultenover (Lewiston, N.Y.: Mellen, 1991), 5–21.

10. For various perspectives, see F. Capra, *The Tao of Physics: An Exploration of the Parallels Between Modern Physics and Eastern Mysticism* (New York: Random House, 1983); D. Bohm, *Wholeness and the Implicate Order* (London: ARK, 1980); G. Zukav, *The Dancing Wu Li Masters: An Overview of the New Physics* (Toronto: Bantam, 1979); P. Davies, *God and the New Physics* (New York: Simon & Schuster, 1983); H. Margenau and R.A. Varghese, eds., *Cosmos, Bios, Theos* (LaSalle, Ill.: Open Court, 1992); and J. Polkinghorne, *Reason and Reality: The Relationship Between Science and Theology* (London: SPCK, 1991).

11. Note, e.g., the present "angel" craze our culture is going through. See, e.g., "Angels Among Us," *Time,* 27 December 1993, 56–65. A similar manifestation of this postmodern trend is the current preoccupation with "near-death experiences." At the time of this writing, the number one best-seller on the nonfiction book list for many weeks running has been B. Eadie's *Embraced by the Light* (Carson City, Nev.: Gold Leaf, 1992) which reports her sup-

posed heavenly journey during a near-death (or post-death) experience. See also E. Taylor, "Desperately Seeking Spirituality," *Psychology Today*, Nov./Dec. 1994, 54–68.

12. See D. Evans, "Academic Skepticism, Spiritual Reality and Transfiguration," in *The Glory of Christ in the New Testament: Studies in Christology in Memory of George Bradford Caird*, ed. L.D. Hurst and N.T. Wright (Oxford/New York: Oxford Univ. Press, 1987), 175–86. See also H. Smith, *Forgotten Truth: The Primordial Tradition* (New York: Harper & Row, 1976); idem, "Bubble Blown and Lived In: A Theological Autobiography," *Dialogue* 33/4 (Fall 1994): 274–79; M. Borg, "Root Images and the Way We See: The Primordial Tradition and the Biblical Tradition," in his *Jesus in Contemporary Scholarship* (Valley Forge, Pa.: Trinity, 1994), 127–39. On contemporary religious experience, see T. Beardsworth, *A Sense of Presence* (Oxford: The Religious Experience Research Unit, Manchester College, Oxford, 1977); M. Maxwell and V. Tschudin, eds., *Seeing the Invisible: Modern Religious and Other Transcendent Experiences* (London: Arkana, 1990); K. Springer, ed., *Power Encounters, Among Christians in the Western World* (San Francisco: Harper & Row, 1988); K.E. Yandell, *The Epistemology of Religious Experience* (Cambridge: Cambridge Univ. Press, 1993). The present resurgence in the belief in the supernatural in non-Christian forms is what is generally called "the New Age movement." While this movement poses many new challenges to Christianity, the positive aspect of this movement is that it clearly signifies the demise of the strictly secular Western worldview of the last two centuries. This point is argued more extensively in G. Boyd, *Satan and the Problem of Evil* (Downers Grove, Ill.: InterVarsity, forthcoming).

13. Mack at times seems hardly aware of other competing theories of religion; e.g., see P.B. Clarke and P. Byrne, *Religion Defined and Explained* (New York: St. Martin's, 1993).

14. Crossan reflects an awareness of the relative subjectivity of the material contents of his methology when he grants that a scholar could in principle accept all the "formal procedures" of his methodology but reject his "material investments." "These are all formal moves," he writes, ". . . inventory, stratigraphy, attestation. . . . Another scholar could accept all of those forms and still diverge completely on whether, say, the *Q Gospel* exists at all or the *Gospel of Thomas* is an independent attestation and, if so, belongs in what stratum" (Crossan, "The Historical Jesus: An Interview with John Dominic Crossan," *The Christian Century* [December 1991], 1201).

15. Crossan, "Responses and Reflection," in *Jesus and Faith: A Conversation on the Work of John Dominic Crossan*, ed. J. Carlson and R.A. Ludwig (Maryknoll, N.Y.: Orbis, 1994), 156.

16. In this vein, F.J. Van Beeck ("The Quest of the Historical Jesus: Origins, Achievements, and the Specter of Diminishing Returns," in *Jesus and Faith*, 83–99), has suggested that Crossan has recovered a Jesus that largely mirrors his own image. Crossan's response ("Responses and Reflections," 159) misses the essential point here when he writes: "how does Frans Jozef Van Beeck know that I agree with or even like my reconstructed Jesus?" (See also *JRB*, xiv). The suspiciousness of Crossan's reconstruction is not that he has recovered a Jesus that he "agrees with" or "likes," but rather one that perfectly fits within the narrow constraints of his religious worldview. Whether he agrees with or likes such a Jesus is beside the point—though it is difficult to take his language about Jesus' glorious paradoxicality in anything but an affectionate way.

17. Mack, *MI*, 73.

18. Crossan, "The Historical Jesus: An Interview," 1202.

19. E.g., see the following reviews of H. Koester's *Introduction to the New Testament*, where one common criticism is the reluctance shown by Koester

to acknowledge other dissenting opinions in the field. R.E. Brown, *Theological Studies* 44 (1983): 694; D.A. Carson, *Journal of the Evangelical Theological Society* 26 (1983): 495; M. Silva, *Westminster Theological Journal* 47 (1985): 115. The thrust of my argument in the last part of this chapter, and more particularly in sections 4 through 6, shall be to show the wealth of scholarship that Crossan and Mack downplay, or ignore, in their research.

20. This post-Bultmannian tendency toward elitism is quite evident in Mack's work, sometimes in a rather striking fashion. For example, in one book review Mack labels "the intelligence" of those who fundamentally disagree with his own approach to the issue of Jesus' resurrection as "very lightweight and extremely embarrassing." See his review of G. Habermas and A. Flew's debate, *Did Jesus Rise from the Dead?* in *History and Theory* 28:2 (1989): 218. Also noteworthy here is the number of times Mack equates his own position – over and against Habermas – with the position of "critical scholarship." Hence, e.g., he holds that "critical scholars recognize diversity among the many experimental movements of early Christianity," and that "reference to Jesus' resurrection was not a common persuasion" among these early movements (p. 219, see also pp. 220–21). This is, however, *Mack's* position, *not* the general position of all "critical scholarship." Because Habermas has a (well-argued!) different approach than Mack, Mack goes so far as to conclude that Habermas "disrespects as a whole the findings of the scholars whom he cites and violates the principles of discourse that allow for membership in their guild" (p. 223). Indeed, he concludes his vitriolic review by stating, "Readers, take care. And Harper and Row: you should really be ashamed. This kind of sensationalism is not worthy of your house" (p. 224). The "in-house" elitism of his position is remarkable. Ironically, only several years later, Mack had this same publishing house put out his own (quite sensationalist!) work, *The Lost Gospel.*

21. In addition, the influence of one's own socio-historical context should not be underestimated in this equation. For a German scholar's reflections upon the manner in which German history itself has predisposed him to suspicions of "continuity," see D. Luehrmann, "Marinus de Jonge's Shaffer Lectures: Where Does Jesus Research Now Stand?" in *From Jesus to John: Essays on Jesus and New Testament Christology in Honour of Marinus de Jonge,* *JSNTSS* 84, ed. M.C. De Boer (Sheffield: JSOT, 1993), 61–64.

22. See R.P.C. Hanson, "The Assessment of Motive in the Study of the Synoptic Gospels," *Modern Churchman* 10 (1967): 265–66; P. Minear, "Gospel History: Celebration or Reconstruction?" in *Jesus and Man's Hope,* 2 vols., ed. D.G. Miller and D.Y. Hadidian (Pittsburgh: Pittsburgh Theological Seminary, 1971), 2:21; G.N. Stanton, *Jesus of Nazareth in New Testament Preaching* (Cambridge: Cambridge Univ. Press, 1974), 186–90; N.T. Wright, "Jesus, Israel, and the Cross," *SBLSP* 1985, ed. K.H. Richards (Atlanta: Scholars, 1985), 90; idem, *New Testament and People of God,* 137, 377–78. I shall address in detail the issue of Mark's historical intention in chap. 10.

23. See N.A. Dahl, "Anamnesis," in his *Jesus in the Memory of the Early Church* (Minneapolis: Augsburg, 1976), 11–29.

24. B. Gerhardsson, *The Gospel Tradition,* CBMTS 15 (Lund, Sweden: Gleerup, 1986), 30. See also R. Stein, *Synoptic Problem: An Introduction* (Grand Rapids: Baker, 1987), 194–96; Wright, *New Testament and the People of God,* 377–78. For a detailed analysis of the Lukan prologue and its ramifications, see L.C.A. Alexander, "Luke's Preface in the Context of Greek Preface-Writing," *Novum Testamentum* 28/1 (1986): 48–74; and esp. idem, *The Preface to Luke's Gospel: Literary Convention and Social Context in Luke 1:1-4 and Acts 1:1* (Cambridge: Cambridge Univ. Press, 1993).

25. This point shall be argued more extensively in relation to Mark's Gospel in chap. 10.

26. See A.W. Mosley, "Historical Reporting in the Ancient World," *New Testament Studies* 12 (1965): 10–26; Wright, *New Testament and the People of God*, 67–69, 83–87, 377–78; contra D. Nineham, *The Use and Abuse of the Bible: A Study of the Bible in an Age of Rapid Cultural Change* (London: Macmillan, 1976), 187–88. Also favoring Mosley's and Wright's generally positive assessments is C. Hemer, *The Book of Acts in the Setting of Hellenistic History* (Tübingen: Mohr, 1989), chap. 3.

27. B. Gerhardsson, *Memory and Manuscript: Oral Tradition and Written Tradition in Rabbinic Judaism and Early Christianity*, 2nd ed. (Lund, Sweden: Gleerup, 1964 [1961]); idem, *Tradition and Transmission in Early Christianity* (Lund, Sweden: Gleerup, 1964); idem, *Gospel Tradition*; idem, "The Path of the Gospel Tradition," in *The Gospel and the Gospels*, ed. P. Stuhlmacher, trans. J. Bowden (Grand Rapids: Eerdmans, 1991 [1983]), 75–96.

28. See M. Smith, "A Comparison of Early Christian and Early Rabbinic Tradition," *Journal of Biblical Literature* 82 (1963): 169–72; J. Neusner, *The Rabbinic Traditions about the Pharisees before 70* (Leiden: Brill, 1971).

29. S. Safrai, "Education and the Study of the Torah," in *The Jewish People in the First Century*, 2 vols., ed. S. Safrai and M. Stern (Amsterdam: Van Gorcum, 1976), 2:952–53. See also, R. Riesner, *Jesus als Lehrer: Eine Untersuchung zum Ursprung der Evangelein-Uberlieferung* (Tübingen: Mohr, 1981); idem, "Jesus as Preacher and Teacher," in *Jesus and the Oral Gospel Tradition*, JSNTSS 64, ed. H. Wansbrough (Sheffield: JSOT, 1991), 185–210; E. Schuerer, *The History of the Jewish People in the Age of Jesus Christ, 175 B.C.–A.D. 135*, 3 vols., rev. and ed. G. Vermes, F. Millar, and M. Black (Edinburgh: T & T Clark, 1973–1987), 2:419; M.R. Wilson, "The Jewish Concept of Learning: A Christian Appreciation," *Christian Scholars' Review* 5 (1975–1976): 350–63; Wright, *New Testament and the People of God*, 233–41.

30. Gerhardsson's more recent writings include *The Origins of the Gospel Traditions*, *The Gospel Tradition*, "The Narrative Meshalim in the Synoptic Gospels," *New Testament Studies* 34 (1988): 339–63, and, "The Path of the Gospel Tradition," in *The Gospel and the Gospels*, 75–96. For important thoughts on, and/or developments of, Gerhardsson's general approach, see B.F. Meyer, "Some Consequences of Birger Gerhardsson's Account of the Origins of the Gospel Tradition," in *Jesus and the Oral Gospel Tradition*, 424–40; Ellis, "Gospels Criticism," 47; idem, "New Directions in Form Criticism," in his *Prophecy and Hermeneutic in Early Christianity: New Testament Essays*, WUNT 18 (Tübingen: Mohr, 1978), 240–41; G. Stanton, "Form Criticism Revisited," in *What About the New Testament? Essays in Honour of Christopher Evans*, ed. M. Hooker and C. Hickling (London: SCM, 1975), 23; and J.D.G. Dunn, *Testing the Foundations: Current Trends in New Testament Study* (Durham: Univ. of Durham, 1984), 16–21. Two other studies that break new ground applying Gerhardsson's insights are, S. Byrskog, *Jesus the Only Teacher: Didactic Authority and Transmission in Ancient Israel, Ancient Judaism and the Matthean Community*, CBNTS 24 (Stockholm: Almqvist & Wiksell, 1994); and F. Zimmermann, *Die urchristlicchen Lehrer: Studien zum Tradentenkreis der didaskaloi im frühen Urchristentum*, WUNT 2:12, 2nd ed. (Tübingen: Mohr, 1988 [1984]). Another important book which argues somewhat along Gerhardsson's lines is the recent *Quaestiones Disputatae* volume by H.-J. Schulz, *Die aposotolische Herkunft der Evangelien*, QD 145 (Freiburg/Basel/Vienna: Herder, 1993). This work, from a liturgical historian in the Eastern Orthodox tradition, challenges the prevailing skepticism regarding the Jesus tradition within critical New Testament studies from presuppositions on down. For a helpful and appreciative review, see W.S. Kurz, S.J., *Catholic Biblical Quarterly* (forthcoming).

31. Riesner, *Jesus als Lehrer*; idem, "Jesus as Preacher and Teacher." For a helpful summary of this material, see C. Blomberg, *The Historical Reliability of*

the Gospels (Downers Grove, Ill.: InterVarsity, 1987), 27–28.

32. See A.B. Lord, *The Singer of Tales* (Cambridge: Harvard Univ. Press, 1960); J. Vansina, *Oral Tradition: A Study in Historical Tradition* (London: Routledge Kegan Paul; Chicago: Aldine, 1965). For a helpful summary of the implications of this work, see Blomberg, *Historical Reliability*, 28–31. See also Schulz, *Die apsotolische Herkunft der Evangelien*, 110–25; L. Alexander, "The Living Voice: Scepticism towards the Written Word in Early Christian and in Graeco-Roman Texts," in *The Bible in Three Dimensions: Essays in Celebration of Forty Years of Biblical Studies in the University of Sheffield, JSOTSS* 87, ed. D.J.A. Clines, S.E. Fowl, and S.E. Porter (Sheffield: JSOT, 1990), 221–47.

33. J. Bradshaw, "Oral Transmission and Human Memory," *Expository Times* 92/10 (1981): 307.

34. W.D. Davies, "Reflections on a Scandinavian Approach to 'The Gospel Tradition,' " in *Neotestamentica et Patristica: Freundesgabe Oscar Cullman, SNT* 6 (Leiden: Brill, 1962), 34.

35. H. Schürmann, "Die vorösterlichen Anfänge der Logientradition," in *Der historische Jesus und der kerygmatische Christus: Beiträge zum Christusverständnis in Forschung und Verkündigung*, ed. H. Ristow and K. Matthiae (Berlin: Evangelische Verlangsanstalt, 1961), 342–70. For a good summary of Schürmann's thesis, see Stein, *Synoptic Problem*, 203–5.

36. Stein, *Synoptic Problem*, 203.

37. For a skeptical view on the issue of eyewitness testimony in the Gospels, see D. Nineham, "Eyewitness Testimony and the Gospel Tradition," *Journal of Theological Studies* 9 (1958): 13–25, 243–52.

38. For a presentation of this position, see the highly influential work of M.E. Boring, *The Continuing Voice of Jesus: Christian Prophecy and the Gospel Tradition*, 2nd rev. ed. (Louisville: Westminster/John Knox, 1991 [1982]).

39. D.E. Aune, *Prophecy in Early Christianity and the Ancient Mediterranean World* (Grand Rapids: Eerdmans, 1983), 245. See also D. Hill, *New Testament Prophecy* (Atlanta: Knox, 1979), 146–85; J.D.G. Dunn, "Prophetic 'I'-Sayings and the Jesus Tradition: The Importance of Testing Prophetic Utterances within Early Christianity," *New Testament Studies* 24 (1978), 175–98.

40. Byrskog's *Jesus the Only Teacher* argues this point extensively. See also, Stein, *Synoptic Problem*, 189–90, and Blomberg, *Historical Reliability*, 31–32.

41. A point many have noted; e.g., see Hanson, "Assessment of Motive in Study of the Synoptic Gospels," 266–67; J.P. Meier, *A Marginal Jew: Rethinking the Historical Jesus*, vol. 1 (New York: Doubleday, 1991), 46.

42. E.g., Ellis, "New Directions in Form Criticism," 243. See also idem, "Gospels Criticism," 39; Riesner, "Jesus as Preacher and Teacher," 196, 203; O. Betz and R. Riesner, *Jesus, Qumran and the Vatican: Clarifications*, trans. J. Bowden (London: SCM, 1994 [1993]), 153–55; Stein, *Synoptic Problem*, 205; J.A. Baird, *Audience Criticism and the Historical Jesus* (Philadelphia: Westminster, 1969), 165–66; R.H. Gundry, *The Use of the Old Testament in St. Matthew's Gospel* (Leiden: Brill, 1967), 181–83; E.J. Goodspeed, *Matthew: Apostle and Evangelist* (Philadelphia: Fortress, 1959), 16–17.

43. Other discoveries, such as the widespread literacy and bilingualism of Palestinian Judaism, have added support to the notion of very early – even pre-Easter – written records behind some of the Jesus traditions. Hence Baird argues that given Jesus' wide audience, from "the most tattered leper to men and women of position . . . the possibilities for literary activity among the disciples becomes enormous." Baird, *Audience Criticism*, 165–66. Baird goes on to conclude that the argument against early literary activity among Jesus' disciples represents "one of the most fatuous examples of special pleading in this whole discussion and needs to be relegated to the limbo reserved for nonscientific methodology" (p. 166).

44. Note, e.g., the reputable Josephus scholar T. Rajack when she argues

that, "as long as what Josephus tells us is *possible*, we have no right to correct it . . ."; and, "If we find no internal grounds for impugning the historian's story, then, in the absence of evidence from the outside, it must have *prima facie* claim on our belief" (T. Rajack, *Josephus: the Historian and His Society* [Philadelphia: Fortress, 1984], 16, 127). If only the Gospels were given this consideration! On the burden of proof question in secular historiography, see L. Gottschalk, *Understanding History: A Primer of Historical Method*, 2nd ed. (New York: Knopf, 1969), 89. For various discussions that support this understanding of the burden of proof question regarding the Gospels, see W. Kümmel, "Jesusforschung seit 1950," *Theologische Rundschau* 31 (1965–1966): 43; idem, "Norman Perrin's 'Rediscovering the Teaching of Jesus,' " *Journal of Religion* 49 (1969): 60–61; Blomberg, *Historical Reliability*, 240–54; R.E. Brown, "After Bultmann, What? – An Introduction to the Post-Bultmannians," *Catholic Biblical Quarterly* 26 (1964): 27; C. Goetz and C. Blomberg, "The Burden of Proof," *Journal for the Study of the New Testament* 11 (1981): 39–63; J. Jeremias, *New Testament Theology*, trans. J. Bowden (London: SCM, 1971), 1:37; I.H. Marshall, *I Believe in the Historical Jesus* (Grand Rapids: Eerdmans, 1977), 199–200; E. Schillebeeckx, *Jesus: An Experiment in Christology*, trans. H. Hoskins (New York: Crossroad, 1991 [1974]), 83; R.H. Stein, "The 'Criteria' for Authenticity," in *Studies of History and Tradition in the Four Gospels*, GP 5, ed. R.T. France and D. Wenham (Sheffield: JSOT, 1980), 227. A middle-of-the-road position has recently emerged that suggests the burden of proof lies with *whoever* makes *any* claim concerning the historicity of an aspect of the Gospel tradition, *one way or the other*. See, e.g., M. Hooker, "Christology and Methodology," *New Testament Studies* 17 (1970–1971): 485; Sanders, *Jesus and Judaism* (Philadelphia: Fortress, 1985), 13. See, however, the discussion by Goetz and Blomberg in "Burden of Proof" concerning the problems of this stance.

45. Funk, et al., *Five Gospels*, 4–5. For others in agreement, see Robinson, *New Quest*, 38–39, n.1; Perrin, *Rediscovering the Teaching of Jesus*, 39ff. See also H.K. McArthur, "The Burden of Proof in Historical Jesus Research," *Expository Times* 82/4 (1971): 116–19, who agrees, but argues that the burden can "shift" in certain circumstances. Incidentally, the now controversial "criterion of dissimilarity," mentioned in chap. 3, is intimately linked to this skeptical bias regarding the burden of proof question. See Goetz and Blomberg, "The Burden of Proof."

46. R.A. Guelich, "The Gospels: Portraits of Jesus and His Ministry," *Journal of the Evangelical Theological Society* 24/2 (1981): 117–25.

47. O. Linton has summarized this last point nicely when he writes, "The evangelists have not arbitrarily rewritten their sources. If they knew only one source they have copied it very faithfully – otherwise there would be no cases of almost total agreement between them. When they deviate from a certain source more or less radically, it is not because they suddenly thought it necessary to rewrite it, but because they used another source, either as it stood or in combination with the 'chief' source. . . ." O. Linton, "The Q-Problem Reconsidered," in *Studies in New Testament and Early Christian Literature: Essays in Honor of Allen P. Wikgren*, SNT 33, ed. D.E. Aune (Leiden: Brill, 1972), 59.

48. Note, e.g., how Rajak works to iron out apparent discrepancies between Josephus' own works and between his account and other sources. See *Josephus the Historian*, 15, 31, 85, 106, 154–55. For helpful, balanced discussions on the issue from the perspective that the Gospels are generally reliable, see C.L. Blomberg, "The Legitimacy and Limits of Harmonization," in Carson and Woodbridge, *Hermeneutics, Authority, and Canon*, 139–74. See also Blomberg, *Historical Reliability*, chaps. 4 and 5; M. Silva, "The Place of Historical Reconstruction in New Testament Criticism," in Carson and Woodbridge, *Hermeneutics, Authority, and Canon*, 109–33.

49. Crossan clearly exhibits his working premise when he argues that, "If you read the four gospels . . . horizontally and comparatively . . . it is disagreement rather than agreement that strikes you most forcibly. And those divergences stem not from the random vagaries of memory and recall but from the coherent and consistent theologies of the individual texts" (*JRB*, x). One who operated from the premise of Gospel reliability could concur that the individual texts sometimes manifest differences even on theological points, but would disagree that it is these sorts of disagreements that "strike you most focibly." For an excellent discussion with ramifications for the handling of Gospel discrepancies throughout the quest, see H. de Jonge, "Loss of Faith in the Historicity of the Gospels." Just as de Jonge demonstrates with regard to Reimarus, so it is the case today that the skeptical questers' claims regarding the irreconcilability of the Gospel accounts derive first and foremost from *a priori* philosophical conclusions, *not* inescapable textual evidence.

50. Our discussion of Mark has positive implications for our assessment of the reliability of Matthew and Luke (assuming, with Mack and Crossan, Markan priority), but not necessarily on the Gospel of John. An investigation of the reliability of John, however, would take us outside the parameters of this study, for this Gospel does not factor centrally into Crossan and Mack's construction of the Cynic thesis. Still, insofar as John can be demonstrated to be a relatively independent reliable witness to the historical Jesus, Crossan and Mack's reconstructed portrait stands further refuted. For a variety of positive assessments regarding John's reliability, see W.F. Albright, "Recent Discoveries in Palestine and the Gospel of John," in *The Background of the New Testament and Its Eschatology*, ed. W.D. Davies and D. Daube (Cambridge: Cambridge Univ. Press, 1959); C. Blomberg, "Problems in the Gospel of John," in his *Historical Reliability*, 153–89; R.E. Brown, "The Problem of Historicity in John," *Catholic Biblical Quarterly* 24 (1962): 1–14; D.A. Carson's excellent essay, "Historical Tradition in the Fourth Gospel: After Dodd, What?" in *Studies of History and Tradition in the Four Gospels, GP* 2, ed. R.T. France and D. Wenham (Sheffield: JSOT, 1981), 83–146; idem, "Historical Tradition in the Fourth Gospel: A Response to J.S. King," *Journal for the Study of the New Testament* 23 (1985): 73–81; idem, *The Gospel According to John* (Grand Rapids: Eerdmans, 1991); C.H. Dodd, *Historical Tradition in the Fourth Gospel* (Cambridge: Cambridge Univ. Press, 1963); L. Morris, "History and Theology in the Fourth Gospel," in his *Studies in the Fourth Gospel* (Grand Rapids: Eerdmans, 1969); J. Murphy-O'Conner, "John the Baptist and Jesus," *New Testament Studies* 36 (1990): 359–74; J.A.T. Robinson, "The New Look on the Fourth Gospel," in his *Twelve New Testament Studies* (Naperville, Ill.: Allenson, 1962), 94–106, as well his groundbreaking work, *The Priority of John*, ed. J.F. Coakley (London: SCM, 1985); D.M. Smith, "Historical Issues and the Problem of John and the Synoptics," in *From Jesus to John*, 252–67. On John as a relatively independent witness to the historical Jesus (a supposition that goes far in accounting for his distinctive style and portrait of Jesus), see, e.g., P.W. Barnett, "The Feeding of the Multitude in Mark 6/John 6," in *The Miracles of Jesus, GP* 6, ed. D. Wenham and C. Blomberg (Sheffield: JSOT, 1986): 273–94; P. Borgen, "John and the Synoptics," in *The Interrelations of the Gospels*, ed. D. Dungan (Leuven, Belgium: Leuven Univ. Press, 1990), 408–37; idem, "The Independence of the Gospel of John: Some Observations," in *The Four Gospels 1992: A Festschrift Frans Neirynck*, 3 vols., ed. F. Van Segbroeck, et al. (Leuven, Belgium: Leuven Univ. Press, 1992), 3:1814–33; R.E. Brown, *The Gospel of John, AB* 29A, 2 vols. (Garden City, N.Y.: Doubleday, 1966, 1970), 1:xliv–vii; H.E. Fagal, "John and the Synoptic Tradition," in *Scripture, Tradition, and Interpretation: Essays Presented to Everett F. Harrison*, ed. W. Ward Gasque and W.S. LaSor (Grand Rapids: Eerdmans, 1978), 127–45; and A.J.B. Higgins, *The Historicity of the Fourth Gospel* (London: Lutterworth, 1960).

Chapter 6: Arguing in Circles and Grasping at Straws

1. For comprehensive critiques, see H.E.W. Turner, *The Pattern of Christian Truth: A Study in the Relations between Orthodoxy and Heresy in the Early Church* (London: Mowbray, 1954); and esp. T.A. Robinson, *The Bauer Thesis Examined: The Geography of Heresy in the Early Christian Church* (Lewiston, N.Y.: Mellen, 1988). See also M. Desjardins, "Bauer and Beyond: On Recent Scholarly Discussions on *Hairesis* in the Early Christian Era," *Second Century* 8 (1991): 65–82.

2. In recent years, a number of scholars along the theological spectrum have called attention to the unity-diversity problematic within early Christianity in general and the New Testament in particular. E.g., see P.J. Achtemeier, *The Quest for Unity in the New Testament Church: A Study in Paul and Acts* (Philadelphia: Fortress, 1987); J.D.G. Dunn, *Unity and Diversity in the New Testament: An Inquiry into the Character of Earliest Christianity*, 2nd ed. (London, SCM; Philadelphia: Trinity, 1990 [1977]); idem, "Earliest Christianity: One Church or Warring Sects?" in his *The Evidence for Jesus* (Philadelphia: Westminster, 1985), 79–102; J. Reumann, *Variety and Unity in New Testament Thought* (Oxford: Oxford Univ. Press, 1991); R.L. Wilken (who, in his first book, very much follows in Bauer's footsteps), *The Myth of Christian Beginnings: History's Impact on Belief* (Garden City, N.Y.: Doubleday, 1971); idem, "Diversity and Unity in Early Christianity," *Second Century* 1/2 (1981): 101–10.

3. I.H. Marshall, "Orthodoxy and Heresy in Earlier Christianity," *Themelios* 2 (1976): 13.

4. See esp. A.J. Hultgren, *The Rise of Normative Christianity* (Minneapolis: Fortress, 1994). For a variety of other discussions that serve to support the contention of an early normative stream of Christian tradition, see D.A. Carson, "Unity and Diversity in the New Testament: The Possibility of Systematic Theology," in *Scripture and Truth*, 2nd ed., ed. D.A. Carson and J.D. Woodbridge (Grand Rapids: Baker, 1992 [1983]), 65–95; Dunn, "Earliest Christianity," 99; W.R. Farmer, *Jesus and the Gospel: Tradition, Scripture, and Canon* (Philadelphia: Fortress, 1982); E.E. Lemcio, "The Unifying Kerygma of the New Testament," *Journal for the Study of the New Testament* (part 1) 33 (1988): 3–17 (part 2) 38 (1990): 3–11; I.H. Marshall, "Jesus, Paul and John," *Aberdeen University Review* 173 (1985): 18–36; idem, "An Evangelical Approach to 'Theological Criticism,' " *Themelios* 13 (April/May 1988): 79–85; idem, "Orthodoxy and Heresy"; J.A. McGuckin, "The Concept of Orthodoxy in Ancient Christianity," *Patristic and Byzantine Review* 8 (1989): 5–23; B.L. Martin, "Some Reflections on the Unity of the New Testament," *Studies in Religion* 8/2 (1979): 143–52; E. Osborn, *The Emergence of Christian Theology* (Cambridge: Cambridge Univ. Press, 1993); H.-J. Schulz, *Die apsotolische Herkunft der Evangelien*; QD 145 (Frieburg/Basel/Vienna: Herder, 1993); E. Schweizer, "The Testimony to Jesus in the Early Christian Community," *Horizons in Biblical Theology* 7 (1985): 77–98; R. Stein, *Synoptic Problem: An Introduction* (Grand Rapids: Baker, 1987), 271–72; R. Williams, "Does It Make Sense to Speak of Pre-Nicene Orthodoxy?" in *The Making of Orthodoxy: Essays in Honour of Henry Chadwick*, ed. R. Williams (Cambridge: Cambridge Univ. Press, 1989), 1–23; W. Willis, "An Irenic View of Christian Origins: Theological Continuity from Jesus to Paul in W.R. Farmer's Writings," in *Jesus, the Gospels, and the Church: Essays in Honor of William R. Farmer*, ed. E.P. Sanders (Macon, Ga.: Mercer Univ. Press, 1987), 265–86.

5. Hultgren, *Rise of Normative Christianity*, 3.

6. Ibid., 53. See also A.J. Hultgren, "The Gospel and the Gospel Traditions in Early Christianity," *Word and World* 11/1 (1991): 23–28; B.F. Meyer, *The Early Christians: Their World Mission and Self-Discovery*, GNS 16 (Wilmington, Del.: Glazier, 1986), 36–39.

7. See M. Hengel, *Between Jesus and Paul* (Philadelphia: Fortress, 1983), chap. 4.

8. For an excellent and exhaustive treatment of this thesis, see R. Hays, *The Faith of Jesus Christ: An Investigation of the Narrative Substructure of Galatians 3:1-4:11*, SBL Dissertation Series (Chicago: Scholars Press, 1983). This point shall be explored more fully in part 4.

9. This is a theme which runs throughout N.T. Wright's *The New Testament and the People of God* (Minneapolis: Fortress, 1992).

10. Again, see C.W. Hedrick, "The Tyranny of the Synoptic Jesus," *Semeia* 44 (1988): 3–8.

11. More than a few scholars have noted this bias in favor of "heretical" streams within the Christian tradition and have noted the dependence of revisionist portraits of Christ on such biases. E.g., see P. Henry, "Why Is Contemporary Scholarship so Enamored of Ancient Heretics?" in *Studia Patristica* 17/1, ed. E.A. Livingstone (Oxford/New York: Pergamon, 1982), 123–26; R.L. Wilken, "The Durability of Orthodoxy," *Word & World* 8/2 (1988): 124–32; P. Meier, *A Marginal Jew: Rethinking the Historical Jesus, Volume 1: The Roots of the Problem and the Person*, ABRL (New York: Doubleday, 1991), 118, 122–23. See also M.J. Edwards, "New Discoveries and Gnosticism: Some Precautions," *Orientalia Christiana Periodica* 55/2 (1989): 257–72. For a balanced discussion of a wide variety of extra-canonical documents, see C.A. Evans, *Noncanonical Writings and New Testament Interpretation* (Peabody, Mass.: Hendrickson, 1992).

12. The late Morton Smith reported that he had found an eighteenth-century copy of a letter of Clement, in which this work was quoted, at the Mar Saba monastery near Jerusalem in 1958. As we shall see, much controversy surrounds both his claim and the import of this cited work. See M. Smith, *Clement of Alexandria and a Secret Gospel of Mark* (Cambridge: Harvard Univ. Press, 1973); idem, *The Secret Gospel: The Discovery and Interpretation of the Secret Gospel According to Mark* (New York: Harper & Row, 1973). For a helpful background discussion to Secret Mark, see S. Levine, "The Early History of Christianity in Light of the 'Secret Gospel' of Mark," in *ANRW* II. 25. 6 (1988): 4270–92.

13. For the initial statement of this position, see H. Koester, "History and Development of Mark's Gospel (From Mark to Secret Mark and 'Canonical' Mark)," in *Colloquy on New Testament Studies: A Time for Reappraisal and Fresh Approaches*, ed. B. Corley (Macon, Ga.: Mercer Univ. Press, 1983), 35–57. See also J.D. Crossan, *Four Other Gospels: Shadows on the Contour of the Canon* (Minneapolis: Winston/Seabury, 1985), 106–10; H. Koester, *Ancient Christian Gospels: Their History and Development* (Philadelphia: Trinity, 1990), 295–303; M.W. Meyer, "The Youth in Secret Mark and the Beloved Disciple in John," in *Gospel Origins and Christian Beginnings: In Honor of James M. Robinson*, ed. J. Goehring, et al. (Sonoma, Calif.: Polebridge, 1990), 94–105; H.M. Schenke, "The Mystery of the Gospel of Mark," *Second Century* 4/2 (1984): 65–82.

14. See R.E. Brown, "The *Gospel of Peter* and Canonical Gospel Priority," *New Testament Studies* 33 (1987): 321–43; J.B. Green, "The Gospel of Peter: Source for a Pre-Canonical Passion Narrative?" *Zeitschrift für die neutestamentliche Wissenschaft* (1987), 293–301; P.M. Head, "On the Christology of the Gospel of Peter," *Vigiliae Christianae* 46 (1992): 209–24; A. Kirk, "Examining Priorities: Another Look at the *Gospel of Peter's* Relationship to the New Testament Gospels," *New Testament Studies* 40 (1994): 572–95; J.W. McCant, "The Gospel of Peter: Docetism Reconsidered," *New Testament Studies* 30 (1984): 258–73; F. Neirynck, "The Apocryphal Gospels and the Gospel of Mark," in *The New Testament in Early Christianity*, BETL 86, ed. J.M. Sevrin (Leuven, Belgium: Leuven Univ. Press, 1989), 140–57; idem, "The Historical Jesus: Reflections on an Inventory," *Ephemerides Theologicae Lovanienses* 70/1

(1994): 226–29; D.F. Wright, "Apocryphal Gospels: The 'Unknown Gospel' (Pap. Egerton 2) and *The Gospel of Peter*," in *The Jesus Tradition Outside the Gospels, GP* 5, ed. D. Wenham (Sheffield: JSOT, 1984), 207–32.

15. See Q. Quesnell, "The Mar Saba Clementine: A Question of Evidence," *Catholic Biblical Quarterly* 37 (1975): 48–67. And see also Smith's reply and Quesnell's rejoinder, *Catholic Biblical Quarterly* 38 (1976): 196–203. Also relevant is Crossan's (*Four Other Gospels*, 101) description of T.J. Talley's frustrated attempt to see the letter at Mar Saba. France reflects an appropriate degree of suspicion regarding Clement's letter when he states, somewhat ironically, "How Clement's letter was preserved from the second or third to the eighteenth century and then lost after the Mar Saba copy was made can only be guessed . . ." (R.T. France, *The Evidence for Jesus* [Downers Grove, Ill.: InterVarsity, 1986], 81).

16. See F.F. Bruce, *The 'Secret' Gospel of Mark* (London: Athlone, 1974); R.M. Grant, "Morton Smith's Two Books," *Anglican Theological Review* 56 (1974): 58–64; Meier, *Marginal Jew*, 120–22; Neirynck, "Apocryphal Gospels and the Gospel of Mark," 168–70; idem, "Reflections on an Inventory," 224–25; France, *Evidence for Jesus*, 82–83. The *conclusions* that Smith drew from Secret Mark regarding the historical Jesus as a homosexual "magician" are so bizarre as to hardly warrant mention. The scholarly consensus – even among those who are sympathetic to the document – has strongly rejected this sort of interpretation. See J.A. Fitzmyer, "How to Exploit a Secret Gospel," *America* 128 (June 23, 1973): 570–72; W. Wink, "Jesus as Magician," *Union Seminary Quarterly Review* 30/1 (1974): 3–14; E.M. Yamauchi, "A Secret Gospel of Jesus as 'Magnus'?: A Review of the Recent Works of Morton Smith," *Christian Scholars Review* 4 (1975): 238–51. Crossan's conclusions from this work, however, are just a bit more guarded than Smith's. He maintains that it was not only the Proto-Carpocratians who interpreted this document in erotic homosexual terms connected with baptism. According to Crossan, the canonical Mark censored this document for this reason. See *HJ*, 329–30.

17. France, *Evidence for Jesus*, 83.

18. W. Schrage, *Das Verhältnis Des Thomas-Evangeliums Zur Synoptischen Tradition Und Zu Den Koptischen Evangelienübersetzungen* (Berlin: Topelmann, 1964). See, e.g., M. Fieger, *Das Thomasevangelium: Einleitung Kommentar und Systematik* (Münster: Aschendorff, 1991).

19. Here, perspectives run from a mixed dependence-independence (assessable only upon a saying-by-saying basis) to strong dependence (as a general thesis) upon the canonical Gospels. See, e.g., C. Blomberg, "Tradition and Redaction in the Parables of the Gospel of Thomas," in *Jesus Tradition Outside the Gospels*, 177–205; B. Chilton, "The Gospel According to Thomas as a Source of Jesus' Teaching," in *Jesus Tradition Outside the Gospels*, 155–75; B. Dehandshutter, "Recent Research on the Gospel of Thomas," in *The Four Gospels 1992: Festschrift Frans Neirynck*, 3 vols., ed. F. Van Segbroeck, et al. (Leuven, Belgium: Leuven Univ. Press, 1992), 3:2257–62; J.E. Menard, *L'Evangile Selon Thomas, NHS* 5 (Leiden: Brill, 1975); Neirynck, "Apocryphal Gospels and the Gospel of Mark," 133–40, 170; K. Snodgrass, "The Gospel of Thomas: A Secondary Gospel," *The Second Century* 7/1 (1989–1990): 19–38; C.M. Tuckett, "Q and Thomas: Evidence of a Primitive 'Wisdom Gospel?' " *Ephemerides Theologicae Lovanienses* 67 (1991): 346–60; idem, "Thomas and the Synoptics," *Novum Testamentum* 30/2 (1988): 132–57.

20. Snodgrass, "Gospel of Thomas," 37–38.

21. See, e.g., G. Quispel, "The *Gospel of Thomas* Revisited," in *Colloque international sur les textes de Nag Hammadi*, ed. B. Barc (Quebec: Laval Univ. Press; Louvain, Belgium: Peeters, 1981), 223. For a historical overview on Gospel of Thomas research, see F. Fallon and R. Cameron, "The Gospel of Thomas: A *Forschungsbericht* and Analysis," *ANRW* 2:25:6 (1988): 4196–4251.

22. E.g., S.L. Davies, *Gospel of Thomas and Christian Wisdom* (New York: Seabury, 1983).

23. E.g., GosThom, 3, 22, 46, 97, 113–14. For a comparison between the Gospels and GosThom, see France, *Evidence for Jesus*, 75ff.

24. Wright, *New Testament and the People of God*, 440.

25. C. Blomberg, *The Historical Reliability of the Gospels* (Downers Grove, Ill.: InterVarsity, 1987), 210.

26. Wright, *New Testament and the People of God*, 440–41.

27. Blomberg, *Historical Reliability*, 212. See Dehandschutter, "Recent Research on Thomas," 2261; P. Perkins, "Pronouncement Stories in the Gospel of Thomas," *Semeia* 20 (1981): 121–32; Snodgrass, "Gospel of Thomas," 27.

28. Dehandschutter, "Recent Research on Thomas," 2258.

29. The following list (though not the surrounding discussion) is taken from M.E. Boring, "The 'First' and 'Lost' Gospel?" a panel paper presented at the SBL Annual Meeting, Q section, 22 November 1993, Washington, D.C.

30. See A. Farrer, "On Dispensing with Q," in *The Two-Source Hypothesis: A Critical Appraisal*, ed. A.J. Bellinzoni (Macon, Ga.: Mercer Univ. Press, 1985), 321–56; M.D. Goulder, *Midrash and Lection in Matthew* (London: SPCK, 1974); idem, *Luke — A New Paradigm*, 2 vols., JSNTSS 20 (Sheffield: JSOT, 1989).

31. See D. Dungan, "Mark — The Abridgement of Matthew and Luke," in *Jesus and Man's Hope*, 1:51–97; Farmer, *The Synoptic Problem: A Critical Analysis* (Dillsboro, N.C.: Western North Carolina, 1976); idem, *The Gospel of Jesus: The Pastoral Relevance of the Synoptic Problem* (Louisville: Westminster/John Knox, 1994); D.B. Orchard, "The Formation of the Synoptic Gospels," *Downside Review* 106 (1988): 1–16. See also T.R. Rosche, "The Words of Jesus and the Future of the 'Q' Hypothesis," *Journal of Biblical Literature* 79 (1960): 210–20.

32. See B. Reike, *The Roots of the Synoptic Gospels* (Philadelphia: Fortress, 1986); J. Wenham, *Redating Matthew, Mark and Luke: A Fresh Assault on the Synoptic Problem* (London: Hodder & Stoughton, 1991); E. Linnemann, *Is There a Synoptic Problem? Rethinking the Literary Dependence of the First Three Gospels* (Grand Rapids: Baker, 1992). On this point see also S. Byrskog, *Jesus the Only Teacher: Didactic Authority and Transmission in Ancient Israel, Ancient Judaism and the Matthean Community*, CENTS 24 (Stockholm: Almqvist & Wiksell, 1994), 337–38; and F. Zimmerman, *Die urchristlichen Lehrer: Studien zum Tradentenkreis der didaskaloi im frühen Urchristentum*, WUNT 2:12, 2nd ed. (Tübingen: Mohr, 1988 [1984]).

33. Neither Crossan nor Mack ever take seriously the hypothetical nature of Q in the light of these scholarly arguments. Mack provides a brief overview of historical obstacles that the Q hypothesis had to overcome (*LG*, 15–27), but does not investigate contemporary objections and hence carries out his work on the ostensive assumption that all obstacles to the thesis have been overcome. The existence of Q thus functions as a starting *assumption* for both Crossan and Mack. But the view of Jesus and the earliest Jesus communities they construct can never be more certain than the questionable foundation they build it upon. Indeed, as we shall see, with each layer of the building it becomes even *less* certain.

34. *LG*, 71, see also 73–102.

35. Ibid., 1.

36. See respectively M.E. Boring, *The Continuing Voice of Jesus: Christian Prophecy and the Gospel Tradition*, 2nd ed. (Louisville: Westminster/John Knox, 1991 [1982]), 191–234; R. Horsley, "Logoi Propheton? Reflections on the Genre of Q," in *The Future of Early Christianity: Essays in Honor of Helmut Koester*, ed. B. Pearson (Minneapolis: Fortress, 1991), 198; idem, "Wisdom Justified by All Her Children: Examining Allegedly Disparate Traditions in Q," in *SBLSP 1994*, ed. E.H. Lovering, Jr. (Atlanta: Scholars, 1994), 733–51.

37. Jacobson, *First Gospel*, 48–51. Others have questioned the scope and

setting of the Near Eastern sayings collections by which Kloppenborg compared Q in terms of genre and from which he constructed his Q-1 hypothesis. See R. Hodgson, Jr., review of Kloppenborg's *Formation of Q, Biblica* 70 (1989): 285.

38. H.M. Humphrey, "Temptation and Authority: Sapiential Narratives in Q," *Biblical Theology Bulletin* 21/2 (1991): 47. See also A.Y. Collins' review of Kloppenborg's *Formation of Q, Catholic Biblical Quarterly* 50 (1988): 722.

39. Wright, *New Testament and the People of God*, 439. For similar conclusions, see J. Collins, "Wisdom, Apocalyptic, and Generic Compatibility," in *In Search of Wisdom: Essays in Memory of John G. Gammie*, ed. L.G. Perdue, B.B. Scott, and W.J. Wisemann (Louisville: Westminster/John Knox, 1993), 182; Horsley, "Wisdom Justified by All Her Children"; G.W.E. Nickelsburg, "Wisdom and Apocalyptic in Early Judaism: Some Points for Discussion," in *SBLSP* 1994, 715–32. The compatibility of sapiential and apocalyptic categories will be addressed more fully below.

40. Koester in particular argues in this fashion. See, e.g., his *Ancient Christian Gospels: Their History and Development* (London: SCM; Philadelphia: Trinity, 1990), 137.

41. See Wright, *New Testament and the People of God*, 438–40.

42. *LG*, 106.

43. Ibid., 108.

44. Ibid., 111.

45. Ibid., 131.

46. For other critiques of the triple-layered Q, see R. Horsley, "Questions about Redactional Strata and the Social Relations Reflected in Q," in *SBLSP* 1989, ed. D.J. Lull (Atlanta: Scholars, 1989), 186–203; C.M. Tuckett, "On the Stratification of Q: A Response," *Semeia* 55 (1992), 213–22. For Kloppenborg's response to Horsley, see *"The Formation of Q Revisited: A Response to Richard Horsley,"* in *SBLSP* 1989, 204–15. See also M.D. Hooker's insightful comments regarding the way in which methodological presuppositions often drive redactional practices and their conclusions, "In His Own Image?" in *What about the New Testament? Essays in Honour of Christopher Evans*, ed. M.D. Hooker and C.J. Hooker (London: SCM, 1975), 28–44.

47. The work of Migaku Sato and David Catchpole is especially noteworthy in this regard. M. Sato, *Q und Prophetie: Studien zur Gattungs- und Traditionsgeschichte der Quelle Q, WUNT* 2:29 (Tübingen: Mohr, 1988); idem, "The Shape of the Q-Source," in *The Shape of Q: Signal Essays on the Sayings Source*, ed. J.S. Kloppenborg (Minneapolis: Fortress, 1994), 156–79; D.R. Catchpole, *The Quest for Q* (Edinburgh: T & T Clark, 1993); idem, "The Beginning of Q: A Proposal," *New Testament Studies* 38 (1992): 205–21; idem, "The Question of Q," *Sewanee Theological Review* 36/1 (1992): 33–44.

48. In addition to the works mentioned in chap. 2, see C.E. Carlston, "On 'Q' and the Cross," in *Scripture, Tradition, and Interpretation: Essays Presented to Everett F. Harrison*, ed. W.W. Gasque and W.S. LaSor (Grand Rapids: Eerdmans, 1978), 27–33.

49. Farmer, *Gospel of Jesus*, 163–73. See also, idem, "The Church's Stake in the Question of 'Q,' " *Perkins Journal* 39 (1986): 9–19. Kloppenborg ("Theological Stakes in the Synoptic Problem," in *The Four Gospels 1992: Festschrift Frans Neirynck*, 3 vols., ed. F. Van Segbroeck, et al. [Leuven, Beglium: Leuven Univ. Press, 1992], 1:93–120) has emphasized the same sort of ramifications, from the other side of the debate.

50. *LG*, 4–5.

51. Hultgren, *Rise of Normative Christianity*, 53.

52. See R. Leivestad, *Jesus in His Own Perspective: An Examination of His Sayings, Actions, and Eschatological Titles*, trans. D.E. Aune (Minneapolis: Augsburg, 1987 [1982]), 19; E. Schweizer, *Jesus Christ: The Man from Nazareth and*

the Exalted Lord (Macon, Ga.: Mercer Univ. Press, 1987), 32; idem, "Testimony to Jesus," 96; G.N. Stanton, "On the Christology of Q," in *Christ and the Spirit in the New Testament: Festschrift C.F.D. Moule*, ed. B. Lindars and S.S. Smalley (Cambridge: Cambridge Univ. Press, 1973), 41–42.

53. Stanton, "Christology of Q," 42. See also M. Hengel, *The Son of God: The Origin of Christology and the History of Jewish-Hellenistic Religion*, trans. J. Bowden (Philadelphia: Fortress, 1976 [1975]), 75, n.132; M. de Jonge, *Christology in Context: The Earliest Christian Response to Jesus* (Philadelphia: Westminster, 1988), 83–84; Kümmel, *Introduction to the New Testament*, ed. and trans. H. Kee (Nashville: Abingdon, 1975 [1973]), 73; P. Pokorny, *The Genesis of Christology: Foundations for a Theology of the New Testament* (Edinburgh: T & T Clark, 1987), 90; A. Polag, "The Theological Center of the Sayings Source," in *The Gospel and the Gospels*, ed. P. Stuhlmacher, trans. J. Bowden (Grand Rapids: Eerdmans, 1991 [1983]), 101–2; O.H. Steck, *Israel und das gewaltsame Geschick der Propheten*, WMANT 23 (Neukirchen-Vluyn: Neukirchener, 1967), 288.

54. Hultgren, *Rise of Normative Christianity*, 33–35; see also idem, *Christ and His Benefits: Christology and Redemption in the New Testament* (Philadelphia: Fortress, 1987), 20–21.

55. E.P. Meadors, "The Orthodoxy of the 'Q' Sayings of Jesus," *Tyndale Bulletin* 43/2 (1992): 255.

56. M. Peel, "The Resurrection in Recent Scholarly Research," *Bible Review* 4 (1989): 21.

57. Downing is an exception here, for he tries to argue that both Jesus and some Cynics were eschatological. He argues, e.g., that Mack has unjustifiably used the Cynic thesis to divest the historical Jesus and Q-1 Christians of "all eschatology" (review of Mack's *A Myth of Innocence*, *Theology* 92 [1989]: 331). He claims to have discovered "Cynic parallels with much of the synoptic apocalyptic material" (p. 331). When, however, one turns to Downing's own sourcebook of early Christian-Cynic parallels (*Christ and the Cynics: Jesus and Other Radical Preachers in First-Century Tradition*, JSOTM 4 [Sheffield: JSOT, 1988]), one finds that he has significant problems coming up with any substantive Cynic analogues! Strangely enough, Downing himself finally admits this: "The Jewish and other early Christian parallels are clearly the more striking. . . . [Eschatology] is one of a limited number of areas where these early Christians may well have seemed least like other Cynics" (p. 9). At another point, Downing notes three strands of thought in early Christianity for which Cynic parallels "failed to emerge . . . miracle, eschatology and 'christology' " (p. 196). This failure coincides with T.F. Glasson's inability to locate any truly viable Hellenistic parallels for the Jewish idea of "a final decisive victory for the God of righteousness, as distinct from cycles of repetition"; see his *Greek Influence in Jewish Eschatology* (London: SPCK, 1961), 75, see also 79–80, 83. In a recent article, Downing refers to two forthcoming articles in which he will apparently argue that an eschatological worldview was fairly common to the first-century East Mediterranean world at large. Downing, "A Genre for Q and a Socio-Cultural Context for Q: Comparing Sets of Similarities with Sets of Differences," *Journal for the Study of the New Testament* 55 [1994]: 22, n.61. One will have to wait and see, though it is difficult to imagine how this will be accomplished.

58. Funk, et al., *Five Gospels*, 4.

59. Charlesworth, "Jesus Research Expands with Chaotic Creativity," in *Images of Jesus Today*, ed. J.H. Charlesworth and W.F. Weaver (Valley Forge, Pa.: Trinity, 1994), 10.

60. For a sampling of scholars who argue that Jesus had a future-oriented eschatology, see D.C. Allison, *The End of the Ages Has Come: An Early Interpretation of the Passion and Resurrection of Jesus* (Philadelphia: Fortress,

1985); G.R. Beasley-Murray, *Jesus and the Kingdom* (Grand Rapids: Eerdmans, 1986); N. Cohn, *Cosmos, Chaos and the World to Come: The Ancient Roots of Apocalyptic Faith* (New Haven: Yale Univ. Press, 1993), 195; J.D.G. Dunn, "Spirit and Kingdom," *Expository Times* 8 (1970–1971): 36–40; R.H. Fuller, "Jesus, Paul and Apocalyptic," *Anglican Theological Review* 71/2 (1989): 134–42; R.H. Hiers, *The Historical Jesus and the Kingdom of God: Present and Future in the Message and Ministry of Jesus* (Gainesville, Fla.: Univ. of Florida Press, 1973); B.F. Meyer, "Jesus' Scenario of the Future," in his *Christus Faber: The Master-Builder and the House of God, PTMS* 29 (Allison Park, Pa.: Pickwick, 1992), 41–58; J.C. O'Neill, *Messiah: Six Lectures on the Ministry of Jesus* (Cambridge: Cochrane, 1980), 26; J.R. Michaels, "The Kingdom of God and the Historical Jesus," in *The Kingdom of God in 20th-Century Interpretation*, ed. W. Willis (Peabody, Mass.: Hendrickson, 1987), 109–18; E. Schweizer, "The Significance of Eschatology in the Teachings of Jesus," in *Eschatology and the New Testament: Essays in Honor of George Raymond Beasley-Murray*, ed. W.H. Gloer (Peabody, Mass.: Hendrickson, 1988), 3; D. Tiede, *Jesus and the Future* (Cambridge: Cambridge Univ. Press, 1990); B. Wiebe, "The Focus of Jesus' Eschatology," in *Self-Definition and Self-Discovery in Early Christianity*, 121–46; B. Witherington III, *Jesus, Paul and the End of the World: A Comparative Study in New Testament Eschatology* (Downers Grove, Ill.: InterVarsity, 1992). Unfortunately, it appears that the word "consensus" has become a tool for argument (based upon a democratic "majority rules" mind-set?), rather than a term reflecting a carefully established conclusion. Neither side of the debate does the field of New Testament scholarship a service by claiming as settled issues that are so obviously in dispute.

61. E.g., the following scholars, a group which would include Bultmann himself, are representative of that school of thought which sees either all or some of the coming Son of Man sayings as authentic to Jesus. F.H. Borsch, *The Son of Man in Myth and History* (London: SCM, 1967); C. Caragounis, *The Son of Man: Vision and Interpretation, WUNT* 38 (Tübingen: Mohr, 1986); O. Cullman, *The Christology of the New Testament* (London: SCM, 1959); R.H. Gundry, *Mark: A Commentary on His Apology for the Cross* (Grand Rapids: Eerdmans, 1993); M. Hooker, *The Son of Man in Mark: A Study of the Background of the Term "Son of Man" and Its Use in St. Mark's Gospel* (London: SPCK, 1967); S. Kim, *The "Son of Man" as the Son of God, WUNT* 30 (Tübingen: Mohr, 1983); I.H. Marshall, "The Synoptic 'Son of Man' Sayings," in *To Tell the Mystery: Essays on New Testament Eschatology in Honor of Robert H. Gundry*, ed. T.E. Schmidt and M. Silva, *JSNTSS* 100 (Sheffield: JSOT, 1994), 72–94; C.D.F. Moule, "Neglected Features in the Problem of 'Son of Man,' " in *Neues Testament und Kirche: für Rudolf Schnackenburg*, ed. J. Gnilka (Frieburg: Herder, 1974), 413–28; Witherington, *Jesus, Paul and the End of the World*, 170–77. See also C.M. Tuckett, "The Son of Man in Q," in *From Jesus to John: Essays on Jesus and New Testament Christology in Honour of Marinus de Jonge*, ed. M.C. de Boer, *JSNTSS* 84 (Sheffield: JSOT, 1993), 196–215, who further argues that the future Son of Man sayings are found in every layer of Q. This view is also argued by A.Y. Collins, "The Son of Man Sayings in the Sayings Source," in *To Touch the Text: Biblical and Related Studies in Honor of Joseph A. Fitzmyer, S.J.*, ed. M. Horgan and P.J. Kobelski (New York: Crossroad, 1989), 369–89.

62. See Funk, "Call for a Canon Council," *Fourth R* (May/June 1993): 13; J.J. Carey, "Apocalypticism as a Bridge Between the Testaments," in *The Old and the New Testaments: Their Relationship and the "Intertestamental" Literature*, ed. J.H. Charlesworth and W.P. Weaver (Valley Forge, Pa.: Trinity, 1993), 97–103; R. Helms, "The Dangers of Apocalyptic Thinking," *Free Inquiry* (Summer 1984): 36–38. A.Y. Collins has chided Mack for his "unsympathetic and romantic view of apocalypticism." See her review of *Myth of Innocence* in *Journal of Biblical Literature* 108 (1989): 727. The point concerning the apocalyptic,

supernatural Jesus as an ongoing embarrassment to the academic community – and thus as a view which many endlessly try to avoid – was strongly emphasized by Paula Fredriksen in her recent lecture, "What You See Is What You Get: Context and Content in Current Research on the Historical Jesus," *Frontiers in Biblical Scholarship Series*, AAR/SBL Annual Meeting, 20 November 1994, Chicago, Illinois.

63. See, e.g., J.C. Beker, "The Promise of Paul's Apocalyptic for Our Time," in *The Future of Christology: Essays in Honor of Leander E. Keck*, ed. A.J. Malherbe and W. Meeks (Minneapolis: Fortress, 1993), 159. Interestingly, even J.M. Robinson has expressed a similar recognition. See his "Jesus as an Apocalypticist," *Free Inquiry* (Summer 1984): 47–49. See also R.J. Bauckham, "The Rise of Apocalyptic," *Themelios* 3/2 (1978): 10–23; P.B. Decock, "The Eclipse and Rediscovery of Eschatology," *Neotestamentica* 22 (1988): 5–16; K. Koch, *The Rediscovery of Apocalyptic*, trans. M. Kohl (London: SCM, 1972 [1970]); A. Koenig, *The Eclipse of Christ in Eschatology: Toward a Christ-Centered Approach* (Grand Rapids: Eerdmans, 1989 [1980]); A. Wilder, "The Eschatology of Jesus in Recent Criticism and Interpretation," *Journal of Religion* 28/3 (1948): 184–85.

64. James Williams raises this issue with regard to the post-Bultmannian "discovery" of a non-eschatological Jesus when he writes, "The element of ideology at work here, in my opinion, is that it is much easier to "save the text" (or *some* texts) and reinterpret the tradition if one comes up with a non-eschatological Jesus who is more congenial to the social location and professional functioning of the biblical scholar." J.G. Williams, "Neither Here Nor There: Between Wisdom and Apocalyptic in Jesus' Kingdom Sayings," *Foundations and Facets Forum* 5/2 (1989): 26. See also A. Buzzard, "The Kingdom of God in the Twentieth-Century Discussion of Scripture," *Evangelical Quarterly* 64/2 (1992): 99–115; D.J. Hawkin, "The Markan Horizon of Meaning," in *Self-Definition and Self-Discovery in Early Christianity*, 27–30; Wilder, "The Eschatology of Jesus," 182; Wright, *New Testament and People of God*, 298–99.

65. I.H. Marshall notes no less than nine shades of meaning in "Slippery Words: I. Eschatology," *Expository Times* 90 (1978): 267. See also R.E. Sturm, "Defining the Word 'Apocalyptic': A Problem in Biblical Criticism," in *Apocalyptic and the New Testament: Essays in Honor of J. Louris Martyn*, ed. J. Marcus and M.L. Soards, *JSNTSS* 24 (Sheffield: JSOT, 1989), 17–48; D. Hellholm, "Introduction," in *Apocalypticism in the Mediterranean World and the Near East*, ed. D. Hellholm (Tübinger: Mohr, 1983), 2.

66. See, e.g., M. Borg, *Jesus in Contemporary Scholarship* (Valley Forge, Pa.: Trinity, 1994), 47 (emphasis added), see also 73–74, 88. There is also much discussion about what "the end of history" which apocalyptic thought anticipates entails. Is it to be taken literally, or does it rather entail the beginning of a new *kind* of world order, as N.T. Wright has (very persuasively) argued? See Wright, *New Testament and the People of God*, 252–53, 280–99, 392–96, 459–64.

67. Unless, of course, his apocalypticism is de-mythologized and given an existential interpretation, as with Bultmann.

68. On the "already-but not yet" or "inaugurated" eschatology, see G. Florovsky, "The Patristic Age and Eschatology: An Introduction," in his *Collected Works, Volume 4: Aspects of Church History* (Belmont, Mass.: Nordland, 1975), 63–78; G.E. Ladd, *The Presence of the Future: The Eschatology of Biblical Realism* (Grand Rapids: Eerdmans, 1974). For a variety of helpful works that highlight Jesus' eschatology – and/or that of the wider New Testament – within this general vein, see Buzzard, "Kingdom of God"; Fuller, "Jesus, Paul and Apocalyptic"; Hawkin, "Markan Horizon of Meaning"; Meyer, "Jesus' Scenario of the Future"; R.H. Stein, *The Method and Message of Jesus' Teachings* (Philadelphia: Westminster, 1978), 68–79; Wiebe, "Focus of Jesus' Eschatolo-

gy," and Witherington, *Jesus, Paul and the End of the World*.

69. In addition to the sources noted previously, see R. Horsley, "The Q People: Renovation, Not Radicalism," *Continuum* 1/3 (1991): 49–63.

70. In "The Q People: Renovation, Not Radicalism," Horsley wonders aloud whether "the attractiveness of the 'stratigraphy' in Q [lies] in the possibility it offers for rescuing the earliest stratum of Jesus-sayings from apocalyptic elements so distasteful to modern sensibilities" (p. 54). Similarly, W. Kelber (review of Mack's *Myth of Innocence, Catholic Biblical Quarterly* 52 [1990]:163) suggests that "the nonapocalyptic, e.g., nonmythological Jesus" — rooted in "the slim and contestable base of 'the earliest layer of Q' " – is little more than "another myth of origin created by modern predilections." Wright suspects the same, and expands it to encompass the post-Bultmannian preference for GosThom in *New Testament and the People of God*, 439.

71. E.g., C. Mearns demonstrates how one can read the apocalyptic in Q as "later," and yet still understand Jesus as fundamentally apocalyptic. "Realized Eschatology in Q? A Consideration of the sayings in Luke 7.22, 11.20 and 16.16," *Scottish Journal of Theology* 40 (1987): 189–210.

72. H. Koester, "The Historical Jesus and the Historical Situation of the Quest: An Epilogue," in *Studying the Historical Jesus: Evaluations of the State of Current Research*, ed. B. Chilton and C.A. Evans, *NTTS* 16 (Leiden/New York: Brill, 1994), 541.

73. Kloppenborg, *The Formation of Q: Trajectories in Ancient Wisdom Collection* (Philadelphia: Fortress, 1987), 244.

74. Nor could Cynic theorists employ Kloppenborg as a means of arriving at their view of the historical Jesus. While Mack seems wholly unaware of the jump he assumes (against Kloppenborg's judgment) from document to history, Crossan is aware of it (e.g., see *HJ*, 229–30), but uses Kloppenborg's work to argue against an apocalyptic historical Jesus nonetheless.

75. Patterson recognizes this polemical aspect in Thomas, but then apparently decides in favor of an original realized/non-apocalyptic eschatology; see *Gospel of Thomas and Jesus* (Sonoma, Calif.: Polebridge, 1993), 212. Such a position, however, is less able to account for the *polemical* tone in question.

76. E.g., see P.W. Hollenbach, "The Conversion of Jesus: From Jesus the Baptizer to Jesus the Healer," in *ANRW* 2.25.1 (1982): 196–219; W.B. Tatum, *John the Baptist and Jesus: A Report of the Jesus Seminar* (Sonoma, Calif.: Polebridge, 1994). The supposition seems plausible only if one accepts a strict double dissimilarity criterion. Few, however, are willing to accept this any longer, though the Jesus/John split speculation seems to be growing in popularity among post-Bultmannians. On the double dissimilarity criterion, see Fuller, "Jesus, Paul and Apocalyptic," 140.

77. Ben Wiebe writes: "Both from the connection to John and to the early church we would expect that in some basic way 'near expectation' marked the message and mission of Jesus" ("Focus of Jesus' Eschatology," 134). See also C. Burchard, "Jesus of Nazareth," in *Christian Beginnings: Word and Community from Jesus to Post-Apostolic Times*, ed. J. Becker, trans. A.S. Kidder and R. Krauss (Louisville Westminster/John Knox, 1993 [1987]), 24–43; A.Y. Collins, "Jesus the Prophet," *Biblical Research* 36 (1991): 30–34; B.F. Meyer, "Appointed Deed, Appointed Doer: Jesus and the Scriptures," in his *Christus Faber*, 64–65.

78. Crossan denies that Jesus ever used the phrase "Son of Man" as a title (e.g., *JRB*, 50–51), though he probably used it in "a generic sense" as being equivalent to "child of humanity." His reason for thinking this is that "*there is only a single instance where two independent sources have the expression in more than a single version*" (*JRB*, 50, emphasis in text). Here, Crossan's criteria for authenticity, I would argue, are overly strict, and his judgments concerning source relations (e.g., independent attestations) are problematic (see chap. 3).

79. By means of this dichotomy the following syllogism is derived, which works beautifully for the Cynic-Jesus thesis: (1) either apocalyptic prophet or subversive sage; (2) not apocalyptic prophet; (3) therefore, subversive sage. E.g., see Mack, *MI*, 67; Crossan, *HJ*, 282–92. But the conclusion only follows if one accepts the original (false) dichotomy, a point to be discussed further in the next chapter.

80. So argues J.J. Collins, summarizing the extant literature, "There is no necessary antithesis between 'apocalyptic' and 'sapiential.' " "Wisdom, Apocalyptic, and Generic Compatibility," in *In Search of Wisdom: Essays in Memory of John G. Gammie*, ed. L.G. Perdue, B.B. Scott, and W.J. Wiseman (Louisville: Westminster/John Knox, 1993), 182. This is a point that even Koester ("Historical Situation of the Quest," 543) acknowledges. See the several relevant essays in J.G. Gammie and L.G. Perdue, eds., *The Sage in Israel and the Ancient Near East* (Winona Lake, Ind.: Eisenbrauns, 1990); E.E. Johnson, "Wisdom and Apocalyptic in Paul," in *In Search of Wisdom*, 263–83; B.B. Scott, "The Gospel of Matthew: A Sapiential Performance of an Apocalyptic Discourse," in *In Search of Wisdom*, 245–62; G. Theissen, *The Miracle Stories of the Early Christian Tradition*, ed. J. Riches, trans. F. McDonagh (Philadelphia: Fortress, 1 983 [1974]), 280; J.A. Trumbower, "The Historical Jesus and the Speech of Gamaliel (Acts 5.35-39)," *New Testament Studies* 39 (1993): 517; W.S. Vorster, "Jesus: Eschatological Prophet and/or Wisdom Teacher," *Hervormde Teologiese Studies* 47/1 (1991): 526–42; Williams, "Neither Here Nor There," 27–29. Note as well B. Witherington, *Jesus the Sage: The Pilgrimage of Wisdom* (Minneapolis: Fortress, 1994); Horsely, "Wisdom Justified by All Her Children"; and Nickelsburg, "Wisdom and Apocalyptic in Early Judaism," against, e.g., Cameron, "*Gospel of Thomas* and Christian Origins," 390–91. One can see Borg, given his tensive affinities for both themes, struggling with this question (e.g., sage vs. prophet) in his "Luke 19:42-44 and Jesus as Prophet?" *Foundations and Facets Forum* 8/1-2 (1992): 99–112.

81. On Jesus as prophet in the Jewish tradition, see H. Anderson, "Jesus: Aspects of the Question of His Authority," in *The Social World of Formative Christianity and Judaism: Essays in Tribute to Howard Clark Kee*, ed. J. Neusner, et al. (Philadelphia: Fortress, 1988), 304; Burchard, "Jesus of Nazareth," 36; Collins, "Jesus the Prophet"; Horsley, "Q and Jesus," 206–9; P. Perkins, *Jesus as Teacher* (Cambridge: Cambridge Univ. Press, 1990), 30–31; E.P. Sanders, *The Historical Figure of Jesus* (London: Lane/Penguin, 1993), 238; G.N. Stanton, *The Gospels and Jesus* (Oxford: Oxford Univ. Press, 1989), 177–88; N.T. Wright, *Jesus and Victory of God* (Minneapolis: Fortress, forthcoming); and R.D. Kaylor, *Jesus the Prophet: His Vision of the Kingdom of Earth* (Louisville: Westminster/John Knox, 1994).

82. The Jesus Seminar, which generally endorses a non-eschatological Jesus while affirming that he was an exorcist, is a good example of this. See *The Fourth R* 5/3 (May 1992) which is devoted to this discussion. At least one member of the seminar, however, has affirmed the connection between Jesus' exorcisms and eschatology. See J.J. Rousseau "Jesus, an Exorcist of a Kind," in *SBLSP* 1993, 151. On this connection, see especially G. Twelftree, *Jesus the Exorcist: A Contribution to the Study of Jesus*, WUNT 2:54 (Tübingen: Mohr, 1993; Peabody, Mass.: Hendrikson, 1994); also C.A. Evans, "From Public Ministry to the Passion: Can a Link Be Found Between the (Galilean) Life and the (Judean) Death of Jesus?" in *SBLSP* 1993, 464–65; R.H. Hiers, "Jesus as Demon-Exorcist: Overpowering Satan," in his *Jesus and the Future: Unresolved Questions for Understanding and Faith* (Atlanta: Knox, 1981), 62–71; idem, *The Kingdom of God in the Synoptic Tradition* (Gainesville, Fla.: Univ. of Florida Press, 1970), 3–9; Horsley, "Q and Jesus," 193, 198–99; J. Kallas' fascinating work, The *Significance of the Synoptic Miracles* (Greenwich, Conn.: Seabury, 1961); J.R. Michaels, "Jesus and the Unclean Spirits," in *Demon Possession*, ed.

J.W. Montgomery (Minneapolis: Bethany, 1976), 41–57; J.J. Rousseau, "Jesus, an Exorcist of a Kind"; Theissen, *Miracle Stories*, 277–80; and Gregory A. Boyd, *Satan and the Problem of Evil* (Downers Grove, Ill.: InterVarsity, forthcoming).

83. Twelftree, *Jesus the Exorcist*, 224 (emphasis in text). Theissen concurs: "He combines two conceptual worlds which had never been combined in this way before, the apocalyptic expectation of universal salvation in the future and the episodic realization of salvation in the present through miracles" *(Miracle Stories, 278).*

Chapter 7: Stretching a Thin Thread Thinner

1. J.S. Kloppenborg, *The Formation of Q: Trajectories in Ancient Wisdom Collections* (Philadelphia: Fortress, 1987), 244. See the discussion in the previous chapter.

2. H.W. Attridge, "Reflections on Research into Q," *Semeia* 55 (1992), 233.

3. Though he admits that his stratification is "crude," Crossan is confident that GosThom I (viz., the earliest strata) "was composed by the fifties C.E., possibly in Jerusalem, under the aegis of James's authority. . . . After his martyrdom in 62 C.E., the collection and maybe also its community, migrated to Syrian Edessa. There a second layer was added, possibly as early as the sixties or seventies, under the aegis of the Thomas authority. . . . The collection is independent of the intracanonical Gospels. . . " *(HJ, 427).* All of this reads like straightforward history, but it is sheer speculation.

4. N.T. Wright, *The New Testament and the People of God* (Minneapolis: Fortress, 1992), 439.

5. The historical work of Martin Hengel has played an important role in this reassessment. See M. Hengel, *Judaism and Hellenism: Studies in Their Encounter in Palestine During the Early Hellenistic Period,* 2 vols., trans. J. Bowden (Philadelphia: Fortress, 1974); idem, *The "Hellenization" of Judea in the First Century After Christ,* trans. J. Bowden (Philadelphia: Trinity; London: SCM, 1989). For other important studies on the issue, see S. Freyne, *Galilee, From Alexander the Great to Hadrian 323 B.C.E. to 135 C.E.: A Study of Second Temple Judaism* (Wilmington, Del.: Glazier; Notre Dame, Ind.: Univ. of Notre Dame Press, 1980); idem, *Galilee, Jesus and the Gospels: Literary Approaches and Historical Investigations* (Philadelphia: Fortress, 1988); E.M. Meyers, "Galilean Regionalism: A Reappraisal," *Approaches to Ancient Judaism,* vol. 5, ed. W.S. Green (Missoula, Mont.: Scholars, 1978), 115–31; idem, "Galilean Regionalism as a Factor of Historical Reconstruction," *ASOR Bulletin* #221 (Fall 1976): 93–101; idem, "The Cultural Setting of Galilee: The Case of Regionalism and Early Judaism," *ANRW* 2.19.1 (1979): 686–701; E.M. Meyers and J.F. Strange, *Archaeology, the Rabbis and Early Christianity* (Nashville: Abingdon, 1981), esp. 26, 42–43, 65, 78–88; D. Edwards, "The Socio-Economic and Cultural Ethos of the Lower Galilee in the First Century: Implications for the Nascent Jesus Movement," in *The Galilee in Late Antiquity,* ed. L.I. Levine (New York/Jerusalem: Jewish Theological Seminary of America; Cambridge: Harvard Univ. Press, 1992), 53–73. Most scholars consider Upper Galilee to have been significantly less influenced by Hellenism than the Lower region. See, e.g., Meyers and Strange, *Archaeology,* 26–27, 42–43; Meyers, "Ancient Synagogues in Galilee: Their Religious and Cultural Setting," *Biblical Archaeologist* 43 (Spring 1980): 97–108.

6. See E.M. Meyer, "Roman Sepphoris in Light of New Archaeological Evidence and Recent Research," in *Galilee in Late Antiquity,* 321–38; idem, "Sepphoris: Ornament of All Galilee," *Biblical Archaeologist* 49/1 (1986): 4–19; R.A. Batey, *Jesus and the Forgotten City: New Light on Sepphoris and the Urban*

World of Jesus (Grand Rapids: Baker, 1991).

7. See Batey, *Jesus and the Forgotten City.* Both Mack (*MI*, 65–67) and Crossan (*HJ*, 15–19) have emphasized this view in constructing their Cynic Jesus.

8. E.g., Eric Meyers, one of the world's leading archaeologists with regard to ancient Galilee and codirector of the Joint Sepphoris Excavation Project for several years, has recently pointed out the need for caution in drawing conclusions from the available evidence. The question of the nature of first-century Galilee, he maintains, ". . . will be answered conclusively only in the course of time when, after considerable excavation, a large enough corpus of early material is finally available for evaluation." Meyer, "Cultural Setting of Galilee," 689. See also idem, "Identifying Religious and Ethnic groups through Archaeology," in *Biblical Archaeology Today, 1990: Proceedings of the Second International Conference on Biblical Archaeology,* ed. A. Biran and J. Aviram (Jerusalem: Israel Exploration Society, 1990), 738–45. Although both Crossan and Mack utilize Meyer's work significantly in arguing their case (e.g., Mack, *MI*, 66, n.9; Crossan, *HJ*, 19), neither show the type of tentativeness in their conclusions that Meyers himself calls for. On the tentativeness of the available data, see also Freyne, *Galilee, From Alexander,* 141; D.E. Groh, review article of Meyers and Strange's *Archaeology, the Rabbis, and Early Christianity, Anglican Theological Review* 64/3 (1982): 396; S. Herbert, "The Greco-Phoenician Settlement at Tel Anafa: A Case Study in the Limits of Hellenization," in *Biblical Archaeology Today, 1990,* 118–25.

9. See S. Applebaum, "Judea as a Roman Province: The Countryside as a Political and Economic Factor," in *ANRW* 2.8 (1977): 371; S. Freyne, "Urban-Rural Relations in First-Century Galilee: Some Suggestions from the Literary Sources," in *Galilee in Late Antiquity,* 75–91; R.A. Horsley, *Jesus and the Spiral of Violence: Popular Jewish Resistance in Roman Palestine* (San Francisco: Harper & Row, 1987); R. McMullen, *Roman Social Relations, 50 B.C. to A.D. 284* (New Haven: Yale Univ. Press, 1974), 28–56; J. Riches, *The World of Jesus: First-Century Judaism in Crisis* (Cambridge: Cambridge Univ. Press, 1990), 16–26, against Edwards, "Socio-Economic and Cultural Ethos," 71–72. On the long-standing tension between the Jews and the Hellenized cities of Palestine through to the first century see A. Kasher, *Jews and Hellenistic Cities in Eretz-Israel: Relations of the Jews in Eretz-Israel with the Hellenistic Cities during the Second Temple Period (332 B.C.E.–70 C.E.), TSAJ* 21 (Tübingen: Mohr, 1990).

10. Meyers, "Roman Sepphoris," 322, 325; Horsley, *Jesus and the Spiral of Violence,* 154.

11. Dio Chrysostom, *Discourse* 32.9. See Downing, "Quite Like Q: A Genre for Q: The 'Lives' of Cynic Philosophers," *Biblica* 69 (1988): 220; Tuckett takes Downing to task at these points. See his "A Cynic Q?" *Biblica* 70 (1989): 357. A.E. Harvey also challenges Downing's identification of Josephus' "fourth philosophy" with Cynic thought as "arbitrary" and notes that this comparison "actually conflicts with his admission that Cynics were uninterested in the use of force"; see Harvey, review of Downing's *Jesus and the Threat of Freedom, Theology* 92 (1989): 553.

12. See G. Theissen, *Sociology of Early Palestinian Christianity,* trans. J. Bowden (Philadelphia: Fortress, 1978): 88–89.

13. Even Theissen, *Sociology of Early Palestinian Christianity,* admits this point, 88.

14. Harvey, review *Threat of Freedom,* 553; Tuckett, "A Cynic Q?" 356–57.

15. See M. Billerbeck, "Greek Cynicism in Imperial Rome," in *Die Kyniker in der modernen Forshung,* BSZF 15, ed. M. Billerbeck (Amsterdam: Grüner, 1991), 147–66. On Demetrius and conjectured dates for his life, see J.F. Kindstrand, "Demetrius the Cynic," *Philologus* 124 (1980): 84–89.

16. See Harvey, *Threat of Freedom,* 553, and H.D. Betz, "Jesus and the Cyn-

ics: Survey and Analysis of a Hypothesis," *Journal of Religion* 74 (October 1994): 471 respectively. See also R. Horsley, "Itinerant Cynic or Israelite Prophet?" in *Images of Jesus Today*, ed. J.H. Charlesworth and W.P. Weaver (Valley Forge, Pa.: Trinity, 1994), 73. Relatedly, R.F. Hock has noted that "problems of evidence constantly dog the student of imperial Cynicism." See "A Dog in a Manger: The Cynic Cynulcus among Athenaeus's Deipnosophists," in *Greeks, Romans, and Christians: Essays in Honor of Abraham J. Malherbe*, ed. D.L. Balch, E. Ferguson, and W.A. Meeks (Minneapolis: Fortress, 1990), 20.

17. See especially Freyne, *Galilee, Jesus and the Gospels*. On the religiously *conservative* nature of Galilean Jews, and their resistance to hellenistic religiophilosophical influence, see Edwards, "Socio-Economic and Cultural Ethos," 71–72; Freyne, "Galilee-Jerusalem Relations According to Josephus' Life," *New Testament Studies* 33 (1987): 600–609; J. Goldstein, "Jewish Acceptance and Rejection of Hellenism," in *Jewish and Christian Self-Definition*, 2:64–87; P.J. Hartin, "The Religious Nature of First-Century Galilee as a Setting for Early Christianity," *Neotestamentica* 27/2 (1993): 339–48; H. Koester, *Introduction to the New Testament*, 2 vols., trans. H. Koester (Philadelphia: Fortress, 1982), 1:218; F. Loftus, "The Anti-Roman Revolts of the Jews and the Galileans," *Jewish Quarterly Review* 68 (1977): 78–98; Meyers and Strange, *Archaeology*, 26–27; E.P. Sanders, "Jesus in Historical Context," *Theology Today* 50/3 (1993): 429–48; E. Schuerer, *A History of the Jewish People in the Time of Christ* (New York: Scribner, n.d.), II, pt. I:29–56; S. Schwartz, "The 'Judaism' of Samaria and Galilee in Josephus's Version of the Letter of Demetrius I to Jonathan (*Antiquities* 13.48-57)," *Harvard Theological Review* 82/4 (1989): 389–91.

18. Meyers, "The Challenge of Hellenism for Early Judaism and Christianity," *Biblical Archaeologist* 55/2 (1992): 86.

19. With regard to the Diaspora, see A.T. Kraabel, "Paganism and Judaism: The Sardis Evidence," in *Paganisme, Judaisme, Christianisme, Influences et affrontements dans le monde antique: Melanges offerts a Marcel Simon* (Paris: de Boccard, 1978), 13–33. Regarding the Palestinian situation, see D. Flusser, "Paganism in Palestine," in *Jewish People in the First Century*, 1065–1100; Sanders, "Jesus in Historical Context," 448.

20. Meyers, "Challenge of Hellenism," 88.

21. L.H. Feldman, "How Much Hellenism in Jewish Palestine?" *Hebrew Union College Annual* 57 (1986): 111.

22. On Cynicism's negative attitude toward religion, see H.W. Attridge, "The Philosophical Critique of Religion under the Early Empire," *ANRW* 2.16.1 (1978): 56–60; R.B. Branham, "Diogenes' Rhetoric and the *Invention* of Cynicism," in *Le Cynisme Ancien et Ses Prolongements*, ed. M.O. Goulet-Caze and R. Goulet (Paris: Presses Universitaires De France, 1993), 461–62; M.O. Goulet-Caze, "Les Premiers Cyniques et la Religion," in *Le Cynisme Ancien*, 117–58 (translated as "Religion and the Early Cynics," in B. Branham, ed., *The Cynics: The Cynic Movement in Antiquity and Its Legacy for Europe* [forthcoming]); J.M. Rist, "Cynicism and Stoicism," in his *Stoic Philosophy* (Cambridge: Cambridge Univ. Press, 1969), 63; L.E. Vaage, "Cynic Epistles," in *Ascetic Behavior in Greco-Roman Antiquity: A Sourcebook*, ed. V.L. Wimbush (Minneapolis: Fortress, 1990), 118; idem, "Like Dogs Barking: Cynic *Parresia* and Shameless Asceticism," *Semeia* 57 (1992), 36. Those who attempt to establish a positive relation between Cynicism and religion often appeal to Epictetus. However, Epictetus' rather unique eclecticism − which does include appreciation for ideal Cynicism − hardly qualifies him as a paradigm Cynic upon which to base such an argument.

23. See the straightforward comments on this point of B.F. Meyer, "Master Builder and Copestone of the Portal: Images of the Mission of Jesus," *Toronto Journal of Theology* 9/2 (1993): 188–89. On the fundamental *Jewishness* of Jesus,

see the host of "Third Quest" authors listed in chap. 2 who emphasize this point.

24. Though he is certainly not a defender of the Cynic thesis, Abraham Malherbe has done much to draw attention to such Pauline-Cynic parallels. See the relevant essays collected in Malherbe, *Paul and the Popular Philosophers* (Minneapolis: Fortress, 1989); also idem, "Hellenistic Moralists and the New Testament," *ANRW* 2.26.1 (1992): 268–333; idem, *Paul and the Thessalonians: The Philosophic Tradition of Pastoral Care* (Philadelphia: Fortress, 1987).

25. See Malherbe, "*Me Genoito* in the Diatribe of Paul," "'Gentle as a Nurse': The Cynic Background to 1 Thessalonians 2," and "Exhortation in First Thessalonians," in his *Paul and the Popular Philosophers*.

26. R.F. Hock, *The Social Context of Paul's Ministry: Tentmaking and Apostleship* (Philadelphia: Fortress, 1980).

27. Malherbe, *Paul and the Popular Philosophers*, 59.

28. Ibid., cf. 48. Those who put great weight on early Christian-Cynic terminological and stylistic parallels without equally emphasizing the all-important differences do a disservice to the comparative project. See, e.g., E.N. O'Neil, "De Cupiditate divitiarum," in *Plutarch's Ethical Writings and Early Christian Literature*, ed. H.D. Betz (Leiden: Brill, 1978), 308–9.

29. In addition to Malherbe's work, see D.W. Palmer, "Thanksgiving, Self-Defense, and Exhortation in 1 Thessalonians 1–3," *Colloquium* 14/1 (1981): 23–31.

30. See V.L. Wimbush, *Paul: The Worldly Ascetic: Response to the World and Self-Understanding According to 1 Corinthians 7* (Macon, Ga.: Mercer Univ. Press, 1987), 96.

31. P.R. Eddy, "Christian and Hellenistic Moral Exhortation: A Literary Comparison Based on 1 Thessalonians 4," in *Directions in New Testament Methods, MST* 2, ed. M.C. Albl, P.R. Eddy, and R. Mirkes (Milwaukee: Marquette Univ. Press, 1993), 50. M.L. Soards has demonstrated the manner in which the pastoral epistles function as a critique of the Cynic notion of self-sufficiency; see "Reframing and Reevaluating the Argument of the Pastoral Epistles Toward a Contemporary New Testament Theology," *Perspectives in Religious Studies* 19 (1992): 389–98. See also Malherbe, "Hellenistic Moralists and the New Testament," 322.

32. Eddy, "Christian and Hellenistic Moral Exhortation," 51. See also P. Perkins, "1 Thessalonians and Hellenistic Religious Practices," in *To Touch the Text: Biblical and Related Studies in Honor of Joseph A. Fitzmyer, S.J.*, ed. M. Horgan and P. Kobelski (New York: Crossroad, 1989), 325–34.

33. Many Cynic-Jesus theorists (and others as well) argue further that a Cynic influence is also discernable in post-apostolic Christian authors. For discussions, see D. Krueger, "Diogenes the Cynic Among the Fourth Century Fathers," *Vigiliae Christianae* 47 (1993): 29–49; idem, *The Life of Symeon the Fool and the Cynic Tradition*," *Journal of Early Christian Studies* 1 (1993): 423–42. On the parallels offered as proof of influence, George Boas' assessment seems generally accurate: "Such resemblances are not proofs that the Christian borrowed his ideas from the [Cynics], or that there was even more than superficial similarities between the two sets of ideas. . . . [For instance] . . . the reduction of wants, common to both Cynicism and early Christianity, was based upon different assumptions in each case" (G. Boas, "Christianity and Cynicism," in his *Essays on Primitivism and Related Ideas in the Middle Ages* [Baltimore: Johns Hopkins Univ. Press, 1948], 108). This observation is a needed corrective to those studies that too easily assume a deep significance regarding the apparent parallels between Cynic and Christian attitudes toward wealth and poverty. See, e.g., R.F. Hock, "Lazarus and Micyllus: Greco-Roman Backgrounds to Luke 16:19-31," *Journal of Biblical Literature* 106/3 (1987): 447–63.

34. On the "secular ethic" within a wisdom view of the world, see D. Cox, "The New Writers: Wisdom's Response to a Changing Society," Studia Missionalia 42 (1993): 1–15.

35. See H.A. Fischel, "Studies in Cynicism and the Ancient Near East: The Transformation of a Chreia," in Religions in Antiquity: Essays in Memory of Erwin Ramsdell Goodenough, SHR 14, ed. J. Neusner (Leiden: Brill, 1968), 407–11. For a very different read on the New Testament chreiai than that of Mack's, see G.W. Buchanan, Jesus: the King and His Kingdom (Macon, Ga.: Mercer Univ. Press, 1984); idem, "Chreiai in the New Testament," in Logia: Les paroles de Jesus—The Sayings of Jesus, BETL 59, ed. J. Delobel (Leuven, Belgium: Leuven Univ. Press, 1982), 501–5. See also J.G. Williams, Those Who Ponder Proverbs: Aphoristic Thinking and Biblical Literature, BLS 2 (Sheffield: Almond, 1981); F. King, "The Chreia: The Return of the Form-Critic," African Theological Journal 22/2 (1993):76–90.

36. The emphasis on Jesus as a sage provides a needed corrective to the tendency among conservative scholars to stress his role as prophet at the expense of his role as sage. As Stein writes, "There is a tendency to overlook and underestimate the role of Jesus as a sage. The evidence in the Gospels that Jesus taught as a wise man, however, is impressive. His abundant use of proverbs, parables, paradox, metaphor, etc., witnesses to a similarity between the forms of his teachings and that of the wise men" (Robert Stein, The Method and Message of Jesus' Teachings [Philadelphia: Westminster, 1978], 2).

37. E. Vaage, Galilean Upstarts: Jesus' First Followers According to Q (Valley Forge, Pa.: Trinity, 1994), 94.

38. Crossan, JRB, 59–60.

39. Stein, Method and Message, 8. See also Horsley, "Itinerant Cynic or Israelite Prophet?" 75.

40. It is, admittedly, also hardly what one would expect from a Jewish sage. It reflects a degree of self-importance that is truly astounding—and this in a saying that almost everyone agrees is authentic (which is why it is utilized to establish Jesus' supposed Cynicism)! The devotion called for here is, in Jewish circles, customarily reserved for God alone. If this much is true in an indisputibly early tradition, one wonders if perhaps the (supposed) later traditions which, according to Mack, attribute to Jesus increasingly "preposterous" attributes (see LG, chap. 11) are necessarily "late," "distorted," and "preposterous" after all. Indeed, perhaps even Paul's perception of Christ as fully divine (see part 4) is rooted in some reliable history. I shall subsequently argue that we have, in fact, good reason to suppose that this is the case.

41. E.E. Ellis, "The Making of Narratives in the Synoptic Gospels," in Jesus and the Oral Gospel Tradition, JSNTSS 64, ed., H. Wansbrough (Sheffield: JSOT, 1991), 329. For more suitable Jewish parallels, see the relevant essays in J. Gammie and L. Perdue, eds., The Sage in Israel and the Ancient Near East (Winona Lake, Ind.: Eisenbrauns, 1990).

42. B.B. Scott, "Jesus as Sage," in The Sage in Israel, 401–2.

43. Malherbe, "Self-Definition," 49.

44. Horsley, Sociology and the Jesus Movement, 117. Horsley is hardly alone in his evaluation here. For others who stress the fundamental differences between the early Christians and Cynics (or other itinerent philosophers), see M. Hengel, The Charismatic Leader and His Followers (New York: Crossroad, 1981), 15, 71; H.C. Kee, Christian Origins in Sociological Perspective: Methods and Resources (Philadelphia: Westminster, 1980), 68–70; W. Michaelis, "pera," in Theological Dictionary of the New Testament, ed. G. Kittel and G. Friedrich (Grand Rapids: Eerdmans, 1964–1976), 6:119–21; J. Stambaugh and D. Balch, The New Testament in Its Social Environment (Philadelphia: Westminster, 1986), 143–45. For a very helpful recent critical analysis of the Cynic-Jesus thesis,

see B. Witherington, "Hokmah Meets Sophia: Jesus the Cynic?" chap. 3 in his *Jesus the Sage: The Pilgrimage of Wisdom* (Minneapolis: Fortress, 1994), 117–45.

Chapter 8: Christ-Cult Leader or Representative Spokesman?

1. A handful of scholars, however, have proposed dating the Gospel of Mark contemporary with, or even prior to, Paul's epistles. A. Harnack, *Date of the Synoptic Gospels* (1911), W.G. Allen, *St. Mark* (1915), and C.C. Torrey, *The Four Gospels: A New Translation* (1933) argued for an early date, possibly even in the 40s, a possibility strongly entertained (for quite different reasons) more recently by J.A.T. Robinson, *Redating the New Testament* (Philadelphia: Westminister, 1976) and J. Wenham, *Redating Matthew, Mark and Luke: A Fresh Assault on the Synoptic Problem* (London: Hodder & Stoughton, 1991). See my discussion of Mark's date in chap. 11. It should also be noted that we are here assuming that Q is not "extant" documentary evidence of earliest Christianity. As discussed above, Q is a *theory*, not a *document*. "Not one scrap of manuscript evidence has turned up which can plausibly be thought of as part of this document" (N.T. Wright, *The New Testament and the People of God* [Minneapolis: Fortress, 1992], 438).

2. For the purpose of this book, we are leaving aside the much discussed issue of whether or not Paul authored 2 Thessalonians, Colossians, Ephesians, and the pastoral epistles and restricting our discussion to only those seven epistles that the vast majority of New Testament scholars accept as Pauline. These are 1 Thessalonians, Galatians, 1 and 2 Corinthians, Philippians, Philemon, and Romans. It is interesting, however, that Crossan, for undisclosed reasons, only cites 1 Thessalonians, Galatians, 1 Corinthians, and Romans in the earliest stratum of Christian witnesses (A.D. 30–60), and he makes almost no use of even these in his reconstruction of the historical Jesus. However, he never even discusses (or dates!) 2 Corinthians, Philippians, and Philemon.

3. For two superb discussions on the origin and theological significance of the title "Christ" in Paul, see N. Dahl, *Jesus the Christ* (Minneapolis: Fortress, 1991), esp. chap. 3; and M. Hengel, *Between Jesus and Paul* (Philadelphia: Fortress, 1983), chap. 4.

4. On the christological significance of the early hymns in the church, echoed in Paul's letters as well as other New Testament documents, see Hengel, *Between Jesus and Paul*, chap. 4.

5. On Bousett's and Bultmann's postulation of a radical split between "Gentile" and "Jewish" Christianity, see Hengel, *Between Jesus and Paul*, 35.

6. Mack, *MI*, 96.

7. Far from being a reliable guide as to what the earliest Christians generally believed, Mack finds evidence in Paul's letters of "an unstable, authoritarian person, eager that 'his' gospel now be recognized as the standard over against all others," and thus says we should not even "assume that Paul's letters provide a clear window into *Hellenistic* Christianity" (*MI*, 98, emphasis mine). Crossan's estimation of the significance of Paul as representing widespread early Christian faith is reflected by the above mentioned fact he makes almost no reference to the epistles in his work, *The Historical Jesus*. There are a few dozen references to 1 Corinthians, four to Galatians, three to 1 Thessalonians, and one to Romans: otherwise he is silent.

8. The term "Hellenistic Christianity" is ambiguous in that it is certainly true that "Jewish Christianity" was influenced by Hellenism as well. Still more ambiguous, however, is the term "Gentile Christianity," for, as we shall see, first-century Christianity was, in all of its forms, more "Jewish" in its outlook than it was "Gentile." Having noted this, however, I shall, for lack of

better phraseology, continue to refer to the Jesus movements centered in and around Palestine as "Jewish Christianity" and those outside this area as "Hellenistic Christianity."

9. Mack, *MI*, 101.

10. Ibid., 105–13, *LG*, 215–18.

11. See, e.g., *MI*, 15.

12. Ibid., 109–10.

13. Ibid., 107–8.

14. Ibid., 122–23.

15. Ibid., 105ff. Crossan has a similar view. Working to explain the literary framework of Mark's passion narrative, he holds that it fuses together the twin themes of "martyrdom vindicated" and "innocence rescued." These motifs were mediated to Mark, according to Crossan, through Paul, the Cross Gospel, and Secret Mark. See *HJ*, 385–91, and *The Cross That Spoke: The Origins of the Passion Narrative* (San Francisco: Harper and Row, 1988), 297–334.

16. Mack, *LG*, 216–17.

17. Mack, *MI*, 107.

18. Ibid., 109.

19. Mack, following a number of other scholars, holds that Jesus' resurrection and exaltation were identical in the orginal kerygma; see *MI*, 113.

20. Mack's treatment of Paul's concept of "God's righteousness" is certainly controversial in the context of recent scholarly reflection on the concept. Käsemann has significantly influenced most recent reflection on the subject with his insistence, against Bultmann, that the concept is essentially eschatological. See E. Käsemann, "The 'Righteousness of God' in Paul," in his *New Testament Questions of Today*, trans. W.J. Montague (Philadelphia: Fortress, 1969), 168–82. See also J.C. Beker, *Paul the Apostle: The Triumph of God in Life and Thought* (Philadelphia: Fortress, 1980); idem, *The Triumph of God: The Essence of Paul's Thought* (Minneapolis: Fortress, 1990).

21. Mack, *MI*, 108, 111–12.

22. Ibid., 109.

23. Ibid., 110.

24. A number of scholars agree with Mack (and Crossan) in his emphasis on the centrality of the mixed fellowship in Paul's thought. E.g., see the compelling work of K. Stendahl, *Paul among Jews and Gentiles* (Philadelphia: Fortress, 1976). It remains to be seen, however, how many will follow Mack in his sociological driven view that it was this concern that *gave rise to* Paul's (and his congregations') mythology. I shall offer a critique of this view below.

25. Mack, *LG*, 218.

26. Ibid., 216.

27. Mack, *MI*, 111.

28. Mack, *LG*, 219.

29. Mack, *MI*, 103.

30. Mack, *LG*, 220.

31. Ibid., 177, 219–20.

32. Ibid., 219.

33. Mack, *MI*, 5.

34. Ibid., 100–11.

35. Mack, *LG*, 221.

36. Ibid., 219.

37. Ibid., 221.

38. See S. Neill and N.T. Wright, *The Interpretation of the New Testament: 1861–1986*, 2nd ed. (Oxford: Oxford Univ. Press, 1988), chap. 5, for an overview of the history of this approach.

39. Hengel, *Between Jesus and Paul*, 40. On this issue see especially A.

Hultgren, *The Rise of Normative Christianity* (Minneapolis: Fortress, 1994).

40. See Mack, *MI*, 99. Walter Bauer's view is expressed in his classic *Orthodoxy and Heresy in Earliest Christianity*, trans. Philadelphia Seminar on Christian Origins, ed. R.A. Kraft and G. Krodel (Philadelphia: Fortress, 1971 [1934]). For a decisive refutation, see J. Munck, *Paul and the Salvation of Mankind*, trans. F. Clarke (Richmond, Va.: John Knox, 1954 [1950]), as well as Hengel, *Acts and Earliest Christianity*, 92, 112–23. On the issue of conflict in early Christianity, see also G. Machen's still valuable discussion in *The Religion of Paul* (Grand Rapids: Eerdmans, 1925), 257–61, cf. 105–13, 119–42.

41. Neill and Wright, *Interpretation of the New Testament*, 196.

42. Hengel, *Between Jesus and Paul*, 44. For a still valuable detailed discussion of this passage, see Machen, *Religion of Paul*, 120–24. In contrast, to both Hengel and Machen, Mack states that Paul's views "alarmed the pillars who apparently decided that Paul was a dangerous man" (*MI*, 99). He does not, however, tell us what his "apparently" is based on. Certainly not on Galatians 2 in which Paul informs us that these pillars gave him "the right hand of fellowship" and "agreed that we [Paul and Titus] should go to the Gentiles, and they to the Jews" (Gal. 2:9; cf. v. 7).

43. From Galatians 2:2, Hengel concludes that for Paul, "a complete break with the earliest community in Jerusalem could have made all previous missionary work towards non-Jews seem meaningless. For him, a division in the church was inconceivable" (Hengel, *Acts and the History of Earliest Christianity*, trans. J. Bowden [Philadelphia: Fortress, 1979], 114).

44. Mack, *MI*, 128. Hengel's insightful work is invaluable in demonstrating how much of contemporary scholarship has not given Acts serious enough consideration, especially as it concerns the relationship between Paul, "Hellenistic Christianity," and the original Palestinian Jesus movement. See esp., M. Hengel, *Acts and Earliest Christianity*, as well as *Between Paul and Jesus*, chaps. 1 and 3. Also significant on this is the brilliant work of the late Colin Hemer. See his *The Book of Acts in the Setting of Hellenistic History*, ed. C.H. Gempf (Tübingen: Mohr, 1989). The reliability of Acts shall be discussed in some detail in chap. 12.

45. See Hengel, *Between Jesus and Paul*, 160 (n. 23).

46. See Hengel, *Between Jesus and Paul*, 37, where he argues against Kramer's argument from the silence of Q. On the general historical invalidity of arguing from silence on historical matters, see J. Lange, "The Argument from Silence," *History and Theology* 5 (1966): 288–301; and D. Fischer, *Historian's Fallacies* (New York: Harper & Row, 1970; London: Routledge and Kegan Paul, 1971), 62–63. If arguing from silence on the basis of an extant document is tenuous, what are we to think of doing so from a hypothetical stratification of a hypothetical document produced by a hypothetical community?

47. Wright, *New Testament and the People of God*, 426.

48. Mack, *MI*, 116.

49. In this light, Mack's concession that "[t]he rapidity with which this happened . . . is astounding" (*MI*, 116) must be read as an incredible understatement.

50. One can, of course, find rare examples of legends quickly springing up about a historical person, even within their own lifetime (e.g., Augustus, Lucian, Martin of Tours). But these do not come close to constituting a "foundational myth" for a community of followers.

51. An attitude reflected in 2 Peter 1:16; 2:3; cf. 1 Tim. 1:4; 2 Tim. 4:4; Titus 1:14. The notion that the ability to think critically about history arose some 200 years ago is a modern "myth" that needs to be abandoned. Ancient Jews and Gentiles were perfectly capable of distinguishing between fact and fable as well as between reliable and unreliable reports. See C.W. Fornara, *The Nature of History in Ancient Greece* (San Francisco: Univ. of California Press,

1983), esp. 16ff, 163; A.W. Mosely, "Historical Reporting in the Ancient World," *New Testament Studies* 12 (1965): 10–26; Wright, *New Testament and the People of God*, 67–69, 83–87, 377–78; and especially Hemer, *Acts in Hellenistic History*, chap. 3.

52. C.F.D. Moule, *The Birth of the New Testament*, 3d ed. (London: A & C Black; San Francisco: Harper and Row, 1982), 4, 10–11, 122, 133.

53. Mack, *MI*, 20.

54. We shall see in chap. 10 that the Gospel of Mark receives similar treatment by both Mack and Crossan.

55. This evidence is rarely given due consideration among post-Bultmannians. C.C. Hill writes of "the customary tendency to minimize (if not vilify) the role of the Jerusalem church in early Christianity. In light of the significance of the Jerusalem church for Paul himself, if for no other reason, this must surely be considered an unfair appraisal." Hence he calls for "a reassessment of Jerusalem's place at all levels in the development of life of the primitive church." *Hellenists and Hebrews: Reappraising Division Within the Earliest Church* (Minneapolis: Fortress, 1992), 196–97. See also J.D.G. Dunn, "The Relationship Between Paul and Jerusalem According to Galatians 1 and 2," *New Testament Studies* 28 (1982): 463–66.

56. This much is true of the society in general, a point that should lead us to expect as much from the early Christians. The mobility of Roman culture and of the early urban Christians is cogently demonstrated by W. Meeks in his *The First Urban Christians: The Social World of the Apostle Paul* (New Haven: Yale Univ. Press, 1983).

57. P. Barnett, *Is the New Testament Reliable? A Look at the Historical Evidence* (Downers Grove, Ill.: InterVarsity, 1986), 82.

58. Neill and Wright, *Interpretation of the New Testament*, 196. .

59. See, e.g., Hengel, *Between Jesus and Paul*, 37–38.

60. See the excellent discussion in Machen, *Religion of Paul*, 46–47. See also, R.A. Martin, *Studies in the Life and Ministry of the Early Paul and Related Issues* (Lewiston, N.Y.: Mellen, 1993), viii, 102.

61. For similar sentiments, see Hengel, *Between Jesus and Paul*, 34–35.

62. Mack, *MI*, 116.

63. See the excellent exposition in O. Cullman, *The Christology of the New Testament*, rev. ed., trans. S. Guthrie and C. Hall (Philadelphia: Westminster, 1963 [1953]), 208ff. See also Hengel, *Acts and Earliest Christianity*, 105. Hengel here further rules out any derivation from Greek mythology. Also significant here is C.F.D. Moule, *The Origin of Christology* (Cambridge: Cambridge Univ. Press, 1977, 35–46).

64. Since the ground-breaking work of J.D.G. Dunn, *The Making of Christology: A New Testament Inquiry into the Origins of the Doctrine of the Incarnation* (Philadelphia: Westminster, 1980), scholars have increasingly questioned the understanding of Philippians 2:5-11 as reflecting a pre-Pauline belief in Christ's preexistence. It is suggested, rather, that it reflects a non-incarnational "Adam-Christology." Wright has convincingly argued, however, that even if an Adam-Christology is granted, the passage yet entails a concept of Christ's preexistence and a strong claim to Christ's divinity. See N.T. Wright, "Adam in Pauline Christology," *SBLSP* 1983, ed. K.H. Richards (Chico, Calif.: Scholars, 1983), 359–89; idem, "Jesus Christ Is Lord: Philippians 2:5-11," in his *The Climax of the Covenant: Christ and Law in Pauline Theology* (Edinburgh: T & T Clark, 1991), 56–98. On the other hand, many scholars dispute the reading of this passage as exemplifying an Adam Christology. See, e.g., T.F. Glasson, "Two Notes on the Philippians Hymn (2:6-11)," *New Testament Studies* 21/1 (1974): 137–39, M. Erickson, *The Word Became Flesh: A Contemporary Incarnational Christology* (Grand Rapids: Baker, 1991), 475–79; and, on a popular level, G.A. Boyd, *Oneness Pentecostals & The Trinity* (Grand

Rapids: Baker, 1992), 106–8. See also I.H. Marshall's review of Dunn's book in *Trinity Journal* 2/2 (1981): 241–45.

65. See N. Dahl, *Jesus the Christ: The Historical Origins of Christological Doctrine*, ed. D. Joel (Minneapolis: Fortress, 1991), who argues that, "It can hardly be doubted today that the basic elements of Paul's Christology were already present in pre-Pauline Christianity." And he concludes from this that the possibility of a major gulf between the Palestinian and Hellenistic communities' christological views is most unlikely (p. 19). Hengel argues in a similar fashion in *Between Jesus and Paul*, 33–34.

66. See M.J. Harris, *Jesus as God: The New Testament Use of Theos in Reference to Jesus* (Grand Rapids: Baker, 1992); R.E. Brown, *Jesus God and Man* (New York: Macmillan; London: Collier Macmillan, 1967), chap. 1; O. Cullmann, *Christology of the New Testament*, 306–14; A.W. Wainwright, "The Confession 'Jesus Is God' in the New Testament," *Scottish Journal of Theology* 10 (1957): 274–99.

67. See Hengel, *Between Jesus and Paul*, 39ff. Hengel allows for some christological development to have taken place between the eighteen years of Jesus' resurrection and Paul's writings, but attributes this incredible development mostly to the impact of Jesus' own ministry and resurrection instead of the assimilation of Hellenistic ideas (pp. 39–47). The roots of this theology probably go back to the resurrection event itself (p. 33). On this point, see also, L.W. Hurtado, *One God, One Lord: Early Christian Devotion and Ancient Jewish Monotheism* (Philadelphia: Fortress, 1988); idem, "The Origins of the Worship of Christ," *Themelios* 19/2 (1994): 4–8.

68. Machen, *Religion of Paul*, 174, cf. 129.

69. Mack, *MI*, 103.

70. Ibid., 101.

71. On the extreme difficulty of working out a cogent naturalistic developmental christology within the early church, see T.C. Oden, *The Word of Life: Systematic Theology: Volume 2* (San Francisco: Harper & Row, 1989), 210, 214; and Wright, *People of God*, 455. Observing how soon the Hellenistic Christians separated themselves from the Jerusalem community, Hengel says, "Here the picture of a differentiated christological development in the earliest period comes under extreme chronological pressure"; see *Between Jesus and Paul*, 37. Also relevant here, against Mack's thesis, is the work of C. Holladay, *Theios Aner in Hellenistic Judaism* (Missoula, Mont.: Scholars, 1977), who meticulously argues that Hellenistic influences among the Jews of the diaspora actually made them *more* resistant to accepting any concept of a "divinized man."

72. For cogent arguments that the term "Christ" was already being applied to Jesus during his earthly ministry, see M. de Jonge, "The Earliest Use of *Christos*: Some Suggestions," *New Testament Studies* 32 (1986): 321–43; I.H. Marshall, *The Origins of New Testament Christology* (Downers Grove, Ill.: InterVarsity, 1976), 83–96, and Moule, *Origin of Christology*, 31–35.

73. For a careful discussion on the martyr motif in Paul and Hellenistic literature, see S. Williams, *Jesus' Death as Saving Event: The Background and Origin of a Concept*, HDR 2 (Missoula, Mont.: Scholars, 1975). For a discussion on the theme of divine vindication, see G.W.E. Nickelsburg, *Resurrection, Immortality, and Eternal Life in InterTestamental Judaism*, HTS 26 (Cambridge: Harvard Univ. Press; London: Oxford Univ. Press, 1972).

74. For a very helpful article that details the parallels—as well as the important differences—between such Greco-Roman notions and the Christian conception of Jesus' death as reflected in the passion accounts, see A.Y. Collins, "From Noble Death to Crucified Messiah," *New Testament Studies* 40 (1994): 481–503.

75. See R.E. Brown, "Appendix VII: The Old Testament Background of the Passion Narratives," in his *The Death of the Messiah: From Gethsemane to the*

Grave (New York: Doubleday, 1994), 2:1445–67; G. Nickelsberg, "The Genre and Function of the Markan Passion Narrative," *Harvard Theological Review* 73 (1980): 153–84; Wright, *Climax of the Covenant*, 137–56. In the light of this it is hard to accept Mack's claim that the notion of a vicarious death "cannot be traced to old Jewish and/or Israelite traditions, for the very idea of a vicarious human sacrifice was anathema in these cultures" (*LG*, 217).

76. For helpful critiques, see M. Hengel, *The Son of God: The Origin of Christology and the History of Jewish-Hellenistic Religion*, trans. J. Bowden (Philadelphia: Fortress, 1976 [1975]); R.H. Nash, *Christianity and the Hellenistic World* (Grand Rapids: Zondervan, 1984), 115–99; A.D. Nock, "Hellenistic Mysteries and Christian Sacraments," in *Early Gentile Christianity and Its Hellenistic Background* (New York: Harper & Row, 1964 [1952]), 109–45; G. Wagner, *Pauline Baptism and the Pagan Mysteries* (London: Oliver and Boyd, 1967); D.H. Wiens, "Mystery Concepts in Primitive Christianity and in Its Environment," *ANRW* 2, 23/2 (1980): 1248–84. Even among those who show signs of sympathy with the old notion, most are quick to qualify their positions. See, e.g., A.J.M. Wedderburn, "Paul and the Hellenistic Mystery-Cults: On Posing the Right Questions," in *La Soteriologia dei culti orientali nell Imperio Romano*, ed. U. Bianchi and M.J. Vermaseren (Leiden: Brill, 1982), 817–33.

77. A good example of this is the much celebrated papyri at Oxyrhynchus which speaks of "the meal of our Lord Sarapis." This was, for a time, read by the proponents of the religio-historical school as providing the background for Paul's concept of eating "at the Lord's table" (1 Cor. 10:21). But the most probable date for this letter is the early third century, and by that time Alexandria was a largely Christian city. Hence, if one wishes to posit a line of influence here at all, the most probable guess is that it runs from Paul, through Christians in Alexandria, to the eastern mystery religions, not the other way around. There is no evidence of anyone referring to "the table of the Lord" before Paul. See Neill and Wright, *Interpretation of the New Testament*, 183–84.

78. For example, when speaking about the methods of the history-of-religions school of his day, Harnack sarcastically comments: "By such methods one can turn Christ into a sun god in the twinkling of an eye, or one can bring up the legends attending the birth of every conceivable god, or one can catch all sorts of mythological doves to keep company with the baptismal dove . . . with the magic wand of 'comparative religion' [one could] trimphantly eliminate every spontaneous trait in any religion." Quoted in Nash, *Christianity and the Hellenistic World*, 118–19. For a trenchant refutation from a conservative perspective, contemporary with Harnack, see Machen, *Religion of Paul*, chap. 7, 211–51. The charge that the history of religions school did not take seriously the uniqueness of Christianity has more recently been made by E. Judge, "St. Paul and Classical Society," *Jahrbuch für Antike und Christentum* 15 (1972), 19–36; and Karl Prumm, *Religionsgeschichtliches Handbuch für den Raum der altchristlichen Umwelt*, 2nd ed. (Rome: Papstliches Bibelinstitut, 1954), 255–307.

79. Even Ian Wilson concludes, "On close inspection the parallels are unimpressive" (I. Wilson, *Jesus: The Evidence* [San Francisco: Harper and Row, 1984], 141). For further discussion on the Christian view of the resurrection in comparison with the resusitation views in mystery religions, see Nash, *Christianity and the Hellenistic World*, 137, 173; and J. Dunn, *The Evidence for Jesus* (Philadelphia: Westminster, 1985), 71. And for a general discussion on the need to exercise caution when drawing parallels between pagan and early Christian concepts, see S. Sandmel, "Parallelomania," *Journal of Biblical Literature* 81 (1962): 1–13; A.D. Nock, "A Note on the Resurrection," in his *Early Gentile Christianity*, 105–8. Wagner, *Pauline Baptism and the Pagan Mysteries*.

80. Mack, *LG*, 220.

81. See esp. Wagner, *Pauline Baptism and the Pagan Mysteries*.

82. See R. Martin, "Pre-Christian Paul: Hellenization of the Pharisees," in his *Life and Ministry of the Early Paul*, 33–102. Even among scholars who emphasize the importance of Greco-Roman culture with regard to understanding Paul, a healthy caution is often voiced lest by pleading "Hellenism" Paul's distinctive Jewish theology be lost. See, e.g., Judge, "St. Paul and Classical Society," 19–36; A.J. Malherbe, "Paul: Hellenistic Philosopher or Christian Pastor?" *Anglican Theological Review* 68/1 (1986): 13.

83. Perhaps the strongest case for the thoroughly Jewish nature of Paul's thought has been carried out in the very influential work of W. Davies, *Paul and Rabbinic Judaism: Some Rabbinic Elements in Pauline Theology*, 4th ed. (London: SPCK; Philadelphia: Fortress, 1980). He here argues that Paul understood his faith in Christ to constitute "the full flowering of Judaism" (p. 323), and as such, he belongs "to the mainstream of first-century Judaism" (p. 2). The thesis has been carried on (in more cautious terms) by E.P. Sanders, *Paul and Palestinian Judaism: A Comparison of Patterns of Religion* (Philadelphia: Fortress, 1977) and Wright, *New Testament and the People of God*.

84. Wright, *New Testament and the People of God*, 453–56.

85. Mack, *MI*, 111.

86. Wright, *New Testament and the People of God*, 453. Machen's discussion on Paul's relationship to Jewish culture still ranks as one of the finest; see *Religion of Paul*, chap. 5, 173–207.

87. Hengel, *Between Jesus and Paul*, 72.

88. Neill and Wright, *Interpretation of the New Testament*, 197.

89. Wright, *New Testament and the People of God*, 456.

90. So Hengel argues when he states: "Anyone who wants to reduce earliest Christianity to often quite different and indeed unconnected 'lines of development' can no longer explain why the church in the second century remained a unity despite all the deviations and how the New Testament canon could come into being. In their view the church should have fallen apart in countless groups" (Hengel, *Between Jesus and Paul*, xi). So too Wright, *New Testament and the People of God*, 454. For Mack and Crossan the question ultimately boils down to a question of how Mark's (fabricated) vision of Jesus won so decisively over the other competing visions? The difficulty they have in presenting a plausible answer to this question will be discussed in the next chapter.

Chapter 9: Imagined in the Mind or Rooted in History?

1. A view made popular in this century by Bultmann, largely on the basis of his questionable exegesis of 2 Corinthians 5:16-17. See his *Theology of the New Testament*, trans. K. Grobel (New York: Scribner's; London: SCM, 1951–1955), 1:237–39. For several critical discussions of his view, see C.F.D. Moule, "Jesus in New Testament Kerygma," in *Verborum Veritas* (für G. Stahlin), ed. O. Bocher and K. Haaker (Wuppental: Brockhaus, 1970), 15–26; and V. Furnish, *2 Corinthians*, AB (New York: Doubleday, 1984), 330–32.

2. Mack, *MI*, 15.

3. J. Bowden, trans., *Acts and the History of Earliest Christianity* (Philadelphia: Fortress, 1979), 44.

4. G.A. Wells sees the force of this line of reasoning; and for this reason in order to defend his thesis that the historical Jesus never existed, attempts to argue that Paul didn't view Jesus as living and dying in the recent past. See *The Historical Evidence for Jesus* (Buffalo: Prometheus, 1988), chap. 1. No reputable New Testament scholar has followed Wells on this matter. Among

a host of other problems, his theory borders on absurdity when he must arbitrarily explain away historical references in Paul's letters to later interpolations (1 Thes. 2:14-15, 24-25) and when he must explain Paul's reference to James as "the Lord's brother" (Gal. 1:19) by postulating the existence of a distinct faction of the early church called "the brothers of the Lord" (167ff). See also his, *Did Jesus Exist?* rev. ed. (London: Pemberton, 1986), 21. The view is, surprisingly, taken up and defended by Michael Martin in his *The Case Against Christianity* (Philadelphia: Temple Univ. Press, 1991), chap. 2. What Wells contributes to the discussion, in my view, is that he sees a genuine problem. If Jesus lived in Paul's recent past, and if Paul had any accurate historical knowledge of him, then not only must one acknowledge that a Jesus actually existed, one must wrestle with the problem of how Paul arrived at such a "mythological" high christology so quickly and in the face of what he knew about this historical Jesus.

5. R.T. France, *The Evidence for Jesus* (Downers Grove, Ill.: InterVarsity, 1986), 100.

6. See, e.g., N. Dahl, *Jesus the Christ: The Historical Origins of Christological Doctrine,* ed. D. Joel (Minneapolis: Fortress, 1991); W.D. Davis, *Paul and Rabbinic Judaism* (New York: Harper and Row, 1955; Harper Torchbook, 1967); D. Dungan, *The Sayings of Jesus in the Churches of Paul* (Oxford: Blackwell, 1971); D.C. Allison, Jr., "The Pauline Epistles and the Synoptic Gospels: The Pattern of the Parallels," *New Testament Studies* 28 (1982): 1–32; F.F. Bruce, *Paul and Jesus* (Grand Rapids: Baker, 1974) as well as his "Paul and the Historical Jesus," in *Paul: An Apostle of the Heart Set Free* (Grand Rapids: Eerdmans, 1977); F. Neirynck, "Paul and the Sayings of Jesus," in *L'Apotre Paul,* ed. A. Vanhoye (Leuven, Belgium: Leuven Univ. Press, 1986); J. Drane, "Patterns of Evangelization in Paul and Jesus: A Way Forward in the Jesus-Paul Debate," and D. Wenham, "The Story of Jesus Known to Paul," both in *Jesus of Nazareth: Lord and Christ: Essays on the Historical Jesus and New Testament Christology,* ed. J. Green and M. Turner (Grand Rapids: Eerdmans, 1994); I.H. Marshall, "Jesus, Paul, and John," *Aberdeen University Review,* 51 (1985): 18–36; and G.N. Stanton, *Jesus of Nazareth in New Testament Preaching* (Cambridge: Cambridge Univ. Press, 1974), 86ff. For a classic statement of the view that the historical Jesus is mostly irrelevant to Paul, see R. Bultmann, "The Significance of the Historical Jesus for the Theology of Paul," in *Faith and Understanding,* trans. L.P. Smith (New York: Harper and Row, 1969), 1:220–46.

7. So Hengel argues in *Acts and Earliest Christianity,* 43.

8. P. Barnett, *Is the New Testament Reliable?* (Downers Grove, Ill.: InterVarsity, 1986), 131.

9. Hengel, *Acts and Earliest Christianity,* 43.

10. France, *Evidence for Jesus,* 91. On the antiquity of 1 Corinthians 15, see T.C. Oden, *The Word of Life: Systematic Theology: Volume 2* (San Francisco: Harper & Row, 1989), 2:211–12.

11. See R. Hays, *The Faith of Jesus Christ: An Investigation of the Narrative Substructure of Galatians 3:1-4:11,* SBL Dissertation Series (Chicago: Scholars, 1983). One of the first and foremost form critics to argue in this direction was C.H. Dodd in his *The Apostolic Preaching and Its Developments* (New York: Harper, 1935). See also "The Framework of the Gospel Narratives," in his *New Testament Studies* (Manchester: Manchester Univ. Press; New York: Scribner, 1952). The general collaboration of the apostolic preaching with the framework of Mark's passion narrative, it is here argued, increases one's estimation of the historical trustworthiness of the latter.

12. N.T. Wright, *The New Testament and the People of God* (Minneapolis: Fortress, 1992), 409. Leonhard Goppelt argues along these lines when he contends that the Jesus traditions are pervasive throughout Paul's epistles, but not in their original form of *geschichtlich* (narrative history) but as

heilsgeschichtlich (salvation history). *Theology of the New Testament*, ed. J. Roloff, trans. J.E. Alsup (Grand Rapids: Eerdmans, 1976), 362–90.

13. On this question, see Wright's discussion in *New Testament and the People of God*, 421–27.

14. See the table of parallels in P. Davids, *The Epistle of James*, NIGTC (Exeter: Paternoster, 1982), 47–49, as well as his article "James and Jesus," in *The Jesus Tradition Outside the Gospels*, GP 5, ed. D. Wenham (Sheffield: JSOT, 1985), 63–84.

15. Even Crossan leans in this direction; see *HJ*, 293–94. For a review of the discussion concerning the uniqueness of the term as coming from Jesus (or at least the Jesus tradition), see L. Hurtado, "God" in *Dictionary of Jesus and the Gospels*, ed. J. Green, S. McKnight and I.H. Marshall (Downers Grove, Ill.: InterVarsity, 1992), 275. Cf. also R.H. Stein, "The 'Criteria' for Authenticity," in *Studies of History and Tradition in the Four Gospels*, GP 1, ed. R.T. France and D. Wenham (Sheffield: JSOT, 1980), 241.

16. See F.F. Bruce's discussion in *The New Testament Documents: Are They Reliable?* 5th ed. (Grand Rapids: Eerdmans; Leicester: Inter-Varsity, 1983), 78.

17. See B. Witherington III, *The Christology of Jesus* (Minneapolis: Fortress, 1990), 12–13; H. Schürman, "Die Vorösterlichen Anfänge der Logien-tradition-Versuch eines Form-geschichtlichen Zugangs zum Leben Jesu," in *Traditions-geschichliche Untersuchungen zu den Synoptischen Evangelion* (Dusseldorf: Patmos, 1968), 39–45. Cf. also Oden, *Word of Life*, 212.

18. Paul's statement that he received this teaching "from the Lord" in all likelihood does not signify direct revelation from the risen Lord, but rather that the tradition he received goes back to the Lord. The customary language of "receiving" and "passing on" a tradition used by Paul supports this view. See C.K. Barrett's helpful discussion in *A Commentary on the First Epistle to the Corinthians*, Black's New Testament Commentary (London: A & C Black, 1971), 264–66. Mack and Crossan avoid acknowledging a passion tradition behind both Paul and the Gospels by arguing that Mark (and the other Gospels following him) adopted the phraseology from Paul. We shall critique this view in the next chapter. For a defense of the authenticity of the Pauline eucharistic tradition, see J. Jeremias, *The Eucharistic Words of Jesus* (London: SCM, 1966), 101–5.

19. *HJ*, 360–67, 398–404; *MI*, 114–23.

20. *HJ*, 361–64, 398; *MI*, 116–20, 375–76; *LG*, 240–41.

21. See G. Bornkamm, *Paul*, trans. D.M. Stalker (New York: Harper and Row, 1971 [1969]), 190–91.

22. Crossan struggles between wanting to place the pre-Pauline eucharistic tradition on "the fourth stage in the eucharistic development" and yet not wanting (because unable) to argue that the Didache preceded this tradition; see *HJ*, 362–65. Coupled with this, to maintain his position he must argue— on very tenuous literary evidence—that the communion material of chap. 10 pre-dates the material of chap. 9 which has "a ritualization of cup and bread" and which reserves communion for those who are baptized (9:5). It is not clear, however, how Crossan can insist that "Didache 10 indicates a eucharistic meal with no ritualization of bread and wine/cup" (*HJ*, 364) when it explicitly contrasts these elements with the ordinary "food and drink men . . . enjoy" by calling them "spiritual food and drink" (10:3). Moreover, it also seems to restrict communion to those who are "holy" (v. 6), hardly the radical egalitarian view Crossan attributes to the earliest communities. See "The Didache" in *The Apostolic Fathers*, trans. J.B. Lightfoot and J.R. Harmer, ed. and rev. by M. Holmes (Grand Rapids: Baker, 1989), 155. In short, neither chaps. 9 or 10 square well with the thesis that the communion meal was originally simply a meal celebrating open commensality.

23. Because he holds that "Jesus enjoined commensality, not alms, wages

. . . or fees," he takes Paul in 9:1-18 to be "arguing with the Jesus *tradition* and not with Jesus himself" (*HJ*, 342, emphasis in text). Two things should be said: (a) in 9:1-18 Paul is refusing a right he sees himself as having (viz., to accept support) partly on the basis of the Lord's command quoted in v. 14. He is not "arguing with" anything; (b) there is no evidence that the tradition he quotes had arrived at an opposite conclusion than what Jesus originally believed, nor an adequate explanation for how it had done so.

24. Crossan believes that Paul is quoting two extra-canonical apocalyptic sayings of Jesus in 1 Corinthians 7:29 and 31b, "The appointed time has grown very short" and "the form of this world is passing away" (Crossan's trans.; *HJ*, 228). Indeed, he holds that Paul is doing so to confront a sapiential interpretation of Jesus at Corinth. Crossan may be correct in locating quotes here (though little evidence is supplied to this effect), but it leaves one wondering why, if he is willing to acknowledge quotes that are this cryptic and concealed, he does not make more use of the many other possible (and explicitly acknowleged!) quotes in Paul that are far less concealed.

25. J. Jeremias, *Unknown Sayings of Jesus* (London: SPCK, 1957), 64–67.

26. For a discussion on the relationship between Paul's eschatology and the apocalyptic discourses in the Synoptics, see D. Wenham, "Paul and the Synoptic Apocalypse," in *Studies of History and Tradition in the Four Gospels, GP* 2, ed. R.T. France and D. Wenham (Sheffield: JSOT, 1981), 345–75. He argues that they have much in common and, on this basis, argues that we have no reason to date the Synoptic discourses late.

27. "[T]here must," argues Erickson, "have been a cause sufficient in effect to account for the presence of each part of the tradition. There must have been something to produce it." This applies to Paul's letters and the Hellenistic communities as it does to the Gospels (*The Word Became Flesh: A Contemporary Incarnational Christology* [Grand Rapids: Baker Book, 1991], 407). Hengel argues along similar lines in *Acts and Earliest Christianity*, 25–26, as does R. Latourelle with his appeal to a "necessary explanation" behind the early Christian traditions in *Finding Jesus Through the Gospels: History and Hermenuetics* (New York: Alba, 1979), 229–32.

Chapter 10: Creative Fabrication or Reliable Report?

1. Mack, *MI*, 23–24.

2. In this limited sense it is perhaps appropriate to speak of the "Christ of faith" being "above history." Such a concept is helpful so long as it is not taken to entail a new epistemological perspective that would divorce the "Christ of faith" from the "Jesus of history," as though one could know the former without any information about the latter. As was argued in chapter 1, this was the fundamental (and very influential) mistake inaugurated by Kähler and propagated by neo-orthodoxy. For a helpful discussion, see J.M. Robinson, *The Problem of History in Mark and Other Marcan Studies* (Philadelphia: Fortress, 1982), 63–68.

3. See Machen's comment in *The Religion of Paul* (Grand Rapids: Eerdmans, 1925), 173.

4. Crossan, *HJ*, xxx.

5. Mack, *MI*, 296.

6. See e.g., Mack, *MI*, 22, 167, 170, 203; Crossan, *HJ*, 390.

7. Mack, *MI*, 238.

8. This is less true of Crossan than it is of Mack, but even Crossan holds that the passion narrative which structures the whole of Mark's narrative is fiction, going back to the prophetic passion of "the Cross Gospel." For several similar perspectives, see W.H. Kelber, ed., *The Passion in Mark: Studies on*

Mark 14–16 (Philadelphia: Fortress, 1976); and J.L. White, "The Way of the Cross: Was There a Pre-Markan Passion Narrative?" *Foundations and Facets Forum* 3:2 (1987): 35–49.

9. See, e.g., Mack, *MI*, 170, 202–3, 204–7, 258, 295; Crossan, *HJ*, 390. This is a recurring theme in Mack's book, appropriately titled, *A Myth of Innocence*. Mark's portrayal of Jesus' trial is "a very vicious fiction" (p. 295), and his reimagined teaching to those who don't understand him is seen as being a malicious rewriting of history (p. 170), "fabricated mockery," and "rhetorical chicanery" (p. 339, cf. p. 202). His pronouncement stories are "fictions because they violate the basic ground rules of human discourse and dialogue. Not even a Cynic would approve" (p. 203). For Mack, the cost of Mark's fabrication was very high in that here the Jesus movement lost its connection to the world and lost its integrity (see p. 204). The original goals of the Jesus movement for "social reform, open borders, the presence of the new social spirit, the affirmation of plural pasts, and invitational discourse," are in Mark all "abrogated, sacrificed to the new desire for self-justification" (p. 331).

10. Mack, *MI*, 280.

11. Ibid., 296.

12. Crossan, *HJ*, 390.

13. For a popular response to Crossan's view, see N.T. Wright, "The New, Unimproved Jesus," *Christianity Today*, September 1993, 25–26. For treatments of the passion narrative that argue that it has a discernably Jewish form and has historical roots in the earliest stages of the church, see G. Nickelsburg, "The Genre and Function of the Markan Passion Narrative," *Harvard Theological Review* 73 (1980): 153–89; G. Theissen, *The Gospel in Context: Social and Political History in the Synoptic Tradition*, trans. L. Maloney (Minneapolis: Fortress, 1991), chap. 4; J.B. Green, *The Death of Jesus: Tradition and Interpretation in the Passion Narrative*, WUNT 33 (Tübingen: Mohr, 1988); A.Y. Collins, "The Genre of the Passion Narrative," *Studia Theologica* 47:1 (1993): 3–28; and idem, "From Noble Death to Crucified Messiah," *New Testament Studies* 40 (1994): 481–503. On the supposed anti-Semitism of the Gospels as well as a defense of the passion as historical reminiscence, see N. Dahl, *Jesus the Christ: The Historical Origin of Christian Doctrine* (Minneapolis: Fortress, 1991), 30–34, as well as M. Silva's excellent essay, "The Place for Historical Reconstruction in New Testament Criticism," in *Hermenuetics, Authority, and Canon*, ed. D.A. Carson and J. Woodbridge (Grand Rapids: Zondervan, 1986), 112–21. And for a solid defense of the historical accuracy of the Gospel accounts of Jesus' trial, see A.N. Sherwin-White, *Roman Society and Roman Law in the New Testament* (Oxford: Clarendon, 1963), 24–47.

14. Mack, *MI*, 66.

15. Ibid., 330.

16. Ibid., 11–12, 205. As we have seen, Crossan holds that Mark used the Cross Gospel, and both he and Mack hold that Mark made use of Secret Mark as well as Q. None of this is widely accepted by contemporary scholarship. Few have made any use of the Gospel of Peter or the Secret Gospel in trying to understand the composition of Mark, and the vast majority argue against the view that Mark knew Q. Chief among the reasons for this latter position is that the only Q we know is the Q arrived at by comparing what Matthew and Luke have in common *over and against Mark!* See B. Throckmorton, "Did Mark Know Q?" *Journal of Biblical Literature* 67 (1948): 319–29; B.H. Streeter, *The Four Gospels* (London: Macmillan, 1925), 186–91; and P. Feine, J. Behm, and W.G. Kümmel, *Introduction to the New Testament*, trans. A.J. Mattill, Jr. (Nashville: Abingdon, 1966), 55.

17. Mack, *MI*, 166–67, cf. 355.

18. Ibid., 328.

19. Ibid., 355.

20. Ibid., 199.

21. Ibid., 331.

22. Ibid., 355.

23. Ibid., 368.

24. Ibid., 368–76.

25. On the criterion of simplicity in historical theories, see N.T. Wright, *The New Testament and the People of God* (Minneapolis: Fortress, 1992), 99–109.

26. Ibid., 426.

27. So, relatedly, Wright argues, "[I]n history, it is getting in the data that really counts." And he asks, "does it really count as 'getting in the data' to say 'this is a creation of the early church?'" (Wright, *New Testament and the People of God*, 106).

28. So Wright charges in *New Testament and the People of God*, 453.

29. M. Hengel, *Between Jesus and Paul*, trans. J. Bowden (Philadelphia: Fortress, 1983), xiv. Cf. R.T. France's insightful comment in *The Evidence for Jesus* (Downers Grove, Ill.: InterVarsity, 1986), 84–85. See as well Wright, *New Testament and the People of God*, 95, who speaks against radical New Testament critics who rearrange or dismiss data to preserve a preconceived notion of who the historical Jesus was.

30. See Wright, *New Testament and the People of God*, 100–101.

31. For a trenchant critique of scholars who confidently appeal to unknown social histories to undermine the historical reliability of Mark, see M. Hengel, *Acts and the History of Earliest Christianity*, trans. J. Bowden (Philadelphia: Fortress, 1979), 25–27, 40. He calls such reconstructions as "the Q community that has become so popular today" "modern fabrications." "[I]n essentials," he adds, "we know far less about the 'communities' which are said to have given rise to such traditions in an unbridled way than we do about Jesus himself" (p. 26). He later castigates that form of radical criticism that exchanges data for "wild reconstructions," saying of it that it "no longer deserves to be called critical, because it completely lacks self-criticism" (p. 40). T.C. Oden raises a similar charge against radical critics for whom "the historical Jesus vanishes in a pile of theories and speculations"; see *The Word of Life: Systematic Theology: Volume 2* (San Francisco: Harper & Row, 1989), 227. See also L.W. Hurtado, "The Gospel of Mark: Evolutionary or Revolutionary Document?" *Journal for the Study of the New Testament* 40 (1990): 15–32.

32. Wright, *New Testament and the People of God*, 99–100.

33. Note Lewis' comment on the implausibility of supposing that "some unknown writer in the second century [or, we could add, first], without known predecessors or successors, suddenly anticipated the whole technique of modern, novelistic, realistic narrative" (C.S. Lewis, "Modern Theology and Biblical Criticism," in *Christian Reflections*, ed. W. Hooper [Grand Rapids: Eerdmans, 1967], 55).

34. See Oden, *Word of Life*, 220–21, in which he argues that "to anyone accustomed to allowing historical documents to speak for themselves," the notion that Jesus' followers were "either disingeneous or stupid or outright liars" is "patently absurd." It is, he argues, more plausible "to believe that God became flesh than to credit such a circuitous series of hypotheses and speculations."

35. So Dahl argues in *Jesus the Christ*, 94–95. From "a purely scientific point of view," he writes, it is "logical to assume that the Master can be known through his disciple's words about him and their historical influence." If this were not true, one wonders where we would get any knowledge of Socrates, Confucius, or any of the other great non-publishing teachers of the past! Relatedly, cf. Oden, *Word of Life*, 223, as he argues, "The most unlikely of all premises is that faith manufactures its own data." The insight applies whether the data is seen as being sincerely or insincerely manufactured.

36. Mack, *MI*, 276.

37. See M. Hengel, *Studies in the Gospel of Mark*, trans. J. Bowden (Philadelphia: Fortress, 1985), 52.

38. Hence Hengel argues that the authoritative acceptance of Mark implies that the early church tradition of Markan authorship based on the preaching of Peter must be reliable (*Studies in Mark*, 83). See also R. Martin, *New Testament Foundations: A Guide for Christian Students*, vol. 1 (Grand Rapids: Eerdmans, 1975), 178.

39. Wright, *New Testament and the People of God*, 397–98.

40. France, *Evidence for Jesus*, 106.

41. Mack perhaps sees the implausibility of suggesting that eyewitnesses could have been won over to Mark's new vision of Jesus, for he insists that, "It is probable that Mark's group did not contain anyone who had known Jesus." Hence, "the past was ripe for reconstruction, full of various fantasies and mythic imageries" (*MI*, 328, 330). It is not clear, however, why he thinks such a supposition is "probable." And it is not clear why such a state of affairs, even if it were granted, would entail that the history of the Jesus people was "ripe for reconstruction." We still have corporate memory and oral tradition to contend with. See the relevant discussion in T.W. Manson, "The Foundations of the Synoptic Tradition: The Gospel of Mark," in *Studies in the Gospels*, ed. M. Black (Philadelphia: Fortress, 1962), 28–45. Manson's basic argument is that the presence of disciples of Jesus in the church would significantly check the amount of creativity allowed in modifying the Jesus traditions.

42. Oden, *Word of Life*, 221.

43. Hengel, *Studies in Mark*, 33.

44. Mack, *MI*, 12.

45. Ibid., 15.

46. Ibid., 21.

47. On the difficulty of arriving at (let alone starting with!) the "why" of an author, see the classic essay by C.S. Lewis, "Fern-Seed and Elephants," in *Fern-Seed and Elephants and Other Essays on Christianity* (Glasgow: William Collins, 1975). On the limitations of redaction criticism and the need for restraint in its employment, see C. Black II, "The Quest of Mark the Redactor: Why Has It Been Used, and What Has It Taught Us?" *Journal for the Study of the New Testament* 33 (1988): 19–39; M.D. Hooker, "On Using the Wrong Tool," *Theology* 75 (1972): 573; and D.A. Carson, "Redaction Criticism: On the Legitimacy and Illegitimacy of a Literary Tool," in *Scripture and Truth*, ed. D.A. Carson and J.D. Woodbridge (Grand Rapids: Zondervan, 1983), 123–28. For a contrasting exemplary restrained use of redaction criticism in discerning the redaction history of Mark, see R.H. Stein, "Ascertaining a Marcan Redactional History: The Proper Methodology," in *Gospels and Tradition: Studies on Redaction Criticism of the Synoptic Gospels* (Grand Rapids: Baker, 1991), 49–67.

48. Significant here is Dahl's observation: "Whoever thinks that the disciples completely misunderstood their Master or even consciously falsified his picture may give fantasy free reign" (Dahl, *Jesus the Christ*, 94–95). Such an approach, he adds, violates common sense and scientific procedure.

49. Mack, *MI*, 203, see also 195–98.

50. Ibid., 294–95.

51. Ibid., 199–202.

52. Ibid., 76, 222–24.

53. Ibid., 238.

54. Ibid., 114.

55. This is not, according to Mack, an original Markan creation. The mythology of the "Christ-cult" had already created this fiction, and Mark's use

of it is "positive proof of his acquaintance with Hellenistic Christianity" (*MI,* 275).

56. Crossan, *JRB,* 35–36; cf. Crossan, *HJ,* 232. See Livy's *History of Rome,* Bk. 39:43:3–4.

57. Crossan, *JRB,* 88–91.

58. Crossan, *JRB,* 140–45; Crossan, *HJ,* 390–91.

59. Crossan, *JRB,* 152–58; Crossan, *HJ,* 393–94. If Mark was concerned with avoiding the ugly aspects of Jesus' death, one wonders why he did not edit out (let alone *create* into) Jesus' cry of 15:34. The point seems to be the opposite of what Crossan suggests — a point emphasized in the early Christian kerygma: Jesus *was* cursed! (Gal. 3:13; cf. also Acts 5:30; 10:37; 13:29; 1 Peter 2:24)

60. Though Martin does not have Crossan or Mack in mind, his comment on this sort of exegetical speculation is to the point: "The elaborateness of such a construction does not argue for its cogency; and its oversubtlety is its weakness" *(Foundations in the New Testament,* 209). Equally to the point (though again neither Crossan nor Mack is in mind) is H. Gardner's argument that we cannot believe that Mark's readers would have understood his text in an overly subtle fashion. See H. Gardner, "The Poetry of St. Mark," in *The Limits of Literary Criticsm: Reflections on the Interpretation of Poetry and Scripture* (London/New York: Oxford Univ. Press, 1956), 34.

61. One is reminded of Hengel's comment, spoken against exegetes who work with the assumption that Mark is not relaying historical information: "It is striking how in their concern to dehistoricize Mark's narrative they have recently found themselves led into an unbounded allegorization of the material, as they have to attribute to it a deeper, unhistorical, symbolic-dogmatic significance" *(Studies in Mark,* 34). Equally to the point is his comment that, "All conjectures about the role of the Galilean communities in the rise of the Gospel of Mark lead to groundless speculations" *(Acts and Earliest Christianity,* 76). See also N. Dahl, *Jesus the Christ,* 94–95.

62. R.H. Stein, "The 'Criteria' for Authenticity," in *Gospels and Tradition,* 156. Cf. also Hengel, *Acts and Earliest Christianity,* 55–56.

63. G.J. Reiner, *History: Its Purpose and Method* (London: Allen & Unwin, 1950), 90–91. Even where a particular account is suspect because of legendary material, Hengel argues, the historian "must look for its historical nucleus, or ask why it was produced in the first place" *(Acts and Earliest Christianity,* 12–13).

64. See Stein, "The 'Criteria' for Authenticity," in *Gospels and Tradition.* See also J. Jeremias, *New Testament Theology: The Proclamation of Jesus* (London: SCM, 1971), 37.

65. For discussions on the nature of the Gospels and their use of traditional material, see Stein, "The 'Criteria' for Authenticity," in *Gospels and Tradition;* K. Nickle, *The Synoptic Gospels: An Introduction* (Atlanta: Knox, 1981; London: SCM, 1982); and D.A. Carson, D. Moo, and L. Morris, "The Synoptic Gospels," in their *An Introduction to the New Testament* (Grand Rapids: Zondervan, 1992), 19–60.

66. A fact that should have significant repercussion on our readiness to postulate errors and contradictions within, and between, the Gospels. See C. Blomberg, "The Legitimacy and Limits of Harmonization," in *Hermenuetics, Authority and Canon,* ed. D.A. Carson and J. Woodbridge (Grand Rapids: Zondervan, 1986), 170–71. For an excellent discussion on ancient historiography, see C. Hemer, *The Book of Acts in the Setting of Hellenistic History,* ed. C.H. Gempf (Tübingen: Mohr, 1989), chap. 3.

67. C. Hemer, *Book of Acts;* I.H. Marshall, *Luke: Historian and Theologian* (Grand Rapids: Zondervan, 1989), 54–55. See my discussion in chap. 5 on this point.

68. *Acts and Earliest Christianity,* 12.

69. Ibid., 27–28.

70. P. Gardener-Smith argues that the quick and universal acceptance of Mark's Gospel as historical means that the burden of proof must rest on contemporary scholars who deny it. See *The Christ of the Gospels* (Cambridge: Heffer, 1938), 36.

71. Indeed, if showing bias itself undermined historical credibility, most modern historiography would have to be discredited as well, for no one writes except out of some perspective or other and with some dominating purpose. See Hemer, *Book of Acts,* 85ff.

72. For arguments along these lines, see Wright, *New Testament and the People of God,* 403; M. Erickson, *The Word Became Flesh: A Contemporary Incarnational Christology* (Grand Rapids: Baker, 1991), 386–88; France, *Evidence for Jesus,* 106; and D.A. Carson, "Historical Tradition in the Fourth Gospel: After Dodd, What?" in *Studies of History and Tradition in the Four Gospels, GP* 2 ed. R.T. France and D. Wenham (Sheffield: JSOT, 1981), 104–7, as well as idem, *The Gospel According to John* (Grand Rapids: Eerdmans, 1991), 40. While a good many New Testament scholars dismiss the historical reliability of the Gospel authors because of their faith perspective, it is perhaps inappropriate to accuse Mack of doing this. The reason why he feels we can derive little information about "Jesus' manner of life, message, and effect upon people" from the Gospel records is because "they were not written for the purpose of keeping alive a memory of an interesting person. They were written to authorize matters held to be important and foundational for their cause" (*MI,* 62). This doesn't seem to constitute a "faith perspective." It is, in any event, certainly clear from his treatment of Mark that he does not think Mark for a moment *actually believed* most of the things he was writing.

73. Hengel, *Acts and Earliest Christianity,* 43. See also his *Studies in Mark,* xii; and Wright, *New Testament and the People of God,* 43.

74. *Jesus the Christ,* 34. Similarly, Hengel writes: "For Mark . . . the 'historical' narrative account of the activity and passion of Jesus as an essential part of the proclamation of the gospel: for him, preaching and historical narrative are not opposites, but are indissolubly connected. For that very reason he can describe his work as *euangelion iasou Christou* – to be understood in the ancient sense as a biography of Jesus" (*Studies in Mark,* 74).

75. Wright, *New Testament and the People of God,* 95.

76. See France, *Evidence for Jesus,* 103; Erickson, *Word of Life,* 387, Carson, *Gospel of John,* 40–41. Carson draws an insightful analogy between this and the historical reports of survivors of Auschwitz. They were intensely passionate and shockingly accurate about what they reported. See "Historical Tradition and the Fourth Gospel," 104–7.

77. Mack, *MI,* 325–31. The extent to which Mark's overall narrative structure should be understood in apocalyptic categories is a matter of much dispute, ranging from S. Schulz, who is convinced that Mark is "anti-apocalyptic," "Mark's Significance for the Theology of Early Christianity," in *The Interpretation of Mark, Issues in Religion and Theology,* no. 7, ed. W.R. Tellford (Philadelphia: Fortress, 1985), to Mack and Crossan, in agreement with H. Kee, *Community and Community of the New Age: Studies in Mark's Gospel* (London: SCM, 1977) and N. Perrin and D. Duling, *The New Testament: An Introduction,* 2nd ed. (New York: Harcourt Brace Jovanovich, 1982), that he is apocalyptic through and through. Mack and Crossan's position seems tenable, but it seems that they have been overly influenced by Bultmann's dualistic understanding of apocalyptic which plays it off against historical interests.

78. See Wright, *New Testament and the People of God,* chap. 10, and (applied especially to Mark), 390–96.

79. Ibid., 391. Far from being a "retrojection of their own Christian experience," Wright argues, a narrative analysis of the Gospels reveals "a sense of dependence upon unique and unrepeatable events which had taken place earlier . . . their intention was to tell stories about events which really took place, and to invest those stories with the significance which, within their total worldview, they irreducibly possessed" (p. 398).

80. See G.N. Stanton, *Jesus of Nazareth in New Testament Preaching* (Cambridge: Cambridge Univ. Press, 1974); C. Talbert, *What Is a Gospel? The Genre of the Canonical Gospels* (Philadelphia: Fortress, 1977); France, *Evidence for Jesus*, 96–97; and esp. R. Burridge, *What Are the Gospels? A Comparison with Graeco-Roman Biography* (Cambridge: Cambridge Univ. Press, 1992). The parallels, however, should not be pressed too far, especially as it concerns the frequent conceptions of divinized heroes found in ancient biographies. See D.E. Aune, "The Problem of the Genre of the Gospels: A Critique of C.H. Talbert's 'What Is a Gospel?' " *GP* 2 (Sheffield: JSOT, 1981), 9–60.

81. Wright, *New Testament and the People of God*, 381–82.

82. Hengel, *Acts and Earliest Christianity*, 12.

83. Mack, *MI*, 208.

84. Hengel, *Acts and Earliest Christianity*, 13.

85. Wright, *New Testament and the People of God*, 92–93.

86. A worldview which, I have noted (chap. 5), is already becoming obsolete even within Western culture! The advent of "postmodernism" is, at both a popular and (more slowly) at an academic level, disintegrating the tyranny of the "closed universe" understanding of reality.

87. Wright, *New Testament and the People of God*, 92. The assumption is particularly unwarranted in the science of academic historiography, says Hugo Staudinger, for here the object of study is always "events which happened once and are not repeatable." See "The Resurrection of Jesus Christ as Saving Event and as 'Object' of Historical Research," *Scottish Journal of Theology* 36:3 (1983), 313.

88. In contrast to Troeltsch's famous "principle of analogy" which dictates that all historical understanding must be arrived at by analogically referencing the events of the past to the present. For a summary of Troeltsch's view, see his "Historiography," in *Encyclopaedia of Religion and Ethics*, vol. 6, ed. James Hastings (New York: Scribner's; Edinburgh: T & T Clark, 1913), 716–23. For critical discussions of this view, see W. Abraham, *Divine Revelation and the Limits of Historical Criticism* (New York/Oxford: Oxford Univ. Press, 1982); and W. Pannenberg, *Basic Questions in Theology*, vol. 1, trans. G. Kehm (Philadelphia: Fortress, 1970), 43–53.

89. J.G. Lloyd, *Alexander the Great: Selections from Arrian* (Cambridge: Cambridge Univ. Press, 1981), 58.

90. See the discussion in Staudinger, "Resurrection of Jesus Christ as Saving Event," 314.

91. One's own experience of the "miraculous" obviously impacts how one evaluates the miraculous dimension of the Gospel narratives. Wolfgang Schadewaldt, e.g., tells of his willingness to believe the Gospel accounts of Jesus feeding the 5,000 partly because of a trustworthy acquaintance of his who reported to him a similar incident while conducting archaeological excavations in Upper Egypt ("The Reliability of the Synoptic Tradition," in Hengel, *Studies in Mark*, 102). For those, such as this author, who have personally witnessed "supernatural" events (such as immediate healings), the Gospel accounts are not all that difficult to believe. For a collection of such stories, see G. Ashe, *Miracle* (London: Routledge & Kegan Paul, 1978). For a comprehensive discussion of the issue of miracles, see C. Brown, *That You May Believe: Miracles and Faith Then and Now* (Grand Rapids: Eerdmans, 1985) as well as his more scholarly *Miracles and the Critical Mind* (Grand

Rapids: Eerdmans, 1984).

92. See Mack, *MI*, 215, 223. Crossan, we have seen (chap. 3), accepts that "Jesus was both an exorcist and a healer" (*HJ*, 332, cf. 311), but nevertheless interprets these displays in social symbolic terms (e.g., *HJ*, 313–18, 397, 404). His sociologically reductionist view is in some respects similar to that of A. Wire in "The Structure of the Gospel Miracle Stories and Their Tellers," *Semeia* 11 (1978), 83–113.

93. So Marcus Borg concludes, e.g., that Jesus was noted by his contemporaries for his healings and exorcism. See *Jesus: A New Vision Spirit: Culture, and the Life of Discipleship* (San Francisco: Harper and Row, 1987), 60. See also G. Theissen's excellent work, *The Miracle Stories of the Early Christian Tradition*, trans. F. McDonagh (Philadelphia: Fortress, 1983), as well as C. Blomberg, *The Historical Reliability of the Gospels* (Downers Grove, Ill.: InterVarsity, 1987), 93–94, and G. Maier, "Zur neutesstamentlichen Wunderexegese im 19. und 20. Jahrhundert," in *The Miracles of Jesus, GP* 6 ed. D. Wenham and C.L. Blomberg (Sheffield: JSOT, 1986), 49–87.

94. E. Best, *Disciples and Discipleship: Studies in the Gospel According to Mark* (Edinburgh: T & T Clark, 1986), 182.

95. In this respect, one is puzzled as to why Crossan dates the Cross Gospel, which he extracts from the mythologically extravagant Gospel of Peter, before the canonical Gospels (*HJ*, 429). For discussions comparing Gospel materials to legendary and magical materials, see W. Nauck, "Die Bedeutung des leeren Grabes für den Glauben an den Auferstnenen," *Zeitschrift für die neutesstaamentliche Wissenschaft* 47 (1956): 243–67, who argues that Mark lacks most of the features found in legendary texts. For other discussions, see Theissen, *Miracle Stories*, 244–45, 76–86; Blomberg, *Reliability of the Gospels*, 80–92; B. Witheringon III, *The Christology of Jesus* (Minneapolis: Fortress, 1990), 156–61; E. Yamauchi, "Magic or Miracle? Diseases, Demons and Exorcisms," in *Miracles of Jesus*, 89–183; C. Holladay, *Theios Aner in Hellenistic Judaism* (Missoula, Mont.: Scholars, 1977); and J. Hull, *Hellenistic Magic and the Synoptic Tradition* (London: SCM, 1974).

96. So W. Schadewald argues in "The Reliability of the Synoptic Tradition," in Hengel, *Studies in Mark*, 100–101, as does Blomberg, *Reliability of Gospels*, 92.

Chapter 11: Obscure Nobody or Apostolic Authority?

1. See M. Hengel, *Studies in the Gospel of Mark*, trans. J. Bowden (Philadelphia: Fortress, 1985), 65. Against many of his contemporaries, B.H. Streeter defended the traditional authorship of Mark. See *The Four Gospels* (New York: Macmillan, 1925), but his defense has found little support among nonconservative New Testament scholars. For an overview, supporting Streeter's views, see R.H. Fuller, *A Critical Introduction to the New Testament* (London: Duckworth, 1966).

2. See Hengel, *Studies in Mark*, 64–84. For related lines of argumentation, see B. Reicke, *The Roots of the Synoptic Gospels* (Philadelphia: Fortress, 1986), 154; R.A. Guelich, *Mark 1-8:26* (Dallas: Word, 1989), xxvi–xxviii.

3. Tertullian, *Against Marcion*, cited in Hengel, *Studies in Mark*, 69. His whole discussion on pages 67–72 is relevant here.

4. Eusebius, *Historica Ecclesiastica* 3:39, 15.

5. Hengel, *Studies in Mark*, 150.

6. I.H. Marshall, *I Believe in the Historical Jesus* (Grand Rapids: Eerdmans, 1976), 146. Cf. Hengel, *Studies in Mark*, 4, who argues against such an apologetic on literary grounds. We might add, if Papias (or those he's relying on) was involved in propaganda, some explanation for why he decided upon

the rather obscure figure of John Mark and limited Peter to a "behind-the-scenes" source must be given. For other favorable assessments of the Papias material, see F.F. Bruce, "The Date and Character of Mark," in *Jesus and the Politics of His Day*, ed. E. Bammel and C.F.D. Moule (Cambridge: Cambridge Univ. Press, 1984), 75–76; D.A. Carson, D.J. Moo, and L. Morris, *An Introduction to the New Testament* (Grand Rapids: Zondervan, 1992), 92–95; C.E.B. Cranfield, *The Gospel According to Saint Mark*, CGTC (Cambridge: Cambridge Univ. Press, 1963), 5; E.E. Ellis, "The Date and Provenance of Mark's Gospel," in *The Four Gospels: Festschrift Frans Neirynck*, vol. 2, ed. F. Van Segbroeck, et al. (Leuven, Belgium: Leuven Univ. Press, 1992), 800–801; J. Kuerzinger, "Der Aussage des Papias von Hierapolis zur literarischen Form des Markusevaangeliums," *Biblische Zeitschrift* 21 (1970): 245–64; A.C. Perumalil, "Are Not Papias and Irenaeus Competent to Report on the Gospels?" *Expository Times* 91 (1980): 332–37; C.S. Petrie, "The Authorship of 'The Gospel According to Matthew,' " *New Testament Studies* 14 (1967–1968): 29; and H. Riley, *The Making of Mark: An Exploration* (Macon, Ga.: Mercer Univ. Press, 1989), 251–52.

7. Hengel, *Studies in Mark*, 47–48. See R.P. Martin, *Mark: Evangelist and Theologian* (Exeter: Paternoster, 1972), 80–83.

8. Marshall, *I Believe in the Historical Jesus*, 146. See also R. Martin, *New Testament Foundations: A Guide for Christian Students*, vol. 1 (Grand Rapids: Eerdmans, 1975), 204–5. If "Babylon" is a reference to Rome, as the majority of scholars contend, this passage also serves to further confirm Papias' location of Rome as the place of origin for this Gospel. See the discussion in D. Guthrie, *New Testament Introduction* (Downers Grove, Ill.: InterVarsity, 1970), 801–3. The fact that Mark explains Jewish customs (e.g., 7:3-4), along with the strong presence of Latinisms in his Gospel, also squares with an origin in Rome, as does Mark's mention of a Rufus (Mark 15:21) who we know from Paul was prominent in Rome (Rom. 16:13). See Guthrie, *New Testament Introduction*, 59–63, and Hengel, *Studies in Mark*, 28–30.

9. P. Barnett, *Is the New Testament Reliable?* (Downers Grove, Ill.: InterVarsity, 1986), 84.

10. F.F. Bruce, *The New Testament Documents: Are They Reliable?* (Grand Rapids: Eerdmans, 1983), 36.

11. Hengel's argument against Papias deriving his source from 1 Peter 5:13 is weak, insofar as it completely hangs on the assumption that 1 Peter is pseudepigraphal and was composed at the time of Domitian. *Studies in Mark*, 69. A sounder approach is to simply point out that Papias has no motive to lie about John as the source of his information, and since we lack any evidence to the contrary, there is virtually no reason not to accept him.

12. Justin, *Dialogue*, 106.3, cf. 103.8, Irenaeus, *Against Heresies*, 3.1.1; Clement, *Hyptyposes*, 6. See the discussion in Hengel, *Studies in Mark*, 1–6, 50–51, and *Acts and Earliest Christianity*, 9. By no means do all scholars accept the dependency of Irenaeus, Origen, and Clement upon Papias. Permalil ("Papias and Irenaeus," 332–35) and Petrie ("Authorship of Matthew," 29) argue for their independence. Even if they are dependent, however, this yet indicates that there was no compelling evidence *against* the historicity of Papias' remark at the time of their writing.

13. On the "stubby fingered" saying in the anti-Marcionite prologue, see Ellis, "Date and Provenance," 802–3 and Geulich, *Mark*, xxiv.

14. Note in this regard Crossan's preference for his own speculative views of how Secret Mark was incorporated into Mark over the testimony of Clement (on whom we depend for any knowledge of this fragment!) that the canonical Gospel came first (*HJ*, 412). It is not being too naive to ask, "Who is in a better position to decide this?" See the discussion in R.T. France, *The Evidence for Jesus* (Downers Grove, Ill.: InterVarsity, 1986), 83.

15. So argues Bruce, "Date and Character," 75–77; Ellis, "Date and Provenance," 806–7; R.H. Gundry, *Mark: A Commentary of His Apology for the Cross* (Grand Rapids: Eerdmans, 1993), 1034–41; B. Orchard, "Mark and the Fusion of Traditions," in *The Four Gospels 1992: Festschrift Frans Neirynck*, BETL 100, ed. F. van Segbroeck, et al. (Leuven, Belgium: Leuven Univ. Press, 1992), II, 779–800; idem, "The Publication of Mark's Gospel," in *The Synoptic Gospels: Source Criticism and the New Literary Criticism*, BETL 110 ed. C. Focant, (Leuven, Belgium: Leuven Univ. Press, 1993), 518–20; and Hengel, *Studies in Mark*, 52, cf. 8–9.

16. Hengel, *Studies in Mark*, 51.

17. "The Portrayal of Peter in the Synoptic Gospels," in Hengel, *Studies in Mark*, 59.

18. In the words of the great classic philologist W. Schadewaldt, "Only Peter himself can have told how directly after his own confession he sought to keep his Lord from suffering, and the same is true of the account of the denial. . . . This basic human fact of commitment followed by failure and then revival indicates Peter's greatness and power and thus at the same time lends truth to what is said of him, and of Jesus." "The Reliability of the Synoptic Tradition," in Hengel, *Studies in Mark*, 108–9. See also R. Martin, *Foundations of the New Testament*, 204.

19. Hengel, *Studies in Mark*, 156.

20. C.H. Turner, *The Gospel According to St. Mark* (London: S.P.C.K., 1928), pt. 3, see esp. 54–55.

21. Vincent Taylor, one of the pioneers of form criticism, argued this point concerning Mark's narrative as well as anyone in *The Gospel Accoring to St. Mark* (London: SPCK, 1959), 135–40. Bultmann, and many form critics following him, argued in the opposite direction, however. The addition of detail, he maintained, signifies lateness in the tradition. See his *Die Erförshung der synoptischen Evangelien*, 4th ed. (Berlin: Alfred Topelmann, 1961), 22. Paradoxically, Bultmann (and the majority of form critics who followed him) nevertheless held to Markan priority, though Mark is the most detailed of the Synoptic Gospels. E.P. Sanders' work, *The Tendencies of the Synoptic Tradition* (Cambridge: Cambridge Univ. Press, 1969), effectively demonstrated the difficulty of speaking confidently of any definitive "tendencies" within the Synoptic tradition. He too held, however, that in a very general way the accrual of detail tended to signify lateness in the tradition and thus was not indicative of an eyewitness influence (see 92ff, 274). His conclusion, however, was largely based on the questionable assumption that we can infer something about the development of the pre-canonical tradition from an analysis of how second- and third-century authors expanded upon the Synoptic tradition. In any case, it is safe to argue that the presence of incidental details in Mark's Gospel serves to confirm an eyewitness influence *if* we have collaborating grounds for believing that an eyewitness is behind this work — which, I am here maintaining, we in fact have.

22. Barnett, *Is the New Testament Reliable?* 92. Even the radical form critic K.L. Schmidt is impressed with 9:14-29 to the point of concluding that the story "can only go back to good tradition." Cited in R. Martin, *New Testament Foundations*, 203.

23. The quotation of Jesus in Aramaic in this passage (5:41) also favors interpreting it as a historical reminiscence. More generally, the Semitic style of Mark's language, and the arguable presence of an Aramaic background to the Greek he uses, also squares well with, if not implies, an early Jewish eyewitness behind the Gospel. See Martin, *New Testament Foundations*, 202–3; F.F. Bruce, *New Testament Documents*, 37.

24. On this passage Rattey comments, "Mark alone tells us all this; but who told Mark? It could only have been one of the Twelve" (B.K. Rattey, *The*

Making of the Synoptic Gospels [New York: Macmillan, 1942], 32). We should perhaps note that form criticism has, for a number of reasons, tended to regard much of the detail we are alluding to here as constituting "Markan seams" — editorial insertions by Mark that serve to string together the narrative he is constructing from traditional material. This frequent form critical position only adversely affects the point I am making if it is assumed that one only editorializes with *fiction*. But there is no good reason to accept this assumption. Indeed, the presence of eyewitness-like detail in the "Markan seams" that string together his narrative is what one might expect if in fact Mark is combining traditional material with eyewitness reminiscences from Peter.

25. So argues Marshall, *I Believe in the Historical Jesus*, 205–6. Even Mack finds "[t]he very human characterization of Jesus" in the Gethsemane story to be 'startling' " (*MI*, 306), though he does not on that account think it relates actual history (*MI*, 307–8). One wonders what *would* count as evidence of historical reliability for Mack.

26. C.F.D. Moule, *The Phenomenon of the New Testament* (Naperville, Ill.: Allenson, 1967), 63, 67. Even Crossan and Mack, we have seen, regard the radically egalitarian style of Jesus as historical.

27. Barnett, *Is the New Testament Reliable?* 96–97.

28. It is sometimes argued that since Mark mentions Dalmanutha (8:10) which is otherwise unknown, his geography must be mistaken. The same argument, however, was frequently used against the Gospels' mention of Nazareth which is not mentioned in any literature of the time and, until recently, had no independent archaeological attestation. Now, however, the existence of Nazareth and the Gospels accurate portrayal of it are universally recognized. See J. Finegan, *The Archeology of the New Testament* (Princeton: Princeton Univ. Press, 1969), 27–29. On the whole, in the few places where archaeology is relevant to Mark's material, it tends to confirm his historical accuracy, even (or esp.) concerning the incidental features of his story. On Mark 1:29-34, e.g., see E.M. Meyers and J.F. Strange, *Archaeology, the Rabbis and Early Christianity* (Nashville: Abingdon, 1981), 60, 129; and R.T. France, *Evidence for Jesus*, 148. Due consideration must, however, be given to Mark's redactional purposes and how his topography structures his Gospel. For discussions, see W. Marxen, *Mark the Evangelist* (New York: Abingdon, 1969), 54–116; G.H. Boobyer, "Galilee and Galileans in St. Mark's Gospel," *Bulletin of the John Rylands University Library of Manchester* 35 (1953): 334–48. For a discussion of other difficulties in geography in Mark, see Guthrie, *New Testament Introduction*, 60–61.

29. "The Reliability of the Synoptic Tradition," in Hengel, *Studies in Mark*, 102.

30. Ibid., 102–4. cf. R.M. Frye, "Literary Criticism and Gospel Criticism," *Theology Today* 36 (1976): 207–19; and T. Oden, *Word of Life*, 223, who argues that radical New Testament criticism is "addicted" to archaic literary techniques.

31. "Jesus' apocalyptic instruction in Mark 13 is the important bit of evidence for a post-70 C.E. date." (*MI*, 315). Sometimes Mark 12:9 and Mark 15:38 which speak of the destruction of the tenants and of the rending of the veil in the temple are seen as prefigurations of this event as well, but this constitutes a highly questionable exegesis of these passages. See Hengel, *Studies in Mark*, 14. As Mack notes (*MI*, 318), there is an increasing trend among contemporary scholars to date Mark and the other Gospels early, with a number of scholars pushing for a pre-70 origin. J.A.T. Robinson's, *Redating the New Testament* (Philadelphia: Westminster, 1976), has been foundational. See also B. Reicke, "Synoptic Problems on the Destruction of Jerusalem," in *Studies in New Testament and Early Christian Literature: Essays in Honor*

of Allen P. Wikgren, Novum Testamentum Supp. 33, ed. D.E. Aune (Leiden: Brill, 1972), 121–34; J. Wenham, *Redating Matthew, Mark, and Luke: A Fresh Assault on the Synoptic Problem* (London: Hodder and Stoughton, 1991); E.E. Ellis, "Dating the New Testament," *New Testament Studies* 26 (1980): 487–502, as well as his "Date and Provenance of Mark's Gospel," 801–16; Bruce, "Date and Character," 77–81; Carson, Moo, and Morris, *New Testament*, 96–99; Riley, *Making of Mark*, 253.

32. Martin, *Foundations of the New Testament*, 214. This is true of the Matthean and Lukan parallels as well, a fact that led C.C. Torrey to date all the Synoptics before A.D. 66. See *The Apocalypse of John* (New Haven: Yale Univ. Press, 1958), 86.

33. Conversely, there are a number of things one would have thought Mark would have *included* had he composed the narrative after the event. See Robinson, *Redating the New Testament*, 15–21; A.E.J. Rawlinson, *The Gospel According to St. Mark*, 7th ed. (London: Methuen, 1949), xxix–xxx; V. Taylor, *Gospel According to St. Mark*, 32; and M. Erickson, *The Word Became Flesh: A Contemporary Incarnational Christology* (Grand Rapids: Baker, 1991), 390–91. We have discussed Wright's uncustomary understanding of apocalyptic in the previous chapter and have found it persuasive. In his view, the cataclysmic nature of apocalyptic language — stars falling from heaven, the Son of man returning, and the like — was never meant to be taken literally (see N.T. Wright, *The New Testament and the People of God* [Minneapolis: Fortress, 1992], 252–53, 280–99, 392–96, 459–64). Still, Mark 13 is laced with references that are difficult to take as nonliteral, such as the prediction that believers will be delivered up before kings and the Gospel preached to the whole world (9, 11–13). Hence, our point against reading it as a *vaticinium ex eventu* remains. For a different approach, one that dates the Synoptic apocalypse early on the basis of its commonalities with Paul, see D. Wenham, "Paul and the Synoptic Apocalypse," in *Studies of History and Tradition in the Four Gospels*, GP 2 (Sheffield: JSOT, 1982); 345–74, as well as Robinson, *Redating the New Testament*, 105–6, and especially his *Jesus and His Coming* (New York: Abingdon, 1958), 105–11.

34. See Hengel's detailed discussion in *Studies in Mark*, 14–28.

35. See Robinson, *Redating the New Testament*, 15.

36. The church tradition is of little help here as it is divided over whether or not the Gospel of Mark was composed during Peter's lifetime or after his death. See Hengel, *Studies in Mark*, 2–6.

37. We know of a Rufus who was prominent in the church at Rome (Rom. 16:13). If this is the same Rufus referred to by Mark, as seems likely, it again supports Papias' contention that Mark composed his Gospel under Peter's tutelage in Rome.

38. Hengel, *Studies in Mark*, 9. Cf. M. Hengel, *Between Jesus and Paul*, trans. J. Bowden (Philadelphia: Fortress, 1983), 148, n.117.

39. An ossuary was recently discovered in a tomb near Jerusalem. Belonging to a Cyrenian Jewish family of the first century, it bore the inscription "Alexander, son of Simon." While "Alexander" and "Simon" were fairly common names, and while it is possible there were other Cyrenian Simon/Alexander, father/son relationships in the late first century, it nevertheless hardly constitutes wild speculation to suppose that we have here the ossuary of the Alexander referred to in Mark 15:21. See France, *Evidence for Jesus*, 145.

40. Pesch goes so far as to maintain that this material only makes sense if we date it back to a time when Caiaphus *was* still high priest! See R. Pesch, *Das Markusevaangelium* II (Dasel: Herder, 1977), 21. He maintains, however, that this material significantly predates Mark's Gospel as a whole. Even if, as a number of scholars conjecture, the passion narrative of Mark substantially

predates Mark, the antiquity of this material, and hence the reliability of this material, remains intact.

41. Hengel, *Studies in Mark*, 9.

42. Ibid., 9, 123–24, n.58.

43. Ibid., 10.

44. Robinson suggests that the omission of any mention of James' death in the Gospels is perhaps indicative that they were written before this event. See *Redating the New Testament*, 107.

Chapter 12: Acts of Luke's Mind, or Acts of the Apostles?

1. The same holds true for all revisionist accounts of the early church. Harnack, who himself "converted" away from a late dating and low estimation of the historical value of Acts, reflects the centrality of this work in one's overall understanding of the early church, including all the documents of the New Testament, when he states: "All the mistakes which have been made in New Testament criticism have been focused into the criticism of the Acts of the Apostles" (Adolf von Harnack, *Luke the Physician*, trans. J.R. Wilkinson [London: Putnam's, 1907], 3).

2. This view of Acts is not so much argued in Crossan's and Mack's works as it is presupposed (see e.g., *LG*, 234–35; *HJ*, 432), though Crossan does make occasional use of it in his own reconstruction of several early traditions (e.g., *HJ*, 201, 401, 414).

3. For Mack and Crossan's account to be accepted, however, not only must their view of Acts be accepted, but their marginalized view of Paul and fictitious understanding of Mark as well. My earlier critiques of these latter positions thus already constitute arguments against their revisionist understanding of early church history.

4. The contemporary trend among historical-critical approaches to Acts is to focus on an analysis of Luke's theology, literary conventions, "creativity," and use of sources, and to do this on the assumption that he is not on the whole conveying reliable history. The literary and source-critical approaches of H. Conzelmann, *The Theology of St. Luke*, trans. G. Buswell (1955; reprint, Philadelphia: Fortress, 1982) and E. Haenchen, *Die Apostelgeschicht neu übersetzt und erklärt* (Göttingen: Vandenhoeck & Ruprecht, 1956) have been especially influential in the last few decades. For an excellent critical review of the history of the historical-critical approach to Acts, see W.W. Gasque, *A History of the Criticism of the Acts of the Apostles*, 2nd ed. (Peabody, Mass.: Hendrickson, 1989 [1975]).

5. F.F. Bruce, *The Acts of the Apostles: The Greek Text with Introduction and Commentary* (Grand Rapids: Eerdmans, 1990), 1–2.

6. A.C. Clark attempted to argue against this in his *The Acts of the Apostles* (Oxford: Clarendon, 1933), but few have followed him. He was effectively answered by W.L. Knox, *The Acts of the Apostles* (Cambridge: Cambridge Univ. Press, 1948), 2–15, 100–109. See also on this issue I.H. Marshall, *The Acts of the Apostles* (Sheffield: JSOT, 1992), 98, and H.-J. Shulz, *Die apostolische Herkunft Evangelien*, QD 145 (Freiburg/Basel/Vienna: Harder, 1993), 243–91. Also on this issue see C.J. Hemer's excellent argument for Lucan authorship in *The Book of Acts in the Setting of Hellenistic History*, ed. C.H. Gempf (Tübingen: Mohr, 1989), 308–34, 413–14. This latter work constitutes the most recent, and certainly the most compelling, comprehensive argument for the historical reliability of Acts. For a summary and appreciative review, see W.W. Gasque, "The Historical Value of Acts," *Tyndale Bulletin* 40 (1989): 136–57.

7. See B.E. Beck, "The Common Authorship of Luke and Acts," *New Testament Studies* 23 (1976–77): 346–52; J.M. Dawsey, "The Literary Question

of Style—a Task for Literary Critics," *New Testament Studies* 35 (1989): 48–66; and esp. Hemer, *Acts in Hellenistic History*, 30–33.

8. For example, Luke alone records Jesus' appearance before Herod Antipas (23:7-12), a fact also mentioned in Acts (4:27).

9. See M. Hengel's discussion in *Acts and the History of Earliest Christianity*, trans. J. Bowden (Philadelphia: Fortress, 1979), 66–67; Hemer, *Acts in Hellenistic Setting*, 312–14; idem, "First-Person Narrative in Acts 27–28," *Tyndale Bulletin* 36 (1985): 79–109; H.J. Cadbury, " 'We' and 'I' Passages in Luke–Acts," *New Testament Studies* 3 (1956–57): 128–32; and P. Barnett, *Is the New Testament Reliable?* (Downers Grove, Ill.: InterVarsity, 1986), 141–42.

10. See V. Robbins, "The We-Passages in Acts and Ancient Sea Voyages," *Bible Review* 20 (1975): 1–14.

11. It also leaves unexplained why a later author would not have named the author of this source if it was regarded as carrying extra authoritative weight. Bruce, *Acts of the Apostles*, 4. It should, however, be noted that even among those who argue along these lines, Acts can still be viewed as containing reliable historical information. See, e.g., G. Lüdemann, "Acts of the Apostles as a Historical Source," in *The Social World of Formative Christianity and Judaism: Essays in Tribute to Howard Clark Kee*, ed. J. Neusner, et al. (Philadelphia: Fortress, 1988), 109–25; idem, *Early Christianity According to the Traditions in Acts* (Minneapolis: Fortress, 1989).

12. So argued Harnack, *Luke the Physician*, 25–120. Cf. J.A.T. Robinson, *Redating the New Testament* (Philadelphia: Westminster, 1976), 87. Indeed, Hengel and others have argued that the amount of geographical and cultural-political detail in the "we" passages is greater than other parts of Luke's narrative. See his *Between Jesus and Paul*, trans. J. Bowden (Philadelphia: Fortress, 1983), 97–128. Even M. Dibelius who largely pioneered the source-critical approach to Acts, and who dated Acts in the 90s, held on this basis that the author was a companion of Paul. See *Studies in the Acts of the Apostles*, trans. M. Ling, ed. H. Greeven (London: SCM, 1956), 104. A number of other arguments have at various times been put forth to prove Lucan authorship, but they are extremely tenuous. Something may yet be said, however, for the old argument of Hobart, Ramsey, and Harnack that the vocabulary of Acts (and the Gospel of Luke) has more technical medical terms than one would normally expect, thus suggesting that it was written by a physician (Col. 4:14). See W.K. Hobart, *The Medical Language of St. Luke* (1882; reprint, Grand Rapids: Baker, 1954); W.M. Ramsey, *Luke the Physician and Other Studies in the History of Religion* (London: Hodder and Stoughton, 1908), 1–68; and A. Harnack, *Luke the Physician*, ed. W.D. Morrison, trans. J.R. Wilkinson (New York: Putnam, 1907); and T. Zahn, *Introduction to the New Testament*, rev. 2nd ed., ed. and trans. J.M. Trout, et al. (New York: Scribners, 1917). While the argument won a lot of credence among scholars at the beginning of this century, it has largely fallen into disfavor since H.J. Cadbury's thorough study, *The Style and Literary Method of Luke* (Cambridge: Harvard Univ. Press, 1928). See also idem, "Lexical Notes on Luke-Acts, II: Recent Arguments for Medical Language," *Journal of Biblical Literature* 45 (1926): 190–209. For more recent defenses, however, see A.T. Robertson, *Luke the Historian in the Light of Research* (Grand Rapids: Baker, 1977), chap. 7, 90–102; and W.G. Marx's cautious assessment in "Luke the Physician, Re-examined," *Expository Times* (1971–80): 168–72.

13. In addition to sources cited below, see Hemer, *Acts in Hellenistic History*, 244–307; and J. Jervell, *The Unknown Paul: Essays on Luke-Acts and the Early Church* (Minneapolis: Augsburg, 1984).

14. See Hengel's discussion in *Acts and the History of Earliest Christianity*, trans. J. Bowden (Philadelphia: Fortress, 1979), 67.

15. Robinson, *Redating the New Testament*, 87. See also Hengel, *Acts and the*

History, 66–67. One must, of course, also give Luke a good deal of leeway in the rather free way he composed his "speeches," a customary practice by ancient historians. See F.F. Bruce, "The Acts of the Apostles: Historical Record or Theological Reconstruction?" *Aufstieg und Niedergang der romischen Welt,* ed. H. Temporini and W. Haase, 25:3 (New York; Berlin, de Gruyter, 1985), 2582–88; Hemer, *Acts in Hellenistic History,* app. 1: "Speeches and Miracles in Acts," 415–43; idem, "The Speeches of Acts: I. The Ephesian Elders at Miletus," *Tyndale Bulletin* 40 (1989): 77–85; and idem, "The Speeches in Acts: II. The Areopagus Address," *Tyndale Bulletin* 40 (1989): 239–59. The complex discussion concerning the extent to which these speeches reflect the general theology of Luke and/or how much they reflect the perspectives of the authors they're attributed to cannot here be entered into, and is of little consequence. For classic discussions representative of the former position, see M. Dibelius, "The Speeches in Acts and Ancient Historiography," in *Studies in the Acts of the Apostles,* ed. H. Greeven, trans. M. Ling (London: SCM, 1956), 138–96. For discussions more representative of the latter position, see Bruce, "Historical Record or Theological Reconstruction?" I.H. Marshall, *Luke Historian and Theologian,* 72–73; Hemer, *Acts in Hellenistic History.*

16. So argues Bruce, "Historical Record or Theological Reconstruction?" 2593. See also J.A. Fitzmyer, "The Authorship of Luke-Acts Reconsidered," in *Luke the Theologian: Aspects of His Teaching* (New York: Paulist, 1989), 1–26; and M.A. Powell, *What Are They Saying about Acts?"* (New York: Paulist, 1991), 36.

17. Hemer, *Acts in Hellenistic History,* 409.

18. Somewhat paradoxically, Crossan dates Luke between 80 and 120, and Acts between 120 and 150, though he agrees that the two were conceived together *(HJ,* 431–32). Others who argue for a second century dating of Acts are H. Koester, *Ancient Christian Gospels: Their History and Development* (Philadelphia: Trinity, 1990), 334; J.C. O'Neill, *The Theology of Acts in Its Historical Setting* (London: SPCK, 1961), 1–28; and J.T. Townsend, "The Date of Luke-Acts," in Luke-Acts: *New Perspectives from the Society of Biblical Literature,* ed. C. Talbert (New York: Crossroad, 1984), 47–62. On the whole, however, this once popular position now has few followers. Robertson's two-decade old summary is yet quite true when he says: "It may now be stated definitely that the second-century date for the Gospel and Acts has been abandoned save by a small number of exceedingly radical critics" *(Luke the Historian,* 30).

19. See F.C. Baur, *Paul, the Apostle of Jesus Christ* (London/Edinburgh: Williams and Norgate, 1876), 4ff.

20. See, e.g., E. Käsemann, "Ephesians and Acts" in Studies in *Luke–Acts: Essays Presented in Honor of Paul Schubert,* ed. L.E. Keck and J.L. Martyn (Nashville: Abingdon, 1966), 288ff. On the parallels between Acts on Justin Martyr as evidence for a mid-second century date, see O'Neill, *Acts in Its Historical Setting.*

21. W.G. Kümmell, *Introduction to the New Testament,* 14th rev. ed., trans. A.J. Mattill, Jr. (Nashville: Abingdon, 1966), 186; Hemer, *Acts in Hellenistic History,* 377; Powell, *What Are They Saying?* 36–37.

22. K. Lake argued against Bauer on this basis in *The Earlier Epistles of St. Paul* (London: Rivingtons, 1914), 116. See also L. Morris, "Luke and Early Catholicism," *Westminster Theological Journal* 35 (1973): 121–36.

23. See Bruce, *Acts of the Apostles,* 10.

24. Bruce, "Historical Record or Theological Reconstruction?" 2599.

25. E.g., C.K. Barrett, *Luke the Historian in Recent Study,* 2nd ed. (Philadelphia: Fortress, 1970), 63; and N.T. Wright, *The New Testament and the People of God* (Minneapolis: Fortress, 1992), 376. By way of comparison, it used to be sometimes argued that Luke was to be dated after Josephus on the basis of supposed parallels with this work. See, e.g., F.C. Burkitt, *The Gospel History*

and Its Transmission (Edinburgh: T & T Clark, 1907), 109–10. The work of A. Plummer at the beginning of this century against this view, however, was generally regarded as decisive, and hence few endorse this argument any longer. See A. Plummer, *A Critical and Exegetical Commentary on the Gospel According to St. Luke,* ICC (Edinburgh: T & T Clark, 1901). For discussions, see Robertson, *Luke the Historian,* 32–33, and Hemer, *Acts in Hellenistic History,* 94–99.

26. See Bruce, "Historical Record or Theological Reconstruction?" 2598.

27. H. Koester, *Introduction to the New Testament, Volume 2: History and Literature of Early Christianity* (Philadelphia: Fortress; Berlin/New York: de Gruyter, 1982), 308–23. This perhaps also reveals the ambiguity in discerning Luke's motive in his portrayal of the Roman government. Is he reflecting a peaceful relationship with the government or trying to remedy a hostile one?

28. A. von Harnack, *Date of the Acts and the Synoptic Gospels* (New York: Putnam, 1911), 95–96. So argues W. Manson, "The Work of St. Luke," *Bulletin of the John Rylands Library* 28 (1944): 403; Robertson, *Luke the Historian,* 34–35; R.T. France, *Evidence for Jesus* (Downers Grove, Ill.: InterVarsity, 1986), 120–21. Hemer cautiously endorses this argument as well, *Acts in Hellenistic History,* 383–408. In view of Luke's apologetic purposes, some earlier commentators argued that Acts was composed in preparation for Paul's defense. See J.I. Still, *St. Paul on Trial* (New York: G.H. Doran, 1923); and G.S. Duncan, *St. Paul's Ephesian Ministry* (London: Hodder and Stoughton, 1929), 97ff. While there is much in Acts that would certainly be superfluous to such an endeavor, as Bruce argues (*Acts of the Apostles,* 15), there is nothing decisive against locating the time of Acts' composition during this period.

29. Robertson, *Luke the Historian,* 35. Harnack utilizes Acts 20:28 in an interesting (but questionable) fashion in arguing for a dating of Acts in the early 60s; see his *Date of Acts,* 103–4.

30. The argument that Luke intended a third book was once popular, but is now generally dismissed. Hemer, *Acts in Hellenistic History,* 385–86; Robertson, *Luke the Historian,* 35–36.

31. For a discussion on the significance of the ending of Acts for locating a date for its composition, see Robinson, *Redating the New Testament,* 89–91; Hemer, *Acts in Hellenistic History,* 406–10.

32. So argues J.P. Moreland, *Scaling the Secular City* (Grand Rapids: Baker, 1987), 153; Robinson, *Redating the New Testament,* 89–90; Hemer, *Acts in Hellenistic History,* 377–78.

33. Robinson, *Redating the New Testament,* 89. Cf. Hemer, *Acts in Hellenistic History.* Of related interest is the fact that James' successor, Symeon, is nowhere mentioned, not only in Luke, but in any of the Gospels. This, according to Robinson, is inexplicable except on the supposition that all of these documents predate James' death. See Robinson, *Redating the New Testament,* 106.

34. The same problems accompany interpreting this apocalyptic discourse as a *vaticinium ex eventu* as accompanied this interpretation concerning Mark's apocalyptic discourse (see chap. 10), upon which it depends if we assume Luke used Mark. Sometimes Luke's (perhaps) addition to Mark's discourse in 21:20 — "when you see Jerusalem surrounded by armies" — is taken to mean that Luke is making Mark's prophecy clearer by adding a detail that could not have been known before A.D. 70. We again cannot rule out that Jesus had either the natural foresight or the supernatural capacity to anticipate the future. But, in any case, the phrase is vague enough, and common enough, to hardly serve as proof of an A.D. post-70 date. See Robertson, *Luke the Historian,* 33–34.

35. See H. Staudinger, *The Trustworthiness of the Gospels* (Edinburgh: Hand-

sel, 1981), 9. Indeed, it has been argued that Luke's irenic stance toward the Roman government is best understood in an atmosphere prior to Nero's persecution. See Hemer, *Acts in Hellenistic History*, 377.

36. Bruce, *Acts of the Apostles*, 17. Interestingly enough, however, Bruce opts for a dating of Acts in the "late 70's or early 80's" (p. 18), though this later dating, in his view, does not adversely affect his estimation of this work's reliability.

37. See Hengel, *Acts and Earliest Christianity*, 63, cf. 106; Moreland, *Scaling the Secular City*, 153; Hemer, *Acts in Hellenistic History*, 381–82. Accounting for the primitive terminology of Acts was in part responsible for Harnack's "conversion" to an early dating of Acts. See his, *Date of Acts*, 104–7.

38. Hemer, *Acts in Hellenistic History*, 380.

39. Robinson, *Redating the New Testament*, 9.

40. France's comment may be to the point: "It is tempting to suggest that the early date has failed to find widespread acceptance not because it is unconvincing in itself but because the results of its acceptance would be too uncomfortable!" See *Evidence for Jesus*, 120–21.

41. On the theology of Luke, see Wright, *New Testament and the People of God*, 378–84; Bruce, *Acts of the Apostles*, 60–66; Marshall, *Luke: Historian and Theologian*, as well as (from a more liberal perspective) J.C. O'Neill, *The Theology of Acts*, 2nd ed. (London: SPCK, 1970). See also R. Maddox, *The Purpose of Luke-Acts* (Edinburgh: T & T Clark, 1982), who locates Luke's primary interests in ecclesiology and eschatology while providing an excellent case against reading of Luke as "an early catholic."

42. Wright, *New Testament and the People of God*, 383. See Hengel, *Between Jesus and Paul*, 2–3, as well as his *Acts and Earliest Christianity*, 67–68.

43. Marshall, *Luke: Historian and Theologian*, 18.

44. See L.C.A. Alexander, "Luke's Preface in the Context of Greek Preface-Writing," *Novum Testamentum* 28 (1986): 48–74; H.J. Cadbury, "The Knowledge Claimed in Luke's Preface," *Expository Times*, 8/24 (1922): 401–22; Bruce, *Acts of the Apostles*, 28–30; Hemer, *Acts in Hellenistic History*, 322–28.

45. For general positive comparisons between Luke and other ancient historians, see C.K. Barrett, *Luke the Historian in Recent Study* (London: Epworth, 1961), 9–12; F. Plümacher, "Lukas als hellenistischer Schriftsteller," *WUNT* 9 (Göttingen: Vandenbhoeck & Ruprecht, 1972), 80ff; Marshall, *Luke: Historian and Theologian*, 54–57; Hengel, *Between Jesus and Paul*, 2–5, 106, 132; idem, *Acts and the History of Earliest Christianity*, 60–62; L.C.A. Alexander, "Luke's Preface in the Context of Greek Preface-Writing," *Novum Testamentum* 25 (1986), 48–74.

46. Indeed, no less an authority than Eduard Meyer, arguably the greatest classical historian in the twentieth century, maintained that Luke should be regarded as one of the greatest historians of classical antiquity on the basis of the evidence. E. Meyer, *Ursprung und Anfänge des Christentums*, I (Stuggart; Berlin, 1921), 2–3. Hengel notes that Meyer's conviction "will seem mad to some 'historical-critical' commentators — if only, perhaps, because they are so unfamiliar with ancient history writing and its problems"; *Between Jesus and Paul*, 2. On Luke's corroboration with other sources, see C.J. Hemer, "Luke the Historian," *Bulletin of the John Ryland's Library* 60 (1977–1978): 28–51; idem, "Paul at Athens: A Topographical Note," *New Testament Studies* 20 (1973–1974): 341–50; idem, "Observations on Pauline Chronology," in *Pauline Studies*, ed. D.A. Hagner and M.J. Harris (Grand Rapids: Eerdmans, 1988), 3–18, and esp. idem, *Acts in Hellenistic Histories*, chap. 5. Much of what follows is indebted to the work of Hemer, Bruce, Hengel, Barnett, Robertson, as well as the older scholars, Harnack, Ramsey, and Sherwin-White.

47. The number of persons killed is much larger in Josephus than in Acts, perhaps owing to Josephus' dominant concern to paint revolutionaries in the

worst possible light.

48. For a helpful discussion of the issues, see Robertson, *Luke the Historian*, chap. 13. Luke has frequently been faulted for not providing more specific fixed reference points to date events within his narrative (only in Luke 3:1). While this is true, it must also be said that he is no worse in this regard than other ancient historians who in general did not share our modern concern for dating. See *Luke the Historian*, 178.

49. As argued, e.g., by R.P.C. Hanson, *Acts* (New York: Oxford Univ. Press, 1967), 86, though Hanson's overall estimation of Acts on matters of history is quite positive.

50. Hemer points out that Theudas was an affectionate form of Theodotus, Theodurus, Theodotion, and other such common names in Jewish culture. See *Acts in Hellenistic History*, 162, n.5.

51. Robertson, *Luke the Historian*, 170.

52. Hemer, *Acts in Hellenistic History*, 163.

53. Crossan, *JRB*, 21.

54. See H.R. Moehring, "The Census in Luke as an Apologetic Device," in *Studies in the New Testament and Early Christian Literature: Essays in Honor of Allen P. Wikgren*, ed. D.E. Aune, *Novum Testamentum* Supp. 33 (Leiden: Brill, 1972), 144–60.

55. Robertson, *Luke the Historian*, 127–29.

56. The translations of these inscriptions, however, is debated. See C. Blomberg, "Quirinius," in *International Standard Bible Encyclopedia*, vol. 4 (Grand Rapids: Eerdmans, 1988) as well as his *The Historical Reliability of the Gospels* (Downers Grove, Ill.: InterVarsity, 1987), 195–96. See also Robertson, *Luke the Historian*, 128.

57. See F.F. Bruce, *The New Testament Documents: Are They Reliable?* (1943; reprint, Grand Rapids: Eerdmans, 1988), 87, and Barnett, *Is the New Testament Reliable?* 149–50.

58. S. Neill and N.T. Wright, *The Interpretation of the New Testament, 1861–1986* (New York: Oxford Univ. Press, 1988), 153–54.

59. Luke correctly identifies six senatorial provinces (Achaia, Asia, Crete and Cyrene, Cyprus, Bithynia and Pontus, and Macedonia), six imperial provinces (Cappadocia, Cilicia, Egypt, Galatia, Lycia, and Pamphylia), and eight Roman colonies (Phillipi, Corinth, Lystra, Pisidian Antioch, Ptolemais, Puteoli, Syracuse, and Troas) though only Phillipi is named as such. Getting this much correct is impressive enough. But to correctly identify various administrative personnel with their differing precise titles within these various regions goes well beyond this in terms of establishing credibility.

60. Achaia had been made an imperial province in A.D. 15, but was reverted to a senatorial province in A.D. 44. The room for error here for a later writer would be significant.

61. *Interpretation of New Testament*, 153. Cf. Barnett, *Is the New Testament Reliable?* 151.

62. *The Bearing of Recent Discovery on the Trustworthiness of the New Testament* (New York: Hodder and Stoughton, 1915), 96–97.

63. See Ramsey's succinct presentation in "Roads and Travel [in the N.T.]," in *Hastings Dictionary of the Bible*, vol. 5, 375–402, as well as his more extensive treatment in *The Church in the Roman Empire* (Grand Rapids: Baker, 1979 [1897]), chaps. 2–8. See also J. Moffatt, *An Introduction to the Literature of the New Testament* (New York: Scribner, 1911), 304; J.B. Lightfoot, *Essays on Supernatural Religion* (New York: Macmillan, 1889), 291–305; and A. Harnack, *The Acts of the Apostles*, trans. J.R. Wilkinson (New York: Putnam, 1909), chap. 2.

64. See Hengel's discussion in *Between Jesus and Paul*, 97ff. While Luke's geographical information on Rome and Asia Minor is excellent, his knowledge of the geography of Palestine is not as precise. See *Between Jesus and*

Paul, 97–128; as well as Marshall, *Luke: Historian and Theologian*, 69–71, who explicitly address problems in Luke's geography of Palestine.

65. Bruce, *Acts of the Apostles*, 319; Hemer, *Acts in Hellenistic History*, 111, 228–30.

66. Hengel, *Between Paul and Jesus*, 114.

67. J. Smith's old but exhaustive treatment of this chapter in his *The Voyage and Shipwreck of St. Paul* (Grand Rapids: Baker, 1970 [1880]) remains one of the best. For a recent, meticulous discussion of the passage, see Hemer, *Acts in Hellenistic History*, 132–52, as well as 388–90.

68. Bruce, quoting H.J. Holtzmann, "Record or Reconstruction?" 2578. See also his *Acts of the Apostles*, 508.

69. For Dibelius' treatment, see his *Studies in the Acts of the Apostles*, trans. Mary Ling, ed. H. Greeven (London: SCM, 1956), 107.

70. See Robertson's discussion, *Luke the Historian*, chap. 16, 206–16. He concludes, "This chapter alone would rank Luke among the great writers of the world" (p. 216).

71. Hemer, *Acts in Hellenistic History*, 389.

72. Robertson, *Luke the Historian*, 187.

73. Bruce, *Acts of the Apostles*, 33. For specifics on Luke's demonstration of local knowledge, and issues that surround various passages, see Hemer, *Acts in Hellenistic History*, 105–58.

74. The work of A.N. Sherwin-White has in particular been influential in this regard. See his *Roman Society and Roman Law in the New Testament* (Oxford: Oxford Univ. Press, 1963), 172–89, *passim*, as well as Robertson, *Luke the Historian*, chap. 15, 190–205; and Hengel, *Between Jesus and Paul*, 97–128.

75. Sherwin-White, *Roman Society and Roman Law*, 173.

76. Hengel, *Between Jesus and Paul*, 119–20.

77. Ibid., 120–21. On the accuracy of Paul's trial, see Hemer, *Acts in Hellenistic History*, 390–404.

78. See Hengel, *Acts and Earliest Christianity*, 66. See Hemer, *Acts in Hellenistic History*, chap. 6.

79. See A.J. Mattill, Jr., "The Value of Acts as a Source for the Study of Paul," in *Perspectives on Luke-Acts*, ed. C.H. Talbert (Danville, Va.: Association of Baptist Professors of Religion, 1978), 76–98.

80. Bruce, "Record or Reconstruction?" 2580.

81. Luke, perhaps in keeping with his apologetic interests, says that Paul escaped because of a conspiracy to kill him by local Jews, whereas Paul only mentions that "the governor under King Aretas had the city of the Damascenes guarded in order to arrest me." There is no contradiction here, as has sometimes been supposed. Indeed, the two accounts complement one another in as much as Luke tells us what Paul does not: namely, *why* the governer wanted to arrest Paul in the first place.

82. Luke cites the disagreement over Barnabas' nephew Mark, while Paul cites Barnabas' inconsistency. Assuming Galatians 2:13 constitutes a "parting of the ways" (which is debatable) and/or assuming that Paul and Barnabas only split once (which is again debatable), the differences between Luke's and Paul's accounts need only amount to a difference of perspectives on what the "final straw" was which set them apart. For an in-depth investigation of the issues in reconciling Acts with Paul's letters to the Galatians, see Hemer, *Acts in Hellenistic History*, chap. 7; and idem, "Acts and Galatians Reconsidered," *Themelios* 2 (1976–1977): 81–88.

83. Paul's first visit to Jerusalem (Gal. 1:18-20), his trip to Syria and Cilicia (Gal. 1:21), and his private meeting with the three Jerusalem leaders (Gal. 2:2-10) are the most difficult pieces of information to fit into Luke's portrait. Still, there are a number of plausible ways of reconciling the accounts, all of which have the advantage of squaring with Luke's otherwise demonstrable

historical veracity. While the issue is frequently discussed, little of significance has been added to J.G. Machen's thorough treatment in The *Origin of Paul's Religion* (Grand Rapids: Eerdmans, 1925), 71–105, 144–47. For more recent discussions, see Robertson, *Luke the Historian*, 171–74; and C.H. Talbert, "Again: Paul's Visits to Jersualem," *Novum Testamentum* 14 (1967), 26–40.

84. Though H.J. Cadbury is certainly not giving Luke's demonstrable accuracy enough due when he will not allow Luke's reliability on depicting the "local color" of various regions to count in favor of his general reliability. See *The Book of Acts in History* (London: Adam & Charles Black, 1955), 120. If accuracy on such points as these doesn't evidence "general reliability," what does?

85. Against C.H. Talbert, e.g., who argues that, "Today the burden of proof rests on anyone who would read Acts as other than theology" [viz., as containing reliable history]. See his essay, "Luke-Acts" in *The New Testament and Its Modern Interpreters*, ed. E.J. Epp and G.W. MacRae (Philadelphia: Fortress; Atlanta: Scholars, 1989), 311. While the consensus of liberal New Testament scholarship is perhaps in Talbert's favor, the actual evidence, we have seen, simply is not.

Chapter 13: Devoured by Beasts or Raised from the Dead?

1. So N.T. Wright argues in *The New Testament and the People of God* (Minneapolis: Fortress, 1992), 400. He further argues that the centrality of the resurrection is inexplicable except on the supposition that "certain things were known, and continued to be known, about the one who had thus been raised after being crucified" (p. 399). In other words, the centrality of the resurrection presupposes a significant continuity in early Christian traditions about Jesus.

2. Crossan, *JRB*, 124–27, 154.

3. Ibid., 158.

4. Ibid., 145.

5. Ibid., 146.

6. J.D. Crossan, *Four Other Gospels: Shadows on the Contour of the Canon* (Minneapolis: Seabury, 1985), 145. This is the central thesis of his *The Cross That Spoke: The Origins of the Passion Narrative* (San Francisco: Harper & Row, 1988).

7. Crossan, *JRB*, 156.

8. Ibid.

9. Ibid., 157.

10. Ibid., 167–69.

11. Ibid., 165–68, *HJ*, 410.

12. Ibid., 172–73.

13. Ibid., 186.

14. Ibid., 187.

15. Ibid., 181.

16. Ibid., 182.

17. Ibid., 183.

18. Ibid., 187.

19. Mack, *MI*, 105–13, *LG*, 216–19, 246.

20. B. Mack, *Review of Did Jesus Rise from the Dead? The Resurrection Debate: Gary Habermas and Anthony G.N. Flew*, ed. T. Miethe (San Francisco: Harper and Row, 1987), in *History and Theology* 28/2 (1989): 221–22.

21. Mack, *LG*, 222.

22. Ibid., see also *MI*, 309.

23. Mack, *LG*, 223.

24. Ibid., 247.

25. For excellent works defending the historicity of the resurrection, see S. Davis, *Risen Indeed: Making Sense of the Resurrection* (Grand Rapids: Eerdmans, 1993); W.L. Craig, *Assessing the New Testament Evidence for the Historicity of the Resurrection of Jesus* (Lewiston, N.Y.: Mellen, 1989); E.L. Bode, *The First Easter Morning* (Rome: Biblical Institute, 1970); R. Brown, *The Virginal Conception and Bodily Resurrection of Jesus* (New York: Paulist, 1973); G. Habermas, *The Resurrection of Jesus: An Apologetic* (Grand Rapids: Baker, 1980); G. O'Collins, *Jesus Risen* (New York: Paulist, 1987); idem, *The Resurrection of Jesus Christ* (Valley Forge, Pa.: Judson, 1973); and G.L. Ladd's excellent succinct work, *I Believe in the Resurrection of Jesus* (Grand Rapids: Eerdmans, 1976).

26. Crossan, *HJ*, 390.

27. G. O'Collins and D. Kendall, "Did Joseph of Arimathea Exist?" *Biblica* 75 (1994): 239. Wright makes a similar point against all redaction critics who emphasize the literary creativity of the evangelists while they nevertheless seek to discover pre-literary forms within them in *New Testament and the People of God*, 424.

28. Crossan, *Four Other Gospels*, 147.

29. J.B. Green, "Review of Crossan's *The Cross That Spoke*," *Journal of Biblical Literature* 109 (1990): 357–58.

30. O'Collins and Kendall, "Did Joseph of Arimathea Exist?" 239.

31. M. Hengel, *Acts in the History of Earliest Christianity*, trans. J. Bowden (Philadelphia: Fortress, 1979), 12–13.

32. On attitudes toward the supernatural among ancient historians, see C. Hemer, *Acts in the Setting of Hellenistic History* (Tübingen: Mohr, 1989), 82–85.

33. See Ladd, *I Believe*, 94ff.

34. For a comparison of the Gospel of Peter and the canonical Gospels, see Ladd, *I Believe*, 95.

35. Davis, *Risen Indeed*, 73.

36. On this, see R. Stein, "Was the Tomb Really Empty?" *Themelios* 5 (Sept. 1979): 20; and Bode, *Easter Morning*, 6, 58, 71.

37. M. Peel, "The Resurrection in Recent Scholarly Research," *Bible Review* 4 (1989): 21. See my earlier discussion in chap. 6.

38. Ladd, *I Believe*, 84.

39. See Davis, *Risen Indeed*, 78–79.

40. See H. Staudinger, "The Resurrection of Jesus Christ As Saving Event and an 'Object' of Historical Research," *Scottish Journal of Theology* 36:3 (1983): 317–18.

41. For a good discussion on the discrepancies between the resurrection accounts and the extent to which they can or cannot be harmonized, see E. Stump, "Visits to the Sepulcher and Biblical Exegesis," *Faith and Philosophy* 6 (Oct. 1989): 353–77. For more exhaustive treatments, see J. Wenham's excellent work, *Easter Enigma* (Exeter: Paternoster, 1984), and Ladd, *I Believe*, 79–93.

42. So argues Ladd, *I Believe*, 84. Even M. Grant argues that the discrepancies between the accounts are incidental and do not significantly affect the basic historicity of the reports; see *Jesus: An Historian's Review of the Gospels* (New York: Scribner's, 1977), 176, 200.

43. Wright, *New Testament and People of God*, 100–104.

44. So argues Staudinger, "The Resurrection As Saving Event," 31–32. See also, Davis, *Risen Indeed*, 73.

45. About this passage Dodd comments, "The story is told with the dramatic realism of which this writer is master. It looks like something as near first-hand evidence as we could hope to get. Perhaps it is, and if so, it becomes the sheet anchor of belief in a 'bodily' resurrection" (C.H. Dodd, *The*

Founder of Christianity [London: Macmillan, 1970], 164). Incidental and irrelevant details are one piece of evidence supporting the influence of eyewitnesses in a report, though, as noted in chap. 11, their presence does not in and of itself prove an eyewitness influence. See the discussion in E.P. Sanders, *The Tendencies of the Synoptic Tradition* (Cambridge: Cambridge Univ. Press, 1969), 143ff.

46. In this light it is interesting to note that Peter's sermon in Acts 2 assumes that the tomb of Jesus, like the tomb of David that is "here to this day" (2:29), could be investigated by the public (2:22-32). The difference between David's tomb and Jesus' tomb is not that one is known and the other not, but that one was empty while the other wasn't! The Gospels' account of Jesus being buried in the tomb of a member of the Sanhedrin squares with this record. It is unlikely that the location of a tomb of a wealthy member of the Sanhedrin would be a secret. And so the refutation of the Christian message of the resurrection would not have been difficult, even if this message was (per hypothesis) first proclaimed forty years after Jesus' death. The point is, if Mark was fabricating his story, then resting the entire credibility of his story on the tomb of a (fictitious) member of the Sanhedrin would be a very foolish move to make. Also significant here is the fact that we have no record of Christianity's opponents disputing the Gospel records on this point. See Brown, *Virginal Conception*, 22.

47. It is perhaps significant to note that, though Crossan discusses at length the release of Barabbas (Mark 15:7-15) and the mocking of Jesus (Mark 15:16-20) that immediately precedes the mentioning of Simon (*HJ*, 390–91, 380–85), he nowhere treats Mark's reference to Simon. One would think that this obviously historical reference would be significant to his treatment of Mark as fiction.

48. See W.L. Craig, *The Son Rises: The Historical Evidence for the Resurrection of Jesus* (Chicago: Moody, 1981), 55–56.

49. See W. Pannenberg, *Jesus – God and Man*, 2nd ed., trans. L. Wilkins and D. Priebe (Philadelphia: Westminster, 1977 [1964]), 88–106. Pannenberg provides a compelling argument for the historicity of the resurrection almost exclusively on the basis of 1 Corinthians 15, for he regards the Gospel narratives to be largely legendary.

50. See Pannenberg's discussion in *Jesus – God and Man*, 90–91. Others who argue in this direction are Craig, *Assessing the New Testament Evidence*, 1–50; C.F. Evans, *Resurrection and the New Testament* (London: SCM, 1970), 41–56; R.H. Fuller, *The Formation of the Resurrection Narratives* (New York: Macmillan, 1971), 9–49; M.J. Harris, *Raised Immortal: Resurrection and Immortality in the New Testament* (Grand Rapids: Eerdmans, 1985), 9–14; Brown, *Virginal Conception*, 81; O. Cullmann, "The Tradition: The Exegetical, Historical, and Theological Problem," in *The Early Church*, ed. A.J.B. Higgins (Philadelphia: Westminster, 1966), 65–66; Ladd, *I Believe*, 141, 161.

51. As W.L. Craig effectively argues in "The Bodily Resurrection of Jesus," *Studies of History and Tradition in the Four Gospels*, GP 1 (Sheffield: JSOT, 1980), 66.

52. Crossan, *JRB*, 166. Crossan has recently expanded upon this argument in a public lecture at the Smithsonian Institute, published as "The Passion, Crucifixion, and Resurrection," in *The Search for Jesus: Modern Scholarship Looks at the Gospels*, ed. H. Shanks (Washington, D.C.: Biblical Archaeological Society, 1994), 109–34.

53. Crossan, *JRB*, 166, cf. 397.

54. Ibid., 167.

55. Ibid., 169. For an excellent discussion on the nature of the resurrection appearances, one that rules out Crossan's interpretation of Paul's experience as a "trance," see Craig, "Bodily Resurrection of Jesus," as well as R. Gundry,

"Soma," in *Biblical Theology* (Cambridge: Cambridge Univ. Press, 1976).

56. Crossan, *JRB*, 169.

57. Ibid., 170.

58. Ibid.

59. Mack, *MI*, 104.

60. Ibid., 104–13; *LG*, 217–20.

61. Mack, *MI*, 98, 103.

62. Mack, Review of *Did Jesus Rise from the Dead?* 221.

63. Ibid., 222.

64. Ibid., 223. So convinced of this is Mack that he maintains that it is an "embarrassment" that "so many critical scholars take this report very seriously" (p. 222). And, before ending by shaming Harper and Row for even publishing the debate between Habermas and Flew on the resurrection, he warns New Testament scholars that, "Fudging on the resurrection can only lead to this dead end" [viz., the one he thinks was arrived at in the book he's reviewing] (p. 224). The intensity of Mack's vitriolic review of this book, especially the inflamatory language used against Habermas (e.g., he calls his debating strategy "dishonest and offensive," [p. 219], and says of the entire debate, "The intelligence presented here is very lightweight and extremely embarrassing." [p. 218]), perhaps reveals the depth of Mack's conviction that any approach which takes seriously the possibility that Paul is telling the truth in 1 Corinthians 15 lies outside the "guild" of New Testament scholarship (see p. 223).

65. E.P. Sanders, *The Historical Figure of Jesus* (New York: Penguin; London: Allen, 1993), 279–80.

66. See D. Guthrie, *New Testament Introduction* (Downers Grove, Ill.: InterVarsity, 1978), 386–91.

67. G. Machen, *The Origins of Paul's Religion* (Grand Rapids: Eerdmans, 1925), 153–69.

68. A view confirmed throughout Acts. See, e.g., 9:16, 23, 25, 29; 16:19-25; 20:22-24; 21:13, 27-33, etc.

69. S. Neill and N.T. Wright, *The Interpretation of the New Testament, 1861–1986*, 2nd ed. (New York: Oxford Univ. Press, 1988), 196–97. See my discussions against the post-Bultmannian postulation of a radically diverse early Christianity in chaps. 5 and 10.

Bibliography

Abraham, W. *Divine Revelation and the Limits of Historical Criticism.* Oxford/ New York: Oxford Univ. Press, 1982.

Alexander, L. "Luke's Preface in the Context of Greek Preface-Writing." *Novum Testamentum* 28/1 (1986): 48–74

———. *The Preface to Luke's Gospel: Literary Convention and Social Context in Luke 1:1-4 and Acts 1:1.* Cambridge: Cambridge Univ. Press, 1993.

Allison, D. *The End of the Ages Has Come: An Early Interpretation of the Passion and Resurrection of Jesus.* Philadelphia: Fortress, 1985.

Anderson, C.C. *Critical Quests of Jesus.* Grand Rapids: Eerdmans, 1969.

Attridge, H. "The Philosophical Critique of Religion under the Early Empire." *ANRW* 2.16.1. (1978): 45–78.

———. "Reflections on Research into Q." *Semeia* 55 (1992): 223–33.

Aulen, G. *Jesus in Contemporary Historical Research.* Translated by I.H. Hjelm. Philadelphia: Fortress, 1976.

Aune, D. *Prophecy in Early Christianity and the Ancient Mediterranean World.* Grand Rapids: Eerdmans, 1983.

Baird, J. *Audience Criticism and the Historical Jesus.* Philadelphia: Westminster, 1969.

Baird, W. *From Deism to Tübingen.* Vol. 1 of *History of New Testament Research.* Minneapolis: Fortress, 1992.

———. *The Quest of the Christ of Faith: Reflections on the Bultmannian Era.* Waco, Texas: Word, 1977.

Barnett, P. *Is the New Testament Reliable? A Look at the Historical Evidence.* Downers Grove, Ill.: InterVarsity, 1986.

Barrett, C.K. *Luke the Historian in Recent Study,* 2nd ed. Philadelphia: Fortress, 1970.

Baur, W. *Orthodoxy and Heresy in Earliest Christianity,* 2nd ed. Edited by R.A. Kraft and G. Krodel. Translated by Philadelphia Seminar on Christian Origins. Philadelphia: Fortress, 1971.

Beardslee, W.A. *Literary Criticism of the New Testament.* Philadelphia: Fortress, 1970.

Beasley-Murray, G.R. *Jesus and the Kingdom of God.* Grand Rapids: Eerdmans, 1986.

Beker, J. *Paul the Apostle: The Triumph of God in Life and Thought.* Philadelphia: Fortress, 1980.

Berger, P.L., and T. Luckmann. *The Social Construction of Reality: A Treatise in the Sociology of Knowledge.* Garden City, N.Y.: Doubleday, 1966.

Best, E. *Disciples and Discipleship: Studies in the Gospel According to Mark.* Edinburgh: T & T Clark, 1986.

Blomberg, C.L. *The Historical Reliability of the Gospels.* Downers Grove, Ill.: InterVarsity, 1987.

_____. *Interpreting the Parables.* Downers Grove, Ill.: InterVarsity, 1990.

_____. "The Legitimacy and Limits of Harmonization." In *Hermeneutics, Authority, and Canon,* edited by D.A. Carson and J.D. Woodbridge. Grand Rapids: Zondervan, 1986.

_____. "The Parables of Jesus: Current Trends and Needs in Research." In *Studying the Historical Jesus: Evaluations of the State of Current Research,* edited by B. Chilton and C.A. Evans. *NTTS* 19. Leiden/New York: Brill, 1994.

_____. "Tradition and Redaction in the Parables of the Gospel of Thomas." In *The Jesus Tradition Outside the Gospels, GP* 5, edited by D. Wenham, 177–205. Sheffield: *JSOT,* 1985.

Borg, M. *Conflict, Holiness and Politics in the Teachings of Jesus, SBEC* 5. Lewiston, N.Y.: Mellen, 1984.

_____. *Jesus in Contemporary Scholarship.* Valley Forge, Pa.: Trinity, 1994.

_____. *Jesus: A New Vision, Spirit, Culture, and the Life of Discipleship.* San Francisco: Harper & Row, 1987.

_____. "Portraits of Jesus in Contemporary North American Scholarship." *Harvard Theological Review* 84/1 (1991): 1–22.

_____. "A Renaissance in Jesus Studies." *Theology Today* 45 (1988): 280–92.

_____. "A Temperate Case for a Non-Eschatological Jesus." *Foundations and Facets Forum* 2/3 (1986): 81–102.

Boring, M. *The Continuing Voice of Jesus: Christian Prophecy and the Gospel Tradition,* 2nd rev. ed. Louisville: Westminster/John Knox, 1991 [1982].

_____. "The 'First' and 'Lost' Gospel?" A panel paper presented at the SBL Annual Meeting, Q section, 22 November 1993, Washington D.C.

Bousset, W. *Kyrios Christos.* Translated by J.E. Seely. Nashville: Abingdon, 1970.

Braaten, C.E. and R.A. Harrisville, eds. *The Historical Jesus and the Kerygmatic Christ: Essays on the New Quest of the Historical Jesus.* Nashville: Abingdon, 1964.

Branham, R. "Diogenes' Rhetoric and the *Invention* of Cynicism." In *Le Cynisme Ancien et Ses Prolongements.* Edited by M.O. Goulet-Cazé and R. Goulet. Paris: Presses Universitaires De France, 1993.

Brice, M. "Reflections on Historical Criticism and Self-Understanding." In *Self-Definition and Self-Discovery in Early Christianity: A Study in Changing Horizons, Essays in Appreciation of Ben F. Meyer from Former Students, SBEC* 26, edited by D.J. Hawkins and T. Robinson, 55–77. Lewiston, N.Y.: Mellen, 1990.

Brown, C. "Historical Jesus, Quest of." In *Dictionary of Jesus and the Gospels*, edited by J. Green, S. McKnight, and I.H. Marshall, 326–41. Downers Grove, Ill.: InterVarsity, 1992.

―――. *Jesus in European Protestant Thought, 1778–1860*. Durham, N.C.: Labyrinth, 1985.

―――. *Miracles and the Critical Mind*. Grand Rapids: Eerdmans, 1984.

―――. *That You May Believe: Miracles and Faith Then and Now*. Grand Rapids: Eerdmans, 1985.

Brown, F.B., and E.S. Malbon, "Parabling as a *Via Negativa:* A Critical Review of the Work of John Dominic Crossan." *Journal of Religion* 64 (1984): 530–38.

Brown, R.E. *The Death of the Messiah: From Gethsemane to the Grave*. New York: Doubleday, 1994.

―――. "The *Gospel of Peter* and Canonical Gospel Priority." *New Testament Studies* 33 (1987): 321–43.

―――. *Jesus, God and Man*. New York: Macmillan; London: Collier Macmillan, 1967.

―――. "The Problem of Historicity in John." *Catholic Biblical Quarterly* 24 (1962): 1–14.

―――. *The Virginal Conception and Bodily Resurrection of Jesus*. New York: Paulist, 1973.

Bruce, F.F. *The Acts of the Apostles: The Greek Text With Introduction and Commentary*. Grand Rapids: Eerdmans, 1990.

―――. "The Acts of the Apostles: Historical Record or Theological Reconstruction?" In *Aufstieg und Niedergang der romischen Welt*, edited by H. Temporini and W. Haase, 2569–2603. New York/Berlin: de Gruyter, 1985.

―――. *The New Testament Documents: Are They Reliable?* 1943. Reprint. Grand Rapids: Eerdmans, 1988.

―――. *Paul and Jesus*. Grand Rapids: Baker, 1974.

―――. *Paul: An Apostle of the Heart Set Free*. Grand Rapids: Eerdmans, 1977.

―――. *The "Secret" Gospel of Mark*. London: Athlone, 1974.

Buchanan, G.W. *Jesus: the King and His Kingdom*. Macon, Ga.: Mercer Univ. Press, 1984.

Bultmann, R.K. "Is Exegesis without Presuppositions Possible?" In *Existence and Faith: Shorter Writings of Rudolf Bultmann*, edited and translated by S.M. Ogden, 289–96. Cleveland: Meridian; New York: World, 1966.

―――. *The History of the Synoptic Tradition*, rev. ed. Oxford: Blackwell, 1963.

―――. *Jesus and the Word*. Translated by L.P. Smith and E.H. Lantero. New York: Scribner's, 1958.

―――. *Jesus Christ and Mythology*. New York: Scribner's, 1958.

―――. *Kerygma and Myth*. Edited by H.W. Bartsch. Translated by R.H. Fuller. London: SPCK, 1953.

―――. *Primitive Christianity in Its Contemporary Setting*. Translated by R.H. Fuller. New York: Meridian, 1956.

―――. "The Significance of the Historical Jesus for the Theology of Paul."

In *Faith and Understanding*, translated by L.P. Smith. New York: Harper & Row, 1969.

Burridge, R. *What Are the Gospels? A Comparison with Graeco-Roman Biography*. Cambridge: Cambridge Univ. Press, 1992.

Butts, J.R. "Probing the Polling: Jesus Seminar Results on the Kingdom Sayings." *Foundations and Facets Forum* 3/1 (1987): 108–11.

Byrskog, S. *Jesus the Only Teacher: Didactic Authority and Transmission in Ancient Israel, Ancient Judaism and the Matthean Community, CBNTS* 24. Stockholm: Almgvist & Wiksell, 1994.

Cadbury, H.J. *The Book of Acts in History*. London: Black, 1955.

Cameron, R., ed. *The Apochryphal Jesus and Christian Origins. Semeia* 49. Atlanta: Scholars, 1990.

_____. "Parable and Interpretation in the Gospel of Thomas." *Foundations and Facets Forum* 2/2 (1986): 3–39.

_____. *The Other Gospels: Non-Canonical Gospel Texts*. Philadelphia: Westminster, 1982.

_____. " 'What have You Come Out to See?': Characterizations of John and Jesus in the Gospels." *Semeia* 49 (1990): 35–69.

Caragounis, C. *The Son of Man: Vision and Interpretation, WUNT* 38. Tübingen: Mohr, 1986.

Carson, D.A. *The Gospel According to John*. Grand Rapids: Eerdmans, 1991.

_____. "Historical Tradition in the Fourth Gospel: After Dodd, What?" In *Studies of History and Tradition in the Four Gospels, GP* 2, edited by R.T. France and D. Wenham, 83–145. Sheffield: JSOT, 1981.

_____. "Historical Tradition in the Fourth Gospel: A Response to J.S. King." *Journal for the Study of the New Testament* 23 (1985): 73–81.

_____. "Unity and Diversity in the New Testament: The Possibility of Systematic Theology." In *Scripture and Truth*, 2nd ed., edited by D.A. Carson and J.D. Woodbridge, 65–95. Grand Rapids: Baker, 1992 [1983].

_____. "Redaction Criticism: On the Legitimacy and Illegitimacy of a Literary Tool." In *Scripture and Truth*, edited by D.A. Carson and J.D. Woodbridge, 119–42. Grand Rapids: Zondervan, 1983.

_____. Moo, D., and L. Morris. *An Introduction to the New Testament*. Grand Rapids: Zondervan, 1992.

Carlston, C. "On 'Q' and the Cross." In *Scripture, Tradition, and Interpretation: Essays Presented to Everett F. Harrison*, edited by W.W. Gasque and W.S. LaSor. Grand Rapids: Eerdmans, 1978.

Catchpole, D. *The Quest for Q*. Edinburgh: Clark, 1993.

Charlesworth, J.H. "From Barren Mazes to Gentle Rappings: The Emergence of Jesus Research." *Princeton Seminary Bulletin* 7 (1986): 221–30.

_____, ed. *Jesus' Jewishness: Exploring the Place of Jesus Within Early Judaism*. New York: Crossroad, 1991.

_____. "Jesus Research Expands with Chaotic Creativity." In *Images of Jesus Today*, edited by J.H. Charlesworth and W.P. Weaver. Valley Forge, Pa.: Trinity, 1994.

————. "Jesus Research: A Paradigm for New Testament Scholars." *Australian Biblical Review* 38 (1990): 18–32.

————, ed. *The Messiah: Developments in Earliest Judaism and Christianity.* Minneapolis: Fortress, 1992.

————. *Jesus Within Judaism: New Light from Exciting Archaeological Discoveries.* New York/London: Doubleday, 1988.

————. "Research on the Historical Jesus Today: Jesus and the Pseudepigrapha, the Dead Sea Scrolls, the Nag Hammadi Codicies, Josephus, and Archaeology." *Princeton Seminary Bulletin* 6/2 (1985): 98–115.

Chilton, B., and C.A. Evans, eds. *Studying the Historical Jesus: Evaluations of the State of Current Research.* Leiden/New York: Brill, 1994.

Cohn, N. *Cosmos, Chaos and the World to Come: The Ancient Roots of Apocalyptic Faith.* New Haven/London: Yale Univ. Press, 1993.

Collins, J. "Wisdom, Apocalyptic, and Generic Compatibility." In *In Search of Wisdom: Essays in Memory of John G. Gammie,* edited by L.G. Perdue, B.B. Scott, and W.J. Wisemann. Louisville: Westminister/John Knox, 1993.

Conzelmann, H. *Jesus.* Edited by J. Reumann. Translated by J.R. Lord. Philadelphia: Fortress, 1973.

————. *The Theology of St. Luke.* 1955. Reprint. Translated by G. Buswell. Philadelphia: Fortress, 1982.

Craig, W. *Assessing the New Testament Evidence for the Historicity of the Resurrection of Jesus.* Lewiston, N.Y.: Mellen, 1989.

————. "The Bodily Resurrection of Jesus." In *Studies of History and Tradition in the Four Gospels,* GP 1. Sheffield: JSOT (1980): 47–74.

Cranfield, C. *The Gospel According to Saint Mark,* CGTC. Cambridge: Cambridge Univ. Press, 1963.

Crossan, J.D. "Almost the Whole Truth." *The Fourth R* (September/October 1993): 3–8.

————. *Cliffs of Fall: Paradox and Polyvalence in the Parables of Jesus.* New York: Crossroad/Seabury, 1980.

————. "The Cross that Spoke: The Earliest Narrative of the Passion and Resurrection." *Foundations and Facets Forum* 3/2 (1987): 3–22.

————. *The Cross that Spoke: The Origins of the Passion Narratives.* San Francisco: Harper & Row, 1988.

————. *The Dark Interval: Towards a Theology of Story.* Niles, Ill.: Argus, 1975.

————. "Difference and Divinity." *Semeia* 23 (1982): 29–40.

————. "Divine Immediacy and Human Immediacy: Towards a New First Principle in Historical Jesus Research." *Semeia* 44 (1988): 121–40.

————. *Finding is the First Act: Trove Folktales and Jesus' Treasure Parable.* Philadelphia: Fortress; Missoula: Scholars, 1979.

————. *Four Other Gospels: Shadows on the Contours of Canon.* Minneapolis: Winston, 1985.

————. *A Fragile Craft: The Work of Amos Niven Wilder,* BSNA 3. Chico, Calif.: Scholars, 1981.

————. "The Historical Jesus: An Interview With John Dominic Crossan."

The Christian Century (December 1991): 1200–1204.

———. *In Fragments: The Aphorisms of Jesus.* San Francisco: Harper & Row, 1983.

———. *In Parables: The Challenge of the Historical Jesus.* New York: Harper & Row, 1973.

———. "Jesus and Gospel." In *The Biblical Heritage in Modern Catholic Scholarship,* edited by J.J. Collins and J.D. Crossan, 106–30. Wilmington, Del.: Glazier, 1986.

———. *The Essential Jesus: Original Sayings and Earliest Images.* SanFrancisco: HarperSanFrancisco, 1994.

———. "Lists in Early Christianity: A Response to Early Christianity, Q and Jesus." *Semeia* 55 (1992): 235–43.

———. "Materials and Methods in Historical Jesus Research." *Foundations and Facets Forum* 4/4 (December 1988): 3–24.

———. "Open Healing and Open Eating: Jesus as a Jewish Cynic?" *Biblical Research* 36 (1991): 6–18.

———. "The Passion, Crucifixion, and Resurrection." In *The Search for Jesus: Modern Scholarship Looks at the Gospels,* edited by H. Shanks, 109–34. Washington D.C.: Biblical Archaeological Society, 1994.

———. "Perspectives and Methods in Contemporary Biblical Criticism." *Biblical Research* 22 (1977): 39–49.

———. *Raid on the Articulate: Comic Eschatology in Jesus and Borges.* New York: Harper & Row, 1976.

———. "Responses and Reflection." In *Jesus and Faith: A Conversation on the Work of John Dominic Crossan,* edited by J. Carlson and R.A. Ludwig, 142–64. Maryknoll, N.Y.: Orbis, 1994.

———. "Stages in Imagination." In *The Archaeology of the Imagination JAARTS* 48/2. Edited by C.E. Winquist. Ann Arbor: Edwards, 1981.

———. "Why We Must Seek the Historical Jesus: His Message Goes Beyond the Gospels." *The Boston Sunday Globe* (26 July 1992): 59.

Cullman, O. *The Christology of the New Testament.* London: SCM, 1959.

———. *The Early Church.* Edited by A.J.B. Higgins. Philadelphia: Westminster, 1966.

Dahl, N. *Jesus in the Memory of the Early Church.* Minneapolis: Augsburg, 1976.

———. *Jesus the Christ: The Historical Origins of Christological Doctrine.* Edited by D. Joel. Minneapolis: Fortress, 1991.

Davids, P. *The Epistle of James, NIGTC.* Exeter: Paternoster, 1982.

———. "James and Jesus." In *The Jesus Tradition Outside the Gospels, GP 5,* edited by D. Wenham. Sheffield: JSOT, 1985.

Davies, D. "The Christology and Protology of the *Gospel of Thomas.*" *Journal of Biblical Literature* 111/4 (1992): 663–82.

———. *The Gospel of Thomas and Christian Wisdom.* New York: Seabury, 1983.

Davies, S. *Gospel of Thomas and Christian Wisdom.* New York: Seabury, 1983.

Davies, S.T. *Risen Indeed: Making Sense of the Resurrection.* Grand Rapids: Eerdmans, 1993.

Davies, W.D. *Paul and Rabbinic Judaism: Some Rabbinic Elements in Pauline Theology*, 4th ed. London: SPCK; Philadelphia: Fortress, 1980.

Decock, P. "The Eclipse and Rediscovery of Eschatology." *Neotestamentica* 22 (1988): 5–16.

Dehandshutter, B. "Recent Research on the Gospel of Thomas." In *The Four Gospels 1992: Festschrift Frans Neirynck*. 3 Vols., edited by F. Van Segbroeck et al., 3.2257–62. Leuven: Leuven Univ. Press, 1992.

de Jonge, M. *Christology in Context: The Earliest Christian Response to Jesus*. Philadelphia: Westminster, 1988.

de Jonge, H.J. "The Loss of Faith in the Historicity of the Gospels: H.S. Reimarus (ca. 1750) on John and the Synoptics." In *John and the Synoptics*, BETL 51, edited by A. Denaux, 409–21. Leuven: Leuven Univ. Press, 1992.

Denaux, A., ed. *John and the Synoptics*, BETL 51. Leuven: Leuven Univ. Press, 1992.

Derrida, J. *Of Grammatology*. Translated by G.C. Spivak. Baltimore: Johns Hopkins Univ. Press, 1976.

deSilva, D. "The Meaning of the New Testament and the *Skandalon* of World Constructions." *Evangelical Quarterly* 64/1 (1992): 3–21.

Dodd, C.H. *The Apostolic Preaching and Its Developments*. New York: Harper, 1935.

———. *The Founder of Christianity*. London: Macmillan, 1970.

———. *New Testament Studies*. Manchester: Manchester Univ. Press; New York: Scribners, 1952.

———. *Historical Tradition in the Fourth Gospel*. Cambridge: Cambridge Univ. Press, 1963.

Downing, F.G. *Christ and the Cynics: Jesus and Other Radical Preachers in First-Century Tradition*, JSOTM 4. Sheffield: JSOT, 1988.

———. *Cynics and Christian Origins*. Edinburgh: Clark, 1992.

———. "Cynics and Early Christianity." In *Le Cynisme Ancien et Ses Prolongements*, edited by M.O. Goulet-Cazè and R. Goulet. Paris: Presses Universitaires De France, 1993, 281–304.

———. "A Genre for Q and a Socio-Cultural Context for Q: Comparing Sets of Similarities with Sets of Differences." *Journal for the Study of the New Testament* 55 (1994): 3–26.

———. *Jesus and the Threat of Freedom*. London: SCM, 1987.

———. "Quite Like Q: A Genre for Q: The 'Lives' of Cynic Philosophers." *Biblica* 69 (1988): 196–225.

Drury, J. *Critics of the Bible, 1724–1873*. Cambridge/New York: Cambridge Univ. Press, 1989.

Dudley, D.B. *A History of Cynicism from Diogenes to the 6th Century A.D.* London: Methuen, 1937.

Dungan, D. *The Sayings of Jesus in the Churches of Paul*. Oxford: Blackwell, 1971.

Dunn, J. "Prophetic 'I'-Sayings and the Jesus Tradition: The Importance of Testing Prophetic Utterances within Early Christianity." *New Testament Studies* 24 (1978): 175–98.

————. *Testing the Foundations: Current Trends in New Testament Study.* Durham: Univ. of Durham, 1984.

————. *Unity and Diversity in the New Testament: An Inquiry into the Character of Earliest Christianity,* 2nd ed. London: SCM; Philadelphia: Trinity, 1990 [1977].

Eddy, P. "Christian and Hellenistic Moral Exhortation: A Literary Comparison Based on 1 Thessalonians 4." In *Directions in New Testament Methods, MST* 2, edited by M.C. Albl, P.R. Eddy, and R. Mirkes. Milwaukee: Marquette Univ. Press, 1993, 45–51.

Elliott, J.H. *What is Social-Scientific Criticism?* Minneapolis: Fortress, 1993.

Ellis, E. "The Date and Provenance of Mark's Gospel." In *The Four Gospels: Festschrift Frans Neirynck,* 3 Vols., edited by F. Van Segbroeck, et al. Leuven: Leuven Univ. Press, 1992, 2:801–15.

————. "Dating the New Testament." *New Testament Studies* 26 (1980): 487–502.

————. "Gospels Criticism: A Perspective on the State of the Art." In *The Gospel and the Gospels,* edited by P. Stuhlamcher, translated by J. Bowden, 26–52. Grand Rapids: Eerdmans, 1991 [1983].

————. *Prophecy and Hermeneutic in Early Christianity: New Testament Essays,* WUNT 18. Tübingen: Mohr, 1978.

Elmore, W.E. "Linguistic Approaches to the Kingdom: Amos Wilder and Norman Perrin." In *The Kingdom of God in 20th-Century Interpretation,* edited by W. Willis, 53–65. Peabody, Mass.: Hendrickson, 1987.

Epp, E.J., and G.W. MacRae, eds. *The New Testement and Its Modern Interpreters.* Philadelphia: Fortress; Atlanta: Scholars, 1989.

Erickson, M. *The Word Became Flesh: A Contemporary Incarnational Christlogy.* Grand Rapids: Baker, 1991.

Evans, C.A. "The Historical Jesus and Christian Faith: A Critical Assessment of a Scholarly Problem." *Christian Scholar's Review* 18/1 (1988): 48–63.

Evans, C.A. *Life of Jesus Research: An Annotated Bibliography, NTTS* 13. Leiden: Brill, 1989.

————. *Jesus, IBRB* 5. Grand Rapids: Baker, 1992.

————. "Life-of-Jesus Research and the Eclipse of Mythology." *Theological Studies* 54 (1993): 3–36.

————. *Noncanonical Writings and New Testament Interpretation.* Peabody, Mass.: Hendrickson, 1992.

Evans, C.F. *Resurrection and the New Testament.* London: SCM, 1970.

Evans, D. *The Glory of Christ in the New Testament: Studies in Christology in Memory of George Bradford Caird.* Edited by L.D. Hurst and N.T. Wright. Oxford/New York: Oxford Univ. Press, 1987.

Farmer, W.R. *Gospel of Jesus: The Pastoral Relevance of the Synoptic Problem.* Louisville: Westminster/John Knox, 1994.

————. *Jesus and the Gospel: Tradition, Scripture, and Canon.* Philadelphia: Fortress, 1982.

————. *The Synoptic Problem: A Critical Analysis.* New York: Macmillan, 1964.

Farrer, A. "On Dispensing with Q." In *The Two-Source Hypothesis: A Critical*

Appraisal, edited by A.J. Bellinzoni. Macon, Ga.: Mercer Univ. Press, 1985.

Feine, P. *Introduction to the New Testament,* 14th ed. Translated by A.J. Mattill, Jr. Nashville: Abingdon, 1966.

Feldman, L. "How Much Hellenism in Jewish Palestine?" *Hebrew Union College Annual* 57 (1986): 83–111.

Ferguson, E. *Backgrounds of Early Christianity.* Grand Rapids: Eerdmans, 1987.

Finegan, J. *The Archeology of the New Testament.* Princeton: Princeton Univ. Press, 1969.

Fischer, D. *Historians' Fallacies.* New York: Harper & Row; London: Routledge and Kegan Paul, 1971.

Fornara, C. *The Nature of History in Ancient Greece.* San Francisco: Univ. of California Press, 1983.

France, R.T. *The Evidence For Jesus.* Downers Grove, Ill.: InterVarsity, 1986.

Frei, H.W. *The Eclipse of Biblical Narrative: A Study in Eighteenth and Nineteenth Century Hermenuetics.* New Haven, Conn.: Yale Univ. Press, 1974.

Freyne, S. *Galilee, from Alexander the Great to Hadrian 323 B.C.E. to 135 C.E.: A Study of Second Temple Judaism.* Wilmington, Del.: Glazier; Notre Dame, Ind.: Univ. of Notre Dame Press, 1980.

———. *Galilee, Jesus and the Gospels: Literary Approaches and Historical Investigations.* Philadelphia: Fortress, 1988.

Fuchs, E. *Studies of the Historical Jesus.* Translated by A. Scobie. London: SCM, 1964.

Fuller, R.H. *A Critical Introduction to the New Testament.* London: Duckworth, 1966.

———. "Jesus, Paul and Apocalyptic." *Anglican Theological Review* 71/2 (1989): 134–42.

———. *The Formation of the Resurrection Narratives.* New York/London: Macmillan, 1971.

Funk, R.W. "Form and Function [of the Jesus Seminar]." *Foundations & Facets Forum* 1/1 (1985): 51–57.

———. "The Issue of Jesus." *Foundations & Facets Forum* 1/1 (1985): 7–12.

———. "The Jesus that Was." *The Fourth R* (November 1992): 1–6.

———. *Language, Hermeneutic, and Word of God: The Problem of Language in the New Testament and Contemporary Theology.* New York: Harper & Row, 1966.

Funk, R.W., R.W. Hoover, and the Jesus Seminar. *The Five Gospels: The Search for the Authentic Words of Jesus.* New York: Macmillan, 1993.

Funk, R.W., and M.H. Smith, eds. *The Gospel of Mark: Red Letter Edition.* Sonoma, Calif.: Polebridge, 1991.

Gammie, J., and L. Perdue, eds. *The Sage in Israel and the Ancient Near East.* Winona Lake, Ind.: Eisenbrauns, 1990.

Gardner, H. *The Limits of Literary Criticism: Reflections on the Interpretation of Poetry and Scripture.* London/New York: Oxford Univ. Press, 1956.

———. "The Poetry of St. Mark." In *The Limits of Literary Criticsm: Reflections on the Interpretation of Poetry and Scripture.* London/New York: Oxford Univ. Press, 1956.

Gardner-Smith, P. *The Christ of the Gospels.* Cambridge: W. Heffer, 1938.

Gasque, W. *A History of the Criticism of the Acts of the Apostles.* Grand Rapids: Eerdmans, 1975.

_____. "The Historical Value of Acts." *Tyndale Bulletin* 40 (1989): 136–57. Gerhardsson, B. *The Gospel Tradition, CBMTS* 15. Lund: Gleerup, 1986.

_____. *Memory and Manuscript: Oral Tradition and Written Tradition in the Rabbinic Judaism and Early Christianity,* 2nd ed. Lund: Gleerup, 1964.

_____. "The Narrative Meshalim in the Synoptic Gospels." *New Testament Studies* 34 (1988): 339–63.

_____. *The Origins of the Gospel Traditions.* Philadelphia: Fortress, 1979.

_____. "The Path of the Gospel Tradition." In *The Gospel and the Gospels,* edited by P. Stuhlmacher, translated by J. Bowden, 75–96. Grand Rapids: Eerdmans, 1991 [1983].

_____. *Tradition and Transmission in Early Christianity.* Lund: Gleerup, 1964.

Girard, R. *Violence and the Sacred.* Translated by P. Gregory. Baltimore: Johns Hopkins Univ. Press, 1977 [1972].

_____. *The Scapegoat.* Translated by Y. Freccero. Baltimore: Johns Hopkins Univ. Press, 1986 [1985].

Goetz, C., and C. Blomberg. "The Burden of Proof" *Journal for the Study of the New Testament* 11 (1981): 39–63.

Goppelt, L. *Theology of the New Testament.* Edited by J. Roloff. Translated by J.E. Alsup. Grand Rapids: Eerdmans, 1976.

Gottschalk, L. *Understanding History: A Primer of Historical Method,* 2nd ed. New York: Knopf, 1969.

Goulder, M. *Luke—A New Paradigm, JSNTSS* 20. Sheffield: JSOT, 1989.

Goulet-Cazé, M. "Le cynisme à l'époque imperiale." *ANRW* II. 36. 4. (1990): 2720–2833.

Goulet-Cazé, M., and R. Goulet, eds. *Le Cynisme Ancien et Ses Prolongements.* Paris: Presses Universitaires De France, 1993.

Grant, M. *Jesus: An Historian's Review of the Gospels.* New York: Scribner's, 1977.

Green, J. *The Death of Jesus: Tradition and Interpretation in the Passion Narrative, WUNT* 33. Tübingen: Mohr, 1988.

_____. "The Gospel of Peter: Source for a Pre-Canonical Passion Narrative?" *Zeitschrift für die neutestamentliche Wissenschaft,* 1987.

Green, J., and M. Turner, eds. *Jesus of Nazareth: Lord and Christ: Essays on the Historical Jesus and New Testament Christology.* Grand Rapids: Eerdmans, 1994.

Guelich, R. "The Gospels: Portraits of Jesus and His Ministry." *Journal of the Evangelical Theological Society* 24/2 (1981): 117–25.

_____. *Mark 1-8:26.* Dallas: Word, 1989.

Gundry, R. *Mark: A Commentary on His Apology for the Cross.* Grand Rapids: Eerdmans, 1993.

Guthrie, D. *New Testament Introduction.* Downers Grove, Ill.: InterVarsity, 1978.

Habermas, G. *The Resurrection of Jesus: An Apologetic*. Grand Rapids: Baker, 1980.

Haenchen, E. *Die Apostelgeschicht neu übersetzt und erklärt*. Gottingen: Vandenhoeck & Ruprecht, 1956.

Hamilton, W. *A Quest for the Post-Historical Jesus*. London: SCM, 1993.

Harnack, A. *The Acts of the Apostles*. Translated by J.R. Wilkinson. New York: Putnam, 1909.

_____. *Date of the Acts and the Synoptic Gospels*. New York: Putnam, 1911.

_____. *Luke the Physician*. Edited by W.D. Morrison. Translated by J.R. Wilkinson. New York: Putnam, 1907.

_____. *New Testament Studies I, Luke the Physician*. London: Williams & Norgate; New York: Putnam, 1907.

Harris, H. *David Friedrich Strauss and His Theology*. Cambridge: Cambridge Univ. Press, 1973.

_____. *The Tübingen School*. Oxford: Clarendon, 1975.

Harris, R.M. *Jesus as God: The New Testament Use of* Theos *in Reference to Jesus*. Grand Rapids: Baker, 1992.

_____. *Raised Immortal: Resurrection and Immortality in the New Testament*. Grand Rapids: Eerdmans, 1985.

Hartlich, C. "Is Historical Criticism Out of Date?" In *Conflicting Ways of Interpreting the Bible*, edited by H.Küng and J. Moltmann, 3–8. *Concilium* 138. Edinburgh: Clark; New York: Seabury, 1980.

Harvey, A. *Jesus and the Constraints of History*. Philadelphia: Westminster, 1982.

Hatch, E. *The Influence of Greek Ideas on Christianity*. New York: Harper & Row, 1957 [1889].

Hays, R. "The Corrected Jesus." *First Things* (May 1994): 43–48.

_____. *The Faith of Jesus Christ: An Investigation of the Narrative Substructure of Galatians 3:1-4:11*, SBL Dissertation Series. Chicago: Scholars Press, 1983.

Head, P. "On the Christology of the Gospel of Peter." *Vigiliae Christianae* 46 (1992): 143–54.

Hedrick, C.W., ed. *The Historical Jesus and the Rejected Gospels, Semeia* 44. Atlanta: Scholars, 1988.

Helm, P. "Understanding Scholarly Presuppositions: A Crucial Tool for Research?" *Tyndale Bulletin* 44/1 (1993): 143–54.

Hemer, C. *The Book of Acts in the Setting of Hellenistic History*. Translated and edited by C.H. Gempf. Tübingen: Mohr, 1989.

_____. "The Speeches of Acts: I. The Ephesian Elders at Miletus." *Tyndale Bulletin* 40 (1989): 77–85.

_____. "The Speeches in Acts: II. The Areopagus Address." *Tyndale Bulletin* 40 (1989): 239–59.

Henaut, B. "Is Q But the Invention of Luke and Mark?: Method and Argument in the Griesbach Hypothesis." *Religious Studies and Theology* 8 (1988): 15–32.

Hengel, M. *Acts and the History of Earliest Christianity.* Translated by J. Bowden. Philadelphia: Fortress, 1979.

_____. *Between Jesus and Paul.* Translated by J. Bowden. Philadelphia: Fortress, 1983.

_____. *The Charismatic Leader and His Followers.* Translated by J. Greig. New York: Crossroad, 1981.

_____. *The "Hellenization" of Judea in the First Century After Christ.* Translated by J. Bowden. Philadelphia: Trinity; London: SCM, 1989.

_____. *Judaism and Hellenism: Studies in Their Encounter in Palestine During the Early Hellenistic Period.* 2 vols. Translated by J. Bowden. Philadelphia: Fortress, 1974.

_____. *The Son of God: The Origin of Christology and the History of Jewish-Hellenistic Religion.* Translated by J. Bowden. Philadelphia: Fortress, 1976 [1975].

_____. *Studies in the Gospel of Mark.* Translated by J. Bowden. Philadelphia: Fortress, 1985.

Henry, C.F.H., ed. *Jesus of Nazareth: Savior and Lord.* Grand Rapids: Eerdmans, 1966.

Henry, P. "Why is Contemporary Scholarship so Enamored of Ancient Heretics?" In *Studia Patristica* 17/1, edited by E.A. Livingstone. Oxford/New York: Pergamon, 1982, 123–26.

Hiers, R. *The Historical Jesus and the Kingdom of God: Present and Future in the Message and Ministry of Jesus.* Gainesville, Fla.: Univ. of Florida Press, 1973.

_____. *The Kingdom of God in the Synoptic Tradition.* Gainesville, Fla.: Univ. of Florida Press, 1970.

Hill, C. *Hellenists and Hebrews: Reappraising Division within the Earliest Church.* Minneapolis: Fortress, 1992.

Hill, D. *New Testament Prophecy.* Atlanta: Knox, 1979.

Hobart, W.K. *The Medical Language of St. Luke.* 1882. Reprint. Grand Rapids: Baker, 1954.

Hock, R.F. "Lazarus and Micyllus: Greco-Roman Backgrounds to Luke 16:19-31." *Journal of Biblical Literature* 106/3 (1987): 447–63.

_____. *The Social Context of Paul's Ministry: Tentmaking and Apostleship.* Philadelphia: Fortress, 1980.

Höistad, R. *Cynic Hero and Cynic King: Studies in the Cynic Conception of Man.* Uppsala, Sweden: Bloms, 1948.

Holladay, C. *Theios Aner in Hellenistic Judaism.* Missoula, Mont.: Scholars, 1977.

Hollenbach, P.W. "The Conversion of Jesus: From Jesus the Baptizer to Jesus the Healer." *ANRW* 2.25.1. 1982: 196–219.

_____. "Recent Historical Jesus Studies and the Social Sciences." In *SBLSP* 1983, edited by K.H. Ricard, 61–78. Chicago: Scholars, 1983.

Holmberg, B. *Sociology and the New Testament: An Appraisal.* Minneapolis: Fortress, 1990.

Holmes, M., ed. *The Apostolic Fathers*. Translated by J.B. Lightfoot and J.R. Harmer. Grand Rapids: Baker, 1989.

Hooker, M.D. *The Son of Man in Mark: A Study of the Background of the Term "Son of Man" and Its Use in St. Mark's Gospel*. London: SPCK, 1967.

Horsley, R. "Itinerant Cynic or Israelite Prophet?" In *Images of Jesus Today*, edited by J.H. Charlesworth and W.P. Weaver, 68–97. Valley Forge, Pa.: Trinity, 1994.

―――. *Jesus and the Spiral of Violence: Popular Jewish Resistance in Roman Palestine*. San Francisco: Harper & Row, 1987.

―――. "Logoi Propheton?: Reflections on the Genre of Q." In *The Future of Early Christianity: Essays in Honor of Helmut Koester*, edited by B. Pearson, 195–209. Minneapolis: Fortress, 1991.

―――. "The Q People: Renovation, Not Radicalism." *Continuum* 1/3 (1991): 49–63.

―――. *Sociology and the Jesus Movement*. New York: Crossroad, 1989.

―――. "Wisdom Justified by All Her Children: Examining Allegedly Disparate Traditions in Q." In *SBLSP 1994*, edited by E.H. Lovering, Jr., 733–51. Atlanta: Scholars, 1994.

Horsley, R., and J.S. Hanson, *Bandits, Prophets, and Messiahs: Popular Movements in the Time of Jesus*. Minneapolis: Winston/Seabury, 1985.

Hull, J. *Hellenistic Magic and the Synoptic Tradition*. London: SCM, 1974.

Hultgren, A. *The Rise of Normative Christianity*. Minneapolis: Fortress, 1994.

Hurtado, L. "God." In *Dictionary of Jesus and the Gospels*, edited by J.Green, S. McKnight, and I.H. Marshall, 270–76. Downers Grove, Ill.: InterVarsity, 1992.

―――. "The Gospel of Mark: Evolutionary or Revolutionary Document?" *Journal for the Study of the New Testament* 40 (1990): 15–32.

―――. *One God, One Lord: Early Christian Devotion and Ancient Jewish Monotheism*. Philadelphia: Fortress, 1988.

Hurth, E. *In His Name: Comparative Studies and the Quest for the Historical Jesus*, EUS. Frankfurt/New York: Lang, 1989.

Jacobson, A. *The First Gospel: An Introduction to Q*. Sonoma, Calif.: Polebridge, 1992.

Jeremias, J. *The Eucharistic Words of Jesus*. London: SCM, 1966.

―――. *New Testament Theology: The Proclamation of Jesus*. Translated by J. Bowden. New York: Scribner's, 1971.

―――. *Unknown Sayings of Jesus*. London: SPCK, 1957.

Jervell, J. *The Unknown Paul: Essays on Luke-Acts and the Early Church*. Minneapolis: Augsburg, 1984.

Johnson, S.E. *A Commentary on the Gospel According to Saint Mark*. New York: Harper, 1961.

Kähler, M. *The So-called Historical Jesus and the Historic, Biblical Christ*. Edited and translated by C.E. Braaten. Philadelphia: Fortress, 1988.

Kallas, J. *The Significance of the Synoptic Miracles*. Greenwich, Conn.: Seabury, 1961.

Kasher, A. *Jews and Hellenistic Cities in Eretz-Israel: Relations of the Jews in Eretz-Israel with the Hellenistic Cities during the Second Temple Period (332 BCE–70 CE),* TSAJ 21. Tübingen: Mohr, 1990.

Käsemann, E. *Essays on New Testament Themes.* Translated by W.J. Montague. London: SCM, 1964.

———. "The 'Righteousness of God' in Paul." In *New Testament Questions of Today,* translated by W.J. Montague. Philadelphia: Fortress, 1969 (1961).

Kaylor, R. *Jesus the Prophet: His Vision of the Kingdom of Earth.* Louisville: Westminster/John Knox, 1994.

Keck, L.C., ed. *Studies in Luke-Acts, Essays Presented in Honor of Paul Schubert.* Nashville: Abingdon, 1966.

Kee, H.C. *Christian Origins in Sociological Perspective: Methods and Resources.* Philadelphia: Westminster, 1980.

Kelber, W., ed. *The Passion in Mark: Studies on Mark 14-16.* Philadelphia: Fortress, 1976.

Kim, S. *The "Son of Man" as the Son of God,* WUNT 30. Tübingen: Mohr, 1983.

King, K. "Kingdom in the Gospel of Thomas." *Foundations and Facets Forum* 3/1 (1987): 48–97.

Kingsbury, J. "The Historical-Critical Method in Perspective." *Currents in Theology and Mission* 2/3 (July 1975): 132–41.

Kirk, A. "Examining Priorities: Another Look at the Gospel of Peter's Relationship to the New Testament Gospels." *New Testament Studies* 40 (1994): 572–95.

Kissenger, W.S. *The Lives of Jesus: A History and Bibliography.* New York/London: Garland, 1985.

Kleinman, A. *Patients and Healers in the Context of Culture: An Exploration on the Borderland Between Anthropology, Medicine, and Psychiatry.* Berkeley: Univ. of California Press, 1980.

Kloppenborg, J. " 'Easter Faith' and the Sayings Gospel Q." *Semeia* 49 (1990): 71–99.

———. *The Formation of Q: Trajectories in Ancient Wisdom Collections.* Philadelphia: Fortress, 1987.

———. "Theological Stakes in the Synoptic Problem." In *The Four Gospels 1992: Festschrift Frans Neirynck,* 3 vols, edited by F. Van Segbroeck, et al., 1:93-120. Leuven, Belgium: Leuven Univ. Press, 1992.

———. *Q Parallels: Synopsis, Critical Notes and Concordance.* Sonoma, Calif.: Polebridge, 1988.

———. *Q-Thomas Reader.* Sonoma Calif.: Polebridge, 1990.

———, ed. and trans. *The Shape of Q: Signal Essays on the Sayings Source.* Minneapolis: Fortress, 1994.

———. "Symbolic Eschatology and the Apocalypticism of Q." *Harvard Theological Review* 80 (1987): 287–306.

———. "Tradition and Redaction in the Synoptic Sayings Source." *Catholic Biblical Quarterly* 46/1 (1984): 34–62.

_____, and L. Vaage, eds. *Early Christianity, Q and Jesus.* Atlanta: Scholars, 1992.

Knox, W. *The Acts of the Apostles.* Cambridge: Cambridge Univ. Press, 1948.

Koch, K. *The Rediscovery of Apocalyptic.* Translated by M. Kohl. London: SCM, 1972 (1970).

Koester, H. *Ancient Christian Gospels: Their History and Development.* Philadelphia: Trinity, 1990.

_____. "Apocryphal and Canonical Gospels." *Harvard Theological Review* 73 (1980): 105–130.

_____. "The Divine Human Being." *Harvard Theological Review* 78 (1985): 143–252.

_____. "Epilogue: Current Issues in New Testament Scholarship." In *The Future of Early Christianity,* edited by B.A. Pearson, 467–76. Minneapolis: Fortress, 1991.

_____. "The Extracanonical Sayings of the Lord as Products of the Christian Community." *Semeia* 44 (1988): 57–77.

_____. "Gnostic Writings as Witnesses for the Development of the Sayings Tradition." In *Rediscovery of Gnosticism.* Vol. 1 of *The School of Valentinus,* edited by B. Layton, 238–56. Leiden: Brill, 1980.

_____. *Introduction to the New Testament.* 2 vols. Translated by H. Koester. Philadelphia: Fortress, 1982 (1980).

_____. "Jesus the Victim." *Journal of Biblical Literature* 111/1 (1992): 3–15.

Koester, H., and J. Robinson, *Trajectories through Early Christianity.* Philadelphia: Fortress, 1971.

Kümmel, W. *Introduction to the New Testament.* Edited and translated by H. Kee. Nashville: Abingdon, 1975 (1973).

_____. *The New Testament: The History of the Investigation of Its Problems.* Translated by S. Gilmour and H.C. Kee. Nashville: Abingdon, 1972.

_____. "Norman Perrin's 'Rediscovering the Teaching of Jesus.'" *The Journal of Religion* 49 (1969): 59–66.

Ladd, G. *I Believe in the Resurrection of Jesus.* Grand Rapids: Eerdmans, 1976.

_____. *The Presence of the Future: The Eschatology of Biblical Realism.* Grand Rapids: Eerdmans, 1974.

Latourelle, R. *Finding Jesus Through the Gospels: History and Hermenuetics.* New York: Alba, 1979.

Lattke, M. "On the Jewish Background of the Synoptic Concept 'Kingdom of God.'" In *The Kingdom of God in the Teaching of Jesus, IRT* 5, edited by B. Chilton, 72–91. Philadelphia: Fortress; London: SPCK, 1984.

Lawler, E.G. *David Friedrich Strauss and His Critics: The Life of Jesus Debate in Early Nineteenth-Century German Journals, TR* 16. New York/Berne: Lang, 1986.

Leivestad, R. *Jesus in His Own Perspective: An Examination of His Sayings, Actions, and Eschatological Titles.* Translated by D.E. Aune. Minneapolis: Augsburg, 1987 (1982).

Lenski, G. *Power and Privilege: A Theory of Social Stratification.* New York: McGraw-Hill, 1966.

Levenson, J. *The Hebrew Bible, the Old Testament, and Historical Criticism: Jews and Christians in Biblical Studies.* Louisville: Westminster/John Knox, 1993.

Levine, S. "The Early History of Christianity in Light of the 'Secret Gospel' of Mark." *ANRW* 2.25.6. (1988): 4270–92.

Lewis, C.S. *Fern-Seed and Elephants and Other Essays on Christianity.* Glasgow: William Collins, 1975.

_____. "Modern Theology and Biblical Criticism." In *Christian Reflections,* edited by W. Hooper. Grand Rapids: Eerdmans, 1967.

Lonergan, B. *Insight: A Study of Human Understanding.* London/New York: Longman's, 1958.

_____. *Method in Theology.* New York: Herder and Herder, 1972.

Lord, A. *The Singer of Tales.* Cambridge: Harvard Univ. Press, 1960.

Lüdemann, G. "Acts of the Apostles as a Historical Source." In *The Social World of Formative Christianity and Judaism: Essays in Tribute to Howard Clark Kee,* edited by J. Neusner, et al., 109–25. Philadelphia: Fortress, 1988.

_____. *Early Christianity According to the Traditions in Acts.* Minneapolis: Fortress, 1989.

Machen, G. *The Origins of Paul's Religion.* Grand Rapids: Eerdmans, 1925.

_____. *The Religion of Paul.* Grand Rapids: Eerdmans, 1925.

Mack, B. "The Christ and Jewish Wisdom." In *The Messiah,* edited by J.H. Charlesworth, 192–221. Minneapolis: Fortress, 1992.

_____ "All the Extra Jesuses: Christian Origins in the Light of the ExtraCanonical Gospels." *Semeia* 49 (1990): 167–76.

_____. "Anecdotes and Arguments: The Chreia in Antiquity and Early Christianity." *Occasional Papers* 10. Claremont, Calif.: Institute for Antiquity and Christianity, 1987, 1–48.

_____. "Decoding the Scripture: Philo and the Rules of Rhetoric." In *Nourished with Peace: Studies in Hellenistic Judaism in Memory of Samuel Sandmel,* SPHS 9, edited by F.E. Greenspahn, E. Hilgert, and B. Mack, 81–115. Chico, Calif.: Scholars, 1984.

_____. "Gilgamesh and the Wizard of Oz: The Scholar as Hero." *Foundations and Facets Forum* 1/2 (June 1985): 3–28.

_____. "Innocence and Power in the Christian Imagination." *Occasional Papers* 17. Claremont, Calif.: *Institute for Antiquity and Christianity,* 1989, 1–12.

_____. "Innocent Transgressor: Jesus in Early Christian Myth and History." *Semeia* 33 (1985): 135–65.

_____. "The Kingdom that Didn't Come: A Social History of the QTradents." In *SBLSP* 1988, edited by D. Lull, 608–635. Atlanta: Scholars, 1988.

_____. "The Kingdom Sayings in Mark." *Foundations and Facets Forum* 3/1 (1987): 3–47.

_____. *Logos und Sophia: Untersuchungen zur Weisheitstheologie im hellenistischen Judentum,* WUNT 10. Güttingen: Vandenhoeck & Ruprecht, 1973.

_____. "Lord of the Logia: Savior or Sage?" In *Gospel Origins and Christian*

Beginnings, in Honor of James M. Robinson, edited by J.E.Goehring, C.W. Hedrick, J.T. Sanders, with H.D. Betz, 3–18. Sonoma, Calif.: Polebridge, 1990.

———. *The Lost Gospel.* San Francisco: HarperSanFrancisco, 1993.

———. *A Myth of Innocence: Mark and Christian Origins.* Philadelphia: Fortress, 1988.

———. "A Myth of Innocence at Sea." *Continuum* 1/2 (1991): 140–57.

———. "Persuasive Pronouncements: An Evaluation of Recent Studies on the Chreia." *Semeia* 64 (1993): 283–87.

———. "Q and the Gospel of Mark: Revising Christian Origins." *Semeia* 55 (1992): 15–39.

———. Review of *Did Jesus Rise From the Dead? The Resurrection Debate: Gary Habermas and Anthony G.N. Flew.* Edited by T. Miethe. SanFrancisco: Harper & Row, 1987. In *History and Theory* 28/2 (1989): 215–24.

———. *Rhetoric and the New Testament.* Minneapolis: Fortress, 1990.

———. "Under the Shadow of Moses: Authorship and Authority in Hellenistic Judaism." In *SBLSP* 1982, edited by K.H. Richards, 299–318. Chico, Calif.: Scholars, 1982.

———. *Wisdom and the Hebrew Epic: Ben Sirach's Hymn in Praise of the Fathers.* Chicago/London: Univ. of Chicago Press, 1985.

———. "Wisdom Makes a Difference: Alternatives to 'Messianic' Configurations." In *Judaisms and Their Messiahs at the Turn of the Christian Era,* edited by J. Neusner, W.S. Green, and E.S. Frerichs, 15–48. Cambridge: Cambridge Univ. Press, 1987.

———. "Wisdom Myth and Mythology: An Essay in Understanding a Theological Tradition." *Interpretation* 24. 1970. 46-60

Mack, B., and R.E. Murphy, "Wisdom Literature." In *Early Judaism and Its Modern Interpreters,* edited by R.A. Kraft and G.W.E. Nickelsburg, 371–410. Philadelphia: Fortress; Atlanta: Scholars, 1986.

Mack, B., and V.K. Robbins, *Patterns of Persuasion in the Gospels.* Sonoma, Calif.: Polebridge, 1989.

Maddox, R. *The Purpose of Luke-Acts.* Edinburgh: T & T Clark, 1982.

Malherbe, A.J. *The Cynic Epistles: A Study Edition, SBLSBS* 12. Missoula, Mont.: Scholars, 1977.

———. "Hellenistic Moralists and the New Testament." *ANRW* II. 26. 1. (1992): 268–333.

———. "Self-Definition among Epicureans and Cynics." In *Self-Definition in the Greco-Roman World.* Vol. 3 of *Jewish and Christian Self-Definition,* edited by B.F. Meyer and E.P. Sanders, 46–59. Philadelphia: Fortress, 1982.

———. *Moral Exhortation, a Greco-Roman Sourcebook.* Philadelphia: Westminster, 1986.

———. *Paul and the Popular Philosophers.* Minneapolis: Fortress, 1989.

Manson, T.W. *The Servant-Messiah.* Cambridge: Cambridge Univ. Press, 1966.

Marshall, I.H. *The Acts of the Apostles.* Sheffield: JSOT, 1992.

———. *Luke: Historian and Theologian.* Grand Rapids: Zondervan, 1989.

_____, ed. *New Testament Interpretation: Essays on Principles and Methods.* Grand Rapids: Eerdmans, 1977.

_____. *The Origins of New Testament Christology.* Downers Grove, Ill.: InterVarsity, 1976.

_____. "Orthodoxy and Heresy in Earlier Christianity." *Themelios* 2 (1976): 5–14.

Martin, B. "Some Reflections on the Unity of the New Testament." *Studies in Religion* 8/2 (1979): 143–52.

Martin, R. *Mark: Evangelist and Theologian.* Exeter: Paternoster, 1972.

_____. *New Testament Foundations: A Guide For Christian Students.* Vol. 1. Grand Rapids: Eerdmans, 1975.

Marxen, W. *Mark the Evangelist.* New York: Abingdon, 1969.

McCant, J. "The Gospel of Peter: Docetism Reconsidered." *New Testament Studies* 30 (1984): 258–73.

McGrath, A. *The Making of Modern German Christology, 1750-1990,* 2nd ed. Grand Rapids: Zondervan, 1994.

McKnight, E.V. *What is Form Criticism?* Philadelphia: Fortress, 1969.

McMullen, R. *Roman Social Relations, 50 B.C. to A.D. 284.* New Haven: Yale Univ. Press, 1974.

Meadors, E. "The Orthodoxy of the 'Q' Sayings of Jesus." *Tyndale Bulletin* 43/2 (1992): 233–57.

Meeks, W. *The First Urban Christians: The Social World of the Apostle Paul.* New Haven: Yale Univ. Press, 1983.

Meier, J.P. *A Marginal Jew: Rethinking the Historical Jesus.* Vol. 1. New York: Doubleday, 1991.

Meijboom, H.U. *A History and Critique of the Origin of the Markan Hypothesis, 1835-1866: A Contemporary Report Rediscovered.* Edited and translated by J.J. Kiwiet. Macon, Ga.: Mercer Univ. Press, 1993.

Menard, J. *L'Evangile Selon Thomas, NHS* 5. Leiden: Brill, 1975.

Meyer, B.F. *The Aims of Jesus.* London: SCM, 1979.

_____. *The Early Christians: Their World Mission and Self-Discovery, GNS* 16. Wilmington, Del.: Glazier, 1986.

_____. "Some Consequences of Birger Gerhardsson's Account of the Origins of the Gospel Tradition." In *Jesus and the Oral Gospel Tradition, JSNTSS* 64, edited by H. Wansbrough. Sheffield: JSOT, 1991.

Meyer, E. *Ursprung und Anfange des Christentums,* I. Stuttgart: J.G. Cotta, 1962.

Meyer, M., ed. and trans. *The Gospel of Thomas: The Hidden Sayings of Jesus.* San Francisco: Harper, 1992

_____. "The Youth in Secret Mark and the Beloved Disciple in John." In *Gospel Origins and Christian Beginnings: In Honor of James M. Robinson,* edited by J. Goehring, et al., 94–105. Sonoma, Calif. Polebridge, 1990.

Meyers, E. "The Challenge of Hellenism for Early Judaism and Christianity." *Biblical Archaeologist* 55/2 (1992): 84–91.

_____. "The Cultural Setting of Galilee: The Case of Regionalism and Early Judaism." *ANRW* 2.19.1. (1979): 686–701.

_____. "Galilean Regionalism as a Factor of Historical Reconstruction." *ASOR Bulletin* 221 (Fall 1976): 93–101.

_____. "Galilean Regionalism: A Reappraisal." In *Approaches to Ancient Judaism*. Vol. 5, edited by W.S. Green, 115–31. Missoula, Mont.: Scholars, 1978.

Meyers, E., and J. Strange. *Archaeology, the Rabbis and Early Christianity*. Nashville: Abingdon, 1981.

Michaels, J. "The Kingdom of God and the Historical Jesus." In *The Kingdom of God in 20th-Century Interpretation*, edited by W. Willis, 109–18. Peabody, Mass.: Hendrickson, 1987.

Miller, M. "How Jesus Became Christ: Probing a Thesis." *Continuum* 2/2-3 (1993): 243–70.

Minear, P. "Gospel History: Celebration or Reconstruction?" In *Jesus and Man's Hope*. 2 vols., edited by D.G. Miller and D.Y. Hadidian, 2:13–27. Pittsburgh: Pittsburgh Theological Seminary, 1971.

Moffatt, J. *An Introduction to the Literature of the New Testament*. New York: Scribner's, 1911.

Moore, S.D. *Poststructuralism and the New Testament: Derrida and Foucault at the Foot of the Cross*. Minneapolis: Fortress, 1994.

Morris, L. *Studies in the Fourth Gospel*. Grand Rapids: Eerdmans, 1969.

Moule, C. *The Birth of the New Testament*, 3rd ed. London: A & C Black; San Francisco: Harper & Row, 1982.

_____. *The Origin of Christology*. Cambridge: Cambridge Univ. Press, 1977.

_____. *The Phenomenon of the New Testament*. Naperville, Ill.: Allenson, 1967.

Nash, R. *Christianity and the Hellenistic World*. Grand Rapids: Zondervan, 1984.

Neill, S., and N.T. Wright, *The Interpretation of the New Testament, 1861–1986*, 2nd ed. Oxford: Oxford Univ. Press, 1988.

Neirynck, F. "The Apocryphal Gospels and the Gospel of Mark." In *The New Testament in Early Christianity, BETL* 86, edited by J.M. Sevrin. Leuven, Belgium: Leuven Univ. Press, 1989.

_____. "The Historical Jesus: Reflections on an Inventory." *Ephemerides Theologicae Lovanienses* 70/1 (1994): 221–34.

Neusner, J., ed. *The Christian and Judaic Invention of History, AARSR* 55. Atlanta: Scholars, 1990.

_____. *The Rabbinic Traditions about the Pharisees before 70*. Leiden: Brill, 1971.

Nickelsberg, G. "Wisdom and Apocalyptic in Early Judaism: Some Points for Discussion." In *SBLSP*, edited by E.H. Lovering, Jr. Atlanta: Scholars, 1994.

Nickle, K. *The Synoptic Gospels: An Introduction*. Atlanta: John Knox; London: SCM, 1981/1982.

Nineham, D. *The Use and Abuse of the Bible*. London: Macmillan, 1976.

Nock, A. *Early Gentile Christianity and Its Hellenistic Background*. New York: Harper & Row, 1964 (1952).

Noll, M. *Between Faith and Criticism: Evangelicals, Scholarship, and the Bible in America*, 2nd ed. Grand Rapids: Baker, 1991.

Norris, C. *Deconstruction: Theory and Practice*. London/New York: Methuen, 1982.

_____. *Derrida*. Cambridge: Harvard Univ. Press, 1987.

O'Collins, G. *Jesus Risen*. New York: Paulist, 1987.

O'Collins, G., and D. Kendall. "Did Joseph of Arimathea Exist?" *Biblica* 75 (1994): 235–41.

Oden, T.C. *After Modernity . . . What? Agenda for Theology*, rev. ed. Grand Rapids: Zondervan, 1990 (1979).

_____. *The Word of Life: Systematic Theology*. Vol. II. San Francisco: Harper & Row, 1989.

O'Neill, J.C. *Messiah: Six Lectures on the Ministry of Jesus*. Cambridge: Cochrane, 1980.

_____. *The Theology of Acts*, 2nd ed. London: SPCK, 1970.

Osborn, E. *The Emergence of Christian Theology*. Cambridge/New York: Cambridge Univ. Press, 1993.

Osiek, C. *What are They Saying about the Social Setting of the New Testament?* Mahwah, N.J.: Paulist, 1992.

Pals, D.L. *The Victorian "Lives" of Jesus*, TUMSR 7. San Antonio: Trinity Univ. Press, 1982.

Pannenberg, W. *Basic Questions in Theology*. Vol. 1. Translated by G. Kehm. Philadelphia: Fortress, 1970.

_____. *Jesus – God and Man*, 2nd ed. Translated by L. Wilkins and D. Priebe. Philadelphia: Westminster, 1977 (1964).

Patterson, S. "The Gospel of Thomas and the Historical Jesus: Retrospectus and Prospectus." In *SBLSP 1990*, edited by D.J. Lull, 614–636. Atlanta: Scholars, 1990.

_____. *The Gospel of Thomas and Jesus*. Sonoma, Calif.: Polebridge, 1993.

_____. "The Gospel of Thomas and Jesus." *The Fourth R* (May/June 1993): 8–13.

_____. "The Gospel of Thomas and the Synoptic Tradition: A Forschungsbericht and Critique." *Foundations and Facets Forum* 8/1-2 (1992): 45–97.

Patterson, S., and H. Koester. "The Gospel of Thomas: Authentic Sayings?" *Bible Review* 6/2 (1990): 28–39.

Peel, M. "The Resurrection in Recent Scholarly Research." *Bible Review* 4 (1989): 14–21, 42–43.

Perkins, P. "1 Thessalonians and Hellenistic Religious Practices." In *To Touch the Text: Biblical and Related Studies in Honor of Joseph A. Fitzmyer, S.J.*, edited by M. Horgan and P. Kobelski, 325–34. New York: Crossroad, 1989.

_____. *Jesus as Teacher*. Cambridge/New York: Cambridge Univ. Press, 1990.

_____. "Pronouncement Stories in the Gospel of Thomas." *Semeia* 20 (1981): 121–32.

Perrin, N. *Rediscovering the Teaching of Jesus*. New York: Harper & Row, 1967.

_____. *What is Redaction Criticism?* Philadelphia: Fortress, 1969.

Perumalil, A. "Are Not Papias and Irenaeus Competent to Report on the Gospels?" *Expository Times* 91 (1980): 332–37.

Pesch, R. *Das Markusevangelium*. Freiburg im Dreisgau: Harder, 1977.

Pokorny, P. *The Genesis of Christology: Foundations for a Theology of the New Testament*. Edinburgh: T & T Clark, 1987.

Polag, A. "The Theological Center of the Sayings Source." In *The Gospel and the Gospels*, edited by P. Stuhlmacher, translated by J. Bowden, 97–105. Grand Rapids: Eerdmans, 1991 (1983).

Powell, M. *What Are They Saying About Acts?* New York: Paulist, 1991.

Quesnell, Q. "The Mar Saba Clementine: A Question of Evidence." *Catholic Biblical Quarterly* 37 (1975): 48–67.

Quispel, G. "The *Gospel of Thomas* Revisited." In *Colloque international sur les textes de Nag Hammadi*, edited by B. Barc, 218–66. Quebec: Laval Univ. Press; Louvain, Belgium: Peeters, 1981.

Rajack, T. *Josephus: the Historian and His Society*. Philadelphia: Fortress, 1984.

Ramsey, W.M. *The Bearing of Recent Discovery on the Trustworthiness of the New Testament*, 2nd ed. London/New York: Hodder and Stoughton, 1915.

_____. *The Church in the Roman Empire before A.D. 170*. Grand Rapids: Baker, 1979 (1897).

_____. *Luke the Physician and Other Studies in the History of Religion*. London: Hodder and Stoughton, 1908.

Ratzinger, J. "Foundations and Approaches of Biblical Exegesis." *Origins* 17/35 (11 February 1988): 593–602.

Rawlinson, A. *The Gospel According to St. Mark*, 7th ed. London: Methuen, 1949.

_____. *St. Mark, with Introduction*, 7th ed. London: Methuen, 1949 (1925).

Reicke, B. "From Strauss to Holtzmann and Meijboom." *Novum Testamentum* 29/1 (1987): 1–21.

_____. *The Roots of the Synoptic Gospels*. Philadelphia: Fortress, 1986.

_____. "Synoptic Prophecies on the Destruction of Jerusalem." In *Studies in New Testament and Early Christian Literature: Essays in Honor of Allen P. Wikgren, Novum Testamentum Supplement* 33, edited by D.E. Aune, 121–34. Leiden: Brill, 1972.

Reiner, G. *History: Its Purpose and Method*. London: Allen & Unwin, 1950.

Reumann, J. *Variety and Unity in New Testament Thought*. Oxford: Oxford Univ. Press, 1991.

Reventlow, H.G. *The Authority of the Bible and the Rise of the Modern World*. Translated by J. Bowden. Philadelphia: Fortress, 1985.

Riches, J. *Jesus and the Transformation of Judaism*. London: Darton, Longman, & Todd, 1980.

_____. *The World of Jesus: First-Century Judaism in Crisis*. Cambridge/New York: Cambridge Univ. Press, 1990.

Riesner, R. *Jesus als Lehrer: Eine Untersuchung zum Ursprung der Evangelein-Uberlieferung*. Tübingen: Mohr, 1981.

_____. "Jesus as Preacher and Teacher." In *Jesus and the Oral Gospel Tradition, JSNTSS* 64, edited by H. Wansbrough, 185–210. Sheffield: JSOT, 1991.

Riley, H. *The Making of Mark: An Exploration.* Macon, Ga.: Mercer Univ. Press, 1989.

Robbins, V.K. "Text and Context in Recent Studies of the Gospel of Mark." *Religious Studies Review* 17/1 (1991): 16–22.

Robertson, A. *Luke the Historian in the Light of Research.* Grand Rapids: Baker, 1977.

Robinson, J.M. "Jesus from Easter to Valentinus or to the Apostles Creed." *Journal of Biblical Literature* 101/11 (1982): 5–37.

_____. *Jesus and His Coming.* New York: Abingdon, 1958.

_____, ed. *The Nag Hammadi Library in English,* 3rd rev. ed. Translated by Coptic Gnostic Library Project. San Francisco: HarperSanFrancisco, 1990.

_____. *A New Quest for the Historical Jesus.* London: SCM, 1959.

_____. *The Problem of History in Mark and Other Marcan Studies.* Philadelphia: Fortress, 1982.

_____. "The Q Trajectory: Between John and Matthew via Jesus." In *The Future of Early Christianity: Essays in Honor of Helmut Koester,* edited B.A. Pearson, 173–94. Minneapolis: Fortress, 1991.

_____. *The Priority of John.* Edited by J.F. Coakley. London: SCM, 1985.

_____. *Redating the New Testament.* Philadelphia: Westminister, 1976.

Robinson J.M., and J.B. Cobb, Jr. eds. *The New Hermeneutic, NFT* 2. New York: Harper & Row, 1964.

Robinson, J., and H. Koester, *Trajectories through Early Christianity.* Philadelphia: Fortress, 1971.

Robinson, T. *The Bauer Thesis Examined: The Geography of Heresy in the Early Christian Church.* Lewiston, N.Y.: Mellen, 1988.

Rousseau, J. "Jesus, an Exorcist of a Kind." In *SBLSP* 1993, edited by E.H. Lovering, Jr., 129–53. Atlanta: Scholars, 1993.

Sabourin, L. "The Miracles of Jesus II: Jesus and the Evil Powers." *Biblical Theology Bulletin* 4/2 (1974): 115–75.

Sanders, E.P. *The Historical Figure of Jesus.* London/New York: Penguin, 1993.

_____. "Jesus in Historical Context." *Theology Today* 50/3 (1993): 429–48.

_____. *Jesus and Judaism.* Philadelphia: Fortress, 1985.

_____. *Paul and Palestinian Judaism: A Comparison of Patterns of Religion.* Philadelphia: Fortress, 1977.

_____. *The Tendencies of the Synoptic Tradition.* London: Cambridge Univ. Press, 1969.

Sandmel, S. "Parallelomania." *Journal of Biblical Literature* 81 (1962): 1–13.

Sarup, M. *An Introductory Guide to Post-structuralism and Postmodernism.* Athens: Univ. of Georgia Press, 1989.

Sato, M. *Q und Prophetie: Studien zur Gattungs- und Traditionsgeschichte der Quelle Q, WUNT* 2:29. Tübingen: Mohr, 1988.

_____. "The Shape of the Q-Source." In *The Shape of Q: Signal Essays on the*

Sayings Source, edited by J.S. Kloppenborg, 156–79. Minneapolis: Fortress, 1994.

Sayre, F. *The Greek Cynics.* Baltimore: Furst, 1948.

Schillebeeckx, E. *Jesus: An Experiment in Christology.* Translated by H. Hoskins. New York: Crossroad, 1991 (1974).

Schrage, W. *Das Verhaltnis Des Thomas-Evangeliums Zur Synoptischen Tradition Und Zu Den Koptischen Evangelienubersetzungen.* Berlin: Topelmann, 1964.

Schulz, H. *Die aposotolische Herkunft der Evangelien,* QD 145. Freiburg/Basel/ Vienna: Herder, 1993.

Schürmann, H. "Die vorösterlichen Anfänge der Logientradition." In *Der historische Jesus und der kerygmatische Christus: Beiträge zum Christusverständnis in Forschung und Verkündigung,* edited by H. Ristow and K. Matthiae, 342–70. Berlin: Evangelische Verlangsanstalt, 1961.

Schüssler Fiorenza, E. "The Ethics of Biblical Interpretation: Decentering Biblical Scholarship." *Journal of Biblical Literature* 107/1 (1988): 3–17.

Schweitzer, A. *The Quest of the Historical Jesus: A Critical Study of Its Progress from Reimarus to Wrede.* Translated by W. Montgomery. New York: Collier/ Macmillan, 1968.

Schweizer, E. *Jesus Christ: The Man From Nazareth and the Exalted Lord.* Macon, Ga.: Mercer Univ. Press, 1987.

––––––. "The Testimony to Jesus in the Early Christian Community." *Horizons in Biblical Theology* 7 (1985): 77–98.

Scott, B.B. *Hear Then the Parable: A Commentary on the Parables of Jesus.* Minneapolis: Fortress, 1989.

Scott, J.C. *Domination and the Arts of Resistance: Hidden Transcripts.* New Haven: Yale Univ. Press, 1990.

Seeley, D. "Blessings and Boundaries: Interpretations of Jesus' Death in Q." *Semeia* 55 (1992): 131–46.

––––––. "Jesus Death in Q." *New Testament Studies* 38 (1992): 222–34.

––––––. *The Noble Death: Graeco-Roman Martyrology and Paul's Concept of Salvation,* JSNTSS 28. Sheffield: JSOT, 1990.

––––––. "Was Jesus Like a Philosopher? The Evidence of Martyrological and Wisdom Motifs in Q, Pre-Pauline Traditions, and Mark." In *SBLSP* 1989, edited by D.J. Lull, 540–49. Atlanta: Scholars, 1989.

Selman, M.J. "The Kingdom of God in the Old Testament." *Tyndale Bulletin* 40/2 (1989): 161–83.

Sherwin-White, A. *Roman Society and Roman Law in the New Testament.* Oxford: Clarendon, 1963.

Sieber, J. "Gospel of Thomas and the New Testament." In *Gospel Origins and Christian Beginnings: In Honor of James M. Robinson,* edited by J. Goehring, et al, 64–73. Sonoma, Calif.: Polebridge, 1990.

––––––. "A Redactional Analysis of the Synoptic Gospels with Regard to the Question of the Sources of the Gospel According to Thomas." Ph.D. diss., Claremont Graduate School, 1964.

Silva, M. "The Place of Historical Reconstruction in New Testament Criticism." In *Hermeneutics, Authority, and Canon,* edited by D.A. Carson and J.D.

Woodbridge, 109–33. Grand Rapids: Zondervan, 1986.

Smith, H. *Forgotten Truth: The Primordial Tradition.* New York: Harper & Row, 1976.

Smith, J. *Drudgery Divine: On the Comparison of Early Christianity and the Religions of Late Antiquity, CSHJ.* Chicago: Univ. of Chicago Press, 1990.

———. *Imagining Religion: From Babylon to Jonestown.* Chicago/London: Univ. of Chicago Press, 1982.

———. *Map is Not Territory: Studies in the History of Religions, SJLA* 23. Leiden: Brill, 1978.

———. *To Take Place: Toward Theory in Ritual.* Chicago/London: Univ. of Chicago Press, 1987.

———. *The Voyage and Shipwreck of St. Paul: With Dissertations on the Life and Writings of St. Luke, and the Ships and Navigation of the Ancients,* 4th ed. Grand Rapids: Baker, 1970.

Smith, M. *Clement of Alexandria and a Secret Gospel of Mark.* Cambridge: Harvard Univ. Press, 1973.

———. "A Comparison of Early Christian and Early Rabbinic Tradition." *Journal of Biblical Studies* 82 (1963): 169–76.

———. *The Secret Gospel: The Discovery and Interpretation of the Secret Gospel According to Mark.* New York: Harper & Row, 1973.

Snodgrass, K. "The Gospel of Thomas: A Secondary Gospel." *The Second Century* 7/1 (1989–1990): 19–38.

Soards, M.L. "Reframing and Reevaluating the Argument of the Pastoral Epistles toward a Contemporary New Testament Theology." *Perspectives in Religious Studies* 19 (1992): 389–398.

Stambaugh, J., and D.L. Balch, *The New Testament and Its Social Environment.* Philadelphia: Westminster, 1986.

Stanton, G. "Form Criticism Revisited." In *What About the New Testament? Essays in Honour of Christopher Evans,* edited by M. Hooker and C. Hickling, 13–27. London: SCM, 1975.

———. *The Gospels and Jesus.* Oxford: Oxford Univ. Press, 1989.

———. *Jesus of Nazareth in New Testament Preaching.* Cambridge: Cambridge Univ. Press, 1974.

———. "On the Christology of Q." In *Christ and the Spirit in the New Testament: Festschrift C.F.D. Moule,* edited by B. Lindars and S.S. Smalley, 27–42. Cambridge: Cambridge Univ. Press, 1973.

Staudinger, H. *The Trustworthiness of the Gospels.* Edinburgh: Handsel, 1981.

Steck, O. *Israel und das gewaltsame Geschick der Propheten, WMANT* 23. Neukirchen-Vluyn: Neukirchener, 1967.

———. *Gospels and Tradition: Studies on Redaction Criticism of the Synoptic Gospels.* Grand Rapids: Baker, 1992.

———. *The Method and Message of Jesus' Teachings.* Philadelphia: Westminster, 1978.

———. *The Synoptic Problem: An Introduction.* Grand Rapids: Baker, 1987.

Stoldt, H. *History and Criticism of the Markan Hypothesis.* Edited and translated by D. L. Niewyk. Edinburgh: T & T Clark; Macon, Ga.: Mercer Univ. Press, 1980.

Strauss, D.F. *The Christ of Faith and the Jesus of History: A Critique of Schleiermacher's The Life of Jesus.* Edited and translated by L.E. Keck. Philadelphia: Fortress, 1977.

_____. *The Life of Jesus Critically Examined.* Edited by P. Hodgson. Translated by G. Eliot. Philadephia: Fortress, 1972.

_____. *A New Life of Jesus.* 2 vols. London: Williams and Norgate, 1865.

_____. *The Old Faith and the New: A Confession.* 2 vols. Translated by M. Blind. New York: Holt, 1874.

Streeter, B. *The Four Gospels.* London: Macmillan, 1925.

Strimple, R. *The Modern Search for the Real Jesus.* Phillipsburg, N.J.: Presbyterian & Reformed, 1995.

Stuhlmacher, P. ed. *The Gospel and the Gospels.* Translated by J. Vriend. Grand Rapids: Eerdmans, 1991.

_____. *Historical Criticism and Theological Interpretation of Scripture: Towards a Hermeneutics of Consent.* Translated by R. A. Harrisville. Philadelphia: Fortress, 1977 (1975).

Sturm, R. "Defining the Word 'Apolocalyptic': A Problem in Biblical Criticism." In *Apocalyptic and the New Testament: Essays in Honor of J. Louris Martyn,* *JSNTSS* 24, edited by J. Marcus and M.L. Soards, 17–48. Sheffield: JSOT, 1989.

Talbert, C.H., ed. *Reimarus: Fragments.* Translated by R.S. Frazer. Philadelphia: Fortress, 1970.

_____. *What is a Gospel? The Genre of the Canonical Gospels.* Philadelphia: Fortress, 1977.

Tannehill, R.C. *The Sword of His Mouth, SBLSS* 1. Philadelphia: Fortress; Missoula: Scholars, 1975.

Tashjian, J.S. "The Social Setting of the Q Mission: Three Dissertations." In *SBLSP* 1988, edited by D. Lull, 636–44. Atlanta: Scholars, 1988.

Tatum, W.B. *John the Baptist and Jesus: A Report of the Jesus Seminar.* Sonoma, Calif.: Polebridge, 1994.

Taussig, H. "The Jesus Seminar and Its Public." *Foundations and Facets Forum* 2/2 (1986): 69–77.

Taylor, V. *The Formation of the Gospel Tradition.* London: Macmillan, 1953.

_____. *The Gospel According to St. Mark,* 2nd ed. Grand Rapids: Baker, 1981.

Telford, W.R. "Major Trends and Interpretive Issues in the Study of Jesus." In *Studying the Historical Jesus: Evaluations of the State of Current Research, NTTS* 19, edited by B. Chilton and C.A. Evans, 33–74. Leiden/New York: Brill, 1994.

Theissen, G. *The Gospel in Context: Social and Political History in the Synoptic Tradition.* Translated by L. Maloney. Minneapolis: Fortress, 1991.

_____. "Itinerant Radicalism: The Tradition of Jesus Sayings from the Perspective of the Sociology of Literature." *Radical Religion* 2 (1975): 84–93.

_____. *The Miracle Stories of the Early Christian Tradition.* Edited by J. Riches.

Translated by F. McDonagh. Philadelphia: Fortress, 1983 (1974).

_____. *Social Reality and the Early Christians: Theology, Ethics, and the World of the New Testament*. Translated by M. Kohl. Minneapolis: Fortress, 1992.

_____. *The Sociology of Early Palestinian Christianity*. Translated by J. Bowden. Philadelphia: Fortress, 1978.

Thiselton, A.C. "The New Hermeneutic." In *New Testament Interpretation: Essays on Principles and Methods,* edited by I. H. Marshall, 308–33. Grand Rapids: Eerdmans, 1971.

_____. *The Two Horizons: New Testament Hermeneutics and Philosophical Description with Special Reference to Heidegger, Bultmann, Gadamer, and Wittgenstein*. Grand Rapids: Eerdmans, 1980.

Tidball, D. *The Social Context of the New Testament: A Sociological Analysis*. Grand Rapids: Zondervan, 1984.

Tiede, D. *Jesus and the Future*. Cambridge: Cambridge Univ. Press, 1990.

Tödt, H.E. *The Son of Man in the Synoptic Tradition*. Translated by D.M. Barton. Philadelphia: Westminster, 1965.

Torrey, C. *The Apocalypse of John*. New Haven: Yale Univ. Press, 1958.

Tuckett, C.M. "A Cynic Q?" *Biblica* 70 (1989): 349–76.

_____. "The Greisbach Hypothesis in the Nineteenth Century." *Journal for the Study of the New Testament*. 3 (1979): 29–60.

_____, ed. *The Messianic Secret, IRT* 1. Philadelphia: Fortress; London: SPCK, 1983.

_____. "On the Stratification of Q: A Response." *Semeia* 55 (1992): 213–22.

_____. "Q and Thomas: Evidence of a Primitive 'Wisdom Gospel?'" *Ephemerides Theologicae Lovaniense* 67 (1991): 346–60.

_____. *The Revival of the Greisbach Hypothesis: An Analysis and Appraisal*. Cambridge/London/New York: Cambridge Univ. Press, 1983.

_____. "The Son of Man in Q." In *From Jesus to John: Essays on Jesus and New Testament Christology in Honour of Marinus de Jonge, JSNTSS* 84, edited by M.C. De Boer, 196–215. Sheffield: JSOT, 1993.

_____. "Thomas and the Synoptics." *Novum Testamentum* 30/2 (1988): 132–57.

Turner, C.H. *The Gospel According to St. Mark*. London: SPCK, 1928.

Turner, H. *The Pattern of Christian Truth: A Study in the Relations between Orthodoxy and Heresy in the Early Church*. London: Mowbray, 1954.

Twelftree, G.H. *Jesus the Exorcist: A Contribution to the Study of the Historical Jesus, WUNT* 2. Tübingen: Mohr, 1993.

Vaage, L. "Cynic Epistles." In *Ascetic Behavior in Greco-Roman Antiquity: A Sourcebook,* edited by V.L. Wimbush, 117–28. Minneapolis: Fortress, 1990.

_____. "Q: The Ethos and Ethics of an Itinerant Intelligence." Ph.D. diss., Claremont Graduate School, 1987.

_____. *Galilean Upstarts: Jesus' First Followers According to Q*. Valley Forge, Pa.: Trinity, 1994.

_____. "Like Dogs Barking: Cynic *Parresia* and Shameless Asceticism." *Semeia* 57 (1992): 25–39.

Vansina, J. *Oral Tradition: A Study in Historical Tradition.* London: Routledge Kegan Paul; Chicago: Aldine, 1965.

Via, D.O. *The Parables: Their Literary and Existential Dimension.* Philadelphia: Fortress, 1967.

Vermes, G. *Jesus the Jew: A Historian's Reading of the Gospels*, 2nd ed. New York/London: Macmillan, 1983 (1973).

————. *Jesus and the World of Judaism.* Philadelphia: Fortress, 1984.

————. *The Religion of Jesus the Jew.* Minneapolis: Fortress, 1993.

Wagner, G. *Pauline Baptism and the Pagan Mysteries.* London: Oliver and Boyd, 1967.

Wansbrough, H., ed. *Jesus and the Oral Gospel Tradition*, JSNT, Supplement 64. Sheffield: JSOT, 1991.

Watson, D.F. "Chreia/Aphorism." In *Dictionary of Jesus and the Gospels,* edited by J.B. Green, S. McKnight, and I.H. Marshall, 104-6. Leicester/Downers Grove, Ill.: InterVarsity, 1992. .

Weaver, W.P. "Reflections on the Continuing Quest for Jesus." In *Images of Jesus Today,* edited by J. Charlesworth and W. Weaver. Valley Forge, Pa.: Trinity, 1994.

Wedderburn, A. "Paul and the Hellenistic Mystery-Cults: On Posing the Right Questions." In *La Soteriologia dei culti orientali nell Imperio Romano,* edited by U. Bianchi and M.J. Vermaseren, 817–33. Leiden: Brill, 1982.

Wiens, D. "Mystery Concepts in Primitive Christianity and in Its Environment." *ANRW* 2.23.2. (1980): 1248–84.

Weiss, J. *Jesus' Proclamation of the Kingdom of God.* Edited and translated by R.H. Hiers and D.L. Holland. Philadelphia: Fortress, 1971.

Welch, C. *Protestant Thought in the Nineteenth Century.* 2 vols. New Haven/London: Yale Univ. Press, 1985.

Wells, G.A. *Did Jesus Exist?* rev. ed. London: Pemberton, 1986.

————. *The Historical Evidence for Jesus.* Buffalo: Prometheus, 1988.

Wenham, D., and C. Blomberg, eds. *The Miracles of Jesus, GP* 6. Sheffield: JSOT, 1986.

Wenham, J. *Easter Enigma.* Exeter: Paternoster, 1984.

————. *Redating Matthew, Mark and Luke: A Fresh Assault on the Synoptic Problem.* London: Hodder & Stoughton, 1991.

White, J. "Jesus as Actant." *Biblical Research* 36 (1991): 19–29.

————. "The Way of the Cross: Was There a Pre-Markan Passion Narrative?" *Foundations and Facets Forum* 3/2 (1987): 35–49.

Wilckens, U. "Die Missionsreden der Apostelgeschichte: Form- und traditions- geschichtliche Untersuchungen," *WUNT* 5. Neukirchen-Vluyn: Neukirchener Verlag, 1961.

Wilder, A.N. "The Eschatology of Jesus in Recent Criticism and Interpretation." *Journal of Religion* 28/3 (1948): 177–87.

————. *The Language of the Gospel: Early Christian Rhetoric.* New York: Harper & Row, 1964.

Wilken, R. "Diversity and Unity in Early Christianity." *Second Century* 1/2 (1981): 101–10.

Wilkens M., and J.P. Moreland, eds. *Jesus Under Fire*. Grand Rapids: Zondervan, 1995.

_____. "The Durability of Orthodoxy." *Word & World* 8/2 (1988): 124–32.

_____. *The Myth of Christian Beginnings: History's Impact on Belief*. Garden City, N.Y.: Doubleday, 1971.

Williams, J.G. "Neither Here Nor There: Between Wisdom and Apocalyptic in Jesus' Kingdom Sayings." *Forum* 5/2 (1989): 7–30.

_____. *Those Who Ponder Proverbs: Aphoristic Thinking and Biblical Literature*, BLS 2. Sheffield: Almond, 1981.

Williams, R. "Does it Make Sense to Speak of Pre-Nicene Orthodoxy?" In *The Making of Orthodoxy: Essays in Honour of Henry Chadwick*, edited by R. Williams, 1–23. Cambridge/New York: Cambridge Univ. Press, 1989.

Williams, S. *Jesus' Death as Saving Event: The Background and Origin of a Concept*, HDR 2. Missoula, Mont.: Scholars, 1975.

Williams, T.C. *The Idea of the Miraculous: The Challenge to Science and Religion*. London/New York: Macmillan, 1990.

Wilson, M. "The Jewish Concept of Learning: A Christian Appreciation." *Christian Scholar's Review* 5 (1975–1976): 350–63.

Wink, W. "Jesus as Magician." *Union Seminary Quarterly Review* 30/1 (1974): 3–14.

Witherington III, B. *The Christology of Jesus*. Minneapolis: Fortress, 1990.

_____. *Jesus, Paul and the End of the World: A Comparative Study in New Testament Eschatology*. Downers Grove, Ill.: InterVarsity, 1992.

_____. *The Jesus Quest: The Third Quest for the Jew of Nazareth*. Downers Grove, Ill.: InterVarsity, forthcoming.

_____. *Jesus the Sage: The Pilgrimage of Wisdom*. Minneapolis: Fortress, 1994.

_____. *Paul's Narrative Thought World: The Tapestry of Tragedy and Triumph*. Louisville: Westminster/John Knox, 1994.

Wrede, W. *The Messianic Secret*. Translated by J.C.G. Greig. Greenwood, S.C.: Attic, 1971.

Wright, N.T. "Adam in Pauline Christlogy," In *SBLSP* 1983, edited by K.H. Richards, 359–89. Chico, Calif.: Scholars, 1983.

_____. *The Climax of the Covenant: Christ and the Law in Pauline Theology*. Edinburgh: T & T Clark, 1991.

_____. "Jesus, Quest for the Historical." In *The Anchor Bible Dictionary*. 6 vols, edited by D.N. Freedman, et al., 3:796–802. New York: Doubleday, 1992.

_____. *Jesus and the Victory of God*. Minneapolis: Fortress Press, 1995.

_____. *The New Testament and the People of God*. Minneapolis: Fortress, 1992.

_____. "The New, Unimproved Jesus." *Christianity Today*. 13 September 1993.

_____. *Who Was Jesus?* London: SPCK, 1992.

Yamauchi, E. "A Secret Gospel of Jesus as 'Magnus'?: A Review of the Recent

Works of Morton Smith." *Christian Scholar's Review* 4 (1975): 238–51.

Yandell, K. *The Epistemology of Religious Experience*. Cambridge: Cambridge Univ. Press, 1993.

Yarbrough Collins, A. "The Son of Man Sayings in the Sayings Source." In *To Touch the Text: Biblical and Related Studies in Honor of Joseph A. Fitzmyer, S.J,* edited by M. Horgan and P.J. Kobelski, 369–89. New York: Crossroad, 1989.

Yieh, J.Y. "The Study of Q: A Survey of Its History and the Current State." *Taiwan Journal of Theology* 8 (1986). 105–39.

Zahrnt, H. *The Historical Jesus.* Translated by J. Bowden. London: Collins, 1963.

Zimmermann, F. *Die urchristlicchen Lehrer: Studien zum Tradentenkreis der didaskaloi im frühen Urchristentum, WUNT* 2:12, 2nd ed. Tübingen: Mohr, 1988 (1984).

Author Index

SUBJECT INDEX